2011
Guide to Literary Agents

includes a 1-year online subscription to
Guide to Literary Agents on **WritersMarket.com**

WritersMarket.com
Where & How to Sell What You Write

THE ULTIMATE MARKET RESEARCH TOOL FOR WRITERS

To register your *2011 Guide to Literary Agents* book and **start your 1-year online genre only subscription**, scratch off the block below to reveal your activation code, then go to www.WritersMarket.com. Click on "Sign Up Now" and enter your contact information and activation code. It's that easy!

UPDATED MARKET LISTINGS FOR YOUR INTEREST AREA

EASY-TO-USE SEARCHABLE DATABASE

RECORD KEEPING TOOLS

INDUSTRY NEWS

PROFESSIONAL TIPS AND ADVICE

Your purchase of *Guide to Literary Agents* gives you access to updated listings related to this genre of writing (valid through 1/31/12). For just $9.99, you can upgrade your subscription and get access to listings from all of our best-selling Market books. Visit **www.WritersMarket.com** for more information.

WritersMarket.com
Where & How to Sell What You Write

ACTIVATE YOUR WRITERSMARKET.COM SUBSCRIPTION TO GET INSTANT ACCESS TO:

11GLI0M

- **UPDATED LISTINGS IN YOUR WRITING GENRE** — Find additional listings that didn't make it into the book, updated contact information and more. WritersMarket.com provides the most comprehensive database of verified markets available anywhere.

- **EASY-TO-USE SEARCHABLE DATABASE** — Looking for a specific magazine or book publisher? Just type in its name. Or widen your prospects with the Advanced Search. You can also search for listings that have been recently updated!

- **PERSONALIZED TOOLS** — Store your best-bet markets, and use our popular record-keeping tools to track your submissions. Plus, get new and updated market listings, query reminders, and more – every time you log in!

- **PROFESSIONAL TIPS & ADVICE** — From pay rate charts to sample query letters, and from how-to articles to Q&A's with literary agents, we have the resources freelance writers need.

- **INDUSTRY UPDATES** — Debbie Ridpath Ohi's Market Watch column keeps you up-to-date on the latest publishing industry news, so you'll always be in-the-know.

YOU'LL GET ALL OF THIS WITH YOUR INCLUDED SUBSCRIPTION TO

WritersMarket.com

To put the full power of WritersMarket.com to work for you, upgrade your subscription and get access to listings from all of our best-selling Market books. Find out more at **www.WritersMarket.com**

2011
Guide to Literary Agents®

20TH ANNUAL EDITION

CHUCK SAMBUCHINO, EDITOR

WITHDRAWN

WRITER'S DIGEST
BOOKS

WritersDigest.com
Cincinnati, Ohio

Publisher & Community Leader: Phil Sexton
Director, Content & Community Development: Jane Friedman

Guide to Literary Agents website: www.guidetoliteraryagents.com
Writer's Market website: www.writersmarket.com
Writer's Digest website: www.writersdigest.com
Writer's Digest Bookstore: www.writersdigestshop.com

Distributed in Canada by Fraser Direct
100 Armstrong Avenue
Georgetown, ON, Canada L7G 5S4
Tel: (905) 877-4411

Distributed in the U.K. and Europe by David & Charles
Brunel House, Newton Abbot, Devon, TQ12 4PU, England
Tel: (Þpl44) 1626 323200, Fax: (Þpl44) 1626 323319
E-mail: mail@davidandcharles.co.uk

Distributed in Australia by Capricorn Link
Loder House, 126 George Street
Windsor, NSW 2756 Australia
Tel: (02) 4577-3555

ISSN: 1078-6945
ISBN-13: 978-1-58297-953-3
ISBN-10: 1-58297-953-7

Cover design by Claudean Wheeler
Production coordinated by Greg Nock
Illustrations © Dominique Bruneton/PaintoAlto

Contents

SEALING THE DEAL

PERSPECTIVES

MARKETS

RESOURCES

INDEXES

From the Editor

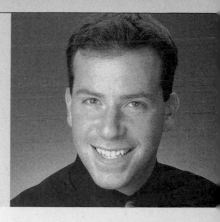

You've finally finished your masterpiece, and you're ready to take the next step—so what happens now? Now you need an agent. Good news: You've come to the right place. *Guide to Literary Agents* turns 20 with this edition, and it's still your one-stop resource for finding an agent. Two decades after its first copy appeared in bookstores, *GLA* is still the most complete and reputable source for literary agents and writers conferences.

Inside this 20th edition, you'll find a wealth of information on agents, such as what they're looking for and how they want to receive submissions from new writers. If you flip through the meat of this book, one thing you may immediately notice is more than 20 new agencies that have never been listed. That's good news for scribes, because newer agents are often building their client list and actively seeking good writers.

Besides its many listings, this book has plenty of informative articles to help you get started in the submission process. Author C. Hope Clark has a fantastic new piece on how researching agents can help make your queries stand out in the slush pile. And as usual, we have several pieces written by literary agents themselves: Rachelle Gardner explains the secrets of composing a book proposal on page 60; Paul S. Levine delves into the different ways writers make money on page 81; and Katharine Sands shines light on all the things agents *don't* want to see in a query or submission (page 96). As a side note, I'm happy to tell you that my own literary agent sold my first book this year to Ten Speed Press (titled *How to Survive a Garden Gnome Attack*)—making me the latest in a long line of *Guide to Literary Agents* success stories. I am living proof that using this book works.

As always, stay in touch with me at www.guidetoliteraryagents.com/blog. Also, please continue to pass along success stories, improvement ideas and news from the ever-changing agent world. In the meantime, good luck—and maybe I'll see you at a writers conference this year!

Chuck Sambuchino
literaryagent@fwmedia.com

How to Use This Book

Searching for a literary agent can be overwhelming, whether you've just finished your first book or you have several publishing credits on your résumé. More than likely, you're eager to start pursuing agents and anxious to see your name on the spine of a book. But before you go directly to the listings of agencies in this book, take time to familiarize yourself with the way agents work and how you should approach them. By doing so, you will be more prepared for your search and ultimately save yourself effort and unnecessary grief.

Read the articles
This book begins with feature articles that explain how to prepare for representation, offer strategies for contacting agents, and provide perspectives on the author/agent relationship. The articles are organized into three sections appropriate for each stage of the search process: **Getting Started**, **Contacting Agents** and **Sealing the Deal**. You may want to start by reading through each article, and then refer back to relevant articles during each stage of your search.

Since there are many ways to make that initial contact with an agent, we've also provided a section called **Perspectives**. These personal accounts from agents and published authors offer information and inspiration for any writer hoping to find representation.

Decide what you're looking for
A literary agent will present your work directly to editors or producers. It's the agent's job to get her client's work published or sold and to negotiate a fair contract. In the **Literary Agents** section, we list each agent's contact information and explain what type of work the agency represents as well as how to submit your work for consideration.

For face-to-face contact, many writers prefer to meet agents at **Conferences**. By doing so, writers can assess an agent's personality, attend workshops and have the chance to get more feedback on their work than they get by mailing submissions and waiting for a response. The conferences section is divided into regions, and lists only those conferences agents and/ or editors attend. In many cases, private consultations are available, and agents attend with the hope of finding new clients to represent.

Utilize the extras
Aside from the articles and listings, the book offers a section of **Resources**. If you come across a term with which you aren't familiar, check out the Resources section for a quick explanation. Also, note the gray tabs along the edge of each page. The tabs block off each section so they are easier to flip to as you conduct your search.

Frequently Asked Questions

1 **Why do you include agents who are not seeking new clients?** Some agents ask that their listings indicate they are currently closed to new clients. We include them so writers know the agents exist and know not to contact them at this time.

2 **Why do you exclude fee-charging agents?** We have received a number of complaints in the past regarding fees, and therefore have chosen to list only those agents who do not charge fees.

3 **Why are some agents not listed in *Guide to Literary Agents*?** Some agents may not have responded to our requests for information. We have taken others out of the book after receiving very serious complaints about them.

4 **Do I need more than one agent if I write in different genres?** It depends. If you have written in one genre and want to switch to a new style of writing, ask your agent if she is willing to represent you in your new endeavor. Most agents will continue to represent clients no matter what genre they choose to write. Occasionally, an agent may feel she has no knowledge of a certain genre and will recommend an appropriate agent to her client. Regardless, you should always talk to your agent about any potential career move.

5 **Why don't you list more foreign agents?** Most American agents have relationships with foreign co-agents in other countries. It is more common for an American agent to work with a co-agent to sell a client's book abroad than for a writer to work directly with a foreign agent. We do, however, list agents in the United Kingdom, Australia, Canada and other countries who sell to publishers both internationally and in the United States. If you decide to query a foreign agent, make sure they represent American writers (if you're American). Some may request to only receive submissions from Canadians, for example, or UK residents.

6 **Do agents ever contact a self-published writer?** If a self-published author attracts the attention of the media or if his book sells extremely well, an agent might approach the author in hopes of representing him.

7 **Why won't the agent I queried return my material?** An agent may not answer your query or return your manuscript for several reasons. Perhaps you did not include a self-addressed, stamped envelope (SASE). Many agents will discard a submission without a SASE. Or, the agent may have moved. To avoid using expired addresses, use the most current edition of *Guide to Literary Agents* or access the information online at www.WritersMarket.com. Another possibility is that the agent is swamped with submissions. An agent can be overwhelmed with queries, especially if the agent has recently spoken at a conference or has been featured in an article or book. Also, some agents specify in their listings that they never return materials of any kind.

Finally—and perhaps most importantly—are the **Indexes** in the back of the book. These can serve as an incredibly helpful way to start your search because they categorize the listings according to different criteria. For example, you can look for literary agents by name or according to their specialties (fiction/nonfiction genres). Plus, there is a General Index that lists every agency and conference in the book.

Listing Policy and Complaint Procedure

Listings in *Guide to Literary Agents* are compiled from detailed questionnaires, phone interviews and information provided by agents. The industry is volatile, and agencies change frequently. We rely on our readers for information on their dealings with agents and changes in policies or fees that differ from what has been reported to the editor of this book. Write to us (Guide to Literary Agents, 4700 E. Galbraith Road, Cincinnati, OH 45236) or e-mail us (literaryagent@fwmedia.com) if you have new information, questions or problems dealing with the agencies listed.

Listings are published free of charge and are not advertisements. Although the information is as accurate as possible, the listings are not endorsed or guaranteed by the editor or publisher of *Guide to Literary Agents*. If you feel you have not been treated fairly by an agent or representative listed in *Guide to Literary Agents*, we advise you to take the following steps:

- First try to contact the agency. Sometimes one phone call, letter or e-mail can clear up the matter. Politely relate your concern.

- Document all your correspondence with the agency. When you write to us with a complaint, provide the name of your manuscript, the date of your first contact with the agency and the nature of your subsequent correspondence.

We will keep your letter on file and attempt to contact the agency. The number, frequency and severity of complaints will be considered when deciding whether or not to delete an agency's listing from the next edition.

Guide to Literary Agents reserves the right to exclude any agency for any reason.

Do I Need an Agent?

Preparing for Representation

A writer's job is to write. A literary agent's job is to find publishers for her clients' books. Because publishing houses receive more and more unsolicited manuscripts each year, securing an agent is becoming increasingly necessary. Finding an eager and reputable agent can be a difficult task. Even the most patient writer can become frustrated or disillusioned. As a writer seeking agent representation, you should prepare yourself before starting your search. Learn when to approach agents, as well as what to expect from an author/agent relationship. Beyond selling manuscripts, an agent must keep track of the ever-changing industry, writers' royalty statements, fluctuating reading habits—and the list goes on.

So, once again, you face the question: Do I need an agent? The answer, much more often than not, is yes.

WHAT CAN AN AGENT DO FOR YOU?

For starters, today's competitive marketplace can be difficult to break into, especially for unpublished writers. Many larger publishing houses will only look at manuscripts from agents—and rightfully so, as they would be inundated with unsatisfactory writing if they did not. In fact, approximately 80 percent of books published by the major houses are acquired through agents.

But an agent's job isn't just getting your book through a publisher's door. The following describes the various jobs agents do for their clients, many of which would be difficult for a writer to do without outside help.

Agents know editors' tastes and needs

An agent possesses information on a complex web of publishing houses and a multitude of editors to ensure her clients' manuscripts are placed in the right hands. This knowledge is gathered through relationships she cultivates with acquisition editors—the people who decide which books to present to their publisher for possible publication. Through her industry connections, an agent becomes aware of the specializations of publishing houses and their imprints, knowing that one publisher only wants contemporary romances while another is interested solely in nonfiction books about the military. By networking with editors, an agent also learns more specialized information—which editor is looking for a crafty Agatha-Christie-style mystery for the fall catalog, for example.

Agents track changes in publishing

Being attentive to constant market changes and shifting trends is another major requirement of an agent. An agent understands what it may mean for clients when publisher A merges

To-Do List for Fiction Writers

1 **Finish your novel** or short story collection. An agent can do nothing for fiction without a finished product.

2 **Revise your novel.** Have other writers offer criticism to ensure your manuscript is as polished as possible.

3 **Proofread.** Don't ruin a potential relationship with an agent by submitting work that contains typos or poor grammar.

4 **Publish** short stories or novel excerpts in literary journals, proving to potential agents that editors see quality in your writing.

5 **Research** to find the agents of writers whose works you admire or are similar to yours.

6 **Use the indexes in the back of this book** to construct a list of agents who are open to new writers and looking for your type of fiction (e.g., literary, romance, mystery).

7 **Rank your list.** Use the listings in this book to determine the agents most suitable for you and your work and to eliminate inappropriate agencies.

8 **Write your synopsis.** Completing this step will help you write your query letter and be prepared for when agents contact you.

9 **Write your query letter.** As an agent's first impression of you, this brief letter should be polished and to the point.

10 **Read about the business** of agents so you are knowledgeable and prepared to act on any offer. Start by reading this book's articles section completely.

with publisher B and when an editor from house C moves to house D. Or what it means when readers—and therefore editors—are no longer interested in Westerns, but instead can't get their hands on enough suspense novels.

Agents get your manuscript read faster

Although it may seem like an extra step to send your manuscript to an agent instead of directly to a publishing house, the truth is an agent can prevent writers from wasting months sending manuscripts that end up in the wrong place or buried in someone's slush pile. Editors rely on agents to save them time as well. With little time to sift through the hundreds of unsolicited submissions arriving weekly in the mail, an editor is naturally going to prefer a work that has already been approved by a qualified reader (i.e., the agent) that knows the editor's preferences. For this reason, many of the larger publishers accept agented submissions only.

Agents understand contracts

When publishers write contracts, they are primarily interested in their own bottom line rather than the best interests of the author. Writers unfamiliar with contractual language may

To-Do List for Nonfiction Writers

1 **Formulate a concrete idea** for your book. Sketch a brief outline making sure you have enough material for an entire book-length manuscript.

2 **Research** works on similar topics to understand the competition and determine how your book is unique.

3 **Write sample chapters.** This step should indicate how much time you will need to finish and if your writing needs editorial help.

4 **Publish** completed chapters in journals and/or magazines. This validates your work to agents and provides writing samples for later in the process.

5 **Polish your outline** so you can refer to it while drafting a query letter and you're prepared when agents contact you.

6 **Brainstorm** three to four subject categories that best describe your material.

7 **Use the indexes in this book** to find agents interested in at least two of your subject areas and who are looking for new clients.

8 **Rank your list.** Narrow your list further by reading the listings of agencies you found in the indexes, and organize the list according to your preferences. Research agent Web sites to be even more selective.

9 **Write your query.** Give an agent an excellent first impression by professionally and succinctly describing your premise and your experience.

10 **Read about the business** of agents so you're knowledgeable and prepared to act on any offer. Start by reading this book's articles section completely.

find themselves bound to a publisher with whom they no longer want to work. Or, they may find themselves tied to a publisher who prevents them from getting royalties on their first book until subsequent books are written. Agents use their experiences and knowledge to negotiate a contract that benefits the writer while still respecting the publisher's needs. After all, more money for the author will almost always mean more money for the agent—another reason they're on your side.

Agents negotiate—and exploit—subsidiary rights

Beyond publication, a savvy agent keeps in mind other opportunities for your manuscript. If your agent believes your book will also be successful as an audio book, a Book-of-the-Month Club selection or even a blockbuster movie, she will take these options into consideration when shopping your manuscript. These additional opportunities for writers are called subsidiary rights. Part of an agent's job is to keep track of the strengths and weaknesses of different publishers' subsidiary rights offices to determine the deposition of these rights regarding your work. After the contract is negotiated, the agent will seek additional moneymaking opportunities for the rights she kept for her client.

Agents get escalators

An escalator is a bonus that an agent can negotiate as part of the book contract. It is commonly given when a book appears on a bestseller list or if a client appears on a popular television show. For example, a publisher might give a writer a $30,000 bonus if he is picked for a book club. Both the agent and the editor know such media attention will sell more books, and the agent negotiates an escalator to ensure the writer benefits from this increase in sales.

Agents track payments

Since an agent only receives payment when the publisher pays the writer, it's in the agent's best interest to make sure the writer is paid on schedule. Some publishing houses are notorious for late payments. Having an agent distances you from any conflict regarding payment and allows you to spend your time writing instead of making phone calls.

Agents are advocates

Besides standing up for your right to be paid on time, agents can ensure your book gets a better cover design, more attention from the publisher's marketing department or other benefits you may not know to ask for during the publishing process. An agent can also provide advice during each step of the process, as well as guidance about your long-term writing career.

ARE YOU READY FOR AN AGENT?

Now that you know what an agent is capable of, ask yourself if you and your work are at a stage where you need an agent. Look at the To-Do Lists for fiction and nonfiction writers on pages 12 and 13, and judge how prepared you are for contacting an agent. Have you spent enough time researching or polishing your manuscript? Does your nonfiction book proposal include everything it should? Is your novel completely finished and thoroughly revised? Sending an agent an incomplete project not only wastes your time, but also may turn off the agent in the process. Literary agents are not magicians, and they can't solve your personal problems. An agent will not be your banker, CPA, social secretary or therapist. Instead, agents will endeavor to sell your book because that's how they earn their living.

Moreover, your material may not be appropriate for an agent. Most agents do not represent poetry, magazine articles, short stories, or material suitable for academic or small presses; the agents' commission does not justify spending time submitting these types of works. Those agents who do take on such material generally represent authors on larger projects first, and then adopt the smaller items as a favor to the client.

If you strongly believe your work is ready to be placed with an agent, make sure you're personally ready to be represented. In other words, consider the direction in which your writing career is headed. Besides skillful writers, agencies want clients with the ability to produce more than one book. Most agents will say they represent careers, not books.

WHEN DON'T YOU NEED AN AGENT?

Although there are many reasons to work with an agent, an author can benefit from submitting his own work directly to a book publisher. For example, if your writing focuses on a very specific area, you may want to work with a small or specialized press. These houses are usually open to receiving material directly from writers. Small presses can often give more attention to a writer than a large house can, providing editorial help, marketing expertise and other advice directly to the writer.

Academic books or specialized nonfiction books (such as a book about the history of Rhode Island) are good bets if you're not with an agent. Beware, though, as you will now be responsible for negotiating all parts of your contract and payment. If you choose this path, it's wise to use a lawyer or entertainment attorney to review all contracts. If a lawyer specializes in intellectual property, he can help a writer with contract negotiations. Instead of giving the lawyer a commission, the lawyer is paid for his time only.

And, of course, some people prefer working independently instead of relying on others to do their work. If you're one of these people, it's probably better to shop your own work instead of constantly butting heads with an agent. Let's say you manage to sign with one of the few literary agents who represent short story collections. If the collection gets shopped around to publishers for several months and no one bites, your agent may suggest retooling the work into a novel or novella(s). Agents suggest changes—some bigger than others—and not all writers think their work is malleable. It's all a matter of what you're writing and how you feel about it.

Agents Tell All

Literary Reps Answer Frequently Asked Questions

by Chuck Sambuchino and Ricki Schultz

ON QUERIES & PITCHING

What are the most common problems you see in a query letter from an unknown author?

First, mistakes in grammar, spelling, word usage or sentence structure. Anything like that is going to put me right off. Second, not saying what the book is about right away. I am only able to spend a minute at most reading your query letter—tell me exactly what I should know immediately, because I may not read all the way to the end. Third, being boring or unoriginal—writers don't seem to realize how many query letters we read in a day or a week. We've seen everything and are looking, more than anything, for our attention to be caught, to be taken by surprise. Be surprising!

— **Ellen Pepus**, *co-founder, Signature Literary*

Let's say you're looking through the slush pile at query letters. What are common elements you see in a query letter that don't truly need to be there?

If your query letter is more than one page long, there are things in there that are superfluous. The most common unnecessary addition is a description of the writer's family/personal life if the book is not a memoir. Some personal background is good, but I would much prefer to know about the amazing novel you wrote. The personal information can come later. The other most common misstep is listing weak qualifications for writing the book. What I mean by that is when someone says, "I have a daughter, so I am qualified to write this very general book about how to raise daughters." In today's very crowded book market, you must have a strong platform to write nonfiction.

— **Abigail Koons**, *literary agent, The Park Literary Group*

I've heard that you shouldn't (can't?) have two different agents represent your work, but what if your varying genres demand it? I write chick lit and thrillers, but my agent handles only the latter. What should I do?

CHUCK SAMBUCHINO (guidetoliteraryagents.com/blog) is the editor of *Guide to Literary Agents*. He is the author of *How to Survive a Garden Gnome Attack* (Ten Speed Press, Sept. 2010) as well as *Formatting & Submitting Your Manuscript* (Writer's Digest Books). **RICKI SCHULTZ** (rickischultz.com) is a Virginia-based freelance writer and recovering high school English teacher. As coordinator of Shenandoah Writers Online, she is an aspiring young adult author and enjoys connecting with other writers.

Most agents handle a smattering of fiction and nonfiction, and so in most cases, there won't be a problem with an agent handling whatever work, categorically, his or her client turns to. However, if one's agent, obviously wanting to serve each and every book optimally, says honestly that he or she truly wouldn't do the job for whatever reason—they don't, let's say, *understand* the genre in question, or they really don't know the editors who publish it to make the proper targeted submissions—then the client should certainly feel free to seek appropriate representation for the book in the "new" genre. What's more, if the situation is succinctly explained to the new agent(s) being approached, they will certainly be understanding (in my view, anyway), and evaluate the submission on merit. And if the writer plans to continue in the new genre, so that the submission in question is not a one-shot, the new agent is even more likely to be open to acting as the writer's "second" agent—even if he or she won't be doing the usual, representing all of that writer's work.

— **John Ware**, *founder, John A. Ware Literary Agency*

Do you see many query letters that come in too long?

Length is an issue, yes. Even though I accept online queries, I still want the query to come in somewhere close to one page. I think that writers often think that because it's online, I have no way of knowing that it's more than a page. Believe me, I do. Queries that are concise and compelling are the most intriguing.

— **Regina Brooks**, *founder, Serendipity Literary Agency*

ON FICTION & GENRES

With literary fiction, what do you look for? What gets you to keep reading?

With literary fiction, I often look for a track record of previous publications. If you've been published in *Tin House* or *McSweeney's* or *Glimmer Train*, I want to know. It tells me that the writer is, in fact, committed to their craft and building an audience out there in the journals. But if you have a good story and are a brilliant writer, I wouldn't mind if you lived in a cave in the Ozarks. For the record, I have yet to sign anyone who lives in a cave in the Ozarks.

— **Michelle Brower**, *literary agent, Folio Literary*

If you were speaking to someone who was sitting down to write a romance book but had never done so before, what would you tell them about the basics of the genre?

The word count should range from 50,000 to about 100,000. There is a formula to writing good romance. The hero must be a man the reader would like to date, and the heroine should be the type of girl who is bigger than life, who the reader would like to be like. They should meet, overcome obstacles and in the end get together. There are dozens of different kinds of romances. The author could join the Romance Writers of America for support and get into critique groups. All my published authors have critique groups.

— **Mary Sue Seymour**, *founder, The Seymour Agency*

How does a writer know if her writing falls into the category of women's fiction, as opposed to perhaps literary fiction?

I think I have a fairly good definition of women's fiction. These are not simply stories with female characters but stories that tell us the female journey. Women's fiction is a way for women to learn and grow, and to relate to others what it is to be a woman. When I think of literary fiction, the emphasis is placed more on the telling of a good story instead of making the female journey the centerpiece.

— **Scott Eagan**, *founder, Greyhaus Literary*

Can you help define the category "Christian Living" and give a few examples?

The Christian Living category of books represents a huge umbrella that covers a multitude of topics. Christian Living works can include books on issues of importance to women, men and teenagers; Christian Living books can be about parenting, marriage, family life, divorce, breast cancer, healing, health, faith journeys, spiritual challenges, leadership and devotionals. [One] series that I've contracted is for three books with a theme of taking faith to the next level. These were written by a pastor of a large church, and the audience will be members of churches across the country who are interested in working through a study program that deals with parenting and other similar topics.

— **Janet Benrey**, *founder, Benrey Literary*

ON NONFICTION & MEMOIR
What do you look for in a memoir?

Memoir is such a tricky genre. Everyone has a story (when I go to writing conferences, memoir writers are usually the overwhelming majority) and unfortunately, few are good and many are overly sentimental. I look for two main things: a unique story and great writing. Memoirs should read like novels; they should have suspense, conflict, emotion, character development, dialogue and narrative arc. On top of all that, it's a tough question to ask about one's own story, but authors should ask it: Why will people be interested in me?

— **Taryn Fagerness**, *founder, Taryn Fagerness Literary Agency*

What's the most important advice you can give for writing nonfiction book proposals?

Three things. 1) Spill the beans. Don't try to tantalize and hold back the juice. 2) No BS! We learn to see right through BS, or we fail rapidly. 3) Get published small. Local papers, literary journals, websites, anything. The more credits you have, the better. And list them all (although not to the point of absurdity) in your query. Why does everyone want to pole-vault from being an unpublished author to having a big book contract? It makes no sense. You have to learn to drive before they'll let you pilot the Space Shuttle.

— **Gary Heidt**, *co-founder, Signature Literary*

Nonfiction writers are always hearing about the importance of building a platform. What does that really mean?

Build your base. I've given workshops at writers conferences about establishing an author platform, and it all boils down to one basic concept: Develop a significant following before you go out with your nonfiction book. If you build it, they (publishers) will come. Think about that word *platform*. What does it mean? If you are standing on a physical platform, it gives you greater visibility. And that's what it's all about: visibility. How visible are you to the world? That's what determines your level of platform. Someone with real platform is the "go to" person in their area of expertise. If a reporter from the *New York Times* is doing a story on what you know about most, they will want to go to you for an interview first. But if you don't make yourself known to the world as the expert in your field, then how will the *NYT* know to reach out to you? RuPaul used to say, "If you don't love yourself, how the hell else is anybody else gonna love you?" I'm not saying be egotistical. I'm just saying, know your strengths, and learn to toot your own horn. Get out there. Make as many connections as you possibly can. We live in a celebrity-driven world. Love it or hate it, either way we all have to live with it. So, celebrate what you have to offer, and if it's genuine and enough people respond to it, then you will become a celebrity in your own right. Get out there and prove to the world that you are the be-all and end-all when it comes to what you know about most. Publishers don't expect you to be as big as Oprah, or Martha, or the Donald, but they do expect you to be the next Oprah, or Martha, or the next Donald in your own field.

— **Jeffery McGraw**, *literary agent, The August Agency*

Your bio says you seek "travel narrative nonfiction." Can you help define this category for writers?

Travel and adventure narrative nonfiction is the type of book that takes you away to another place. It is often a memoir, but can be a journalistic story of a particular event or even a collection of essays. The key here is that it tells an interesting and engaging story. It is also very important these days that the story is fresh and new—you'd be surprised at how many people have had the exact same experience with the rickshaw in Bangkok that you had. Some successful examples of this genre are Jon Krakauer's *Into Thin Air*, Elizabeth Gilbert's *Eat, Pray, Love*, and most things by Paul Theroux and Bill Bryson.

— **Abigail Koons**, *literary agent, The Park Literary Group*

What stands out for you in a nonfiction book proposal? What immediately draws you into a project?

There are several factors that can help a book's ultimate prospects: great writing, great platform or great information, and ideally all three. For narrative works, the writing should be gorgeous, not just functional. For practical works, the information should be insightful, comprehensive and preferably new. And for any work of nonfiction, of course, the author's platform is enormously important.

— **Ted Weinstein**, *founder, Ted Weinstein Literary*

What's a common mistake writers make when composing book proposals?

Nonfiction proposals should be fairly easy to write. There's a lot of information available to writers on how to write "the greatest," "the most compelling," "the no-fail" nonfiction proposal, so I'm often surprised when authors fail to mention their reasons and credentials for writing the work. Like publishers, I often jump to the credentials section of the proposal before getting to the meat of the proposal. I need to know why an author is qualified to write what they're writing and how their work differs from what has already been published on the topic they've chosen.

— **Janet Benrey**, *founder Benrey Literary*

When you receive a nonfiction book proposal, how detailed should the author's promotional plan be?

As long as it needs to be and still be realistic. I see marketing plans all the time along the lines of "I'll be happy to be on Oprah," or other things that the author hopes will happen. I just want to hear what the author can really do that will help sell the book, not pie-in-the-sky wishful thinking.

— **Jim Donovan**, *founder, Jim Donovan Literary*

ON CHILDREN'S & YOUNG ADULT

Can you offer some basic tips for writing children's nonfiction?

You can write about almost anything when it comes to children's nonfiction, even if it's been done before. But you need to come at the subject from a different angle. If there is already a book on tomatoes and how they grow, then try writing about tomatoes from a cultural angle. There are a ton of books on slavery, but not many on slaves in Haiti during the Haitian Revolution (Is there even one? There's an idea—someone take it and query me!). Another thing to always consider is your audience. Kids already have textbooks at school, so you shouldn't write your book like one. Come at the subject in a way that kids can relate to and find interesting. Humor is always a useful tool in nonfiction for kids.

— **Joanna Stampfel-Volpe**, *literary agent, Nancy Coffey Literary & Media Representation*

Where are writers going wrong in picture book submissions?

Rhyming! So many writers think picture books need to rhyme. There are some editors who won't even look at books in rhyme, and a lot more who are extremely wary of them, so it limits an agent on where it can go and the likelihood of it selling. It's also particularly hard to execute perfectly. Aside from rhyming, I see way too many picture books about a family pet or bedtime.

— **Kelly Sonnack**, *literary agent, Andrea Brown Literary Agency*

I've heard that nothing is taboo anymore in young adult books, and you can write about topics such as sex and drugs. Is this true?

I would say this: Nothing is taboo if it's done well. Each scene needs to matter in a novel. I've read a number of "edgy" young adult books where writers seem to add in scenes just for shock value, and it doesn't work with the flow of the rest of the novel. "Taboo" subjects need to have a purpose in the progression of the novel—and of course, need to be well written! Taboo topics do, however, affect whether the school and library market will pick up the book—and this can have an effect on whether a publisher feels they can sell enough copies.

— **Jessica Regel**, *literary agent, Jean V. Naggar Literary Agency*

Simply put, concerning middle grade and young adult—how are they different? Subject matter? Length?

As a disclaimer, there are exceptions to these rules, with the fantasy genre being a big one. But, typically, middle grade novels run between 20,000–40,000 words and feature protagonists ages 9–13. Young adult novels run between 40,000–75,000 words and feature protagonists ages 14–17. The type of relationship at the core of a project can also tell you how to characterize it: MG often revolves around a protagonist's relationships with family and friends, while a story heavily driven by a romantic relationship is going to be YA.

— **Michelle Andelman**, *literary agent, Lynn C. Franklin & Associates*

What are some reasons you stop reading a young adult manuscript?

Once I've determined that the writing is strong enough, it's usually a question of plot (we receive many works that are derivative or otherwise unoriginal) or voice. As we know from the young adults in our lives, anything that sounds even vaguely parental will not be well received. And there's nothing worse than narration that reads like a text message from a grandmother. In the past month, I've received 29 YA partials. Looking back on my notes, I see that I rejected eight for writing, seven for voice, six for derivative or unoriginal plots, four because they were inappropriate for the age group, and two that simply weren't a good fit for the agency but may find a home elsewhere. Then there were two I liked and passed them on to others in my office. Also, I think a lot of writers, seeing the success of *Twilight*, have tried to force their manuscripts into this genre. I know you've heard it before, but it's so true: Write what you love—don't write what you think will sell.

— **Jessica Sinsheimer**, *literary agent, Sarah Jane Freymann Literary Agency*

Are there any subjects you feel are untapped and would, therefore, be a refreshing change from the typical YA story?

When I was a (buyer for a bookstore), I was tired of certain subject matters only because those subjects have been explored so well, so often, that you really needed to bring something special to the page to make anyone take notice. Send me some modern immigrant stories, some multi-generational stuff, like the forthcoming (in the U.S.) YA novels of Carlos Ruiz Zafón. There are deeply rich stories about being an outsider, and yet how assimilation means a compromise and loss. I'd also love to see more issues of race discussed in modern terms, where there is the melting pot happening across the U.S., yet the tensions are still there. I think these stories, when done well, are universal stories, as we all feel that way at some point. Look at Junot Diaz's *The Brief Wondrous Life of Oscar Wao* as exhibit A.

— **Joe Monti**, *literary agent, Barry Goldblatt Literary*

What can writers do to enhance their chances of getting a picture book published?

I know it sounds simplistic, but write the very best picture books you can. I think the market contraction has been a good thing, for the most part. I'm only selling the very best picture books my clients write—but I'm definitely selling them. Picture books are generally skewing young, and have been for some time, so focus on strong read-alouds and truly kid-friendly styles. I'm having a lot of luck with projects that have the feel of being created by an author-illustrator even if the author is not an artist, in that they're fairly simple, have all kinds of room for fun and interpretation in the illustrations, and have a lot of personality. I see a lot of picture book manuscripts that depend too heavily on dialogue, which tends to give them the feel of a chapter book or middle grade novel. The style isn't a picture book style.

— **Erin Murphy**, *founder, Erin Murphy Literary Agency*

Does "tween" exist as a category?

Tween *does* exist, and various publishers even have specific tween imprints in place. As for queries, the same standard holds true for me in terms of tween as it does with YA or MG: If the voice is authentic, then I'm probably interested. However, I do look more at plot with tween novels: right now, it's not enough just to have a great tween voice—the storyline also needs to be unique enough to stand out in the marketplace.

— **Meredith Kaffel**, *literary agent, Charlotte Sheedy Literary Agency*

ON OTHER AGENT MATTERS

Do agents usually hold out for a good deal on a book, or do they take the first acceptable offer that comes along?

Well, an offer in your pocket is always better than none. Certainly, if an agent feels she can demand more for a book, she should hold out; however, usually the editor who makes the first offer is the most enthusiastic and thoroughly understands the book, and may turn out to be the best editor and in-house advocate for that book. The most money is not necessarily the best deal for an author. That enthusiasm, commitment and support from all divisions within a publishing house often means more than those dollars in your bank account. An agent's experience regarding what editors are looking to buy, what publishers are currently paying and what the marketplace is like should lead that agent to advise her client regarding whether or not an offer on the table is the *best* (whatever its true meaning) that can be expected. We do *see* editors on a regular basis. Again, working from experience, an agent helps her client make the best possible decision. We all want our authors to accomplish their goals.

— **Laura Langlie**, *founder, Laura Langlie, Literary Agent*

Do you need a conservative agent to represent a conservative-minded book about religion or politics? A liberal agent to represent a liberal book? Do agents cross over?

I suspect many agents prefer to work only with political authors whose views are at least in the same quadrant as their own. Some, though, including myself, are open to and enjoy the chance to work with clients whose views challenge us, and are no less effective at selling those books to the right editor and publisher. I have represented a number of liberal, conservative and libertarian authors writing on a range of interesting topics, and sold their books to a mix of publishers. As always, the best way for an author to see if an agent might be right for them, regardless of their political views, is to read the good directories/guides to agents and then visit any prospective agent's website to get a more thorough understanding of their work with other clients.

— **Ted Weinstein**, *founder, Ted Weinstein Literary*

What advice would you give writers who have had work rejected by agents?

It still surprises me how many writers are angry or defensive when agents reject their work. It's a wasted opportunity. We invest countless hours reading book proposals and giving each proposal careful thought. We have firsthand knowledge of what's selling (or easy to sell) and what's not. Rather than firing off a counter-response (which has probably never convinced an agent in the history of agenting), authors should use the opportunity to find out why they were rejected and improve their future chances of success. It is not rude to ask for more detailed feedback following a rejection, as long as the request is polite. We may be able to give advice or point out character, dialogue, pacing, pitch or structural issues that you might have missed. It could also lead to a referral or a request to resubmit.

— **Brandi Bowles**, *literary agent, Howard Morhaim Literary*

I've read some articles that say "Agents agent," meaning that their job is to sell your work, rather than do other tasks such as assisting to edit a manuscript. But other articles say agents are now responsible for lots of editing throughout the process. Which is correct?

I can only speak for what we do at our agency, but it's been a long time since any good agent I know has *just* sold books. Agenting is a full-service business and, in this day and age, when editors sometimes seem to be playing musical chairs and projects are orphaned almost as soon as they're bought, providing editorial feedback for our clients is increasingly important. Here at Dystel & Goderich, we edit an author's work before it goes out on submission in order to optimize its chances in the marketplace. Occasionally, we also offer editorial support once the book is sold and the acquiring editor is unable or unwilling to edit. We like to think that our role is to "cause" books to be published, and for that to happen, we need to be involved at every step of the way.

— **Miriam Goderich**, *founding agent, Dystel & Goderich Literary Management*

I'm talking with an agent who politely refused to share a list of who he represents and what he's recently sold. Is this normal?

I understand agencies that don't list clients in directories and public access places. That's a personal choice. Hartline (my agency) lists authors and books sold right on its website. To get down to the point of considering representation, however, not knowing anything about who an agent has represented and what success he's had would, to me, be like agreeing to surgery without knowing for sure that my doctor has a medical degree. If someone applies for a job, she has to provide a résumé and show her experience and qualifications. An agent is not going to take on a client without knowing the critical details about him, and I believe the client is entitled to the same consideration. Before you sign with an agent, know who he is, who he represents and what titles he's sold.

— **Terry W. Burns**, *literary agent, Hartline Literary Agency*

What are the most common things you see writers do wrong during an in-person pitch at a writers conference?

Two things: One, some authors don't seem to understand their true "hook," or most interesting aspect of their work. One writer I met spoke about his young adult fantasy novel, but it wasn't until the end of his pitch that he mentioned how his book was inspired by Japanese folklore and myths. How cool! That is what I would have wanted to hear first. Until then, it sounded like just another young adult fantasy. Two: Some authors over-praise their work. Some people told me how wonderful, great, amazing, funny, etc. their projects are. Coming from the author, such statements make me a bit skeptical. Of course the writer thinks his or her own work is amazing, but what is it about your work that makes it so fabulous? Why is it wonderful? I want more concrete information about an author's work so I can really think about where the book might fit in the market.

— **Taryn Fagerness**, *founder, Taryn Fagerness Literary Agency*

If I envision a five-book series for my story and even have three manuscripts completed, is it still best to query regarding the first one only? Will the "series talk" come later?

We've been seeing a lot more of these types of "series" presentations lately—the feeling being that the author needs to present a future "franchise" for the agent and publisher to get them more interested in representation and publishing their work. This is not necessarily the case. In fact, it may send up a red flag about the author's expectations. I always try to downplay the series pitch (to publishers) unless there has already been a strong brand presence established in the marketplace. My advice to writers is to sell the first one; when it sells well, the editor and publisher will be very happy to listen to ideas for books two and three. Also, feedback can come from the publisher's sales and marketing teams, who will suggest (based on the success of book one) that the author write another book or make a series out of the original. With that in mind, stick to pitching one book at a time.

— **John Willig**, *founder, Literary Services Inc.*

Let's say an acquaintance calls you and says, "An agent wants to represent me, but she's new to the scene and has no sales. Is that OK?" How would you answer that?

An agent with little or no sales who has been an assistant at a leading agency will have just as much clout getting to an editor perhaps as an established agent, at least initially. One of the things I always advise writers to do is to ask an interested agent—that is, one who's made an offer of representation—"Why do you want to be my agent?" They will then hear a very clear thumbnail sketch of how that agent will sound agenting.

— **Katharine Sands**, *literary agent, Sarah Jane Freymann Literary Agency*

Assessing Credibility

The Scoop on Researching Agents

Many people wouldn't buy a used car without at least checking the odometer, and savvy shoppers would consult the blue books, take a test drive and even ask for a mechanic's opinion. Much like the savvy car shopper, you want to obtain the best possible agent for your writing, so you should do some research on the business of agents before sending out query letters. Understanding how agents operate will help you find an agent appropriate for your work, as well as alert you about the types of agents to avoid.

Many writers take for granted that any agent who expresses interest in their work is trustworthy. They'll sign a contract before asking any questions and simply hope everything will turn out all right. We often receive complaints from writers regarding agents *after* they have lost money or have work bound by contract to an ineffective agent. If writers put the same amount of effort into researching agents as they did writing their manuscripts, they would save themselves unnecessary grief.

The best way to educate yourself is to read all you can about agents and other authors. Organizations such as the Association of Authors' Representatives (AAR; www.aar-online. org), the National Writers Union (NWU; www.nwu.org), American Society of Journalists and Authors (ASJA; www.asja.org) and Poets & Writers, Inc. (www.pw.org), all have informational material on finding and working with an agent.

Publishers Weekly (www.publishersweekly.com) covers publishing news affecting agents and others in the publishing industry. The Publishers Lunch newsletter (www. publishersmarketplace.com) comes free via e-mail every workday and offers news on agents and editors, job postings, recent book sales and more.

Even the Internet has a wide range of sites where you can learn basic information about preparing for your initial contact, as well as specific details on individual agents. You can also find online forums and listservs, which keep authors connected and allow them to share experiences they've had with different editors and agents. Keep in mind, however, that not everything printed on the Web is solid fact; you may come across the site of a writer who is bitter because an agent rejected his manuscript. Your best bet is to use the Internet to supplement your other research.

Once you've established what your resources are, it's time to see which agents meet your criteria. Below are some of the key items to pay attention to when researching agents.

LEVEL OF EXPERIENCE

Through your research, you will discover the need to be wary of some agents. Anybody can go to the neighborhood copy center and order business cards that say "literary agent," but that title doesn't mean she can sell your book. She may lack the proper connections with others in the publishing industry, and an agent's reputation with editors can be a major strength or weakness.

Agents who have been in the business awhile have a large number of contacts and carry the most clout with editors. They know the ins and the outs of the industry and are often able to take more calculated risks. However, veteran agents can be too busy to take on new clients or might not have the time to help develop the author. Newer agents, on the other hand, may be hungrier, as well as more open to unpublished writers. They probably have a smaller client list and are able to invest the extra effort to make your book a success.

If it's a new agent without a track record, be aware that you're taking more of a risk signing with her than with a more established agent. However, even a new agent should not be new to publishing. Many agents were editors before they were agents, or they worked at an agency as an assistant. This experience is crucial for making contacts in the publishing industry and learning about rights and contracts. The majority of listings in this book explain how long the agent has been in business, as well as what she did before becoming an agent. You could also ask the agent to name a few editors off the top of her head who she thinks may be interested in your work and why they sprang to mind. Has she sold to them before? Do they publish books in your genre?

If an agent has no contacts in the business, she has no more clout than you do. Without publishing prowess, she's just an expensive mailing service. Anyone can make photocopies, slide them into an envelope and address them to "Editor." Unfortunately, without a contact name and a familiar return address on the envelope, or a phone call from a trusted colleague letting an editor know a wonderful submission is on its way, your work will land in the slush pile with all the other submissions that don't have representation. You can do your own mailings with higher priority than such an agent could.

PAST SALES

Agents should be willing to discuss their recent sales with you: how many, what type of books and to what publishers. Keep in mind, though, that some agents consider this information confidential. If an agent does give you a list of recent sales, you can call the publishers' contracts department to ensure the sale was actually made by that agent. While it's true that even top agents are not able to sell every book they represent, an inexperienced agent who proposes too many inappropriate submissions will quickly lose her standing with editors.

You can also find out details of recent sales on your own. Nearly all of the listings in this book offer the titles and authors of books with which the agent has worked. Some of them also note to which publishing house the book was sold. Again, you can call the publisher and affirm the sale. If you don't have the publisher's information, simply go to your local library or bookstore to see if they carry the book. Consider checking to see if it's available on Web sites like Amazon.com, too. You may want to be wary of the agent if her books are nowhere to be found or are only available through the publisher's website. Distribution is a crucial component to getting published, and you want to make sure the agent has worked with competent publishers.

TYPES OF FEES

Becoming knowledgeable about the different types of fees agents may charge is vital to conducting effective research. Most agents make their living from the commissions they receive after selling their clients' books, and these are the agents we've listed. Be sure to ask about any expenses you don't understand so you have a clear grasp of what you're paying for. Described below are some types of fees you may encounter in your research.

Office fees

Occasionally, an agent will charge for the cost of photocopies, postage and long-distance phone calls made on your behalf. This is acceptable, so long as she keeps an itemized account of the expenses and you've agreed on a ceiling cost. The agent should only ask for office expenses after agreeing to represent the writer. These expenses should be discussed up front, and the writer should receive a statement accounting for them. This money is sometimes returned to the author upon sale of the manuscript. Be wary if there is an up-front fee amounting to hundreds of dollars, which is excessive.

Reading fees

Agencies that charge reading fees often do so to cover the cost of additional readers or the time spent reading that could have been spent selling. Agents also claim that charging reading fees cuts down on the number of submissions they receive. This practice can save the agent time and may allow her to consider each manuscript more extensively. Whether such promises are kept depends upon the honesty of the agency. You may pay a fee and never receive a response from the agent, or you may pay someone who never submits your manuscript to publishers.

Officially, the Association of Authors' Representatives' (AAR) Canon of Ethics prohibits members from directly or indirectly charging a reading fee, and the Writers Guild of America (WGA) does not allow WGA signatory agencies to charge a reading fee to WGA members, as stated in the WGA's Artists' Manager Basic Agreement. A signatory may charge you a fee if you are not a member, but most signatory agencies do not charge a reading fee as an across-the-board policy.

Warning Signs! Beware of . . .

Important

- Excessive typos or poor grammar in an agent's correspondence.

- A form letter accepting you as a client and praising generic things about your book that could apply to any book. A good agent doesn't take on a new client very often, so when she does, it's a special occasion that warrants a personal note or phone call.

- Unprofessional contracts that ask you for money up front, contain clauses you haven't discussed or are covered with amateur clip-art or silly borders.

- Rudeness when you inquire about any points you're unsure of. Don't employ any business partner who doesn't treat you with respect.

- Pressure, by way of threats, bullying or bribes. A good agent is not desperate to represent more clients. She invites worthy authors but leaves the final decision up to them.

- Promises of publication. No agent can guarantee you a sale. Not even the top agents sell everything they choose to represent. They can only send your work to the most appropriate places, have it read with priority and negotiate you a better contract if a sale does happen.

- A print-on-demand book contract or any contract offering you no advance. You can sell your own book to an e-publisher any time you wish without an agent's help. An agent should pursue traditional publishing routes with respectable advances.

Reading fees vary from $25 to $500 or more. The fee is usually nonrefundable, but sometimes agents agree to refund the money if they take on a writer as a client, or if they sell the writer's manuscript. Keep in mind, however, that payment of a reading fee does not ensure representation.

No literary agents who charge reading fees are listed in this book. It's too risky of an option for writers, plus non-fee-charging agents have a stronger incentive to sell your work. After all, they don't make a dime until they make a sale. If you find that a literary agent listed in this book charges a reading fee, please contact the editor at literaryagent@fwmedia.com.

Critique fees

Sometimes a manuscript will interest an agent, but the agent will point out areas requiring further development and offer to critique it for an additional fee. Like reading fees, payment of a critique fee does not ensure representation. When deciding if you will benefit from having someone critique your manuscript, keep in mind that the quality and quantity of comments varies from agent to agent. The critique's usefulness will depend on the agent's knowledge of the market. Also be aware that agents who spend a significant portion of their time commenting on manuscripts will have less time to actively market work they already represent.

In other cases, the agent may suggest an editor who understands your subject matter or genre and has some experience getting manuscripts into shape. Occasionally, if your story is exceptional or your ideas and credentials are marketable but your writing needs help, you will work with a ghostwriter or co-author who will share a percentage of your commission, or work with you at an agreed upon cost per hour.

An agent may refer you to editors she knows, or you may choose an editor in your area. Many editors do freelance work and would be happy to help you with your writing project. Of course, before entering into an agreement, make sure you know what you'll be getting for your money. Ask the editor for writing samples, references or critiques he's done in the past. Make sure you feel comfortable working with him before you give him your business.

An honest agent will not make any money for referring you to an editor. We strongly advise writers not to use critiquing services offered through an agency. Instead, try hiring a freelance editor or joining a writer's group until your work is ready to be submitted to agents who don't charge fees.

Revisions and Self-Editing

Get Your Work Ready for Submission

by James Scott Bell

Submitting a novel without rewriting is like playing hockey naked. You're just not equipped to put your best, um, face on things. And sooner rather than later, a well-placed puck is going to hit you where it hurts most. That puck is editors' and agents' built-in prejudice against weak material. They are tuned to say *No*. That's why you rewrite. You want to take out all those *No* reasons.

Rewriting is one of the most important—if the not *the* most important—parts of writing. In that first draft you've completed is plenty of gold, but also plenty of waste that needs excising. So it's time to get to work.

THE TIME TO REVISE

So you have a completed manuscript. This is a crucial time. What you must avoid is any temptation to stop and do wholesale revisions *before you have read the entire manuscript once*.

Think of this process as Google Earth. You want to get a complete overview of your "earth." Your novel. Your story as a whole. You can spin the earth a little here and there to get a better view, but stay up top. You'll tag a few places to visit later, to zoom in on. That'll be the nuts and bolts of revision.

First, it's essential to give yourself a break from the first draft. At least two weeks. During this "cooling phase," try to forget about your book completely. Then try to read the manuscript through in a couple of sittings—three or four at the most. What you want to create is the feeling of being a fresh reader, getting into this book for the first time.

Don't stop to make changes at this point. You may jot a few things down, notes to yourself and the like, but keep going to get the overall impression of the book. Too many writers just sit down and read a manuscript page by page, making changes as they come up. Big or small, each item is dealt with the moment it's seen. Much better is to go from large to small. To start with the most crucial aspects and work your way down to the final step, which is *The Polish*.

MAKING BIG-PICTURE REVISIONS

When it comes to revision, I've found that most writers need a systematic approach. Think of this, then, as your ultimate revision checklist. Apply these questions to every manuscript you write.

JAMES SCOTT BELL is a novelist and writer. This article excerpted with permission from *Write Great Fiction: Revision and Self-Editing* (Writer's Digest Books).

Lead Character

- Is my Lead worth following for a whole novel? Why?
- How can I make my Lead "jump off the page" more?
- Do my characters sufficiently contrast? Are they interesting enough on their own?
- Will readers bond to my Lead because he:
  - . . . cares for someone other than himself?
  - . . . is funny, irreverent, or a rebel with a cause?
  - . . . is competent at something?
  - . . . is an underdog facing long odds without giving up?
  - . . . has a dream or desire readers can relate to?
  - . . . has undeserved misfortune, but doesn't whine about it?
  - . . . is in jeopardy or danger?

Opposition Character

- Is the opposition character just as fully realized as the Lead?
- Is his behavior justified (in his own mind)?
- Are you being "fair" with the opposition?
- Is he as strong or (preferably) stronger than the Lead, in terms of ability to win the fight?

Plot

- Is there any point where a reader might feel like putting the book down?
- Does the plot feel forced or unnatural?
- Is the story out of balance? Too much action? Too much reaction?

The Opening

- Do I open with some part of the story engine running? Or am I spending too much time warming up?
- How do my opening pages conform to Hitchcock's axiom ("A good story is life with the dull parts taken out")? What is the *story world* I'm trying to present?
- What mood descriptions bring that story world to life for the reader?
- What is the tone of my novel going to be? Are the descriptions consistent with that mood?
- What happens in Act I that's going to compel the reader to keep reading? What danger to the Lead? Is there enough conflict in the setup to run through the whole book?
- Do I deepen character relationships? Why should the reader care what's happening?
- Have I justified the final battle or final choice that will wrap things up at the end? Is there a sense of death (physical, professional, or psychological) that overhangs?
- Is there a strong adhesive keeping the characters together (such as moral or professional duty, physical location, or other reasons characters can't just walk away)?

Endings

- Are there loose threads left dangling? (You must either resolve these in a way that doesn't distract from the main plotline, or go back and snip them out.)
- Do I give a feeling of resonance? (The best endings leave a sense of something beyond the confines of the book covers.)
- Will the readers *feel* the way I want them to feel?

Scenes

- Is there conflict or tension in every scene?
- Do I establish a viewpoint character?
- If the scene is action, is the objective clear?

• If the scene is reaction, is the emotion clear?

Exposition
• Do I have large chunks of information dumped in one spot?
• Is my exposition doing *double duty*? Cut out any exposition that doesn't also add to the mood or tone of your novel.

Voice, Style, & Point of View
• Are there sections where the style seems forced or stilted? (Try reading it out loud. Hearing it will often help identify places to be cut or modified.)
• Is the POV consistent in every scene?
• If writing in first person, can the character see and feel what it is I describe?
• If writing in third person, do I slip into the thoughts of other characters rather than sticking to the POV character in the scene? Do I describe something the character can't see or feel?

Setting & Description
• Have I brought the setting to life for the reader?
• Does the setting operate as a "character"?
• Are my descriptions of places and people too generic?
• Are my descriptions doing "double duty" by adding to the mood or tone?

Dialogue
• Can I put in non-sequiturs, or answer a question with a question, and so on?
• Can I change some attributions—*he said, she said*—to action beats?
• Does my dialogue have conflict or tension, even between allies?

Theme
• Do I know what my theme is?
• Has a different theme emerged in the writing? Am I fighting it?
• Have I woven in thematic elements naturally?
• Have I avoided "the lecture"?

THE POLISH
Now, before you send off the manuscript, give it one more going over. This won't take long in comparison, but it will add that extra sparkle that could make all the difference.

Chapter Openings
• Can you begin a little further in?
• Does the opening grab? Have a hint of conflict or action?
• Do most of your chapters begin the same way? Vary them.

Chapter Endings
• Do most of your chapters end the same way? Vary them.
• Can you end the chapter earlier? How does it feel? If it's better, use it.

Dialogue
• Is there plenty of "white space" in your dialogue exchanges?
• Can you cut any words to make the dialogue tighter?

Word Search
• Do a word search for those repeated words and phrases you tend to overuse, then

modify them accordingly.
- Look for overuse of the words "very," "really," and "suddenly."
- Adverbs are usually not necessary, and the emotion you're trying to clarify can be better shown through action.

Big Moments
- Identify five big moments in your manuscript. After each moment, make a list of 10 ways you can heighten that moment, make it more intense, and give it more juice.

WHAT THE PROCESS LOOKS LIKE

Below are two versions of a section from my novel, *Sins of the Fathers*. The first is my original. The second shows a little of the thinking process that goes into self-editing.

Original Version

First came the children.

In Lindy's dream they were running and screaming, dozens of them, in some sunlit field. A billowing surge of terrified kids, boys and girls, some in baseball garb, others in variegated ragtag clothes that gave the impression of a Dickens novel run amok.

What was behind them, what was causing the terror, was something dark, unseen. In the hovering over visions that only dreams afford, Lindy sought desperately the source of the fear.

There was a black forest behind the field, like you'd see in fairy tales. Or nightmares.

She moved toward the forest, knowing who it was, who was in there, and she'd meet him coming out. It would be Darren DiCinni, and he would have a gun, and in the dream she kept low to avoid being shot herself.

Moving closer and closer now, the screams of the scattering children fading behind her. Without having to look behind she knew that a raft of cops was pulling up to the scene.

She wondered if she was going to warn DiCinni, or was she just going to look at him?

Would he say anything to her, or she to him?

The dark forest had the kind of trees that come alive at night, with gnarly arms and knotted trunks. It was the place where the bad things lived.

Lindy didn't want to go in, but she couldn't stop herself.

That's when the dark figure started to materialize, from deep within the forest, and he was running toward her.

Edited Version

First came the children.

In Lindy's dream they were running and screaming, dozens of them, in some sunlit field. A billowing surge of terrified kids, boys and girls, some in baseball garb, others in variegated ragtag clothes that gave the impression of a Dickens novel run amok.

~~What was behind them, what was causing the terror, was something dark, unseen.~~ [Weak sentence structure. Rethink. Check "dark." I use it a lot!] ~~In the hovering over visions~~ [Confusing.] that only dreams afford, Lindy sought desperately the source of the fear.

There was [Sentences starting with "There" are generally weak. Rethink.] a black forest behind the field, like you'd see [Using "you" in this way can be effective in some places, but overuse is not good. Rethink.] in fairy tales. Or nightmares.

She moved toward the forest, ~~knowing who it was, who was in there,~~ [Awkward.] and she'd meet him coming out. ~~It would be Darren DiCinni, and he would have a gun, and in the dream she kept low to avoid being shot herself.~~ [See if I can strengthen this dramatic image.]

Moving closer and closer now, the screams of the scattering children fading behind her. Without having to look behind she knew that a raft of cops was pulling up to the scene.

~~She wondered if she was going to warn DiCinni, or was she just going to look at him?~~ [Tighten.]

Would he say anything to her, or she to him?

~~The dark forest had the kind of trees that come alive at night, with gnarly arms and knotted trunks. It was the place where the bad things lived.~~ [Rethink. There's "dark" again.]

Lindy didn't want to go in, but she couldn't stop herself.

~~That's when~~ [Unneeded verbiage.] the dark figure started to materialize, from deep within the forest, and ~~he~~ [How do we know it's *he*?] was running toward her.

LEARNING TO BE A REAL WRITER

Self-editing is the ability to *know* what makes fiction work. You learn to be your own guide so you may, as Renni Browne and Dave King put it in *Self-Editing for Fiction Writers*, "See your manuscript the way an editor might see it—to do for yourself what a publishing house editor once might have done."

By practicing self-editing exercises and revising your work, you'll be operating on all cylinders. This is how you become a real writer. Cutting, shaping, adding, subtracting, working it, making it better, that's what real writing is all about. This is how unpublished writers become published.

Beginnings

The Writing Chore that
Demands Perfection

by Maralys Wills

There is no job more difficult than penning the opening lines of a book. Whatever the genre, it's as though you've been granted one minute to sell a reader on your 400-page manuscript. With each discarded attempt, you recognize anew the difficulty of capturing the soul of your work in only a few lines. Or if not the soul, at least a tantalizing moment, an outrageous attitude, a startling event or a compelling story question. Worse, the requirement intensifies if the book is a novel or memoir—meaning if your opening's no good, you might as well toss out the rest of the book.

Opening lines are so demanding that I've learned to loathe, fear, deplore and agonize over them. Are these few sentences good enough? Can they be made better still? Shall I ruthlessly delete them and start over? I'm not alone; all striving authors quake before the Almighty Opening Lines.

The importance of openings is preached endlessly by speakers at writers conferences, who impart as a dark secret what few editors or agents will admit publicly: If you don't hook readers in the first few lines, the rest of your book doesn't matter. No one will read on. So what constitutes a good beginning, anyway? The quick, useless answer is anything that makes you eager to read on—anything that raises irresistible story questions. With that in mind, let's look at some examples of story beginnings that worked.

ATTITUDE

Good beginnings employ all sorts of tactics. One of the best tactics is to display attitude—meaning an opinion or mind-set or emotional bias for or against something. Examine *The Catcher in the Rye* by J.D. Salinger:

> "If you really want to hear about it, the first thing you'll probably want to know is where I was born, and what my lousy childhood was like, and how my parents were occupied and all before they had me, and all that David Copperfield kind of crap, but I don't feel like going into it."

Or *Keys to Rebecca* by Ken Follett:

> "The last camel collapsed at noon. It was the five-year-old white bull he had bought in Gialo, the youngest and strongest of the three beasts, and the least

MARALYS WILLS (DamntheRejections.com) is the author of *Damn the Rejections, Full Speed Ahead: The Bumpy Road to Getting Published* (Stephens Press), the book from which this article is excerpted. She has also written another dozen books in multiple genres. She talks on writing subjects at conferences and workshops around the country.

ill-tempered. He liked the animal as much as a man could like a camel, which is to say that he hated it only a little."

AN ELEMENT OF SURPRISE

An element of surprise—catching a reader off guard and wanting to know more—is a tried-and-true method of beginning a work. Consider this example from an unknown romance author:

"From the waist down, he looked promising."

Or *Windmills of the Gods* by Sidney Sheldon:

"Stanton Rogers was destined to be President of the United States. He was a charismatic politician, highly visible to an approving public, and backed by powerful friends. Unfortunately for Rogers, his libido got in the way of his career. Or, as the Washington mavens put it: 'Old Stanton fucked himself out of the presidency.' "

Or *Through the Narrow Gate* by Karen Armstrong:

"It was 14 September 1962, the most important day of my life. On the station platform, my parents and my sister, Lindsey, were clustered together in a sad little knot, taking their last look at me. I was seventeen years old and was leaving them forever to become a nun."

Or *Running from the Law* by Lisa Scottoline:

"Any good poker player will tell you the secret to a winning bluff is believing it yourself."

TRAGEDY

A tragedy of some kind (or hint of a tragedy), especially a death, can be a compelling hook. Examine *The Lovely Bones* by Alice Sebold:

"My name was Salmon, like the fish; first name, Susie. I was fourteen when I was murdered on December 6, 1973."

Or *Eric*, by Doris Lund:

"Good friends have said, 'But how did it begin? You must have seen it coming.' No one could have seen it coming. This had been a summer like many others . . ."

Or *The Joy Luck Club* by Amy Tan:

"My father has asked me to be the fourth corner at the Joy Luck Club. I am to replace my mother, whose seat at the mah jong table has been empty since she died two months ago. My father thinks she was killed by her own thoughts. 'She had a new idea inside her head,' said my father. 'But before it could come out of her mouth the thought grew too big and burst. It must have been a very bad idea.'"

STRONG ATMOSPHERE

Beware description to start a novel. A cliché novel opening involves describing the weather and light from the sunset. But *atmosphere*, if down well, is something different. A strong mood or atmosphere can provide a compelling start. See this example from *The Old Man and the Sea* by Ernest Hemingway:

"He was an old man who fished alone in a skiff in the Gulf Stream and he had gone eighty-four days now without taking a fish."

Or *The Summer of the Barshinskeys* by Diane Pearson:

"The first time I saw Mr. Barshinskey he was strolling across Tyler's meadow with a fiddle under his arm. He was singing at the top of his voice in a language none of us could understand, and around the crown of his black hat was a garland of buttercups."

Or *Angela's Ashes* by Frank McCourt:

"My father and mother should have stayed in New York where they met and married and where I was born. Instead, they returned to Ireland when I was four, my brother, Malachy, three, the twins, Oliver and Eugene, barely one, and my sister, Margaret, dead and gone. When I look back on my childhood I wonder how I survived at all. It was, of course, a miserable childhood: the happy childhood is hardly worth your while. Worse than the ordinary miserable childhood is the miserable Irish childhood, and worse yet is the miserable Irish Catholic childhood."

And I shamelessly offer one of my own books, *Scatterpath* by Maralys Wills:

"James Higgins was suddenly fed up with disasters. Eleven consecutive months of viewing charred bodies and reconstructing the mangled chunks of jet engines had left him drained and ready to hang up his job."

INTERESTING OBSERVATION

A thoughtful, interesting observation helps establish the writer's style/voice and makes for an intriguing start. See this example from *Onions in the Stew* by Betty MacDonald:

"For twelve years we MacDonalds have been living on an island in Puget Sound. There is no getting away from it, life on an island is different from life in the St. Francis hotel."

Or try *The Firm* by John Grisham:

"The senior partner studied the résumé for the hundredth time and again found nothing he disliked about Mitchell Y. McDeere, at least not on paper. He had the brains, the ambition, the good looks. And he was hungry; with his background, he had to be."

IRONY OR HUMOR

A final opening ploy is the use of irony or humor. See this example from *Horowitz and Mrs. Washington* by Henry Denker:

"'Mister, a man your age does not resist muggers! You could have got yourself killed!' the irritated cop rebuked Samuel Horowitz in a quite forceful tone. Horowitz sat silent while the nervous young black intern attempted to suture the ugly wound. But he could not keep from thinking, Some doctor! Where did anyone ever get the idea that a black kid could be a good doctor? To be a good doctor, a man had to be Jewish."

Or *Why I'm Like This* by Cynthia Kaplan:

"There was always one girl at camp whom everyone hated. It had nothing to do with cliques or teams or personal dislikes, and it was not even that everyone had discussed it and a consensus had been raised upon certain irrefutable evidence.

It was just like everyone hated lima beans and the color brown. It was obvious and it was universal, so it didn't require organization."

START WITH DRAMA

Okay, so not all the examples above are from famous writers. But it doesn't matter, because each of these books has a beginning that is different in some way from the ordinary conversation you'd hear on the street. Each poses questions that are so compelling they grab the reader's hand and drag him into the story. One element they all have in common is *immediacy*—an ability to drop the reader quickly into the world of the story. The story seems to be already in progress when the reader gets there. Fists are flying, curses fill the air, and the reader just makes it to the balcony, he's just started to peer down. Furthermore, the story has arrived, or is about to arrive, at some dramatic moment—the beginning of great change, a turning point, a dramatic highlight that will alter the characters forever. It's as though we've happened in at a critical time and are witnessing a vital event—and nothing will ever be the same again.

When one of my students asks, "Where shall I begin my book?" I always ask in return, "What is the most dramatic thing that happens in your story?" then tell them to start at that moment. Notice how not one of the above books begins with background information, and none begin at the "actual start" of the events that make up the story. Almost every beginning is dramatic or hints at drama: a boy hates his parents; the last essential camel dies; a man loses his chance at the presidency; a girl leaves home to become a nun; a son dies; a girl is murdered; a Chinese mother dies. High drama everywhere.

In a class I teach, we discuss beginnings a lot. Sometimes, when defending a slow start, a student will protest: "But the reader has to know all these details. He has to know the facts before he'll understand what's going on." Not true, I say. "The reader doesn't need to be told most of these things at all. Just relax. Drop your reader into the middle of your story and tell him only as much as he absolutely must know at that moment." Whatever else the reader needs to know, he'll find out as he goes. And whatever facts are not vitally important, he may never learn at all.

If you can excite agents at the beginning, you'll hold their attention and force them to read on.

100 Writing Prompts

Looking for Ideas? We've Got You Covered

by E.L. Collins

1. A teenager finds out that his father was a priest and his mother a nun.

2. "I'm here to answer the ad in the paper."

3. "Seriously, I was eating at the same restaurant as him, and let me tell you, he didn't look like such a 'badass' to me."

4. A woman awakens to find herself levitating above the bed.

5. During the State Fair Opening Ceremonies, a prize-winning animal is kidnapped.

6. A group of salesmen on their way to a company retreat decide to stop and investigate a strange-looking suitcase on the side of the road.

7. "If we have this conversation, it's going to end badly for you. Consider that a fair warning."

8. "I'm sorry, sir, but she checked out last night."

9. A stay-at-home dad joins the neighborhood "mommies club."

10. "C'mon, let's try it. They test this stuff all the time to make sure it's safe."

11. "Do you ever feel like you just haven't got the common sense that everyone else was born with?"

12. While traveling abroad, a nurse finds herself on a tour bus with an expectant mother who begins to go into labor.

13. "I'm sure that's an urban legend."

14. A PR firm's newest client becomes a public relations nightmare.

15. "I've seen enough monkeys for one day, thank you very much."

16. A young woman must run errands while wearing an embarrassing and inappropriate outfit.

17. You arrive at your office to find that your personal belongings have been boxed up.

18. "Thanks for seeing me. I need to discuss something important, and I didn't want to do it over the phone."

E.L. COLLINS is a Virginia-based writer and freelancer. These prompts excerpted with permission from *The Writer's Book of Matches: 1,001 Prompts to Ignite Your Fiction* (Writer's Digest Books).

19. "Mom, Principal Sanderson is on the phone. He wants to talk to you."

20. A journalist doing a story on what it's like to live on death row begins to fall for one of the inmates she's been interviewing.

21. What appears to be the fuselage of a strange aircraft is uncovered during the site excavation for a future strip mall.

22. A nurse in a mental hospital discovers that a well-known missing person is being held there against her will.

23. "I think you're out of options."

24. "Are you following me?"

25. You win a seat on the first commercial space shuttle flight.

26. After a near-death experience, a young man is haunted by visions of a beautiful yet terrifying afterlife.

27. While serving a long tour of duty overseas, a soldier becomes distraught that he can't remember his wife's face.

28. A family member disappears while vacationing on a cruise ship.

29. "It would be best if you put that back where you found it, sir."

30. An alcoholic attends his first social event since leaving rehab.

31. Though paralyzed by his fear of heights, a man considers bungee jumping to impress someone.

32. A renowned psychic finds that her powers of precognition have vanished.

33. It is a discovered that the pie in a small-town diner has curative properties.

34. After watching Eminem's movie *8 Mile*, a mild-mannered businessman is inspired to participate in a rap battle.

35. "If you can guess what I have in my pocket, you can have it."

36. A philanthropist's plane crashes in the jungle, where the native tribe he has fought so hard to protect begins hunting him.

37. "I just want to kiss him. I know it's the wrong time, the wrong place, but I don't care."

38. The morning after a heavy snowfall, a single man sees a set of footprints leading away from his house.

39. After falling asleep on his shift, a prison guard awakens to find that all of the cells are empty.

40. After completing a solo camping trip, a woman gets her film developed and discovers that several of the photos are of her … sleeping.

41. A man's doorbell rings. He looks through the peephole to see a figure wearing a yellow jumpsuit and a motorcycle helmet with wings painted on each side.

42. "At least I'm walking out of this alive."

43. A psychiatrist is offered a large sum of money to treat a patient, but he must first sign a contract stating that he will never reveal the patient's identity to anyone. If he does, the consequences will be severe.

44. "Helpful hint: Wait until you're sober before trying that again."

45. "So they can't get the landing gear down and we were up there just circling for, like, three hours."

46. "I can't believe you've taken up jogging. What about our pact?"

47. A young woman loses her ability to speak, save for one word.

48. "Oh I'll propose a toast to happy couple, all right..."

49. In the middle of the night, a man rolls over just in time to see his wife pull on a pajama top. In the moonlight, he notices bruises/marks on her arms that weren't there when they went to bed.

50. "It's always the quiet ones, you know."

51. "You have ten seconds..."

52. Two high school sweethearts arrange to meet for a drink fifteen years after graduation.

53. "Mom, you've got to stop dragging me into the middle of things."

54. A man in a business suit, briefcase handcuffed to his wrist, stands on a quiet beach watching the sunrise.

55. "Yeah, she's got two kids, but so what?"

56. An unstable, institutionalized woman believes herself to be a time traveler. She vows to escape to return to her own era.

57. An infertile woman wants a child so badly that she starts to contemplate some unthinkable options.

58. "I'm going to disappoint you. But you knew that already."

59. "None of that 'eye for an eye' bullshit. I just want him dead."

60. While surfing porn on the Internet, a man comes across a picture of his wife.

61. "You'll notice my wife doesn't drink."

62. A woman discovers that her boyfriend's apartment is bugged with surveillance equipment.

63. "Who are these women who keep calling the house? And why do they call you 'Mr. President'?"

64. On his way to propose to his girlfriend, a man is approached on the subway by four youths.

65. A married woman attends a teamwork training retreat with several co-workers. Upon arriving, an attractive man from her office suggests that they start an affair.

66. A radio talk jock plans a farewell show as his station prepares to change to a soft rock format.

67. A drug addict's only supplier is killed in a police raid.

68. A woman learns that one of her young daughters has used a home pregnancy test.

69. "Whatever you do, don't go outside."

70. A telemarketer begins to receive telephone threats from the customer she just called moments before.

71. "You need special permission to view this material."

72. Two friends decide to ditch school for the day and explore the nearby sewer tunnels.

73. After practicing his act for years, a man finally gets the chance to audition for a television variety show.

74. A riot breaks out at a candlelight vigil for a dead rock star.

75. "Remember how you said my marriage wouldn't last a year? Well…"

76. "How much do you know about guns?"

77. A young man of North-African descent, but who has lived in the United States almost his whole life, is deported back to the country he never knew.

78. A therapist at a battered women's shelter is beaten up by her boyfriend.

79. "She lost the baby."

80. Big tobacco announces that smoking increases penis size.

81. A Florida game warden volunteers to work undercover to apprehend members of an alligator-poaching ring.

82. "Can you *please* turn the camera off?"

83. A young man works his way into an apprenticeship with a slick salesman.

84. An architect is informed that his current project bears an uncanny resemblance to a "haunted" hotel destroyed decades earlier.

85. "Well, he said we were pretty drunk at the time."

86. Faced with poverty, a retired exotic dancer concocts a plan to take Broadway by storm.

87. An ant decides to take his revenge upon the man who stepped on his family.

88. "Is it true what they say about you?"

89. A frustrated artist finds himself temporarily inspired after committing an act of violence.

90. You're secretly in love with your best friend's wife, and you suspect she feels the same way about you.

91. A woman walks into a grocery store, but when she walks out, many things have changed.

92. A teenage girl's dead grandmother starts appearing in her dreams and revealing family secrets.

93. "How am I supposed to go to the bathroom with this on?"

94. A man gets out of bed one morning and discovers that he's a foot shorter that the day before.

95. Believing the floating lights in his backward to be fireflies, a young boy accidentally traps a fairy in a Mason jar.

96. An accountant believes that his "sick" co-worker has been killed by her husband.

97. "You won't believe what I just got in the mail."

98. "They said I'd never walk again. Ha—what did they know?"

99. While on a camping trip, a little boy strays from his family and happens upon a carnival in the middle of nowhere.

100. "I don't care if this is a recorded threat. If you come near my wife again, I will kill you."

Avenues to an Agent

Getting Your Foot in the Door

Once your work is prepared and you have a solid understanding of how literary agents operate, the time is right to contact an agent. Your initial contact determines the agent's first impression of you, so you want to be professional and brief.

Again, research plays an important role in getting an agent's attention. You want to show the agent you've done your homework. Read the listings in this book to learn agents' areas of interest, check out agents' websites to learn more details on how they do business, and find out the names of some of their clients. If there is an author whose book is similar to yours, call the author's publisher. Someone in the contracts department can tell you the name of the agent who sold the title, provided an agent was used. Contact that agent, and impress her with your knowledge of the agency.

Finding an agent can often be as difficult as finding a publisher. Nevertheless, there are four ways to maximize your chances of finding the right agent: submit a query letter or proposal; obtain a referral from someone who knows the agent; meet the agent in person at a writers conference; or attract the agent's attention with your own published writing.

SUBMISSIONS

The most common way to contact an agent is through a query letter or a proposal package. Most agents will accept unsolicited queries. Some will also look at outlines and sample chapters. Almost none want unsolicited complete manuscripts. Check the "How to Contact" subhead in each listing to learn exactly how an agent prefers to be solicited.

Agents agree to be listed in directories such as *Guide to Literary Agents* to indicate what they want to see and how they wish to receive submissions from writers. As you start to query agents, make sure you follow their individual submission directions. This, too, shows an agent you've done your research.

Like publishers, agencies have specialties. Some are only interested in novel-length works. Others are open to a variety of subjects and may actually have member agents within the company who specialize in only a handful of the topics covered by the entire agency.

Before querying any agent, first consult the Agent Specialties Indexes in the back of this book for your manuscript's subject, and identify those agents who handle what you write. Then, read the agents' listings to see which are appropriate for you and your work.

REFERRALS

The best way to get your foot in an agent's door is through a referral from one of her clients, an editor or another agent she has worked with in the past. Since agents trust their clients, they'll usually read referred work before over-the-transom submissions. If you are friends

Communication Etiquette

Via Mail
- Address the agent formally and make sure her name is spelled correctly.
- Double-check the agency's address.
- Include a SASE.
- Use a clear font and standard paragraph formatting.
- A short handwritten thank-you note can be appropriate if the agent helped you at a conference or if she provided editorial feedback along with your rejection.
- Don't include any extraneous materials.
- Don't try to set yourself apart by using fancy stationery. Standard paper and envelopes are preferable.

Via E-mail
- Address the agent as you would in a paper letter—be formal.
- If it's not listed on the website, call the company to get the appropriate agent's e-mail address.
- Include a meaningful subject line.
- Keep your emotions in check: Resist the temptation to send an angry response after being rejected, or to send a long, mushy note after being accepted. Keep your e-mails businesslike.
- Don't type in all caps or all lower case. Use proper punctuation and pay attention to grammar and spelling.
- Don't overuse humor—it can be easily misinterpreted.
- Don't e-mail about trivial things.

On the Phone
- Be polite: Ask if she has time to talk, or set up a time to call in advance.
- Get over your "phone phobia." Practice your conversation beforehand if necessary.
- Resist the urge to follow up with an agent too quickly. Give her time to review your material.
- Never make your first contact over the phone unless the agent calls you first or requests you do so in her submission guidelines.
- Don't demand information from her immediately. Your phone call is interrupting her busy day and she should be given time to respond to your needs.
- Don't call to get information you could otherwise obtain from the Internet or other resources.
- Don't have your spouse, secretary, best friend or parent call for you.

In Person
- Be clear and concise.
- Shake the agent's hand and greet her with your name.
- Be yourself, but be professional.
- Maintain eye contact.
- Don't monopolize her time. Either ask a brief question or ask if you can contact her later (via phone/mail/e-mail) with a more in-depth question.
- Don't get too nervous—agents are human!

with anyone in the publishing business who has connections with agents, ask politely for a referral. However, don't be offended if another writer will not share the name of his agent.

CONFERENCES

Going to a conference is your best bet for meeting an agent in person. Many conferences invite agents to give a speech or simply be available for meetings with authors, and agents view conferences as a way to find writers. Often agents set aside time for one-on-one discussions with writers, and occasionally they may even look at material writers bring to the conference. These critiques may cost an extra fee, but if an agent is impressed with you and your work, she'll ask to see writing samples after the conference. When you send your query, be sure to mention the specific conference where you met and that she asked to see your work.

When you're face to face with an agent, it's an important time to be friendly, prepared and professional. Always wait for the agent to invite you to send work to them. Saying "I'll send it to your office tomorrow" before they've offered to read it comes off wrong. Don't bring sample chapters or a copy of your manuscript unless you've got a professional critique arranged beforehand. Agents will almost never take writers' work home (they don't have the suitcase space), and writers nervously asking agents to take a look at their work and provide some advice could be considered gauche.

Remember, at these conferences, agents' time is very valuable—as is yours. If you discover that agent who's high on your list recently stopped handling your genre, don't hunt her down and try to convince her to take it on again. Thank the agent for her time and move on to your next target.

If you plan to pitch agents, practice your speech—and make sure you have a pitch that clocks in at less than one minute. Also have versions of your pitch for 2-minute pitches and 3-minute pitches, depending on the conference. Keep your in-person pitch simple and exciting—letting the agent become interested and ask the follow-up questions.

Because this is an effective way to connect with agents, we've asked agents to indicate in their listings which conferences they regularly attend. We've also included a section of Conferences, starting on page 266, where you can find more information about a particular event.

PUBLISHING CREDITS

Some agents read magazines or journals to find writers to represent. If you have had an outstanding piece published in a periodical, an agent wanting to represent you may make contact. In such cases, make sure the agent has read your work. Some agents send form letters to writers, and such representatives often make their living entirely from charging reading fees and not from commissions on sales.

However, many reputable and respected agents do contact potential clients in this way. For them, you already possess attributes of a good client: You have publishing credits and an editor has validated your work. To receive a letter from a reputable agent who has read your material and wants to represent you is an honor.

Occasionally, writers who have self-published or who have had their work published electronically may attract an agent's attention, especially if the self-published book has sold well or received a lot of positive reviews.

Recently, writers have been posting their work on the Internet with the hope of attracting an agent's eye. With all the submissions most agents receive, they probably have little time to peruse writers' websites. Nevertheless, there are agents who do consider the Internet a resource for finding fresh voices.

Contacting Agents

Research Agents

Get Personal Using Resources and the Web

by C. Hope Clark

I clicked from website to website, one blog to another, all telling me my chances of finding an agent were slim in the current publishing environment. Statistics spouted success rates of one half of one percent. One agent read 8,000 queries in a year and only signed five new clients. Some agents even posted the number of queries they received each week versus the number of manuscripts requested. All too often the percentage equaled zero. Hell-bent on beating the odds, I devised a plan to find my agent.

Throughout the course of twenty months, I submitted 72 queries, opened 55 rejections, and received invitations for seven complete manuscripts. I landed an 88-percent response rate, and finally, a contract with an agent. How did I do it? I got personal.

WHERE TO FIND AGENTS

Many writers cringe at the thought of researching the publishing business. You must be better than that. Embrace the research, especially if it leads to representation. The more you analyze the rules, the players, the successes and failures, the more you increase your chances of signing a contract with a representative. Set aside time (i.e., days, weeks) to educate yourself about these professionals. You have your manuscript, your synopsis, a list of published books like yours, and a biography. You've edited and re-edited your query so it's tight as a drum. Now focus. Who do you see as your handler, your mentor, your guide through the publishing maze? And where do you find him or her?

Agency websites

Most literary houses maintain a website. They post guidelines and books they've pushed into the marketplace. They also inform you about the individual agents on staff—including bios, favorite reads, writing styles they prefer, photos, and maybe where they attended school. Read all the notes have to offer, taking notes. If any agent represents your type of work, record what they prefer in a query and move on to their blog, if they keep one.

Blogs

Agent blogs reveal clues about what agents prefer. While websites are static in design, blogs allow comments. Here agents offer information about publishing changes, new releases—even their vacations and luncheons with movers and shakers in the industry. Some agents

---

C. HOPE CLARK is founder of FundsforWriters.com, a ten-year winner of *Writer's Digest*'s 101 Best Websites for Writers. She writes commercial nonfiction by day and mysteries by night from her lakeside home in South Carolina.

solicit feedback with dynamic dilemmas or ethical obstacles. Nathan Bransford of Curtis Brown, Mary Kole of the Andrea Brown Literary Agency, and Rachelle Gardner of WordServe Literary Agency have been known to post short contests for their blog readers, if for no other reason than to emphasize what they seek in a client. For a complete list of agent blogs, go to the GLA blog (guidetoliteraryagents.com/blog) and see them on the left.

Guidebooks and Databases

The *Guide to Literary Agents* is a premier example of a guidebook resource. Use it to cull the agents who don't suit your taste and those who seek writers just like you. PublishersMarketplace.com and WritersMarket.com offer online, fingertip access to the websites, addresses and desires of most agents—and also point you in other directions to learn more.

Facebook and Twitter

Social networking has enabled writers to see yet another side of agents. These mini-versions of agents' lives can spark ideas for you to use in a query as well as help you digest the publishing world through professional eyes.

Conferences

Margot Starbuck, author of *The Girl in the Orange Dress* and *Unsqueezed: Springing Free from Skinny Jeans*, met her agent at a writers conference. "He had given a seminar that was essentially themed, 'My Perfect Client,' describing the type of writer he'd want to represent. When I got home, I crafted my letter to his own specs!"

It's easier to query an agent you've met, who you've heard, who has articulated what he likes. That subtle Midwestern accent you would not have heard otherwise might trigger you to pitch about your travel book or romance set in Nebraska. A one-hour class might empower you to query a particular agent after hearing her pet peeves and desires.

Online Interviews

Google an agent's name and the word "interview." Authors, writers' organizations, magazines, and commercial writing sites post such interviews to attract readers. A current Q&A might prompt you to reword that query opening and tag an agent's interest. The agent might express a wish to read less women's fiction and more young adult novels these days— information not spelled out on her website profile. She might reveal a weakness for Southern writing. Reps also hop from agency to agency, and a timely interview might let you know she's changed location.

THE PLAN

Not wanting to collaborate with a complete stranger, I began dissecting agents' information to get a better feel for them. After noting 1) name, 2) agency, 3) query preferences, and 4) an address for each potential agent on a spreadsheet column, I dug down more for what I deemed the "zing" factor—the human factor. As a previous human resource director, I knew the power of connection. An applicant attending the same university as the manager often warranted a second glance. A first-time interviewee who played golf might reap a return invitation. Why couldn't this concept apply to literary agents? I was a job seeker; they were hiring. How could I make them take a second look at me and the fabulous writing I offered?

I reread bios and Googled deeper; I studied interviews and deciphered blogs. I read between the lines, earnestly seeking what made these people more than agents. Just like I canvassed the doctors and hairdressers in my life, I investigated these people for characteristics that bridged their preferences with mine.

The Zing Factors

The human connection between you and an agent is what I call the "zing" factor. These agents receive hundreds of queries per week, most skimmed or unread. You never know when an agent has been up all night with a sick child or arrived at work fighting the flu. You have no control over the timing that places your query in an agent's hands. What you can control is a creative opening that doesn't echo like the thirty before it and the twenty after, and rises to the top even if the reader hasn't had his coffee.

Agents hate to be taken for granted or treated like an anonymous personality (i.e., Dear Agent). The attention you give to zing factors will demonstrate that you respect the agent as a person. Suddenly you have that magical connection that holds his attention at least long enough to read your dead-on synopsis.

What makes for a great conduit between you and your agent? Anything and everything.

Clientele—Signing good authors and landing great contracts make an agent proud. If you intend to become part of an agency's stable of authors, become familiar with who occupies the neighboring stalls. Recognize agents for what they have accomplished.

Author Tanya Egan Gibson not only emphasized her knowledge of Susan Golomb's clients, but she contacted one of the authors and asked permission to use him as a reference after meeting at a conference. The query won her representation and, later, a contract with Dutton Publishers.

Christine Chitnis introduced herself to other authors at a retreat where they shared critiques and ideas. Once she completed her manuscript, she pitched to the agents of those authors, knowing they could vouch for the quality of her work. She acquired an agent after two attempts.

Previous Meetings—A dinner table discussion with an agent at a conference could provide the lead for your next query. Make a point to meet and greet agents at these functions. They expect it. Give and take in the conversations. Don't smother them with your views. Listen for advice. Be polite. Afterward, before the experience evaporates, record notes about the topics discussed, the locale, maybe even the jokes or awkward speaker. The zing factor becomes instant recall when you remind an agent you met over dinner, during a fast-pitch, or over drinks. You evolve into a person instead of another faceless query.

Recognition—In your query, include where you found the agent's name. Congratulate him or her on recent contracts for books that sound similar to yours. You'll find this information through a website called PublishersMarketplace or on the agency's website, blog, tweets, or Facebook page.

Favorite Reads—Agents are voracious readers, and, like any word geeks, they have favorite genre, authors, and styles. Website bios often mention what sits on their nightstand, and blogs might post writers they admire. Note where you uncovered this information and marvel at your similarities, particularly if your work parallels the subjects.

Geography—All agents aren't born and reared in New York. With the ease of communication these days, agents live everywhere and telecommute. They also come from other places, and those roots might marry with yours. A New York agent who grew up in Smyrna, Georgia might have a soft spot for Civil War nonfiction.

Personal Interests—Agents have lives and off-duty pastimes. When author Nina Amir first contacted her agent, she also noted a mutual love of horses—in particular, a desire to save ex-racehorses from slaughter. The agent immediately called her.

In pitching to literary agent Verna Dreisbach, I revealed a common interest in mentoring teenage writers, knowing Verna founded Capitol City Young Writers, a nonprofit for youth interested in writing and publishing. Since my proposal was a mystery and I married a federal agent, I also admired her past work in law enforcement. Later, when asked if those initial items caught her attention, Verna responded in the positive. "Of course it made an impact. Writing with a degree of expertise in any field is crucial, including law enforcement. I looked forward to reading your work. I choose to represent authors that I have a connection with, and your interests and aspirations certainly fit well with mine. As I expected, we hit it off immediately."

PASSION

Nothing, however, replaces the ability to show passion in your work. Genuine excitement over your book is contagious, and agents spot it in an instant. Carole Bartholomeaux unknowingly personalized her query through her passion. Her agent, an expectant father at the time, was touched by her story about a small town putting their lives on the line to save a group of Jewish children during World War II. You are the biggest advocate for your book, with your agent a close second. Everyone in your path should feel that energy. When agents sense it, they jump on your bandwagon knowing that readers will do the same.

When asked which grabbed her attention more, the personalization or the writing, Dreisbach replied diplomatically yet succinctly: "Both are equally important—authors who are personal and professional. Just as in any business, it is important to stand out from the crowd. I do not mean by being bizarre or unusual, but through the expression of a writer's passion, honesty and talent."

Don't cheapen yourself, though. Nathan Bransford, agent and award-winning blogger, gives his opinion about personalizing a query: "The goal of personalization isn't to suck up to the agent and score cheap points. As much as some people think we agents just want people to suck up to us, it's really not true. There is an art to personalization. Dedication and diligence are important, so if you query me, I hope you'll do your homework, and sure, if you've read books by my clients, mention that. Just don't try and trick me."

So be genuine. Be your passionate self and the person who obviously has done the research. A relationship with an agent is to be entered seriously and practically, with both parties sharing excitement for a common goal.

Contacting agents

How Not to Write Your Chapter 1

Agents Spill the Beans

Ask literary agents what they're looking for in a first chapter and they'll all say the same thing: "Good writing that hooks me in." Agents appreciate the same elements of good writing that readers do. They want action; they want compelling characters and a reason to read on; they want to see your voice come through in the work and feel an immediate connection with your writing style.

Sure, the fact that agents look for great writing and a unique voice is nothing new. But, for as much as you know about what agents want to see in chapter one, what about all those things they don't want to see? Obvious mistakes such as grammatical errors and awkward writing aside, writers need to be conscious of first-chapter clichés and agent pet peeves—any of which can sink a manuscript and send a form rejection letter your way.

Have you ever begun a story with a character waking up from a dream? Or opened chapter one with a line of salacious dialogue? Both clichés! Chances are, you've started a story with a cliché or touched on a pet peeve (or many!) in your writing and you don't even know it—and nothing turns off an agent like what agent Cricket Freeman of the August Agency calls "nerve-gangling, major turn-off, ugly-as-sin, nails-on-the-blackboard pet peeves."

To help compile a grand list of these poisonous chapter one no-no's, dozens of established literary agents were more than happy to chime in and vent about everything that they can't stand to see in that all-important first chapter. Here's what they had to say.

DESCRIPTION

"I dislike endless 'laundry list' character descriptions. For example: 'She had eyes the color of a summer sky and long blonde hair that fell in ringlets past her shoulders. Her petite nose was the perfect size for her heart-shaped face. Her azure dress—with the empire waist and long, tight sleeves—sported tiny pearl buttons down the bodice and ivory lace peeked out of the hem in front, blah, blah, blah.' Who cares! Work it into the story."
—**Laurie McLean**, Larsen/Pomada, Literary Agents

"Slow writing with a lot of description will put me off very quickly. I personally like a first chapter that moves quickly and draws me in so I'm immediately hooked and want to read more."
—**Andrea Hurst**, Andrea Hurst & Associates Literary Management

VOICE AND POINT-OF-VIEW

"A pet peeve of mine is ragged, fuzzy point-of-view. How can a reader follow what's happening? I also dislike beginning with a killer's POV. What reader would want to be in such an ugly place? I feel like a nasty voyeur."
—**Cricket Freeman**, The August Agency

"An opening that's predictable will not hook me in. If the average person could have come up with the characters and situations, I'll pass. I'm looking for a unique outlook, voice, or character and situation."
—**Debbie Carter**, Muse Literary Management

"Avoid the opening line 'My name is …,' introducing the narrator to the reader so blatantly. There are far better ways in chapter one to establish an instant connection between narrator and reader."
—**Michelle Andelman**, Lynn C. Franklin Associates

"I hate reading purple prose, taking the time to set up—to describe something so beautifully and that has nothing to do with the actual story. I also hate when an author starts something and then says '(the main character) would find out later.' I hate gratuitous sex and violence anywhere in the manuscript. If it is not crucial to the story then I don't want to see it in there, in any chapters."
—**Cherry Weiner**, Cherry Weiner Literary

"I recently read a manuscript when the second line was something like, 'Let me tell you this, Dear Reader …' What do you think of that?"
—**Sheree Bykofsky**, Sheree Bykofsky Literary

ACTION (OR LACK THEREOF)
"I don't really like first-day-of-school beginnings, or the 'From the beginning of time,' or 'Once upon a time' starts. Specifically, I dislike a chapter one where nothing happens."
—**Jessica Regel**, Jean V. Naggar Literary Agency

"'The Weather' is always a problem—the author feels he has to take time to set up the scene completely and tell us who the characters are, etc. I like starting a story in media res."
—**Elizabeth Pomada**, Larsen/Pomada, Literary Agents

"I want to feel as if I'm in the hands of a master storyteller, and starting a story with long, flowery, overly-descriptive sentences (kind of like this one) makes the writer seem amateurish and the story contrived. Of course, an equally jarring beginning can be nearly as off-putting, and I hesitate to read on if I'm feeling disoriented by the fifth page. I enjoy when writers can find a good balance between exposition and mystery. Too much accounting always ruins the mystery of a novel, and the unknown is what propels us to read further. It is what keeps me up at night saying, 'Just one more chapter, then I'll go to sleep.' If everything is explained away in the first chapter, I'm probably putting the book down and going to sleep."
—**Peter Miller**, Peter Miller Literary

"Characters that are moving around doing little things, but essentially nothing. Washing dishes and thinking, staring out the window and thinking, tying shoes, thinking. Authors often do this to transmit information, but the result is action in a literal sense but no real energy in a narrative sense. The best rule of thumb is always to start the story where the story starts."
—**Dan Lazar**, Writers House

CLICHÉS AND FALSE BEGINNINGS
"I hate it when a book begins with an adventure that turns out to be a dream at the end of the chapter."
—**Mollie Glick**, Foundry Literary + Media

"Anything cliché such as 'It was a dark and stormy night' will turn me off. I hate when a narrator or author addresses the reader (e.g., 'Gentle reader')."
—**Jennie Dunham**, Dunham Literary

"Sometimes a reasonably good writer will create an interesting character and describe him in a compelling way, but then he'll turn out to be some unimportant bit player. I also don't want to read about anyone sleeping, dreaming, waking up or staring at anything. Other annoying, unoriginal things I see too often: some young person going home to a small town for a funeral, someone getting a phone call about a death, a description of a psycho lurking in the shadows, or a terrorist planting a bomb."

—**Ellen Pepus**, Signature Literary Agency

"I don't like it when the main character dies at the end of chapter one. Why did I just spend all this time with this character? I feel cheated."

—**Cricket Freeman**, The August Agency

"1. Squinting into the sunlight with a hangover in a crime novel. Good grief—been done a million times. 2. A sci-fi novel that spends the first two pages describing the strange landscape. 3. A trite statement ('Get with the program' or 'Houston, we have a problem' or 'You go girl' or 'Earth to Michael' or 'Are we all on the same page?'), said by a weenie sales guy, usually in the opening paragraph. 4. A rape scene in a Christian novel, especially in the first chapter. 5. 'Years later, Monica would look back and laugh ...' 6. 'The [adjective] [adjective] sun rose in the [adjective] [adjective] sky, shedding its [adjective] light across the [adjective] [adjective] [adjective] land.' "

—**Chip MacGregor**, MacGregor Literary

"A cheesy 'hook' drives me nuts. I know that they say 'Open with a hook!'—something to grab the reader. While that's true, there's a fine line between a hook that's intriguing and a hook that's just silly. An example of a silly hook would be opening with a line of overtly sexual dialogue. Or opening with a hook that's just too convoluted to be truly interesting."

—**Dan Lazar**, Writers House

"Here are things I can't stand: Cliché openings in fantasy novels can include an opening scene set in a battle (and my peeve is that I don't know any of the characters yet so why should I care about this battle) or with a pastoral scene where the protagonist is gathering herbs (I didn't realize how common this is). Opening chapters where a main protagonist is in the middle of a bodily function (jerking off, vomiting, peeing or what have you) is usually a firm no right from the get-go. Gross. Long prologues that often don't have anything to do with the story. (So common in fantasy, again.) Opening scenes that are all dialogue without any context. I could probably go on ..."

—**Kristin Nelson**, Nelson Literary

CHARACTERS AND BACKSTORY

"I don't like descriptions of the characters where writers make the characters seem too perfect. Heroines (and heroes) who are described physically as being unflawed come across as unrelatable and boring. No 'flowing, windswept golden locks'; no 'eyes as blue as the sky'; no 'willowy, perfect figures.'"

—**Laura Bradford**, Bradford Literary Agency

"Many writers express the character's backstory before they get to the plot. Good writers will go back and cut that stuff out and get right to the plot. The character's backstory stays with them—it's in their DNA—even after the cut. To paraphrase Bruno Bettelheim: The more the character in a fairy tale is described, the less the audience will identify with him ... The less the character is characterized and described, the more likely the reader is to identify with him."

—**Adam Chromy**, Artists and Artisans

"I'm really turned off when a writer feels the need to fill in all the backstory before starting the story; a story that opens on the protagonist's mental reflection of their situation is (usually) a red flag."
—**Stephany Evans**, FinePrint Literary Management

"One of the biggest problems I encounter is the 'information dump' in the first few pages, where the author is trying to tell us everything we supposedly need to know to understand the story. Getting to know characters in a story is like getting to know people in real life. You find out their personality and details of their life over time."
—**Rachelle Gardner**, WordServe Literary

OTHER PET PEEVES

"The most common opening is a grisly murder scene told from the killer's point of view. While this usually holds the reader's attention, the narrative drive often doesn't last once we get into the meat of the story. A catchy opening scene is great, but all too often it falls apart after the initial pages. I often refer people to the opening of *Rosemary's Baby* by Ira Levin, which is about nothing more than a young couple getting an apartment. It is masterfully written and yet it doesn't appear to be about anything sinister at all. And it keeps you reading."
—**Irene Goodman**, Irene Goodman Literary

"Things I dislike include: 1) Telling me what the weather's like in order to set atmosphere. OK, it was raining. It's always raining. 2) Not starting with action. I want to have a sense of dread quite quickly—and not from rain! 3) Sending me anything but the beginning of the book; if you tell me that it 'starts getting good' on page 35, then I will tell you to start the book on page 35, because if even you don't like the first 34, neither will I or any other reader."
—**Josh Getzler**, Russell & Volkening, Inc.

"One of my biggest pet peeves is when writers try to stuff too much exposition into dialogue rather than trusting their abilities as storytellers to get information across. I'm talking stuff like the mom saying, 'Listen, Jimmy, I know you've missed your father ever since he died in that mysterious boating accident last year on the lake, but I'm telling you, you'll love this summer camp!'"
—**Chris Richman**, Upstart Crow Literary

"I hate to see a whiny character who's in the middle of a fight with one of their parents, slamming doors, rolling eyes, and displaying all sorts of other stereotypical behavior. I also tend to have a hard time bonding with characters who address the reader directly."
—**Kelly Sonnack**, Andrea Brown Literary Agency

Contacting Agents

Write a Killer Query Letter

How to Hook an Agent

by Mollie Glick

At conferences, I often meet worried writers who think they've got to be well connected in order to find an agent—thinking that agents don't pay any attention to query letters. But the truth is that I've found some of my favorite clients through unsolicited queries, and almost every agency I know has someone on staff whose job it is to sort through the queries and let their higher-ups know if they spot one that looks promising. The trick is to write a query letter strong enough to catch that person's attention.

A good query letter accomplishes two things: it makes an agent want to read your book, and it makes it easy for them to contact you to request sample material. Sounds pretty easy, right? Well, if you follow the following guidelines it can be.

PROFESSIONALISM

The first thing to think about when you sit down to write a query letter is that, in a lot of ways, it's similar to writing a cover letter for a job application. You're addressing your letter to a person who's never met you before, and who sorts through hundreds of such letters a day. This crucial first contact is your chance to demonstrate that you're smart, professional, and interesting. The way to convey those traits is through the tone and content of your letter. The tone should be professional, specific and engaging—never general, overly familiar or abrasive. Make sure your letter is well written and grammatically correct. And make sure to include all of your contact information, including your mailing address, phone number and e-mail address.

These suggestions may sound obvious, but you'd be surprised how many letters I get that leave out vital contact information, start out with "Hi Mollie—" instead of "Dear Ms. Glick:", or include unprofessional phrases such as, "You'll probably just throw this letter out like the other agents have." Occasionally, I get a letter written in a lighter, more humorous tone, and that's OK—as long as the letter reflects the kind of book the author is querying me about (i.e., a humorous nonfiction book or funny novel) and it still includes all the information I need to know. But if in doubt, stick with a professional tone, and include a one- or two-line quote from the book to give the agent a taste of its voice.

Like a cover letter, your query letter should be no longer than a page. It should include your contact information, a salutation, a paragraph describing your book, and a paragraph explaining why you're the perfect person to write that book. Lets take a closer look at each of these components.

MOLLIE GLICK is a literary agent with Foundry Literary + Media in New York.

CONTACT INFORMATION

To be perfectly honest, it doesn't really matter where you include the information on a snail mail query; it just matters that the information is complete and easily located. That said, you can't go wrong by putting your contact information at the top of a letter, centered.

What's more important to note is that the location of your contact information in e-mail correspondence is very important. Whereas a snail mail letter would have your information (as well as the agent's address) at the top, an e-query should include your information at the bottom, following your signature. The reasoning is simple. When an agent opens up your e-mail, they only see part of the letter in the e-mail window. It's most effective if we can just jump into the meat of the query rather than scrolling down past ten lines. (See the e-query example on page 57.)

THE SALUTATION

You should address the agent by his/her last name, or at the very least as "Dear Agent"— never by their first name unless you've met them previously in person and they've invited you to do so. At the start of your letter, feel free to explain why you've chosen to query this particular agent (i.e., "I read on the *Writer's Digest* website that you're particularly interested in acquiring smart, funny women's fiction," or "I noticed that you represent both Greg Olear and Ames Holbrook and thought you would be an excellent fit for my humorous political memoir"). If you were referred by a current client or an editor, or recently heard the author speak at a conference, this is also a good place to mention it.

If the agent has a name such as Chris or Pat and you're unsure of the gender, feel free to use the rep's full name: "Dear Pat Richardson:".

ABOUT THE BOOK

This is the trickiest part of the query letter—your chance to summarize, in one paragraph, what your book is about and who it will appeal to. Before you sit down to write this paragraph, you might want to start by developing a hook or "elevator pitch." This is a one- or two-sentence description that sums up what you're hoping to achieve—the kind of thing you'd say to a Hollywood exec if you bumped into them on an elevator and had 30 seconds to get them interested in your project.

One approach to an elevator pitch is to capture the theme of the novel. For example, if you were my author, Dorothy Hearst, pitching her first novel, *Promise of the Wolves*, you might say: "*Promise of the Wolves* is a debut novel that tells the story of the first wolves who became dogs, from the wolf's point of view."

Another approach is to give a brief summary of the plot. So if you were Brenda Janowitz, pitching *Jack with a Twist*, you could write something like "When NY attorney Brooke Miller lands her first big case, and finds out that her opposing attorney is her fiancé, Jack, she realizes that she's going to have to decide between the case of her life and actually having a life."

If you're writing a nonfiction book, you might lead with your audience. For example, you might say something like "over the past year, more than 10,000 new cases of autism have been diagnosed, and parents are hungry for information about dealing with this devastating diagnosis."

An elevator pitch is a good way to start off your About the Book paragraph, immediately grabbing the attention of the agent, but whether you're writing fiction or nonfiction, it's also a good idea to make a case in this paragraph that there's going to be a large, appreciative audience for your book. One way to do that is to compare your book to other books that have already been successfully published. For example, if you were my client Ellen Bryson pitching her fiction debut, you might say something like this: "A historical novel set in the Barnum and Bailey Museum in New York at the turn of the century, *The Transformation of Bartholomew Fortuno* will appeal to fans of Sara Gruen's *Water for Elephants* and Elizabeth McCracken's *The*

Giant's House." Just make sure you don't overreach by saying you're the next Dan Brown, J.K. Rowling or Elizabeth Gilbert. No agent wants to hear that you've got the next *Da Vinci Code*, *Harry Potter*, or *The Secret*. Make sure you've earned any comparisons you make and that they're not the same two "hot" books everyone else in the world is using as comparisons.

If you're writing nonfiction, you could also make an argument for the timeliness and relevance of your subject. For example, nonfiction writer John Park's query for *The Last Farmer* starts out with the following paragraph:

> Five years ago, no one in America was talking about farmers, and most of us were blissfully ignorant about the origins of our food. Sure, the occasional bestseller like *Fast Food Nation* lifted a section of the veil from time to time, but agriculture itself was not a sexy subject. That's about to change. With the price of food escalating to record heights, increasing concern over the safety of genetically modified foods, the terrifyingly rapid spread of E. coli outbreaks, and new research into ethanol as an alternative to oil, farming is about to move into the mainstream. Last month there were more news stories about farmers than there were about Britney Spears, and recently even magazines like *Vanity Fair* and *New York Magazine* have featured articles about farmers. Books such as Paul Roberts's *The End of Food* and Michael Pollan's *The Omnivore's Dilemma* have piqued the public's interest in learning more about the origins of the food they eat, but the real story is just beginning to surface.

ABOUT THE AUTHOR

In addition to introducing your book, your query letter should also introduce you. Agents aren't interested in hearing your full life history, but we do want to know who you are in relation to the project you're submitting. Why are you uniquely qualified to write the book you're writing? Do you have academic credentials (and MFA or journalism degree, PhD or MD) in a related subject? Did you have a real-life experience that your book is based upon? What's your publishing history? Have you ever been written about in national publications, or been interviewed on TV or on the radio? The term "platform" gets bandied about quite frequently in publishing, and it can be confusing, but it really means two things: 1) Why do you have the particular expertise to write on a certain subject, and 2) do you have the media connections to get attention for your book? It's more important for a nonfiction author to prove that he's got a strong platform, but if you're a fiction author who went to a great MFA program or has published articles on a topic related to your novel, there's no harm in saying so.

RESEARCHING AGENTS

Once you've written your query letter, the next step is to do some research into the best agents to approach, and whether those agents prefer to be queried via e-mail or via snail mail. If you're querying a bunch of agents at once ("simultaneous submissions"), take extra care not to mix up the names and addresses of agents you're querying; and if you're sending your letters out via e-mail, make sure to send each of them individually. You'd be amazed how many letters I get with my address but another agent's name in the salutation, and how many e-mail queries get sent out with every agent in town CC'd.

It may take a few weeks for you to hear back from agents (and you should check their websites to get a sense of whether they respond to all queries received, or just the ones they're interested in) but if you've done a good job with your query letter, and your project is viable, your query letter will have done its job and you'll soon receive requests for sample material—usually a "partial." If your letter is really good, your agent may later cull from it in his/her pitch letter, and your editor will pull lines from it for your back cover copy. But first things first, you've got to catch an agent's eye. So get cracking on those elevator pitches … and don't forget to check your spelling!

More Query Tips

WHAT WORKS BEST

- Taking a polite, professional tone.

- Including multiple forms of contact information.

- Mentioning why you chose to query a particular agent.

- If you've got a connection, were referred by a client, or met the agent at a conference, make sure to point that out early in your letter.

- Developing a killer "elevator pitch" based on theme, plot, or importance of your topic.

- Making a case for the book's built-in audience.

- Showing why your expertise and media contacts make you the best author for your project.

- Including blurbs or references from established, well-respected authors.

WHAT DOESN'T

- Querying an agent who doesn't handle the kind of book you're writing.

- Overly familiar, aggressive, or incorrect salutations.

- Pitching more than one book at a time.

- Overreaching with your comparisons.

- Outlining the full plot of your book—save it for your synopsis, if the agent has indicated that she'd like to see one. Your query should not give away the ending, for example.

- Querying agents about incomplete novels. (While it's preferable to query with an unfinished nonfiction project as long as you've written a proposal, novels should be finished before you start contacting agents.)

- Including personal information that isn't related to the topic of your book.

- Telling your agent that your writers' group, your congregants, or your mother's next-door neighbor's cockerspaniel loved your book.

Good Query Example #1

Dr. Doreen Orion
123 Author Road
Authorville, NM 21290
DoreenOrion@email.com
(212)555-2345

April 5, 2006

Full contact information

Dear Ms. Glick:

Demonstrating that you have researched and handpicked this agent

I am a psychiatrist, published author, and expert for the national media seeking representation for my memoir titled, *Queen of the Road: The True Tale of 47 States, 22,000 Miles, 200 Shoes, 2 Cats, 1 Poodle, a Husband, and a Bus with a Will of Its Own.* Because you are interested in unique voices, I thought we might be a good match.

An entertaining but professional tone

A quick, catchy hook or "elevator pitch"

When Tim first announced he wanted to "chuck it all" and travel around the country in a converted bus for a year, I gave this profound and potentially life-altering notion all the thoughtful consideration it deserved. "Why can't you be like a normal husband with a midlife crisis and have an affair or buy a Corvette?" I asked, adding, "I will never, ever, EVER live on a bus." What do you get when you cram married shrinks—one in a midlife crisis, the other his materialistic, wise-cracking wife—two cats who hate each other and a Standard Poodle who loves licking them all, into a bus for a year? *Queen of the Road* is a memoir of my dysfunctional, multi-species family's travels to and travails in the 49 continental states. (Tim insisted on seeing them all, despite my assurances that there were a few we could skip.)

An author bio that demonstrates your platform and why you're the right author for this project

As a psychiatrist, award-winning author (*I Know You Really Love Me*, Macmillan/Dell) and frequent media expert on psychiatric topics, (including *Larry King*, GMA, *48 Hours*, *The New York Times* and *People Magazine*), my life has centered on introspection, analysis and storytelling. Yet, I count among my greatest accomplishments that last year, our bus was featured as the centerfold of *Bus Conversions Magazine*, thus fulfilling my life-long ambition of becoming a Miss September. The story of our year-long adventure is already garnering interest in the media and has been mentioned in AMA News (circulation 250,000, and this journal of the American Medical Association has already agreed to review the book with an author interview when it comes out), *Woman's Day*, *Quick and Simple*, Match.com and *Best Life Magazine*. An upcoming *Parade Magazine* article on the growing phenomenon of mid-life career breaks (who knew I was a trend setter?) will include a photo of Tim and me, along with our story. My blog of our trip has also been mentioned in Andy Serwer's *Street Life* ecolumn *(Fortune Magazine)*. I hope you are interested in seeing the proposal and if so, would be most happy to send it to you via e-mail or snail mail.

Short and simple

Best wishes,

Signature

Doreen Orion

Good Query Example #2

① Name, address, e-mail address, and phone number. In an e-mail query, your contact info should be at the lower left.

② Notes the personal connection and a reason to query this agent.

③ The word count is right there with the standards for cozy mysteries. Also, her description fits her genre.

④ Establishes voice and a feeling for the book.

⑤ Impressive credentials. She's obviously been writing for a while and I really like the addition of her summers in Maine. I think it's a personal touch, but one that's perfectly related to the book.

⑥ Polite wrap up; offers to send more.

⑦ You would usually want to pitch only one book, but Karen knew that I liked to handle mystery series, so this worked well in her case.

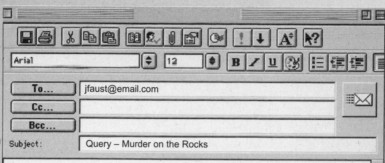

To... jfaust@email.com
Cc...
Bcc...
Subject: Query – Murder on the Rocks

Dear Ms. Faust:

I enjoyed meeting you at the conference in Austin **②** this past weekend. As I mentioned, I have had my eye on BookEnds **②** for quite some time; when I discovered you would be at the conference, I knew I had to attend. We met during the final pitch session and discussed how the series I am working on might fit in with your current line of mystery series **⑦**. Per your request, I have enclosed a synopsis and first three chapters of *Murder on the Rocks*, an **③** 80,000-word cozy mystery that was a finalist in this year's Writers' League of Texas manuscript contest and includes several bed-and-breakfast recipes.

Thirty-eight-year-old Natalie Barnes has quit her job, sold her house and gambled everything she has on the Gray Whale Inn on Cranberry Island, Maine. But she's barely fired up the stove when portly developer Bernard Katz rolls into town and starts mowing through her morning glory muffins **④**. Natalie needs the booking, but Katz is hard to stomach—especially when he unveils his plan to build an oversized golf resort on top of the endangered tern colony next door. When the town board approves the new development not only do the terns face extinction, but Natalie's Inn might just follow along. Just when Natalie thinks she can't face more trouble, she discovers Katz's body at the base of the cliff and becomes the number one suspect in the police's search for a murderer. If Natalie doesn't find the killer fast she stands to lose everything—maybe even her life.

I am a former public relations writer, a graduate of Rice University, a member of the Writers' League of Texas **⑤**, and founder of the Austin Mystery Writers critique group. I have spent many summers in fishing communities in Maine and Newfoundland, and escape to Maine as often as possible. The second Gray Whale Inn mystery, *Dead and Berried*, is currently in the computer.

If you would like to see the manuscript, I can send it via e-mail or snail mail. Thank you for your time and attention; I look forward to hearing from you soon. **⑥**

Sincerely,

Karen Swartz MacInerney **①**
123 Author Lane
Writerville, CA
(323) 555-0000
Karen@email.com

Query critique provided by Jessica Faust of BookEnds, LLC.

Good Query Example #3

Mary Timmins
1458 Ion Lane
Los Angeles, CA
(323) 555-0000
marytwriter@email.com

October 31, 2008

Steven T. Murray, Editor-in-Chief
Fjord Press
P.O. Box 16349
Seattle, WA 98116

Dear Mr. Murray:

Plenty Good Room concerns the emotional struggles a thirteen-year-old African-American boy endures when his mother declares that he must leave his native Harlem and move down south (Florida) to live with a father he has never known. The three stages of the story show the young man's life: His time in New York and the events that subsequently lead to his mother's insistence that the father shoulder the remaining responsibility of rearing him; the not so clear-cut path he takes to become part of his father's life; and his life with father and the ultimate unraveling of a dream he thought had come true.

The story is written entirely from the viewpoint of the teen protagonist (à la *The Catcher in the Rye*) and is a first-person account replete with emotion and stingingly blunt dialogue. Despite the age of the protagonist, *Plenty Good Room* is not a children's book. The language is contemporary and often raw and unrelenting. The book is, however, a timely exposé on a young black male growing up in a single-parent home where the parent is too young, too inexperienced, and too poor to adequately parent and where the father is not at all involved.

I have enclosed the first twenty pages of my thirteen-chapter manuscript. Please notify me if you are interested in reviewing the complete text. Thank you for your consideration.

Sincerely,

Teresa McClain
Encl.: SASE

Annotations (margin notes):

- 1" margin
- Addressed to a specific editor
- The query jumps right into the pitch, which is perfectly acceptable
- Good that she gives a clear idea of the overall structure of the novel
- Effective pitch thus far shows map of the novel
- Single-spaced text
- Signature
- Details enclosures

Bad Query Example

The strange date here is either a mistake, or a sign that this letter has been circulating for quite some time. Neither is a good thing

Querying an agent who doesn't represent the kind of book you're writing

Making broad claims that you can't back up

Giving references from people outside the publishing industry

Failing to demonstrate a platform

Don't ask for a phone call or in-person meeting before the agent has requested one

Where's the rest of the contact information?

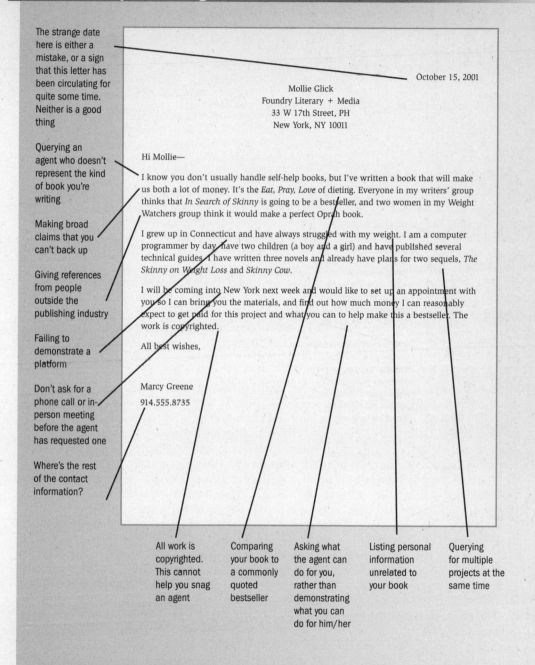

October 15, 2001

Mollie Glick
Foundry Literary + Media
33 W 17th Street, PH
New York, NY 10011

Hi Mollie—

I know you don't usually handle self-help books, but I've written a book that will make us both a lot of money. It's the *Eat, Pray, Love* of dieting. Everyone in my writers' group thinks that *In Search of Skinny* is going to be a bestseller, and two women in my Weight Watchers group think it would make a perfect Oprah book.

I grew up in Connecticut and have always struggled with my weight. I am a computer programmer by day, have two children (a boy and a girl) and have published several technical guides. I have written three novels and already have plans for two sequels, *The Skinny on Weight Loss* and *Skinny Cow*.

I will be coming into New York next week and would like to set up an appointment with you so I can bring you the materials, and find out how much money I can reasonably expect to get paid for this project and what you can to help make this a bestseller. The work is copyrighted.

All best wishes,

Marcy Greene
914.555.8735

All work is copyrighted. This cannot help you snag an agent

Comparing your book to a commonly quoted bestseller

Asking what the agent can do for you, rather than demonstrating what you can do for him/her

Listing personal information unrelated to your book

Querying for multiple projects at the same time

Nonfiction Book Proposals

Why You Need One, and How to Write It

by Rachelle Gardner

As a literary agent, I receive queries every day. When one interests me, I ask to see more material. If it's fiction, I'll ask for the manuscript, but if it's nonfiction, I'll ask for a book proposal. Occasionally I receive an e-mail back from the writer: What's a book proposal? Needless to say, that's not the answer I want. A book proposal is the basic sales tool for a nonfiction book—a business plan, if you will. An agent can't sell your book to a publisher without it. You've got to have one, and it's got to be good. Let me put it to you straight: If you don't know what a book proposal is, you're not quite ready to approach an agent. You shouldn't even query an agent with your nonfiction project until your proposal is complete. So if the proposal is your key tool to getting an agent's attention for your book, let's review why you need one and how to compose it.

THE NEED FOR PROPOSALS

If you have a completed manuscript, you may be tempted to think that's enough. It's not. You still need a proposal. Here are a few reasons why:

Publishers usually don't look at nonfiction manuscripts. The proposal itself provides information publishers need in order to make a purchasing decision. Before they even want to read sample chapters, they will review elements such as the author's platform, how the book fits into the marketplace, and what titles already exist on your topic.

The book proposal can be used throughout the publishing process—to help the editorial, marketing, and sales teams understand your book. They'll refer to it when they write copy for your book—copy that goes on to your book cover or into marketing, advertising, and sales pieces. Therefore you'll want to write the best and most effective "sell language" into your proposal.

A proposal helps your own understanding of the project—its structure, theme, and execution—and you may be able to identify and correct any problems. If done correctly, your proposal will also help you understand and be able to explain who your audience is and why they would buy your book.

The proposal shows the publisher that you've done your homework. It shows you're a professional, and you have a good understanding of the business of publishing. Alternatively, a shoddy proposal makes it easy for an editor to quickly say "No" and toss it in the reject pile.

RACHELLE GARDNER (cba-ramblings.blogspot.com) is a literary agent at WordServe Literary Group. Her publishing experience dates back to 1995 and has encompassed positions in sales, subrights, editorial, and collaborative writing.

Reading entire manuscripts is extremely time-consuming. Proposals give editors the information they need to make decisions as quickly and effectively as possible.

ELEMENTS OF A PROPOSAL

Here's a basic rundown of what you should include. The four questions agents and editors will be asking when they sit down to review your project are: What is the project? What is its place in the market? Why is this writer the best individual to write it? And, finally: Can the writer write?

Addressing "What is the project?"

Title page: Title, authors' names, phone numbers, and e-mail addresses. Contact information for your agent if you have one. If you've had books traditionally published, you can list them under your name.

One-sentence summary: It's the first sentence of your overview and it captures your book in 25 words or fewer. It should be more hook than description. This could also be a tagline that you might see across the top of the back cover.

Brief overview: This should read similar to back-cover copy. It should be exciting, informative, and make someone want to read your book. It tells the publisher in a succinct form what the book is about, why this project is necessary and unique, and who the market is. Aim for one page single-spaced, or two at the most.

Felt need: What needs will your book fulfill that your audience is already aware of? What questions are they asking that your book will answer? What do they want that you can give them?

Details: How many words will your book be? (Words, not pages.) Is the book complete? If not, how long after the signing of a contract will it take you to complete the book? Two to six months is typical. Are you envisioning photos or illustrations as part of the project? Will you be responsible for collecting art or illustrations for the book?

Addressing "What is its place in the market?"

The market: Whom do you see as the audience for the book? Make sure you identify whether it's a larger, general audience or a niche market. More is not always better. What's important is whether you've accurately identified your audience(s). Don't say your book is for "all adults ages 18 to 68." Find a way to identify and categorize specific groups of people who will want your book. Is it for skateboard enthusiasts? New moms? Pop culture junkies? Fans of college football?

You'll also want to answer such questions as: Why would somebody buy this book? How is this audience reached? Do you have any special relationships to the market? What books and magazines does this audience already read? What radio and TV programs do they tune into? Demonstrate an understanding of exactly who will buy your book and why. For example, instead of naming a potential audience group as "new moms," can you further delve into the audience and describe as "new moms who are on the cutting edge of parenting techniques and read upscale parenting magazines like *Cookie*."

Competitive analysis: What other books are in print on the same subject? How is your book different and better? (Never say there are no books like yours. There is always competition.) List four to eight books that could be considered most comparable to yours. List the title, author, ISBN and year of publication. (Books in the last two to three years are best.) Then write a couple of sentences explaining what that book is about, and how yours is different, better, and/or a good complement to it. If possible, add book sale numbers. If you see online that a comparative book passed a half million sales in January 2010, say so.

This section is more important than you might think. It forces you to become familiar with what's already been written along the same lines as your book. It shows you whether there is a hole in the market that your book can fill, or whether the topic has already been

What About Fiction?

If you're writing a novel, don't worry about creating a proposal when you're looking for an agent. Concentrate on writing your book and then a terrific query. If your agent prefers to submit fiction business proposals to publishers, he or she will let you know. However, before querying, you should at least have these three things ready: The hook: one sentence. The pitch: This is the one- or two-paragraph pitch for the book that you probably used in your query. The synopsis: These are difficult to write without it being awful to read, but necessary nonetheless. Aim for one to three pages, single-spaced—giving the gist of the entire story, including the main plot twists and the ending.

done to death (in which case, you go back to the drawing board and tweak your idea so that it takes a different approach or says something other than what everyone else is saying). It shows the publisher that you know your genre or category well. It alerts your publisher to any possible sales issues regarding competition. It helps everyone (editors, marketing, sales, design) to capture a vision for your book, to understand it a little better, to know which section of the bookstore it goes in. To find all comparative titles, use Amazon and Google to search for books using a variety of means; don't limit yourself to one particular search term or one method. Go deeper than the titles to make sure you're not missing anything; search using different keywords. I recommend an actual trip to the bookstore (strange concept, I know) rather than solely online research. Lastly, don't criticize the other books or say they're terrible (even if you think they are). Simply highlight the differences.

Addressing "Why is this writer the best individual to write it?"

About the authors: Half page to a full page on each author. Why are you qualified to write this book? Make a good case for you as the best possible author for a book on this topic. Be sure to include any academic or professional credentials, as well as work or life experiences that qualify you. Have you won awards? Possess relevant degrees? This is also where you list any previously published books along with sales figures. Be sure to include the title, publisher, year published, and number of copies sold. You can also include your published magazine or journal articles here. If you have a large number of these, don't list them all individually, but find a way to convey the breadth of your work. For example, one bullet point could be something like, "From 2002 to 2010, (Author) had sixteen articles appear in *Money* magazine."

Author marketing: This is where you'll talk about your platform. How are you able to reach your target audience to market your book? This is not the place for expressing your willingness to participate in marketing. This is the place for concrete facts: what you've already done, what contacts you already have, and what plans you've already made to help market your book.

Feel free to mention things such as speaking engagements already booked, radio or television programs on which you're scheduled to appear (or have in the past), a newsletter you're already sending out regularly, or a blog or website that gets an impressive number of daily page views. This section should be specific, and include numbers wherever possible. For example, on your biggest speaking engagements, list the size of each audience; also, give specific stats on your blog or website traffic. This is not the place to say that your book would be terrific on the "Today" show, unless you can document that the "Today" show has already contacted you.

Addressing "Can the writer write?"

Annotated chapter outline: This is where it becomes crucial that your book is well organized and completely thought out. You will need chapter titles and a couple of sentences capturing each chapter's theme. From this outline, the editor will gain an understanding of your book as a whole. You'll need to make sure the outline communicates that you will deliver on what your proposal promises.

Sample chapters: Include the Introduction (if you have one) and Chapter 1, along with one other chapter (either Chapter 2, or one from later in the book). Make sure they're polished and perfect! The two sample chapters should not only be well written, but each one should have a high degree of interest and be designed to grab an editor's attention. Ideally the two chapters should highlight different aspects of your writing. For example, if one is general, the other one can be more specific, covering one aspect of your topic. If one of the chapters is more personal, the other can be instructive or professional. Your goal is to give the editor an idea of your range as an author. The execution—the quality of writing in the sample chapters—is extremely important. The editor might love your book idea, but they also need to know you can deliver a well-written book.

SOME LAST TIPS

There are many acceptable formats for book proposals, so don't be overly stressed about it. Just make sure it looks nice and is easy to read and well organized. Always err on the side of more white space—i.e., don't crunch everything together on the page. Aim for a pleasing reading experience. Double-space the overview and sample chapters.

Make sure to demonstrate that you have enough material to fill an entire book. One pitfall of many nonfiction authors is presenting a topic that doesn't seem to warrant a book but rather a long magazine article. Prove you have the content to fill a book.

Remember that the book proposal is a sales tool. Like any good salesperson, you'll need to anticipate all possible objections to your book, and overcome them in your proposal. Imagine the questions the editor will be asking, and answer them.

Lastly, be yourself in the proposal! Just because a book proposal is a professional document and a sales tool does not mean it should be dry and boring. Bring your personality to the page. Whatever voice you've used in your book, be sure to use it in your proposal, too. If you're seeking more information about proposals, seek out either *Write the Perfect Book Proposal* by Jeff Herman and Deborah Levine Herman, or *How to Write a Book Proposal*, 4th Ed., by Michael Larsen. Both address and dissect real proposals that sold.

Contacting Agents

Make the Most of a Writers Conference

Meet Agents, Editors and Peers

by Ricki Schultz

I f you've picked up this book, chances are, you're serious about writing and want to know how to advance to the next level. That said, no matter what the stage of your writing career, as a serious professional, you should attend writers conferences.

Writers conferences are events where writers gather together to see presentations and seminars from accomplished people in the industry. Some events last a day; others last a weekend. Other events may even last longer—but those are most likely retreats, which focus on sitting down to relax and write, rather than conferences, which are about mingling and learning. This article will address conferences—and all the reasons you should think about heading out to one (or more) this year.

REASONS TO ATTEND

Networking

First off, writing is a business. If you're looking to land an agent or sign a book deal with such-and-such publisher, the chances of that happening without networking are slim to nonexistent; you have to get out there and make things happen. Conferences are golden opportunities to connect not only with industry professionals but other writers, too.

As well, writing can be a lonely business. Although you might get on a roll, you can also lose your flow in an instant. It's during those times that writers most need the advice, ideas, and companionship of other writers. Conferences are chock-full of people—just like you—who know what it's like to consider setting their manuscripts ablaze after yet another revision. If you've ever been rereading your story and wished you had a friend who could give a critique, conferences are where you meet such friends.

Seminars

Other than providing you with a place to rub elbows with industry professionals and other write-minded folks, writers conferences offer myriad opportunities for you to learn more about the craft and business of writing. Published authors, as well as editors and agents, teach seminars and sit on panels. Presentation schedules vary, but they usually include sessions on everything from drafting query letters to developing characters.

Some presenters assign in-class exercises or homework; some divulge secrets on how they

RICKI SCHULTZ (rickischultz.com) is a Virginia-based freelance writer and recovering high school English teacher. As coordinator of Shenandoah Writers Online, she is an aspiring young adult author and enjoys connecting with other writers.

structure plot; but every conference is packed with tips on how to shape your writing. In addition, most offer group or one-on-one critique sessions with authors, agents, and editors, so you can get specific feedback on how to attack your current project.

HOW TO CHOOSE AN EVENT

If you've made up your mind that you want to attend a conference but have no idea what to do now, it's all a matter of asking yourself two simple questions.

Do you want a general event, specialized conference, or retreat?

General conferences are just what you think they are—events that are geared toward all categories and levels of writers. There are hundreds of these nationwide every year, and most of the biggest gatherings fall under this category. Just as there are plenty of general events, there are also conferences that focus on a particular category of writing. If you are writing kids books, romance, Christian themes, or mystery/thriller, there are specialized conferences out there for you. Lastly, retreats are longer events designed to let writers write, rather than sit in on seminars or pitch agents.

What do you want to get out of the experience?

This question, obviously, is key. Perhaps you want to just sit down and write—maybe finally finish that novel. If so, then an intensive retreat is just what you need. Do you want to sit in on presentations and learn? Are you ready to pitch agents? If so, then you want to look for conferences that not only have agents in attendance, but have agents in attendance who represent the category you're writing. This is where a specialized conference comes in handy. If you're writing Christian fiction, then all agents in attendance at a Christian conference should be interested in your pitch. Bigger conferences often have a slew of editors and agents in attendance—but they also cost more. Start by looking local. You may find an event nearby that has a solid list of seminars and professionals as part of the conference.

MAXIMIZE THE EXPERIENCE

Here are some tips on how to maximize your conference experience and make a lasting impression on the industry's finest.

Be prepared

This involves doing some homework before the conference; however, it's worth the time and effort.

1. Business cards. Cards are a quick, inexpensive way to assert professionalism. Don't hand them out to literary agents, editors, or authors (unless someone specifically requests one), but do distribute them whenever you make a connection with another writer. Agents and editors will generally hand you a card if they're interested, and they will quickly give instructions on what to send them and how.

2. Have work handy. Even though it's extremely rare for agents and editors to request material from you (outside a pitch session), you want to be prepared for anything and everything—which means having your work handy at a moment's notice. Because agents vary in terms of preferences, print out a few hard copies of your first chapter and synopsis and stick them on your person at all times. For a "green" option, carry a thumb drive with your first chapter and synopsis on it. That way, you can raid your hotel's business center and print or e-mail your work, should the need arise.

3. Study the faculty. Another way to stand out is to read up on the presenters. Not only will this prior knowledge aid you in choosing which sessions to attend, but it will also help you decide with whom to schmooze. Likewise, having studied up on the industry pros will ease the daunting task of talking to them. When you run into the editor from Your Dream Publisher, you'll have something more to say than just an awkward hello.

My Experiences at Two Conferences

I attended two conferences in 2009: the **Southeastern Writers Association Conference** (SWA; southeasternwriters.com) as well as the **South Carolina Writers Workshop** (SCWW; www.myscww.org). SWA was intimate, with around 60 annual attendees, and is held in the serene atmosphere of St. Simons Island, Ga.; SCWW is more of a networking hub, as it welcomes 300 attendees and is held in Myrtle Beach, S.C. Here's what I did right.

With SCWW hosting agents, editors, and a *New York Times* best-selling author, I did my homework before arriving. At a cocktail hour, I approached some fellow writer folks. Because I'd done my research, I was able to give my new pals the scoop on who's who around the patio. At dinner, I ended up sitting next to an agent with whom I had scheduled a pitch session for the next day (eek!). Sharing the meal with her actually helped take the edge off when it came time for my pitch.

On day two of SCWW, a woman asked me if I was a literary agent. When I told her I wasn't, she asked me what sessions I was teaching. This was all because I simply dressed up. I struck the book sale woman as someone of more importance than just the conference attendee I was.

When researching presenters for SWA, I saw that Chuck Sambuchino (editor of the book you hold in your hands) and I actually shared a mutual friend. I used this fact to start up a conversation. That led to an invitation to dinner with other presenters and attendees. That dinner led to talk of freelance work (and this article you're now reading!). As well, at an after-dinner social at SCWW, I invited one of the agents, who was alone at the bar, to join our table of writers. When some of his fellow presenters showed, they joined us, as well. This translated into an agent offering to review some of my pages—all without ever pitching.

In the days since both conferences, I have followed up with many of the people I met. Some have become critique partners as well as friends. What's more, I later blogged about the events, and agents commented on my posts!

Dress the part

It's the oldest business advice in the world, but this simple cliché can help you stand out at writing conferences: Dress for success. As much as we might resist it because we're writers (and, therefore, averse to anything as cold and unfeeling as the business world), writing is a business. You have to be able to sell your writing—and the first way to do that at a conference is to sell people on you. You want to stand out in a positive way—and if you achieve that from something as simple as not wearing jeans, good for you. Your attire won't get you a book deal, but dressing in professional garb will make you pop against all the schlubs who didn't.

Be visible

Sign up for any and all extras the conference offers, such as critiques, pitch sessions, slush fests, and contests. Some of these things cost extra money, but they make the experience that much more worth it. Think of them as your takeaways, because you can gain much in terms of feedback, networking, and experience from each of them. As well, go to as many sessions as possible while you're there. You can't go to everything, but the more activities you attend, the more people you'll meet, the more you'll learn, and the more visible you'll become. After all, how can those agents fall in love with you if they never see you? You can sleep when you get home. In addition, don't hide in the corner during sessions. Ask questions. You've got a unique opportunity to pick this pro's brain, so take advantage of it.

Be open
No one said going to these things isn't scary at first, but the more assertive you are, the more you'll get out of a conference.

ATTENDEES
Walking up to complete strangers may threaten your comfort levels—particularly because you might fear everyone there is more accomplished than you—but you need to do it anyway. If you can't think of a conversation starter, simply ask, "What do you write?" Every attendee fears the same things you do, and they're all dying to talk about what they're writing, what they're reading, whom they've queried, etc. If you overcome your initial nervousness, you'll stand out from the wallflowers and make connections.

Furthermore, talk to anyone and everyone. No matter where you are in your writing journey, be just as open to meeting folks with less experience than you as you are to meeting those with more. Who knows? The guy who just asked you what a literary agent does might be the next Stephen King. If you blow him off to schmooze with someone else, that will make just as much of an impression on him as if you'd been friendly; it just won't make the kind of impression you want.

INDUSTRY PROFESSIONALS
Even more frightening than chatting up conference attendees is approaching the agents, editors and authors of the faculty. Some of these people are famous; some of these people are from—gasp—New York City, and they all hold your publishing career in their hands.

One common misconception is that these people do not want to be bothered; on the contrary, agents and editors expect to field questions and hear pitches at conferences. If there is an opportunity to sit with one of them, take it. Don't stalk the person; just use your best judgment about appropriate times. Often at meals, the faculty will distribute themselves among the conference-goers, so these are perfect opportunities to get to know them.

FOLLOW THROUGH
A last way you can stand out and make the most of a writers conference happens after you return home—and it lies in the follow-through. If you got to know someone well enough to exchange information, take a few minutes to shoot your conference buddy an e-mail, saying how much you enjoyed chatting with her. Not only is this important in terms of fostering those sanity-saving writer groups, but you never know: The lady from Wichita, with whom you split the last sugar cookie, might snag an agent before you do—and if you stay in touch with her, you might have a potential referral to her agency within your grasp.

Ultimately, however, to start making splashes at a writers conference, you first need to scrape together the dough and get to one. You already consider yourself to be a serious writer—now prove it.

Contacting Agents

Sign on the Dotted Line

Research Your Options and Beware Scams

O nce you've received an offer of representation, you must determine if the agent is right for you. As flattering as any offer may be, you need to be confident that you are going to work well with the agent and that she is going to work hard to sell your manuscript.

EVALUATE THE OFFER

You need to know what to expect once you enter into a business relationship. You should know how much editorial input to expect from your agent, how often she gives updates about where your manuscript has been and who has seen it, and what subsidiary rights the agent represents.

More importantly, you should know when you will be paid. The publisher will send your advance and any subsequent royalty checks directly to the agent. After deducting her commission—usually 10 to 15 percent—your agent will send you the remaining balance. Most agents charge a higher commission of 20 to 25 percent when using a co-agent for foreign, dramatic or other specialized rights. As you enter into a relationship with an agent, have her explain her specific commission rates and payment policy.

Some agents offer written contracts and some do not. If your prospective agent does not, at least ask for a "memorandum of understanding" that details the basic relationship of expenses and commissions. If your agent does offer a contract, be sure to read it carefully, and keep a copy for yourself. Since contracts can be confusing, you may want to have a lawyer or knowledgeable writer friend check it out before signing anything.

The National Writers Union (NWU) has drafted a Preferred Literary Agent Agreement and a pamphlet, *Understand the Author-Agent Relationship,* which is available to members. The union suggests clauses that delineate such issues as:

- the scope of representation (One work? One work with the right of refusal on the next? All work completed in the coming year? All work completed until the agreement is terminated?)
- the extension of authority to the agent to negotiate on behalf of the author
- compensation for the agent and any co-agent, if used
- manner and time frame for forwarding monies received by the agent on behalf of the client
- termination clause, allowing client to give about 30 days to terminate the agreement
- the effect of termination on concluded agreements as well as ongoing negotiations
- arbitration in the event of a dispute between agent and client

If you have any concerns about the agency's practices, ask the agent about them before

What Should I Ask?

The following is a list of topics the Association of Authors' Representatives suggests authors discuss with literary agents who have offered to represent them. Please bear in mind that most agents are not going to be willing to spend time answering these questions unless they have already read your material and wish to represent you.

1. Are you a member of the Association of Authors' Representatives or do you adhere to their basic canon of ethics?

2. How long have you been in business as an agent?

3. Do you have specialists at your agency who handle movie and television rights? Foreign rights?

4. Do you have subagents or corresponding agents in Hollywood and overseas?

5. Who in your agency will actually be handling my work? Will the other staff members be familiar with my work and the status of my business at your agency?

6. Will you oversee or at least keep me apprised of the work that your agency is doing on my behalf?

7. Do you issue an agent/author agreement? May I review the language of the agency clause that appears in contracts you negotiate for your clients?

8. How do you keep your clients informed of your activities on their behalf?

9. Do you consult with your clients on any and all offers?

10. What are your commission rates? What are your procedures and time frames for processing and disbursing client funds? Do you keep different bank accounts separating author funds from agency revenue? What are your policies about charging clients for expenses incurred by your agency?

11. When you issue 1099 tax forms at the end of each year, do you also furnish clients—upon request—with a detailed account of their financial activity, such as gross income, commissions and other deductions and net income for the past year?

12. In the event of your death or disability, what provisions exist for my continued representation?

13. If we should part company, what is your policy about handling any unsold subsidiary rights to my work?

Reprinted with the permission of the Association of Authors' Representatives (www.aar-online.org).

Sealing the Deal

you sign. Once an agent is interested in representing you, she should be willing to address any questions or concerns that you have. If the agent is rude or unresponsive, or tries to tell you that the information is confidential or classified, the agent is uncommunicative at best and, at worst, is already trying to hide something from you.

AVOID GETTING SCAMMED

The number of literary agents in the country, as well as the world, is increasing. This is because each year, aspiring authors compose an increasing number of manuscripts, while publishing houses continue to merge and become more selective as well as less open to working directly with writers. With literary agents providing the crucial link between writers and publishers, it's no wonder dozens of new agencies sprout up each year in the United States alone.

While more agencies may seem like a good thing, writers who seek to pair up with a successful agent must beware when navigating the murky waters of the Internet. Because agents are such a valuable part of the process, many unethical persons are floating around the online publishing world, ready to take advantage of uninformed writers who desperately want to see their work in print.

To protect yourself, you must familiarize yourself with common agent red flags and keep your radar up for any other warning signs. First of all, it can't be stressed enough that you should never pay agents any fees just so they consider your work. Only small fees (such as postage and copying) are acceptable—and those miniscule costs are administered *after* the agent has contacted you and signed you as a client.

A typical scam goes something like this: You send your work to an agency and they reply with what seems like a form letter or e-mail, telling you they love your story. At some point, they ask for money, saying it has to do with distribution, production, submissions, analysis or promotion. By that point, you're so happy with the prospect of finding an agent (you probably already told family and friends) that you nervously hand over the money. Game over. You've just been scammed. Your work may indeed end up in print, but you're likely getting very little if any money. To be a successful author, publishers must pay you to write; you must never pay them.

When a deal seems too good to be true, it likely is. If you want to learn more about a particular agent, look at her website. If she doesn't have a website (some small agents do not), look in this book to see if she has legitimate sales in the industry. Google her name: You'll likely find a dozen writers just like you discussing this agent on an Internet forum asking questions such as "Does anyone know anything about agent so-and-so?" These writer-oriented websites exist so writers like you can meet similar persons and discuss their good/bad experiences with publications, agents and publishing houses.

Protect yourself from scams by getting questions answered before you make any deals. When an abundance of research material is not available, you must be cautious. Ask around, ask questions and never pay upfront fees.

If you've been scammed

If you have trouble with your agent and you've already tried to resolve it to no avail, it may be time to call for help. Please alert the writing community to protect others. If you find agents online, in directories or in this book who aren't living up to their promises or are charging you money when they're listed as non-fee-charging agents, please let the Web master or editor of the publication know. Sometimes they can intervene for an author, and if no solution can be found, they can at the very least remove a listing from their directory so that no other authors will be scammed in the future. All efforts are made to keep scam artists out, but in a world where agencies are frequently bought and sold, a reputation can change overnight.

If you have complaints about any business, consider contacting The Federal Trade

Commission, The Council of Better Business Bureaus or your state's attorney general. (For full details, see Reporting a Complaint below). Legal action may seem like a drastic step, but sometimes people do it. You can file a suit with the attorney general and try to find other writers who want to sue for fraud with you. The Science Fiction & Fantasy Writers of America's website offers sound advice on recourse you can take in these situations. For more details, visit www.sfwa.org/beware/.

If you live in the same state as your agent, it may be possible to settle the case in small claims court. This is a viable option for collecting smaller damages and a way to avoid lawyer fees. The jurisdiction of the small claims court includes cases in which the claim is $5,000 or less. (This varies from state to state, but should still cover the amount for which you're suing.) Keep in mind that suing takes a lot of effort and time. You'll have to research all the necessary legal steps. If you have lawyers in the family, that could be a huge benefit if they agree to help you organize the case, but legal assistance is not necessary.

Above all, if you've been scammed, don't waste time blaming yourself. It's not your fault if someone lies to you. Respect in the literary world is built on reputation, and word gets around about agents who scam, cheat, lie and steal. Editors ignore their submissions and writers avoid them. Without clients or buyers, a swindling agent will find her business collapsing.

Meanwhile, you'll keep writing and believing in yourself. One day, you'll see your work in print, and you'll tell everyone what a rough road it was to get there, but how you wouldn't trade it for anything in the world.

Reporting a Complaint

If you feel you've been cheated or misrepresented, or you're trying to prevent a scam, the following resources should be of help.

- The Federal Trade Commission, Bureau of Consumer Protection. While the FTC won't resolve individual consumer problems, it does depend on your complaints to help them investigate fraud, and your speaking up may even lead to law enforcement action. Visit www.ftc.gov.

- Volunteer Lawyers for the Arts is a group of volunteers from the legal profession who assist with questions of law pertaining to the arts. Visit www.vlany.org.

- The Council of Better Business Bureau is the organization to contact if you have a complaint or if you want to investigate a publisher, literary agent or other business related to writing and writers. Contact your local BBB or visit www.bbb.org.

- Your state's attorney general. Don't know your attorney general's name? Go to www.attorneygeneral.gov. This site provides a wealth of contact information, including a complete list of links to each state's attorney general website.

Sealing the Deal

Copyrights and Wrongs

Know the Lingo of Legalese

by Chuck Sambuchino and Brian A. Klems

Imagine you're at a writers conference. You're getting ready to pitch that great novel idea to a bunch of powerful agents. As you walk up to the microphone, you start to notice all the other writers in the room staring, pens and pads in their hands. That's when the questions start flooding your head. Should you have secured a copyright before spilling your idea like this? Will other writers steal your concept? Can they do that? Will the agents ignore your pitch because the book title comes from a Billy Joel song?

Don't panic—a little paranoia is almost expected. It's natural for you to want to protect your work from others. Along with protecting your work from pilferers, you also have to protect yourself from being sued for legal infringement. As you compose your work and enter into the publishing world, it's vital to know how to navigate the murky waters of copyrights, libel and other contractual small print. Here's the scoop on some commonly asked questions about copyrights and other rights.

What is a copyright?

A copyright is a proprietary right designed to give the creator of a work the power to control that work's reproduction, distribution and public display or performance, as well as its adaptation into other forms. If another artist copies your work, the copyright will help you sue for proper compensation.

How long does a copyright last?

Usually, a copyright is valid until 70 years after the creator's death, but rare circumstances can cause this to fluctuate. Works written before 1978 do not adhere to current copyright laws. It's best to ask the U.S. Copyright Office about pre-1978 works and your specific circumstances. (You may have to pay to have the records checked for you.) The office's online site—copyright.gov—lists all copyright records dating back to 1978.

Do I need to register my work with the U.S. Copyright Office to hold a copyright on the work?

No. Your work is copyrighted the moment it hits a tangible medium—everything from your scribbles on a piece of paper to your musings on your Internet blog are protected. Putting

CHUCK SAMBUCHINO (guidetoliteraryagents.com/blog) is the editor of *Guide to Literary Agents*. He is the author of *How to Survive a Garden Gnome Attack* (Ten Speed Press, Sept. 2010) as well as *Formatting & Submitting Your Manuscript* (Writer's Digest Books). **BRIAN A. KLEMS** is the online community editor for *Writer's Digest*.

the word "Copyright" or the copyright symbol at the front of your text is also advisable, as it will prevent those who steal your work from pleading innocence down the road. Using the Copyright symbol on your manuscript is a topic of contention, though, as agents and editors tend to see it as the sign of an amateur—because they obviously know your work is protected. Try to avoid inserting the symbol or the word "Copyright" when querying agents and editors, but remember to use it when passing your work around—such as to peers, other writers or on public forums (e.g. the Internet).

Though it's not mandatory, formally registering your work will certainly help your cause in court should that scenario occur. If someone steals your work and you take the thief to court, the possible compensation and damages awarded to you are greater if your work is registered.

"Poor man's copyright" is a questionably effective tactic where you mail yourself a manuscript and never open the envelope, thereby "proving" that you had written your work by a specific date. This is what the U.S. Copyright Office said about the idea: "The practice of sending a copy of your own work to yourself is sometimes called a 'poor man's copyright.' There is no provision in the copyright law regarding any such type of protection, and it is not a substitute for registration."

Does a copyright protect ideas?

No. Let's say you write a sci-fi story about a soldier who battles aliens on the moons of Neptune. Your idea—or concept—cannot be copyrighted, and therefore, can be used by anyone. If someone wants to try their hand at the same basic premise (soldier, aliens, our solar system), they may, but they can't use your characters, dialogue or passages from your text. If specific things from your story are stolen or copied, you can sue—but just because someone ripped off your basic concept doesn't make them culpable.

What are the legal ramifications of reproducing song lyrics in a manuscript? Also, can I use a song title as the title of my book?

Song lyrics are copyrighted, which means you need permission to use them. Although there isn't any specific law about how much you can take under fair use, it's common for the music industry to say you need permission for even one line of a song. One way you can check to see if the song is still under copyright protection is to visit copyright.gov. Publishers will usually assist in securing necessary permissions for you during the publishing process.

Differently, song and book titles of any kind generally aren't copyrightable—the only exception being those rare titles subject to trademark or unfair competition laws. Titles that fall in this small category are closely tied to a specific artist. (Think "Yellow Submarine" or "Stairway to Heaven.")

Can I use a minor character from a famous work as the protagonist of my novel?

Original characters—from Atticus Finch to Hermione Granger—are protected by copyright as long as the characters are both original and well defined. You can't use them without permission from the copyright holder. Now, just because you can't use someone else's work doesn't mean you can't be inspired by it. If the character has a rather common name and isn't particularly fleshed out, she's up for grabs (e.g., a perky young college student named Jennifer who used to baby-sit the main character and doesn't play much of a role in the book).

According to *Writer's Digest* legal expert Amy Cook, character names can even warrant trademark protection, depending on how distinctive the name is and to what extent the public associates the name with the original author. It's in your best interest to avoid names like Buzz Lightyear or James Bond.

Sealing the Deal

What's the difference between slander and libel?

Simple: Slander is spoken; libel is written. Note that to be considered either, the words must inflict defamation of character—thereby falsely and negatively reflecting on a living person's reputation. Whenever concerned that your work may contain libelous material (such as in a memoir), always consult an attorney. Better safe than sued.

This is as good a place as ever to note that, although publishers should help purge libelous material in pre-production, they still will likely want you to an agreement that indemnifies them against all claims, suits and judgments.

In a work of fiction, what restrictions exist on using the names of professional sports teams, TV networks or real people?

If your character is a Dodgers fan that watches CNN and walks past Rupert Murdoch on the street, you generally won't have lawyers calling for your head. You can use these well-known proper names in your text as long as you don't intentionally try to harm the reputation of that person or product.

Normally you won't catch much grief for writing neutral or positive words about real people, places and things. It's the negative press you provide that could be considered trade libel or commercial disparagement—both ugly phrases that could cost you plenty of cash in a court of law.

Once an agent wants to take me on as a client and sends me a contract, do I need to have the agreement looked at by a contract lawyer before I sign to protect my rights?

It would probably be wise to have a lawyer who knows a thing or two about publishing look over the contract. Most contracts vary from agent to agent, and it's important to know exactly what agreements you make by signing. If you don't read the fine print or understand the legal language, months down the road you could find out that you gave up the right to profits from international sales.

About 20 years ago, I sold a short story to a magazine. One line in my contract stated the payment was for "full rights." Does this mean I can't sell the story ever again?

Selling full rights to your work is like selling your car—once the contract is signed, you have no rights to the piece and can't sell it again. The new owner has that copyright protection, even if the original publication went defunct. The best option is to find the former publisher and buy back the copyright.

Who holds the copyright in a work-for-hire?

With a work-for-hire, the buyer is usually obtaining the copyright. (Read your contract thoroughly to know for sure.) Also note: When a writer works for an organization as an employee and produces creative works as part of his job, the copyright to those works belongs to the employer.

Improve Your Book Contract

Nine Negotiating Tips

by The Authors Guild

Even if you're working with an agent, it's crucial to understand the legal provisions associated with book contracts. After all, you're the one ultimately responsible for signing off on the terms set forth by the deal. Below are nine clauses found in typical book contracts. Reading the explanation of each clause, along with the negotiating tips, will help clarify what you are agreeing to as the book's author.

1. Grant of Rights

The Grant of Rights clause transfers ownership rights in, and therefore control over, certain parts of the work from the author to the publisher. Although it's necessary and appropriate to grant some exclusive rights (e.g., the right to print, publish and sell print-book editions), don't assign or transfer your copyright and use discretion when granting rights in languages other than English and territories other than the United States, its territories and Canada. Also, limit the publication formats granted to those that your publisher is capable of exploiting adequately.
* Never transfer or assign your copyright or "all rights" in the work to your publisher.
* Limit the languages, territories and formats in which your publisher is granted rights.

2. Subsidiary Rights

Subsidiary rights are uses that your publisher may make of your manuscript other than issuing its own hardcover or paperback print book editions. Print-related subsidiary rights include book club and paperback reprint editions, publication of selections, condensations or abridgments in anthologies and textbooks and first and second serial rights (i.e., publication in newspapers or magazines either before or after publication of the hardcover book). Subsidiary rights not related to print include motion picture, television, stage, audio, animation, merchandising and electronic rights.

Subsidiary rights may be directly exploited by your publisher or licensed to third parties. Your publisher will share licensing fees with you in proportion to the ratios set forth in your contract. You should receive at least 50 percent of the licensing proceeds.
* Consider reserving rights outside the traditional grant of primary print book publishing rights, especially if you have an agent.
* Beware of any overly inclusive language, such as "in any format now known or hereafter developed," used to describe the scope of the subsidiary rights granted.

- Make sure you are fairly compensated for any subsidiary rights granted. Reputable publishers will pay you at least 50 percent of the proceeds earned from licensing certain categories of rights, much higher for others.

3. Delivery and Acceptance

Most contracts stipulate that the publisher is only obligated to accept, pay for and publish a manuscript that is "satisfactory to the publisher in form and content." It may be difficult to negotiate a more favorable, objective provision, but you should try. Otherwise, the decision as to whether your manuscript is satisfactory, and therefore publishable, will be left to the subjective discretion of your publisher.

- If you cannot do better, indicate that an acceptable manuscript is one which your publisher deems editorially satisfactory.
- Obligate your publisher to assist you in editing a second corrected draft before ultimately rejecting your manuscript.
- Negotiate a nonrefundable advance or insert a clause that would allow you to repay the advance on a rejected book from re-sale proceeds paid by a second publisher.

4. Publication

Including a publication deadline in your contract will obligate your publisher to actually publish your book in a timely fashion. Be sure that the amount of time between the delivery of the manuscript and the publication of the book isn't longer than industry standard.

- Make sure you're entitled to terminate the contract, regain all rights granted and keep the advance if your publisher fails to publish on or before the deadline.
- Carefully limit the conditions under which your publisher is allowed to delay publication.

5. Copyright

Current copyright law doesn't require authors to formally register their copyright in order to secure copyright protection. Copyright automatically arises in written works created in or after 1978. However, registration with the Copyright Office is a prerequisite to infringement lawsuits and important benefits accrue when a work is registered within three months of initial publication.

- Require your publisher to register your book's copyright within three months of initial publication.
- As previously discussed in Grant of Rights, don't allow your publisher to register copyright in its own name.

6. Advance

An advance against royalties is money that your publisher will pay you prior to publication and subsequently deduct from your share of royalty earnings. Most publishers will pay, but might not initially offer, an advance based on a formula which projects the first year's income.

- Bargain for as large an advance as possible. A larger advance gives your publisher greater incentive to publicize and promote your work.
- Research past advances paid by your publisher in industry publications such as *Publishers Weekly*.

7. Royalties

You should earn royalties for sales of your book that are in line with industry standards. For example, many authors are paid 10 percent of the retail price of the book on the first 5,000 copies sold, 12.5 percent of the retail price on the next 5,000 copies sold, and 15 percent of the retail price on all copies sold thereafter.

- Base your royalties on the suggested retail list price of the book, not on net sales income earned by your publisher. Net-based royalties are lower than list-based royalties of the same percentage, and they allow your publisher room to offer special deals or write off bad debt without paying you money on the books sold.
- Limit your publisher's ability to sell copies of your book at deep discounts—quantity discount sales of more than 50 percent—or as remainders.
- Limit your publisher's ability to reduce the percentage of royalties paid for export, book club, mail order and other special sales.

8. Accounting and Payments

Your accounting clause should establish the frequency with which you should expect to receive statements accounting for your royalty earnings and subsidiary rights licensing proceeds. If you are owed money in any given accounting period, the statement should be accompanied by a check.

- Insist on at least a bi-annual accounting.
- Limit your publisher's ability to withhold a reserve against returns of your book from earnings that are otherwise owed to you.
- Include an audit clause in your contract which gives you or your representative the right to examine the sales records kept by the publisher in connection with your work.

9. Out of Print

Your publisher should only have the exclusive rights to your work while it is actively marketing and selling your book (i.e., while your book is "in print"). An out-of-print clause will allow you to terminate the contract and regain all rights granted to your publisher after the book stops earning money.

It is crucial to actually define the print status of your book in the contract. Stipulate that your work is in print only when copies are available for sale in the United States in an English language hardcover or paperback edition issued by the publisher and listed in its catalog. Otherwise, your book should be considered out of print and all rights should revert to you.

- Don't allow the existence of electronic and print-on-demand editions to render your book in print. Alternatively, establish a floor above which a certain amount of royalties must be earned or copies must be sold during each accounting period for your book to be considered in print. Once sales or earnings fall below this floor, your book should be deemed out of print and rights should revert to you.
- Stipulate that as soon as your book is out of print, all rights will automatically revert to you regardless of whether or not your book has earned out the advance.

Sealing the Deal

The Next Steps

So You Have an Agent—Now What?

by Chuck Sambuchino

In this book, we've told you all about contacting and securing agents. Details on everything from writing to pitching to getting the most out of your subsidiary rights are included in these pages. But should your hard work and passion pay off in a signed deal with a big-shot agent, the journey isn't over. Now it's time to learn what lies in store after the papers are signed.

LET YOUR AGENT WORK

In the time leading up to signing a contract, you may have bantered around plenty with your agent—realizing you both love the New York Yankees and Kung Pao Chicken. But don't let this camaraderie allow you to forget that the relationship is a business one first and foremost. Does this mean you can't small talk occasionally and ask your agent how her children are doing? No. But don't call every day complaining about the traffic and your neighbor's habit of mowing his lawn before the sun comes up.

Your agent is going to read your work again (and again . . .) and likely suggest possible changes to the manuscript. "When you sign with an agent, you should go over next steps, and talk about what the agent expects from you," says Sorche Fairbank, principal of the Fairbank Literary Agency. "This can vary with each author-agent relationship, and on the type of book project. We (at the Fairbank agency) are fairly hands-on with shaping and polishing a proposal or manuscript, and there often is quite a bit of work to be done before we and the author feel it's ready to send out.

"If you have a nonfiction project, there is certain to be some final tweaking of the proposal and sample chapter(s)," Fairbank says. "If you have a novel, then I hope you would be . . . taking any agent advice on tightening and polishing it. Go through it one more time and weed out extraneous words, overused pet words and phrases, and stock descriptions."

KEEP WRITING

If you're not working with your agent on rewrites and revisions, it's your responsibility to continue creating. One challenge is over—another begins. As your agent is trying hard to sell your work and bring home a nice paycheck, you're expected to keep churning out material for her to sell. Keep her informed of what you're working on and when it'll be ready.

Stay passionate. Once you've convinced yourself that your first book was not a fluke,

---

CHUCK SAMBUCHINO (guidetoliteraryagents.com/blog) is the editor of *Guide to Literary Agents*. He is the author of *How to Survive a Garden Gnome Attack* (Ten Speed Press, Sept. 2010) as well as *Formatting & Submitting Your Manuscript* (Writer's Digest Books).

you've convinced yourself that you're a capable writer—and a capable writer needs to keep writing and always have material to sell. Always be considering new projects and working on new things, but give preference to the first work that got you a contract. Rewrites and revisions—wanted by agents and editors alike—will likely take months and become somewhat tedious, but all that frustration will melt away when you have that first hardcover book in your hands.

SELLING THE BOOK

When the book is as perfect as can be, it's time for your agent to start shopping it to her publishing contacts. During this process, she'll likely keep you abreast of all rejections. Don't take these to heart—instead, learn from each one, especially those with editors who have kindly given a specific reason as to why they don't want the book." When the project is being shopped around, discuss rejections with your agent. There may be patterns that point to a fixable weak spot," Fairbank says.

Your book may be bought in a pre-empt. That's when a publishing house tries to beat other potential buyers to your work and offers a solid price in the hopes of securing your book early and avoiding a bidding war. An actual bidding war—or "auction"—happens when a work is so stunningly marvelous that every house in town wants it bad enough to compete against each other, offering different perks such as a large advance and guaranteed ad dollars. Traditionally, the best deal (read: most money and enthusiasm) wins and signs. After the auction was finished for Elizabeth Kostova's *The Historian*, her advance was a cool $2 million. (Note: First-time novelists will likely get an advance of $20,000 to $60,000, but hey, anything can happen!)

Your agent will submit the work to publishers (either exclusively or simultaneously, depending on her opinion) and hold a private auction if need be to secure the best deal possible. Fairbank says it's important for writers to relax during the auction process and not call every 30 minutes for an update. "In an auction, everything should go through the agent, but writers may be called upon to do a few things," she says. "I have had some cases where it made sense to bring the author around to meet with the various interested houses, usually to drive home the author's expertise and promotability. In every instance, it increased the size of the offers. There have also been times where a particular house asked for more specifics on something, and I needed my author ready to respond ASAP."

PROMOTE YOURSELF

Besides continuing to write and revise, the most important thing a writer needs to focus on is promotion. It's likely your work will not have the benefit of countless publicists setting up interviews for you. How you want to promote your work is up to you.

According to Regina Brooks, president of Serendipity Literary Agency, "It's always a great time to research who you might want on your team once the book is published (e.g., publicists, Web developers, graphic artists, etc.). Often times, authors wait until the last minute to start researching these options. The more lead time a publicist has to think about your project, the better. This is also an ideal time to attend conferences to network and workshops to tighten your writing skills."

GO WITH THE FLOW

An agent's job is to agent. That means knowing which people are buying what, and where they're headed if a move is in the works. Throughout the editing process, you'll work hand-in-hand with your agent and editor to revise and polish the manuscript. But let's say the editor makes the not-so-uncommon decision to switch jobs or switch houses. Ideally, an agent will shepherd you through the change.

"It happens more often than we'd like," says Brooks. "When it does, you hope that someone in-house will be as excited about the project as the acquiring editor initially was, but there's no guarantee." Fairbank agrees: "The most important thing the author and agent can do in that case is take a deep breath, pick up the phone, and wholeheartedly welcome the new editor to the book team. Once they have their feet under them and have reviewed your work, ask them what they think, and listen to any questions or comments they may have."

In addition to switching editors at publishing houses, a writer must concern himself with the possibility of his agent hitting the lottery and quitting (or just quitting without hitting the lottery, which is more probable). To protect yourself, make sure that this scenario is clearly addressed in your contract with the agent. "It really depends on the initial written agreement between the agent and the author," says Brooks. "It's important that the agreement cover such situations in their termination language. This assures that all parties including the publishing company know how to proceed with royalty statements, notices, etc."

AND WHAT IF . . . ?

A difficult question that may come up is this: What should you do if you think your agent has given up on you, or isn't fulfilling her end of the bargain? (In other words, how do you get out? *Can* you get out?) First, consider that if an agent is trying and failing to sell your manuscript, then at least the *trying* part is there. It could just be an unfortunate instance where you and an agent both love a work but can't find anyone else who feels the same. This is no one's fault. As far as simply quitting an agent is concerned, you can't opt out of a contract until the contract says so.

A similar dilemma involves authors who have a satisfactory agent but want out in favor of one perceived to be better. If you already have an agent, but others are calling in hopes to work with you, the new agents likely don't know you already possess representation. Obviously, you need to tell them you are currently represented. That said, you most likely can't just switch agents because you're under contract. When the time comes when you can legally opt out of a contract (and you think your agent has had ample time to make a sale), consider your options then.

GET READY FOR YOUR RIDE

Hopefully, you'll never need to experience the difficulty and confusion of switching agents and/or editors. Hopefully, your work will smoothly find a house and then a large audience once it's published. Just remember that the smoother things go, the less excuses exist for you not to keep writing then promote the heck out of your work. Simply do what you do best (write) and continue to learn what you can about the publishing world. As Fairbank puts it so simply, "Be available, willing, and ready to help your agent."

Sealing the Deal

How Authors Make Money

Advances, Royalties, Rights, and Bonuses

by Paul S. Levine, Esq.

In this article, I'm going to discuss four ways authors make money from book publishers. When I give lectures to beginning writers, I find that they have very little idea of how they can go from slaving away on their keyboards at night to actually quitting their day job.

I'm going to discuss here not only ways in which authors make money from publishers, but also ways publishers try not to pay, or try to postpone paying for as long as possible, monies authors are owed. Of course, there are other avenues outside of these four ways in which authors can make money, but they don't involve getting paid by the publisher. Other money can come from third parties, such as the sale of movie and television rights to Hollywood, or foreign rights to overseas territories (countries)—but those are subjects for other articles. So for right now, let's focus on advances, royalties, serialization rights, and best-seller bonuses.

ADVANCES

Advances are just what the term implies: monies paid in advance of something being paid later. In this case, an *advance against royalties* to be paid once your book is actually published (and, hopefully, sells a gazillion copies). Advances can range from a thousand dollars to several hundred thousand or even millions of dollars. In general, the smaller the publishing house, the smaller the upfront paycheck; many small houses don't even pay advances at all. At the other end of the spectrum, when two or more large houses get into a "bidding war" (an *auction*) over your book, the sky is the limit on the size of the advance could be paid.

Advances are non-refundable. This is a detail many writers inquire about—fearing that poor book sales will force them to forfeit the money they received prior to the book's release. But rest assured, an advance is yours to keep. So even if your publisher sells only five copies of the book to your immediate family and no one else buys it, you don't have to return the advance paid to you. That's the good news. The bad news is that if your book fairs poorly and the publisher's investment is a loss—that is to say, the advance paid to you is not recouped—you could be branded as a writer who is not financially worthwhile.

Advances are typically paid in installments. For example, one-third on signing the publishing agreement; one-third on "acceptance" of your manuscript (i.e., when your editor and you have agreed that "this" is the version of your manuscript which will be published); and one-third when your book is actually published. One way in which publishers delay paying your advance, or at least the first "installment," is by holding on to the publishing

PAUL S. LEVINE, ESQ. (paulslevine.com and paulslevinelit.com) is a literary agent and publishing and intellectual property attorney based in Venice, Calif. He has been representing writers for more than 28 years.

agreement you've signed and not counter-signing it. Remember, the first portion of the advance is payable "on signing," and, until the publisher counter-signs it, the agreement is not final.

You can avoid this problem by asking your agent to change the contract language to read that the first part of the advance is payable within a certain number of days (5 or 10 business days is typical) after the publisher receives the agreement that you've signed and your agent has sent back.

ROYALTIES

Royalties are an author's share of a book's selling price. In other words, every time a copy of your book sells, you get a small percentage of the profit: a royalty. The amount you receive per book sold depends on the book's price as well as the language in your contract.

Flat fees vs. an advance against royalties

A "flat fee" is when an author gets no royalties per book but rather a set payment for the entire job. The upside to a flat fee is that authors do not have to worry about earning out an advance. The downside is that payment is set, so if the book sells half a million copies, there are no extra royalties to be had.

We already talked about advances, and how that money is yours to keep. What writers must keep in mind is that money paid in advance needs to be earned back before you start earning royalties. Let's break down an example: You sell a book and the publishing house gives you a $15,000 advance. According to your contract, you earn $1 per book in royalties. What that means is that you will have to sell 15,000 copies of your book (15,000 x $1 = $15,000) to earn out the advance. Upon selling copy 15,001, you begin earning royalties: $1 per book. You can continue earning royalties, in theory, forever—and the royalty amount will increase with stellar sales.

Royalty percentages

In order to compare offers from various houses, royalties should always be expressed in the same way—as a percentage of the Suggested Retail List Price ("SRLP"), or "cover price," of the book. Note that this is *not* the price at which the retailer sells the book to the consumer, which may be 30% or more off the SRLP, but rather the price on the cover of the book.

A typical royalty structure for a hardcover book is 10 percent of the first 5,000 copies sold; 12.5 percent of the next 5,000 copies sold; and 15 percent for all copies sold in excess of 10,000. Once again, remember that this is *always* a percentage of the same thing—the SRLP. So, if your book has a SRLP of $29.99, and more than 10,000 copies of your book have been sold, you will receive a royalty of $4.50 per book.

Payment

Royalties are usually paid twice a year—as stated in the contract, "within 60 (or 90) days after the close of the semi-annual accounting period." So, for example, for the period January through June, your agent will receive the royalty statement (and, of course, any money due), on March 1 or April 1.

Clever accounting

One way for the publisher to try to "cheat" you out of your full royalty is to have a provision in the publishing agreement (usually buried where you and your agent won't find it) that says something like "If the book is purchased by the retailer [*i.e.* when the retailer sells it to the consumer] at other than our usual and customary discount [which is almost always 50 percent of the SRLP] we will cut your royalty rate by one-half." What this means is if the retailer pays the publisher $14.97 instead of $15.00 for that book which has a SRLP of $30,00, you will receive a royalty check for $2.25 instead of $4.50. Your agent should be able to solve this problem by specifying the percentage off the SRLP that triggers the royalty cut, and by minimizing the actual cut

Royalties are paid on all books sold, except for promotional copies and the like. It is rare, but not unheard of, for a publisher to "mis-count" the number of books sold. So, it is usually wise to add a provision to the "audit" clause of the contract, which says that if you have to hire an auditor to examine the publisher's records, and the auditor finds a discrepancy of five percent or more in your favor, then the publisher, and not you, pays for the cost of the audit.

Speaking of the number of books actually sold, watch out for a clause in the publishing agreement that allows the publisher to "hold" a "reserve against returns." Because books are on the shelves at retailers on a consignment basis, they can be returned to the publisher if they are not sold. Publishers can, and do, estimate the amount of books likely to be returned, and hold back a certain amount of money from royalties otherwise due. (Note that when your agent receives your royalty statement, it will show the amount of books actually *shipped* to the retailers, and the number of books *actually returned* during the period covered by the statement. Because there is no way for the publisher to know how many books will be returned during the *next* accounting period, the publisher usually takes a reserve against returns.)

What you don't want is for the publisher to keep taking that reserve indefinitely. The reserve should be "liquidated," or credited to you, during the third or fourth accounting period. By then, the publisher should have a good idea of the amount of returns it is likely to receive, because it will have received most, if not nearly all, of the returns it is going to receive. There is therefore no need, or continuing justification, for the publisher to keep taking the reserve against returns.

FIRST AND SECOND SERIALIZATION RIGHTS

Say you've written a cookbook, and a magazine wants to publish your chapter on desserts (i.e., an *excerpt* from your book) in an upcoming edition of its magazine. If the magazine hits to the newsstands *before* your book is published, this is called "first serialization," and, by long-standing custom (as well as by a provision in your contract), you will usually receive 90 percent of whatever money the magazine pays the publisher. This can be quite a substantial amount of money if the magazine is a major one (think *Bon Appetit* or *Forbes*) and is especially valuable promotion for your book. There will usually be a blurb at the end of the magazine article that says something to the effect of "Excerpted with permission from the upcoming book [*Title*] by [Author] to be published by [Publisher] in [Pub Date]."

If the magazine is issued *after* your book is published, the publicity and promotional value diminishes somewhat. For these "second serialization" rights, you and your publisher will usually equally split whatever money the magazine pays the publisher. Publications may contact you asking for an excerpt, or you the author may query and pitch them an article that involves excerpting your book. Traditionally, magazines and other publications pay less for an excerpt than they would for a new, assigned article.

BEST-SELLER BONUSES

For each week your book is in the "Top 10" or Top 15" of a "best-seller list," such as the one issued by the *New York Times*, you will receive a "bonus" of a certain amount of money, typically $5,000 or $10,000. Every once in a great while, the publisher forgets to "cap" the total amount of this bonus which you receive (typically $50,000), so, if your book is on the list for 293 weeks, you can expect to receive an additional $2,930,000 over your royalties and other monies. We all live for that day!

Sealing the Deal

10 Hidden Gifts of Rejection Letters

See the Silver Lining

by Debra Darvick

1. Rejection letters take you out of submission limbo. Familiar with that hell whose name is Waiting? Is the agent reading your submission? Chortling with her cronies over it? Using it as a doorstop or drink coaster? With that rejection letter in hand, you now know where you stand. No more wondering. No more worry. Of course, no more hope either. Time to move on. Next.

2. All it takes is one rejection letter to make you an instant life member of a club whose luminaries include Walt Whitman, J.K. Rowling and Dr. Seuss. What published writer has never received a rejection letter? These are our badges of determination. Of striving. And on bad days, of lunacy. Take heart. No one's, and I mean no one's, first query snags an agent and a book contract. Unless of course you are Madonna, Jamie Lee Curtis or Fergie.

3. Rejection letters strengthen you and build courage. Where would you be if you didn't rail at your most recent rejection letter: "Agent Babe, you are wrong! I will *not* make my overweight heroine svelte, my gay character straight or turn my borzoi into a chihuahua!" Rejection letters give you practice taking a hit and moving on. Are you going to let one agent's (or one dozen's) opinion make you give up your intention to publish your book? Hell no.

4. Rejection letters can be stockpiled for future use: wallpaper; bonfire kindling; shredded material as an environmentally sound substitute for Styrofoam peanuts. Personally, I'm going to turn them into a necklace. My other creative outlet is beaded jewelry. I've just found a way to roll paper strips into beads. I plan to make a necklace from paper strips cut from my rejection letters and wear it to my book signings, the National Book Awards Ceremony, and the Academy Awards. OK, OK, I'll start with the signings and take it from there.

5. The good ones (offering constructive criticism) help you develop as a writer. And you *will* get some good ones in amongst the ones who used your manuscript as coffee coasters and doorstops. Thoughtful rejection letters, in addition to being a balm to your weary writer's soul, afford the opportunity to revisit your work, to consider it through another's lens. Such letters may lead you in a new direction. Or you might just add them to your stack of kindling. Good rejection letters are a clue that you are on the right track and getting closer. Take heart.

DEBRA DARVICK (debradarvick.wordpress.com) is a journalist, essayist and author of *This Jewish Life: Stories of Discovery, Connection and Joy*. Her book, *I Love Jewish Faces* (a children's picture book celebrating Jewish diversity) was published by the URJ Press in May 2009.

6. Get a few rejection letters beneath your belt and you can blog authoritatively on sites such as absolutewrite.com's Water Cooler. There are more web-based communities devoted to the world of submissions than you can shake a keyboard at. At the abovementioned Water Cooler, bloggers share their agent experiences. Which ones don't follow through? Which ones are reputable? Which ones should be drawn and quartered for asking for a full and then never getting back to you? Rejection letter in hand, you can add your voice to the fray.

7. All it takes is one good one to renew your faith in agents. Number Seven is a corollary to Number Five. There are good agents out there—human beings who love books as much as you do. Why else would they be in the business of trying to link their authors with publishers? Or take home reams of manuscripts to read over the weekend when they could be training for the New York City Marathon instead? A good rejection letter, whose tone is sincere and offers advice, can revive your flagging spirit.

8. Rejection letters keep the USPS in business. The Internet has taken a huge toll on the USPS. Mail carriers may go the way of the Maytag man. And then what will happen to the stamp designers? To the workers who assemble all those annoying circulars that come through the slot as fourth class mail? To the Neiman-Marcus Christmas catalog? Rejection letters might mean you can't quit your day job but they do help others keep theirs.

9. Rejection letters let you know who your true allies are. Are your loved ones sympathetic when a dreaded rejection letter falls through the slot? Do they bring flowers or send sweet e-mails of encouragement? Or do they chide you and say, "*Now* will you get serious and put this silliness away?" Rejection letters let you know who you want on your team in this endeavor.

10. The number of rejection letters you receive is proportional to the euphoria that will envelop you when you do get The Call. Think about it. If an agent signs you up three queries into your search, you'll be ecstatic. And perhaps kind of blasé. But get that call after slugging it out for a year or so, and man will success be sweet. So sweet you can taste it even now, can't you?

Perspectives

Does Location Matter?

Three Colorado Agents Weigh In

by Kerrie Flanagan

 location is not as important as many writers think when it comes to finding a good literary agent. The explosion of technology and social media over the past decade make it easy for agents to stay connected with editors regardless of where the agent lives. Literary agents Kristin Nelson, Kate Schafer Testerman and Rachelle Gardner agree that living in New York, the Emerald City of the publishing world, isn't what makes a successful agent. Residing at the foot of the snow-capped Rocky Mountains, these three Colorado-based agents have all found success outside of the Big Apple.

KRISTIN NELSON

Kristin Nelson, founder and president of Nelson Literary agency, has her office in the heart of downtown Denver. In 2002, after working with another Colorado agent, she decided to strike out on her own. "I actually opened my own company because the previous agency did nonfiction almost exclusively and I wanted to do fiction," said Nelson. "I wanted all kinds of fiction, including genre stuff like romance and science-fiction and fantasy. That definitely would not have fit at that agency."

Nelson Literary also represents women's fiction, chick lit, YA, middle grade and memoir. Nelson would love to see more literary fiction with that strong commercial bent—like Jamie Ford, author of *Hotel on the Corner of Bitter and Sweet*; a novel with great storytelling, lovely writing, and a dynamic plot to really drive the story.

For Nelson, reputation, not location, is an agent's greatest asset. "The reality is that I network with editors almost about the same amount of time as any New York City agent, and any New York editor will tell you that an agent's location matters less than his/her reputation in terms of how serious a project is considered, how fast a project is read, how much money will be negotiated for it."

Since the beginning, Nelson has worked diligently to gain the respect and confidence of editors and it shows. In less than ten years, the Nelson Agency has sold more than 100 books and landed several film deals. Many of their authors became national bestsellers, RITA-award winners, and appeared on bestseller lists such as *The New York Times*, *USA Today*, Barnes & Noble, *The Wall Street Journal*, and *The Denver Post*.

KERRIE FLANAGAN is a freelance writer and the Director of Northern Colorado Writers (NorthernColoradoWriters. com), an organization that supports and encourages writers of all levels and genres. Each spring her conference draws agents, editors and writers from all over the country.

KATE SCHAFER TESTERMAN

Another agent, Kate Schafer Testerman, founder of KT Literary, worked for Janklow & Nesbit Associates in New York for over a decade. In 2008 she left the agency, the city and sea level behind to start her own agency in Highlands Ranch, Colo. She represents middle grade and YA fiction as well as some adult commercial fiction and narrative nonfiction. Testerman would love to see more fantastic middle grade novels: "I feel like my cup runneth over a bit in terms of the quality and quantity of YA submissions I receive, but I would love to see more great middle grade novels, particularly those you'd call 'boy books.'"

Leaving the big city did not affect her relationships with editors. "I actually know more about some editors now than I did when I was in New York City, where I worked for more than 12 years. Plus, each trip I take back to refresh my face time, I see more editors in a single week than I would otherwise see in months."

RACHELLE GARDNER

A little further south in Monument, you will find Rachelle Gardner of WordServe literary. For more than a decade, Gardner worked for both the Christian and mainstream publishing industries in various capacities including marketing, sales, international rights, acquisitions and editorial. A few years back, she worked as a freelance editor and writer. Her agent, Greg Johnson, was looking to bring in another agent. "I finally realized that as an agent, I could still do what I loved—work with authors and help them with their books," said Gardner. "I decided to make the switch, and it turned out to be perfect for me."

When it comes to being a successful agent outside of New York, Gardner has another reason why this works for her. "Some agents specialize in an area of publishing that's not quite so concentrated in New York. My primary area of interest is Christian publishing, and 99% of Christian publishers are located outside of New York— Chicago, Nashville and Colorado Springs are the main cities. So being in Colorado works great for me."

CONNECTED THROUGH TECHNOLOGY

Nelson, Testerman and Gardner state that the boom in technology has allowed them and other agents more freedom to operate outside of New York City. Testerman states that in the past few months, her Twitter and Facebook connections with editors and other agents have quadrupled. Gardner also likes the way social media has given her regular, everyday contact with agents on the east coast. Nelson stays in contact with others in the industry via private Yahoo chat rooms. Testerman goes on to say, "With technology such as it is, it's almost easier today for me to stay in touch with people 1,600 miles away than a few years ago, when I was only six blocks away."

All three women have successful blogs they update daily, which helps them not only stay in contact with other agents and editors, but also with current and potential clients. They share publishing news, industry advice, answer questions and share what they'd like to see more and less of. Even with the blogs and other social media, authors still have misperceptions about where an agent should live and do business. Many still feel that a good agent needs to live in New York City.

"I think the greatest misperception writers hold about New York agents," said Nelson, "is that they are always going to lunch or popping by the publisher's office to be 'in touch and in the know;' that you have to be there to throw your weight around."

Testerman adds, "They might think that agents outside of New York can't sell books as effectively, or maintain strong relationships with editors. That's a misperception because these days, most day-to-day business is done electronically whether you live across the street from the publisher or half a continent away."

Testerman has also come across another issue in regards to location. Some authors believe that it is good if their agent lives in the same state. For her, it doesn't matter if a potential client lives in Denver or Barrow, Alaska. She bases her decision to sign an author based on the writing, not on where they live. She believes authors should do the same thing when choosing an agent. The decision should be based on the reputation and abilities of the agent, not their location.

VISITING NEW YORK

Technology aside, nothing replaces face-to-face meeting—and each of these agents sets aside time annually to visit New York. "For the weeks that I'm there, we are usually doing our big marketing meetings with my marketing director, the author, and the publisher's in-house marketing and promotion team," says Nelson. "We lay all the groundwork for our upcoming releases. I also do a lot of breakfast, lunch, tea, evening drinks or dinner meetings with editors I either have projects with or editors I want to know better."

Testerman heads there somewhere between three and five times a years, for about a week at a time. "When I'm prepping a New York trip," she says, "I start making lots of phone calls and sending e-mails, setting up appointments. On a given day in New York City, I may see an average of 7 or 8 editors—more if some of my meetings involve multiple editors at once. I'm meeting people over breakfast, lunch, and drinks, seeing authors for dinners, and meeting for coffee or in publishers' offices all day."

For Gardner, who focuses mainly on the Christian market, other locations like Nashville and Chicago are also important to her business. But she still schedules a trip or two to New York where she meets with editors.

New York City is still the hub of the publishing world, but technology has opened up other options for agents. Savvy agents no longer need to live and work in Manhattan in order to stay connected to editors and publishers. For Gardner, Nelson and Testerman, there is no place like home—in Colorado.

Perspectives

My First Year with an Agent and Editor

One Novelist Looks Back

by Karen Dionne

I write science thrillers. My debut was published from Berkley Books in October 2008. *Freezing Point* is about a solar energy company that uses microwaves from orbiting satellites to melt Antarctic icebergs into drinking water while environmental extremists plot to stop them—neither realizing that the water is contaminated with an unknown, deadly disease. (Think *Jurassic Park* on ice.)

Except … *Freezing Point* was *not* my first novel. In 1998, I wrote a science thriller set in the South American jungle. *That* was my first novel. I finished the first draft in three months, and because I knew nothing about the publishing industry except that I wanted to place the book with a major publisher, I prematurely began looking for an agent. The initial results were not pretty.

THE FIRST NOVEL

When an agent reads your query and requests material, they don't want to receive your first draft. They want edited, polished work that has already gone through multiple drafts and readers. (Of course, I know that *now*.) Now I can say that querying agents with my first draft was a grievous mistake. The odds of an author's first efforts catching the eye of an agent are incredibly small. A bad idea a dozen years ago, it's an even worse one now. In today's publishing climate, agents and editors are more cautious than ever about what they take on. It's foolhardy to query with anything less than your absolute best.

But at the time, authors didn't have the wealth of resources that are available now, and I was woefully naive. In 1999, only a handful of literary agents even accepted e-queries when, after my snail mail efforts didn't pan out, I decided to give them a try. I searched through my copy of *Guide to Literary Agents*, then e-mailed 19 prospective agents on an optimistic Thursday morning. Within the hour, I had two requests for the full. One agent's e-mail opened with, "Dear Ms. Dionne: I would be pleased to consider your novel." The other began, "Dear Ms. Dionne: Your novel sounds wonderful!"

THE CALL

One enthusiastic response was from Jeff Kleinman (then of Graybill & English, now of Folio Literary Management). I printed the manuscript per his instructions and sent it off. Four days later, I received an e-mail. Mr. Kleinman had begun reading the manuscript as soon

---

KAREN DIONNE (karendionne.net) is the author of *Freezing Point*. She is a member of Sisters in Crime, Mystery Writers of America, and the International Thriller Writers.

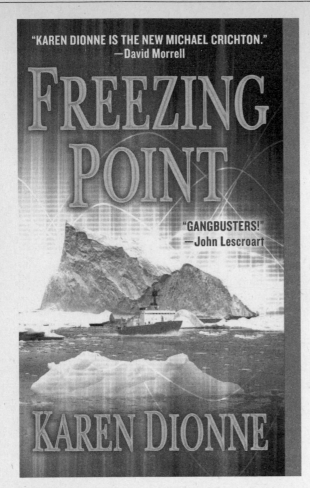

"KAREN DIONNE IS THE NEW MICHAEL CRICHTON."
—David Morrell

FREEZING POINT

"GANGBUSTERS!"
—John Lescroart

KAREN DIONNE

as it arrived, but the story was running into some snags. He asked me to call him the next day at my convenience to discuss. I fretted all night. Is a snag bigger than a problem? He said "snags"—plural. Does that mean there's more than one? If you're a writer, you know this fretting drill.

I called first thing the next morning. Jeff assured me he loved my novel's premise, and thought my writing was strong. The plotting, however, was a mess. As he detailed where I'd gone wrong, it became apparent that he was being charitable when he'd used the term "snags." However, I knew immediately that he was right. Far more than the proverbial light bulb, it was like a bank of floodlights on a movie set had gone off. So when Jeff said he wanted to take me on as a client if I was willing to rewrite the book, I immediately said yes.

It was a bittersweet moment. I'd gone from having a book, but no agent, to having an agent, but no book. However, I knew what I needed to do, and couldn't wait to dive in. But I hadn't yet learned how to write a novel. Jeff has a marvelous editorial eye, but even with his help, it took me three and a half years and three complete rewrites before we were satisfied. In the final version, only two of the original 62 chapters remained. In his book, *Writing the Breakout Novel*, Donald Maass says that "a novel is a large, complex, fluid, and difficult-to-manage undertaking. It is a tough art form to get right, one tougher still to master." My experience certainly proved that true.

THE SECOND NOVEL

Ultimately, after all the work, that first novel didn't sell. So I went back to the story I'd begun during my agent search—a science thriller about an environmental disaster in Antarctica.

In July 2006, *Freezing Point* was ready. We recast the story as an environmental thriller because it had a strong environmental theme, and technothrillers were currently out of vogue. My agent sent the manuscript to fifteen editors. Within days, rejections came in. "I think ecological thrillers are always somewhat difficult," one editor wrote. "Certainly, there is always Michael Crichton, but by and large I think it's a difficult category," wrote another. "These environmental/techno thrillers just don't seem to work unless they come from a more established author," from another. And even, "I actually ended up reading this entire book because the premise really sucked me in—imagine that! Even I, a self-professed non-fan of eco-thrillers..."

At first, I wasn't worried. All we needed was one editor to fall in love. But by the end of two months, all of the editors passed on *Freezing Point*. Believing the submission process was over, I did what novelists do: started another.

Dream Agent

I have a theory about authors and agents, and it goes like this: Authors write passionately on the subjects they care about most. Their writing also reflects their personality. Tender and romantic, sly and witty, acerbic and cynical, who they are, what they believe, and their approach to life—it all comes through in their work. When an agent asks to represent an author, ostensibly, it's because they've fallen in love with the author's story. But I maintain that because the author's work is so intrinsically a part of them, in a literary sense, the agent has actually fallen in love with the author.

It's no coincidence that the agent-author relationship is often likened to a marriage. When two people love each other, they understand each other, trust each other, and work well together. I know many authors who say they love their agent. I certainly adore mine.

When I began my agent search, I had no idea that my dream agent would turn out to be Jeff Kleinman (then of Graybill & English, now of Folio Literary Management). If I had, Jeff would not have been the 54th agent I queried. Like many new writers, I'd set my sights on well-known agents at the big-name agencies. What I now understand is that a new author and a new agent at an established agency are very often an ideal fit. New agents more readily take on new clients because they're actively building their lists. And while they're less experienced, when they need advice, they can easily tap the other agents at their agency. Because a new agent is in the process of establishing their career and reputation, they actually have more at stake when they take on a project, and are thus more invested in seeing their clients succeed.

When I signed with Jeff Kleinman, we were both just starting out. As I became a better writer, he became a better agent. Over the years, our careers have both grown. I started a writers organization that now has more than 1,200 members in a dozen countries. Jeff partnered with two other agents to form his own agency, which quickly became one of the most respected and successful in the biz. (Folio now has nine agents as of 2010.) I've heard aspiring writers say my agent is on their "A-list." If I were querying today, he'd be at the top of mine. By signing with him when he was a new agent, I got in on the ground floor.

THE CALL (REDUX)

Six months later, in January 2007, I happened to be in a bookstore when Jeff called. He asked if I could talk, and wouldn't tell me more until I sat down. By that time, I was so deeply immersed in writing the new story, I couldn't imagine what he had to say that was so important I had to sit to hear it. I resisted. It went like this.

"Just tell me what you want."

"No, I'm not going to tell you until you're sitting down. Are you sitting down?"

"I'm sitting down," I finally said after I found an empty chair, annoyed that he was making me play such a ridiculous game.

But after Jeff told me we had an offer for *Freezing Point* from Berkley, my knees actually did get weak. It was such an incredible, once-in-a-lifetime, life-changing moment. My girls bought me flowers and fixed a lovely celebration dinner, and my husband and I broke open the gift bottle of champagne I'd been saving for this occasion for years.

What changed? Why did an editor suddenly want to publish my novel? I believe it was simply a matter of timing. Between the time *Freezing Point* went on submission and my editor

Perspectives

read the novel, Al Gore's documentary *An Inconvenient Truth* had come out. Environmental issues had become the darlings of the day. Eco-thrillers were now a hot commodity.

After *Freezing Point* published, a number of trade magazines and reviewers commented on my novel's timeliness. "The scientific and ethical themes are fascinating and timely" (*Publishers Weekly*). "The storyline is as disturbing as it is chilling when you think that something like this could actually happen" (*Fresh Fiction*). "A timely, terrifying thriller" (*Dame Magazine*). This for a novel I began writing a full ten years before the book hit the shelves.

BOOK THREE—AND BEYOND

Shortly after *Freezing Point* published, my editor signed on for another environmental thriller from me. Scheduled for October 2010, *Boiling Point* brings back two characters from *Freezing Point*, and features an erupting volcano, a missing researcher, and a radical scheme to end global warming. Because I hadn't yet written the novel, I was able to take a research trip to the location where the story takes place: Chaitén Volcano in Northern Patagonia, Chile. The volcano actually erupted on May 2, 2008, for the first time in 9,000 years, and since then has never stopped. I stayed in the town at the volcano's base, even though the volcano is on Red Alert and the town is without electricity and running water, and hiked to within one mile of the lava dome, where I saw steam vents, heard explosions coming from the caldera, and felt a small earthquake.

Visiting Chaitén Volcano was an amazing experience that brought a level of authority and detail to my novel I never would have been able to otherwise achieve. It's hard to imagine any research trip I might take in the future that could possibly top a trip to an active volcano—unless I write a thriller about a lunar landing gone wrong!

My journey from aspiring novelist to internationally published thriller author began the day my future dream agent fell in love with the first draft of my first book. The dedication to *Freezing Point* reads simply, "For Jeff, for everything." Now you know why. Literary love. It's a beautiful thing.

Self-Publishing and Agents

Make Your Project Interest Agents

by Chuck Sambuchino

Between subsidy publishers, vanity presses, print-on-demand companies, Lulu.com and other options, plenty of avenues exist for writers to see their work brought to life outside of the traditional publishing route. While writers young and old will argue all day about the benefits and downsides of self-publishing, one thing is fairly certain. It's very difficult for a self-published book to be available in bookstores all across the country and break out. That's why acquiring a literary agent to rep the book is seen as a logical step in the process.

As inspiring as it is to stare at that copy of *Eragon* on your bookshelves, know that getting an agent to take on a self-published book and take it to best-seller lists is no easy task. In fact, the odds are very slim. Some agents won't even consider your book, no matter what. The many that *will* consider it are already deluged in slush—so your submission better stand out. Before you send out any more queries (or worse, the whole book), keep reading to find out what agents said about what they look for—and what they absolutely must see—when considering to take on a self-published book.

FOR YOUR CONSIDERATION, MS. AGENT

Let's go straight to the good news: Many agents are open to representing self-published books and trying to see those books get a new contract. "Most agents will at least hear out an author with a self-published book to the same extent that they would hear out any query letter," says agent Stephany Evans, president of FinePrint Literary Management.

Make sure that, as always, you follow agency submission guidelines to a T. If the agency says "Query only," then don't send the book. Also be certain that the rep you're contacting does indeed handle works in your particular genre or category. (If you haven't defined what your work is—e.g., memoir, thriller—you need to identify it before starting the query process, or else you'll waste a lot of money sending out books.)

As you might expect, some agents, on the other hand, won't consider self-published works of any kind. Those closed to submissions include high-brow reps in the literary world with a full list of clients. And then there are just a small number of agents who pass on self-published books because they take pleasure of finding "fresh" projects. "A self-published book is already viewed as a 'used product.' There are so many great new manuscripts out there for editors to choose from, so why take on one that already has some community?" says Andrea Brown, founder of Andrea Brown Literary Agency.

CHUCK SAMBUCHINO (guidetoliteraryagents.com/blog) is the editor of *Guide to Literary Agents*. He is the author of *How to Survive a Garden Gnome Attack* (Ten Speed Press, Sept. 2010) as well as *Formatting & Submitting Your Manuscript* (Writer's Digest Books).

Michelle Andelman, an associate agent at Brown's agency, echoes the same opinion: "I won't consider self-published books, because they deflate that great sense of 'discovery' for me. I always feel I can most enthusiastically champion something brand new to editors, who I think are eager to feel that sense of discovery as well."

MAKE YOUR PROJECT STAND OUT

When an author sends in a query for a novel, the *hook* is the crucial element. An agent wants to know what makes this particular book unique. Queries for self-published books have the disadvantage of immediately being scanned for not only a clever hook, but also a promising track record of sales.

In fact, your sales may be *the* most important factor in the query, because agents are looking for proof that the book has markets into which to tap. Concerning how many sales constitute a number impressive enough to attract attention, the answer varies greatly; however, a general rule of thumb would be to start querying after you've sold no fewer than 3,000 books. Another guideline to consider is that nonfiction sells easier than fiction. A lower number of sales for a novel would be somewhat equal to a higher number of nonfiction sales. Agent Adam Chromy of Artists and Artisans says he also weighs the number of books sold against how long the book has been available for purchase. "It's about momentum," he says. "If it's out two months and has sold 5,000 copies and it's getting press, that's great. If it's out for years, the number would have to be higher."

When Sharlene Martin, principal of Martin Literary Management, sits down to consider a self-published book, she's looking not only for sales information, but also for a mention that the author self-published by choice, not default by rejection of agents and editors on previous submission rounds. Agents are looking for authors who self-published *before* drowning in rejections who sold enough books to warrant the project a new life with traditional publishing.

Whether your work is fiction or nonfiction, agents will definitely be looking for a solid platform—meaning all the avenues you possess to sell/market your book to the identified markets of readers who will buy it. "A couple of aspects of a query letter for a self-published book will get me interested," says Jennie Dunham of Dunham Literary. "How much of an expert is the author? Really strong credentials help. Also, what type of platform does the author have? An author who can promote and sell a book is valuable."

If the writer's platform is good, and the book is on its way up (rather than fizzling out sales-wise), then your odds are improved. Agent Andrea Hurst, who founded an agency in Sacramento, came across a proposal from a self-published nonfiction author who had recently appeared on the Dr. Laura Show. Hurst signed the client and made a deal. Other writers have successfully signed with Hurst the same way, she says, though self-published books she reps may sometimes need an overhaul before a publisher's review. "We have taken on a few where we had the author add chapters, possibly change the title, and update it before it sold," she says.

In addition to detailing out your platform and how you intend to sell the book, include independent praise of your work. Awards, accolades, reviews, press and endorsements can all help stir the buzzstorm. Evans says she took on a self-published project when the book picked up several high-profile endorsements that helped trigger a few thousand sales. Diane Freed, another agent at FinePrint, noticed an article in a Maine newspaper about an award-winning self-published book written by a local librarian. The article was enough to get Freed's attention, and that librarian just signed a two-book deal with Freed's help.

RECOGNIZING A POSSIBLE DEAD END

Knowing that agents immediately look for sales, you may be tempted to head outside right this moment and peddle your wares at the nearest independent bookstore. But the flipside problem to not selling enough copies of your book is selling *too* many. Believe it or not, that's actually a bad thing. "There's a bit of a Catch-22 here," says Jessica Regel, agent at the Jean

V. Naggar Literary Agency. "If they haven't sold very many copies and the book was just self-published, then you try to convince a mainstream publisher that the book hasn't hit its market yet, because it had no marketing/publicity. If the book has sold a good number of copies—let's say more than 10,000—then a publisher will worry that it has already hit its market, so you need to convince them that there is still an untapped audience out there."

For example, let's say you printed a book about the history of Mobile, Ala. After five months, you've sold several thousand copies—to local historians, community members, as well as your friends and relatives. Impressive, sure—but there isn't much of a point finding an agent or publisher, as you're probably close to maxing out your sales. Dunham agrees that very strong sales can be a deterrent: "I want to know that the author is off to a solid start. I also have to be convinced, however, that there's a wider audience beyond that," she says. "I've seen a couple of books where I felt there were strong sales, but then I felt like there wouldn't be many more."

Memoir is one of the most common categories where writers self-publish their work. With memoirs in particular, getting an agent to take on the book is a steep hill to climb, as there are just *too many* self-published memoirs out there to compete against. If writing the memoir gave you a new vigor for writing, then set the self-published book aside and start on a new book that you will take to agents first. Get the first book out of your system and keep writing. "I have only taking on a couple of self-published books and have sold almost all of them, but I will often look at a self-published author and see if we can't just let the self-pub book go and work on the next book in their career," says Chromy.

BATTLING (YET RECOGNIZING) THE STIGMA

Perhaps the biggest reason why the odds are against self-published books catching the eye of an agent is this: "Often they have not sold well, are not professionally edited, and have been out for quite a while," says Hurst.

Self-published books are constantly fighting against assumptions. Agents and editors will assume that the work was turned down by dozens (or hundreds) of people already—even if this is not the case. If your work is print-on-demand, they will assume it sold the average amount of copies: 75. They will assume the writing is below average and the author has no ability to market the work—even if these thoughts, too, are not the case. That's why your query letter that introduces the self-published book must squelch all misconceptions immediately—and that includes the assumption that you, the writer, will be difficult to work with. Books are changed and edited and some drastically reworked throughout the publishing process. Just because your literary fiction book has already sold 2,500 copies won't make it immune to major suggestions from agents and editors on how to rework it.

"I've found that a lot of self-published writers don't want to revise their books," says Debbie Carter of Muse Literary. "These projects can be a waste of time for agents and editors who are looking to develop new talent."

ADDRESSING PREVIOUS SELF-PUBLISHED BOOKS

If you've decided to go the route of letting your self-published book stay self-published and move on to Work No. 2, then how do you address your prior books when crafting that next query?

Previous self-published works can easily be found and analyzed if they have ISBN numbers. Nielson's BookScan allows the publishing industry to search sales records of books and authors. You must mention all your self-published books upfront in the interest of full disclosure. If you're worried because sales were weak, then include mentions of them at the bottom of the query letter in your "bio" paragraph. Don't even include the titles just yet. This way, you're honest about your publishing past, but not drawing a whole lot of attention to it. If you mention your self-published books in the first line or two, the agent may stop reading simply because of the stigma. Let the agent see your pitch and get hooked. If they are interested enough, your bio details—including a list of any self-published books in your arsenal—should have little effect.

Agents' Pet Peeves

Avoid These Peeves and Get Your Story Read

by Katharine Sands

To peeve or not to peeve … that is the question. For the savvy wordsmith, this means heeding agent peeves, the universally cited blights any writer would do well to avoid. Some peeves are decades old, while the advent of technology has created new ones. For a new understanding of how to attract and how not to annoy, here are examples of *querial killers*: the mistakes writers make that we agents see and dislike on a daily basis. When you set out to woo, win and work with a literary agent, avoid these peeves to make sure your manuscript gets read.

QUERY LETTER PET PEEVES

OK. First that granddaddy of gripes: How writers misaddress agents. For example, let's say you're writing a cold query letter to agent Ivana Schmooze. The correct salutation is: "Dear Ms. Schmooze"; it is not "Dear Ivana Schmooze," "Dear Ivana," "Dear Agent," "Dear Meredith Bernstein," or "Dear Sirs." An anonymous agent once addressed this peeve by saying: "No addressing me as Sir/Madam. To my mind, there are only several agents who can pull this one off, and it's usually after hours."

On to the Cadillac of classic peeves: submitting your work to dozens of agents at the same time. While this may seem like a surefire way to reach out to many potential agents and up your chances for success, it will end up working against you. Yes, getting an agent to represent you *is* a numbers game, but an e-mail blast to countless reps dings the place in the agent brain marked auto-reject and this is guaranteed to land your submission in the circular file (recycle bin). Why? This is the mark of the obvious amateur—a writer who doesn't respect basic submitting-to-an-agent etiquette. If you're thinking about e-blasting agents, remember that it may be a timesaver, but we ourselves save some time by deleting these submissions. When introducing your work (or yourself) to an agent, show you are ready for the literary marketplace by selecting your agent candidates with a serious and intelligent eye. Sending to multiple agents scattershot does not attract their attention. If your e-query doesn't end up in the trash, it's likely stuck in a spam filter. Make sure your submission does not become spam-a-lot.

TECHNOLOGY AND THE INTERNET

A query letter is designed to hook an agent; what it's not supposed to do is simply point them to websites. "My new peeve is a query made up of links," says Rita Rosenkranz, who

KATHARINE SANDS is an agent with the Sarah Jane Freymann Literary Agency in New York City. She is the author of *Making the Perfect Pitch: How to Catch a Literary Agent's Eye* (Watson-Guphill, 2004).

has an agency in New York. "I think a submission, especially via e-mail, should have at least a basic description about the work and the author, duplicating the content of a query letter sent through the mail. I feel the author is taking a self-defeating shortcut when the correspondence is made up only of links or attachments, requiring the agent to investigate these one by one."

Breakout success stories from the blogosphere where writers are blogging their way into agents' hearts is indeed happening, but blog-like submissions where the query is chatty and unfocused is a turn-off for agents. One has to kiss a lot of frogs to find a prince, and we have to riff a lot of blogs to find a print.

Even though it may seem like an agent needs only invest a few seconds to find a viable client, agents do not see a cyber scavenger hunt quite this way. To an agent, a writer stands out from the throng and shows preparedness by a crisp perfect pitch—one that gets the agent to say *yes*. A pitch is not the beginning of your book; it is the introduction to your potential as an author. The best pitches create a moment, pose a provocative question, or give a flavor for the project. Sarah Jane Freymann, who has her own agency in Manhattan, shares: "If you are able to sum up your entire book with a title or one-line description, that's gold."

On that note, avoid the tendency to use lines that sound like they came right out of *The Player*, such as "It's *Sex and the City* meets *Silence of the Lambs*." Titles or ideas that are derivative do not fly; for example, we still see a spate of Dan Brown-inspired ones—*The Michelangelo Zone* or *The Cellini Code*. These are easy to decline.

CONCERNING REJECTIONS AND CRITICISM

Reactions to rejection spawn several agent peeves. Says agent Janet Reid of FinePrint Literary Management: "(Writers) just have to get over the idea that our response of 'It's not right for me' is some sort of comment on the value or quality of your work. It's not. It's only a comment about whether it resonates with me *and* whether I can sell it. I pass on really good stuff all the time."

Ah, but here is a new nettle: Writers posting comments on a website from a letter of rejection to create the impression of a blurb. This is false advertising since, the agent is, in fact, declining to represent the work, not extolling it. This is fast becoming a big no-no; plus, publishing pros know these are probably from rejection letters, so it really doesn't serve a writer to claim a host of agents is championing their work, when they are merely being polite and encouraging.

At a conference, some writers react badly to being critiqued. If you are ready for an agent meeting, steady yourself for the hot seat. Your work will be deconstructed in a way unlike that of a supportive writing group, retreat, MFA program, or workshop. Best use of the time is to 1) understand where and why the agent suggests next steps about what to do, and 2) listen to feedback, whether or not it's agreeable. Agents do strive to be sensitive when rendering professional opinions about personal stories and we understand how emotional it can be to be reviewed, but our most helpful evaluation is an honest one.

AND THE REST

For more ways not to vex, consider this potpourri of peeves:

We see a lot of channeled and cosmic-inspired material. Hey, maybe your spirit guides did select the agency, but all forms of faith are a matter between you and your god, not you and your agent. (Besides, how do I know my spirit guides are simpatico with yours?) Connection with the divine is best left to the heavens and out of your pitch.

Red flags wave when a writer starts to huff and puff for any reason. Always behave professionally. Remember that how you interact is an important indicator of how you will work with your publisher. An agent is an author advocate, but functions a bit like an officer of the court. We do not swear oaths, but are instead bound to represent to each side honestly. You want your agent to act like a tigress on the prowl? Not likely in today's publishing climate. The martini-swilling dragon lady of your dreams who fights on your behalf for every deal point has been replaced by increasingly impersonal dealings with the corporate politics of a publishing imprint of a media behemoth. The new criteria: not how tough agents are, but how effective we can be as ambassadors for your writing.

Your attorney (a cousin in Florida who practices maritime law and has never seen a publishing contract) is unlikely to be a welcome part of the negotiation process. Agents not only have experience in negotiating contracts, but also a vested interest in your success and legal protections. It is not in your interest to obtain inaccurate legal advice, or to want the agent to address every issue that might arise for the Slovakian theme park rights from your 15th international bestseller (when you are really just starting out).

SO NOW YOU KNOW...

Whether meeting with you or reading your pitch letter, agents want to be engaged—to zero in on the zeitgeist, find hooks and sales engines, identify the intended audience, and be impressed by a writer's voice. We need to determine the answer to two pressing questions: *Why you? Why now?* The guiding principle is to remember that agents are looking first for a reason to keep reading, and then for a reason to represent you. Be certain you give us crystal clear answers—fast. We cherry-pick our clients, and want things to progress smoothly and happily. We want writers to get as close to their ultimate dreams and goals as possible, and a good way to start is to avoid agent pet peeves and make sure your next submission isn't sunk by a *querial killer*.

Literary Agents

Agents listed in this section generate 98-100 percent of their income from commission on sales. They do not charge for reading, critiquing or editing your manuscript or book proposal. It's the goal of an agent to find salable manuscripts: Her income depends on finding the best publisher for your manuscript.

Since an agent's time is better spent meeting with editors, she will have little or no time to critique your writing. Agents who don't charge fees must be selective and often prefer to work with established authors, celebrities or those with professional credentials in a particular field.

Some agents in this section may charge clients for office expenses such as photocopying, foreign postage, long-distance phone calls or express mail services. Make sure you have a clear understanding of what these expenses are before signing any agency agreement.

SUBHEADS

Each agency listing is broken down into subheads to make locating specific information easier. In the first section, you'll find contact information for each agency. You'll also learn if the agents within the agency belong to any professional organizations; membership in these organizations can tell you a lot about an agency. For example, members of the Association of Authors' Representatives (AAR) are prohibited from charging reading or evaluating fees. Additional information in this section includes the size of each agency, its willingness to work with new or unpublished writers, and its general areas of interest.

Member Agents: Agencies comprised of more than one agent list member agents and their individual specialties. This information will help you determine the appropriate person to whom you should send your query letter.

Represents: This section allows agencies to specify what nonfiction and fiction subjects they represent. Make sure you query only those agents who represent the type of material you write.

Look for the key icon to quickly learn an agent's areas of specialization. In this portion of the listing, agents mention the specific subject areas they're currently seeking, as well as those subject areas they do not consider.

How to Contact: Most agents open to submissions prefer an initial query letter that briefly describes your work. While some agents may ask for an outline and a specific number of sample chapters, most don't. You should send these items only if the agent requests them. In this section, agents also mention if they accept queries by fax or e-mail, if they consider simultaneous submissions, and how they prefer to obtain new clients.

Recent Sales: To give you a sense of the types of material they represent, the agents list specific titles they've sold, as well as a sampling of clients' names. Note that some agents consider their client list confidential and may only share client names once they agree to represent you.

Terms: Provided here are details of an agent's commission, whether a contract is offered and for how long, and what additional office expenses you might have to pay if the agent agrees to represent you. Standard commissions range from 10-15 percent for domestic sales and 15-20 percent for foreign or dramatic sales (with the difference going to the co-agent who places the work).

Writers' Conferences: A great way to meet an agent is at a writers' conference. Here agents list the conferences they usually attend. For more information about a specific conference, check the Conferences section starting on page 266.

Tips: In this section, agents offer advice and additional instructions for writers.

SPECIAL INDEXES

Literary Agents Specialties Index: This index (page 287) organizes agencies according to the subjects they are interested in receiving. This index should help you compose a list of agents specializing in your areas. Cross-referencing categories and concentrating on agents interested in two or more aspects of your manuscript might increase your chances of success.

Agents Index: This index (page 358) provides a list of agents' names in alphabetical order, along with the name of the agency for which they work. Find the name of the person you would like to contact, and then check the agency listing.

General Index: This index (page 363) lists all agencies and conferences appearing in the book.

Quick Reference Icons

At the beginning of some listings, you will find one or more of the following symbols:

N Agency new to this edition

⚷ Canadian agency

🌐 International agency

◖ Agency actively seeking clients

◑ Agency seeking both new and established writers

◉ Agency seeking mostly established writers through referrals

◎ Agency specializing in certain types of work

⊘ Agency not currently seeking new clients

Find a pull-out bookmark with a key to symbols on the inside cover of this book.

◎ A+B WORKS

E-mail: query@aplusbworks.com; literary@aplusbworks.com. Website: www.aplusbworks.com/literary/submissions. **Contact:** Amy Jameson.

• Prior to her current position, Ms. Jameson worked at Janklow & Nesbit Associates.

Represents Nonfiction books, novels. **Considers these fiction areas:** young adult and middle grade fiction, women's fiction, and select narrative nonfiction.

    ☛ This agency specializes in middle grade and YA fiction, women's fiction and some adult nonfiction. We are only interested in established writers at this time. We do not represent thrillers, literary fiction, erotica, cook books, picture books, poetry, short fiction, or screenplays. Due to the high volume of queries we receive, we cannot guarantee a response to unsolicited queries. We accept very few new clients in order to ensure the best possible representation for each of our authors.

How to Contact Query via e-mail only. Please review our submissions policies first. Send queries to query@aplusbworks.com.

◖ DOMINICK ABEL LITERARY AGENCY, INC.

146 W. 82nd St., #1A, New York NY 10024. (212)877-0710. Fax: (212)595-3133. E-mail: agency@dalainc.com. Member of AAR. Represents 100 clients. Currently handles: adult fiction and nonfiction.

How to Contact Query via e-mail.

Terms Agent receives 15% commission on domestic sales. Agent receives 20% commission on foreign sales.

ABOUT WORDS AGENCY

Website: agency.aboutwords.org. **Contact:** Susan Graham. Currently handles: nonfiction books 40%, novels 60%.

    ☛ Does not want true crime, religious market, poetry.

How to Contact Only accepts e-mail queries now.

Terms Agent receives 15% commission on domestic sales. Agent receives 20% commission on foreign sales. Offers written contract.

⚊ ◖ ACACIA HOUSE PUBLISHING SERVICES, LTD.

62 Chestnut Ave., Brantford ON N3T 4C2 Canada. (519)752-0978. **Contact:** (Ms.) Frances Hanna or Bill Hanna. Represents 100 clients. Currently handles: nonfiction books 30%, novels 70%.

• Ms. Hanna has been in the publishing business for 30+ years, first in London as a fiction editor with Barrie & Jenkins and Pan Books, and as a senior editor with a packager of mainly illustrated books. She was condensed books editor for 6 years for *Reader's Digest* in Montreal and senior editor and foreign rights manager for William Collins & Sons (now HarperCollins) in Toronto. Mr. Hanna has more than 40 years of experience in the publishing business.

Member Agents Frances Hanna; Bill Hanna, vice president (self-help, modern history, military history).

Represents Nonfiction books, novels. **Considers these nonfiction areas:** animals, biography, language, memoirs, military, music, nature, film, travel. **Considers these fiction areas:** adventure, detective, literary, mainstream, mystery, thriller.

    ☛ This agency specializes in contemporary fiction—literary or commercial. Actively seeking outstanding first novels with literary merit. Does not want to receive horror, occult or science fiction.

How to Contact Query with outline, SASE. *No unsolicited mss.* No phone queries. Responds in 6 weeks to queries.

Terms Agent receives 15% commission on English language sales; 20% commission on dramatic sales; 25% commission on foreign sales. Charges clients for photocopying, postage, courier.

Recent Sales This agency prefers not to share information on specific sales.

Tips "We prefer that writers be previously published, with at least a few short stories or articles to their credit. Strongest consideration will be given to those with three or more published books. However, we would take on an unpublished writer of outstanding talent."

◖ ADAMS LITERARY

7845 Colony Road C4, #215, Charlotte NC 28226. (704)542-1440. Fax: (704)542-1450. E-mail:

info@adamsliterary.com. Website: www.adamsliterary.com. **Contact:** Tracey Adams, Josh Adams, Quinlan Lee. Member of AAR. Other memberships include SCBWI and WNBA.

Member Agents Tracey Adams; Josh Adams; Quinlan Lee.

⚬ Adams Literary is a full-service literary agency exclusively representing children's book authors and artists.

How to Contact "Guidelines are posted (and frequently updated) on our website."

BRET ADAMS LTD. AGENCY

448 W. 44th St., New York NY 10036. (212)765-5630. E-mail: literary@bretadamsltd.net. Website: bretadamsltd.net. **Contact:** Bruce Ostler, Mark Orsini. Member of AAR. Currently handles: movie scripts, TV scripts, stage plays.

Member Agents Bruce Ostler, Mark Orsini.

Represents Movie scripts, TV scripts, TV movie of the week, theatrical stage play.

⚬ Handles theatre/film and TV projects. No books. Cannot accept unsolicited material.

How to Contact Professional recommendation.

☷ THE AGENCY GROUP, LLC

142 West 57th St., 6th Floor, New York NY 10019. (212)581-3100. E-mail: sasharaskin@theagencygroup.com. Website: www.theagencygroup.com. **Contact:** Marc Gerald, Sasha Raskin. Represents 50 clients. 10% of clients are new/unpublished writers. Currently handles: nonfiction books 60%, novels 30%, multimedia 10%.

• Prior to becoming an agent, Mr. Gerald owned and ran an independent publishing and entertainment agency.

Member Agents Marc Gerald; Sarah Stephens; Sasha Raskin.

Represents Nonfiction books, novels. **Considers these nonfiction areas:** anthropology, archeology, architecture, art, autobiography, biography, business, child guidance, cooking, cultural interests, dance, decorating, design, economics, environment, ethnic, finance, foods, government, health, history, how-to, humor, interior design, investigative, law, medicine, memoirs, money, nature, nutrition, parenting, personal improvement, popular culture, politics, psychology, satire, self-help, sports, true crime. **Considers these fiction areas:** action, adventure, cartoon, comic books, commercial, confession, contemporary issues, crime, detective, erotica, ethnic, experimental, family saga, feminist, frontier, gay, glitz, hi-lo, historical, horror, humor, inspirational, juvenile, lesbian, literary, mainstream, metaphysical, military, multicultural, multimedia, mystery, New Age, occult, picture books, plays, poetry, poetry in translation, police, psychic, regional, religious, romance, satire, short story collections, spiritual, sports, supernatural, suspense, thriller, translation, war, westerns, women's, young adult.

⚬ "While we admire beautiful writing, we largely represent recording artists, celebrities, authors, and pop culture and style brands with established platforms. When we represent fiction, we work almost exclusively in genre and in areas of expertise. We tend to take a non-linear approach to content—many of our projects ultimately have a TV/film or digital component." This agency is only taking on new clients through referrals.

How to Contact Accepts simultaneous submissions. Responds in 1 month to queries. Responds in 3 months to mss. Obtains most new clients through recommendations from others.

Terms Agent receives 15% commission on domestic sales. Agent receives 20% commission on foreign sales. Offers written contract. Charges clients for office fees (only for mss that have been sold).

☐ THE AHEARN AGENCY, INC.

2021 Pine St., New Orleans LA 70118. E-mail: pahearn@aol.com. Website: www.ahearnagency.com. **Contact:** Pamela G. Ahearn. Other memberships include MWA, RWA, ITW. Represents 35 clients. 20% of clients are new/unpublished writers. Currently handles: novels 100%.

• Prior to opening her agency, Ms. Ahearn was an agent for 8 years and an editor with Bantam Books.

Represents Considers these nonfiction areas: animals, child guidance, cultural interests, current affairs, ethnic, film, gay, health, history, investigative, lesbian, medicine, parenting, personal improvement, popular culture, self-help, theater, true crime, women's issues. **Considers these fiction areas:** action, adventure, contemporary issues, crime, detective, ethnic, family saga, feminist, glitz, historical, humor, literary, mainstream, mystery, police, psychic, regional, romance, supernatural, suspense, thriller.

○┐ "This agency specializes in historical romance and is also very interested in mysteries and suspense fiction. Does not want to receive category romance, science fiction or fantasy."

How to Contact Query with SASE. Accepts simultaneous submissions. Responds in 8 weeks to queries. Responds in 10 weeks to mss. Obtains most new clients through recommendations from others, solicitations, conferences.

Terms Agent receives 15% commission on domestic sales. Agent receives 20% commission on foreign sales. Offers written contract, binding for 1 year; renewable by mutual consent.

Recent Sales *Red Chrysanthemum,* by Laura Rowland; *Only a Duke Will Do*, by Sabrina Jeffries; *The Alexandria Link*, by Steve Berry.

Writers Conferences Moonlight & Magnolias; RWA National Conference; Thriller Fest; Florida Romance Writers; Bouchercon; Malice Domestic.

Tips "Be professional! Always send in exactly what an agent/editor asks for—no more, no less. Keep query letters brief and to the point, giving your writing credentials and a very brief summary of your book. If one agent rejects you, keep trying—there are a lot of us out there!"

AITKEN ALEXANDER ASSOCIATES

18-21 Cavaye Place, London England SW10 9PT UK. (44)(207)373-8672. Fax: (44)(207)373-6002. E-mail: reception@aitkenalexander.co.uk. Website: www.aitkenalexander.co.uk. **Contact:** Submissions Department. Estab. 1976. Represents 300+ clients. 10% of clients are new/unpublished writers.

Member Agents Gillon Aitken, agent; Clare Alexander, agent; Andrew Kidd, agent; Lesley Thorne, film/television.

Represents Nonfiction books, novels. **Considers these nonfiction areas:** current affairs, government, history, law, memoirs, popular culture, politics. **Considers these fiction areas:** historical, literary.

○┐ "We specialize in literary fiction and nonfiction."

How to Contact Query with SASE. Submit synopsis, first 30 pages. Responds in 6-8 weeks to queries. Obtains most new clients through recommendations from others, solicitations.

Terms Agent receives 15% commission on domestic sales. Agent receives 20% commission on foreign sales. Offers written contract; 28-day notice must be given to terminate contract. Charges for photocopying and postage.

Recent Sales Sold 50 titles in the last year. *My Life With George*, by Judith Summers (Voice); *The Separate Heart*, by Simon Robinson (Bloomsbury); *The Fall of the House of Wittgenstein*, by Alexander Waugh (Bloomsbury); *Shakespeare's Life*, by Germane Greer (Picador); *Occupational Hazards*, by Rory Stewart.

Tips "Before submitting to us, we advise you to look at our existing client list to establish whether your work will be of interest. Equally, you should consider whether the material you have written is ready to submit to a literary agency. If you feel your work qualifies, then send us a letter introducing yourself. Keep it relevant to your writing (e.g., tell us about any previously published work, be it a short story or journalism; you may be studying or have completed a post-graduate qualification in creative writing; when it comes to nonfiction, we would want to know what qualifies you to write about the subject)."

ALIVE COMMUNICATIONS, INC.

7680 Goddard St., Suite 200, Colorado Springs CO 80920. (719)260-7080. Fax: (719)260-8223. E-mail: submissions@alivecom.com. Website: www.alivecom.com. Member of AAR. Other memberships include Authors Guild. Represents 100+ clients. 5% of clients are new/unpublished writers. Currently handles: nonfiction books 50%, novels 40%, juvenile books 10%.

Member Agents Rick Christian, president (blockbusters, bestsellers); Lee Hough (popular/commercial nonfiction and fiction, thoughtful spirituality, children's); Andrea Heineke (thoughtful/inspirational nonfiction, women's fiction/nonfiction, popular/commercial nonfiction & fiction); Joel Kneedler popular/commercial nonfiction and fiction, thoughtful spirituality, children's).

Represents Nonfiction books, novels, short story collections, novellas. **Considers these nonfiction areas:** autobiography, biography, business, child guidance, economics, how-to, inspirational, parenting, personal improvement, religious, self-help, women's issues, women's studies. **Considers**

these fiction areas: action, adventure, contemporary issues, crime, detective, family saga, historical, humor, inspirational, literary, mainstream, mystery, police, religious, satire, suspense, thriller.

○┳ This agency specializes in fiction, Christian living, how-to and commercial nonfiction. Actively seeking inspirational, literary and mainstream fiction, and work from authors with established track records and platforms. Does not want to receive poetry, scripts or dark themes.

How to Contact Query via e-mail. "Be advised that this agency works primarily with well-established, best-selling, and career authors." Obtains most new clients through recommendations from others.

Terms Agent receives 15% commission on domestic sales. Offers written contract; 2-month notice must be given to terminate contract.

Recent Sales Sold 300 + titles in the last year. A spiritual memoir by Eugene Peterson (Viking); A biography of Rwandan president Paul Kagame, by Stephen Kinzaya (St. Martin's Press); *Ever After*, by Karen Klingsbury (Zondervan).

Tips Rewrite and polish until the words on the page shine. Endorsements and great connections may help, provided you can write with power and passion. Network with publishing professionals by making contacts, joining critique groups, and attending writers conferences in order to make personal connections and to get feedback. Alive Communications, Inc., has established itself as a premiere literary agency. We serve an elite group of authors who are critically acclaimed and commercially successful in both Christian and general markets.

☑ ALLEN O'SHEA LITERARY AGENCY

615 Westover Road, Stamford CT 06902. (203)359-9965. Fax: (203)357-9909. E-mail: marilyn@allenoshea.com. Website: www.allenoshea.com. **Contact:** Marilyn Allen. Represents 100 clients. 20% of clients are new/unpublished writers. Currently handles: nonfiction books 99%.

• Prior to becoming agents, both Ms. Allen and Ms. O'Shea held senior positions in publishing.

Member Agents Marilyn Allen; Coleen O'Shea.

Represents Nonfiction books. **Considers these nonfiction areas:** biography, business, cooking, current affairs, health, history, how-to, humor, military, money, popular culture, psychology, sports, interior design/decorating.

○┳ "This agency specializes in practical nonfiction including cooking, sports, business, pop culture, etc. We look for clients with strong marketing platforms and new ideas coupled with strong writing." Actively seeking narrative nonfiction, health and history writers; very interested in writers who have large blog following and interesting topics. Does not want to receive fiction, memoirs, poetry, textbooks or children's.

How to Contact Query with via e-mail or mail with SASE. Submit outline, author bio, marketing page. No phone or fax queries. Accepts simultaneous submissions. Responds in 1 week to queries. Responds in 1-2 months to mss. Obtains most new clients through recommendations from others, conferences.

Terms Agent receives 15% commission on domestic sales. Offers written contract, binding for 2 years; 1-month notice must be given to terminate contract. Charges for photocopying large mss, and overseas postage—"typically minimal costs."

Recent Sales Sold 45 titles in the last year. "This agency prefers not to share information about specific sales, but see our website."

Writers Conferences ASJA, Publicity Submit for Writers, Connecticut Authors and Publishers, Mark Victor Hansen Mega Book Conference.

Tips "Prepare a strong overview, with competition, marketing and bio. We will consider when your proposal is ready."

☑ MIRIAM ALTSHULER LITERARY AGENCY

53 Old Post Road N., Red Hook NY 12571. (845)758-9408. Website: www.miriamaltshulerliterary agency.com. **Contact:** Miriam Altshuler. Estab. 1994. Member of AAR. Represents 40 clients. Currently handles: nonfiction books 45%, novels 45%, story collections 5%, juvenile books 5%.

• Ms. Altshuler has been an agent since 1982.

Represents Nonfiction books, novels, short story collections, juvenile. **Considers these nonfiction areas:** biography, ethnic, history, language, memoirs, multicultural, music, nature, popular culture, psychology, sociology, film, women's. **Considers these fiction areas:** literary, mainstream, multicultural, some selective children's books.

> ⚭ Actively seeking literary commercial fiction and nonfiction. Does not want self-help, mystery, how-to, romance, horror, spiritual, fantasy, poetry, screenplays, science fiction or techno-thriller, western.

How to Contact Send query; If we want to see your ms we will respond via e-mail (if you do not have an e-mail address, please send an SASE. We will only respond if interested in materials. Submit contact info with e-mail address. Prefers to read materials exclusively. Accepts simultaneous submissions. Responds in 3 weeks to mss. Obtains most new clients through recommendations from others.

Terms Agent receives 15% commission on domestic sales. Agent receives 20% commission on foreign sales. Charges clients for overseas mailing, photocopies, overnight mail when requested by author.

Writers Conferences Bread Loaf Writers' Conference; Washington Independent Writers Conference; North Carolina Writers' Network Conference.

Tips See the website for specific submission details.

⌧ AMBASSADOR LITERARY AGENCY

P.O. Box 50358, Nashville TN 37205. (615)370-4700. E-mail: Wes@AmbassadorAgency.com. Website: www.AmbassadorAgency.com. **Contact:** Wes Yoder. Represents 25-30 clients. 10% of clients are new/unpublished writers. Currently handles: nonfiction books 95%, novels 5%.

> • Prior to becoming an agent, Mr. Yoder founded a music artist agency in 1973; he established a speakers bureau division of the company in 1984.

Represents Nonfiction books, novels. **Considers these nonfiction areas:** biography, current affairs, ethnic, government, history, how-to, memoirs, popular culture, religion, self-help, women.

> ⚭ "This agency specializes in religious market publishing dealing primarily with A-level publishers." Actively seeking popular nonfiction themes, including the following: practical living; Christian spirituality; literary fiction. Does not want to receive short stories, children's books, screenplays or poetry."

How to Contact Query with SASE. Submit proposal package, outline, synopsis, 6 sample chapters, author bio. Accepts simultaneous submissions. Responds in 2-4 weeks to queries. Obtains most new clients through recommendations from others.

Terms Agent receives 15% commission on domestic sales. Agent receives 20% commission on foreign sales. Offers written contract.

Recent Sales Sold 20 titles in the last year. *The Death and Life of Gabriel Phillips*, by Stephen Baldwin (Hachette); *Amazing Grace: William Wilberforce and the Heroic Campaign to End Slavery*, by Eric Mataxas (Harper San Francisco); *Life@The Next Level*, by Courtney McBath (Simon and Schuster); *Women, Take Charge of Your Money*, by Carolyn Castleberry (Random House/Multnomah).

⌧ MARCIA AMSTERDAM AGENCY

41 W. 82nd St., Suite 9A, New York NY 10024-5613. (212)873-4945. **Contact:** Marcia Amsterdam. Signatory of WGA. Currently handles: nonfiction books 15%, novels 70%, movie scripts 5%, TV scripts 10%.

> • Prior to opening her agency, Ms. Amsterdam was an editor.

Represents Novels, movie scripts, feature film, sitcom. **Considers these fiction areas:** adventure, detective, horror, mainstream, mystery, romance (contemporary, historical), science, thriller, young adult. **Considers these script areas:** comedy, romantic comedy.

How to Contact Query with SASE. Responds in 1 month to queries.

Terms Agent receives 15% commission on domestic sales. Agent receives 20% commission on foreign sales. Agent receives 10% commission on film sales. Offers written contract, binding for 1 year. Charges clients for extra office expenses, foreign postage, copying, legal fees (when agreed upon).

Recent Sales *Hidden Child,* by Isaac Millman (FSG); *Lucky Leonardo*, by Jonathan Canter (Sourcebooks).

Tips "We are always looking for interesting literary voices."

☑ BETSY AMSTER LITERARY ENTERPRISES

P.O. Box 27788, Los Angeles CA 90027-0788. **Contact:** Betsy Amster. Estab. 1992. Member of AAR. Represents more than 65 clients. 35% of clients are new/unpublished writers. Currently handles: nonfiction books 65%, novels 35%.

- Prior to opening her agency, Ms. Amster was an editor at Pantheon and Vintage for 10 years, and served as editorial director for the Globe Pequot Press for 2 years.

Represents Nonfiction books, novels. **Considers these nonfiction areas:** art & design, biography, business, child guidance, cooking/nutrition, current affairs, ethnic, gardening, health/medicine, history, memoirs, money, parenting, popular culture, psychology, science/technology, self-help, sociology, travelogues, social issues, women's issues. **Considers these fiction areas:** ethnic, literary, women's, high quality.

- ☞ "Actively seeking strong narrative nonfiction, particularly by journalists; outstanding literary fiction (the next Richard Ford or Jhumpa Lahiri); witty, intelligent commerical women's fiction (the next Elinor Lipman or Jennifer Weiner); mysteries that open new worlds to us; and high-profile self-help and psychology, preferably research based." Does not want to receive poetry, children's books, romances, Western, science fiction, action/adventure, screenplays, fantasy, techno thrillers, spy capers, apocalyptic scenarios, or political or religious arguments.

How to Contact For adult titles: b.amster.assistant@gmail.com. See submission requirements online at website. The requirements have changed and only e-mail submissions are accepted. Accepts simultaneous submissions. Responds in 1 month to queries. Responds in 2 months to mss. Obtains most new clients through recommendations from others, solicitations, conferences.

Terms Agent receives 15% commission on domestic sales. Agent receives 20% commission on foreign sales. Offers written contract, binding for 1 year; 3-month notice must be given to terminate contract. Charges for photocopying, postage, long distance phone calls, messengers, galleys/books used in submissions to foreign and film agents and to magazines for first serial rights.

Writers Conferences USC Masters in Professional Writing; San Diego State University Writers' Conference; UCLA Extension Writers' Program; Los Angeles Times Festival of Books; The Loft Literary Center.

☑ ANDERSON LITERARY MANAGEMENT, LLC

12 W. 19th St., New York NY 10011. (212)645-6045. Fax: (212)741-1936. E-mail: info@andersonliterary. com. Website: www.andersonliterary.com/. **Contact:** Kathleen Anderson. Estab. 2006. Member of AAR. Represents 100+ clients. 20% of clients are new/unpublished writers. Currently handles: nonfiction books 50%, novels 50%.

Represents Nonfiction books, novels, short story collections, juvenile. **Considers these nonfiction areas:** anthropology, archeology, architecture, art, autobiography, biography, cultural interests, current affairs, dance, design, education, environment, ethnic, gay, government, history, law, lesbian, memoirs, music, nature, politics, psychology, women's issues, women's studies. **Considers these fiction areas:** action, adventure, ethnic, family saga, feminist, frontier, gay, historical, lesbian, literary, mystery, suspense, thriller, westerns, women's, young adult.

- ☞ "Specializes in adult and young adult literary and commercial fiction, narrative nonfiction, American and European history, literary journalism, nature and travel writing, memoir, and biography." We do not represent science fiction, cookbooks, gardening, craft books or children's picture books. While we love literature in translation, we cannot accept samples of work written in languages other than English.

How to Contact Query with SASE. Submit synopsis, first 3 sample chapters, proposal (for nonfiction). Snail mail queries only. Accepts simultaneous submissions. Responds in 6 weeks to queries. Obtains most new clients through recommendations from others, solicitations, conferences.

Terms Agent receives 15% commission on domestic sales. Offers written contract.

Writers Conferences Squaw Valley Conference.

Tips "We do not represent plays or screenplays."

⊕ ANUBIS LITERARY AGENCY

7 Birdhaven Close Lighthorne Heath, Banbury Road, Warwick Warwickshire CV35 0BE United Kingdom. Phone/Fax: (44)(192)664-2588. E-mail: anubis.agency2@btopenworld.com. **Contact:** Steve Calcutt. Estab. 1994. Represents 15 clients. 50% of clients are new/unpublished writers. Currently handles: novels 100%.

- In addition to being an agent, Mr. Calcutt teaches creative writing and American history (U.S. Civil War) at Warwick University.

Represents Novels. **Considers these nonfiction areas:** historical. **Considers these fiction areas:** crime, horror, literary fiction, mainstream, science fiction, women's, dark fantasy.

- ⚓ "Actively seeking horror fiction." Does not want to receive children's books, nonfiction, journalism or TV/film scripts.

How to Contact Query with proposal package. Send 50 pp. with one-page synopsis. Returns materials only with SASE/IRCs. Responds in 6 weeks to queries. Responds in 3 months to mss. Obtains most new clients through personal recommendation.

Terms Agent receives 15% commission on domestic sales. Agent receives 20% commission on foreign sales.

⬢ ARCADIA

31 Lake Place N., Danbury CT 06810. E-mail: arcadialit@sbcglobal.net. **Contact:** Victoria Gould Pryor. Member of AAR.

Represents Nonfiction books, literary and commercial fiction. **Considers these nonfiction areas:** biography, business, current affairs, health, history, psychology, science, true crime, women's, investigative journalism; culture; classical music; life transforming self-help.

- ⚓ "I'm a very hands-on agent, which is necessary in this competitive marketplace. I work with authors on revisions until whatever we present to publishers is as strong as possible. I represent talented, dedicated, intelligent and ambitious writers who are looking for a long-term relationship based on professional success and mutual respect." Does not want to receive science fiction/fantasy, horror, humor or children's/YA. "We are only able to read fiction submissions from previously published authors."

How to Contact Query with SASE. This agency accepts e-queries (no attachments).

⬢ EDWARD ARMSTRONG LITERARY AGENCY

Fiction, PO Box 3343, Fayville MA 01745. (401)569-7099. **Contact:** Edward Armstrong. Currently handles: other 100% fiction.

- Prior to becoming an agent, Mr. Armstrong was a business professional specializing in quality and regulatory compliance. **This agency has not been taking submissions since 2007.** Please continue to check back.

Represents Novels, short story collections, novellas. **Considers these fiction areas:** mainstream, romance, science, thriller, suspense.

- ⚓ **This agency is not taking submissions at this time.** Please continue to check back. Does not want to receive nonfiction or textbooks.

How to Contact Obtains most new clients through solicitations.

Terms Agent receives 5% commission on domestic sales. Agent receives 5% commission on foreign sales. This agency charges for photocopying and postage.

⬢ ARTISTS AND ARTISANS INC.

244 Madison Ave., Suite 334, New York NY 10016. Website: www.artistsandartisans.com. **Contact:** Adam Chromy and Jamie Brenner. Represents 70 clients. 80% of clients are new/unpublished writers. Currently handles: nonfiction books 50%, fiction 50%.

Member Agents Adam Chromy (fiction and narrative nonfiction); Jamie Brenner (thrillers, commercial and literary fiction, memoir, narrative nonfiction, Young Adult); Gwendolyn Heasley (Young Adult).

Represents Nonfiction books, novels. **Considers these nonfiction areas:** biography, business, child, current affairs, ethnic, health, how to, humor, language, memoirs, money, music, popular culture, religion, science, self-help, sports, film, true crime, women's, fashion/style. **Considers these fiction areas:** confession, family, humor, literary, mainstream.

- ⚓ "My education and experience in the business world ensure that my clients' enterprise as authors gets as much attention and care as their writing." Working journalists for nonfiction books. No scripts.

How to Contact Query by e-mail only. Accepts simultaneous submissions. Responds to queries only if interested. Obtains most new clients through recommendations from others, solicitations, conferences.

Terms Agent receives 15% commission on domestic sales. Agent receives 25% commission on foreign sales. Offers written contract; 1-month notice must be given to terminate contract. "We only charge for extraordinary expenses (e.g., client requests check via FedEx instead of regular mail)."

Recent Sales *New World Monkeys*, (Shaye Areheart); *World Made by Hand* (Grove Atlantic); *House of Cards*, by David Ellis Dickerson (Penguin).

Writers Conferences ASJA Writers Conference, Pacific Northwest Writers Conference, Newbury Port Writers Conference.

Tips "Please make sure you are ready before approaching us or any other agent. If you write fiction, make sure it is the best work you can do and get objective criticism from a writing group. If you write nonfiction, make sure the proposal exhibits your best work and a comprehensive understanding of the market."

☑ ROBERT ASTLE AND ASSOCIATES LITERARY MANAGEMENT, INC.

419 Lafayette Street, 3rd Floor, New York NY 10003. (212)277-8014. Fax: (212)228-6149. E-mail: robert@astleliterary.com. Website: www.astleliterary.com. **Contact:** Robert Astle.

• Prior to becoming an agent, Mr. Astle spent 25 years in theater.

Represents Nonfiction books, novels.

    ⚬ "We are especially interested in receiving nonfiction projects with a wide range of topics, including narrative nonfiction, popular culture, arts and culture, theater and performance, sports, travel, celebrity, biography, politics, memoir, history, new media and multi-ethnic. We are actively seeking writers of literary fiction and commercial fiction—mysteries and suspense, thrillers, mainstream literary fiction, historical fiction, women's fiction, humor/satire and graphic novels. We will also seek writers in the genre of young audiences: middle grade and teen."

How to Contact Use the online form to query. Specifications for nonfiction and fiction submissions are online. Obtains most new clients through recommendations from others, solicitations.

Tips "Please read the submission guidelines carefully, and make sure your query letter is the best it can be."

☑ THE AUGUST AGENCY, LLC

E-mail: submissions@augustagency.com. Website: www.augustagency.com. **Contact:** Cricket Freemain, Jeffery McGraw. Estab. 2004. Represents 25-40 clients. 50% of clients are new/unpublished writers. Currently handles: nonfiction books 75%, novels 20%, other 5% other.

• Before opening The August Agency, Ms. Freeman was a freelance writer, magazine editor and independent literary agent; Mr. McGraw worked as an editor for HarperCollins and publicity manager for Abrams.

Member Agents Jeffery McGraw (politics/current affairs, entertainment, business, psychology, self-help, narrative nonfiction, contemporary women's fiction, literary fiction); Cricket Freeman (mystery/crime fiction, chick lit, thrillers).

Represents Nonfiction books, novels. **Considers these nonfiction areas:** interior design, biography, business, child guidance, cooking, current affairs, ethnic, gay, government, health, history, how to, humor, memoirs, military, money, music, pop culture, psychology, self-help, sociology, sports, film, true crime, women's, inspirational. **Considers these fiction areas:** psychic, adventure, detective, ethnic, family, gay, historical, humor, literary, mainstream, mystery, thriller, smart chick lit (non-genre romance).

    ⚬ "An array of fiction and nonfiction, with an emphasis in media (seasoned journalists receive special favor here), popular culture/entertainment, political science, diet/fitness, health, cookbooks, psychology, business, memoir, highly creative nonfiction, accessible literary fiction, women's fiction, and high-concept mysteries and thrillers. When it comes to nonfiction, we favor persuasive and prescriptive works with a narrative command and contemporary relevance. We like storytelling defined—by its extraordinary power to resonate universally on a deeply emotional level." Does not want academic textbooks, children's books, cozy mysteries, horror, poetry, science fiction/fantasy, short story collections, Westerns, screenplays, genre romance or previously self-published works.

How to Contact Submit book summary (1-2 paragraphs), chapter outline (nonfiction only), first 1,000 words or first chapter, total page/word count, brief paragraph on why you have chosen to write the book. Send via e-mail only (no attachments). Responds in 2-3 weeks to queries if we are interested. Responds in 3 months to mss. Obtains most new clients through recommendations from others, solicitations, conferences.

Terms Agent receives 15% commission on domestic sales. Agent receives 20% commission on foreign sales. Offers written contract; 1-month notice must be given to terminate contract.

Writers Conferences Surrey International Writers' Conference; Southern California Writers' Conference; Naples Writers' Conference, et al.

☐ AVENUE A LITERARY

419 Lafayette St., Second Floor, New York NY 10003. Fax: (212)228-6149. E-mail: submissions@ avenuealiterary.com. Website: www.avenuealiterary.com. **Contact:** Jennifer Cayea. Represents 20 clients. 75% of clients are new/unpublished writers. Currently handles: nonfiction books 40%, novels 45%, story collections 5%, juvenile books 10%.

- Prior to opening her agency, Ms. Cayea was an agent and director of foreign rights for Nicholas Ellison, Inc., a division of Sanford J. Greenburger Associates. She was also an editor in the audio and large print divisions of Random House.

Represents Nonfiction books, novels, short story collections, juvenile. **Considers these nonfiction areas:** cooking, cultural interests, current affairs, dance, ethnic, film, foods, health, history, medicine, memoirs, music, nutrition, personal improvement, popular culture, self-help, sports, theater. **Considers these fiction areas:** contemporary issues, family saga, feminist, historical, literary, mainstream, thriller, young adult, women's/chick lit.

- ⚬ "Our authors are dynamic and diverse. We seek strong new voices in fiction and nonfiction, and are fiercely dedicated to our authors." We are actively seeking new authors of fiction and nonfiction.

How to Contact Query via e-mail only. Submit synopsis, publishing history, author bio, full contact info. Paste info in e-mail body. No attachments. Accepts simultaneous submissions. Responds in 8 weeks to queries. Obtains most new clients through recommendations from others, solicitations, conferences.

Terms Agent receives 15% commission on domestic sales. Agent receives 15% commission on foreign sales. Offers written contract; 30-day notice must be given to terminate contract.

Recent Sales *Gunmetal Black*, by Daniel Serrano.

Tips "Build a résumé by publishing short stories if you are a fiction writer."

☑ THE AXELROD AGENCY

55 Main St., P.O. Box 357, Chatham NY 12037. (518)392-2100. E-mail: steve@axelrodagency. com. **Contact:** Steven Axelrod. Member of AAR. Represents 15-20 clients. 1% of clients are new/ unpublished writers. Currently handles: novels 95%.

- Prior to becoming an agent, Mr. Axelrod was a book club editor.

Represents Novels. **Considers these fiction areas:** mystery, romance, women's.

How to Contact Query with SASE. Accepts simultaneous submissions. Responds in 3 weeks to queries. Responds in 6 weeks to mss. Obtains most new clients through recommendations from others.

Terms Agent receives 15% commission on domestic sales. Agent receives 20% commission on foreign sales. No written contract.

Writers Conferences RWA National Conference.

☑ BAKER'S MARK LITERARY AGENCY

P.O. Box 8382, Portland OR 97207. (503)432-8170. E-mail: info@bakersmark.com. Website: www. Bakersmark.com. **Contact:** Bernadette Baker-Baughman or Gretchen Stelter. Currently handles: nonfiction books 35%, novels 25%, 40% graphic novels.

Represents Nonfiction books, novels, scholarly books, graphic novels. **Considers these nonfiction areas:** anthropology, archeology, autobiography, biography, business, cultural interests, economics, ethnic, gay, government, how-to, humor, investigative, law, lesbian, popular culture, politics, satire, true crime, women's issues, women's studies, comics/graphic novels. **Considers these fiction areas:** cartoon, comic books, contemporary issues, crime, detective, erotica, ethnic, experimental, fantasy, feminist, gay, glitz, historical, horror, humor, lesbian, literary, mainstream, mystery, police, psychic, regional, satire, supernatural, suspense, thriller, women's, chick literature.

- ⚬ "Baker's Mark specializes in graphic novels and popular nonfiction with an extremely selective taste in commercial fiction." Actively seeking graphic novels, nonfiction, fiction

(YA/Teen and magical realism in particular). Does not want to receive Westerns, poetry, sci-fi, novella, high fantasy, or children's picture books.

How to Contact Query with 1 page with no attachments and no chapters in the e-mail. Send SASE if mailing by post. "If interested, we will request representative materials from you." Accepts simultaneous submissions. Responds in 4-6 weeks. Obtains most new clients through recommendations from others, solicitations.

Terms Agent receives 15% commission on domestic sales. Agent receives 20% commission on foreign sales. Offers written contract, binding for 18 months; 30-day notice must be given to terminate contract.

Recent Sales *Never After*, by Dan Elconin (Simon Pulse); *Boilerplate: History's Mechanical Marvel*, by Paul Guinan and Anina Bennet (Abrams Image); *War Is Boring*, by David Axe with illustration by Matt Bors (New American Library); *The Choyster Generation*, by Amalia mcGibbon, Claire Williams, and Lara Vogel (Seal Press).

Writers Conferences New York Comic Convention, BookExpo of America, San Diego Comic Con, Stumptown Comics Fest, Emerald City Comic Con.

Tips "Baker's Mark is also looking to help pioneer new media models for books, and is especially interested in books that experiment with social media, open source software (and other digital technologies) as we help establish new business paradigms for the ebook revolution."

◨ THE BALKIN AGENCY, INC.

P.O. Box 222, Amherst MA 01004. Phone/Fax: (413)322-8697. E-mail: rick62838@crocker.com. **Contact:** Rick Balkin, president. Member of AAR. Represents 50 clients. 10% of clients are new/unpublished writers. Currently handles: nonfiction books 85%, 5% reference books.

• Prior to opening his agency, Mr. Balkin served as executive editor with Bobbs-Merrill Company.

Represents Nonfiction books. **Considers these nonfiction areas:** animals, anthropology, current affairs, health, history, how to, nature, popular culture, science, sociology, translation, biography, et alia.

    ⚬ This agency specializes in adult nonfiction. Does not want to receive fiction, poetry, screenplays, children's books or computer books.

How to Contact Query with SASE. Submit proposal package, outline. Responds in 1 week to queries. Responds in 2 weeks to mss. Obtains most new clients through recommendations from others.

Terms Agent receives 15% commission on domestic sales. Agent receives 20% commission on foreign sales. Offers written contract, binding for 1 year. This agency charges clients for photocopying and express or foreign mail.

Recent Sales Sold 15 titles in the last year. *No Tongue Shall Speak*, by Utpal Sandesara/Tom Wooten (Prometheus Books); *Wrong*, by David H. Freedman (Little, Brown); *The Musical Vision of Gustavo Dudamel*, by Tricia Tunstall, W.W. Norton & Co.

Tips "I do not take on books described as bestsellers or potential bestsellers. Any nonfiction work that is either unique, paradigmatic, a contribution, truly witty, or a labor of love is grist for my mill."

◨ THE PAULA BALZER AGENCY

55 Eastern Parkway, #5H, Brooklyn NY 11238. (347)787-4131. E-mail: info@pbliterary.com. Website: http://pbliterary.com. **Contact:** Paula Balzer. Member of AAR. Represents 35 clients. 50% of clients are new/unpublished writers. Currently handles: nonfiction books 50%, novels 50%.

• Prior to her current position, Ms. Balzer was with Carlisle & Company, as well as Sarah Lazin Books.

Represents Nonfiction books, novels. **Considers these nonfiction areas:** autobiography, biography, child guidance, cooking, current affairs, education, foods, gay, government, history, humor, law, lesbian, memoirs, nutrition, parenting, personal improvement, popular culture, politics, psychology, satire, science, self-help, technology, women's issues, women's studies. **Considers these fiction areas:** contemporary issues, erotica, family saga, gay, glitz, historical, horror, humor, lesbian, literary, mainstream, mystery, satire, suspense, thriller, women's.

    ⚬ Humor and popular culture.

How to Contact Query with e-mail or by post with SASE. Submit proposal package, author bio, 50 sample pages. Responds in 3 weeks to queries. Responds in 4-6 weeks to mss. Obtains most new clients through recommendations from others.

Terms Agent receives 15% commission on domestic sales. Agent receives 20% commission on foreign sales. Offers written contract.

Recent Sales *What's Up Dawg?* by Randy Jackson and K. C. Baker, *Pledged: The Secret Life of Sororities* by Alexandra Robbins, *Dear Mrs. Lindbergh: A Novel* by Kathleen Hughes, *Confessions of a Nervous Shiksa* by Tracy McArdle.

☑ BARER LITERARY, LLC

270 Lafayette St., Suite 1504, New York NY 10012. Website: www.barerliterary.com. **Contact:** Julie Barer. Estab. 2004. Member of AAR.

- Before becoming an agent, Julie worked at Shakespeare & Co. Booksellers in New York City. She is a graduate of Vassar College.

Member Agents Julie Barer.

Represents Nonfiction books, novels, short story collections. Julie Barer is especially interested in working with emerging writers and developing long-term relationships with new clients. **Considers these nonfiction areas:** biography, ethnic, history, memoirs, popular culture, women's. **Considers these fiction areas:** contemporary issues, ethnic, historical, literary, mainstream.

- ☞ This agency no longer accepts young adult submissions. No Health/Fitness, Business/Investing/Finance, Sports, Mind/Body/Spirit, Reference, Thrillers/Suspense, Military, Romance, Children's Books/Picture Books, Screenplays.

How to Contact Query with SASE; no attachments if query by e-mail. We do not respond to queries via phone or fax.

Terms Agent receives 15% commission on domestic sales. Agent receives 20% commission on foreign sales. Offers written contract. Charges for photocopying and books ordered.

Recent Sales *The Unnamed*, by Joshua Ferris (Reagan Arthur Books); *Tunneling to the Center of the Earth*, by Kevin Wilson (Ecco Press); *A Disobedient Girl*, by Ru Freeman (Atria Books); *A Friend of the Family*, by Lauren Grodstein (Algonquin); *City of Veils*, by Zoe Ferraris (Little, Brown).

BAROR INTERNATIONAL, INC.

P.O. Box 868, Armonk NY 10504. E-mail: danny@barorint.com; heather@barorint.com. Website: www.barorint.com. **Contact:** Danny Baror; Heather Baror. Represents 300 clients.

- ☞ "This agency represents authors and publishers in the international market. Currently representing all genres ranging from thrillers to science fiction/fantasy, self-help, spiritual, young adult, commercial fiction, and more."

Tips "No further information on this agency is available."

☑ LORETTA BARRETT BOOKS, INC.

220 E. 23rd St., 11th Floor, New York NY 10010. (212)242-3420. E-mail: query@lorettabarrettbooks.com. Website: www.lorettabarrettbooks.com. **Contact:** Loretta A. Barrett, Nick Mullendore. Estab. 1990. Member of AAR. Currently handles: nonfiction books 50%, novels 50%.

- Prior to opening her agency, Ms. Barrett was vice president and executive editor at Doubleday and editor-in-chief of Anchor Books.

Member Agents Loretta A. Barrett; Nick Mullendore.

Represents Nonfiction books, novels. **Considers these nonfiction areas:** biography, child guidance, current affairs, ethnic, government, health/nutrition, history, memoirs, money, multicultural, nature, popular culture, psychology, religion, science, self-help, sociology, spirituality, sports, women's, young adult, creative nonfiction. **Considers these fiction areas:** contemporary, psychic, adventure, detective, ethnic, family, fantasy, historical, literary, mainstream, mystery, thriller, young adult.

- ☞ "The clients we represent include both fiction and nonfiction authors for the general adult trade market. The works they produce encompass a wide range of contemporary topics and themes including commercial thrillers, mysteries, romantic suspense, popular science, memoirs, narrative fiction and current affairs." No children's, juvenile, cookbooks, gardening, science fiction, fantasy novels, historical romance.

How to Contact See guidelines online. Use e-mail or if by post, query with SASE. Accepts simultaneous submissions. Responds in 3-6 weeks to queries.

Terms Agent receives 15% commission on domestic sales. Agent receives 20% commission on foreign sales. Offers written contract. Charges clients for shipping and photocopying.

☑ BARRON'S LITERARY MANAGEMENT

4615 Rockland Drive, Arlington TX 76016. E-mail: barronsliterary@sbcglobal.net. **Contact:** Adele Brooks, president.

Represents Nonfiction books, novels. **Considers these nonfiction areas:** business/investing/ finance, health/exercise/nutrition, history, cook books, psychology, science, true crime. **Considers these fiction areas:** historical, horror, all mysteries, detective/pi/police, romance: suspense, paranormal, historical, chick lit and lady lit, science fiction, thriller, crime thriller, medical thriller.

> ☞ Barron's Literary Management is a small Dallas/Fort Worth-based agency with good publishing contacts. Seeks tightly written, fast moving fiction, as well as authors with a significant platform or subject area expertise for nonfiction book concepts.

How to Contact Contact by e-mail initially. Send bio and a brief synopsis of your story or a nonfiction proposal. Obtains most new clients through e-mail submissions.

Tips "Have your book tightly edited, polished and ready to be seen before contacting agents. I respond quickly and if interested may request an electronic or hard copy mailing."

▦ ☑ LORELLA BELLI LITERARY AGENCY

54 Hartford House, 35 Tavistock Crescent, Notting Hill, London England W11 1AY United Kingdom. (44)(207)727-8547. Fax: (44)(870)787-4194. E-mail: info@lorellabelliagency.com. Website: www. lorellabelliagency.com. **Contact:** Lorella Belli. Other memberships include AAA.

Represents Nonfiction books, novels. **Considers these nonfiction areas:** business, current affairs, economics, history, personal improvement, politics, science, self-help, technology, travel, women's issues, women's studies, food/wine; popular music; lifestyle. **Considers these fiction areas:** historical, literary, genre fiction; women's; crime.

> ☞ "We are interested in first-time novelists, journalists, multicultural and international writing, and books about Italy." Does not want children's books, fantasy, science fiction, screenplays, short stories, or poetry.

How to Contact For fiction, send query letter, first 3 chapters, synopsis, brief CV, SASE. For nonfiction, send query letter, full proposal, chapter outline, 2 sample chapters, SASE.

Terms Agent receives 15% commission on domestic sales. Agent receives 20% commission on foreign sales.

☑ FAYE BENDER LITERARY AGENCY

337 W. 76th St., #E1, New York NY 10023. E-mail: info@fbliterary.com. Website: www.fbliterary. com. **Contact:** Faye Bender. Estab. 2004. Member of AAR.

Represents Nonfiction books, novels, juvenile. **Considers these nonfiction areas:** biography, memoirs, popular culture, women's issues, women's studies, young adult, narrative; health; popular science. **Considers these fiction areas:** commercial, literary, women's, young adult (middle-grade).

> ☞ "I choose books based on the narrative voice and strength of writing. I work with previously published and first-time authors." Faye does not represent picture books, genre fiction for adults (western, romance, horror, science fiction, fantasy), business books, spirituality or screenplays.

How to Contact Query with SASE and 10 sample pages via mail or e-mail. Guidelines online.

Tips "Please keep your letters to the point, include all relevant information, and have a bit of patience."

☑ BENREY LITERARY

P.O. Box 12721, New Bern NC 28561. (252)638-5787. Fax: (886)297-9483. E-mail: query@ benreyliterary.com. Website: www.benreyliterary.com. **Contact:** Janet Benrey. Represents 20 clients. 5% of clients are new/unpublished writers. Currently handles: nonfiction books 20%, novels 80%.

• Prior to her current position, Ms. Benrey was with the Hartline Literary Agency.

Represents Novels, nonfiction books with a narrow focus. **Considers these nonfiction areas:** religious, true crime. **Considers these fiction areas:** literary, mystery, religious, romance, thriller, women's.

☞ This agency's specialties include inspirational romance, women's fiction, mystery, true crime, thriller (secular and Christian), as well as Christian living, church resources, inspirational.
How to Contact Query via e-mail only. Submit proposal package, synopsis, 3 sample chapters, author bio. More submission details available online. Accepts simultaneous submissions. Responds only if there is interest. Obtains most new clients through recommendations from others, conferences.
Terms Agent receives 15% commission on domestic sales. Agent receives 20% commission on foreign sales. Offers written contract; 30-day notice must be given to terminate contract.
Tips Understand the market as best you can. Attend conferences and network. Don't create a new genre.

◙ MEREDITH BERNSTEIN LITERARY AGENCY

2095 Broadway, Suite 505, New York NY 10023. (212)799-1007. Fax: (212)799-1145. Member of AAR. Represents 85 clients. 20% of clients are new/unpublished writers. Currently handles: nonfiction books 50%, other 50% fiction.

• Prior to opening her agency, Ms. Bernstein served at another agency for 5 years.
Represents Nonfiction books, novels. **Considers these fiction areas:** literary, mystery, romance, thriller, young adult.

☞ "This agency does not specialize. It is very eclectic."
How to Contact Query with SASE. Accepts simultaneous submissions. Obtains most new clients through recommendations from others, conferences, developing/packaging ideas.
Terms Agent receives 15% commission on domestic sales. Agent receives 20% commission on foreign sales. Charges clients $75 disbursement fee/year.
Recent Sales *House of Night* series, by P.C. Cast and Kristin Cast; *The No Cry Separation Anxiety Solution*, by Elizabeth Pantrey; and *Following the Waters*, by David Carroll (a McArthur Genius Award Winner) and nominee for National Book Award in 2009.
Writers Conferences Southwest Writers' Conference; Rocky Mountain Fiction Writers' Colorado Gold; Pacific Northwest Writers' Conference; Willamette Writers' Conference; Surrey International Writers' Conference; San Diego State University Writers' Conference.

BIDNICK & COMPANY

E-mail: bidnick@comcast.net. Currently handles: 100% Nonfiction books.
• Founding member of Collins Publishers. Vice President of HarperCollins, San Francisco.
Member Agents Carole Bidnick.
Represents Nonfiction books.

☞ This agency specializes in cookbooks and narrative nonfiction.
How to Contact Send queries via e-mail only.

◙ VICKY BIJUR LITERARY AGENCY

333 West End Ave., Apt. 5B, New York NY 10023. E-mail: assistant@vickybijuragency.com. Estab. 1988. Member of AAR.
• Vicky Bijur worked at Oxford University Press and with the Charlotte Sheedy Literary Agency. Books she represents have appeared on the New York Times Bestseller List, in the New York Times Notable Books of the Year, Los Angeles Times Best Fiction of the Year, Washington Post Book World Rave Reviews of the Year.
Represents Nonfiction books, novels. **Considers these nonfiction areas:** cooking, government, health, history, psychology, psychiatry, science, self-help, sociology, biography; child care/development; environmental studies; journalism; social sciences.

☞ Does not want science fiction, fantasy, horror, romance, poetry, children's or YA.
How to Contact Accepts e-mail queries. Fiction: query and first chapter (if e-mailed, please paste chapter into body of e-mail as I don't open attachments from unfamiliar senders). Nonfiction: query and proposal. No phone or fax queries.
Recent Sales *Left Neglected* and *Love, Anthony* by Lisa Genova (Pocket Books, 2011 and 2012); *I'd Know You Anywhere* and two untitled books by Laura Lippman (William Morrow, 2010, 2011, 2012); *The Serious Eats Guide* by Ed Levine (Clarkson Potter, 2012); *The Cartoon Guide to Calculus* by Larry Gonick (HarperCollins, 2012); *Relaxation Revolution* by Herbert Benson, M.D., and William Proctor (Scribner, 2010).

◙ DAVID BLACK LITERARY AGENCY

156 Fifth Ave., Suite 608, New York NY 10010-7002. (212)242-5080. Fax: (212)924-6609. **Contact:** David Black, owner. Member of AAR. Represents 150 clients. Currently handles: nonfiction books 90%, novels 10%.

Member Agents David Black; Susan Raihofer (general nonfiction, literary fiction); Gary Morris (commercial fiction, psychology); Joy E. Tutela (general nonfiction, literary fiction); Leigh Ann Eliseo; Linda Loewenthal (general nonfiction, health, science, psychology, narrative).

Represents Nonfiction books, novels. **Considers these nonfiction areas:** autobiography, biography, business, economics, finance, government, health, history, inspirational, law, medicine, military, money, multicultural, psychology, religious, sports, war, women's issues, women's studies. **Considers these fiction areas:** literary, mainstream, commercial.

  ⚷ This agency specializes in business, sports, politics, and novels.

How to Contact Query with SASE. For nonfiction works, send a formal proposal that includes an overview, author bio, chapter outline, a marketing/publicity section, a competition section, and at least one sample chapter. Please also include writing samples, such as newspaper or magazine clips if relevant. (See questions in Guidelines online.) When submitting fiction, please include a synopsis, author bio, and the first 3 chapters of the book (25-50 pages). Accepts simultaneous submissions. Responds in 2 months to queries.

Terms Agent receives 15% commission on domestic sales. Charges clients for photocopying and books purchased for sale of foreign rights.

Recent Sales Some of the agency's best-selling authors include: Mitch Albom, Erik Larson, Ken Davis, Bruce Feiler, Dan Coyle, Jane Leavy, Randy Pausch, Steve Lopez, Jenny Sanford, David Kidder and Noah Oppenheim.

BLEECKER STREET ASSOCIATES, INC.

532 LaGuardia Place, #617, New York NY 10012. (212)677-4492. Fax: (212)388-0001. E-mail: bleeckerst@hotmail.com. **Contact:** Agnes Birnbaum. Member of AAR. Other memberships include RWA, MWA. Represents 60 clients. 20% of clients are new/unpublished writers. Currently handles: nonfiction books 75%, novels 25%.

  • Prior to becoming an agent, Ms. Birnbaum was a senior editor at Simon & Schuster, Dutton/ Signet, and other publishing houses.

Represents Nonfiction books, novels. **Considers these nonfiction areas:** New Age, animals, biography, business, child, computers, cooking, current affairs, ethnic, government, health, history, how to, memoirs, military, money, nature, popular culture, psychology, religion, science, self-help, sociology, sports, true crime, women's. **Considers these fiction areas:** ethnic, historical, literary, mystery, romance, thriller, women's.

  ⚷ "We're very hands-on and accessible. We try to be truly creative in our submission approaches. We've had especially good luck with first-time authors." Does not want to receive science fiction, westerns, poetry, children's books, academic/scholarly/professional books, plays, scripts, or short stories.

How to Contact Query with SASE. No e-mail, phone, or fax queries. Accepts simultaneous submissions. Responds in 2 weeks to queries. Responds in 1 month to mss. "Obtains most new clients through recommendations from others, solicitations, conferences, plus, I will approach someone with a letter if his/her work impresses me."

Terms Agent receives 15% commission on domestic sales. Agent receives 25% commission on foreign sales. Offers written contract; 1-month notice must be given to terminate contract. Charges for postage, long distance, fax, messengers, photocopies (not to exceed $200).

Recent Sales Sold 14 titles in the last year. *Following Sarah*, by Daniel Brown (Morrow); *Biology of the Brain*, by Paul Swingle (Rutgers University Press); *Santa Miracles*, by Brad and Sherry Steiger (Adams); *Surviving the College Search*, by Jennifer Delahunt (St. Martin's).

Tips "Keep query letters short and to the point; include only information pertaining to the book or background as a writer. Try to avoid superlatives in description. Work needs to stand on its own, so how much editing it may have received has no place in a query letter."

BLISS LITERARY AGENCY INTERNATIONAL, INC.

1601 N. Sepulveda Blvd, #389, Manhattan Beach CA 90266. E-mail: info@blissliterary.com. Website: www.blissliterary.com. **Contact:** Jenoyne Adams.

Member Agents Prior to her current position, Ms. Adams was with Levine Greenberg Literary Agency.

Represents Nonfiction books, novels, juvenile. **Considers these nonfiction areas:** parenting, narrative nonfiction, women's. **Considers these fiction areas:** literary, multicultural, commercial.

☞ "Middle grade, YA fiction and nonfiction, young reader? Bring it on. We are interested in developing and working on projects that run the gamut—fantasy, urban/edgy, serious, bling-blingy? SURE. We love it all." "I haven't found it yet, but with a deep appreciation for anime and martial arts flicks, we are looking for the perfect graphic novel."

How to Contact Query via e-mail or snail mail. Send query, synopsis, one chapter, contact info. No attachments. One Word document via e-mail is preferred. No pdf files. Responds in 6-8 weeks to queries, sometimes longer.

Tips "Non-query related matters can be addressed by e-mailing info@blissliterary.com."

REID BOATES LITERARY AGENCY

69 Cooks Crossroad, Pittstown NJ 08867. (908)797-8087. Fax: (908)788-3667. E-mail: reid.boates@gmail.com. **Contact:** Reid Boates. Represents 45 clients. 5% of clients are new/unpublished writers. Currently handles: nonfiction books 85%, novels 15%, story collections very rarely.

How to Contact No unsolicited queries of any kind. Obtains new clients by personal referral only.

Terms Agent receives 15% commission on domestic sales. Agent receives 20% commission on foreign sales.

Recent Sales Sold 15 titles in the last year. New sales include placements at HarperCollins, Wiley, Random House, and other major general-interest publishers.

⊘ BOND LITERARY AGENCY

4340 E Kentucky Ave, Suite 471, Denver CO 80246. E-mail: sbbond@aol.com. **Contact:** Sandra Bond.

• Prior to her current position, Ms. Bond worked with agent Jody Rein.

Represents Nonfiction books, novels. **Considers these nonfiction areas:** business, health, history, science, narrative nonfiction. **Considers these fiction areas:** literary, general fiction, mystery, juvenile fiction.

How to Contact Submit query by mail or e-mail (no attachments). "She will let you know if she is interested in seeing more material. No unsolicited manuscripts." Accepts simultaneous submissions.

⊘ BOOK CENTS LITERARY AGENCY, LLC

2011 Quarrier Street, Charleston WV 25311. (304)347-2330, ext. 1105. E-mail: cw@bookcentsliteraryagency.com. Website: www.bookcentsliteraryagency.com. **Contact:** Christine Witthohn.

☞ Actively seeking "single title romance (contemporary, romantic comedy, paranormal, mystery/suspense), women's lit (must have a strong hook), mainstream mystery/suspense, medical or legal fiction, literary fiction. For nonfiction, seeking women's issues/experiences, fun/quirky topics (particularly those of interest to women), cookbooks (fun, ethnic, etc.), gardening (herbs, plants, flowers, etc.), books with a "save-the-planet" theme, how-to books, travel and outdoor adventure." Does not want to receive category romance, erotica, inspirational, historical, sci-fi/fantasy, horror/dark thrillers, short stories/novella, children's picture books, poetry, screenplays.

How to Contact "We prefer and respond faster to e-mail queries and submissions."

Tips "Sponsors *International Women's Fiction Festival* in Matera, Italy. See: womensfictionfestival.com for more information."

⊘ BOOKENDS, LLC

136 Long Hill Rd., Gillette NJ 07933. Website: www.bookends-inc.com; bookendslitagency.blogspot.com. **Contact:** Jessica Faust, Kim Lionetti. Member of AAR. RWA, MWA. Represents 50 + clients. 10% of clients are new/unpublished writers. Currently handles: nonfiction books 50%, novels 50%.

Member Agents Jessica Faust (fiction: romance, erotica, women's fiction, mysteries and suspense; nonfiction: business, finance, career, parenting, psychology, women's issues, self-help, health, sex); Kim Lionetti (women's fiction, mystery, true crime, pop science, pop culture, and all areas of romance).

Represents Nonfiction books, novels. **Considers these nonfiction areas:** business, child, ethnic, gay, health, how to, money, psychology, religion, self-help, sex, true crime, women's. **Considers these fiction areas:** detective, cozies, mainstream, mystery, romance, thriller, women's.

O→ "BookEnds is currently accepting queries from published and unpublished writers in the areas of romance (and all its sub-genres), erotica, mystery, suspense, women's fiction, and literary fiction. We also do a great deal of nonfiction in the areas of self-help, business, finance, health, pop science, psychology, relationships, parenting, pop culture, true crime, and general nonfiction." BookEnds does not want to receive children's books, screenplays, science fiction, poetry, or technical/military thrillers.

How to Contact Review website for guidelines, as they change.

◯ BOOKS & SUCH LITERARY AGENCY

52 Mission Circle, Suite 122, PMB 170, Santa Rosa CA 95409. E-mail: representation@booksandsuch. biz. Website: www.booksandsuch.biz. **Contact:** Janet Kobobel Grant, Wendy Lawton, Etta Wilson, Rachel Zurakowski. Member of AAR. Member of CBA (associate), American Christian Fiction Writers. Represents 150 clients. 5% of clients are new/unpublished writers. Currently handles: nonfiction books 50%, novels 50%.

• Prior to becoming an agent, Ms. Grant was an editor for Zondervan and managing editor for *Focus on the Family*; Ms. Lawton was an author, sculptor and designer of porcelain dolls. Ms. Wilson emphasizes middle grade children's books. Ms. Zurakowski concentrates on material for 20-something or 30-something readers.

Represents Nonfiction books, novels, juvenile books. **Considers these nonfiction areas:** child, humor, religion, self-help, womens. **Considers these fiction areas:** contemporary, family, historical, mainstream, religious, romance, African American adult.

O→ This agency specializes in general and inspirational fiction, romance, and the Christian booksellers market. Actively seeking well-crafted material that presents Judeo-Christian values, if only subtly.

How to Contact Query via e-mail only, no attachments. Accepts simultaneous submissions. Responds in 1 month to queries. "If you don't hear from us asking to see more of your writing within 30 days after you have sent your e-mail, please know that we have read and considered your submission but determined that it would not be a good fit for us." Obtains most new clients through recommendations from others, conferences.

Terms Agent receives 15% commission on domestic sales. Agent receives 20% commission on foreign sales. Offers written contract; 2-month notice must be given to terminate contract. No additional charges.

Recent Sales Sold 125 titles in the last year. *One Simple Act*, by Debbie Macomber (Howard Books); *Victim of Grace*, by Robin Jones Gunn (Zondervan); *Paradise Valley*, by Dale Cramer (Bethany House). Other clients include: Lauraine Snelling, Lori Copeland, Rene Gutteridge, Dale Cramer, BJ Hoff, Diann Mills.

Writers Conferences Mount Hermon Christian Writers' Conference; Society of Childrens' Book Writers and Illustrators Conference; Writing for the Soul; American Christian Fiction Writers' Conference; San Francisco Writers' Conference.

Tips "The heart of our agency's motivation is to develop relationships with the authors we serve, to do what we can to shine the light of success on them, and to help be a caretaker of their gifts and time."

◯ GEORGES BORCHARDT, INC.

136 E. 57th St., New York NY 10022. Member of AAR.

Member Agents Anne Borchardt; Georges Borchardt; Valerie Borchardt.

O→ This agency specializes in literary fiction and outstanding nonfiction.

How to Contact *No unsolicited mss.* Obtains most new clients through recommendations from others.

Terms Agent receives 15% commission on domestic sales. Agent receives 20% commission on foreign sales. Offers written contract.

⊌ THE BARBARA BOVA LITERARY AGENCY

3951 Gulf Shore Blvd. No. PH 1-B, Naples FL 34103. (239)649-7263. Fax: (239)649-7263. E-mail: michaelburke@barbarabovaliteraryagency.com. Website: www.barbarabovaliteraryagency.com. **Contact:** Ken Bova, Michael Burke. Represents 30 clients. Currently handles: nonfiction books 20%, fiction 80%.

Represents Nonfiction books, novels. **Considers these nonfiction areas:** biography, history, science, self-help, true crime, women's, social sciences. **Considers these fiction areas:** adventure, crime, detective, mystery, police, science fiction, suspense, thriller, women's, young adult, teen lit.

⁐ This agency specializes in fiction and nonfiction, hard and soft science.

How to Contact Query through website. Obtains most new clients through recommendations from others.

Terms Agent receives 15% commission on domestic sales. Agent receives 20% commission on foreign sales. Charges clients for overseas postage, overseas calls, photocopying, shipping.

Recent Sales Sold 24 titles in the last year. *The Green Trap* and *The Aftermath*, by Ben Bova; *Empire and A War of Gifts*, by Orson Scott Card; *Radioman*, by Carol E. Hipperson.

Tips "We also handle foreign, movie, television, and audio rights."

◪ BRADFORD LITERARY AGENCY

5694 Mission Center Road, #347, San Diego CA 92108. (619)521-1201. E-mail: laura@bradfordlit. com. Website: www.bradfordlit.com. **Contact:** Laura Bradford. Represents 35 clients. 20% of clients are new/unpublished writers. Currently handles: nonfiction books 10%, novels 90%.

- Ms. Bradford started with her first literary agency straight out of college and has 14 years of experience as a bookseller in parallel.

Represents Nonfiction books, novels, novellas, stories within a single author's collection, anthology. **Considers these nonfiction areas:** business, child care, current affairs, health, history, how-to, memoirs, money, popular culture, psychology, self-help, women's interest. **Considers these fiction areas:** adventure, detective, erotica, ethnic, historical, humor, mainstream, mystery, romance, thriller, psychic/supernatural.

⁐ Actively seeking romance (including category), romantica, women's fiction, mystery, thrillers and young adult. Does not want to receive poetry, short stories, children's books (juvenile) or screenplays.

How to Contact Query with SASE. Submit cover letter, first 30 pages of completed ms., synopsis and SASE. Send no attachments via e-mail; only send a query letter. Accepts simultaneous submissions. Responds in 10 weeks to queries. Responds in 10 weeks to mss. Obtains most new clients through solicitations.

Terms Agent receives 15% commission on domestic sales. Agent receives 20% commission on foreign sales. Offers written contract, non-binding for 2 years; 45-day notice must be given to terminate contract. Charges for photocopies, postage, extra copies of books for submissions.

Recent Sales Sold 53 titles in the last year. *Tempting Eden*, by Margaret Rowe (Berkley Heat); *Princess Poltergeist*, by Stacey Kade (Hyperion Children's); *Ruthless Heart*, by Emma Lang (Kensington Brava); *Deadly Fear*, by Cynthia Eden (Grand Central); *Precious and Fragile Things*, (Mira Books); *Cruel Enchantment*, by Anya Bast (Berkley Sensation); *Razorland*, by Elisabeth Naughton (Dorchestser); *His Darkest Craving*, by Juliana Stone (Avon).

Writers Conferences RWA National Conference; Romantic Times Booklovers Convention.

◎ BRANDS-TO-BOOKS, INC.

419 Lafayette St., New York NY 10003. E-mail: agents@brandstobooks.com. Website: www. brandstobooks.com. **Contact:** Robert Allen. Estab. 2003. 70% of clients are new/unpublished writers. Currently handles: nonfiction books 100%.

- Prior to co-founding Brands-to-Books, Mr. Allen was president and publisher of the Random House Audio Division; Ms. Spinelli was vice president/director of marketing for Ballantine Books.

Member Agents Kathleen Spinelli, kspinelli@brandstobooks.com (lifestyle, design, business, personal finance, health, pop culture, sports, travel, cooking, crafts, how-to, reference); Robert Allen, rallen@brandstobooks.com (business, motivation, psychology, how-to, pop culture, self-help/personal improvement, narrative nonfiction).

Represents Nonfiction books, ghostwriters. **Considers these nonfiction areas:** anthropology, archeology, architecture, art, autobiography, biography, business, child guidance, computers, cooking, crafts, criticism, cultural interests, current affairs, dance, decorating, design, economics, electronic, ethnic, film, finance, foods, gay, government, health, history, hobbies, how-to, humor, interior design, language, law, lesbian, literature, medicine, memoirs, money, music, nutrition, parenting, personal improvement, photography, popular culture, politics, psychology, satire, self-help, sports, theater, books based from brands.

> ⚏ "We concentrate on brand-name businesses, products, and personalities whose platform, passion, and appeal translate into successful publishing ventures. We offer more than literary representation—we provide clients a true marketing partner, pursuing and maximizing every opportunity for promotion and sales within the publishing process." "Actively seeking nonfiction proposals supported by strong media platforms and experienced ghostwriters—especially those who have worked with brands/personalities." Does not want fiction or poetry.

How to Contact E-query with book overview, résumé/platform. Accepts simultaneous submissions. Responds in 3 weeks to queries. Obtains most new clients through recommendations from others, outreach to brand managers and the licensing industry.

Terms Agent receives 15% commission on domestic sales. Agent receives 20% commission on foreign sales. Offers written contract; 3-month written notice must be given to terminate contract. Charges for office expenses (copying, messengers, express mail).

Tips "In your query, clearly show your passion for the subject and why you are the best person to write this book. Establish your media experience and platform. Indicate you have done your market research and demonstrate how this book is different from what is already on the shelves."

◪ BRANDT & HOCHMAN LITERARY AGENTS, INC.

1501 Broadway, Suite 2310, New York NY 10036. (212)840-5760. Fax: (212)840-5776. **Contact:** Gail Hochman. Member of AAR. Represents 200 clients.

Member Agents Carl Brandt; Gail Hochman; Marianne Merola; Charles Schlessiger; Bill Contardi; Joanne Brownstein.

Represents Nonfiction books, novels, short story collections, juvenile, journalism. **Considers these nonfiction areas:** autobiography, biography, cultural interests, current affairs, ethnic, government, history, law, politics, women's issues, women's studies. **Considers these fiction areas:** contemporary issues, ethnic, historical, literary, mystery, romance, suspense, thriller, young adult.

How to Contact Submit through e-mail or if by post, query with SASE. Accepts simultaneous submissions. Responds in 1 month to queries. Obtains most new clients through recommendations from others.

Terms Agent receives 15% commission on domestic sales. Agent receives 20% commission on foreign sales. Charges clients for ms duplication or other special expenses agreed to in advance.

Tips "Write a letter which will give the agent a sense of you as a professional writer—your long-term interests as well as a short description of the work at hand."

◪ THE JOAN BRANDT AGENCY

788 Wesley Drive, Atlanta GA 30305-3933. (404)351-8877. **Contact:** Joan Brandt.

- Prior to her current position, Ms. Brandt was with Sterling Lord Literistic.

Represents Nonfiction books, novels, short story collections. **Considers these nonfiction areas:** investigative, true crime. **Considers these fiction areas:** family saga, historical, literary, mystery, suspense, thriller, women's.

How to Contact Query letter with SASE. Accepts simultaneous submissions.

Terms Agent receives 15% commission on domestic sales. Agent receives 20% commission on foreign sales. No written contract.

◪ THE HELEN BRANN AGENCY, INC.

94 Curtis Road, Bridgewater CT 06752. Fax: (860)355-2572. Member of AAR.

How to Contact Query with SASE.

◎ BARBARA BRAUN ASSOCIATES, INC.

151 West 19th St., 4th floor, New York NY 10011. Fax: (212)604-9041. E-mail: bbasubmissions@ gmail.com. Website: www.barbarabraunagency.com. **Contact:** Barbara Braun. Member of AAR.
Member Agents Barbara Braun; John F. Baker.
Represents Nonfiction books, novels. **Considers these nonfiction areas:** We represent both literary and commercial and serious nonfiction, including psychology, biography, history, women's issues, social and political issues, cultural criticism, as well as art, architecture, film, photography, fashion and design. **Considers these fiction areas:** literary and commercial.

- ☞ "Our fiction is strong on women's stories, historical and multicultural stories, as well as mysteries and thrillers. We're interested in narrative nonfiction and books by journalists. We do not represent poetry, science fiction, fantasy, horror, or screenplays. Look online for more details."

How to Contact E-mail submissions only marked "query" in subject line. We no longer accept submissions by regular mail. Your query should include: a brief summary of your book, word count, genre, any relevant publishing experience, and the first 5 pages of your manuscript pasted into the body of the e-mail. (NO attachments – we will not open these.)
Terms Agent receives 15% commission on domestic sales. Agent receives 20% commission on foreign sales.
Tips "Our clients' books are represented throughout Europe, Asia and Latin America by various sub-agents. We are also active in selling motion picture rights to the books we represent, and work with various Hollywood agencies."

◎ PAUL BRESNICK LITERARY AGENCY, LLC

115 W. 29th St., Third Floor, New York NY 10001. (212)239-3166. Fax: (212)239-3165. E-mail: paul@ bresnickagency.com. **Contact:** Paul Bresnick, Polly Bresnick.

- Prior to becoming an agent, Mr. Bresnick spent 25 years as a trade book editor.

Represents Nonfiction books, novels. **Considers these nonfiction areas:** autobiography/memoir, biography, health, history, humor, memoirs, multicultural, popular culture, sports, travel, true crime, celebrity-branded books, narrative nonfiction, pop psychology, relationship issues. **Considers these fiction areas:** general fiction.
How to Contact For fiction, submit query/SASE and 2 chapters. For nonfiction, submit query/SASE with proposal.

◎ BRICK HOUSE LITERARY AGENTS

80 Fifth Ave., Suite 1101, New York NY 10011. Website: www.brickhouselit.com. **Contact:** Sally Wofford-Girand. Member of AAR.

- Jenni holds an MFA in fiction from the University of Michigan and a BA from Oberlin College. She taught creative writing at the University of Michigan and the Gotham Writers Workshop. She has worked as a reader for *The Paris Review*, and a bookseller at Housing Works. Her short fiction and food writing have been published in numerous magazines. She is the editor of *Alone in the Kitchen With an Eggplant* and a member of the International Association of Culinary Professionals.

Member Agents Sally Wofford-Girand; Jenni Ferrari-Adler; Melissa Sarver, assistant.
Represents Nonfiction books, narrative nonfiction. **Considers these nonfiction areas:** cultural interests, ethnic, history, memoirs, nature, science, women's issues, women's studies, biography; food writing; lifestyle; science; natural history. **Considers these fiction areas:** literary, general & juvenile fiction.

- ☞ Sally's particular areas of interest are: history, memoir, women's issues, cultural studies, and fiction that is both literary and hard to put down (novels like *The Road* or *Blindness*). Jenni Ferrari-Adler specializes in representing novels, food narrative and cookbooks, and narrative nonfiction. Actively seeking history, memoir, women's issues, cultural studies, literary fiction and quality commerical fiction.

How to Contact "E-mail query letter (in body of e-mail—not as attachment) and first page to either Sally or Jenni. We will ask to see more if interested and are sorry that we cannot respond to all queries."

RICK BROADHEAD & ASSOCIATES LITERARY AGENCY

501-47 St. Clair Ave. W., Toronto ON M4V 3A5 Canada. (416)929-0516. Fax: (416)927-8732. E-mail:

submissions@rbaliterary.com; rba@rbaliterary.com. Website: www.rbaliterary.com. **Contact:** Rick Broadhead, president. Other memberships include Authors Guild. Represents 50 clients. 50% of clients are new/unpublished writers. Currently handles: nonfiction books 100%.

- Prior to becoming an agent in 2002, Mr. Broadhead discovered his passion for books at a young age and co-authored his first bestseller at the age of 23. In addition to being one of the few literary agents with a business background, he has the rare distinction of having authored and co-authored more than 34 books.

Represents Nonfiction books. **Considers these nonfiction areas:** crafts, animals, anthropology, biography, business, child, cooking, current affairs, government, health, history, how to, humor, memoirs, military, money, music, nature, popular culture, psychology, science, self-help, sports, true crime, womens, politics, business, natural history/environment, national security/intelligence, pop science, relationships, medicine.

- ⚷ "Rick Broadhead & Associates is an established literary agency that represents primarily nonfiction projects in a wide variety of genres. Priority is given to original, compelling proposals as well as proposals from experts in their fields who have a strong marketing platform. The agency represents American authors to American and foreign publishers in a wide variety of nonfiction genres. The agency is deliberately small, which allows clients to receive personalized service to maximize the success of their book projects and brands." Actively seeking compelling nonfiction proposals, especially narrative nonfiction (history, current affairs, business) from authors with relevant credentials and an established media platform (TV, radio, print exposure). Does not want to receive novels, television scripts, movie scripts, children's or poetry.

How to Contact Query with SASE. Submit publishing history, author bio. E-mail queries preferred. Agency will reply only to projects of interest and request a full ms. Accepts simultaneous submissions. Obtains most new clients through recommendations from others, solicitations.

Terms Agent receives 15% commission on domestic sales. Agent receives 20% commission on foreign sales. Offers written contract. Charges for postage and photocopying expenses.

Tips "The agency has excellent relationships with New York publishers and editors and many of the agency's clients are American authors. The agency has negotiated many six-figure deals for its clients and has sold numerous unsolicited submissions to large publishers. We're good at what we do! E-mail queries are welcome."

CURTIS BROWN, LTD.

10 Astor Place, New York NY 10003-6935. (212)473-5400. Website: www.curtisbrown.com. Alternate address: Peter Ginsberg, president at CBSF, 1750 Montgomery St., San Francisco CA 94111. (415)954-8566. Member of AAR. Signatory of WGA.

Member Agents Ginger Clark; Katherine Fausset; Holly Frederick; Emilie Jacobson, senior vice president; Elizabeth Hardin; Ginger Knowlton, vice president; Timothy Knowlton, CEO; Laura Blake Peterson; Maureen Walters, senior vice president; Mitchell Waters. San Francisco Office: Nathan Bransford, Peter Ginsberg (President).

Represents Nonfiction books, novels, short story collections, juvenile. **Considers these nonfiction areas:** agriculture horticulture, Americana, crafts, interior, juvenile, New Age, young, animals, anthropology, art, biography, business, child, computers, cooking, current affairs, education, ethnic, gardening, gay, government, health, history, how to, humor, language, memoirs, military, money, multicultural, music, nature, philosophy, photography, popular culture, psychology, recreation, regional, religion, science, self-help, sex, sociology, software, spirituality, sports, film, translation, travel, true crime, women's, creative nonfiction. **Considers these fiction areas:** contemporary, glitz, New Age, psychic, adventure, comic, confession, detective, erotica, ethnic, experimental, family, fantasy, feminist, gay, gothic, hi lo, historical, horror, humor, juvenile, literary, mainstream, military, multicultural, multimedia, mystery, occult, picture books, plays, poetry, regional, religious, romance, science, short, spiritual, sports, thriller, translation, western, young, womens.

How to Contact Prefers to read materials exclusively. *No unsolicited mss.* Responds in 3 weeks to queries. Responds in 5 weeks to mss. Obtains most new clients through recommendations from others, solicitations, conferences.

Terms Offers written contract. Charges for some postage (overseas, etc.).

Recent Sales This agency prefers not to share information on specific sales.

Literary Agents

MARIE BROWN ASSOCIATES, INC.

412 W. 154th St., New York NY 10032. (212)939-9725. Fax: (212)939-9728. E-mail: mbrownlit@ aol.com. **Contact:** Marie Brown. Estab. 1984. Represents 60 clients. Currently handles: nonfiction books 75%, juvenile books 10%, other 15% other.

Member Agents Janell Walden Agyeman (Miami).

Represents Nonfiction books, juvenile. **Considers these nonfiction areas:** juvenile, biography, business, ethnic, history, music, religion, womens. **Considers these fiction areas:** ethnic, juvenile, literary, mainstream.

☌ This agency specializes in multicultural and African-American writers.

How to Contact Query with SASE. Prefers to read materials exclusively. Reports in 6-10 weeks on queries. Obtains most new clients through recommendations from others.

Terms Agent receives 15% commission on domestic sales. Agent receives 20% commission on foreign sales. Offers written contract.

☷ ☑ CURTIS BROWN (AUST) PTY LTD

P.O. Box 19, Paddington NSW 2021 Australia. (61)(2)9361-6161. Fax: (61)(2)9360-3935. E-mail: info@curtisbrown.com.au. Website: www.curtisbrown.com.au. **Contact:** Submissions Department. 10% of clients are new/unpublished writers. Currently handles: nonfiction books 30%, novels 30%, juvenile books 25%, other 15% other.

• Prior to joining Curtis Brown, most of our agents worked in publishing or the film/theatre industries in Australia and the United Kingdom.

Member Agents Fiona Inglis, managing director; Fran Moore, agent/deputy managing director; Tara Wynne, agent; Pippa Masson, agent; Clare Forster, agent.

Represents Nonfiction books, novels, novellas, juvenile.

☌ "We are the oldest and largest literary agency in Australia and we look after a wide variety of clients." No poetry, short stories, film scripts, picture books or translations.

How to Contact Submit 3 sample chapters, cover letter with biographical information, synopsis (2-3 pages), SASE.

☑ BROWNE & MILLER LITERARY ASSOCIATES

410 S. Michigan Ave., Suite 460, Chicago IL 60605-1465. (312)922-3063. E-mail: mail@ browneandmiller.com. Website: www.brownandmiller.com. **Contact:** Danielle Egan-Miller. Estab. 1971. Member of AAR. Other memberships include RWA, MWA, Author's Guild. Represents 150 clients. 2% of clients are new/unpublished writers. Currently handles: nonfiction books 25%, novels 75%.

Represents Nonfiction books, most genres of commercial adult fiction and nonfiction, as well as select young adult projects. **Considers these nonfiction areas:** agriculture, animals, anthropology, archeology, autobiography, biography, business, child guidance, cooking, crafts, cultural interests, current affairs, economics, environment, ethnic, finance, foods, health, hobbies, horticulture, how-to, humor, inspirational, investigative, medicine, memoirs, money, nature, nutrition, parenting, personal improvement, popular culture, psychology, religious, satire, science, self-help, sociology, sports, technology, true crime, women's issues, women's studies. **Considers these fiction areas:** contemporary issues, crime, detective, erotica, ethnic, family saga, glitz, historical, inspirational, literary, mainstream, mystery, police, religious, romance, sports, suspense, thriller, paranormal.

☌ "We are partial to talented newcomers and experienced authors who are seeking hands-on career management, highly personal representation, and who are interested in being full partners in their books' successes. We are editorially focused and work closely with our authors through the whole publishing process, from proposal to after publication." "We are most interested in commercial women's fiction, especially elegantly crafted, sweeping historicals; edgy, fresh teen/chick/mom/lady lit; and CBA women's fiction by established authors. We are also very keen on literary historical mysteries and literary YA novels. Topical, timely nonfiction projects in a variety of subject areas are also of interest, especially prescriptive how-to, self-help, sports, humor, and pop culture." Does not represent poetry, short stories, plays, original screenplays, articles, children's picture books, software, horror or sci-fi novels.

How to Contact Query with SASE. *No unsolicited mss.* Prefers to read material exclusively. Put submission in the subject line. Send no attachments. Responds in 6 weeks to queries. Obtains most new clients through referrals, queries by professional/marketable authors.

Terms Agent receives 15% commission on domestic sales. Agent receives 20% commission on foreign sales. Offers written contract, binding for 2 years. Charges clients for photocopying, overseas postage.

Writers Conferences BookExpo America; Frankfurt Book Fair; RWA National Conference; ICRS; London Book Fair; Bouchercon, regional writers conferences.

Tips "If interested in agency representation, be well informed."

⊘ PEMA BROWNE, LTD.

11 Tena Place, Valley Cottage NY 10989. E-mail: ppbltd@optonline.net. Website: www.pemabrowneltd.com. **Contact:** Pema Browne. Signatory of WGA. Other memberships include SCBWI, RWA. Represents 30 clients.

• Prior to opening her agency, Ms. Browne was an artist and art buyer.

Represents Nonfiction books, novels, juvenile, reference books. **Considers these nonfiction areas:** business, child guidance, cooking, cultural interests, economics, ethnic, finance, foods, gay, health, how-to, inspirational, juvenile nonfiction, lesbian, medicine, metaphysics, money, New Age, nutrition, parenting, personal improvement, popular culture, psychology, religious, self-help, spirituality, women's issues, women's studies, reference. **Considers these fiction areas:** contemporary, glitz, adventure, feminist, gay, historical, juvenile, literary, mainstream, commercial, mystery, picture books, religious, romance, contemporary, gothic, historical, regency, young.

☛ "We are not accepting any new projects or authors until further notice."

How to Contact Query with SASE. No attachments for e-mail.

Terms Agent receives 20% commission on domestic sales. Agent receives 20% commission on foreign sales.

Recent Sales *The Champion*, by Heather Grothaus (Kensington/Zebra); *The Highlander's Bride*, by Michele Peach (Kensington/Zebra); *The Daring Harriet Quimby*, by Suzanne Whitaker (Holiday House); *One Night to Be Sinful*, by Samantha Garver (Kensington); *Taming the Beast*, by Heather Grothaus (Kensington/Zebra); *Kisses Don't Lie,* by Alexis Darin (Kensington/Zebra).

Tips "We do not review manuscripts that have been sent out to publishers. If writing romance, be sure to receive guidelines from various romance publishers. In nonfiction, one must have credentials to lend credence to a proposal. Make sure of margins, double-space, and use clean, dark type."

⊘ BROWN LITERARY AGENCY

410 Seventh St. NW, Naples FL 34120. Website: www.brownliteraryagency.com. **Contact:** Roberta Brown. Member of AAR. Other memberships include RWA, Author's Guild. Represents 45 clients. 5% of clients are new/unpublished writers.

Represents Novels. **Considers these fiction areas:** erotica, romance, women's, single title and category.

☛ "This agency is selectively reading material at this time."

How to Contact Query via e-mail only. Send synopsis and two chapters in Word attachment. Response time varies.

Terms Agent receives 15% commission on domestic sales. Agent receives 20% commission on foreign sales. Offers written contract; 30-day notice must be given to terminate contract.

Writers Conferences RWA National Conference.

Tips "Polish your manuscript. Be professional."

⊘ ANDREA BROWN LITERARY AGENCY, INC.

1076 Eagle Drive, Salinas CA 93905. E-mail: andrea@andreabrownlit.com; caryn@andreabrownlit.com. Website: www.andreabrownlit.com. **Contact:** Andrea Brown, president. 10% of clients are new/unpublished writers.

• Prior to opening her agency, Ms. Brown served as an editorial assistant at Random House and Dell Publishing and as an editor with Knopf.

Member Agents Andrea Brown; Laura Rennert (laura@andreabrownlit.com); Kelly Sonnack; Caryn Wiseman; Jennifer Rofé; Jennifer Laughran, associate agent; Jamie Weiss Chilton, associate agent; Jennifer Mattson, associate agent; Mary Kole.

Represents Juvenile nonfiction books, novels. **Considers these nonfiction areas:** juvenile nonfiction, memoirs, young adult, narrative. **Considers these fiction areas:** juvenile, literary, picture books, women's, young adult, middle-grade, all juvenile genres.

➤ This agency specializes in children's books, though each agent has differing tastes.
How to Contact For picture books, submit complete ms, SASE. For fiction, submit short synopsis, SASE, first 3 chapters. For nonfiction, submit proposal, 1-2 sample chapters. For illustrations, submit 4-5 color samples (no originals). "We only accept queries via e-mail. No attachments, with the exception of jpeg illustrations from illustrators." Visit the agents' bios on our website and choose only one agent to whom you will submit your e-query. Send a short e-mail query letter to that agent with QUERY in the subject field. Accepts simultaneous submissions. If we are interested in your work, we will certainly follow up by e-mail or by phone. However, if you haven't heard from us within 6 to 8 weeks, please assume that we are passing on your project. Obtains most new clients through referrals from editors, clients and agents. Check website for guidelines and information.
Terms Agent receives 15% commission on domestic sales. Agent receives 20% commission on foreign sales. Offers written contract.
Recent Sales *Chloe*, by Catherine Ryan Hyde (Knopf); Sasha Cohen Autobiography (HarperCollins); *The Five Ancestors*, by Jeff Stone (Random House); *Thirteen Reasons Why*, by Jay Asher (Penguin); *Identical*, by Ellen Hopkins (S&S)
Writers Conferences SCBWI; Asilomar; Maui Writers' Conference; Southwest Writers' Conference; San Diego State University Writers' Conference; Big Sur Children's Writing Workshop; William Saroyan Writers' Conference; Columbus Writers' Conference; Willamette Writers' Conference; La Jolla Writers' Conference; San Francisco Writers' Conference; Hilton Head Writers' Conference; Pacific Northwest Conference; Pikes Peak Conference.

🄼 TRACY BROWN LITERARY AGENCY
P.O. Box 88, Scarsdale NY 10583. (914)400-4147. Fax: (914)931-1746. E-mail: tracy@brownlit.com. **Contact:** Tracy Brown. Represents 35 clients. Currently handles: nonfiction books 90%, novels 10%.
• Prior to becoming an agent, Mr. Brown was a book editor for 25 years.
Represents Nonfiction books, novels, anthologies. **Considers these nonfiction areas:** animals, autobiography, biography, business, cooking, current affairs, dance, economics, environment, finance, foods, government, health, history, how-to, humor, inspirational, law, medicine, memoirs, military, money, music, nature, nutrition, personal improvement, popular culture, politics, psychology, religious, satire, science, self-help, sociology, sports, technology, war, women's issues, women's studies. **Considers these fiction areas:** contemporary issues, feminist, literary, mainstream, women's.
➤ Specializes in thorough involvement with clients' books at every stage of the process from writing to proposals to publication. Actively seeking serious nonfiction and fiction. Does not want to receive YA, sci-fi or romance.
How to Contact Submit outline/proposal, synopsis, author bio. Accepts simultaneous submissions. Responds in 2 weeks to queries. Obtains most new clients through referrals.
Terms Agent receives 15% commission on domestic sales. Agent receives 20% commission on foreign sales. Offers written contract.
Recent Sales *Super in the City: A Novel*, by Daphne Uviller (Bantam); *The Purity Myth*, by Jessica Valenti (Seal Press); *Jane Addams: Spirit In Action*, by Louise W. Knight (Norton).

🄲 🌐 THE BUKOWSKI AGENCY
14 Prince Arthur Ave., Suite 202, Toronto Ontario M5R 1A9 Canada. (416)928-6728. Fax: (416)963-9978. E-mail: assistant@thebukowskiagency.com; info@thebukowskiagency.com. Website: www.thebukowskiagency.com. **Contact:** Denise Bukowski. Represents 70 clients.
• Prior to becoming an agent, Ms. Bukowski was a book editor.
Represents Nonfiction books, novels.
➤ "The Bukowski Agency specializes in international literary fiction and up-market nonfiction for adults. Bukowski looks for Canadian writers whose work can be marketed in many media and territories, and who have the potential to make a living from their work." Actively seeking nonfiction and fiction works from Canadian writers. Does not want submissions from American authors, as well as genre fiction, poetry, children's literature, picture books, film scripts or television scripts.

How to Contact Query with SASE. Submit proposal package, outline/proposal, synopsis, publishing history, author bio. Send submissions by snail mail only. See online guidelines for nonfiction and fiction specifics. Responds in 6 weeks to queries.

☑ SHEREE BYKOFSKY ASSOCIATES, INC.

PO Box 706, Brigantine NJ 08203. E-mail: submitbee@aol.com. Website: www.shereebee.com. **Contact:** Sheree Bykofsky. Member of AAR. Other memberships include ASJA, WNBA. Currently handles: nonfiction books 80%, novels 20%.

- Prior to opening her agency, Ms. Bykofsky served as executive editor of The Stonesong Press and managing editor of Chiron Press. She is also the author or co-author of more than 20 books, including *The Complete Idiot's Guide to Getting Published*. Ms. Bykofsky teaches publishing at NYU and SEAK, Inc.

Member Agents Janet Rosen, associate.

Represents Nonfiction books, novels. **Considers these nonfiction areas:** Americana, animals, architecture, art, autobiography, biography, business, child guidance, cooking, crafts, creative nonfiction, cultural interests, current affairs, dance, design, economics, education, environment, ethnic, film, finance, foods, gardening, gay, government, health, history, hobbies, humor, language, law, lesbian, memoirs, metaphysics, military, money, multicultural, music, nature, New Age, nutrition, parenting, philosophy, photography, popular culture, politics, psychology, recreation, regional, religious, science, sex, sociology, spirituality, sports, translation, travel, true crime, war, anthropology; creative nonfiction. **Considers these fiction areas:** contemporary issues, literary, mainstream, mystery, suspense.

- ☛ This agency specializes in popular reference nonfiction, commercial fiction with a literary quality, and mysteries. "I have wide-ranging interests, but it really depends on quality of writing, originality, and how a particular project appeals to me (or not). I take on fiction when I completely love it—it doesn't matter what area or genre." Does not want to receive poetry, material for children, screenplays, westerns, horror, science fiction, or fantasy.

How to Contact E-mail short queries to submitbee@aol.com. Please, no attachments, snail mail, or phone calls. Accepts simultaneous submissions. Responds in 3 weeks to queries with SASE. Responds in 1 month to requested mss. Obtains most new clients through recommendations from others.

Terms Agent receives 15% commission on domestic sales. Agent receives 20% commission on foreign sales. Offers written contract, binding for 1 year. Charges for postage, photocopying, fax.

Recent Sales *Red Sheep: The Search for my Inner Latina*, by Michele Carlo (Citadel/Kensington); *Bang the Keys: Four Steps to a Lifelong Writing Practice*, by Jill Dearman (Alpha, Penguin); *Signed, Your Student: Celebrities on the Teachers Who Made Them Who They Are Today*, by Holly Holbert (Kaplan); *The Five Ways We Grieve*, by Susan Berger (Trumpeter/Shambhala).

Writers Conferences ASJA Writers Conference; Asilomar; Florida Suncoast Writers' Conference; Whidbey Island Writers' Conference; Florida First Coast Writers' Festival; Agents and Editors Conference; Columbus Writers' Conference; Southwest Writers' Conference; Willamette Writers' Conferece; Dorothy Canfield Fisher Conference; Maui Writers' Conference; Pacific Northwest Writers' Conference; IWWG.

Tips "Read the agent listing carefully and comply with guidelines."

Ⓝ ☑ KIMBERLEY CAMERON & ASSOCIATES

1550 Tiburon Blvd., #704, Tiburon CA 94920. Fax: (415)789-9177. E-mail: info@kimberleycameron. com. Website: www.kimberleycameron.com. **Contact:** Kimberley Cameron. Member of AAR. 30% of clients are new/unpublished writers. Currently handles: nonfiction books 50%; fiction 50%.

- Kimberley Cameron & Associates (formerly The Reece Halsey Agency) has had an illustrious client list of established writers, including the estate of Aldous Huxley, and has represented Upton Sinclair, William Faulkner, and Henry Miller.

Member Agents Kimberley Cameron, April Eberhardt, Amy Burkhardt.

Represents Nonfiction, fiction. **Considers these nonfiction areas:** biography, current affairs, foods, humor, language, memoirs, popular culture, science, true crime, women's issues, women's studies, lifestyle. **Considers these fiction areas:** adventure, contemporary issues, ethnic, family saga, historical, horror, mainstream, mystery, interlinked short story collections, thriller, women's, and sophisticated/crossover young adult.

- ☛ "We are looking for a unique and heartfelt voice that conveys a universal truth."

How to Contact Query via e-mail. See our website for submission guidelines. Obtains new clients through recommendations from others, solicitations.

Terms Agent receives 15% on domestic sales; 10% on film sales. Offers written contract, binding for 1 year.

Writers Conferences Pacific Northwest Writers Association Conference, Aspen Summer Words, Willamette Writers Conference, San Diego State University Writers Conference, San Francisco Writers Conference, Killer Nashville, Left Coast Crime, Bouchercon, Book Passage Mystery and Travel Writers Conferences, Antioch Writers Workshop, Florida Writers Association Conference, and others.

Tips "Please consult our submission guidelines and send a polite, well-written query to our e-mail address."

⊘ CYNTHIA CANNELL LITERARY AGENCY

833 Madison Ave., New York NY 10021. Fax: (212)396-9797. **Contact:** Cynthia Cannell. Member of AAR.

⌐ Not accepting new clients at this time.

⊠ MARIA CARVAINIS AGENCY, INC.

1270 Avenue of the Americas, Suite 2320, New York NY 10019. (212)245-6365. Fax: (212)245-7196. E-mail: mca@mariacarvainisagency.com. **Contact:** Maria Carvainis, Chelsea Gilmore. Member of AAR. Signatory of WGA. Other memberships include Authors Guild, Women's Media Group, ABA, MWA, RWA. Represents 75 clients. 10% of clients are new/unpublished writers. Currently handles: nonfiction books 35%, novels 65%.

- Prior to opening her agency, Ms. Carvainis spent more than 10 years in the publishing industry as a senior editor with Macmillan Publishing, Basic Books, Avon Books, and Crown Publishers. Ms. Carvainis has served as a member of the AAR Board of Directors and AAR Treasurer, as well as serving as chair of the AAR Contracts Committee. She presently serves on the AAR Royalty Committee. Ms. Gilmore started her publishing career at Oxford University Press, in the Higher Education Group. She then worked at Avalon Books as associate editor. She is most interested in women's fiction, literary fiction, young adult, pop culture, and mystery/suspense.

Member Agents Maria Carvainis, president/literary agent; Chelsea Gilmore, literary agent.

Represents Nonfiction books, novels. **Considers these nonfiction areas:** autobiography, biography, business, economics, history, memoirs, science, technology, women's issues, women's studies. **Considers these fiction areas:** contemporary issues, historical, literary, mainstream, mystery, suspense, thriller, women's, young adult, middle grade.

⌐ Does not want to receive science fiction or children's picture books.

How to Contact Query with SASE. Responds in up to 3 months to mss and to queries. Obtains most new clients through recommendations from others, conferences, query letters.

Terms Agent receives 15% commission on domestic sales. Agent receives 20% commission on foreign sales. Offers written contract. Charges clients for foreign postage and bulk copying.

Recent Sales *A Secret Affair*, by Mary Balogh (Delacorte); *Tough Customer*, by Sandra Brown (Simon & Schuster); *A Lady Never Tells*, by Candace Camp (Pocket Books); *The King James Conspiracy*, by Phillip Depoy (St. Martin's Press).

Writers Conferences BookExpo America; Frankfurt Book Fair; London Book Fair; Mystery Writers of America; Thrillerfest; Romance Writers of America.

⊠ CASTIGLIA LITERARY AGENCY

1155 Camino Del Mar, Suite 510, Del Mar CA 92014. (858)755-8761. Fax: (858)755-7063. Website: home.earthlink.net/~mwgconference/id22.html. Member of AAR. Other memberships include PEN. Represents 50 clients. Currently handles: nonfiction books 55%, novels 45%.

Member Agents Julie Castiglia; Winifred Golden; Sally Van Haitsma; Deborah Ritchken.

Represents Nonfiction books, novels. **Considers these nonfiction areas:** animals, anthropology, archeology, autobiography, biography, business, child guidance, cooking, cultural interests, current affairs, economics, environment, ethnic, finance, foods, health, history, inspirational, language, literature, medicine, money, nature, nutrition, psychology, religious, science, technology, women's issues, women's studies. **Considers these fiction areas:** contemporary issues, ethnic, literary, mainstream, mystery, suspense, women's.

⌐ Does not want to receive horror, screenplays, poetry or academic nonfiction.

How to Contact Query with SASE. Obtains most new clients through recommendations from others, solicitations, conferences.

Terms Agent receives 15% commission on domestic sales. Agent receives 25% commission on foreign sales. Offers written contract; 6-week notice must be given to terminate contract.

Recent Sales *Germs Gone Wild*, by Kenneth King (Pegasus); *The Insider*, by Reece Hirsch (Berkley/Penguin); *The Leisure Seeker*, by Michael Zadoorian (Morrow/HarperCollins); *Beautiful: The Life of Hedy Lamarr*, by Stephen Shearer (St. Martin's Press); *American Libre*, by Raul Ramos y Sanchez (Grand Central); *The Two Krishnas*, by Ghalib Shiraz Dhalla (Alyson Books).

Writers Conferences Santa Barbara Writers' Conference; Southern California Writers' Conference; Surrey International Writers' Conference; San Diego State University Writers' Conference; Willamette Writers' Conference.

Tips "Be professional with submissions. Attend workshops and conferences before you approach an agent."

CHAMEIN CANTON AGENCY

E-mail: cantonsmithagency@cantonsmithagency.com; chamein@cantonsmithagency.com. Website: www.cantonsmithagency.com. **Contact:** Eric Smith, senior partner (esmith@cantonsmithagency.com); Chamein Canton, partner (chamein@cantonsmithagency.com); Netta Beckford, associate (nettab@cantonsmithagency.com). Estab. 2001. Represents 28 clients. 100% of clients are new/unpublished writers.

• Prior to becoming agents, Mr. Smith was in advertising and bookstore retail; Ms. Canton was a writer and a paralegal.

Member Agents Chamein Canton, managing partner, chamein@cantonsmithagency (women's fiction, chick-lit, business, how-to, fashion, romance, erotica, African American, Latina, women's issues, health, relationships, decorating, cookbooks, lifestyle, literary novels, astrology, numerology, New Age); Eric Smith, senior partner, ericsmith@cantonsmithagency.com (science fiction, sports, literature); James Weil, reviewer, jamesw@cantonsmithagency.com.

Represents Nonfiction books, novels, juvenile, scholarly, textbooks, movie. **Considers these nonfiction areas:** architecture, art, business, child guidance, cooking, cultural interests, dance, design, economics, education, ethnic, foods, health, history, how-to, humor, language, literature, medicine, memoirs, military, music, nutrition, parenting, photography, psychology, satire, sports, translation, war, women's issues, women's studies. **Considers these fiction areas:** fantasy, humor, juvenile, multicultural, romance, young adult, Latina fiction, chick lit, African-American fiction, entertainment. **Considers these script areas:** action/adventure, comedy, romantic comedy, romantic drama, science fiction.

⌐ "We specialize in helping new and established writers expand their marketing potential for prospective publishers. We are currently focusing on women's fiction (chick lit), Latina fiction, African American fiction, multicultural, romance, memoirs, humor and entertainment, in addition to more nonfiction titles (cooking, how to, fashion, home improvement, etc)."

How to Contact Only accepts e-queries. Send a query with synopsis only—include title and genre in subject line. Accepts simultaneous submissions. Responds in 8-12 weeks to queries. Responds in 3-5 months to mss. Obtains most new clients through recommendations from others.

Terms Agent receives 15% commission on domestic sales. Agent receives 20% commission on foreign sales. Offers written contract; 2-month notice must be given to terminate contract.

Tips "Know your market. Agents, as well as publishers, are keenly interested in writers with their finger on the pulse of their market."

☑ JANE CHELIUS LITERARY AGENCY

548 Second St., Brooklyn NY 11215. (718)499-0236. Fax: (718)832-7335. E-mail: queries@janechelius.com; jane@janechelius.com. Website: www.janechelius.com. Member of AAR.

Represents Nonfiction books, novels. **Considers these nonfiction areas:** biography, humor, medicine, parenting, popular culture, satire, women's issues, women's studies, natural history; narrative. **Considers these fiction areas:** literary, mystery, suspense, women's, men's adventure.

⌐ Does not want to receive fantasy, science fiction, children's books, stage plays, screenplays, or poetry.

How to Contact Please see website for submission procedures. We do not consider e-mail queries with attachments. No unsolicited sample chapters or mss. Responds in 3-4-weeks usually.

☑ ◎ ELYSE CHENEY LITERARY ASSOCIATES, LLC

270 Lafayette St., Suite 1504, New York NY 10012. Website: www.cheneyliterary.com. **Contact:** Elyse Cheney, Nicole Steen.

- Prior to her current position, Ms. Cheney was an agent with Sanford J. Greenburger Associates.

Represents Nonfiction, novels. **Considers these nonfiction areas:** autobiography, biography, business, cultural interests, current affairs, finance, history, memoirs, multicultural, politics, science, sports, women's issues, women's studies, narrative; journalism. **Considers these fiction areas:** commercial, family saga, historical, literary, romance, short story collections, suspense, thriller, women's.

How to Contact Query this agency with a referral. Include SASE or IRC. No fax queries. Snail mail or e-mail (submissions@cheneyliterary.com) only.

Recent Sales *Moonwalking with Einstein: A Journey into Memory and the Mind*, by Joshua Foer; *The Coldest Winter Ever*, by Sister Souljah (Atria); *A Heartbreaking Work of Staggering Genius*, by Dave Eggers (Simon and Schuster).

THE CHOATE AGENCY, LLC

1320 Bolton Road, Pelham NY 10803. E-mail: mickey@thechoateagency.com. Website: www.thechoateagency.com. **Contact:** Mickey Choate. Estab. 2004. Member of AAR.

Represents Nonfiction books, novels. **Considers these nonfiction areas:** history; memoirs by journalists, military or political figures; biography; cookery/food; journalism; military science; narrative; politics; general science; natural science, wine/spirits. **Considers these fiction areas:** historical, mystery, thriller, select literary fiction, strong commercial fiction.

- ⚬⊸ The agency does not handle genre fiction, chic-lit, cozies, romance, self-help, confessional memoirs, spirituality, pop psychology, religion, how-to, New Age titles, children's books, poetry, self-published works or screenplays.

How to Contact Query with brief synopsis and bio. This agency prefers e-queries, but accepts snail mail queries with SASE.

☑ ◎ THE CHUDNEY AGENCY

72 North State Road, Suite 501, Briarcliff Manor NY 10510. (914)488-5008. E-mail: steven@thechudneyagency.com. Website: www.thechudneyagency.com. **Contact:** Steven Chudney. Estab. 2001. Other memberships include SCBWI. 90% of clients are new/unpublished writers.

- Prior to becoming an agent, Mr. Chudney held various sales positions with major publishers.

Represents Novels, juvenile. **Considers these nonfiction areas:** juvenile. **Considers these fiction areas:** historical, juvenile, literary, mystery, suspense, young adult.

- ⚬⊸ This agency specializes in children's and teens books, and wants to find authors who are illustrators as well. "At this time, the agency is only looking for Author/Illustrators (one individual), who can both write and illustrate wonderful picture books. The author/illustrator must really know and understand the prime audience's needs and wants—the child reader! Storylines should be engaging, fun, with a hint of a life lesson and cannot be longer than 800 words." Does not want to receive board books or lift-the-flap books, fables, folklore, or traditional fairytales, poetry or mood pieces, stories for all ages (as these ultimately are too adult oriented), message-driven stories that are heavy-handed, didactic or pedantic.

How to Contact Query with SASE. Submit proposal package, 4-6 sample chapters. For children's, submit full text and 3-5 illustrations. Accepts simultaneous submissions. Responds in 2-3 weeks to queries. Responds in 3-4 weeks to mss.

Terms Agent receives 15% commission on domestic sales. Agent receives 20% commission on foreign sales. Offers written contract, binding for 1 year; 30-day notice must be given to terminate contract.

Tips "If an agent has a website, review it carefully to make sure your material is appropriate for that agent. Read lots of books within the genre you are writing; work hard on your writing; don't follow trends—most likely, you'll be too late."

◙ EDWARD B. CLAFLIN LITERARY AGENCY, LLC

128 High Ave., Suite #2, Nyack NY 10960. (845)358-1084. E-mail: edclaflin@aol.com. **Contact:** Edward Claflin. Represents 30 clients. 10% of clients are new/unpublished writers.
- Prior to opening his agency, Mr. Claflin worked at Banbury Books, Rodale and Prentice Hall Press. He is the co-author of 13 books.

Represents Nonfiction books. **Considers these nonfiction areas:** business, cooking, current affairs, economics, finance, foods, health, history, how-to, medicine, military, money, nutrition, psychology, sports, war.
- ⛏ This agency specializes in consumer health, narrative history, psychology/self-help and business. Actively seeking compelling and authoritative nonfiction for specific readers. Does not want to receive fiction.

How to Contact Query with synopsis, bio, SASE or e-mail attachment in Word. Responds in 1 month to queries. Obtains most new clients through recommendations from others.
Terms Agent receives 15% commission on domestic sales.

◙ WM CLARK ASSOCIATES

186 Fifth Avenue, Second Floor, New York NY 10010. (212)675-2784. Fax: (347)-649-9262. E-mail: general@wmclark.com. Website: www.wmclark.com. Estab. 1997. Member of AAR. 50% of clients are new/unpublished writers. Currently handles: nonfiction books 50%, novels 50%.
- Prior to opening WCA, Mr. Clark was an agent at the William Morris Agency.

Represents Nonfiction books, novels. **Considers these nonfiction areas:** architecture, art, autobiography, biography, cultural interests, current affairs, dance, design, ethnic, film, history, inspirational, memoirs, music, politics, popular culture, religious, science, sociology, technology, theater, translation, travel memoir, Eastern Philosophy. **Considers these fiction areas:** contemporary issues, ethnic, historical, literary, mainstream, Southern fiction.
- ⛏ William Clark represents a wide range of titles across all formats to the publishing, motion picture, television, and new media fields on behalf of authors of first fiction and award-winning, best-selling narrative nonfiction, international authors in translation, chefs, musicians, and artists. Offering individual focus and a global presence, the agency undertakes to discover, develop, and market today's most interesting content and the talent that create it, and forge sophisticated and innovative plans for self-promotion, reliable revenue streams, and an enduring creative career. Referral partners are available to provide services including editorial consultation, media training, lecture booking, marketing support, and public relations. Agency does not respond to screenplays or screenplay pitches. It is advised that before querying you become familiar with the kinds of books we handle by browsing our Book List, which is available on our website.

How to Contact Accepts queries via online form only at www.wmclark.com/queryguidelines. html. E-mail queries will be deleted. Responds in 1-2 months to queries.
Terms Agent receives 15% commission on domestic sales. Agent receives 20% commission on foreign sales. Offers written contract.
Tips "WCA works on a reciprocal basis with Ed Victor Ltd. (UK) in representing select properties to the US market and vice versa. Translation rights are sold directly in the German, Italian, Spanish, Portuguese, Latin American, French, Dutch, and Scandinavian territories in association with Andrew Nurnberg Associates Ltd. (UK); through offices in China, Bulgaria, Czech Republic, Latvia, Poland, Hungary, and Russia; and through corresponding agents in Japan, Greece, Israel, Turkey, Korea, Taiwan, and Thailand."

◙ NANCY COFFEY LITERARY & MEDIA REPRESENTATION

240 W. 35th St., Suite 500, New York NY 10001. Fax: (212)279-0927. E-mail: assist@ nancycoffeyliterary.com. Website: www.nancycoffeyliterary.com. **Contact:** Nancy Coffey. Member of AAR. Currently handles: nonfiction books 5%, novels 90%, juvenile books 5%.
Member Agents Nancy Coffey (hard copy queries only); Joanna Stampfel-Volpe (joanna@ nancycoffeyliterary.com).
Represents Nonfiction books, novels, juvenile, young adult, from cutting edge material to fantasy. **Considers these fiction areas:** family, fantasy, military, espionage, mystery, romance, science, thriller, young adult, women's.
How to Contact Query with SASE, e-mail.

⊘ COLCHIE AGENCY, GP

324 85th St., Brooklyn NY 11209. (718)921-7468. E-mail: ColchieLit@earthlink.net. **Contact:** Thomas or Elaine Colchie. Currently handles: 100% fiction.

Represents Novels.

⚬⟶ Does not want to receive nonfiction.

How to Contact This listing does not take or respond to unsolicited queries or submissions.

Recent Sales *The Prince of Mist*, by Carlos Ruizz Zafon (Little Brown Books); *White Masks*, by Elias Khoury (Archipelago); *The Philosopher's Kiss*, by Peter Prange (Atria); *The Woman Who Dove Into the Heart of the World*, by Sabina Berman (Holt).

⊘ FRANCES COLLIN, LITERARY AGENT

P.O. Box 33, Wayne PA 19087-0033. Website: www.francescollin.com. **Contact:** Sarah Yake, associate agent. Member of AAR. Represents 90 clients. 1% of clients are new/unpublished writers. Currently handles: nonfiction books 50%, fiction 50%.

Represents Nonfiction books, fiction, young adult.

⚬⟶ Does not want to receive cookbooks, craft books, poetry, screenplays, or books for young children.

How to Contact Query via e-mail describing project (text in the body of the e-mail only, no attachments) to queries@francescollin.com. "Please note that all queries are reviewed by both agents." No phone or fax queries. Accepts simultaneous submissions.

Terms Agent receives 15% commission on domestic sales. Agent receives 20% commission on foreign sales. Offers written contract.

CONNOR LITERARY AGENCY

2911 W. 71st St., Minneapolis MN 55423. (612)866-1486. E-mail: connoragency@aol.com; coolmkc@aol.com. **Contact:** Marlene Connor Lynch. Represents 50 clients. 30% of clients are new/unpublished writers. Currently handles: nonfiction books 50%, novels 50%.

- Prior to opening her agency, Ms. Connor served at the Literary Guild of America, Simon & Schuster and Random House. She is author of *Welcome to the Family: Memories of the Past for a Bright Future* (Broadway Books) and *What is Cool: Understanding Black Manhood in America* (Crown).

Member Agents Marlene Connor Lynch (all categories with an emphasis on these nonfiction areas: Child guidance/parenting; cooking/foods/nutrition; crafts/hobbies; current affairs; ethnic/cultural interests; government/politics/law; health/medicine; how-to; humor/satire; interior design/decorating; language/literature/criticism; money/finance; photography; popular culture; self-help/personal improvement; women's issues/studies; relationships. Considers these fiction areas: historical; horror; literary; mainstream/contemporary; multicultural; thriller; women's; suspense); Deborah Coker (mainstream and literary fiction, multicultural fiction, children's books, humor, politics, memoirs, narrative nonfiction, true crime/investigative); Nichole L. Shields/Chicago (multicultural fiction and nonfiction with an emphasis on African-American literature, poetry and children's content).

Represents Nonfiction books, novels.

⚬⟶ Actively seeking illustrated books. We are currently accepting manuscripts; and we are expanding our interest to include more mainstream and multicultural fiction.

How to Contact Query with one page and synopsis, SASE. All unsolicited mss returned unopened. Obtains most new clients through recommendations from others, conferences, grapevine.

Terms Agent receives 15% commission on domestic sales. Agent receives 25% commission on foreign sales. Offers written contract, binding for 1 year.

Recent Sales *Beautiful Hair at Any Age*, by Lisa Akbari; *12 Months of Knitting*, by Joanne Yordanou; *The Warrior Path: Confessions of a Young Lord,* by Felipe Luciano.

Writers Conferences National Writers Union, Midwest Chapter; Agents, Agents, Agents; Texas Writers' Conference; Detroit Writers' Conference; Annual Gwendolyn Brooks Writers' Conference for Literature and Creative Writing; Wisconsin Writers' Festival.

Tips "Previously published writers are preferred; new writers with national exposure or potential to have national exposure from their own efforts preferred."

◙ THE DOE COOVER AGENCY

P.O. Box 668, Winchester MA 01890. (781)721-6000. Fax: (781)721-6727. E-mail: info@ doecooveragency.com. Website: http://doecooveragency.com. Represents more than 100 clients. Currently handles: nonfiction books 80%, novels 20%.

Member Agents Doe Coover (general nonfiction, including business, cooking/food writing, health and science); Colleen Mohyde (literary and commercial fiction, general nonfiction), Member AAR; Amanda Lewis (YA & children's books); Associate: Frances Kennedy.

Represents Considers these nonfiction areas: autobiography, biography, business, cooking, economics, foods, gardening, health, history, nutrition, science, technology, social issues, narrative nonfiction. **Considers these fiction areas:** commercial, literary.

> ⚬┅ This agency specializes in general nonfiction, particularly biography, business, cooking and food writing, health, history, popular science, social issues, gardening, and humor. The agency does not accept romance, fantasy, science fiction, poetry or screenplays.

How to Contact Query with SASE. E-mail queries are acceptable—please check website for submission guidelines. No unsolicited manuscripts, please. Accepts simultaneous submissions. Responds in 4-6 weeks to queries. Obtains most new clients through recommendations from others, solicitations.

Terms Agent receives 15% commission on domestic sales. Agent receives 10% of original advance commission on foreign sales. No reading fees.

Recent Sales Sold 25-30 titles in the last year. *As Always, Julia, Letters of Julia Child and Avis De Voto—Food, Friendship and the Making of a Masterpiece*, selected and edited by Joan Reardon (Houghton Mifflin Harcourt); *Confessions of a Tarot Card Reader*, by Jane Stern (The Globe Pequot Press); *The Farm*, by Ian Knauer (Houghton Mifflin Harcourt); *Bottling the Gods: Why Global Development has gone Unnecessarily Wrong for So Long*, by Edward Carr (Palgrave/St. Martin's); *The Sewing Book*, by Tanya Whelan (Potter Craft); *The Gourmet Cookie Book: The Single Best Cookie Recipe from 1941-2009*, by Gourmet Magazine (Houghton Mifflin Harcourt); *Shades of Grey*, by Clea Simon (Severn House UK); *Cloud County Revival: How Wind Energy is Breathing New Life into America's Heartland*, by Philip Warburg (Beacon Press). Movie/TV MOW script(s) optioned/sold: *Keeper of the House*, by Rebecca Godwin; *Mr. White's Confession* by Robert Clark. Other clients include: WGBH, New England Aquarium, Blue Balliett, David Allen, Jacques Pepin, Deborah Madison, Rick Bayless, Suzanne Berne, Adria Bernardi, Paula Poundstone.

◙ CORNERSTONE LITERARY, INC.

4525 Wilshire Blvd., Ste. 208, Los Angeles CA 90010. (323)930-6039. Fax: (323)930-0407. E-mail: info@cornerstoneliterary.com. Website: www.cornerstoneliterary.com. **Contact:** Helen Breitwieser. Member of AAR. Other memberships include Author's Guild, MWA, RWA, PEN, Poets & Writers. Represents 40 clients. 30% of clients are new/unpublished writers.

> • Prior to founding her own boutique agency, Ms. Breitwieser was a literary agent at The William Morris Agency.

Represents Novels. **Considers these fiction areas:** crime, detective, erotica, ethnic, family saga, glitz, graphic novels, historical, literary, mainstream, memoirs, multicultural, mystery, police, romance, suspense, thriller, women's fiction, Christian fiction.

> ⚬┅ "We are not taking new clients at this time. We do not respond to unsolicited e-mail inquiries. All unsolicited manuscripts will be returned unopened." Does not want to receive science fiction, Western, poetry, screenplays, fantasy, gay/lesbian, horror, self-help, psychology, business or diet.

How to Contact Obtains most new clients through recommendations from others.

Terms Agent receives 15% commission on domestic sales. Agent receives 20% commission on foreign sales. Offers written contract, binding for 1 year; 2-month notice must be given to terminate contract.

CRAWFORD LITERARY AGENCY

92 Evans Road, Barnstead NH 03218. (603)269-5851. Fax: (603)269-2533. E-mail: crawfordlit@ att.net. **Contact:** Susan Crawford. Winter Office: 3920 Bayside Rd., Fort Myers Beach FL 33931. (239)463-4651. Fax: (239)463-0125.

Represents Nonfiction books, novels.

○┯ This agency specializes in celebrity and/or media-based books and authors. Actively seeking action/adventure stories, medical thrillers, self-help, inspirational, how-to, and women's issues. No short stories, or poetry.

How to Contact Query with SASE. Accepts simultaneous submissions. Obtains most new clients through recommendations from others, solicitations, conferences.

Terms Agent receives 15% commission on domestic sales. Agent receives 20% commission on foreign sales. Offers written contract.

Recent Sales *Thriving After Divorce*, by Tonja Weimer; *Something About You*, by Julie James; *The Golden Temple*, by Mingmei Yip; *Untitled Memoir*, by John Travolta; *Final Finesse,* by Karna Bodman; *Tunnel Vision*, by Gary Braver; *White House Doctor*, by Dr. Connie Mariano.

Writers Conferences International Film & Television Workshops; Maui Writers Conference; Emerson College Conference; Suncoast Writers Conference; San Diego Writers Conference; Simmons College Writers Conference; Cape Cod Writers Conference; Writers Retreats on Maui; Writers Alaskan Cruise; Western Caribbean Cruise and Fiji Island.

Tips "Keep learning to improve your craft. Attend conferences and network."

◪ THE CREATIVE CULTURE, INC.

47 E. 19th St., Third Floor, New York NY 10003. (212)680-3510. Fax: (212)680-3509. Website: www. thecreativeculture.com. **Contact:** Debra Goldstein. Estab. 1998. Member of AAR.

• Prior to opening her agency, Ms. Goldstein and Ms. Gerwin were agents at the William Morris Agency; Ms. Naples was a senior editor at Simon & Schuster.

Member Agents Debra Goldstein (self-help, creativity, fitness, inspiration, lifestyle); Mary Ann Naples (health/nutrition, lifestyle, narrative nonfiction, practical nonfiction, literary fiction, animals/vegetarianism); Laura Nolan (literary fiction, parenting, self-help, psychology, women's studies, current affairs, science); Karen Gerwin; Matthew Elblonk (literary fiction, humor, pop culture, music and young adult. Interests also include commercial fiction, narrative nonfiction, science, and he is always on the lookout for something slightly quirky or absurd).

Represents Nonfiction books, novels.

○┯ We are known for our emphasis on lifestyle books that enhance readers' overall wellbeing— be it through health, inspiration, entertainment, thought-provoking ideas, life management skills, beauty and fashion, or food. Does not want to receive children's books, poetry, screenplays or science fiction.

How to Contact Query with bio, book description, 4-7 sample pages (fiction only), SASE. We only reply if interested. Please see the titles page to get a sense of the books we represent. Responds in 2 months to queries.

◪ CRICHTON & ASSOCIATES

6940 Carroll Ave., Takoma Park MD 20912. (301)495-9663. Fax: (202)318-0050. E-mail: query@ crichton-associates.com. Website: www.crichton-associates.com. **Contact:** Sha-Shana Crichton. 90% of clients are new/unpublished writers. Currently handles: nonfiction books 50%, fiction 50%.

• Prior to becoming an agent, Ms. Crichton did commercial litigation for a major law firm.

Represents Nonfiction books, novels. **Considers these nonfiction areas:** child guidance, cultural interests, ethnic, gay, government, investigative, law, lesbian, parenting, politics, true crime, women's issues, women's studies, African-American studies. **Considers these fiction areas:** ethnic, feminist, inspirational, literary, mainstream, mystery, religious, romance, suspense, chick lit.

○┯ Actively seeking women's fiction, romance, and chick lit. Looking also for multicultural fiction and nonfiction. Does not want to receive poetry.

How to Contact For fiction, include short synopsis and first 3 chapters with query. Send no e-attachments. For nonfiction, send a book proposal. Responds in 3-5 weeks to queries.

Terms Agent receives 15% commission on domestic sales. Agent receives 20% commission on foreign sales. Offers written contract, binding for 45 days. Only charges fees for postage and photocopying.

Recent Sales *The African American Entrepreneur*, by W. Sherman Rogers (Praeger); *The Diversity Code*, by Michelle Johnson (Amacom); *Secret & Lies*, by Rhonda McKnight (Urban Books); *Love on the Rocks*, by Pamela Yaye (Harlequin). Other clients include Kimberley White, Beverley Long, Jessica Trap, Altonya Washington, Cheris Hodges.

Writers Conferences Silicon Valley RWA; BookExpo America.

⊙ RICHARD CURTIS ASSOCIATES, INC.

171 E. 74th St., New York NY 10021. (212)772-7363. Fax: (212)772-7393. Website: www.curtisagency. com. Other memberships include RWA, MWA, SFWA. Represents 100 clients. 1% of clients are new/unpublished writers. Currently handles: nonfiction books 50%, other 50% genre fiction.

• Mr. Curtis authored more than 50 published books.

Represents Considers these nonfiction areas: autobiography, biography, business, economics, health, history, medicine, science, technology.

How to Contact Send 1-page query letter and no more than a 5-page synopsis. Include SASE. Don't send ms unless specifically requested. Responds in 6 weeks to queries.

Terms Agent receives 15% commission on domestic sales. Agent receives 25% commission on foreign sales. Offers written contract. Charges for photocopying, express mail, international freight, book orders.

Recent Sales Sold 100 titles in the last year. *Morpheus*, by DJ MacHale; *Hull 03*, by Greg Bear; *Black Magic Sanction*, by Kim Harrison.

Writers Conferences RWA National Conference.

D4EO LITERARY AGENCY

7 Indian Valley Road, Weston CT 06883. (203)544-7180. Fax: (203)544-7160. E-mail: d4eo@ optonline.net. **Contact:** Bob Diforio. Represents more than 100 clients. 50% of clients are new/unpublished writers. Currently handles: nonfiction books 70%, novels 25%, juvenile books 5%.

• Prior to opening his agency, Mr. Diforio was a publisher.

Represents Nonfiction books, novels. **Considers these nonfiction areas:** juvenile, art, biography, business, child, current affairs, gay, health, history, how-to, humor, memoirs, military, money, psychology, religion, science, self-help, sports, true crime, women's. **Considers these fiction areas:** adventure, detective, erotica, historical, horror, humor, juvenile, literary, mainstream, mystery, picture books, romance, science, sports, thriller, western, young adult.

How to Contact Query with SASE. Accepts and prefers e-mail queries. Prefers to read material exclusively. Responds in 1 week to queries. Obtains most new clients through recommendations from others.

Terms Agent receives 15% commission on domestic sales. Agent receives 25% commission on foreign sales. Offers written contract, binding for 2 years; 60-day notice must be given to terminate contract. Charges for photocopying and submission postage.

⊙ LAURA DAIL LITERARY AGENCY, INC.

350 Seventh Ave., Suite 2003, New York NY 10010. (212)239-7477. Fax: (212)947-0460. E-mail: queries@ldlainc.com. Website: www.ldlainc.com. Member of AAR.

Member Agents Laura Dail; Tamar Rydzinski.

Represents Nonfiction books, novels.

⊶ "Due to the volume of queries and manuscripts received, we apologize for not answering every e-mail and letter. Specializes in historical, literary and some young adult fiction, as well as both practical and idea-driven nonfiction." None of us handles children's picture books or chapter books. No New Age. We do not handle screenplays or poetry.

How to Contact Query with SASE or e-mail. This agency prefers e-queries. Include the word "query" in the subject line.

⊙ DANIEL LITERARY GROUP

1701 Kingsbury Drive, Suite 100, Nashville TN 37215. (615)730-8207. E-mail: submissions@ danielliterarygroup.com. Website: www.danielliterarygroup.com. **Contact:** Greg Daniel. Represents 45 clients. 30% of clients are new/unpublished writers. Currently handles: nonfiction books 85%, novels 15%.

• Prior to becoming an agent, Mr. Daniel spent 10 years in publishing—six at the executive level at Thomas Nelson Publishers.

Represents Nonfiction books, novels. **Considers these nonfiction areas:** autobiography, biography, business, child guidance, current affairs, economics, environment, film, health, history, how-to, humor, inspirational, medicine, memoirs, nature, parenting, personal improvement, popular culture, religious, satire, self-help, sports, theater, women's issues, women's studies. **Considers these**

fiction areas: action, adventure, contemporary issues, crime, detective, family saga, historical, humor, inspirational, literary, mainstream, mystery, police, religious, satire, suspense, thriller.

- The agency currently accepts all fiction topics, except for children's, romance and sci-fi. "We take pride in our ability to come alongside our authors and help strategize about where they want their writing to take them in both the near and long term. Forging close relationships with our authors, we help them with such critical factors as editorial refinement, branding, audience, and marketing." The agency is open to submissions in almost every popular category of nonfiction, especially if authors are recognized experts in their fields. No screenplays, poetry or short stories.

How to Contact Query via e-mail only. Submit publishing history, author bio, brief synopsis of work, key selling points. E-queries only. Send no attachments. For fiction, send first 5 pages pasted in e-mail. Responds in 2-3 weeks to queries.

DARHANSOFF, VERRILL, FELDMAN LITERARY AGENTS

236 W. 26th St., Suite 802, New York NY 10001. (917)305-1300. Fax: (917)305-1400. Website: www. dvagency.com. Member of AAR. Represents 120 clients. 10% of clients are new/unpublished writers. Currently handles: nonfiction books 25%, novels 60%, story collections 15%.

Member Agents Liz Darhansoff; Charles Verrill; Leigh Feldman.

Represents Nonfiction books, novels, short story collections.

How to Contact Query with SASE. Obtains most new clients through recommendations from others. Only Leigh Feldman accepts unsolicited submissions.

CAROLINE DAVIDSON LITERARY AGENCY

5 Queen Anne's Gardens, London England W4 ITU United Kingdom. (44)(208)995-5768. Fax: (44)(208)994-2770. E-mail: caroline@cdla.co.uk. Website: www.cdla.co.uk. **Contact:** Caroline Davidson.

Represents Nonfiction books, serious material only, novels.

- Does not consider autobiographies, chick lit, children's, crime, erotica, fantasy, horror, local history, murder mysteries, occult, self-help, short stories, sci-fi, thrillers, individual short stories, or memoir.

How to Contact Query with SASE. See website for additional details and what to include for fiction and nonfiction. Responds in 2 weeks to queries. Obtains most new clients through recommendations from others, solicitations.

Tips "Visit our website before submitting any work to us."

DAVIS WAGER LITERARY AGENCY

419 N. Larchmont Blvd., #317, Los Angeles CA 90004. E-mail: submissions@daviswager.com. Website: www.daviswager.com. **Contact:** Timothy Wager. Estab. 2004. Represents 12 clients.

- Prior to his current position, Mr. Wager was with the Sandra Dijkstra Literary Agency, where he worked as a reader and associate agent.

Represents Nonfiction books, novels. **Considers these fiction areas:** literary.

- Actively seeking: literary fiction and general-interest nonfiction. "I do not handle screenplays, children's books, romance, or science fiction. Memoirs and most genre fiction (other than crime or noir) are a serious long shot, too."

How to Contact Query with SASE. Submit author bio, synopsis for fiction, book proposal or outline for nonfiction. Query via e-mail. No author queries by phone.

LIZA DAWSON ASSOCIATES

350 7th Ave., Ste. 2003, New York NY 10001. (212)465-9071. Fax: (212)947-0460. Website: www. lizadawsonassociates.com. Member of AAR. Other memberships include MWA, Women's Media Group. Represents 50+ clients. 15% of clients are new/unpublished writers. Currently handles: nonfiction books 60%, novels 40%.

- Prior to becoming an agent, Ms. Dawson was an editor for 20 years, spending 11 years at William Morrow as vice president and 2 years at Putnam as executive editor. Ms. Bladell was a senior editor at HarperCollins and Avon. Ms. Miller is an *Essence*-best-selling author and niche publisher. Ms. Olswanger is an author.

Member Agents Liza Dawson (plot-driven literary fiction, historicals, thrillers, suspense, parenting books, history, psychology (both popular and clinical), politics, narrative nonfiction and memoirs);

Caitlin Blasdell (science fiction, fantasy [both adult and young adult], parenting, business, thrillers and women's fiction); Anna Olswanger (gift books for adults, young adult fiction and nonfiction, children's illustrated books, and Judaica); Havis Dawson (business books, how-to and practical books, spirituality, fantasy, Southern-culture fiction and military memoirs); David Austern (fiction and nonfiction, with an interest in young adult, pop culture, sports, and male-interest works). **Represents** Nonfiction books, novels, and gift books (Olswanger only). **Considers these nonfiction areas:** autobiography, biography, business, health, history, medicine, memoirs, parenting, politics, psychology, sociology, women's issues, women's studies. **Considers these fiction areas:** literary, mystery, regional, suspense, thriller, African-American (Miller only), fantasy and science fiction (Blasdell only).

   ☛ "This agency specializes in readable literary fiction, thrillers, mainstream historicals, women's fiction, academics, historians, business, journalists and psychology."

How to Contact Query only with SASE. Individual query e-mails are query[agentfirstname]@lizadawsonassociates.com. Responds in 3 weeks to queries. Responds in 6 weeks to mss. Obtains most new clients through recommendations from others, conferences.

Terms Agent receives 15% commission on domestic sales. Agent receives 20% commission on foreign sales. Offers written contract. Charges clients for photocopying and overseas postage.

☑ THE JENNIFER DECHIARA LITERARY AGENCY

31 East 32nd St., Suite 300, New York NY 10016. (212)481-8484. E-mail: jenndec@aol.com. Website: www.jdlit.com. **Contact:** Jennifer DeChiara, Stephen Fraser. Represents 100 clients. 50% of clients are new/unpublished writers. Currently handles: nonfiction books 25%, novels 25%, juvenile books 50%.

• Prior to becoming an agent, Ms. DeChiara was a writing consultant, freelance editor at Simon & Schuster and Random House, and a ballerina and an actress.

Member Agents Jennifer DeChiara, Stephen Fraser, Dorothy Spencer (adult fiction and nonfiction).

Represents Nonfiction books, novels, juvenile. **Considers these nonfiction areas:** autobiography, biography, child guidance, cooking, crafts, criticism, cultural interests, current affairs, dance, decorating, education, environment, ethnic, film, finance, foods, gay, government, health, history, hobbies, how-to, humor, interior design, investigative, juvenile nonfiction, language, law, lesbian, literature, medicine, memoirs, military, money, music, nature, nutrition, parenting, personal improvement, photography, popular culture, politics, psychology, satire, science, self-help, sociology, sports, technology, theater, true crime, war, women's issues, women's studies, celebrity biography. **Considers these fiction areas:** confession, crime, detective, ethnic, family saga, fantasy, feminist, gay, historical, horror, humor, juvenile, lesbian, literary, mainstream, mystery, picture books, police, regional, satire, sports, suspense, thriller, young adult, chick lit; psychic/supernatural; glitz.

   ☛ "We represent both children's and adult books in a wide range of ages and genres. We are a full-service agency and fulfill the potential of every book in every possible medium—stage, film, television, etc. We help writers every step of the way, from creating book ideas to editing and promotion. We are passionate about helping writers further their careers, but are just as eager to discover new talent, regardless of age or lack of prior publishing experience. This agency is committed to managing a writer's entire career. For us, it's not just about selling books, but about making dreams come true. We are especially attracted to the downtrodden, the discouraged, and the downright disgusted." Actively seeking literary fiction, chick lit, young adult fiction, self-help, pop culture, and celebrity biographies. Does not want westerns, poetry, or short stories.

How to Contact Query with SASE. Accepts simultaneous submissions. Responds in 3-6 months to queries. Responds in 3-6 months to mss. Obtains most new clients through recommendations from others, conferences, query letters.

Terms Agent receives 15% commission on domestic sales. Agent receives 20% commission on foreign sales. Offers written contract.

Recent Sales Sold over 100 titles in the past year. *The Chosen One*, by Carol Lynch Williams (St. Martin's Press); *The 30-Day Heartbreak Cure*, by Catherine Hickland (Simon & Schuster); *Naptime for Barney*, by Danny Sit (Sterling Publishing); *The Screwed-Up Life of Charlie the Second*, by Drew Ferguson (Kensington); *Heart of a Shepherd*, by Rosanne Parry (Random House); *Carolina*

Harmony, by Marilyn Taylor McDowell (Random House); *Project Sweet Life*, by Brent Hartinger (HarperCollins). Movie/TV MOW scripts optioned/sold: *The Elf on the Shelf*, by Carol Aebersold and Chanda Bell (Waddell & Scorsese); *Heart of a Shepherd*, by Rosanne Parry (Tashtego Films); *Geography Club*, by Brent Hartinger (The Levy Leder Company). Other clients include Sylvia Browne, Matthew Kirby, Sonia Levitin, Susan Anderson, Michael Apostolina.

◙ DEFIORE & CO.

47 E. 19th St., 3rd Floor, New York NY 10003. (212)925-7744. Fax: (212)925-9803. E-mail: info@defioreandco.com; submissions@defioreandco.com. Website: www.defioreandco.com. **Contact:** Lauren Gilchrist. Member of AAR. Represents 75 clients. 50% of clients are new/unpublished writers. Currently handles: nonfiction books 70%, novels 30%.

- Prior to becoming an agent, Mr. DeFiore was publisher of Villard Books (1997-1998), editor-in-chief of Hyperion (1992-1997), and editorial director of Delacorte Press (1988-1992).

Member Agents Brian DeFiore (popular nonfiction, business, pop culture, parenting, commercial fiction); Laurie Abkemeier (memoir, parenting, business, how-to/self-help, popular science).

Represents Nonfiction books, novels. **Considers these nonfiction areas:** autobiography, biography, business, child guidance, cooking, economics, foods, how-to, inspirational, money, multicultural, parenting, popular culture, psychology, religious, self-help, sports, young adult, middle grade. **Considers these fiction areas:** ethnic, literary, mainstream, mystery, suspense, thriller.

- ⚬⇥ "Please be advised that we are not considering children's picture books, poetry, adult science fiction and fantasy, romance, or dramatic projects at this time."

How to Contact Query with SASE or e-mail to submissions@defioreandco.com. Please include the word "Query" in the subject line. All attachments will be deleted; please insert all text in the body of the e-mail. For more information about our agents, their individual interests, and their query guidelines, please visit our "About Us" page. Accepts simultaneous submissions. Responds in 3 weeks to queries. Responds in 2 months to mss. Obtains most new clients through recommendations from others.

Terms Agent receives 15% commission on domestic sales. Agent receives 20% commission on foreign sales. Offers written contract; 10-day notice must be given to terminate contract. Charges clients for photocopying and overnight delivery (deducted only after a sale is made).

Writers Conferences Maui Writers Conference; Pacific Northwest Writers Conference; North Carolina Writers' Network Fall Conference.

◙ JOELLE DELBOURGO ASSOCIATES, INC.

101 Park St., 3rd Floor, Montclair NJ 07042. (973)783-6800. Fax: (973)783-6802. E-mail: info@delbourgo.com. Website: www.delbourgo.com. **Contact:** Joelle Delbourgo, Molly Lyons, Jacquie Flynn. Represents more than 100 clients. Currently handles: nonfiction books 75%, novels 25%.

- Prior to becoming an agent, Ms. Delbourgo was an editor and senior publishing executive at HarperCollins and Random House.

Member Agents Joelle Delbourgo (narrative nonfiction, serious "expert-driven" nonfiction, self-help, psychology, business, history, science, medicine, quality fiction); Molly Lyons (memoir, narrative nonfiction, biography, current events, cultural issues, pop culture, health, psychology, smart, fresh practical nonfiction, fiction, young adult and middle grade); Jacquie Flynn (thought-provoking and practical business, parenting, education, personal development, current events, science and other select nonfiction and fiction titles).

Represents Nonfiction books, novels. **Considers these nonfiction areas:** autobiography, biography, business, child guidance, cooking, cultural interests, current affairs, decorating, diet/nutrition, economics, education, environment, ethnic, foods, gay/lesbian, government, health, history, how-to, inspirational, interior design, investigative, law, medicine, metaphysics, money, New Age, popular culture, politics, psychology, religious, science, sociology, technology, true crime, women's issues, women's studies, New Age/metaphysics, interior design/decorating. **Considers these fiction areas:** historical, literary, mainstream, mystery, suspense.

- ⚬⇥ "We are former publishers and editors, with deep knowledge and an insider perspective. We have a reputation for individualized attention to clients, strategic management of authors' careers, and creating strong partnerships with publishers for our clients." Actively seeking history, narrative nonfiction, science/medicine, memoir, literary fiction, psychology, parenting, biographies, current affairs, politics, young adult fiction and nonfiction. Does not want to receive genre fiction, science fiction, fantasy, or screenplays.

How to Contact Query by mail with SASE. Accepts simultaneous submissions. Responds in 3 weeks to queries. Responds in 2 months to mss.

Terms Agent receives 15% commission on domestic sales. Agent receives 20% commission on foreign sales. Offers written contract. Charges clients for postage and photocopying.

Recent Sales *Tabloid Medicine*, by Robert Goldberg, Ph.D. (Kaplan); *The Lost Gospel*, by Simcha Jacobovichi (represented by the Elaine Markson Agency) and Barrie Wilson (Overlook Press); *Risk and the Smart Investor*, by David Martin (McGraw-Hill); *Dragon Bone Hill*, by Lindsay Tam Holland (Simon and Schuster Books for Young Readers).

Tips "Do your homework. Do not cold call. Read and follow submission guidelines before contacting us. Do not call to find out if we received your material. No e-mail queries. Treat agents with respect, as you would any other professional, such as a doctor, lawyer or financial advisor."

JACQUES DE SPOELBERCH ASSOCIATES

9 Shagbark Road, Wilson Point, South Norwalk CT 06854. (203)838-7571. Fax: (203)866-2713. E-mail: Jdespoel@aol.com. **Contact:** Jacques de Spoelberch. Represents 50 clients.

Member Agents Jacques de Spoelberch.

Represents Nonfiction books, novels.

How to Contact Query with SASE. Responds in 2 months to queries. Obtains most new clients through recommendations from others.

Terms Agent receives 15% commission on domestic sales. Agent receives 20% commission on foreign sales.

◙ DH LITERARY, INC.

P.O. Box 805, Nyack NY 10960-0990. **Contact:** David Hendin. Member of AAR. Represents 10 clients. Currently handles: nonfiction books 80%, novels 10%, scholarly books 10%.

- Prior to opening his agency, Mr. Hendin served as president and publisher for Pharos Books/ World Almanac, as well as senior VP and COO at sister company United Feature Syndicate.
- ⚷ *Not accepting new clients. Please do not send queries or submissions.*

Terms Agent receives 15% commission on domestic sales. Agent receives 20% commission on foreign sales. Offers written contract, binding for 1 year. Charges for out-of-pocket expenses for overseas postage specifically related to the sale.

Recent Sales *Big Nate, In a Class By Himself* (plus 5 additional titles) and *Zacula* (3 titles), by Lincoln Peirce to Harper Collins; *Miss Manners Guide to a Surprisingly Dignified Wedding*, by Judith and Jacobina Martin (Norton); *Killer Cuts*, by Elaine Viets (NAL/Signet); *The New Time Travelers*, by David Toomey (Norton).

◙ DHS LITERARY, INC.

10711 Preston Road, Suite 100, Dallas TX 75230. (214)363-4422. Fax: (214)363-4423. Website: www. dhsliterary.com. **Contact:** David Hale Smith, president. Represents 35 clients. 15% of clients are new/unpublished writers. Currently handles: nonfiction books 60%, novels 40%.

- Prior to opening his agency, Mr. Smith was an agent at Dupree/Miller & Associates.

Represents Nonfiction books, novels. **Considers these nonfiction areas:** autobiography, biography, business, child guidance, cooking, cultural interests, current affairs, diet/nutrition, economics, ethnic, foods, investigative, parenting, popular culture, sports, true crime. **Considers these fiction areas:** crime, detective, ethnic, frontier, literary, mainstream, mystery, police, suspense, thriller, westerns.

- ⚷ This agency is not actively seeking clients and usually takes clients on by referral only.

How to Contact We accept new material by referral only. Only responds if interested. *No unsolicited mss.*

Terms Agent receives 15% commission on domestic sales. Agent receives 25% commission on foreign sales. Offers written contract; 10-day notice must be given to terminate contract. This agency charges for postage and photocopying.

Recent Sales *Safer*, by Sean Doolittle; *Person of Interest*, by Theresa Schwegel; *Monday Morning Choices*, by David Cottrell.

Tips "Remember to be courteous and professional, and to treat marketing your work and approaching an agent as you would any formal business matter. If you have a referral, always query first via e-mail. Sorry, but we cannot respond to queries sent via mail, even with a SASE. Visit our website for more information."

☑ SANDRA DIJKSTRA LITERARY AGENCY

1155 Camino del Mar, PMB 515, Del Mar CA 92014. (858)755-3115. Fax: (858)794-2822. E-mail: elise@dijkstraagency.com. Website: www.dijkstraagency.com. Member of AAR. Other memberships include Authors Guild, PEN West, Poets and Editors, MWA. Represents 100 + clients. 30% of clients are new/unpublished writers. Currently handles: nonfiction books 50%, novels 45%, juvenile books 5%.

Member Agents Sandra Dijkstra; Elise Capron; Natalie Fischer; Jill Marr; Taylor Martindale.

Represents Nonfiction books, novels. **Considers these nonfiction areas:** Americana, animals, anthropology, archeology, art, business, child guidance, cooking, cultural interests, diet/nutrition, economics, environment, ethnic, foods, gay/lesbian, government, health, history, inspirational, language, law, literature, medicine, memoirs, military, money, parenting, politics, psychology, regional, science, self-help, sociology, technology, travel, war, women's issues, women's studies, Asian studies, juvenile nonfiction, accounting, transportation. **Considers these fiction areas:** erotica, ethnic, fantasy, juvenile, literary, mainstream, mystery, picture books, science fiction, suspense, thriller, graphic novels.

➤ Does not want to receive Western, screenplays, short story collections or poetry.

How to Contact "Please see guidelines on our website. Due to the large number of unsolicited submissions we receive, we are now ONLY able to respond those submissions in which we are interested. Unsolicited submissions in which we are not interested will receive no response. (Therefore, please do not enclose a self addressed stamped envelope [SASE], and do not send any pages or material you need returned to you. In your materials, please be sure to include all your contact information, including your e-mail address. We accept hard copy submissions only, and will not read or respond to e-mailed submissions." Responds in 6 weeks to queries. Obtains most new clients through recommendations from others, solicitations, conferences.

Terms Agent receives 15% commission on domestic sales. Agent receives 20% commission on foreign sales. Offers written contract. Charges clients for expenses for foreign postage and copying costs if a client requests a hard copy submission to publishers.

Tips Be professional and learn the standard procedures for submitting your work. Be a regular patron of bookstores, and study what kind of books are being published and will appear on the shelves next to yours. Read! Check out your local library and bookstores—you'll find lots of books on writing and the publishing industry that will help you. At conferences, ask published writers about their agents. Don't believe the myth that an agent has to be in New York to be successful. We've already disproved it!

◑ THE JONATHAN DOLGER AGENCY

49 E. 96th St., Suite 9B, New York NY 10128. Fax: (212)369-7118. Member of AAR.

Represents Nonfiction books, novels. **Considers these nonfiction areas:** biography, history, womens, cultural/social. **Considers these fiction areas:** women's, commercial.

How to Contact Query with SASE. No e-mail queries.

Terms Agent receives 15% commission on domestic sales. Agent receives 25% commission on foreign sales.

Tips "Writers must have been previously published if submitting fiction. We prefer to work with published/established authors, and work with a small number of new/previously unpublished writers."

◎ DONADIO & OLSON, INC.

121 W. 27th St., Suite 704, New York NY 10001. (212)691-8077. Fax: (212)633-2837. E-mail: mail@donadio.com. **Contact:** Neil Olson. Member of AAR.

Member Agents Neil Olson (no queries); Edward Hibbert (no queries); Carrie Howland (query via snail mail or e-mail).

Represents Nonfiction books, novels.

➤ This agency represents mostly fiction, and is very selective.

How to Contact Query by snail mail is preferred; for e-mail use mail@donadio.com; only send submissions to open agents. Obtains most new clients through recommendations from others.

☑ JANIS A. DONNAUD & ASSOCIATES, INC.

525 Broadway, Second Floor, New York NY 10012. (212)431-2664. Fax: (212)431-2667. E-mail: jdonnaud@aol.com; donnaudassociate@aol.com. **Contact:** Janis A. Donnaud. Member of AAR. Signatory of WGA. Represents 40 clients. 5% of clients are new/unpublished writers. Currently handles: nonfiction books 100%.

- Prior to opening her agency, Ms. Donnaud was vice president and associate publisher of Random House Adult Trade Group.

Represents Nonfiction books. **Considers these nonfiction areas:** autobiography, African-American, biography, business, celebrity, child guidance, cooking, current affairs, diet/nutrition, foods, health, humor, medicine, parenting, psychology, satire, women's issues, women's studies, lifestyle.

- ⚬ This agency specializes in health, medical, cooking, humor, pop psychology, narrative nonfiction, biography, parenting, and current affairs. We give a lot of service and attention to clients. Does not want to receive "fiction, poetry, mysteries, juvenile books, romances, science fiction, young adult, religious or fantasy."

How to Contact Query with SASE. Submit description of book, 2-3 pages of sample material. Prefers to read materials exclusively. No phone calls. Responds in 1 month to queries. Responds in 1 month to mss. Obtains most new clients through recommendations from others.

Terms Agent receives 15% commission on domestic sales. Agent receives 20% commission on foreign sales. Agent receives 20% commission on film sales. Offers written contract; 1-month notice must be given to terminate contract. Charges clients for messengers, photocopying and purchase of books.

Recent Sales *The Coupon Mom's Guide to Cutting Your Grocery Bill in Half,* by Stephanie Nelson; *Jim Lahey's Pizza Book,* by Jim Lahey and Rick Flaste; *Cook Like a Rock Star: At the Stove with America's Favorite Girl Chef,* by Anne Burrell; *Savannah Style,* by Paula Deen and Brandon Branch.

☑ 📷 JIM DONOVAN LITERARY

4515 Prentice St., Suite 109, Dallas TX 75206-5028. E-mail: jdlqueries@sbcglobal.net. **Contact:** Melissa Shultz, agent. Represents 30 clients. 10% of clients are new/unpublished writers. Currently handles: nonfiction books 75%, novels 25%.

Member Agents Jim Donovan (history—particularly American, military and Western; biography; sports; popular reference; popular culture; fiction—literary, thrillers and mystery); Melissa Shultz (parenting, women's issues, memoir).

Represents Nonfiction books, novels. **Considers these nonfiction areas:** autobiography, biography, business, child guidance, current affairs, economics, environment, health, history, how-to, investigative, law, medicine, memoirs, military, money, music, parenting, popular culture, politics, sports, true crime, war, women's issues, women's studies. **Considers these fiction areas:** action, adventure, crime, detective, literary, mainstream, mystery, police, suspense, thriller.

- ⚬ This agency specializes in commercial fiction and nonfiction. "Does not want to receive poetry, children's, short stories, inspirational or anything else not listed above."

How to Contact "For nonfiction, I need a well-thought query letter telling me about the book: What it does, how it does it, why it's needed now, why it's better or different than what's out there on the subject, and why the author is the perfect writer for it. For fiction, the novel has to be finished, of course; a short (2 to 5 page) synopsis—not a teaser, but a summary of all the action, from first page to last—and the first 30-50 pages is enough. This material should be polished to as close to perfection as possible." Accepts simultaneous submissions. Responds in 3 weeks to queries. Responds in 1 month to mss. Obtains most new clients through recommendations from others.

Terms Agent receives 15% commission on domestic sales. Agent receives 20% commission on foreign sales. Offers written contract, binding for 1 year; 30-day notice must be given to terminate contract. This agency charges for things such as overnight delivery and manuscript copying. Charges are discussed beforehand.

Recent Sales Sold 27 titles in the last year. *The Last Gunfight,* by Jeff Guinn (Simon and Schuster); *Resurrection,* by Jim Dent (St. Martin's Press); *The Battling Bastards of Bataan,* by Bill Sloan (Simon and Schuster); *Perfect,* by Lew Paper (NAL); *Honor in the Dust,* by Gregg Jones (NAL);

First in War, by David Clary (Simon and Schuster); *Desperadoes,* by Mark Gardner (HarperCollins); *Apocalypse of the Dead,* by Joe McKinney (Kensington).

Tips "Get published in short form—magazine reviews, journals, etc.—first. This will increase your credibility considerably, and make it much easier to sell a full-length book."

◙ DOYEN LITERARY SERVICES, INC.

1931 660th St., Newell IA 50568-7613. (712)272-3300. Website: www.barbaradoyen.com. **Contact:** (Ms.) B.J. Doyen, president. Represents over 100 clients. 20% of clients are new/unpublished writers. Currently handles: nonfiction books 100%.

- Prior to opening her agency, Ms. Doyen worked as a published author, teacher, guest speaker, and wrote and appeared in her own weekly TV show airing in 7 states. She is also the co-author of *The Everything Guide to Writing a Book Proposal* (Adams 2005) and *The Everything Guide to Getting Published* (Adams 2006).

Represents Nonfiction for adults, no children's. **Considers these nonfiction areas:** agriculture, Americana, animals, anthropology, archeology, architecture, art, autobiography, biography, business, child guidance, computers, cooking, crafts, cultural interests, current affairs, diet/ nutrition, design, economics, education, environment, ethnic, film, foods, gardening, government, health, history, hobbies, horticulture, language, law, medicine, memoirs, metaphysics, military, money, multicultural, music, parenting, photography, popular culture, politics, psychology, recreation, regional, science, self-help, sex, sociology, software, technology, theater, true crime, women's issues, women's studies, creative nonfiction, computers, electronics.

- ☞ This agency specializes in nonfiction. Actively seeking business, health, science, how-to, self-help—all kinds of adult nonfiction suitable for the major trade publishers. Does not want to receive pornography, children's books, fiction, or poetry.

How to Contact Prefer e-mail query through our website, using the contact button. Please read the wesite before submitting a query. Include your background information in a bio. Send no unsolicited attachments. Accepts simultaneous submissions. Responds immediately to queries. Responds in 3 weeks to mss.

Terms Agent receives 15% commission on domestic sales. Agent receives 20% commission on foreign sales. Offers written contract, binding for 2 years.

Recent Sales *Stem Cells For Dummies,* by Lawrence S.B. Goldstein and Meg Schneider; T*he Complete Idiot's Guide to Country Living,* by Kimberly Willis; *The Complete Illustrated Pregnancy Companion,* by Robin Elise Weiss; *The Complete Idiot's Guide to Playing the Fiddle,* by Ellery Klein; *Healthy Aging for Dummies,* by Brent Agin, M.D. and Sharon Perkins, R.N.

Tips "Our authors receive personalized attention. We market aggressively, undeterred by rejection. We get the best possible publishing contracts. We are very interested in nonfiction book ideas at this time and will consider most topics. Many writers come to us from referrals, but we also get quite a few who initially approach us with query letters. Do not call us regarding queries. It is best if you do not collect editorial rejections prior to seeking an agent, but if you do, be upfront and honest about it. Do not submit your manuscript to more than 1 agent at a time—querying first can save you (and us) much time. We're open to established or beginning writers—just send us a terrific letter!"

Ｎ DREISBACH LITERARY MANAGEMENT

PO Box 5379, El Dorado Hills CA 95762. (916)804-5016. E-mail: verna@dreisbachliterary.com. Website: www.dreisbachliterary.com. **Contact:** Verna Dreisbach. Estab. 2007.

Represents Considers these nonfiction areas: animals, biography, business, health, multicultural, parenting, religious, spirituality, travel, true crime, women's issues. **Considers these fiction areas:** literary, mystery, thriller.

- ☞ "The agency has a particular interest in books with a political, economic or social context. Verna's first career as a law enforcement officer gives her a genuine interest and expertise in the genres of mystery, thriller and true crime." Does not want to receive children's books.

How to Contact E-mail queries only please. No attachments in the query. They will not be opened. No unsolicited manuscripts. Indicate whether or not this is an exclusive or simultaneous submission, or if a partial or full manuscript is out to other agencies or publishers.

Recent Sales *Why We Ride:Women Writers on the Horses in Their Lives,* by Verna Dreisbach (Seal Press/Perseus); *The Short Sale Savior,* by Elizabeth Weintraub (Archer Ellison); *The Power of Memoir:Writing Your Healing Story,* by Linda Joy Myers (Jossey-Bass/Wiley).

◪ DUNHAM LITERARY, INC.

156 Fifth Ave., Suite 625, New York NY 10010-7002. (212)929-0994. Website: www.dunhamlit. com. **Contact:** Jennie Dunham. Member of AAR. Represents 50 clients. 15% of clients are new/ unpublished writers. Currently handles: nonfiction books 25%, novels 25%, juvenile books 50%.

- Prior to opening her agency, Ms. Dunham worked as a literary agent for Russell & Volkening. The Rhoda Weyr Agency is now a division of Dunham Literary, Inc.

Represents Nonfiction books, novels, short story collections, juvenile. **Considers these nonfiction areas:** anthropology, archeology, autobiography, biography, cultural interests, environment, ethnic, government, health, history, language, law, literature, medicine, popular culture, politics, psychology, science, technology, women's issues, women's studies. **Considers these fiction areas:** ethnic, juvenile, literary, mainstream, picture books, young adult.

How to Contact Query with SASE. Responds in 1 week to queries. Responds in 2 months to mss. Obtains most new clients through recommendations from others, solicitations.

Terms Agent receives 15% commission on domestic sales. Agent receives 20% commission on foreign sales.

Recent Sales *America the Beautiful*, by Robert Sabuda; *Dahlia*, by Barbara McClintock; *Living Dead Girl*, by Tod Goldberg; *In My Mother's House*, by Margaret McMulla; *Black Hawk Down*, by Mark Bowden; *Look Back All the Green Valley*, by Fred Chappell; *Under a Wing*, by Reeve Lindbergh; *I Am Madame X*, by Gioia Diliberto.

◪ DUNOW, CARLSON, & LERNER AGENCY

27 W. 20th St., #1107, New York NY 10011. E-mail: mail@dclagency.com. Website: www.dclagency. com/. **Contact:** Jennifer Carlson, Henry Dunow, Betsy Lerner. Member of AAR.

Member Agents Jennifer Carlson (young adult and middle grade, some fiction and nonfiction); Henry Dunow (quality fiction – literary, historical, strongly written commercial – and with voice-driven nonfiction across a range of areas – narrative history, biography, memoir, current affairs, cultural trends and criticism, science, sports); Erin Hosier (nonfiction: popular culture, music, sociology and memoir); Betsy Lerner (nonfiction writers in the areas of psychology, history, cultural studies, biography, current events, business; fiction: literary, dark, funny, voice driven); Yishai Seidman (broad range of fiction: literary, postmodern, and thrillers; nonfiction: sports, music, and pop culture).

Represents Nonfiction books, novels, juvenile.

How to Contact Query with SASE or by e-mail to mail@dclagency.com. No attachments. Unable to respond to queries except when interested.

◪ DUPREE/MILLER AND ASSOCIATES INC. LITERARY

100 Highland Park Village, Suite 350, Dallas TX 75205. (214)559-BOOK. Fax: (214)559-PAGE. Website: www.dupreemiller.com. **Contact:** Submissions Department. Other memberships include ABA. Represents 200 clients. 20% of clients are new/unpublished writers. Currently handles: nonfiction books 90%, novels 10%.

Member Agents Jan Miller, president/CEO; Shannon Miser-Marven, senior executive VP; Annabelle Baxter; Nena Madonia; Cheri Gillis.

Represents Nonfiction books, novels, scholarly, syndicated, religious.inspirational/spirituality. **Considers these nonfiction areas:** animals, anthropology, archeology, architecture, art, autobiography, biography, business, child guidance, cooking, crafts, current affairs, dance, diet/ nutrition, design, economics, education, environment, ethnic, film, foods, gardening, government, health, history, how-to, humor, language, literature, medicine, memoirs, money, multicultural, music, parenting, philosophy, photography, popular culture, psychology, recreation, regional, satire, science, self-help, sex, sociology, sports, technology, theater, translation, true crime, women's issues, women's studies. **Considers these fiction areas:** action, adventure, crime, detective, ethnic, experimental, family saga, feminist, glitz, historical, humor, inspirational, literary, mainstream, mystery, picture books, police, psychic, religious, satire, sports, supernatural, suspense, thriller.

- ♀ This agency specializes in commercial fiction and nonfiction.

How to Contact Submit 1-page query, outline, SASE. Obtains most new clients through recommendations from others, conferences, lectures.

Terms Agent receives 15% commission on domestic sales. Offers written contract.

Writers Conferences Aspen Summer Words Literary Festival.

Tips "If interested in agency representation, it is vital to have the material in the proper working format. As agents' policies differ, it is important to follow their guidelines. Work on establishing a strong proposal that provides sample chapters, an overall synopsis (fairly detailed), and some biographical information on yourself. Do not send your proposal in pieces; it should be complete upon submission. Your work should be in its best condition."

✍ DWYER & O'GRADY, INC.

Agents for Writers & Illustrators of Children's Books, P.O. Box 790, Cedar Key FL 32625-0790. (352)543-9307. Fax: (603)375-5373. Website: www.dwyerogrady.com. **Contact:** Elizabeth O'Grady. Estab. 1990. Other memberships include SCBWI. Represents 30 clients. Currently handles: juvenile books 100%.

- Prior to opening their agency, Mr. Dwyer and Ms. O'Grady were booksellers and publishers.

Member Agents Elizabeth O'Grady; Jeff Dwyer.

Represents Juvenile. **Considers these nonfiction areas:** juvenile. **Considers these fiction areas:** juvenile, picture books, young.

- ⚓ "We are not accepting new clients at this time. This agency represents only writers and illustrators of children's books."

How to Contact *No unsolicited mss.* Obtains most new clients through recommendations from others, direct approach by agent to writer whose work they've read.

Terms Agent receives 15% commission on domestic sales. Agent receives 20% commission on foreign sales. Offers written contract; 1-month notice must be given to terminate contract. This agency charges clients for photocopying of longer mss or mutually agreed upon marketing expenses.

Writers Conferences BookExpo America; American Library Association Annual Conference; SCBWI.

Tips "This agency previously had an address in New Hampshire. Mail all materials to the new Florida address."

✍ DYSTEL & GODERICH LITERARY MANAGEMENT

1 Union Square W., Suite 904, New York NY 10003. (212)627-9100. Fax: (212)627-9313. E-mail: mbourret@dystel.com. Website: www.dystel.com. **Contact:** Michael Bourret and Jim McCarthy. Member of AAR, SCBWI. Represents 617 clients. 50% of clients are new/unpublished writers. Currently handles: nonfiction books 65%, novels 35%.

- Dystel & Goderich Literary Management recently acquired the client list of Bedford Book Works.

Member Agents Jane Dystel; Stacey Glick; Michael Bourret; Jim McCarthy; Jessica Papin; Lauren Abramo; Chasya Milgrom; Rachel Oakley.

Represents Nonfiction books, novels, cookbooks. **Considers these nonfiction areas:** animals, anthropology, archeology, autobiography, biography, business, child guidance, cultural interests, current affairs, economics, ethnic, gay/lesbian, health, history, humor, inspirational, investigative, medicine, metaphysics, military, New Age, parenting, popular culture, psychology, religious, science, technology, true crime, women's issues, women's studies. **Considers these fiction areas:** action, adventure, crime, detective, ethnic, family saga, gay, lesbian, literary, mainstream, mystery, police, suspense, thriller.

- ⚓ "This agency specializes in cookbooks and commercial and literary fiction and nonfiction."

How to Contact Query with SASE. Please include the first 3 chapters in the body of the e-mail. E-mail queries preferred (Michael Bourret only accepts e-mail queries); will accept mail. See website for full guidelines. Accepts simultaneous submissions. Responds in 6 to 8 weeks to queries. Responds within 8 weeks to mss. Obtains most new clients through recommendations from others, solicitations, conferences.

Terms Agent receives 15% commission on domestic sales. Agent receives 19% commission on foreign sales. Offers written contract.

Writers Conferences Backspace Writers' Conference; Pacific Northwest Writers' Association; Pike's Peak Writers' Conference; Writers League of Texas; Love Is Murder; Surrey International Writers Conference; Society of Children's Book Writers and Illustrators; International Thriller Writers; Willamette Writers Conference; The South Carolina Writers Workshop Conference; Las Vegas Writers Conference; Writer's Digest; Seton Hill Popular Fiction; Romance Writers of America; Geneva Writers Conference.

Tips "DGLM prides itself on being a full-service agency. We're involved in every stage of the publishing process, from offering substantial editing on mss and proposals, to coming up with book ideas for authors looking for their next project, negotiating contracts and collecting monies for our clients. We follow a book from its inception through its sale to a publisher, its publication, and beyond. Our commitment to our writers does not, by any means, end when we have collected our commission. This is one of the many things that makes us unique in a very competitive business."

TOBY EADY ASSOCIATES
Third Floor, 9 Orme Court, London England W2 4RL United Kingdom. (44)(207)792-0092. Fax: (44) (207)792-0879. E-mail: Jamie@tobyeady.demon.co.uk. Website: www.tobyeadyassociates.co.uk. **Contact:** Jamie Coleman. Estab. 1968. Represents 53 clients. 13% of clients are new/unpublished writers. Currently handles: nonfiction books 50%, novels 50%.

Member Agents Toby Eady (China, the Middle East, Africa, politics of a Swiftian nature); Laetitia Rutherford (fiction and nonfiction from around the world).

Represents Nonfiction books, novels, short story collections, novellas, anthologies. **Considers these nonfiction areas:** architecture, art, cooking, cultural interests, current affairs, diet/nutrition, design, ethnic, foods, government, health, history, law, medicine, memoirs, popular culture, politics. **Considers these fiction areas:** action, adventure, confession, historical, literary, mainstream.

⦿ "We handle fiction and nonfiction for adults and we specialize in China, the Middle East and Africa." Actively seeking "stories that demand to be heard." Does not want to receive poetry, screenplays or children's books.

How to Contact Send the first 50 pages of your work, double-spaced and unbound, with a synopsis and a brief bio attn: Jamie Coleman. Accepts simultaneous submissions. Responds in 2 weeks to queries. Responds in 2 weeks to mss. Obtains most new clients through recommendations from others, solicitations, conferences.

Terms Agent receives 15% commission on domestic sales. Agent receives 20% commission on foreign sales. Offers written contract; 3-month notice must be given to terminate contract.

Writers Conferences City Lit; Winchester Writers' Festival.

Tips "Send submissions to this address: Jamie Coleman, Third Floor, 9 Orme Court, London W2 4RL."

EAMES LITERARY SERVICES
4117 Hillsboro Road, Suite 251, Nashville TN 37215. Fax: (615)463.9361. E-mail: info@eamesliterary. com; John@eamesliterary.com; Ahna@eamesliterary.com. Website: www.eamesliterary.com. **Contact:** John Eames.

Member Agents John Eames, Jonathan Rogers.

Represents Nonfiction books, novels. **Considers these nonfiction areas:** inspirational, memoirs, religious, young adult. **Considers these fiction areas:** inspirational, religious, young adult.

⦿ This agency specializes in the Christian marketplace. Actively seeking "adult and young adult fiction that sparks the imagination, illuminates some angle of truth about the human condition, causes the reader to view the world with fresh eyes, and supports a Christian perspective on life in all its complexities. Stories might be redemptive, or tragic. Characters might be noble, or flawed. Situations might be humorous, or dark. And many manuscripts might contain some combination of all of the above. We also seek adult and young adult nonfiction that is anecdotal as well as instructional, utilizes a 'show, don't tell' philosophy of writing, and offers a unique and biblically sound perspective on a given topic. If the submission is a nonfiction narrative (e.g., memoir), the work should follow most of the same recommendations for a work of fiction, as listed above. We look for proposals that are very well written and (especially for nonfiction) are from authors with an expansive platform and processing some literary notoriety."

How to Contact Query through e-mail along with a book proposal; author bio (including publishing history); plot synopsis or chapter summary; and 2-3 chapters of sample content (attached as a Microsoft Word document). Responds in 3-5 weeks.

EAST/WEST LITERARY AGENCY, LLC
1158 26th St., Suite 462, Santa Monica CA 90403. (310)573-9303. Fax: (310)453-9008. E-mail:

query@eastwestliteraryagency.com. Estab. 2000. Represents 100 clients. 70% of clients are new/unpublished writers. Currently handles: nonfiction books 25%, juvenile books 75%.

Member Agents Deborah Warren, founder; Mary Grey James, partner literary agent (special interest: southern writers and their stories, literary fiction); Rubin Pfeffer, partner content agent and digital media strategist.

How to Contact By referral only. Submit proposal and first 3 sample chapters, table of contents (2 pages or fewer), synopsis (1 page). For picture books, submit entire ms. Requested submissions should be sent by mail as a Word document in Courier, 12-pt., double-spaced with 1.20 inch margin on left, ragged right text, 25 lines per page, continuously paginated, with all your contact info on the first page. Only responds if interested, no need for SASE. Responds in 60 days. Obtains new clients through recommendations from others.

Terms Agent receives 15% commission on domestic sales. Agent receives 25% commission on foreign sales. Offers written contract; 30-day notice must be given to terminate contract. Charges for out-of-pocket expenses, such as postage and copying.

☑ THE EBELING AGENCY

P.O. Box 790267, Pala HI 96779. (808)579-6414. Fax: (808)579-9294. E-mail: kristina@ebelingagency.com; ebothat@yahoo.com. Website: www.ebelingagency.com. **Contact:** Michael Ebeling or Kristina Holmes. Represents 6 clients. 50% of clients are new/unpublished writers. Currently handles: nonfiction books 100%.

- Prior to becoming an agent, Mr. Ebeling established a career in the publishing industry through long-term author management. He has expertise in sales, platforms, publicity and marketing. Ms. Holmes joined the agency in 2005, and considers many types of projects. She is interested in books that take a stand, bring an issue to light or help readers.

Member Agents Michael Ebeling, ebothat@yahoo.com; Kristina Holmes, kristina@ebelingagency.com.

Represents Nonfiction books. **Considers these nonfiction areas:** animals, anthropology, archeology, architecture, art, autobiography, biography, business, child guidance, cooking, cultural interests, current affairs, dance, diet/nutrition, design, economics, education, environment, ethnic, foods, gay/lesbian, government, health, history, how-to, humor, inspirational, law, medicine, memoirs, money, music, parenting, photography, popular culture, politics, psychology, religious, satire, science, self-help, spirituality, sports, technology, travel, women's issues, women's studies, food/fitness, computers.

- ⚷ "We accept very few clients for representation. To be considered, an author needs a very strong platform and a unique book concept. We represent nonfiction authors, most predominantly in the areas of business and self-help. We are very committed to our authors and their messages, which is a main reason we have such a high placement rate. We are always looking at new ways to help our authors gain the exposure they need to not only get published, but develop a successful literary career." Actively seeking well-written nonfiction material with fresh perspectives written by writers with established platforms. Does not want to receive fiction.

How to Contact E-mail query and proposal to either Michael or Kristina. E-queries only. Accepts simultaneous submissions. Responds in 4-6 weeks to queries. Obtains most new clients through recommendations from others, solicitations.

Terms Agent receives 15% commission on domestic sales. Agent receives 20% commission on foreign sales. Offers written contract; 60-day notice must be given to terminate contract. There is a charge for normal out-of-pocket fees, not to exceed $200 without client approval.

Writers Conferences BookExpo America; San Francisco Writers' Conference.

Tips "Approach agents when you're already building your platform, you have a well-written book, you have a firm understanding of the publishing process, and have come up with a complete competitive proposal. Know the name of the agent you are contacting. You're essentially selling a business plan to the publisher. Make sure you've made a convincing pitch throughout your proposal, as ultimately, publishers are taking a financial risk by investing in your project."

☑ ANNE EDELSTEIN LITERARY AGENCY

20 W. 22nd St., Suite 1603, New York NY 10010. (212)414-4923. Fax: (212)414-2930. E-mail: info@aeliterary.com. Website: www.aeliterary.com. Member of AAR.

Member Agents Anne Edelstein; Krista Ingebretson.

Represents Nonfiction books, fiction. **Considers these nonfiction areas:** history, inspirational, memoirs, psychology, religious, Buddhist thought. **Considers these fiction areas:** literary.

⚲ This agency specializes in fiction and narrative nonfiction.

How to Contact Query with SASE; submit 25 sample pages.

Recent Sales *Confessions of a Buddhist Atheist*, by Stephen Batchelor (Spiegel & Grau); *April & Oliver*, by Tess Callahan (Doubleday).

◎ EDUCATIONAL DESIGN SERVICES, LLC

5750 Bou Ave., Suite 1508, Bethesda MD 20852. (301)881-8611. E-mail: blinder@educationaldesignservices.com. Website: www.educationaldesignservices.com. **Contact:** Bertram L. Linder, president. Represents 14 clients. 95% of clients are new/unpublished writers. Currently handles: 100% textbooks and professional materials for education.

• Prior to becoming an agent, Mr. Linder was an author and a teacher.

Member Agents Bertram Linder (textbooks and professional materials for education).

Represents Scholarly, textbooks.

⚲ "We are one of the few agencies that specialize exclusively in materials for the education market. We handle text materials for grades pre K-12, text materials for college/university use, and materials for professionals in the field of education, staff development and education policy." Does not want to receive children's fiction and nonfiction, or picture books.

How to Contact Query with SASE. Submit proposal package, outline, outline/proposal, 2-3 sample chapters, SASE. Prefers e-mail submission. Accepts simultaneous submissions. Responds in 3-4 weeks to queries and mss. Obtains most new clients through recommendations from others, solicitations, conferences.

Terms Agent receives 15% commission on domestic sales. Agent receives 25% commission on foreign sales. Offers written contract; 30 days notice must be given to terminate contract. Charges clients for extraordinary expenses in postage and shipping, as well as long distance telephone calls.

Recent Sales Sold 5 titles in the last year. *No Parent Left Behind*, by P. Petrosino and L. Spiegel (Rowman & Littlefield Education); *Preparing for the 8th Grade Test in Social Studies*, by E. Farran and A. Paci (Amsco Book Company); *Teaching Test-Taking Skills*, by G. Durham (Rowman & Littlefield Education); *Teacher's Quick Guide to Communicating*, by G. Sundem (Corwin Press); *Being Grown Up In a Teenage World*, by Susan Porter (R&L Education).

☑ JUDITH EHRLICH LITERARY MANAGEMENT, LLC

880 Third Ave., Eighth Floor, New York NY 10022. (646)505-1570. E-mail: jehrlich@JudithEhrlichLiterary.com. Website: www.judithehrlichliterary.com. Other memberships include Author's Guild, the American Society of Journalists and Authors.

• Prior to her current position, Ms. Ehrlich was an award-winning journalist; she is the co-author of *The New Crowd: The Changing of the Jewish Guard on Wall Street* (Little, Brown). Emmanuelle Alspaugh was an agent at Wendy Sherman Associates and an editor at Fodor's, the travel division of Random House.

Member Agents Judith Ehrlich, jehrlich@judithehrlichliterary.com; Emmanuelle Alspaugh (upmarket fiction, historical fiction, women's fiction and romance, urban fantasy, thrillers, young adult fiction, and select memoir, narrative nonfiction, and how-to projects); Sophia Seidner (strong literary fiction and nonfiction including self-help, narrative nonfiction, memoir, and biography. Areas of special interest include medical and health-related topics, science [popular, political and social], animal welfare, current events, politics, law, history, ethics, parody and humor, sports, art and business self-help).

Represents Nonfiction books, novels.

⚲ "Special areas of interest include compelling narrative nonfiction, outstanding biographies and memoirs, lifestyle books, works that reflect our changing culture, women's issues, psychology, science, social issues, current events, parenting, health, history, business, and prescriptive books offering fresh information and advice." Does not want to receive children's or young adult books, novellas, poetry, textbooks, plays or screenplays.

How to Contact Query with SASE. Queries should include a synopsis and some sample pages. Send e-queries to jehrlich@judithehrlichliterary.com. The agency will respond only if interested.

Recent Sales Fiction: *Breaking the Bank*, by Yona Zeldis McDonough (Pocket); *Sinful Surrender*, by Beverley Kendall (Kensington); Nonfiction: *Strategic Learning: How to be Smarter Than Your Competition and Turn Key Insights Into Competitive Advantage*, by William Pieterson (Wiley); *Paris Under Water: How the City of Light Survived the Great Flood of 1910*, by Jeffrey Jackson (Palgrave Macmillan); *When Growth Stalls: How It Happens, Why You're Stuck & What to Do About It*, by Steve McKee (Jossey-Bass); *I'm Smarter Than My Boss. Now What?* by Diane Garnick (Bloomberg Press).

THE LISA EKUS GROUP, LLC

57 North St., Hatfield MA 01038. (413)247-9325. Fax: (413)247-9873. E-mail: LisaEkus@lisaekus.com. Website: www.lisaekus.com. **Contact:** Lisa Ekus-Saffer. Member of AAR.
Represents Nonfiction books. **Considers these nonfiction areas:** cooking, diet/nutrition, foods, occasionally health/well-being and women's issues.
How to Contact Submit a one-page query via e-mail or submit your complete hard copy proposal with title page, proposal contents, concept, bio, marketing, TOC, etc. Include SASE for the return of materials.
Recent Sales Please see the regularly updated client listing on website.
Tips "Please do not call. No phone queries."

ETHAN ELLENBERG LITERARY AGENCY

548 Broadway, #5-E, New York NY 10012. (212)431-4554. Fax: (212)941-4652. E-mail: agent@ethanellenberg.com. Website: ethanellenberg.com. **Contact:** Ethan Ellenberg. Estab. 1984. Represents 80 clients. 10% of clients are new/unpublished writers. Currently handles: nonfiction books 25%, novels 75%.
- Prior to opening his agency, Mr. Ellenberg was contracts manager of Berkley/Jove and associate contracts manager for Bantam.

Represents Nonfiction books, novels, children's books. **Considers these nonfiction areas:** biography, current affairs, health, history, medicine, military, science, technology, war, narrative. **Considers these fiction areas:** commercial, fantasy, mystery, romance, science fiction, suspense, thriller, young adult, children's (all types).
- "This agency specializes in commercial fiction—especially thrillers, romance/women's, and specialized nonfiction. We also do a lot of children's books." "Actively seeking commercial fiction as noted above—romance/fiction for women, science fiction and fantasy, thrillers, suspense and mysteries. Our other two main areas of interest are children's books and narrative nonfiction. We are actively seeking clients, follow the directions on our website." Does not want to receive poetry, short stories, Western's, autobiographies or screenplays.

How to Contact For fiction, send introductory letter, outline, first 3 chapters, SASE. For nonfiction, send query letter, proposal, 1 sample chapter, SASE. For children's books, send introductory letter, up to 3 picture book mss, outline, first 3 chapters, SASE. Accepts simultaneous submissions. Responds in 2 weeks to queries (no attachments); 4-6 weeks to mss.
Terms Agent receives 15% commission on domestic sales. Agent receives 10% commission on foreign sales. Offers written contract. Charges clients (with their consent) for direct expenses limited to photocopying and postage.
Writers Conferences RWA National Conference; Novelists, Inc.; and other regional conferences.
Tips We do consider new material from unsolicited authors. Write a good, clear letter with a succinct description of your book. We prefer the first 3 chapters when we consider fiction. For all submissions, you must include a SASE or the material will be discarded. It's always hard to break in, but talent will find a home. Check our website for complete submission guidelines. We continue to see natural storytellers and nonfiction writers with important books.

THE NICHOLAS ELLISON AGENCY

Affiliated with Sanford J. Greenburger Associates, 55 Fifth Ave., 15th Floor, New York NY 10003. (212)206-5600. Fax: (212)463-8718. E-mail: nellison@sjga.com. Website: www.greenburger.com. **Contact:** Nicholas Ellison. Represents 70 clients. Currently handles: nonfiction books 50%, novels 50%.
- Prior to becoming an agent, Mr. Ellison was an editor at Minerva Editions and Harper & Row, and editor-in-chief at Delacorte.

Member Agents Nicholas Ellison; Sarah Dickman.

Represents Nonfiction books, novels. **Considers these fiction areas:** literary, mainstream.
How to Contact Query with SASE. Responds in 6 weeks to queries.
Terms Agent receives 15% commission on domestic sales. Agent receives 20% commission on foreign sales.

⊙ ANN ELMO AGENCY, INC.

305 Seventh Avenue, # 1101, New York NY 10001. (212)661-2880. Fax: (212)661-2883. E-mail: aalitagent@sbcgobal.net. **Contact:** Lettie Lee. Member of AAR. Other memberships include Authors Guild.
Member Agents Lettie Lee; Mari Cronin (plays); A.L. Abecassis (nonfiction).
Represents Nonfiction books, novels. **Considers these nonfiction areas:** biography, current affairs, health, history, how to, popular culture, science. **Considers these fiction areas:** ethnic, family, mainstream, romance, contemporary, gothic, historical, regency, thriller, women's.
How to Contact Only accepts mailed queries with SASE. Do not send full ms unless requested. Responds in 3 months to queries. Obtains most new clients through recommendations from others.
Terms Agent receives 15% commission on domestic sales. Agent receives 20% commission on foreign sales. Offers written contract.
Tips "Query first, and only when asked send a double-spaced, readable manuscript. Include a SASE, of course."

⊙ THE ELAINE P. ENGLISH LITERARY AGENCY

4710 41st St. NW, Suite D, Washington DC 20016. (202)362-5190. Fax: (202)362-5192. E-mail: elaine@elaineenglish.com; naomi@elaineenglish.com. Website: www.elaineenglish.com. **Contact:** Elaine English; Naomi Hackenberg. Member of AAR. Represents 20 clients. 25% of clients are new/unpublished writers. Currently handles: novels 100%.
  • Ms. English has been working in publishing for more than 20 years. She is also an attorney specializing in media and publishing law.
Member Agents Elaine English (novels); Naomi Hackenberg (Young Adult fiction).
Represents Novels. **Considers these fiction areas:** historical, multicultural, mystery, suspense, thriller, women's, romance (single title, historical, contemporary, romantic, suspense, chick lit, erotic), general women's fiction. The agency is slowly but steadily acquiring in all mentioned areas.
  ☞ Actively seeking women's fiction, including single-title romances, and young adult fiction. Does not want to receive any science fiction, time travel, or picture books.
How to Contact Generally prefers e-queries sent to queries@elaineenglish.com or YA sent to naomi@elaineenglish.com. If requested, submit synopsis, first 3 chapters, SASE. Please check website for further details. Responds in 4-8 weeks to queries; 3 months to requested submissions. Obtains most new clients through recommendations from others, conferences, submissions.
Terms Agent receives 15% commission on domestic sales. Agent receives 20% commission on foreign sales. Offers written contract; 30-day notice must be given to terminate contract. Charges only for shipping expenses; generally taken from proceeds.
Recent Sales Have been to Sourcebooks, Tor, Harlequin.
Writers Conferences RWA National Conference; Novelists, Inc.; Malice Domestic; Washington Romance Writers Retreat, among others.

◻ THE EPSTEIN LITERARY AGENCY

P.O. Box 392, Avon MA 02368. (781)718-4025. E-mail: kate@epsteinliterary.com. Website: www.epsteinliterary.com. **Contact:** Kate Epstein. Member of AAR. Represents 30 clients. 70% of clients are new/unpublished writers. Currently handles: nonfiction books 100%.
  • Prior to opening her literary agency, Ms. Epstein was an acquisitions editor at Adams Media.
Member Agents Kate Epstein represents: practical nonfiction, memoir, narrative nonfiction, YA fiction, popular science, sociology, and psychology.
Represents Nonfiction books for adults and young adults and fiction for young adults (12 and up). **Considers these nonfiction areas:** animals, autobiography, biography, business, child guidance, cooking, crafts, current affairs, diet/nutrition, economics, foods, health, hobbies, how-to, humor, medicine, memoirs, metaphysics, New Age, parenting, popular culture, psychology, satire, self-help, sociology, travel, women's issues, women's studies.

☞ "My background as an editor means that I'm extremely good at selling to them. It also means I'm a careful and thorough line editor. I'm particularly skilled at hardening concepts to make them sellable and proposing the logical follow-up for any book. Most of my list is practical nonfiction, and I have a particular affinity for pets." Actively seeking commercial nonfiction for adults. Does not want scholarly works.

How to Contact Query via e-mail (no attachments). Accepts simultaneous submissions. Responds in 3 months to queries. Obtains most new clients through solicitations.

Terms Agent receives 15% commission on domestic sales. Agent receives 20% commission on foreign sales. Offers written contract; 30-day notice must be given to terminate contract.

Recent Sales *Austentatious Crochet*, by Melissa Horozewski (Running Press); *The Buddha in the Classroom*, by Donna Quesada (Skyhorse); *An Eagle Named Freedom*, by Jeffery Guidry (William Morrow).

☑ FELICIA ETH LITERARY REPRESENTATION

555 Bryant St., Suite 350, Palo Alto CA 94301-1700. (650)375-1276. Fax: (650)401-8892. E-mail: feliciaeth@aol.com. **Contact:** Felicia Eth. Member of AAR. Represents 25-35 clients. Currently handles: nonfiction books 85%, novels 15% adult.

Represents Nonfiction books, novels. **Considers these nonfiction areas:** animals, anthropology, autobiography, biography, business, child guidance, cultural interests, current affairs, economics, ethnic, gay/lesbian, government, health, history, investigative, law, medicine, parenting, popular culture, politics, psychology, science, sociology, technology, true crime, women's issues, women's studies. **Considers these fiction areas:** literary, mainstream.

☞ This agency specializes in high-quality fiction (preferably mainstream/contemporary) and provocative, intelligent, and thoughtful nonfiction on a wide array of commercial subjects.

How to Contact Query with SASE. Accepts simultaneous submissions. Responds in 3 weeks to queries. Responds in 4-6 weeks to mss.

Terms Agent receives 15% commission on domestic sales. Agent receives 20% commission on foreign sales. Agent receives 20% commission on film sales. Charges clients for photocopying and express mail service.

Recent Sales Sold 70-10 titles in the last year. *Bumper Sticker Philosophy*, by Jack Bowen (Random House); *Boys Adrift*, by Leonard Sax (Basic Books); *A War Reporter*, by Barbara Quick (HarperCollins); Pantry, by Anna Badkhen (Free Press/S&S).

Writers Conferences "Wide Array - from Squaw Valley to Mills College."

Tips "For nonfiction, established expertise is certainly a plus—as is magazine publication—though not a prerequisite. I am highly dedicated to those projects I represent, but highly selective in what I choose."

☑ MARY EVANS INC.

242 E. Fifth St., New York NY 10003. (212)979-0880. Fax: (212)979-5344. Website: www.maryevansinc.com. Member of AAR.

Member Agents Mary Evans (no unsolicited queries); Devin McIntyre, devin@maryevansinc.com (commericial and literary fiction, narrative nonfiction, pop culture, graphic novels, multicultural, pop science, sports, food).

Represents Nonfiction books, novels.

How to Contact Query with SASE. Query by snail mail. Non-query correspondence can be sent to info(at)maryevansinc.com. Obtains most new clients through recommendations from others, solicitations.

🅽 ☑ The Taryn Fagerness Agency, LLC

302 Washington St. #944, San Diego California 92103. E-mail: taryn.fagerness@gmail.com. Website: www.tarynfagernessagency.com. **Contact:** Taryn Fagerness.

How to Contact *This agency does not accept unsolicited submissions.*

☑ FAIRBANK LITERARY REPRESENTATION

199 Mount Auburn St., Suite 1, Cambridge MA 02138-4809. (617)576-0030. Fax: (617)576-0030. E-mail: queries@fairbankliterary.com. Website: www.fairbankliterary.com. **Contact:** Sorche Fairbank. Member of AAR. Represents 45 clients. 20% of clients are new/unpublished

writers. Currently handles: nonfiction books 60%, novels 22%, story collections 3%, other 15% illustrated.

Member Agents Sorche Fairbank (narrative nonfiction, commercial and literary fiction, memoir, food and wine); Matthew Frederick (scout for sports nonfiction, architecture, design).

Represents Nonfiction books, novels, short story collections. **Considers these nonfiction areas:** agriculture, architecture, art, autobiography, biography, cooking, crafts, cultural interests, current affairs, decorating, diet/nutrition, design, environment, ethnic, foods, gay/lesbian, government, hobbies, horticulture, how-to, interior design, investigative, law, memoirs, photography, popular culture, politics, science, sociology, sports, technology, true crime, women's issues, women's studies. **Considers these fiction areas:** action, adventure, feminist, gay, lesbian, literary, mainstream, mystery, sports, suspense, thriller, women's, Southern voices.

> ⚲ "I have a small agency in Harvard Square, where I tend to gravitate toward literary fiction and narrative nonfiction, with a strong interest in women's issues and women's voices, international voices, class and race issues, and projects that simply teach me something new about the greater world and society around us. We have a good reputation for working closely and developmentally with our authors and love what we do." Actively seeking literary fiction, international and culturally diverse voices, narrative nonfiction, topical subjects (politics, current affairs), history, sports, architecture/design and pop culture. Does not want to receive romance, poetry, science fiction, young adult or children's works.

How to Contact Query with SASE. Submit author bio. Accepts simultaneous submissions. Responds in 6 weeks to queries. Responds in 10 weeks to mss. Obtains most new clients through recommendations from others, solicitations, conferences, ideas generated in-house.

Terms Agent receives 15% commission on domestic sales. Agent receives 20% commission on foreign sales. Offers written contract, binding for 12 months; 45-day notice must be given to terminate contract.

Writers Conferences San Francisco Writers' Conference, Muse and the Marketplace/Grub Street Conference, Washington Independent Writers' Conference, Murder in the Grove, Surrey International Writers' Conference.

Tips "Be professional from the very first contact. There shouldn't be a single typo or grammatical flub in your query. Have a reason for contacting me about your project other than I was the next name listed on some website. Please do not use form query software! Believe me, we can get a dozen or so a day that look identical—we know when you are using a form. Show me that you know your audience—and your competition. Have the writing and/or proposal at the very, very best it can be before starting the querying process. Don't assume that if someone likes it enough they'll 'fix' it. The biggest mistake new writers make is starting the querying process before they—and the work—are ready. Take your time and do it right."

☑ FARRIS LITERARY AGENCY, INC.

P.O. Box 570069, Dallas TX 75357. (972)203-8804. E-mail: farris1@airmail.net. Website: www. farrisliterary.com. **Contact:** Mike Farris, Susan Morgan Farris. Represents 30 clients. 60% of clients are new/unpublished writers. Currently handles: nonfiction books 40, novels 60.

- Both Mr. Farris and Ms. Farris are attorneys.

Represents Nonfiction books, novels. **Considers these nonfiction areas:** autobiography, biography, business, child guidance, cooking, current affairs, dance, economics, government, health, history, how-to, humor, inspirational, memoirs, military, music, parenting, popular culture, religious, satire, self-help, sports, war, women's issues, women's studies. **Considers these fiction areas:** action, adventure, crime, detective, frontier, historical, humor, inspirational, mainstream, mystery, police, religious, romance, satire, sports, suspense, thriller, westerns.

> ⚲ "We specialize in both fiction and nonfiction books. We are particularly interested in discovering unpublished authors. We adhere to AAR guidelines." Does not want to receive science fiction, fantasy, gay and lesbian, erotica, young adult or children's.

How to Contact Query with SASE or by e-mail. Accepts simultaneous submissions. Responds in 2-3 weeks to queries. Responds in 4-8 weeks to mss. Obtains most new clients through recommendations from others, solicitations, conferences.

Terms Agent receives 15% commission on domestic sales. Agent receives 20% commission on foreign sales. Offers written contract; 30-day notice must be given to terminate contract. Charges clients for postage and photocopying.

Recent Sales *The Yard Dog* and The Insane Train, by Sheldon Russell (St. Martin's Press); *Eurostorm*, by Payne Harrison (Variance Publishing); *Relative Chaos*, by Kay Finch (Avalon Books); *Call Me Lucky: A Texan in Hollywood*, by Robert Hinkle and Mike Farris (University of Oklahoma Press); *Sketch Me If You Can* (the first book in a three book deal for the A Portrait of Crime mystery series), by Sharon Pape (Berkley Books); film rights options for *Balaam Gimble's Gumption*, by Mike Nichols (John M. Hardy Publishing).

Writers Conferences The Screenwriting Conference in Santa Fe; La Jolla Writers Conference; East Texas Christian Writers Conference.

☑ ☛ THE FIELDING AGENCY, LLC

269 S. Beverly Drive, No. 341, Beverly Hills CA 90212. (323)461-4791. E-mail: wlee@fieldingagency. com; query@fieldingagency.com. Website: www.fieldingagency.com. **Contact:** Whitney Lee. Currently handles: nonfiction books 25%, novels 35%, juvenile books 35%, other 5% other.

  • Prior to her current position, Ms. Lee worked at other agencies in different capacities.

Represents Nonfiction books, novels, short story collections, juvenile. **Considers these nonfiction areas:** animals, anthropology, archeology, architecture, art, autobiography, biography, business, child guidance, cooking, crafts, cultural interests, current affairs, decorating, diet/nutrition, design, economics, education, environment, ethnic, foods, gay/lesbian, government, health, history, hobbies, how-to, humor, investigative, juvenile nonfiction, language, law, literature, medicine, memoirs, military, money, parenting, popular culture, politics, psychology, satire, science, self-help, sociology, sports, technology, translation, true crime, war, women's issues, women's studies. **Considers these fiction areas:** action, adventure, cartoon, comic books, crime, detective, ethnic, family saga, fantasy, feminist, gay, glitz, historical, horror, humor, juvenile, lesbian, literary, mainstream, mystery, picture books, police, romance, satire, suspense, thriller, women's, young adult.

  ☛ "We specialize in representing books published abroad and have strong relationships with foreign co-agents and publishers. For books we represent in the U.S., we have to be head-over-heels passionate about it because we are involved every step of the way." Does not want to receive scripts for TV or film.

How to Contact Query with SASE. Submit synopsis, author bio. Accepts queries by e-mail and snail mail. Accepts simultaneous submissions. Obtains most new clients through recommendations from others.

Terms Agent receives 15% commission on domestic sales. Agent receives 20% commission on foreign sales. Offers written contract, binding for 9-12 months.

Writers Conferences London Book Fair; Frankfurt Book Fair; Bologna Book Fair.

☑ DIANA FINCH LITERARY AGENCY

116 W. 23rd St., Suite 500, New York NY 10011. (646)375-2081. E-mail: diana.finch@verizon. net. Website: dianafinchliteraryagency.blogspot.com/. **Contact:** Diana Finch. Member of AAR. Represents 40 clients. 20% of clients are new/unpublished writers. Currently handles: nonfiction books 65%, novels 25%, juvenile books 5%, multimedia 5%.

  • Prior to opening her agency, Ms. Finch worked at Ellen Levine Literary Agency for 18 years.

Represents Nonfiction books, novels, scholarly. **Considers these nonfiction areas:** autobiography, biography, business, child guidance, computers, cultural interests, current affairs, dance, economics, environment, ethnic, film, government, health, history, how-to, humor, investigative, juvenile nonfiction, law, medicine, memoirs, military, money, music, parenting, photography, popular culture, politics, psychology, satire, science, self-help, sports, technology, theater, translation, true crime, war, women's issues, women's studies, computers, electronic. **Considers these fiction areas:** action, adventure, crime, detective, ethnic, historical, literary, mainstream, police, thriller, young adult.

  ☛ Actively seeking narrative nonfiction, popular science, and health topics. "Does not want romance, mysteries, or children's picture books."

How to Contact Query with SASE or via e-mail (no attachments). Accepts simultaneous submissions. Obtains most new clients through recommendations from others.

Terms Agent receives 15% commission on domestic sales. Agent receives 20% commission on foreign sales. Offers written contract. "I charge for photocopying, overseas postage, galleys, and books purchased, and try to recap these costs from earnings received for a client, rather than charging outright."

Recent Sales *Genetic Rounds* by Robert Marion, M.D. (Kaplan); *Honeymoon In Tehran* by Azadeh Moaveni (Random House); *Darwin Slept Here* by Eric Simons (Overlook); *The Tyranny of Oil* by Antonia Juhasz (HarperCollins); *Stalin's Children* by Owen Matthews (Bloomsbury); *Radiant Days* by Michael Fitzgerald (Shoemaker & Hoard); *The Queen's Soprano* by Carol Dines (Harcourt Young Adult); *What To Say to a Porcupine* by Richard Gallagher (Amacom).

Tips "Do as much research as you can on agents before you query. Have someone critique your query letter before you send it. It should be only 1 page and describe your book clearly—and why you are writing it—but also demonstrate creativity and a sense of your writing style."

FINEPRINT LITERARY MANAGEMENT

240 West 35th St., Suite 500, New York NY 10001. (212)279-1282. E-mail: stephany@fineprintlit. com. Website: www.fineprintlit.com. Member of AAR.

Member Agents Peter Rubie, CEO (nonfiction interests include narrative nonfiction, popular science, spirituality, history, biography, pop culture, business, technology, parenting, health, self-help, music, and food; fiction interests include literate thrillers, crime fiction, science fiction and fantasy, military fiction and literary fiction); Stephany Evans, president (nonfiction interests include health and wellness - especially women's health, spirituality, lifestyle, home renovating/ decorating, entertaining, food and wine, popular reference, and narrative nonfiction; fiction interests include stories with a strong and interesting female protagonist, both literary and upmarket commercial—including chick lit, romance, mystery, and light suspense); June Clark (nonfiction: entertainment, self-help, parenting, reference/how-to books, teen books, food and wine, style/ beauty, and prescriptive business titles); Diane Freed (nonfiction: health/fitness, women's issues, memoir, baby boomer trends, parenting, popular culture, self-help, humor, young adult, and topics of New England regional interest); Meredith Hays (both fiction and nonfiction: commercial and literary; she is interested in sophisticated women's fiction such as urban chick lit, pop culture, lifestyle, animals, and absorbing nonfiction accounts); Janet Reid (mysteries and offbeat literary fiction); Colleen Lindsay; Marissa Walsh; Ward Calhoun; Laura Wood.

Represents Nonfiction books, novels. **Considers these nonfiction areas:** business, child guidance, cooking, dance, diet/nutrition, economics, foods, government, health, history, humor, law, medicine, memoirs, music, parenting, politics, psychology, science, spirituality, true crime, women's issues, women's studies, narrative nonfiction, young adult, popular science. **Considers these fiction areas:** crime, detective, fantasy, literary, military, mystery, police, romance, science fiction, suspense, war, women's, young adult.

How to Contact Query with SASE. Submit synopsis and first two chapters for fiction; proposal for nonfiction. Do not send attachments or manuscripts without a request. Obtains most new clients through recommendations from others, solicitations.

Terms Agent receives 15% commission on domestic sales. Agent receives 20% commission on foreign sales.

☻ JAMES FITZGERALD AGENCY

80 E. 11th St., Suite 301, New York NY (212)308-1122. E-mail: submissions@jfitzagency.com. Website: www.jfitzagency.com. **Contact:** James Fitzgerald.

- Prior to his current position, Mr. Fitzgerald was an editor at St. Martin's Press, Doubleday, and the New York Times.

Member Agents James Fitzgerald.

Represents Books that reflect the popular culture of today being in the forms of fiction, nonfiction, graphic and packaged books.

⎲ Does not want to receive poetry or screenplays.

How to Contact Query with SASE. Submit proposal package, outline/proposal, publishing history, author bio, overview.

Recent Sales *Gimme Something Better: The Profound, Progressive, and Occasionally Pointless History of Punk in the Bay Area,* by Jack Boulware and Silke Tudor (Viking/Penguin); *Black Dogs: The Possibly Story of Classic Rock's Greatest Robbery,* by Jason Buhrmester (Three Rivers/Crown); *Theo Gray's Med Science: Experiments You Can Do at Home—But Probably Shouldn't* (Black Dog and Loenthal).

Tips "Please submit all information in English, even if your manuscript is in Spanish."

☑ FLAMING STAR LITERARY ENTERPRISES

11 Raup Rd., Chatham NY 12037. E-mail: flamingstarlit@aol.com; janvall@aol.com. Website: www.flamingstarlit.com for Joseph Vallely; www.janisvallely.com for Janis Vallely. **Contact:** Joseph B. Vallely, Janis C. Vallely. Represents 100 clients. 25% of clients are new/unpublished writers. Currently handles: nonfiction books 100%.

- Prior to opening the agency, Mr. Vallely served as national sales manager for Dell; Ms. Vallely was V.P. and Associate Publisher of Doubleday.

Represents Nonfiction books. **Considers these nonfiction areas:** current affairs, diet/nutrition, government, health, law, memoirs, politics, psychology, self-help.

○┅ This agency specializes in upscale commercial nonfiction.

How to Contact E-mail only (no attachments). Responds in one week to queries. Obtains most new clients through recommendations from others, solicitations.

Terms Agent receives 15% commission on domestic sales. Agent receives 20% commission on foreign sales. Offers written contract. Charges clients for photocopying and postage only.

Recent Sales *Diabetes Without Drugs*, by Suzy Cohen (Rodale).

Tips "See website."

☑ FLANNERY LITERARY

1140 Wickfield Ct., Naperville IL 60563. (630)428-2682. Fax: (630)428-2683. E-mail: FlanLit@aol.com. **Contact:** Jennifer Flannery. Represents 40 clients. 50% of clients are new/unpublished writers. Currently handles: juvenile books 100%.

○┅ This agency specializes in children's and young adult fiction and nonfiction. It also accepts picture books.

How to Contact Query with SASE. No e-mail submissions or queries. Responds in 2 weeks to queries. Responds in 1 month to mss. Obtains most new clients through recommendations from others, submissions.

Terms Agent receives 15% commission on domestic sales. Agent receives 20% commission on foreign sales. Offers written contract, binding for life of book in print; 1-month notice must be given to terminate contract.

Tips "Write an engrossing, succinct query describing your work. We are always looking for a fresh new voice."

☑ PETER FLEMING AGENCY

P.O. Box 458, Pacific Palisades CA 90272. (310)454-1373. E-mail: peterfleming@earthlink.net. **Contact:** Peter Fleming. Currently handles: nonfiction books 100%.

○┅ This agency specializes in nonfiction books that unearth innovative and uncomfortable truths with bestseller potential. "Greatly interested in journalists in the free press (the Internet)."

How to Contact Query with SASE. Obtains most new clients through a different, one-of-a-kind idea for a book often backed by the writer's experience in that area of expertise.

Terms Agent receives 15% commission on domestic sales. Agent receives 25% commission on foreign sales. Offers written contract, binding for 1 year. Charges clients only those fees agreed to in writing.

Recent Sales *Stop Foreclosure*, by Lloyd Segol; *Rulers of Evil*, by F. Tupper Saussy (HarperCollins); *Why Is It Always About You—Saving Yourself from the Narcissists in Your Life*, by Sandy Hotchkiss (Free Press)

Tips "You can begin by starting your own blog."

FLETCHER & COMPANY

78 Fifth Ave., 3rd Floor, New York NY 10011. (212)614-0778. Fax: (212)614-0728. E-mail: mail@fletcherparry.com. Website: www.fletcherandco.com. **Contact:** Christy Fletcher. Member of AAR.

Member Agents Melissa Chinchilla (current affairs/politics, multicultural literature, smart women's fiction, horror, thrillers, crime and the paranormal—as well as select, high concept children's books, academic/trade books); Swanna MacNair (Southern literature and music, literary fiction, nonfiction, narrative journalism, investigative journalism, international fictions, thrillers, crime, paranormal, cultural studies, medical investigation, Young Adult, self-help, minority literature and smart romance; Grainne Fox (looking for Irish literary fiction and more smart, upmarket fiction) Rebecca Gradinger (literary fiction, upmarket commercial fiction, narrative nonfiction, self-help, memoir, humor, parenting, YA, and pop culture, health and medicine, women's issues, cultural studies, and fiction); Donald Lamm (history, biography, investigative journalism, politics, current affairs, and business books for the trade); Anne Loder (nonfiction, literary fiction, popular culture, poetry, and narrative journalism); Lucinda Blumenfeld (reps journalists, specialists, and emerging, young voices. Specific categories include: narrative and prescriptive nonfiction, business, memoir, YA, cultural studies, commercial and literary fiction).

Represents Nonfiction books, novels. **Considers these nonfiction areas:** biography, business, current affairs, health, history, memoirs, science, sports, travel, African American, narrative, lifestyle. **Considers these fiction areas:** literary, young adult, commercial.

☋ Does not want genre fiction.

How to Contact Query with SASE or e-mail according to our guidelines. NO ATTACHMENTS. Responds in 6 weeks to queries.

◐ THE FOLEY LITERARY AGENCY

34 E. 38th St., New York NY 10016-2508. (212)686-6930. **Contact:** Joan Foley, Joseph Foley. Estab. 1956. Represents 10 clients. Currently handles: nonfiction books 75%, novels 25%.

Represents Nonfiction books, novels. **Considers these nonfiction areas:** business services.

How to Contact Query with letter, brief outline, SASE. Responds promptly to queries. Obtains most new clients through recommendations from others (rarely taking on new clients).

Terms Agent receives 10% commission on domestic sales. Agent receives 15% commission on foreign sales.

◐ FOLIO LITERARY MANAGEMENT, LLC

505 Eighth Ave., Suite 603, New York NY 10018. Website: www.foliolit.com. Member of AAR. Represents 100+ clients.

- Prior to creating Folio Literary Management, Mr. Hoffman worked for several years at another agency; Mr. Kleinman was an agent at Graybill & English; Ms. Wheeler was an agent at Creative Media Agency; Ms. Fine was an agent at Vigliano Associates and Trident Media Group; Ms. Brower was an agent at Wendy Sherman Associates; Ms. Niumata was an editor at Simon & Schuster, HarperCollins, and Avalon Books.

Member Agents Scott Hoffman; Jeff Kleinman; Paige Wheeler; Celeste Fine; Erin Niumata; Rachel Vater; Michelle Brower, Marcy Posner, Steve Troha, Molly Jaffa.

Represents Nonfiction books, novels, short story collections. **Considers these nonfiction areas:** animals, art, biography, business, child guidance, economics, environment, health, history, how-to, humor, inspirational, memoirs, military, parenting, popular culture, politics, psychology, religious, satire, science, self-help, technology, war, women's issues, women's studies, animals (equestrian), narrative nonfiction, espionage; fitness, lifestyle, relationship, culture, cookbooks. **Considers these fiction areas:** erotica, fantasy, literary, mystery, religious, romance, science, thriller, psychological, young, womens, Southern; legal; edgy crime, young adult, middle grade, women's nonfiction, popular sociology.

How to Contact Query via e-mail only (no attachments). Read agent bios online for specific submission guidelines. Responds in 1 month to queries.

Tips "Please do not submit simultaneously to more than one agent at Folio. If you're not sure which of us is exactly right for your book, don't worry. We work closely as a team, and if one of our agents gets a query that might be more appropriate for someone else, we'll always pass it along. It's important that you check each agent's bio page for clear directions as to how to submit, as well as when to expect feedback."

FOUNDRY LITERARY + MEDIA

33 West 17th St., PH, New York NY 10011. (212)929-5064. Fax: (212)929-5471. Website: www.foundrymedia.com.

Member Agents Peter H. McGuigan (smart, offbeat nonfiction, particularly works of narrative nonfiction on pop culture, niche history, biography, music and science; fiction interests include commercial and literary, across all genres, especially first-time writers); Yfat Reiss Gendell (favors nonfiction books focusing on all manners of prescriptive: how-to, science, health and well-being, memoirs, adventure, travel stories and lighter titles appropriate for the gift trade genre. Yfat also looks for commercial fiction highlighting the full range of women's experiences—young and old— and also seeks science fiction, thrillers and historical fiction); Stéphanie Abou (in fiction and

nonfiction alike, Stéphanie is always on the lookout for authors who are accomplished storytellers with their own distinctive voice, who develop memorable characters, and who are able to create psychological conflict with their narrative. She is an across-the-board fiction lover, attracted to both literary and smart upmarket commercial fiction. In nonfiction she leans towards projects that tackle big topics with an unusual approach. Pop culture, health, science, parenting, women's and multicultural issues are of special interest); Chris Park (memoirs, narrative nonfiction, Christian nonfiction and character-driven fiction); David Patterson (outstanding narratives and/or idea-driven works of nonfiction); Hannah Brown Gordon (fiction, YA, memoir, narrative nonfiction, history, current events, science, psychology and pop-culture); Lisa Grubka; Mollie Glick (literary fiction, narrative nonfiction, YA, and a bit of practical nonfiction); Stephen Barbara (all categories of books for young readers in addition to servicing writers for the adult market); Brandi Bowles (idea and platform-driven nonfiction in all categories, including music and pop-culture, humor, business, sociology, philosophy, health, and relationships. Quirky, funny, or contrarian proposals are always welcome in her inbox, as are big-idea books that change the way we think about the world. Brandi also represents fiction in the categories of literary fiction, women's fiction, urban fantasy, and YA).
Represents Considers these nonfiction areas: biography, child, health, memoirs, multicultural, music, popular culture, science. **Considers these fiction areas:** literary, religious.
How to Contact Query with SASE. Should be addressed to one agent only. Submit synopsis, 3 sample chapters, author bio, For nonfiction, submit query, proposal, sample chapter, TOC, bio. Put submisssions on your snail mail submission.

🌑 ◎ FOX CHASE AGENCY, INC.
701 Lee Road, Suite 102, Chesterbrook Corporate Center, Chesterbrook PA 19087. Member of AAR.
Member Agents A.L. Hart; Jo C. Hart.
Represents Nonfiction books, novels.
How to Contact Query with SASE.

FOX LITERARY
168 Second Ave., PMB 180, New York NY 10003. E-mail: submissions@foxliterary.com. Website: www.foxliterary.com.
Represents Considers these nonfiction areas: memoirs, biography, pop culture, narrative nonfiction, history, science, spirituality, self-help, celebrity, dating/relationships, women's issues, psychology, film & entertainment, cultural/social issues, journalism. **Considers these fiction areas:** erotica, fantasy, literary, romance, science, young adult, science fiction, thrillers, historical fiction, literary fiction, graphic novels, commercial fiction, women's fiction, gay & lesbian, erotica, historical romance.
  ⚠ Does not want to receive screenplays, poetry, category Westerns, horror, Christian/inspirational, or children's picture books.
How to Contact E-mail query and first five pages in body of e-mail. E-mail queries preferred. For snail mail queries, must include an e-mail address for response. Do not send SASE.

LYNN C. FRANKLIN ASSOCIATES, LTD.
1350 Broadway, Suite 2015, New York NY 10018. (212)868-6311. Fax: (212)868-6312. **Contact:** Lynn Franklin, President; Claudia Nys, Foreign Rights; Michelle Andelman, Agent/Children's. Other memberships include PEN America. Represents 30-35 clients. 50% of clients are new/unpublished writers. Currently handles: nonfiction books 90%, novels 10%.
Represents Nonfiction books, novels. **Considers these nonfiction areas:** New Age, biography, current affairs, health, history, memoirs, psychology, religion, self-help, spirituality. **Considers these fiction areas:** literary, mainstream, commercial; juvenile, middle-grade, and young adult.
  ⚠ "This agency specializes in general nonfiction with a special interest in self-help, biography/memoir, alternative health, and spirituality."
How to Contact Query via e-mail to agency@franklinandsiegal.com. No unsolicited mss. No attachments. For nonfiction, query letter with short outline and synopsis. For fiction, query letter with short synopsis and a maximum of 10 sample pages (in the body of the e-mail). Please indicate "query adult" or "query children's" in the subject line. Accepts simultaneous submissions.

Responds in 2 weeks to queries. Responds in 6 weeks to mss. Obtains most new clients through recommendations from others, solicitations.

Terms Agent receives 15% commission on domestic sales. Agent receives 20% commission on foreign sales. Offers written contract.

Recent Sales Adult: *Made for Goodness*, by Archbishop Desmond Tutu and Reverend Mpho Tutu (HarperOne); *Children of God Storybook Bible*, by Archbishop Desmond Tutu (Zondervan for originating publisher Lux Verbi); *Playing Our Game: Why China's Economic Rise Doesn't Threaten the West*, by Edward Steinfeld (Oxford University Press); *The 100 Year Diet*, by Susan Yager (Rodale); Children's/YA: *I Like Mandarin*, by Kirsten Hubbard (Delacorte/Random House); *A Scary Scene in a Scary Movie*, by Matt Blackstone (Farrar, Straus & Giroux).

◙ JEANNE FREDERICKS LITERARY AGENCY, INC.

221 Benedict Hill Road, New Canaan CT 06840. (203)972-3011. Fax: (203)972-3011. E-mail: jeanne.fredericks@gmail.com. Website: jeannefredericks.com/. **Contact:** Jeanne Fredericks. Member of AAR. Other memberships include Authors Guild. Represents 90 clients. 10% of clients are new/unpublished writers. Currently handles: nonfiction books 100%.

- Prior to opening her agency, Ms. Fredericks was an agent and acting director with the Susan P. Urstadt, Inc. Agency.

Represents Nonfiction books. **Considers these nonfiction areas:** animals, autobiography, biography, child guidance, cooking, decorating, finance, foods, gardening, health, history, how-to, interior design, medicine, money, nature, nutrition, parenting, personal improvement, photography, psychology, self-help, sports (not spectator sports), women's issues.

- ๑ This agency specializes in quality adult nonfiction by authorities in their fields. Does not want to receive children's books or fiction.

How to Contact Query first with SASE, then send outline/proposal, 1-2 sample chapters, SASE. See submission guidelines online first. Accepts simultaneous submissions. Responds in 3-5 weeks to queries. Responds in 2-4 months to mss. Obtains most new clients through recommendations from others, solicitations, conferences.

Terms Agent receives 15% commission on domestic sales. Agent receives 25% commission on foreign sales with co-agent. Offers written contract, binding for 9 months; 2-month notice must be given to terminate contract. Charges client for photocopying of whole proposals and mss, overseas postage, priority mail, express mail services.

Recent Sales *The Green Market Baking Book*, by Laura Martin (Sterling); *Tales of the Seven Seas*, by Dennis Powers (Taylor); *The Monopoly® Guide to Real Estate*, by Carolyn Janik (Sterling); The Generosity Plan, by Kathy LeMay (Beyond Words/Atria); *Canadian Vegetable Gardening*, by Doug Green (Cool Springs).

Writers Conferences Connecticut Authors and Publishers Association-University Conference; ASJA Writers' Conference; BookExpo America; Garden Writers' Association Annual Symposium; Harvard Medical School CME Course in Publishing.

Tips "Be sure to research competition for your work and be able to justify why there's a need for your book. I enjoy building an author's career, particularly if he/she is professional, hardworking, and courteous. Aside from 17 years of agenting experience, I've had 10 years of editorial experience in adult trade book publishing that enables me to help an author polish a proposal so that it's more appealing to prospective editors. My MBA in marketing also distinguishes me from other agents."

◖ GRACE FREEDSON'S PUBLISHING NETWORK

375 North Broadway, Suite 102, Jericho NY 11753. (516)931-7757. Fax: (516)931-7759. E-mail: gfreedson@worldnet.att.net. **Contact:** Grace Freedson. Represents 100 clients. 10% of clients are new/unpublished writers. Currently handles: nonfiction books 90%, juvenile books 10%.

- Prior to becoming an agent, Ms. Freedson was a managing editor and director of acquisition for Barron's Educational Series.

Represents Nonfiction books, juvenile. **Considers these nonfiction areas:** animals, business, cooking, crafts, current affairs, diet/nutrition, economics, education, environment, foods, health, history, hobbies, how-to, humor, medicine, money, popular culture, psychology, satire, science, self-help, sports, technology.

- ๑ "In addition to representing many qualified authors, I work with publishers as a packager of unique projects—mostly series." Does not want to receive fiction.

How to Contact Query with SASE. Submit synopsis, SASE. Responds in 2-6 weeks to queries. Obtains most new clients through recommendations from others.

Terms Agent receives 15% commission on domestic sales. Offers written contract; 30-day notice must be given to terminate contract.

Recent Sales Sold 50 titles in the last year. *The Dangers Lurking Beyond the Glass Ceiling*, by D. sherr bourierg Carter (Prometheus); *Threats, Lies and Intimidation: Inside Debt Collection*, by Fred Williams (FT Press); *Plastic Planet*, by Kathryn Jones (FT Press).

Writers Conferences BookExpo of America.

Tips "At this point, I am only reviewing proposals on nonfiction topics by credentialed authors with platforms."

✷ ◎ FRESH BOOKS LITERARY AGENCY

231 Diana St., Placerville CA 95667. E-mail: matt@fresh-books.com. Website: www.fresh-books. com. **Contact:** Matt Wagner. Represents 30+ clients. 5% of clients are new/unpublished writers. Currently handles: nonfiction books 95%, multimedia 5%.

- Prior to becoming an agent, Mr. Wagner was with Waterside Productions for 15 years.

Represents Nonfiction books. **Considers these nonfiction areas:** animals, anthropology, archeology, architecture, art, business, child guidance, computers, cooking, crafts, cultural interests, current affairs, dance, design, economics, education, environment, ethnic, gay/lesbian, government, health, history, hobbies, humor, law, medicine, military, money, music, parenting, photography, popular culture, politics, psychology, satire, science, sports, technology.

 ⚭ "I specialize in tech and how-to. I love working with books and authors, and I've repped many of my clients for upwards of 15 years now." Actively seeking popular science, natural history, adventure, how-to, business, education and reference. Does not want to receive fiction, children's books or poetry.

How to Contact Query with SASE. No phone calls. Accepts simultaneous submissions. Responds in 1-4 weeks to queries. Responds in 1-4 weeks to mss. Obtains most new clients through recommendations from others.

Terms Agent receives 15% commission on domestic sales. Agent receives 20% commission on foreign sales.

Recent Sales *The Myth of Multitasking: How Doing It All Gets Nothing Done* (Jossey-Bass); *Wilderness Survival for Dummies* (Wiley); and *The Zombie Combat Manual* (Berkley).

Tips "Do your research. Find out what sorts of books and authors an agent represents. Go to conferences. Make friends with other writers—most of my clients come from referrals."

◐ SARAH JANE FREYMANN LITERARY AGENCY

59 W. 71st St., Suite 9B, New York NY 10023. (212)362-9277. E-mail: sarah@sarahjanefreymann. com; Submissions@SarahJaneFreymann.com. Website: www.sarahjanefreymann.com. **Contact:** Sarah Jane Freymann, Steve Schwartz. Represents 100 clients. 20% of clients are new/unpublished writers. Currently handles: nonfiction books 75%, novels 23%, juvenile books 2%.

Member Agents Sarah Jane Freymann; (nonfiction books, novels, illustrated books); Jessica Sinsheimer, Jessica@sarahjanefreymann.com (young adult fiction).

Represents Considers these nonfiction areas: animals, anthropology, architecture, art, autobiography, biography, business, child guidance, cooking, current affairs, decorating, diet/ nutrition, design, economics, ethnic, foods, health, history, interior design, medicine, memoirs, parenting, psychology, self-help, women's issues, women's studies, lifestyle. **Considers these fiction areas:** ethnic, literary, mainstream.

How to Contact Query with SASE. Responds in 2 weeks to queries. Responds in 6 weeks to mss. Obtains most new clients through recommendations from others.

Terms Agent receives 15% commission on domestic sales. Agent receives 20% commission on foreign sales. Offers written contract. Charges clients for long distance, overseas postage, photocopying. 100% of business is derived from commissions on ms sales.

Recent Sales *How to Make Love to a Plastic Cup: And Other Things I Learned While Trying to Knock Up My Wife*, by Greg Wolfe (Harper Collins); *I Want to Be Left Behind: Rapture Here on Earth*, by Brenda Peterson (a Merloyd Lawrence Book); *That Bird Has My Name: The Autobiography of an Innocent Man on Death Row*, by Jarvis Jay Masters with an Introduction by Pema Chodrun (HarperOne); *Perfect One-Dish Meals*, by Pam Anderson (Houghton Mifflin); *Birdology*, by Sy Montgomery (Simon & Schuster); *Emptying the Nest: Launching Your Reluctant Young Adult*, by Dr.

Brad Sachs (Macmillan); *Tossed & Found*, by Linda and John Meyers (Steward, Tabori & Chang); *32 Candles*, by Ernessa Carter; *God and Dog*, by Wendy Francisco.

Tips "I love fresh, new, passionate works by authors who love what they are doing and have both natural talent and carefully honed skill."

☑ FREDRICA S. FRIEDMAN AND CO., INC.

136 E. 57th St., 14th Floor, New York NY 10022. (212)829-9600. Fax: (212)829-9669. E-mail: info@ fredricafriedman.com; submissions@fredricafriedman.com. Website: www.fredricafriedman. com/. **Contact:** Ms. Chandler Smith. Represents 75 + clients. 50% of clients are new/unpublished writers. Currently handles: nonfiction books 95%, novels 5%.

Represents Nonfiction books, novels, anthologies. **Considers these nonfiction areas:** art, biography, business, child, cooking, current affairs, education, ethnic, gay, government, health, history, how to, humor, language, memoirs, money, music, photography, popular culture, psychology, self-help, sociology, film, true crime, womens, interior design/decorating. **Considers these fiction areas:** literary.

- ⚬┯ "We represent a select group of outstanding nonfiction and fiction writers. We are particularly interested in helping writers expand their readership and develop their careers." Does not want poetry, plays, screenplays, children's books, sci-fi/fantasy, or horror.

How to Contact Submit e-query, synopsis; be concise, and include any pertinent author information, including relevant writing history. If you are a fiction writer, we also request a one-page sample from your manuscript to provide its voice. We ask that you keep all material in the body of the e-mail. Accepts simultaneous submissions. Responds in 4-6 weeks to queries. Responds in 4-6 weeks to mss. Obtains most new clients through recommendations from others.

Terms Agent receives 15% commission on domestic sales. Agent receives 25% commission on foreign sales. Offers written contract. Charges for photocopying and messenger/shipping fees for proposals.

Recent Sales *A World of Lies: The Crime and Consequences of Bernie Madoff*, by Diana B. Henriques (Times Books/Holt); *Polemic and Memoir: The Nixon Years*, by Patrick J. Buchanan (St. Martin's Press); *Angry Fat Girls: Five Women, Five Hundred Pounds, and a Year of Losing It...Again*, by Frances Kuffel (Berkley/Penguin); *Life With My Sister Madonna*, by Christopher Ciccone with Wendy Leigh (Simon & Schuster Spotlight); *The World Is Curved: Hidden Dangers to the Global Economy*, by David Smick (Portfolio/Penguin); *Going to See the Elephant*, by Rodes Fishburne (Delacorte/Random House); *Seducing the Boys Club: Uncensored Tactics from a Woman at the Top*, by Nina DiSesa (Ballantine/Random House); *The Girl from Foreign: A Search for Shipwrecked Ancestors, Forgotten Histories, and a Sense of Home*, by Sadia Shepard (The Penguin Press).

Tips "Spell the agent's name correctly on your query letter."

THE FRIEDRICH AGENCY

136 East 57th St., 18th Floor, New York NY 10022. Website: www.friedrichagency.com. **Contact:** Molly Friedrich. Member of AAR. Represents 50 + clients.

- Prior to her current position, Ms. Friedrich was an agent at the Aaron Priest Literary Agency.

Member Agents Molly Friedrich, Founder and Agent (open to queries); Paul Cirone, Foreign Rights Director and Agent(open to queries); Lucy Carson, assistant.

Represents Full-length fiction and nonfiction.

How to Contact Query with SASE by mail, or e-mail. See guidelines on website.

Recent Sales *Vanished* by Joseph Finder, *T is for Trespass* by Sue Grafton, *Look Again* by Lisa Scottoline, *Olive Kitteridge* by Elizabeth Strout. Other clients include Frank McCourt, Jane Smiley, Esmeralda Santiago, Terry McMillan, Cathy Schine, and more.

☑ FULL CIRCLE LITERARY, LLC

7676 Hazard Center Dr., Suite 500, San Diego CA 92108. E-mail: submissions@fullcircleliterary.com. Website: www.fullcircleliterary.com. **Contact:** Lilly Ghahremani, Stefanie Von Borstel. Represents 55 clients. 60% of clients are new/unpublished writers. Currently handles: nonfiction books 70%, novels 10%, juvenile books 20%.

- Before forming Full Circle, Ms. Von Borstel worked in both marketing and editorial capacities at Penguin and Harcourt; Ms. Ghahremani received her law degree from UCLA, and has experience in representing authors on legal affairs.

Member Agents Lilly Ghahremani (young adult, pop culture, crafts, "green" living, narrative nonfiction, business, relationships, Middle Eastern interest, multicultural); Stefanie Von Borstel (Latino interest, crafts, parenting, wedding/relationships, how-to, self-help, middle grade/teen fiction/YA, green living, multicultural/bilingual picture books); Adriana Dominguez (fiction areas of interest: children's books - picture books, middle grade novels, and (literary) young adult novels; on the adult side, she is looking for literary, women's, and historical fiction. Nonfiction areas of interest: multicultural, pop culture, how-to, and titles geared toward women of all ages).

Represents Nonfiction books, juvenile. **Considers these nonfiction areas:** animals, autobiography, biography, business, child guidance, crafts, cultural interests, current affairs, dance, diet/nutrition, ethnic, foods, health, hobbies, how-to, humor, juvenile nonfiction, medicine, parenting, popular culture, satire, self-help, women's issues, women's studies. **Considers these fiction areas:** ethnic, literary, young adult.

O— "Our full-service boutique agency, representing a range of nonfiction and children's books (limited fiction), provides a one-stop resource for authors. Our extensive experience in the realms of law and marketing provide Full Circle clients with a unique edge." "Actively seeking nonfiction by authors with a unique and strong platform, projects that offer new and diverse viewpoints, and literature with a global or multicultural perspective. We are particularly interested in books with a Latino or Middle Eastern angle and books related to pop culture." Does not want to receive "screenplays, poetry, commercial fiction or genre fiction (horror, thriller, mystery, Western, sci-fi, fantasy, romance, historical fiction)."

How to Contact Agency accepts e-queries. See website for fiction guidelines, as they are in flux. For nonfiction, send full proposal. Accepts simultaneous submissions. Responds in 1-2 weeks to queries. Responds in 4-6 weeks to mss. Obtains most new clients through recommendations from others, solicitations, conferences.

Terms Agent receives 15% commission on domestic sales. Agent receives 20% commission on foreign sales. Offers written contract; up to 30-day notice must be given to terminate contract. Charges for copying and postage.

Tips "Put your best foot forward. Contact us when you simply can't make your project any better on your own, and please be sure your work fits with what the agent you're approaching represents. Little things count, so copyedit your work. Join a writing group and attend conferences to get objective and constructive feedback before submitting. Be active about building your platform as an author before, during, and after publication. Remember this is a business and your agent is a business partner."

◎ NANCY GALLT LITERARY AGENCY

273 Charlton Ave., South Orange NJ 07079. (973)761-6358. Fax: (973)761-6318. E-mail: nancy@nancygallt.com; marietta@nancygallt.com. Website: www.nancygalltliteraryagency.com. **Contact:** Nancy Gallt. Represents 40 clients. 30% of clients are new/unpublished writers. Currently handles: juvenile books 100%.

• Prior to opening her agency, Ms. Gallt was subsidiary rights director of the children's book division at Morrow, Harper and Viking.

Member Agents Nancy Gallt; Marietta Zacker.

Represents Juvenile.

O— "I only handle children's books." Actively seeking picture books, middle-grade and young adult novels. Does not want to receive rhyming picture book texts.

How to Contact Submit a novel or chapter book by copying and pasting the first 5 pages onto the body of the e-mail and attach the first three chapters to submissions@nancygallt.com. Do not send to individual e-mail address, but do address submission to specific agent. If submitting a picture book: please copy and paste the entire manuscript into the body of the e-mail and attach it as well. A response from one agent is a response from the entire company. Please see website for more submission details. Accepts simultaneous submissions. Responds in 3 months to queries. Responds in 3 months to mss. Obtains most new clients through recommendations from others, solicitations.

Terms Agent receives 15% commission on domestic sales. Agent receives 20% commission on foreign sales. Offers written contract; 30-day notice must be given to terminate contract.

Recent Sales Sold 50 titles in the last year. *Kane Chronicles* series, by Rick Riordan (Hyperion); *Nightshade City*, by Hilary Wagner (Holiday House); *Cinderella Smith*, by Stephanie Barden

(HarperCollins); *The Square Cat*, by Elizabeth Schoonmaker (Simon & Schuster); *Granddaughter's Necklace*, illustrated by Bagram Ibatoulline (Scholastic).

Tips "Writing and illustrations stand on their own, so submissions should tell the most compelling stories possible—whether visually, in words, or both."

⊚ THE GARAMOND AGENCY, INC.

12 Horton St., Newburyport MA 01950. E-mail: query@garamondagency.com. Website: www. garamondagency.com. Other memberships include Author's Guild.

Member Agents Lisa Adams; David Miller.

Represents Nonfiction books. **Considers these nonfiction areas:** business, economics, government, history, law, politics, psychology, science, technology, social science, narrative nonfiction.

- ⊶ "We work closely with our authors through each stage of the publishing process, first in developing their books and then in presenting themselves and their ideas effectively to publishers and to readers. We represent our clients throughout the world in all languages, media, and territories through an extensive network of subagents." No proposals for children's or young adult books, fiction, poetry, or memoir.

How to Contact See website.

Recent Sales *Fifty-Nine in '84*, by Edward Achorn (Harper Collins); *Counterclockwise*, by Ellen J. Langer (Ballantine); *Too Big To Know*, by David Weinberger (Basic Books); *The Complete Psalms*, by Pamela Greenberg (Bloomsbury). See website for other clients.

Tips "Query us first if you have any questions about whether we are the right agency for your work."

MAX GARTENBERG LITERARY AGENCY

912 N. Pennsylvania Ave., Yardley PA 19067. (215)295-9230. Website: www.maxgartenberg.com. **Contact:** Anne Devlin. Estab. 1954. Represents 50 clients. 5% of clients are new/unpublished writers. Currently handles: nonfiction books 90%, novels 10%.

Member Agents Max Gartenberg, president, (biography, environment, and narrative nonfiction); Anne G. Devlin (current events, women's issues, health, lifestyle, literary fiction, romance, and celebrity); Will Devlin (sports, popular culture, humor and politics).

Represents Nonfiction books, novels. **Considers these nonfiction areas:** agriculture horticulture, animals, art, biography, child, current affairs, health, history, money, music, nature, psychology, science, self-help, sports, film, true crime, women's.

How to Contact Writers desirous of having their work handled by this agency should first send a one- or two-page query letter directed to an agent on staff. Send queries via snail mail with SASE. Accepts simultaneous submissions. Responds in 2 weeks to queries. Responds in 6 weeks to mss. Obtains most new clients through recommendations from others, following up on good query letters.

Terms Agent receives 15% commission on domestic sales. Agent receives 20% commission on foreign sales.

Recent Sales *What Patients Taught Me*, by Audrey Young, MD (Sasquatch Books); *Unorthodox Warfare: The Chinese Experience*, by Ralph D. Sawyer (Westview Press); *Encyclopedia of Earthquakes and Volcanoes*, by Alexander E. Gates (Facts on File); *Homebirth in the Hospital*, by Stacey Kerr, MD (Sentient Publications).

Tips "We have recently expanded to allow more access for new writers."

DON GASTWIRTH & ASSOCIATES

265 College St., New Haven CT 06510. (203)562-7600. Fax: (203)562-4300. E-mail: Donlit@snet. net. **Contact:** Don Gastwirth. Signatory of WGA. Represents 26 clients. 10% of clients are new/unpublished writers. Currently handles: nonfiction books 30%, scholarly books 60%, other 10% other.

- Prior to becoming an agent, Mr. Gastwirth was an entertainment lawyer and law professor.

Represents Nonfiction books, scholarly. **Considers these nonfiction areas:** business, current affairs, history, military, money, music, nature, popular culture, psychology, translation, true crime. **Considers these fiction areas:** mystery, thriller.

- ⊶ This is a selective agency and is rarely open to new clients that do not come through a referral.

How to Contact Query with SASE.

Terms Agent receives 15% commission on domestic sales. Agent receives 10% commission on foreign sales.

◙ GELFMAN SCHNEIDER LITERARY AGENTS, INC.

250 W. 57th St., Suite 2122, New York NY 10107. (212)245-1993. Fax: (212)245-8678. E-mail: mail@ gelfmanschneider.com. **Contact:** Jane Gelfman, Deborah Schneider. Member of AAR. Represents 300+ clients. 10% of clients are new/unpublished writers.

Represents Fiction and Nonfiction books. **Considers these fiction areas:** literary, mainstream, mystery, women's.

> ⚲ Does not want to receive romance, science fiction, westerns, or children's books.

How to Contact Query with SASE. Send queries via snail mail only. Responds in 1 month to queries. Responds in 2 months to mss.

Terms Agent receives 15% commission on domestic sales. Agent receives 20% commission on foreign sales. Agent receives 15% commission on film sales. Offers written contract. Charges clients for photocopying and messengers/couriers.

◙ BARRY GOLDBLATT LITERARY, LLC

320 Seventh Ave., #266, Brooklyn NY 11215. Fax: (718)360-5453. Website: www.bgliterary.com/ contactme.html. **Contact:** Barry Goldblatt. Member of AAR. SCBWI

Member Agents Barry Goldblatt, Joe Monti, Beth Fleisher (kids work and graphic novels; she is particularly interested in finding new voices in middle grade and young adult fantasy, science fiction, mystery, historicals and action adventure).

Represents Juvenile books. **Considers these fiction areas:** picture books, young adult, middle grade, all genres.

> ⚲ This agency specializes in children's books of all kinds.

How to Contact E-mail queries query@bgliterary.com, and include the first five pages and a synopsis of the novel pasted into the text of the e-mail. No attachments or links.

Recent Sales *The Infernal Devices* trilogy, by Cassandra Clare (McElderry Books); *Kat by Moonlight* trilogy, by Stephanie Burgis (Atheneum Books); *Giving Up a Ghost*, by Samantha Schutz (Scholastic).

◙ FRANCES GOLDIN LITERARY AGENCY, INC.

57 E. 11th St., Suite 5B, New York NY 10003. (212)777-0047. Fax: (212)228-1660. E-mail: agency@ goldinlit.com. Website: www.goldinlit.com. Estab. 1977. Member of AAR. Represents over 100 clients.

Member Agents Frances Goldin, principal/agent; Ellen Geiger, agent (commercial and literary fiction and nonfiction, cutting-edge topics of all kinds); Matt McGowan, agent/rights director (innovative works of fiction and nonfiction); Sam Stoloff, agent (literary fiction, memoir, history, accessible sociology and philosophy, cultural studies, serious journalism, narrative and topical nonfiction with a progressive orientation); Sarah Bridgins, agent/office manager (literary fiction and nonfiction).

Represents Nonfiction books, novels.

> ⚲ "We are hands on and we work intensively with clients on proposal and manuscript development." Does not want anything that is racist, sexist, agist, homophobic, or pornographic. No screenplays, children's books, art books, cookbooks, business books, diet books, self-help, or genre fiction.

How to Contact Query with SASE. No unsolicited mss or work previously submitted to publishers. Prefers hard-copy queries. If querying by e-mail, put word "query" in subject line. Responds in 6 weeks to queries.

◙ THE SUSAN GOLOMB LITERARY AGENCY

875 Avenue of the Americas, Suite 2302, New York NY 10001. Fax: (212)239-9503. E-mail: susan@ sgolombagency.com. **Contact:** Susan Golomb. Represents 100 clients. 20% of clients are new/ unpublished writers. Currently handles: nonfiction books 50%, novels 40%, story collections 10%.

Member Agents Susan Golomb (accepts queries); Sabine Hrechdakian (accepts queries); Kim Goldstein (no unsolicited queries).

Represents Nonfiction books, novels, short story collections, novellas. **Considers these nonfiction areas:** animals, anthropology, archeology, autobiography, biography, business, current affairs, economics, environment, government, health, history, law, memoirs, military, money, popular culture, politics, psychology, science, sociology, technology, war, women's issues, women's studies. **Considers these fiction areas:** ethnic, historical, humor, literary, mainstream, satire, thriller, women's, young adult, chick lit.

> ☞ "We specialize in literary and upmarket fiction and nonfiction that is original, vibrant and of excellent quality and craft. Nonfiction should be edifying, paradigm-shifting, fresh and entertaining." Actively seeking writers with strong voices. Does not want to receive genre fiction.

How to Contact Query with SASE. Submit outline/proposal, synopsis, 1 sample chapters, author bio, SASE. Query via mail or e-mail. Responds in 2 week to queries. Responds in 8 weeks to mss. Obtains most new clients through recommendations from others, solicitations.

Terms Agent receives 15% commission on domestic sales. Agent receives 20% commission on foreign sales. Offers written contract.

Recent Sales Sold 20 titles in the last year. *Sunnyside*, by Glen David Gold (Knopf); *How to Buy a Love of Reading*, by Tanya Egan Gibson (Dutton); *Telex From Cuba*, by Rachel Kushner (Scribner); *The Imperfectionists*, by Tom Rachman (Dial).

◎ GOODMAN ASSOCIATES

500 West End Ave., New York NY 10024-4317. (212)873-4806. Member of AAR.

> ☞ Accepting new clients by recommendation only.

◪ IRENE GOODMAN LITERARY AGENCY

27 W. 24th Street, Suite 700B, New York NY 10010. E-mail: queries@irenegoodman.com. Website: www.irenegoodman.com. **Contact:** Irene Goodman, Miriam Kriss. Member of AAR.

Member Agents Irene Goodman; Miriam Kriss; Barbara Poelle; Jon Sternfeld.

Represents Nonfiction books, novels. **Considers these nonfiction areas:** narrative nonfiction dealing with social, cultural and historical issues; an occasional memoir and current affairs book, parenting, social issues, francophilia, anglophilia, Judaica, lifestyles, cooking, memoir. **Considers these fiction areas:** historical, intelligent literary, modern urban fantasies, mystery, romance, thriller, women's.

> ☞ "Specializes in the finest in commercial fiction and nonfiction. We have a strong background in women's voices, including mysteries, romance, women's fiction, thrillers, suspense. Historical fiction is one of Irene's particular passions and Miriam is fanatical about modern urban fantasies. In nonfiction, Irene is looking for topics on narrative history, social issues and trends, education, Judaica, Francophilia, Anglophilia, other cultures, animals, food, crafts, and memoir." Barbara is looking for commercial thrillers with strong female protagonists; Miriam is looking for urban fantasy and edgy sci-fi/young adult.

How to Contact Query. Submit synopsis, first 10 pages. E-mail queries only! See the website submission page. No e-mail attachments. Responds in 2 months to queries.

Recent Sales *The Ark*, by Boyd Morrison; *Isolation*, by C.J. Lyons; *The Sleepwalkers*, by Paul Grossman; *Dead Man's Moon*, by Devon Monk; *Becoming Marie Antoinette*, by Juliet Grey; *What's Up Down There*, by Lissa Rankin; *Beg for Mercy*, by Toni Andrews; *The Devil Inside*, by Jenna Black.

Tips "We are receiving an unprecedented amount of e-mail queries. If you find that the mailbox is full, please try again in two weeks. E-mail queries to our personal addresses will not be answered. E-mails to our personal in-boes will be deleted."

Ⓝ ◪ DOUG GRAD LITERARY AGENCY, INC.

156 Prospect Park West, Brooklyn NY 11215. (718)788.6067. E-mail: doug.grad@dgliterary.com. Website: www.dgliterary.com. **Contact:** Doug Grad. Estab. 2008.

- Prior to being an agent, Doug Grad spent the last twenty-two years as an editor at four major publishing houses.

How to Contact Query by e-mail first at query@dgliterary.com. No sample material unless requested.

Recent Sales *Drink the Tea*, by Thomas Kaufman (St. Martin's); *15 Minutes: The Impossible Math of Nuclear War*, by L. Douglas Keeney (St. Martin's)

⊞ ☐ GRAHAM MAW CHRISTIE LITERARY AGENCY

19 Thornhill Crescent, London England N1 1BJ United Kingdom. (44)(207)812-9937. E-mail: info@grahammawchristie.com. Website: www.grahammawchristie.com. Represents 40 clients. 30% of clients are new/unpublished writers. Currently handles: nonfiction books 100%.

- Prior to opening her agency, Ms. Graham Maw was a publishing director at HarperCollins and worked in rights, publicity and editorial. She has ghostwritten several nonfiction books, which gives her an insider's knowledge of both the publishing industry and the pleasures and pitfalls of authorships. Ms. Christie has a background in advertising and journalism.

Member Agents Jane Graham Maw; Jennifer Christie.

Represents Nonfiction books. **Considers these nonfiction areas:** autobiography, biography, child guidance, cooking, diet/nutrition, foods, health, how-to, medicine, memoirs, parenting, popular culture, psychology, self-help.

- ⟀ "We aim to make the publishing process easier and smoother for authors. We work hard to ensure that publishing proposals are watertight before submission. We aim for collaborative relationships with publishers so that we provide the right books to the right editor at the right time. We represent ghostwriters as well as authors." Actively seeking work from UK writers only. Does not want to receive fiction, poetry, plays or e-mail submissions.

How to Contact Query with synopsis, chapter outline, bio, SASE. Responds in 2 weeks to queries. Obtains most new clients through recommendations from others.

Terms Agent receives 15% commission on domestic sales. Agent receives 20% commission on foreign sales. Offers written contract; 30-day notice must be given to terminate contract.

Writers Conferences London Book Fair, Frankfurt Book Fair.

Tips "UK clients only!"

◐ ASHLEY GRAYSON LITERARY AGENCY

1342 W. 18th St., San Pedro CA 90732. Fax: (310)514-1148. E-mail: graysonagent@earthlink.net. Website: www.graysonagency.com/blog. Estab. 1976. Member of AAR. Represents 100 clients. 5% of clients are new/unpublished writers. Currently handles: nonfiction books 20%, novels 50%, juvenile books 30%.

Member Agents Ashley Grayson (fantasy, mystery, thrillers, young adult); Carolyn Grayson (chick lit, mystery, children's, nonfiction, women's fiction, romance, thrillers); Denise Dumars (mind/body/spirit, women's fiction, dark fantasy/horror); Lois Winston (women's fiction, chick lit, mystery).

Represents Nonfiction books, novels. **Considers these nonfiction areas:** business, computers, economics, history, investigative, popular culture, science, self-help, sports, technology, true crime, mind/body/spirit, lifestyle. **Considers these fiction areas:** fantasy, juvenile, multicultural, mystery, romance, science fiction, suspense, women's, young adult, chick lit.

- ⟀ "We prefer to work with published (traditional print), established authors. We will give first consideration to authors who come recommended to us by our clients or other publishing professionals. We accept a very small number of new, previously unpublished authors."

How to Contact As of early 2008, the agency was only open to fiction authors with publishing credits (no self-published). For nonfiction, only writers with great platforms will be considered.

Terms Agent receives 15% commission on domestic sales. Agent receives 20% commission on foreign sales.

◐ SANFORD J. GREENBURGER ASSOCIATES, INC.

55 Fifth Ave., New York NY 10003. (212)206-5600. Fax: (212)463-8718. E-mail: queryHL@sjga.com. Website: www.greenburger.com. Member of AAR. Represents 500 clients.

Member Agents Heide Lange; Faith Hamlin; Dan Mandel; Matthew Bialer; Courtney Miller-Callihan, Michael Harriot, Brenda Bowen (authors and illustrators of children's books for all ages as well as graphic novelists); Lisa Gallagher.

Represents Nonfiction books and novels. **Considers these nonfiction areas:** Americana, animals, anthropology, archeology, architecture, art, biography, business, computers, cooking, crafts, current affairs, decorating, diet/nutrition, design, education, environment, ethnic, film, foods, gardening, gay/lesbian, government, health, history, horticulture, how-to, humor, interior design, investigative, juvenile nonfiction, language, law, literature, medicine, memoirs, metaphysics, military, money, multicultural, music, New Age, philosophy, photography, popular culture, psychology, recreation, regional, science, sex, sociology, software, sports, theater, translation, travel, true crime, women's issues, women's studies, young adult, software. **Considers these fiction areas:** action, adventure, crime, detective, ethnic, family saga, feminist, gay, glitz, historical, humor, lesbian, literary, mainstream, mystery, police, psychic, regional, satire, sports, supernatural, suspense, thriller.

⚬ No romances or Westerns.

How to Contact Submit query, first 3 chapters, synopsis, brief bio, SASE. Accepts simultaneous submissions. Responds in 2 months to queries and mss. Responds to mss. Obtains most new clients through recommendations from others.

Terms Agent receives 15% commission on domestic sales. Agent receives 20% commission on foreign sales. Charges for photocopying and books for foreign and subsidiary rights submissions.

⚬ ⚪ THE GREENHOUSE LITERARY AGENCY

11308 Lapham Drive, Oakton VA 22124. E-mail: submissions@greenhouseliterary.com. Website: www.greenhouseliterary.com. **Contact:** Sarah Davies. Other memberships include SCBWI. Represents 20 clients. 100% of clients are new/unpublished writers. Currently handles: juvenile books 100%.

- Prior to becoming an agent, Ms. Davies was the publishing director of Macmillan Children's Books in London.

Represents Juvenile. **Considers these fiction areas:** juvenile, young adult.

⚬ "We exclusively represent authors writing fiction for children and teens. The agency has offices in both the USA and UK, and Sarah Davies (who is British) personally represents authors to both markets. The agency's commission structure reflects this—taking 15% for sales to both US and UK, thus treating both as 'domestic' market." All genres of children's and YA fiction—ages 5+ . Does not want to receive nonfiction, poetry, picture books (text or illustration) or work aimed at adults.

How to Contact E-queries only as per guidelines given on website. Query should contain one-paragraph synopsis, one-paragraph bio, up to 5 sample pages pasted into e-mail. Replies to all submissions mostly within 2 weeks, but leave 6 weeks before chasing for response. Responds in 6-8 weeks to requested full manuscripts. Responds in 6 week to queries. Obtains most new clients through recommendations from others, solicitations, conferences.

Terms Agent receives 15% commission on domestic sales. Agent receives 25% commission on foreign sales. Offers written contract. This agency charges very occasionally for copies for submission to film agents or foreign publishers.

Writers Conferences Bologna Children's Book Fair, SCBWI conferences, BookExpo America.

Tips "Before submitting material, authors should read the Greenhouse's 'Top 10 Tips for Authors of Children's Fiction,' which can be found on our website."

⚬ KATHRYN GREEN LITERARY AGENCY, LLC

250 West 57th St., Suite 2302, New York NY 10107. (212)245-2445. Fax: (212)245-2040. E-mail: query@kgreenagency.com. **Contact:** Kathy Green. Other memberships include Women's Media Group. Represents approximately 20 clients. 50% of clients are new/unpublished writers. Currently handles: nonfiction books 50%, novels 25%, juvenile books 25%.

- Prior to becoming an agent, Ms. Green was a book and magazine editor.

Represents Nonfiction books, novels, short story collections, juvenile (middle grade and young adult only). **Considers these nonfiction areas:** autobiography, biography, business, child guidance, cooking, current affairs, diet/nutrition, economics, education, foods, history, how-to, humor, interior design, investigative, juvenile nonfiction, memoirs, parenting, popular culture, psychology, satire, self-help, sports, true crime, women's issues, women's studies, juvenile. **Considers these fiction areas:** crime, detective, family saga, historical, humor, juvenile, literary, mainstream, mystery, police, romance, satire, suspense, thriller, women's, young adult, women's.

⚬ Keeping the client list small means that writers receive my full attention throughout the process of getting their project published. Does not want to receive science fiction or fantasy.

How to Contact Query to query@kgreenagency.com. Send no samples unless requested. Accepts simultaneous submissions. Responds in 1-2 months to mss. Obtains most new clients through recommendations from others, solicitations, conferences.

Terms Agent receives 15% commission on domestic sales. Agent receives 20% commission on foreign sales. No written contract.

Recent Sales *The Touch Series,* by Laurie Stolarz; *How Do You Light a Fart,* by Bobby Mercer; *Creepiosity,* by David Bickel; *Hidden Facets: Diamonds For the Dead,* by Alan Orloff; *Don't Stalk the Admissions Officer,* by Risa Lewak; *Designed Fat Girl,* by Jennifer Joyner.
Tips "This agency offers a written agreement."

GREGORY & CO. AUTHORS' AGENTS

3 Barb Mews, Hammersmith, London W6 7PA England. (44)(207)610-4676. Fax: (44)(207)610-4686. E-mail: info@gregoryandcompany.co.uk. Website: www.gregoryandcompany.co.uk. **Contact:** Jane Gregory. Other memberships include AAA. Represents 60 clients. Currently handles: nonfiction books 10%, novels 90%.
Member Agents Stephanie Glencross.
Represents Nonfiction books, novels. **Considers these nonfiction areas:** autobiography, biography, history. **Considers these fiction areas:** crime, detective, historical, literary, mainstream, police, thriller, contemporary women's fiction.
➤ As a British agency, we do not generally take on American authors. Actively seeking well-written, accessible modern novels. Does not want to receive horror, science fiction, fantasy, mind/body/spirit, children's books, screenplays, plays, short stories or poetry.
How to Contact Query with SASE. Submit outline, first 10 pages by e-mail or post, publishing history, author bio. Send submissions to Mary Jones, submissions editor: maryjones@gregoryandcompany. co.uk. Accepts simultaneous submissions. Returns materials only with SASE. Obtains most new clients through recommendations from others, conferences.
Terms Agent receives 15% commission on domestic sales. Agent receives 20% commission on foreign sales. Offers written contract; 1-month notice must be given to terminate contract. Charges clients for photocopying of whole typescripts and copies of book for submissions.
Recent Sales *Ritual,* by Mo Hader (Bantam UK/Grove Atlantic); *A Darker Domain,* by Val McDermid (HarperCollins UK); *The Chameleon's Shadow,* by Minette Walters (Macmillan UK/ Knopf Inc); *Stratton's War,* by Laura Wilson (Orion UK/St. Martin's).
Writers Conferences CWA Conference; Bouchercon.

BLANCHE C. GREGORY, INC.

2 Tudor City Place, New York NY 10017. (212)697-0828. E-mail: info@bcgliteraryagency.com. Website: www.bcgliteraryagency.com. Member of AAR.
Represents Nonfiction books, novels, juvenile.
➤ This agency specializes in adult fiction and nonfiction; children's literature is also considered. Does not want to receive screenplays, stage plays or teleplays.
How to Contact Submit query, brief synopsis, bio, SASE. No e-mail queries. Obtains most new clients through recommendations from others.

GREYHAUS LITERARY

3021 20th St., PL SW, Puyallup WA 98373. E-mail: scott@greyhausagency.com. Website: www. greyhausagency.com. **Contact:** Scott Eagan. Member RWA.
Represents Fiction, novels. **Considers these fiction areas:** romance, women's, young adult.
➤ "We specialize in romance, women's fiction and YA romance." Actively seeking contemporary romance, and stories that are 75,000-100,000 words in length. Does not want sci-fi, fantasy, inspirational, literary, futuristic.
How to Contact Send a query, the first 3 pages and a synopsis of no more than 3 pages. There is also a submission form on this agency's website.

JILL GRINBERG LITERARY AGENCY

244 Fifth Ave., Floor 11, New York NY 10011. (212)620-5883. Fax: (212)627-4725. E-mail: info@ grinbergliterary.com. Website: www.grinbergliterary.com.
• Prior to her current position, Ms. Grinberg was at Anderson Grinberg Literary Management.
Member Agents Jill Grinberg; Kirsten Wolf (foreign rights).
Represents Nonfiction books, novels. **Considers these nonfiction areas:** autobiography, biography, business, current affairs, economics, government, health, history, law, medicine, multicultural, politics, psychology, science, spirituality, technology, travel, women's issues, women's studies.
Considers these fiction areas: commercial, fantasy, historical, juvenile, literary, romance, science fiction, women's, young adult, middle grade.

How to Contact Query with SASE. Send a proposal and author bio for nonfiction; send a query, synopsis and the first 50 pages for fiction.
Tips "We prefer submissions by mail."

⊘ JILL GROSJEAN LITERARY AGENCY

1390 Millstone Road, Sag Harbor NY 11963-2214. (631)725-7419. Fax: (631)725-8632. E-mail: jill6981@aol.com. **Contact:** Jill Grosjean. Represents 40 clients. 100% of clients are new/ unpublished writers. Currently handles: novels 100%.

- Prior to becoming an agent, Ms. Grosjean was manager of an independent bookstore. She has also worked in publishing and advertising.

Represents Novels. **Considers these fiction areas:** historical, literary, mainstream, mystery, regional, romance, suspense.

- ⊶ This agency offers some editorial assistance (i.e., line-by-line edits). Actively seeking literary novels and mysteries.

How to Contact E-mail queries only, no attachments. No cold calls, please. Accepts simultaneous submissions. Responds in 1 week to queries. Responds in 1 month to mss. Obtains most new clients through recommendations from others, solicitations.

Terms Agent receives 15% commission on domestic sales. Agent receives 20% commission on foreign sales. No written contract. Charges clients for photocopying and mailing expenses.

Recent Sales *Single Thread* and *Thread of Truth, A Thread So Thin, Snow Angels*, by Marie Bostwick (Kensington); *Greasing the Pinata* and *Jump*, by Tim Maleeny (Poison Pen Press); *Stealing the Dragon and Beating the Babushka, Midnight Ink, Emma and the Vampires*, by Wayne Josephson; *Shame and No Idea*, by Greg Garrett, David C. Cook; *The Reluctant Journey* of David Conners; *The Summer the Wind Whispered My Name*, by Don Locke; *Cyber Crime Fighters*, by Felicia Donovan and Kristyn Bernier.

Writers Conferences Book Passage's Mystery Writers' Conference; Agents and Editors Conference; Texas Writers' and Agents' Conference.

◖ LAURA GROSS LITERARY AGENCY

75 Clinton Pl., Newton MA 02459. (617)964-2977. Fax: (617)964-3023. E-mail: query@ lauragrossliteraryagency.com; lgross@lauragrossliteraryagency.com. **Contact:** Laura Gross. Represents 30 clients. Currently handles: nonfiction books 40%, novels 50%, scholarly books 10%.

- Prior to becoming an agent, Ms. Gross was an editor.

Represents Nonfiction books, novels. **Considers these nonfiction areas:** autobiography, biography, child guidance, cultural interests, current affairs, ethnic, government, health, history, law, medicine, memoirs, parenting, popular culture, politics, psychology, sports, women's issues, women's studies. **Considers these fiction areas:** historical, literary, mainstream, mystery, suspense, thriller.

How to Contact Query with SASE or by e-mail. Submit author bio. Responds in several days to queries. Obtains most new clients through recommendations from others.

Terms Agent receives 15% commission on domestic sales. Agent receives 20% commission on foreign sales. Offers written contract.

THE GUMA AGENCY

PO Box 503 Kensington, MD 20895, New York NY E-mail: matthew@gumaagency.com. **Contact:** Matthew Guma.

Represents Considers these nonfiction areas: Autobiography/Biography, Business/Economics, Celebrity, Child Guidance/Parenting, Health/Fitness, Narrative, Relationships/Dating, Religious/ Inspirational, Science, Spirituality.

How to Contact Accepts e-mail queries.

◷ HALSTON FREEMAN LITERARY AGENCY, INC.

140 Broadway, 46th Floor, New York NY 10005. E-mail: queryhalstonfreemanliterary@hotmail. com. **Contact:** Molly Freeman, Betty Halston. Currently handles: nonfiction books 65%, novels 35%.

- Prior to becoming an agent, Ms. Halston was a marketing and promotion director for a local cable affiliate; Ms. Freeman was a television film editor and ad agency copywriter.

Member Agents Molly Freeman, Betty Halston.

Represents Nonfiction books, novels. **Considers these nonfiction areas:** autobiography, biography, business, child guidance, cultural interests, current affairs, economics, ethnic, gay/lesbian, government, health, history, horticulture, how-to, humor, investigative, law, medicine, memoirs, metaphysics, New Age, parenting, politics, psychology, satire, self-help, true crime, women's issues, women's studies. **Considers these fiction areas:** action, adventure, crime, detective, ethnic, feminist, frontier, historical, horror, humor, literary, mainstream, mystery, police, romance, satire, science fiction, suspense, thriller, westerns, women's.

☙ "We are a hands-on agency specializing in quality nonfiction and fiction. As a new agency, it is imperative that we develop relationships with good writers who are smart, hardworking and understand what's required of them to promote their books." Does not want to receive children's books, textbooks or poetry. Send no e-mail attachments.

How to Contact Query with SASE. For nonfiction, include sample chapters, synopsis, platform, bio and competitive titles. For fiction, include synopsis, bio and three sample chapters. No e-mail attachments. Accepts simultaneous submissions. Responds in 2-6 weeks to queries. Responds in 1-2 months to mss. Obtains most new clients through recommendations from others, solicitations, conferences.

Terms Agent receives 15% commission on domestic sales. Agent receives 20% commission on foreign sales. This agency charges clients for copying and postage directly related to the project.

◉ HALYARD LITERARY AGENCY

Chicago IL E-mail: submissions@halyardagency.com. Website: www.halyardagency.com. **Contact:** Alaina Grayson.

Member Agents Alaina Grayson.

Represents Nonfiction books, novels. **Considers these nonfiction areas:** autobiography, biography, history, science, technology. **Considers these fiction areas:** fantasy, historical, juvenile, science fiction, young adult, general, paranormal.

☙ Based out of Chicago, Halyard Literary Agency is a new agency on the lookout for authors who have the same passion for innovation that we do. Halyard is small, but provides assistance through every stage of book production. We're dedicated to building relationships with our authors, not just for one book or one year, but throughout their publishing life.

How to Contact *Closed to all submissions currently.* Query with SASE. E-mail queries only to submissions@halyardagency.com. Send requested materials as e-mail attachments only if requested from query.

THE MITCHELL J. HAMILBURG AGENCY

149 S. Barrington Ave., #732, Los Angeles CA 90049. (310)471-4024. Fax: (310)471-9588. **Contact:** Michael Hamilburg. Estab. 1937. Signatory of WGA. Represents 70 clients. Currently handles: nonfiction books 70%, novels 30%.

Represents Nonfiction books, novels. **Considers these nonfiction areas:** anthropology, biography, business, child, cooking, current affairs, education, government, health, history, memoirs, military, money, psychology, recreation, regional, self-help, sex, sociology, spirituality, sports, travel, womens, creative nonfiction; romance; architecture; inspirational; true crime. **Considers these fiction areas:** glitz, New Age, adventure, experimental, feminist, humor, military, mystery, occult, regional, religious, romance, sports, thriller, crime; mainstream; psychic.

How to Contact Query with outline, 2 sample chapters, SASE. Responds in 1 month to mss. Obtains most new clients through recommendations from others, conferences, personal search.

Terms Agent receives 10-15% commission on domestic sales.

◉ THE JOY HARRIS LITERARY AGENCY, INC.

156 Fifth Ave., Suite 617, New York NY 10010. (212)924-6269. Fax: (212)924-6609. Website: joyharrisliterary.com. **Contact:** Joy Harris. Member of AAR. Represents more than 100 clients. Currently handles: nonfiction books 50%, novels 50%.

Represents Nonfiction books, novels, and young adult. **Considers these fiction areas:** ethnic, experimental, family saga, feminist, gay, glitz, hi-lo, historical, humor, lesbian, literary, mainstream, multicultural, multimedia, mystery, regional, satire, short story collections, spiritual, suspense, translation, women's, young adult.

☙ No screenplays.

Literary Agents

How to Contact Visit our website for guidelines. Query with sample chapter, outline/proposal, SASE. Accepts simultaneous submissions. Responds in 2 months to queries. Obtains most new clients through recommendations from clients and editors.

Terms Agent receives 15% commission on domestic sales. Agent receives 20% commission on foreign sales. Charges clients for some office expenses.

⬤ HARTLINE LITERARY AGENCY

123 Queenston Dr., Pittsburgh PA 15235-5429. (412)829-2483. Fax: (412)829-2432. E-mail: joyce@ hartlineliterary.com. Website: www.hartlineliterary.com. **Contact:** Joyce A. Hart. Represents 40 clients. 20% of clients are new/unpublished writers. Currently handles: nonfiction books 40%, novels 60%.

Member Agents Joyce A. Hart, principal agent; Terry Burns; Tamela Hancock Murray; Diana Flegal.

Represents Nonfiction books, novels. **Considers these nonfiction areas:** business, child guidance, cooking, diet/nutrition, economics, foods, inspirational, money, parenting, religious, self-help, women's issues, women's studies. **Considers these fiction areas:** action, adventure, contemporary issues, family saga, historical, inspirational, literary, mystery, regional, religious, suspense, thriller, amateur sleuth, cozy, contemporary, gothic, historical, and regency romances.

> ⚲ This agency specializes in the Christian bookseller market. Actively seeking adult fiction, self-help, nutritional books, devotional, and business. Does not want to receive erotica, gay/lesbian, fantasy, horror, etc.

How to Contact Submit summary/outline, author bio, 3 sample chapters. Accepts simultaneous submissions. Responds in 2 months to queries. Responds in 3 months to mss. Obtains most new clients through recommendations from others.

Terms Agent receives 15% commission on domestic sales. Offers written contract.

Recent Sales *Aurora, An American Experience in Quilt, Community and Craft*, and *A Flickering Light*, by Jane Kirkpatrick (Waterbrook Multnomah); *Oprah Doesn't Know My Name*, by Jane Kirkpatric (Zondervan); *Paper Roses, Scattered Petals, and Summer Rains*, by Amanda Cabot (Revell Books); *Blood Ransom*, by Lisa Harris (Zondervan); *I Don't Want a Divorce*, by David Clark (Revell Books); *Love Finds You in Hope, Kansas*, by Pamela Griffin (Summerside Press); *Journey to the Well*, by Diana Wallis Taylor (Revell Books); *Paper Bag Christmas, The Nine Lessons*, by Kevin Milne (Center Street); *When Your Aging Parent Needs Care*, by Arrington & Atchley (Harvest House); *Katie at Sixteen*, by Kim Vogel Sawyer (Zondervan); *A Promise of Spring*, by Kim Vogel Sawyer (Bethany House); *The Big 5-OH!*, by Sandra Bricker (Abingdon Press); *A Silent Terror & A Silent Stalker*, by Lynette Eason (Steeple Hill); Extreme Devotion series, by Kathi Macias (New Hope Publishers); *On the Wings of the Storm*, by Tamira Barley (Whitaker House); *Tribute*, by Graham Garrison (Kregel Publications); *The Birth to Five Book*, by Brenda Nixon (Revell Books); *Fat to Skinny Fast and Easy*, by Doug Varrieur (Sterling Publishers).

▦ ✒ ANTONY HARWOOD LIMITED

103 Walton St., Oxford OX2 6EB England. +44 01865 559 615. Fax: +44 01865 310 660. E-mail: mail@antonyharwood.com. Website: www.antonyharwood.com. **Contact:** Antony Harwood, James Macdonald Lockhart. Estab. 2000. Represents 52 clients.

- Prior to starting this agency, Mr. Harwood and Mr. Lockhart worked at publishing houses and other literary agencies.

Member Agents Antony Harwood, James Macdonald Lockhart, Jo Williamson (children's).

Represents Nonfiction books, novels. **Considers these nonfiction areas:** Americana, animals, anthropology, archeology, architecture, art, autobiography, biography, business, child guidance, computers, cooking, current affairs, design, economics, education, environment, ethnic, film, gardening, gay/lesbian, government, health, history, horticulture, how-to, humor, language, memoirs, military, money, multicultural, music, parenting, philosophy, photography, popular culture, psychology, recreation, regional, science, self-help, sex, sociology, software, spirituality, sports, technology, translation, travel, true crime, war, women's issues, women's studies. **Considers these fiction areas:** action, adventure, cartoon, comic books, confession, crime, detective, erotica, ethnic, experimental, family saga, fantasy, feminist, frontier, gay, hi-lo, historical, horror, humor, lesbian, literary, mainstream, military, multicultural, multimedia, mystery, occult, picture books, plays, police, regional, religious, romance, satire, science fiction, spiritual, sports, suspense, thriller, translation, war, westerns, young adult, gothic.

⚓ "We accept every genre of fiction and nonfiction except for children's fiction for readers ages 10 and younger." No poetry or screenplays.

How to Contact Submit outline, 2-3 sample chapters via e-mail in a Word or RTF format or postal mail (include SASE or IRC). Responds in 2 months to queries.

Terms Agent receives 15% commission on domestic sales. Agent receives 20% commission on foreign sales.

🖲 JOHN HAWKINS & ASSOCIATES, INC.

71 W. 23rd St., Suite 1600, New York NY 10010. (212)807-7040. Fax: (212)807-9555. E-mail: jha@jhalit.com. Website: www.jhalit.com. **Contact:** Moses Cardona (moses@jhalit.com). Member of AAR. Represents over 100 clients. 5-10% of clients are new/unpublished writers. Currently handles: nonfiction books 40%, novels 40%, juvenile books 20%.

Member Agents Moses Cardona; Anne Hawkins (ahawkins@jhalit.com); Warren Frazier (frazier@jhalit.com); William Reiss (reiss@jhalit.com).

Represents Nonfiction books, novels, young adult. **Considers these nonfiction areas:** agriculture, Americana, anthropology, archeology, architecture, art, autobiography, biography, business, cultural interests, current affairs, design, economics, education, ethnic, film, gardening, gay/lesbian, government, health, history, horticulture, how-to, investigative, language, law, medicine, memoirs, money, multicultural, music, philosophy, popular culture, politics, psychology, recreation, science, self-help, sex, sociology, software, theater, travel, true crime, young adult, music, creative nonfiction. **Considers these fiction areas:** action, adventure, crime, detective, ethnic, experimental, family saga, feminist, frontier, gay, glitz, hi-lo, historical, inspirational, lesbian, literary, mainstream, military, multicultural, multimedia, mystery, police, psychic, religious, short story collections, sports, supernatural, suspense, thriller, translation, war, westerns, women's, young adult.

How to Contact Submit query, proposal package, outline, SASE. Accepts simultaneous submissions. Responds in 1 month to queries. Obtains most new clients through recommendations from others.

Terms Agent receives 15% commission on domestic sales. Agent receives 20% commission on foreign sales. Charges clients for photocopying.

Recent Sales *Celebration of Shoes*, by Eileen Spinelli; *Chaos*, by Martin Gross; *The Informationist*, by Taylor Stevens; *The Line*, by Olga Grushin

🖲 HEACOCK HILL LITERARY AGENCY, INC.

West Coast Office, 1020 Hollywood Way #439, Burbank CA 91505. (505)585-0111. E-mail: agent@heacockhill.com. Website: www.heacockhill.com. **Contact:** Catt LeBaigue. Member of AAR. Other memberships include SCBWI.

- Prior to becoming an agent, Ms. LeBaigue spent 18 years with Sony Pictures and Warner Bros.

Member Agents Tom Dark (adult fiction, nonfiction); Catt LeBaigue (juvenile fiction, adult nonfiction including arts, crafts, anthropolgy, astronomy, nature studies, ecology, body/mind/spirit, humanities, self-help).

Represents Nonfiction, fiction. **Considers these nonfiction areas:** hiking.

How to Contact E-mail queries only. No unsolicited manuscripts. No e-mail attachments. Obtains most new clients through recommendations from others, solicitations.

Terms Offers written contract.

Tips "Write an informative original e-query expressing your book idea, your qualifications, and short excerpts of the work. No unfinished work, please."

🖲 HELEN HELLER AGENCY INC.

253 Eglinton Ave W., Suite 202, Toronto Ontario M4R 1B1 Canada. (416)489-0396. E-mail: info@helenhelleragency.com. Website: www.helenhelleragency.com. **Contact:** Helen Heller. Represents 30+ clients.

- Prior to her current position, Ms. Heller worked for Cassell & Co. (England), was an editor for Harlequin Books, a senior editor for Avon Books, and editor-in-chief for Fitzhenry & Whiteside.

Member Agents Helen Heller, helen@helenhelleragency.com; Daphne Hart, daphne.hart@sympatico.ca; Sarah Heller, sarah@helenhelleragency.com.

Represents Nonfiction books, novels.

⚬ Actively seeking adult fiction and nonfiction (excluding children's literature, screenplays or genre fiction). Does not want to receive screenplays, poetry, or young children's picture books.

How to Contact Query with SASE. Submit synopsis, publishing history, author bio. Responds in 6 weeks. Obtains most new clients through recommendations from others, solicitations.

Recent Sales *Break on Through*, by Jill Murray (Doubleday Canada); *Womankind: Faces of Change Around the World*, by Donna Nebenzahl (Raincoast Books); *One Dead Indian: The Premier, The Police, and the Ipperwash Crisis*, by Peter Edwards (McClelland & Stewart); a full list of deals is available online.

Tips "Whether you are an author searching for an agent, or whether an agent has approached you, it is in your best interest to first find out who the agent represents, what publishing houses has that agent sold to recently and what foreign sales have been made. You should be able to go to the bookstore, or search online and find the books the agent refers to. Many authors acknowledge their agents in the front or back or their books."

⬤ RICHARD HENSHAW GROUP

22 West 23rd St., Fifth Floor, New York NY 10010. (212)414-1172. Fax: (212)414-1182. E-mail: submissions@henshaw.com. Website: www.rich.henshaw.com. **Contact:** Rich Henshaw. Member of AAR. Other memberships include SinC, MWA, HWA, SFWA, RWA. Represents 35 clients. 20% of clients are new/unpublished writers. Currently handles: nonfiction books 35%, novels 65%.

• Prior to opening his agency, Mr. Henshaw served as an agent with Richard Curtis Associates, Inc.

Represents Nonfiction books, novels. **Considers these nonfiction areas:** animals, autobiography, biography, business, child guidance, computers, cooking, current affairs, dance, diet/nutrition, economics, environment, foods, gay/lesbian, government, health, humor, investigative, law, metaphysics, military, money, music, New Age, parenting, popular culture, politics, psychology, science, self-help, sociology, sports, technology, true crime, women's issues, women's studies, electronic. **Considers these fiction areas:** action, adventure, crime, detective, ethnic, family saga, fantasy, glitz, historical, horror, humor, literary, mainstream, mystery, police, psychic, romance, satire, science fiction, sports, supernatural, suspense, thriller.

⚬ This agency specializes in thrillers, mysteries, science fiction, fantasy and horror.

How to Contact Query with SASE. Accepts multiple submissions. Responds in 3 weeks to queries. Responds in 6 weeks to mss. Obtains most new clients through recommendations from others, solicitations, conferences.

Terms Agent receives 15% commission on domestic sales. Agent receives 20% commission on foreign sales. No written contract. Charges clients for photocopying and book orders.

Recent Sales *A Night Too Dark* by Dana Stabenow; *The Silent Spirit* by Margaret Coel; *Diving Into the Wreck* series by Kristine Kathryn Rusch; *History of the World* series by Susan Wise Bauer; *Wicked Intentions* series by Elizabeth Hoyt.

Tips "While we do not have any reason to believe that our submission guidelines will change in the near future, writers can find up-to-date submission policy information on our website. Always include a SASE with correct return postage."

Ⓝ ⬤ Herman Agency

350 Central Park West, New York NY 10025. (212)749-4907. E-mail: Ronnie@HermanAgencyInc.com. Website: www.hermanagencyinc.com. Estab. 1999. Currently handles: books for young readers.

Member Agents Ronnie Ann Herman, Jill Corcoran.

Represents Children's books. **Considers these fiction areas:** picture books, middle grade and young adult, fiction and nonfiction for all ages.

How to Contact Submit via e-mail to one of the agents listed above. See website for specific agents' specialties.

⬤ THE JEFF HERMAN AGENCY, LLC

P.O. Box 1522, Stockbridge MA 01262. (413)298-0077. Fax: (413)298-8188. E-mail: jeff@jeffherman.com. Website: www.jeffherman.com. **Contact:** Jeffrey H. Herman. Represents 100 clients. 10% of clients are new/unpublished writers. Currently handles: nonfiction books 85%, scholarly books 5%, textbooks 5%.

- Prior to opening his agency, Mr. Herman served as a public relations executive.

Member Agents Deborah Levine, vice president (nonfiction book doctor); Jeff Herman.

Represents Nonfiction books. **Considers these nonfiction areas:** business, economics, government, health, history, how-to, law, medicine, politics, psychology, self-help, spirituality, technology, popular reference.

⌐ This agency specializes in adult nonfiction.

How to Contact Query with SASE. Accepts simultaneous submissions.

Terms Agent receives 15% commission on domestic sales. Offers written contract. Charges clients for copying and postage.

Recent Sales Sold 35 titles in the last year. This agency prefers not to share information on specific sales.

⦾ HIDDEN VALUE GROUP

1240 E. Ontario Ave., Ste. 102-148, Corona CA 92881. (951)549-8891. Fax: (951)549-8891. E-mail: bookquery@hiddenvaluegroup.com. Website: www.hiddenvaluegroup.com. **Contact:** Nancy Jernigan. Represents 55 clients. 10% of clients are new/unpublished writers.

Member Agents Jeff Jernigan, jjernigan@hiddenvaluegroup.com (men's nonfiction, fiction, Bible studies/curriculum, marriage and family); Nancy Jernigan, njernigan@hiddenvaluegroup.com (nonfiction, women's issues, inspiration, marriage and family, fiction).

Represents Nonfiction books and adult fiction. **Considers these nonfiction areas:** autobiography, biography, business, child guidance, economics, history, how-to, inspirational, juvenile nonfiction, language, literature, memoirs, money, parenting, psychology, religious, self-help, women's issues, women's studies. **Considers these fiction areas:** action, adventure, crime, detective, fantasy, frontier, inspirational, literary, police, religious, thriller, westerns, women's.

⌐ "The Hidden Value Group specializes in helping authors throughout their publishing career. We believe that every author has a special message to be heard and we specialize in getting that message out." Actively seeking established fiction authors, and authors who are focusing on women's issues. Does not want to receive poetry or short stories.

How to Contact Query with SASE. Submit synopsis, 2 sample chapters, author bio, and marketing and speaking summary. Accepts queries to bookquery@hiddenvaluegroup.com. No fax queries. Accepts simultaneous submissions. Responds in 1 month to queries. Responds in 1 month to mss. Obtains most new clients through recommendations from others, solicitations.

Terms Agent receives 15% commission on domestic sales. Agent receives 15% commission on foreign sales. Offers written contract.

Writers Conferences Glorieta Christian Writers' Conference; CLASS Publishing Conference.

⦿ JULIE A. HILL AND ASSOC, LLC

1155 Camino Del Mar, #530, Del Mar CA 92014. (858)259-2595. Fax: (858)259-2777. **Contact:** Julie Hill. Represents 50 clients. 20% of clients are new/unpublished writers. Currently handles: nonfiction books 90%, story collections 5%, other 5% books that accompany films.

Member Agents Julie Hill, agent/publicist; Anette Farrell, agent.

Represents Nonfiction books. **Considers these nonfiction areas:** biography, cooking, ethnic, health, history, how-to, language, memoirs, music, New Age, popular culture, psychology, religious, self-help, women's issues.

⌐ "Check your ego at the door. If we love your book, we mean it. If we are so-so, we also mean that. If we cannot place it, we tell you ASAP." Currently interested in finding memoir from wives and adult children of drug lords, known criminals, and those in polygamist marriages. Actively seeking travel, health, and media tie-ins. Does not want to receive horror, juvenile, sci-fi, thrillers or autobiographies of any kind.

How to Contact Query with SASE. Submit outline/proposal, SASE. Send all submissions via snail mail. Never send a complete ms unless requested. Accepts simultaneous submissions. Responds in 4-6 weeks to queries. Obtains most new clients through recommendations from others, solicitations, conferences.

Recent Sales TV: *Cracking Up*, from the book *The Happy Neurotic*, by David Granirer, to GRBTV. Travel: multiple titles to Frommers (Wiley) for kids travel and theme parks guides, by Laura Lea Miller, Barnes and Noble travel bestsellers. Falcon (Globe Pequot) hiking guides: Best Easy Day Hikes to Long Island, and others by Susan Finch. Insiders Guides, Off the Beaten Path, Best Day

Trips to multiple US cities by multiple authors, including New York City, Chicago, Seattle, Houston, and many more.

◪ FREDERICK HILL BONNIE NADELL, INC.

8899 Beverly Blvd., Suite 805, Los Angeles CA 90048. (310)860-9605. Fax: (310)860-9672. Represents 100 clients.

Member Agents Bonnie Nadell; Elise Proulx, associate.

Represents Nonfiction books, novels. **Considers these nonfiction areas:** biography, current affairs, environment, government, health, history, language, literature, medicine, popular culture, politics, science, technology, biography; government/politics, narrative. **Considers these fiction areas:** literary, mainstream.

How to Contact Query with SASE. Keep your query to one page. Send via snail mail. Do not send the same query to multiple locations. Accepts simultaneous submissions.

Terms Agent receives 15% commission on domestic sales. Agent receives 20% commission on foreign sales. Agent receives 15% commission on film sales. Charges clients for photocopying and foreign mailings.

Recent Sales *Living the Sweet Life in Paris* by David Lebovitz (memoir); *Next Stop, Reloville: Inside America's New Rootless Professional Class* by Peter Kilborn.

◪ BARBARA HOGENSON AGENCY

165 West End Ave., Suite 19-C, New York NY 10023. (212)874-8084. Fax: (212)362-3011. E-mail: bhogenson@aol.com. **Contact:** Barbara Hogenson, Nicole Verity. Member of AAR.

Represents **Considers these fiction areas:** mystery.

How to Contact Query with SASE. Obtains most new clients through recommendations from other clients.

HOPKINS LITERARY ASSOCIATES

2117 Buffalo Rd., Suite 327, Rochester NY 14624-1507. (585)352-6268. **Contact:** Pam Hopkins. Member of AAR. Other memberships include RWA. Represents 30 clients. 5% of clients are new/unpublished writers. Currently handles: novels 100%.

Represents Novels. **Considers these fiction areas:** mostly women's genre romance, historical, contemporary, category, women's.

    ⌐ This agency specializes in women's fiction, particularly historical, contemporary, and category romance, as well as mainstream work.

How to Contact Regular mail with synopsis, 3 sample chapters, SASE. Accepts simultaneous submissions. Responds in 2 weeks to queries. Responds in 1 month to mss. Obtains most new clients through recommendations from others, solicitations, conferences.

Terms Agent receives 15% commission on domestic sales. Agent receives 20% commission on foreign sales. No written contract.

Recent Sales Sold 50 titles in the last year. *The Wilting Bloom Series*, by Madeline Hunter (Berkley); *The Dead Travel Fast*, by Deanna Raybourn; *Baggage Claim*, by Tanya Michna (NAL).

Writers Conferences RWA National Conference.

◪ HORNFISCHER LITERARY MANAGEMENT

P.O. Box 50544, Austin TX 78763. E-mail: queries@hornfischerlit.com. Website: www.hornfischerlit.com. **Contact:** James D. Hornfischer, president. Represents 45 clients. 10% of clients are new/unpublished writers. Currently handles: nonfiction books 100%.

    • Prior to opening his agency, Mr. Hornfischer held editorial positions at HarperCollins and McGraw-Hill. "My New York editorial background working with a variety of best-selling authors, such as Erma Bombeck, Jared Diamond, and Erica Jong, is useful in this regard. In 17 years as an agent, I've handled twelve *New York Times* nonfiction bestsellers, including three No. 1's."

Represents Nonfiction books. **Considers these nonfiction areas:** anthropology, archeology, autobiography, biography, business, child guidance, current affairs, economics, environment, government, health, history, how-to, humor, inspirational, investigative, law, medicine, memoirs, military, money, multicultural, parenting, popular culture, politics, psychology, religious, satire, science, self-help, sociology, sports, technology, true crime, war.

    ⌐ Actively seeking the best work of terrific writers. Does not want poetry or genre fiction.

How to Contact E-mail queries only. Submit proposal package, outline, 2 sample chapters. Accepts simultaneous submissions. Responds in 8 weeks to queries. Obtains most new clients through referrals from clients, reading books and magazines, pursuing ideas with New York editors.

Terms Agent receives 15% commission on domestic sales. Agent receives 25% commission on foreign sales. Offers written contract. Reasonable expenses deducted from proceeds after book is sold.

Recent Sales *The Next 100 Years*, by George Friedman (Doubleday); *Traitor to His Class,* by H. W. Brands (Doubleday); *Scent of the Missing,* by Susannah Charleson (Houghton Mifflin Harcourt); *Red November*, by W. Craig Reed (Morrow); and *Abigail Adams,* by Woody Holton (Free Press). See agency website for more sales information.

Tips "When you query agents and send out proposals, present yourself as someone who's in command of his material and comfortable in his own skin. Too many writers have a palpable sense of anxiety and insecurity. Take a deep breath and realize that—if you're good—someone in the publishing world will want you."

ANDREA HURST LITERARY MANAGEMENT

P.O. Box 19010, Sacramento CA 95819. E-mail: andrea@andreahurst.com. Website: www. andreahurst.com. **Contact:** Andrea Hurst, Judy Mikalonis, Amberly Finarelli, Gordon Warnock. Represents 100 + clients. 50% of clients are new/unpublished writers. Currently handles: nonfiction books 50%, novels 50%.

- Prior to becoming an agent, Ms. Hurst was an acquisitions editor as well as a freelance editor and published writer; Ms. Mikalonis was in marketing and branding consulting; Amberly Finarelli was a freelance editor, and Gordon Warnock was a freelance editor and marketing consultant.

Member Agents Andrea Hurst, andrea@andreahurst.com (adult fiction, women's fiction, nonfiction—including personal growth, health and wellness, science, business, parenting, relationships, women's issues, animals, spirituality, women's issues, metaphysical, psychological, cookbooks and self-help); Judy Mikalonis, judy@andreahurst.com (YA fiction, Christian fiction, Christian nonfiction); Amberly Finarelli, amberly@andreahurst.com (Nonfiction: humor/gift books, crafts, how-to, Relationships/advice, Self-help, psychology, Travel writing, Narrative nonfiction. Fiction: Commercial women's fiction, Comic and cozy mysteries, Literary fiction with a focus on the arts, culture, and/or history, Contemporary young adult); Represents Nonfiction books. Considers these nonfiction areas: crafts, interior, juvenile, New Age, animals, art, biography, business, child, cooking, education, health, humor, memoirs, military, money, music, business, child. Represents Nonfiction books, true crime, women's, gift books, nature, photography, popular culture, psychology, religion, science, self-help, sociology, true crime, women's, gift books. Gordon Warnock, gordon@andreahurst.com, PO Box 29380, Sacramento CA 95829. Gordon represents nonfiction: Memoir, political and current affairs, health, humor and cookbooks. Fiction: Commercial narrative with a literary edge. Writers Conferences: San Francisco Writers Conference, Willamette, American Independent Writers Conference, Wyoming Writers Conference, East of Eden, Algonkian Write and Pitch.

Represents Nonfiction books, novels, juvenile. **Considers these fiction areas:** inspirational, juvenile, literary, mainstream, psychic, religious, romance, supernatural, thriller, women's, young adult.

- "We work directly with our signed authors to help them polish their work and their platform for optimum marketability. Our staff is always available to answer phone calls and e-mails from our authors and we stay with a project until we have exhausted all publishing avenues." Actively seeking "well written nonfiction by authors with a strong platform; superbly crafted fiction with depth that touches the mind and heart and all of our listed subjects." Does not want to receive sci-fi, horror, Western, poetry or screenplays.

How to Contact E-mail query with SASE. Submit outline/proposal, synopsis, 2 sample chapters, author bio. Query a specific agent after reviewing website. Use (agentfirstname)@andreahurst. com. Accepts simultaneous submissions. Obtains most new clients through recommendations from others, solicitations, conferences.

Terms Agent receives 15% commission on domestic sales. Agent receives 20% commission on foreign sales. Offers written contract, binding for 6 to 12 months; 30-day notice must be given to terminate contract. This agency charges for postage. No reading fees. Visit our new blog. www.andreahurst.com.

Recent Sales *A Year of Miracles*, by Dr. Bernie Siegel, NWL; *Selling Your Crafts on Etsy* (St. Martins); *The Underground Detective Agency*, (Kensington); *Alaskan Seafood Cookbook*, (Globe Pequot); *Faith, Hope and Healing*, by Dr. Bernie Siegel (Rodale); *Code Name: Polar Ice*, by Jean-Michel Cousteau and James Fraioli (Gibbs Smith); *How to Host a Killer Party*, by Penny Warner (Berkley/Penguin).

Writers Conferences San Francisco Writers' Conference; Willamette Writers' Conference; PNWA; Whidbey Island Writers Conference.

Tips "Do your homework and submit a professional package. Get to know the agent you are submitting to by researching their website or meeting them at a conference. Perfect your craft: Write well and edit ruthlessly over and over again before submitting to an agent. Be realistic: Understand that publishing is a business and be prepared to prove why your book is marketable and how you will market it on your own. Be persistent!"

☑ INKWELL MANAGEMENT, LLC

521 Fifth Ave., 26th Floor, New York NY 10175. (212)922-3500. Fax: (212)922-0535. E-mail: info@inkwellmanagement.com. Website: www.inkwellmanagement.com. Represents 500 clients. Currently handles: nonfiction books 60%, novels 40%.

Member Agents Michael Carlisle; Richard Pine; Kimberly Witherspoon; George Lucas; Catherine Drayton; David Forrer; Susan Arellano; Alexis Hurley; Patricia Burke, Susan Hobson; Nat Jacks; Ethan Bassoff, Julie Schilder, Libby O'Neill; Elisa Petrini, Mairead Duffy.

Represents Nonfiction books, novels.

How to Contact Query with SASE or via e-mail to submissions@inkwellmanagement.com. Obtains most new clients through recommendations from others.

Terms Agent receives 15% commission on domestic sales. Agent receives 20% commission on foreign sales. Offers written contract.

Tips "We will not read manuscripts before receiving a letter of inquiry."

☑ INTERNATIONAL CREATIVE MANAGEMENT

825 Eighth Ave., New York NY 10019. (212)556-5600. Website: www.icmtalent.com. **Contact:** Literary Department. Member of AAR. Signatory of WGA.

Member Agents Lisa Bankoff, lbankoff@icmtalent.com (fiction interests include: literary fiction, family saga, historical fiction, offbeat/quirky; nonfiction interests include: history, biography, memoirs, narrative); Patrick Herold, pherold@icmtalent.com; Jennifer Joel, jjoel@icmtalent.com (fiction interests include: literary fiction, commercial fiction, historical fiction, thrillers/suspense; nonfiction interests include: history, sports, art, adventure/true story, pop culture); Esther Newberg; Sloan Harris; Amanda Binky Urban; Heather Schroder; Kristine Dahl; Andrea Barzvi, abarzvi@icmtalent.com (fiction interests include: chick lit, commercial fiction, women's fiction, thrillers/suspense; nonfiction interests include: sports, celebrity, self-help, dating/relationships, women's issues, pop culture, health and fitness); Tina Dubois Wexler, twexler@icmtalent.com (literary fiction, chick lit, young adult, middle grade, memoir, narrative nonfiction); Kate Lee, klee@icmtalent.com (mystery, commercial fiction, short stories, memoir, dating/relationships, pop culture, humor, journalism).

Represents Nonfiction books, novels.

☞ *We do not accept unsolicited submissions.*

How to Contact Query with SASE. Send queries via snail mail and include an SASE. Target a specific agent. Obtains most new clients through recommendations from others.

Terms Agent receives 15% commission on domestic sales. Agent receives 20% commission on foreign sales.

☑ INTERNATIONAL LITERARY ARTS

RR 5, Box 5391 A, Moscow PA 18444. E-mail: query@InternationalLiteraryArts.com. Website: www.InternationalLiteraryArts.com. **Contact:** Pamela K. Brodowsky.

- Prior to her current position, Ms. Fazio worked at Prentice Hall, Random House, M.E. Sharpe and Baker & Taylor; Ms. Brodowsky is a public speaker, as well as the author of *Secrets of Successful Query Letters* and *Bulletproof Book Proposals*.

Member Agents Pamela K. Brodowsky; Evelyn Fazio.

Represents Nonfiction books, movie. **Considers these nonfiction areas:** autobiography, biography, business, cooking, current affairs, diet/nutrition, economics, foods, health, history, humor, medicine, money, parenting, satire, science, self-help, sports, technology, travel, reference, lifestyle.

- ⊶ "ILA is a full service literary property agency representing authors in all areas of nonfiction across the creative spectrum. The agency is committed to the clients it represents and to the publishers with whom we match our talent. Our goal is to provide for our publishers talented authors with long-term career goals. Our mission is to create the continuance of the discovery of new talent and thriving careers for our represented clients." No longer accepting fiction.

How to Contact Query with SASE. For nonfiction, send an e-mail cover letter, contact info, proposal and sample chapter. Send no e-attachments. Responds in 4-6 weeks to queries.

Writers Conferences BookExpo America.

Tips "If you are inquiring about a nonfiction book project, please address your material to the attention of the Book Department. For screenplays, please address your material to the attention of the Motion Picture Department. Due to the enormous amount of submissions we receive, we will only respond to queries that we feel are a good fit for our agency."

◙ INTERNATIONAL TRANSACTIONS, INC.

P.O. Box 97, Gila NM 88038-0097. (845)373-9696. Fax: (845)373-7868. E-mail: info@intltrans.com. Website: www.intltrans.com. **Contact:** Peter Riva. Represents 40+ clients. 10% of clients are new/unpublished writers. Currently handles: nonfiction books 60%, novels 25%, story collections 5%, juvenile books 5%, scholarly books 5%.

Member Agents Peter Riva (nonfiction, fiction, illustrated; television and movie rights placement); Sandra Riva (fiction, juvenile, biographies); JoAnn Collins (fiction, women's fiction, medical fiction).

Represents Nonfiction books, novels, short story collections, juvenile, scholarly, illustrated books, anthologies. **Considers these nonfiction areas:** anthropology, archeology, architecture, art, autobiography, biography, computers, cooking, cultural interests, current affairs, diet/nutrition, design, ethnic, foods, gay/lesbian, government, health, history, humor, investigative, language, law, literature, medicine, memoirs, military, music, photography, politics, satire, science, sports, translation, true crime, war, women's issues, women's studies. **Considers these fiction areas:** action, adventure, crime, detective, erotica, experimental, family saga, feminist, gay, historical, humor, lesbian, literary, mainstream, mystery, police, satire, spiritual, sports, suspense, thriller, women's, young adult, chick lit.

- ⊶ "We specialize in large and small projects, helping qualified authors perfect material for publication." Actively seeking intelligent, well-written innovative material that breaks new ground. Does not want to receive material influenced by TV (too much dialogue); a rehash of previous successful novels' themes or poorly prepared material.

How to Contact First, e-query with an outline or synopsis. E-queries only! Responds in 3 weeks to queries. Responds in 5 weeks to mss. Obtains most new clients through recommendations from others, solicitations.

Terms Agent receives 15% (25% on illustrated books) commission on domestic sales. Agent receives 20% commission on foreign sales. Offers written contract; 120-day notice must be given to terminate contract.

Tips "'Book'—a published work of literature. That last word is the key. Not a string of words, not a book of (TV or film) 'scenes,' and never a stream of consciousness unfathomable by anyone outside of the writer's coterie. A writer should only begin to get 'interested in getting an agent' if the work is polished, literate and ready to be presented to a publishing house. Anything less is either asking for a quick rejection or is a thinly disguised plea for creative assistance—which is often given but never fiscally sound for the agents involved. Writers, even published authors, have difficulty in being objective about their own work. Friends and family are of no assistance in that process either. Writers should attempt to get their work read by the most unlikely and stern critic as part of the editing process, months before any agent is approached. In another matter: the economics of our job have changed as well. As the publishing world goes through the transition to e-books (much as the music industry went through the change to downloadable music)—a transition we expect to see at 95% within 10 years—everyone is nervous and wants "assured bestsellers" from which to eke out a living until they know what the new e-world will bring. This makes the sales rate and, especially, the advance royalty rates, plummet. Hence, our ability to take risks and take on new clients' work is increasingly perilous financially for us and all agents."

◙ JABBERWOCKY LITERARY AGENCY

P.O. Box 4558, Sunnyside NY 11104-0558. (718)392-5985. Website: www.awfulagent.com. **Contact:** Joshua Bilmes. Other memberships include SFWA. Represents 40 clients. 15% of clients are new/ unpublished writers. Currently handles: nonfiction books 15%, novels 75%, scholarly books 5%, other 5% other.

Member Agents Joshua Bilmes; Eddie Schneider.

Represents Novels. **Considers these nonfiction areas:** autobiography, biography, business, cooking, current affairs, diet/nutrition, economics, film, foods, gay/lesbian, government, health, history, humor, language, law, literature, medicine, money, popular culture, politics, satire, science, sociology, sports, theater, war, women's issues, women's studies, young adult. **Considers these fiction areas:** action, adventure, contemporary issues, crime, detective, ethnic, family saga, fantasy, gay, glitz, historical, horror, humor, lesbian, literary, mainstream, police, psychic, regional, satire, science fiction, sports, supernatural, thriller.

  ○━ This agency represents quite a lot of genre fiction and is actively seeking to increase the amount of nonfiction projects. It does not handle children's or picture books. Book-length material only—no poetry, articles, or short fiction.

How to Contact Query with SASE. Please check our website as there may be times during the year when we are not accepting queries. Query letter only; no manuscript material unless requested. Accepts simultaneous submissions. Responds in 3 weeks to queries. Obtains most new clients through solicitations, recommendation by current clients.

Terms Agent receives 15% commission on domestic sales. Agent receives 20% commission on foreign sales. Offers written contract, binding for 1 year. Charges clients for book purchases, photocopying, international book/ms mailing.

Recent Sales Sold 30 US and 100 foreign titles in the last year. *Dead in the Family*, by Charlaine Harris; *The Way of Kings*, by Brandon Sanderson; *The Desert Spear*, by Peter V. Brett; *Oath of Fealty*, by Elizabeth Moon. Other clients include Tanya Huff, Simon Green, Jack Campbell, Kat Richardson and Jon Sprunk.

Writers Conferences World SF Convention, September 2009; World Fantasy, October 2009; Boucheron, September 2009; full schedule of appearances can be found on our website.

Tips "In approaching with a query, the most important things to us are your credits and your biographical background to the extent it's relevant to your work. I (and most agents) will ignore the adjectives you may choose to describe your own work."

◙ JAMES PETER ASSOCIATES, INC.

P.O. Box 358, New Canaan CT 06840. (203)972-1070. E-mail: gene_brissie@msn.com. **Contact:** Gene Brissie. Represents 75 individual and 6 corporate clients. 15% of clients are new/unpublished writers. Currently handles: nonfiction books 100%.

Represents Nonfiction books. **Considers these nonfiction areas:** anthropology, archeology, architecture, art, biography, business, current affairs, dance, design, ethnic, film, gay/lesbian, government, health, history, language, literature, medicine, military, money, music, popular culture, psychology, self-help, theater, travel, war, women's issues, women's studies, memoirs (political, business).

  ○━ "We are especially interested in general, trade and reference nonfiction." Does not want to receive children's/young adult books, poetry or fiction.

How to Contact Submit proposal package, outline, SASE. Prefers to read materials exclusively. Responds in 1 month to queries. Obtains most new clients through recommendations from others, solicitations, contact with people who are doing interesting things.

Terms Agent receives 15% commission on domestic sales. Agent receives 20% commission on foreign sales. Offers written contract.

◙ JANKLOW & NESBIT ASSOCIATES

445 Park Ave., New York NY 10022. (212)421-1700. Fax: (212)980-3671. **Contact:** Morton L. Janklow, Lynn Nesbit.

o→ Does not want to receive unsolicited submissions or queries.

How to Contact Obtains most new clients through recommendations from others.

JCA LITERARY AGENCY

27 West 20th St., New York NY 10011. (212)727-0190. E-mail: tonyouthwaite@yahoo.com. Website: www.jcalit.com. **Contact:** Tony Outhwaithe. Tony's mailing address: Midpoint Trade Books, 27 West 20th Street, New York, NY 10011; Member of AAR. Represents 100 clients.

Member Agents Tony Outhwaite, Tom Cushman.

Represents Nonfiction books, novels. **Considers these nonfiction areas:** autobiography, biography, current affairs, film, government, history, investigative, language, law, literature, memoirs, popular culture, politics, sociology, sports, theater, translation, true crime. **Considers these fiction areas:** action, adventure, contemporary issues, crime, detective, family saga, historical, literary, mainstream, mystery, police, sports, suspense, thriller.

o→ Does not want to receive screenplays, poetry, children's books, science fiction/fantasy, textbooks, or genre romance.

How to Contact Query with SASE. No unsolicited mss. Materials not returned without proper envelope/postage.

Terms Agent receives 15% commission on domestic sales. Agent receives 20% commission on foreign sales. No written contract.

J DE S ASSOCIATES, INC.

9 Shagbark Road, Wilson Point, South Norwalk CT 06854. (203)838-7571. **Contact:** Jacques de Spoelberch. Represents 50 clients. Currently handles: nonfiction books 50%, novels 50%.

• Prior to opening his agency, Mr. de Spoelberch was an editor with Houghton Mifflin.

Represents Nonfiction books, novels. **Considers these nonfiction areas:** biography, business, cultural interests, current affairs, economics, ethnic, government, health, history, law, medicine, metaphysics, military, New Age, personal improvement, politics, self-help, sociology, sports, translation. **Considers these fiction areas:** crime, detective, frontier, historical, juvenile, literary, mainstream, mystery, New Age, police, suspense, westerns, young adult.

How to Contact Query with SASE. Responds in 2 months to queries. Obtains most new clients through recommendations from authors and other clients.

Terms agent receives 15% commission on domestic sales. Agent receives 20% commission on foreign sales. Charges clients for foreign postage and photocopying.

JET LITERARY ASSOCIATES

2570 Camino San Patricio, Santa Fe NM 87505. (505)474-9139. E-mail: etp@jetliterary.com. Website: www.jetliterary.com. **Contact:** Liz Trupin-Pulli. Represents 75 clients. 35% of clients are new/unpublished writers.

Member Agents Liz Trupin-Pulli (adult and YA fiction/nonfiction; romance, mysteries, parenting); Jim Trupin (adult fiction/nonfiction, military history, pop culture); Jessica Trupin, associate agent based in Seattle (adult fiction and nonfiction, children's and young adult, memoir, pop culture).

Represents Nonfiction books, novels, short story collections. **Considers these nonfiction areas:** autobiography, biography, business, child guidance, cultural interests, current affairs, economics, ethnic, gay/lesbian, government, humor, investigative, law, memoirs, military, parenting, popular culture, politics, satire, sports, true crime, war, women's issues, women's studies. **Considers these fiction areas:** action, adventure, crime, detective, erotica, ethnic, gay, glitz, historical, humor, lesbian, literary, mainstream, mystery, police, romance, suspense, thriller, women's, young adult.

o→ "JET was founded in New York in 1975, so we bring a wealth of knowledge and contacts, as well as quite a bit of expertise to our representation of writers." Actively seeking women's fiction, mysteries and narrative nonfiction. Does not want to receive sci-fi, fantasy, horror, poetry, children's or religious.

How to Contact An e-query is preferred; if sending by snail mail, include an SASE. Responds in 1 week to queries. Responds in 8 weeks to mss. Obtains most new clients through recommendations from others, solicitations, conferences.

Terms Agent receives 15% commission on domestic sales. Agent receives 10% commission on foreign sales. Offers written contract, binding for 3 years. This agency charges for reimbursement of mailing and any photocopying.

Recent Sales Sold 22 books in 2009 including several ghostwriting contracts. *Mom-In-Chief*, by Jamie Woolf (Wiley, 2009); *Dangerous Games*, by Charlotte Mede (Kensington, 2009); *So You Think You Can Spell!*, by David Grambs and Ellen Levine (Perigee, 2009); *Cut, Drop & Die*, by Joanna Campbell Slan (Midnight Ink, 2009).

Writers Conferences Women Writing the West; Southwest Writers Conference; Florida Writers Association Conference.

Tips Do not write 'cute' queries—stick to a straightforward message that includes the title and what your book is about, why you are suited to write this particular book, and what you have written in the past (if anything), along with a bit of a bio.

✉ CAREN JOHNSON LITERARY AGENCY

132 East 43rd St., No. 216, New York NY 10017. Fax: (718)228-8785. E-mail: caren@johnsonlitagency. com. Website: www.johnsonlitagency.com. **Contact:** Caren Johnson Estesen, Elana Roth. Represents 20 clients. 50% of clients are new/unpublished writers. Currently handles: nonfiction books 35%, juvenile books 35%, romance/women's fiction 30%.

- Prior to her current position, Ms. Johnson was with Firebrand Literary and the Peter Rubie Agency.

Member Agents Caren Johnson Estesen, Elana Roth.

Represents Nonfiction books, novels. **Considers these nonfiction areas:** history, popular culture, science, technology. **Considers these fiction areas:** detective, erotica, ethnic, romance, young adult, middle grade, women's fiction.

- ☞ Does not want to receive poetry, plays or screenplays/scripts. Elana Roth will consider picture books but is very selective of what she takes on.

How to Contact Query via e-mail only, "directing your query to the appropriate person; responds in 12 weeks to all materials sent. Include 4-5 sample pages withing the body of your e-mail when pitching us. Accepts simultaneous submissions. Responds in 4-6 weeks to queries. Responds in 6-8 weeks to mss. Obtains most new clients through recommendations from others.

Terms Agent receives 15% commission on domestic sales. Agent receives 20% commission on foreign sales. Offers written contract; 30-day notice must be given to terminate contract. This agency charges for postage and photocopying, though the author is consulted before any charges are incurred.

Recent Sales Please check out website for a complete client list.

Writers Conferences RWA National; BookExpo America; SCBWI.

LAWRENCE JORDAN LITERARY AGENCY

231 Lenox Ave., Suite One, New York NY 10027. (212)662-7871. Fax: (212)865-7171. E-mail: ljlagency@aol.com. **Contact:** Lawrence Jordan, president.

- Prior to opening his agency, Mr. Jordan served as an editor with Doubleday & Co.

Represents Nonfiction books, novels.

- ☞ This agency specializes in general adult fiction and nonfiction. Handles spiritual and religious books, mystery novels, action suspense, thrillers, biographies, autobiographies, and celebrity books. Does not want to receive poetry, movie scripts, stage plays, juvenile books, fantasy novels, or science fiction.

How to Contact Online submissions only. Please note that the agency takes on only a few new clients each year.

Terms Agent receives 15% commission on domestic sales. Agent receives 20% commission on foreign sales. Agent receives 20% commission on film sales. Charges for long-distance calls, photocopying, foreign submission costs, postage, cables, messengers.

JUDY BOALS, INC.

307 W. 38th Street, #812, New York NY 10018. 212-500-1424. Fax: 212-500-1426. E-mail: info@ judyboals.com. Website: www.judyboals.com/. **Contact:** Judy Boals.

✉ ◎ KELLER MEDIA INC.

23852 West Pacific Coast Hwy., Suite 701, Malibu CA 90265. (800)278-8706. E-mail: query@ KellerMedia.com. Website: www.KellerMedia.com. **Contact:** Megan Collins, associate agent. Other memberships include National Speakers Association. 25% of clients are new/unpublished writers. Currently handles: nonfiction books 100%.

- Prior to becoming an agent, Ms. Keller was an award-winning journalist and worked for PR Newswire and several newspapers.

Represents Nonfiction. **Considers these nonfiction areas:** business, current affairs, finance, health, history, nature, politics, psychology, science, self-help, sociology, spirituality, women's issues.

- ⌐ "We focus a great deal of attention on authors who want to also become paid professional speakers, and current speakers who want to become authors. All of our authors are highly credible experts, who have or want a significant platform in media, academia, politics, paid professional speaking, syndicated columns or regular appearances on radio/TV." Does not want (and absolutely will not respond to) fiction, scripts, teleplays, poetry, juvenile, anything Christian, picture books, illustrated books, first-person stories of mental or physical illness, wrongful incarceration, or abduction by aliens, books channeled by aliens, demons, or dead celebrities (I wish I was kidding!).

How to Contact Accepts e-mail queries only. Make sure to include your credentials and a good, short overview of the proposed book. Do not send attachments; just a simple, succinct e-mail. Accepts simultaneous submissions. Responds in 7 days. Obtains most new clients through referral.

Terms Agent receives 15% commission on domestic sales. Agent receives 20% commission on foreign sales.

Tips "Don't send a query to any agent unless you're certain they handle the type of book you're writing. 90% of all rejections happen because what you offered us doesn't fit our established, advertised, printed, touted and shouted guidelines. Be organized! Have your proposal in order before you query. Never make apologies for 'bad writing' or sloppy content—get it right before you waste your one shot with us. Have something new, different or interesting to say and be ready to dedicate your whole heart to marketing it."

◪ NATASHA KERN LITERARY AGENCY

P.O. Box 1069, White Salmon WA 98672. (509)493-3803. E-mail: agent@natashakern.com. Website: www.natashakern.com. **Contact:** Natasha Kern. Other memberships include RWA, MWA, SinC, The Authors Guild, and American Society of Journalists and Authors

- Prior to opening her agency, Ms. Kern worked as an editor and publicist for Simon & Schuster, Bantam, and Ballantine. This agency has sold more than 700 books.

Member Agents Natasha Kern.

Represents Considers these nonfiction areas: animals, child guidance, cultural interests, current affairs, environment, ethnic, gardening, health, inspirational, medicine, metaphysics, New Age, parenting, popular culture, psychology, religious, self-help, spirituality, women's issues, women's studies, investigative journalism. **Considers these fiction areas:** commercial, historical, inspirational, mainstream, multicultural, mystery, religious, romance, suspense, thriller, women's.

- ⌐ "This agency specializes in commercial fiction and nonfiction for adults. We are a full-service agency." Historical novels from any country or time period; contemporary fiction including novels with romance or suspense elements; and multi-cultural fiction. We are also seeking inspirational fiction in a broad range of genres including: suspense and mysteries, historicals, romance, and contemporary novels. Does not represent horror, true crime, erotica, children's books, short stories or novellas, poetry, screenplays, technical, photography or art/craft books, cookbooks, travel, or sports books.

How to Contact See submission instructions online. Send query to queries@natashakern.com. Please include the word QUERY in the subject line. "We do not accept queries by snail mail or phone." Accepts simultaneous submissions. Responds in 3 weeks to queries.

Terms Agent receives 15% commission on domestic sales. Agent receives 20% commission on foreign sales. Agent receives 15% commission on film sales.

Recent Sales Sold 43 titles in the last year. *China Dolls*, by Michelle Yu and Blossom Kan (St. Martin's); *Bastard Tongues*, by Derek Bickerton (Farrar Strauss); *Bone Rattler*, by Eliot Pattison; *Wicked Pleasure*, by Nina Bangs (Berkley); *Inviting God In*, by David Aaron (Shambhala); *Unlawful Contact*, by Pamela Clare (Berkley); *Dead End Dating*, by Kimberly Raye (Ballantine); *A Scent of Roses*, by Nikki Arana (Baker Book House); *The Sexiest Man Alive*, by Diana Holquist (Warner Books).

Writers Conferences RWA National Conference; MWA National Conference; ACFW Conference; and many regional conferences.

Tips "Your chances of being accepted for representation will be greatly enhanced by going to our website first. Our idea of a dream client is someone who participates in a mutually respectful business relationship, is clear about needs and goals, and communicates about career planning. If we know what you need and want, we can help you achieve it. A dream client has a storytelling gift, a commitment to a writing career, a desire to learn and grow, and a passion for excellence. We want clients who are expressing their own unique voice and truly have something of their own to communicate. This client understands that many people have to work together for a book to succeed and that everything in publishing takes far longer than one imagines. Trust and communication are truly essential."

LOUISE B. KETZ AGENCY

414 E. 78th St., Suite 1B, New York NY 10075. (212)249-0668. E-mail: ketzagency@aol.com. **Contact:** Louise B. Ketz. Represents 25 clients. 15% of clients are new/unpublished writers. Currently handles: nonfiction books 100%.

Represents Nonfiction books. **Considers these nonfiction areas:** business, current affairs, history, military, science, sports, economics.

- This agency specializes in science, history and reference.

How to Contact Query with SASE. Submit outline, 1 sample chapter, author bio (with qualifications for authorship of work). Responds in 6 weeks to mss. Obtains most new clients through recommendations from others, idea development.

Terms Agent receives 15% commission on domestic sales.

VIRGINIA KIDD AGENCY, INC.

538 E. Harford St., P.O. Box 278, Milford PA 18337. (570)296-6205. Fax: (570)296-7266. Website: www.vk-agency.com. Other memberships include SFWA, SFRA. Represents 80 clients.

Member Agents Christine Cohen.

Represents Novels. **Considers these fiction areas:** fantasy, historical, mainstream, mystery, science fiction, suspense, women's, speculative.

- This agency specializes in science fiction and fantasy.

How to Contact *This agency is not accepting unpublished authors at this time.* Query with SASE. Submit synopsis (1-3 pages), cover letter, first chapter, SASE. Snail mail queries only. Responds in 6 weeks to queries.

Terms Agent receives 15% commission on domestic sales. Agent receives 20-25% commission on foreign sales. Agent receives 20% commission on film sales. Offers written contract; 2-month notice must be given to terminate contract. Charges clients occasionally for extraordinary expenses.

Recent Sales *Sagramanda*, by Alan Dean Foster (Pyr); *Incredible Good Fortune*, by Ursula K. Le Guin (Shambhala); *The Wizard and Soldier of Sidon*, by Gene Wolfe (Tor); *Voices and Powers*, by Ursula K. Le Guin (Harcourt); *Galileo's Children*, by Gardner Dozois (Pyr); *The Light Years Beneath My Feet* and *Running From the Deity*, by Alan Dean Foster (Del Ray); *Chasing Fire*, by Michelle Welch. Other clients include Eleanor Arnason, Ted Chiang, Jack Skillingstead, Daryl Gregory, Patricia Briggs, and the estates for James Tiptree, Jr., Murray Leinster, E.E. "Doc" Smith, R.A. Lafferty.

Tips "If you have a completed novel that is of extraordinary quality, please send us a query."

KIRCHOFF/WOHLBERG, INC., AUTHORS' REPRESENTATION DIVISION

897 Boston Post Road, Madison CT 06443. (203)245-7308. Fax: (203)245-3218. E-mail: trade@kirchoffwohlberg.com. **Contact:** Ronald Zollshan. Member of AAR. Other memberships include SCBWI, AAP, Society of Illustrators, SPAR, Bookbuilders of Boston, New York Bookbinders' Guild, AIGA. 10% of clients are new/unpublished writers. Currently handles: nonfiction books 5%, novels 25%, other 5% young adult.

- Kirchoff/Wohlberg has been in business for over 60 years.
- This agency specializes in juvenile fiction and nonfiction through Young Adult.

How to Contact Submit by mail to address above. Include SASE. Accepts simultaneous submissions.

Terms Offers written contract, binding for at least 1 year. Agent receives standard commission, depending upon whether it is an author only, illustrator only, or an author/illustrator book.

HARVEY KLINGER, INC.

300 W. 55th St., Suite 11V, New York NY 10019. (212)581-7068. E-mail: queries@harveyklinger.com. Website: www.harveyklinger.com. **Contact:** Harvey Klinger. Member of AAR. Represents 100

clients. 25% of clients are new/unpublished writers. Currently handles: nonfiction books 50%, novels 50%.

Member Agents David Dunton (popular culture, music-related books, literary fiction, young adult, fiction, and memoirs); Sara Crowe (children's and young adult authors, adult fiction and nonfiction, foreign rights sales); Andrea Somberg (literary fiction, commercial fiction, romance, sci-fi/fantasy, mysteries/thrillers, young adult, middle grade, quality narrative nonfiction, popular culture, how-to, self-help, humor, interior design, cookbooks, health/fitness).

Represents Nonfiction books, novels. **Considers these nonfiction areas:** autobiography, biography, cooking, diet/nutrition, foods, health, investigative, medicine, psychology, science, self-help, spirituality, sports, technology, true crime, women's issues, women's studies. **Considers these fiction areas:** action, adventure, crime, detective, family saga, glitz, literary, mainstream, mystery, police, suspense, thriller.

⎰ This agency specializes in big, mainstream, contemporary fiction and nonfiction.

How to Contact Query with SASE. No phone or fax queries. Don't send unsolicited manuscripts or e-mail attachments. Responds in 2 months to queries and mss. Obtains most new clients through recommendations from others.

Terms Agent receives 15% commission on domestic sales. Agent receives 25% commission on foreign sales. Offers written contract. Charges for photocopying mss and overseas postage for mss.

Recent Sales *Woman of a Thousand Secrets*, by Barbara Wood; *I am Not a Serial Killer*, by Dan Wells; untitled memoir, by Bob Mould; *Children of the Mist*; by Paula Quinn; *Tutored*, by Allison Whittenberg; *Will You Take Me As I Am*, by Michelle Mercer. Other clients include: George Taber, Terry Kay, Scott Mebus, Jacqueline Kolosov, Jonathan Maberry, Tara Altebrando, Alex McAuley, Eva Nagorski, Greg Kot, Justine Musk, Alex McAuley, Nick Tasler, Ashley Kahn, Barbara De Angelis.

☑ KNEERIM & WILLIAMS AT FISH & RICHARDSON

90 Canal St., Boston MA 02114. (617)542-5070. Fax: (617)542-8906. Website: http://www.kwlit. com. **Contact:** John Taylor Williams. Also located in New York and Washington D.C. Estab. 1990. Represents 200 clients. 5% of clients are new/unpublished writers. Currently handles: nonfiction books 80%, novels 15%, movie scripts 5%.

- Prior to becoming an agent, Mr. Williams was a lawyer; Ms. Kneerim was a publisher and editor; Mr. Wasserman was an editor and journalist; Ms. Grosvenor was an editor.

Member Agents John Taylor "Ike" Williams (accepts queries); Jill Kneerim (not actively looking for clients); Steve Wasserman; Brettne Bloom (not currently accepting submissions); Deborah C. Grosvenor (not accepting submissions); Ike Williams; Leslie Kaufmann.

Represents Nonfiction books, novels. **Considers these nonfiction areas:** anthropology, archeology, autobiography, biography, business, child guidance, current affairs, economics, environment, government, health, history, inspirational, language, law, literature, medicine, memoirs, parenting, popular culture, politics, psychology, religious, science, sociology, sports, technology, women's issues, women's studies. **Considers these fiction areas:** historical, literary, mainstream.

⎰ "This agency specializes in narrative nonfiction, history, science, business, women's issues, commercial and literary fiction, film, and television. We have 5 agents and 4 scouts in Boston, New York, Washington DC and Santa Fe." Actively seeking distinguished authors, experts, professionals, intellectuals, and serious writers. Does not want to receive blanket multiple submissions, genre fiction or original screenplays.

How to Contact Submit query via e-mail only at: submissions@kwlit.com. No hard copies will be accepted. Submissions should contain a cover letter explaining your book and why you are qualified to write it, a two-page synopsis of the book, one sample chapter, and your c.v. or a history of your publications. Responds in 2 weeks to queries. Responds in 2 months to mss. Obtains most new clients through recommendations from others.

Recent Sales *Nuclear Terrorism, The Ultimate Preventable Catastrophe* by Graham Allison; *Thieves of Bagdad* by Matthew Bogdanos with William Patrick.

☑ LINDA KONNER LITERARY AGENCY

10 W. 15th St., Suite 1918, New York NY 10011-6829. (212)691-3419. E-mail: ldkonner@cs.com. Website: www.lindakonnerliteraryagency.com. **Contact:** Linda Konner. Member of AAR. Signatory

of WGA. Other memberships include ASJA. Represents 85 clients. 30-35% of clients are new/unpublished writers. Currently handles: nonfiction books 100%.

Represents Nonfiction books. **Considers these nonfiction areas:** diet/nutrition, gay/lesbian, health, medicine, money, parenting, popular culture, psychology, self-help, women's issues, biography (celebrity), African American and Latino issues, relationships.

   ○━ This agency specializes in health, self-help, and how-to books. Authors/co-authors must be top experts in their field with a substantial media platform.

How to Contact Query with SASE, synopsis, author bio, sufficient return postage. Prefers to read materials exclusively for 2 weeks. Accepts simultaneous submissions. Obtains most new clients through recommendations from others, occasional solicitation among established authors/journalists.

Terms Agent receives 15% commission on domestic sales. Agent receives 25% commission on foreign sales. Offers written contract. Charges one-time fee for domestic expenses; additional expenses may be incurred for foreign sales.

Recent Sales *Organize Your Mind, Organize Your Life*, by Paul Hammerness, PhD, Margaret Moore and John Hanc, with the editors of Harvard Health Publications; *Southern Plate: Cherished Recipes and Stories From My Grandparents*, by Christy Jordan (Harper Studio); *Second Acts: Finding a Passionate New Career*, by Kerry Hannon (Chronicle Books); *Who Do You Think You Are?: Tracing Your Family History*, a tie-in to the NBC tv series, by Megan Smolenyak (Viking).

Writers Conferences ASJA Writers Conference, Harvard Medical School's "Publishing Books, Memoirs, and Other Creative Nonfiction" Annual Conference.

◙ ELAINE KOSTER LITERARY AGENCY, LLC

55 Central Park W., Suite 6, New York NY 10023. (212)362-9488. Fax: (212)712-0164. **Contact:** Elaine Koster, Stephanie Lehmann, Ellen Twaddell. Estab. 1998. Member of AAR. Other memberships include MWA, Author's Guild, Women's Media Group. Represents 40 clients. 10% of clients are new/unpublished writers. Currently handles: nonfiction books 10%, novels 90%.

   • Prior to opening her agency, Ms. Koster was president and publisher of Dutton-NAL, part of the Penguin Group.

Represents Nonfiction books, novels. **Considers these nonfiction areas:** autobiography, biography, business, child guidance, cooking, current affairs, diet/nutrition, economics, environment, ethnic, foods, health, history, how-to, medicine, money, parenting, popular culture, psychology, self-help, spirituality, women's issues, women's studies. **Considers these fiction areas:** contemporary issues, crime, detective, ethnic, family saga, feminist, historical, literary, mainstream, mystery, police, regional, suspense, thriller, young adult, chick lit.

   ○━ This agency specializes in quality fiction and nonfiction. Does not want to receive juvenile, screenplays, or science fiction.

How to Contact Fiction: a query letter (hard copy only) which includes publishing credentials, 3 sample chapters, outline and a SASE. Nonfiction: query letter (hard copy only) with proposal and SASE. Prefers to read materials exclusively. Responds in 3 weeks to queries. Responds in 1 month to mss. Obtains most new clients through recommendations from others.

Terms Agent receives 15% commission on domestic sales. Bills back specific expenses incurred doing business for a client.

Recent Sales *The Lost and Forgotten Languages of Shanghai*, by Ruiyan Xu (St. Martin's Press);

Tips "We prefer exclusive submissions. Don't e-mail or fax submissions. Please include biographical information and publishing history."

BARBARA S. KOUTS, LITERARY AGENT

P.O. Box 560, Bellport NY 11713. (631)286-1278. Fax: (631) 286-1538. **Contact:** Barbara S. Kouts. Member of AAR. Represents 50 clients. 10% of clients are new/unpublished writers.

Represents Juvenile.

   ○━ This agency specializes in children's books.

How to Contact Query with SASE. Accepts simultaneous submissions. Responds in 1 week to queries. Responds in 2 months to mss. Obtains most new clients through recommendations from others, solicitations, conferences.

Terms Agent receives 10% commission on domestic sales. Agent receives 20% commission on foreign sales. This agency charges clients for photocopying.

Tips "Write, do not call. Be professional in your writing."

☑ KRAAS LITERARY AGENCY

E-mail: irenekraas@sbcglobal.net. Website: www.kraasliteraryagency.com. **Contact:** Irene Kraas. Represents 35 clients. 75% of clients are new/unpublished writers. Currently handles: novels 100%.

Member Agents Irene Kraas, principal.

Represents Novels. **Considers these fiction areas:** literary, thriller, young adult.

- ☛ This agency is interested in working with published writers, but that does not mean self-published writers. "Actively seeking psychological thrillers, medical thrillers, some literary fiction and young adult. With each of these areas, I want something new. No *Da Vinci Code* or *Harry Potter* ripoffs. I am especially not interested in storylines that include the Mafia or government. Not interested in personal stories of growth, stories about generation hangups and stories about drugs, incest, etc." Does not want to receive short stories, plays or poetry. This agency no longer represents adult fantasy or science fiction.

How to Contact Query and e-mail the first 10 pages of a completed ms. Requires exclusive read on mss. Accepts simultaneous submissions.

Terms Offers written contract.

Tips "I am interested in material—in any genre—that is truly, truly unique."

☑ BERT P. KRAGES

6665 SW Hampton St., Suite 200, Portland OR 97223. (503)597-2525. E-mail: krages@onemain. com. Website: www.krages.com. **Contact:** Bert Krages. Represents 10 clients. 80% of clients are new/unpublished writers. Currently handles: nonfiction books 95%, scholarly books 5%.

- Mr. Krages is also an attorney.

Represents Nonfiction books. **Considers these nonfiction areas:** agriculture, animals, anthropology, archeology, architecture, art, autobiography, biography, business, child guidance, computers, cultural interests, current affairs, design, economics, education, environment, ethnic, health, history, horticulture, medicine, memoirs, military, parenting, psychology, science, self-help, sociology, technology, war.

- ☛ "I handle a small number of literary clients and concentrate on trade nonfiction (science, health, history)." No fiction submissions until further notified—check the website.

How to Contact Keep queries to one page—nonfiction only. E-mail submissions preferred. Accepts simultaneous submissions. Responds in 1-6 weeks to queries. Obtains most new clients through solicitations.

Terms Agent receives 15% commission on domestic sales. Agent receives 20% commission on foreign sales. Offers written contract, binding for 1 year; 60-day notice must be given to terminate contract. Charges for photocopying and postage only if the book is placed.

Tips Read at least 2 books on how to prepare book proposals before sending material. An extremely well-prepared proposal will make your material stand out.

☑ STUART KRICHEVSKY LITERARY AGENCY, INC.

381 Park Ave. S., Suite 914, New York NY 10016. (212)725-5288. Fax: (212)725-5275. E-mail: query@ skagency.com. Website: www.skagency.com. Member of AAR.

Member Agents Stuart Krichevsky; Shana Cohen (science fiction, fantasy); Jennifer Puglisi (assistant).

Represents Nonfiction books, novels.

How to Contact Submit query, synopsis, 1 sample page via e-mail (no attachments). Snail mail queries also acceptable. Obtains most new clients through recommendations from others, solicitations.

EDITE KROLL LITERARY AGENCY, INC.

20 Cross St., Saco ME 04072. (207)283-8797. Fax: (207)283-8799. E-mail: ekroll@maine.rr.com. **Contact:** Edite Kroll. Represents 45 clients. 20% of clients are new/unpublished writers. Currently handles: nonfiction books 40%, novels 5%, juvenile books 40%, scholarly books 5%, other.

- Prior to opening her agency, Ms. Kroll served as a book editor and translator.

Represents Nonfiction books, novels, very selective, juvenile, scholarly. **Considers these nonfiction areas:** juvenile, selectively, biography, current affairs, ethnic, gay, government, health, no diet books, humor, memoirs, selectively, popular culture, psychology, religion, selectively, self-help, selectively, womens, issue-oriented nonfiction. **Considers these fiction areas:** juvenile, literary, picture books, young adult, middle grade, adult.

- ☛ "We represent writers and writer-artists of both adult and children's books. We have a special focus on international feminist writers, women writers and artists who write their own books (including children's and humor books)." Actively seeking artists who write their own books and international feminists who write in English. Does not want to receive genre (mysteries, thrillers, diet, cookery, etc.), photography books, coffee table books, romance or commercial fiction.

How to Contact Query with SASE. Submit outline/proposal, synopsis, 1-2 sample chapters, author bio, entire ms if sending picture book. No phone queries. Responds in 2-4 weeks to queries. Responds in 4-8 weeks to mss. Obtains most new clients through recommendations from others.

Terms Agent receives 15% commission on domestic sales. Agent receives 20% commission on foreign sales. Offers written contract; 30-day notice must be given to terminate contract. Charges clients for photocopying and legal fees with prior approval from writer.

Recent Sales Sold 12 domestic/30 foreign titles in the last year. This agency prefers not to share information on specific sales. Clients include Shel Silverstein estate, Suzy Becker, Geoffrey Hayes, Henrik Drescher, Charlotte Kasl, Gloria Skurzynski, Fatema Mernissa.

Tips "Please do your research so you won't send me books/proposals I specifically excluded."

☐ KT LITERARY, LLC

9249 S. Broadway, #200-543, Highlands Ranch CO 80129. (720)344-4728. Fax: (720)344-4728. E-mail: queries@ktliterary.com. Website: www.ktliterary.com. **Contact:** Kate Schafer Testerman. Member of AAR. Other memberships include SCBWI. Represents 20 clients. 60% of clients are new/unpublished writers. Currently handles: nonfiction books 5%, novels 5%, juvenile books 90%.

- Prior to her current position, Ms. Schafer was an agent with Janklow & Nesbit.

Represents Nonfiction books, novels, juvenile books. **Considers these nonfiction areas:** popular culture. **Considers these fiction areas:** action, adventure, fantasy, historical, juvenile, romance, science fiction, women's, young adult.

- ☛ "I'm bringing my years of experience in the New York publishing scene, as well as my lifelong love of reading, to a vibrant area for writers, proving that great work can be found, and sold, from anywhere." "Actively seeking brilliant, funny, original middle grade and young adult fiction, both literary and commercial; witty women's fiction (chick lit); and pop-culture, narrative nonfiction. Quirky is good." Does not want picture books, serious nonfiction, and adult literary fiction.

How to Contact E-mail queries only. Responds in 2 weeks to queries. Responds in 2 months to mss. Obtains most new clients through recommendations from others, solicitations, conferences.

Terms Agent receives 15% commission on domestic sales. Agent receives 20% commission on foreign sales. Offers written contract; 30-day notice must be given to terminate contract.

Writers Conferences Various SCBWI conferences, BookExpo.

Tips "If we like your query, we'll ask for (more). Continuing advice is offered regularly on my blog 'Ask Daphne', which can be accessed from my website."

☐ KT PUBLIC RELATIONS & LITERARY SERVICES

1905 Cricklewood Cove, Fogelsville PA 18051. (610)395-6298. Fax: (610)395-6299. Website: www. ktpublicrelations.com; Blog: http://newliteraryagents.blogspot.com. **Contact:** Jon Tienstra. Represents 12 clients. 75% of clients are new/unpublished writers. Currently handles: nonfiction books 50%, novels 50%.

- Prior to becoming an agent, Kae Tienstra was publicity director for Rodale, Inc. for 13 years and then founded her own publicity agency; Mr. Tienstra joined the firm in 1995 with varied corporate experience and a master's degree in library science.

Member Agents Kae Tienstra (health, parenting, psychology, how-to, women's fiction, general fiction); Jon Tienstra (nature/environment, history, cooking/foods/nutrition, war/military, automotive, health/medicine, gardening, general fiction, science fiction/contemporary fantasy, popular fiction).

Represents Nonfiction books, novels. **Considers these nonfiction areas:** animals, child guidance, cooking, decorating, diet/nutrition, environment, foods, health, history, hobbies, horticulture, how-to, interior design, medicine, military, parenting, popular culture, psychology, science, self-help, technology, interior design/decorating. **Considers these fiction areas:** action, adventure, crime, detective, family saga, historical, literary, mainstream, mystery, police, romance, science fiction, suspense, thriller, contemporary fantasy (no swords or dragons).

- ⚬⌐ "We have worked with a variety of authors and publishers over the years and have learned what individual publishers are looking for in terms of new acquisitions. We are both mad about books and authors and we look forward to finding publishing success for all our clients. Specializes in parenting, history, cooking/foods/nutrition, war, health/medicine, psychology, how-to, gardening, science fiction, contemporary fantasy, women's fiction, and popular fiction." Does not want to see unprofessional material.

How to Contact Query with SASE. Prefers snail mail queries. Will accept e-mail queries. Responds in 3 months to chapters; 6-9 months for mss. Accepts simultaneous submissions. Responds in 4 weeks to queries.

Terms Agent receives 15% commission on domestic sales. Agent receives 20% commission on foreign sales. Offers written contract. Charges clients for long-distance phone calls, fax, postage, photocopying (only when incurred). No advance payment for these out-of-pocket expenses.

⊘ LADNERBOND LITERARY MANAGEMENT

500 E. 77th St., #422, New York NY 10021. **Contact:** Christopher Ladner. Other memberships include adheres to AAR canon of ethics.

- • Prior to his current position, Mr. Ladner began his career in publishing as an associate at Writers House.

Represents Nonfiction books, novels. **Considers these nonfiction areas:** autobiography, biography, health, history, medicine, memoirs, popular culture, sports, lifestylel.

How to Contact Query with SASE. As of early 2008, this agency was closed to queries. Check the website for more info. Responds in 4 weeks to queries. Responds in 6-8 weeks to mss. Obtains most new clients through recommendations from others, solicitations.

◐ ALBERT LaFARGE LITERARY AGENCY

Fax: (270)512-5179. E-mail: office@thelafargeagency.com. Website: www.thelafargeagency.com. **Contact:** Albert LaFarge. Represents 24 clients. 50% of clients are new/unpublished writers. Currently handles: nonfiction books 90%, novels 10%.

- • Prior to becoming an agent, Mr. LaFarge was an editor.

Represents Nonfiction books, novels. **Considers these nonfiction areas:** architecture, art, autobiography, biography, current affairs, dance, design, environment, health, history, medicine, memoirs, music, photography, psychology, sports. **Considers these fiction areas:** literary.

- ⚬⌐ This agency specializes in helping clients to develop nonfiction.

How to Contact Query with SASE. Submit outline and sample chapters. Obtains most new clients through recommendations from others.

Terms Agent receives 15% commission on domestic sales. Agent receives 20% commission on foreign sales. Offers written contract. Charges for photocopying.

◐ THE LA LITERARY AGENCY

P.O. Box 46370, Los Angeles CA 90046. (323)654-5288. E-mail: laliteraryag@mac.com. **Contact:** Ann Cashman, Eric Lasher.

- • Prior to becoming an agent, Mr. Lasher worked in publishing in New York and Los Angeles.

Represents Nonfiction books, novels. **Considers these nonfiction areas:** animals, anthropology, archeology, architecture, art, autobiography, biography, business, child guidance, cooking, cultural interests, current affairs, diet/nutrition, design, economics, environment, ethnic, foods, government, health, history, how-to, investigative, law, medicine, parenting, popular culture, politics, psychology, science, self-help, sociology, sports, technology, true crime, women's issues, women's studies, narrative nonfiction. **Considers these fiction areas:** action, adventure, crime, detective, family saga, feminist, historical, literary, mainstream, police, sports, thriller.

How to Contact Query with outline, 1 sample chapter. No fax or e-mail queries.

Recent Sales *Full Bloom: The Art and Life of Georgia O'Keeffe*, by Hunter Druhojowska-Philp (Norton); *And the Walls Came Tumbling Down*, by H. Caldwell (Scribner); *Italian Slow & Savory*, by Joyce Goldstein (Chronicle); *A Field Guide to Chocolate Chip Cookies*, by Dede Wilson (Harvard Common Press); *Teen Knitting Club* (Artisan); *The Framingham Heart Study*, by Dr. Daniel Levy (Knopf).

⬤ PETER LAMPACK AGENCY, INC.

551 Fifth Ave., Suite 1613, New York NY 10176-0187. (212)687-9106. Fax: (212)687-9109. E-mail: alampack@verizon.net. **Contact:** Andrew Lampack. Represents 50 clients. 10% of clients are new/unpublished writers. Currently handles: nonfiction books 20%, novels 80%.

Member Agents Peter Lampack (president); Rema Delanyan (foreign rights); Andrew Lampack (new writers).

Represents Nonfiction books, novels. **Considers these fiction areas:** adventure, crime, detective, family saga, literary, mainstream, mystery, police, suspense, thriller, contemporary relationships.

> ⚬ "This agency specializes in commercial fiction and nonfiction by recognized experts." Actively seeking literary and commercial fiction, thrillers, mysteries, suspense, and psychological thrillers. Does not want to receive horror, romance, science fiction, westerns, historical literary fiction or academic material.

How to Contact Query via e-mail. *No unsolicited mss.* Responds within 2 months to queries. Obtains most new clients through referrals made by clients.

Terms Agent receives 15% commission on domestic sales. Agent receives 20% commission on foreign sales.

Recent Sales *Spartan Gold*, by Clive Cussler with Grant Blackwood; *The Wrecker*, by Clive Cussler with Justin Scott; *Medusa*, by Clive Cussler and Paul Kemprecos; *Silent Sea,* by Clive Cussler with Jack Dubrul; *Summertime*, by J.M. Coetzee; *Dreaming in French*, by Megan McAndrew; *Time Pirate*, by Ted Bell.

Writers Conferences BookExpo America; Mystery Writers of America.

Tips "Submit only your best work for consideration. Have a very specific agenda of goals you wish your prospective agent to accomplish for you. Provide the agent with a comprehensive statement of your credentials—educational and professional accomplishments."

⬤ LAURA LANGLIE, LITERARY AGENT

239 Carroll St., Garden Apartment, Brooklyn NY 11231. (718)855-8102. Fax: (718)855-4450. E-mail: laura@lauralanglie.com. **Contact:** Laura Langlie. Represents 25 clients. 50% of clients are new/unpublished writers. Currently handles: nonfiction books 15%, novels 58%, story collections 2%, juvenile books 25%.

- Prior to opening her agency, Ms. Langlie worked in publishing for 7 years and as an agent at Kidde, Hoyt & Picard for 6 years.

Represents Nonfiction books, novels, short story collections, novellas, juvenile. **Considers these nonfiction areas:** autobiography, biography, cultural interests, current affairs, environment, film, history, language, law, literature, memoirs, popular culture, politics, psychology, satire, theater, women's issues, women's studies, history of medicine and science, animals (not how-to). **Considers these fiction areas:** crime, detective, ethnic, feminist, historical, humor, juvenile, literary, mainstream, mystery, police, suspense, thriller, young adult, mainstream.

> ⚬ "I'm very involved with and committed to my clients. I also employ a publicist to work with all my clients to make the most of each book's publication. Most of my clients come to me via recommendations from other agents, clients and editors. I've met very few at conferences. I've often sought out writers for projects, and I still find new clients via the traditional query letter." Does not want to receive how-to, children's picture books, science fiction, poetry, men's adventure or erotica.

How to Contact Query with SASE. Accepts queries via fax. Accepts simultaneous submissions. Responds in 1 week to queries. Responds in 1 month to mss. Obtains most new clients through recommendations, submissions.

Terms Agent receives 15% commission on domestic sales. Agent receives 20% commission on foreign and dramatic sales. No written contract.

Recent Sales Sold 15 titles in the last year. *Alice I Have Been*, by Melanie Benjamin (Delacorte Press); *Here Lies Linc*, by Delia Ray (Alfred A. Knopf Books for Young Readers); *Livvie Owen Lived Here*, by Sarah Dooley (Feiwel & Friends/Macmillan); *Miss Dimple Disappears*, by Mignon F. Ballard (St. Martin's Press); *Insatiable*, by Meg Cabot (William Morrow); *Gemma*, by Meg Tilly (St. Martin's Press); *Girl's Best Friend*, by Leslie Margolis (Bloomsbury); *The Elite Gymnasts*, by Dominique Moceanu and Alicia Thompson (Disney/Hyperion); *Safe From the Sea*, by Peter Geye (Unbridled Books).

Tips "Be complete, forthright and clear in your communications. Do your research as to what a particular agent represents."

LANGTONS INTERNATIONAL AGENCY

124 West 60th St., #42M, New York NY 10023. (646)344-1801. E-mail: langtonsinternational@ gmail.com. Website: www.langtonsinternational.com. **Contact:** Linda Langton, President.

- Prior to becoming an agent, Ms. Langton was a co-founding director and publisher of the international publishing company, The Ink Group.

Represents Nonfiction books and literary fiction. **Considers these nonfiction areas:** biography, health, history, how-to, politics, self-help, true crime. **Considers these fiction areas:** literary, political thrillers, young adult and middle grade books.

- ⌐ "Langtons International Agency is a multi-media literary and licensing agency specializing in nonfiction, thrillers and children's middle grade and young adult books as well as the the visual world of photography."

How to Contact Query with SASE. Submit outline/proposal, synopsis, publishing history, author bio. Only published authors should query this agency. Accepts simultaneous submissions.

Recent Sales *Talking With Jean-Paul Sartre: Conversations and Debates*, by Professor John Gerassi (Yale University Press); *The Obama Presidency and the Politics of Change*, by Professor Stanley Renshon (Routledge Press); *I Would See a Girl Walking*, by Diana Montane and Kathy Kelly (Berkley Books); *Begin 1913-1992*, by Avi Shilon (Yale University Press); *This Borrowed Earth*, by Robert Emmet Hernan (Palgrave McMillan); *The Perfect Square*, by Nancy Heinzen (Temple Uni Press); *The Honey Trail*, by Grace Pundyk (St. Martins Press); *Dogs of Central Park,* by Fran Reisner (Rizzoli/Universe Publishing).

☑ MICHAEL LARSEN/ELIZABETH POMADA, LITERARY AGENTS

1029 Jones St., San Francisco CA 94109-5023. (415)673-0939. E-mail: larsenpoma@aol.com. Website: www.larsen-pomada.com. **Contact:** Mike Larsen, Elizabeth Pomada. Member of AAR. Other memberships include Authors Guild, ASJA, PEN, WNBA, California Writers Club, National Speakers Association. Represents 100 clients. 40-45% of clients are new/unpublished writers. Currently handles: nonfiction books 70%, novels 30%.

- Prior to opening their agency, Mr. Larsen and Ms. Pomada were promotion executives for major publishing houses. Mr. Larsen worked for Morrow, Bantam and Pyramid (now part of Berkley); Ms. Pomada worked at Holt, David McKay and The Dial Press. Mr. Larsen is the author of the 4th edition of *How to Write a Book Proposal* and *How to Get a Literary Agent* as well as the coauthor of *Guerilla Marketing for Writers: 100 Weapons for Selling Your Work*, which was republished in September 2009.

Member Agents Michael Larsen (nonfiction); Elizabeth Pomada (fiction & narrative nonfiction).

Represents Considers these nonfiction areas: anthropology, archeology, architecture, art, autobiography, biography, business, current affairs, diet/nutrition, design, economics, environment, ethnic, film, foods, gay/lesbian, health, history, how-to, humor, inspirational, investigative, law, medicine, memoirs, metaphysics, money, music, New Age, popular culture, politics, psychology, religious, satire, science, self-help, sociology, sports, travel, women's issues, women's studies, futurism. **Considers these fiction areas:** action, adventure, contemporary issues, crime, detective, ethnic, experimental, family saga, feminist, gay, glitz, historical, humor, inspirational, lesbian, literary, mainstream, mystery, police, religious, romance, satire, suspense, chick lit.

- ⌐ We have diverse tastes. We look for fresh voices and new ideas. We handle literary, commercial and genre fiction, and the full range of nonfiction books. Actively seeking commercial, genre and literary fiction. Does not want to receive children's books, plays, short stories, screenplays, pornography, poetry or stories of abuse.

How to Contact Query with SASE. Responds in 8 weeks to pages or submissions.

Terms Agent receives 15% commission on domestic sales. Agent receives 20% (30% for Asia) commission on foreign sales. May charge for printing, postage for multiple submissions, foreign mail, foreign phone calls, galleys, books, legal fees.

Recent Sales Sold at least 15 titles in the last year. *Secrets of the Tudor Court*, by D. Bogden (Kensington); *Zen & the Art of Horse Training*, by Allan Hamilton, M.D. (Storey Pub.); *The Solemn Lantern Maker,* by Merlinda Bobis (Delta); *Bite Marks*, the fifth book in an urban fantasy series by J.D. Rardin (Orbit/Grand Central); *The Iron King*, by Julie Karawa (Harlequin Teen).

Writers Conferences This agency organizes the annual San Francisco Writers' Conference (www. sfwriters.org).

Tips "We love helping writers get the rewards and recognition they deserve. If you can write books that meet the needs of the marketplace and you can promote your books, now is the best time ever to be a writer. We must find new writers to make a living, so we are very eager to hear from new writers whose work will interest large houses, and nonfiction writers who can promote their books. For a list of recent sales, helpful info, and three ways to make yourself irresistible to any publisher, please visit our website."

◎ THE STEVE LAUBE AGENCY

5025 N. Central Ave., #635, Phoenix AZ 85012. (602)336-8910. E-mail: krichards@stevelaube.com. Website: www.stevelaube.com. **Contact:** Steve Laube. Other memberships include CBA. Represents 60+ clients. 5% of clients are new/unpublished writers. Currently handles: nonfiction books 48%, novels 48%, novella 2%, scholarly books 2%.

- Prior to becoming an agent, Mr. Laube worked 11 years as a Christian bookseller and 11 years as editorial director of nonfiction with Bethany House Publishers.

Represents Nonfiction books, novels. **Considers these nonfiction areas:** religious. **Considers these fiction areas:** religious.

- ⚷ Primarily serves the Christian market (CBA). Actively seeking Christian fiction and religious nonfiction. Does not want to receive children's picture books, poetry or cookbooks.

How to Contact Submit proposal package, outline, 3 sample chapters, SASE. No e-mail submissions. Consult website for guidelines. Accepts simultaneous submissions. Responds in 6-8 weeks to queries. Obtains most new clients through recommendations from others, solicitations, conferences.

Terms Agent receives 15% commission on domestic sales. Agent receives 20% commission on foreign sales. Offers written contract; 30-day notice must be given to terminate contract.

Recent Sales Sold 80 titles in the last year. Other clients include Deborah Raney, Bright Media, Allison Bottke, H. Norman Wright, Ellie Kay, Jack Cavanaugh, Karen Ball, Tracey Bateman, Susan May Warren, Lisa Bergren, John Rosemond, David Gregory, Cindy Woodsmall, Karol Ladd, Judith Pella, Michael Phillips, Margaret Daley, William Lane Craig, Vicki Hinze, Tosca Lee, Ginny Aiken.

Writers Conferences Mount Hermon Christian Writers' Conference; American Christian Fiction Writers' Conference.

▢ LAUNCHBOOKS LITERARY AGENCY

566 Sweet Pea Place, Encinitas CA 92024. (760)944-9909. E-mail: david@launchbooks.com. Website: www.launchbooks.com. **Contact:** David Fugate. Represents 45 clients. 35% of clients are new/unpublished writers. Currently handles: nonfiction books 100%.

- Prior to his current position, Mr. Fugate was hired by the Margret McBride Agency to handle its submissions. In 1994, he moved to Waterside Productions, Inc., where he was an agent for 11 years and successfully represented more than 600 book titles before leaving to form LaunchBooks in 2005.

Represents Nonfiction books, novels, textbooks. **Considers these nonfiction areas:** anthropology, archeology, autobiography, biography, business, child guidance, computers, cooking, cultural interests, current affairs, dance, diet/nutrition, economics, education, environment, ethnic, foods, government, health, history, how-to, humor, investigative, law, medicine, memoirs, military, money, music, parenting, popular culture, politics, satire, science, sociology, sports, technology, true crime, war.

- ⚷ Actively seeking a wide variety of nonfiction, including business, technology, adventure, popular culture, science, creative nonfiction, current events, history, politics, reference, memoirs, health, how-to, lifestyle, parenting and more.

How to Contact E-mail query is preferred, or query with SASE. Submit outline/proposal, synopsis, 1 sample chapter, author bio. Accepts simultaneous submissions. Responds in 1 week to queries. Responds in 4 weeks to mss. Obtains most new clients through recommendations from others, solicitations.

Terms Agent receives 15% commission on domestic sales. Agent receives 25% commission on foreign sales. Offers written contract; 30-day notice must be given to terminate contract. Charges occur very seldom and typically only if the author specifically requests overnight or something of that nature. This agency's agreement limits any charges to $50 unless the author gives a written consent.

Recent Sales *$20 per Gallon*, by Christopher Steiner (Grand Central); *Kingpin*, by Kevin Poulsen (Crown); *Inventing Green*, by Alexis Madrigal (Da Capo); *The Revenge of Everyday Things*, by Robert Vamosi (Basic Books); *SLOW: Life in a Tuscan Town*, by Douglas Gayeton (Welcome Books); *The Art of Non-Conformity*, by Chris Guillebeau (Perigee); *When A Billion Chinese Jump*, by Jonathan Watts (Scribner); *The Hyper-Social Organization*, by Francois Gossieaux and Ed Moran (McGraw-Hill Business); *Truth, Lies & Kevin Mitnick* (Little Brown).

◙ SARAH LAZIN BOOKS

126 Fifth Ave., Suite 300, New York NY 10011. (212)989-5757. Fax: (212)989-1393. **Contact:** Sarah Lazin. Member of AAR. Represents 75 + clients. Currently handles: nonfiction books 80%, novels 20%.

Member Agents Sarah Lazin; Rebecca Ferreira.

Represents Nonfiction books, novels. **Considers these nonfiction areas:** biography, cultural interests, dance, ethnic, gay/lesbian, history, inspirational, memoirs, music, popular culture, religious, Works with companies who package their books; handles some photography.

How to Contact Query with SASE. No e-mail queries.

Terms Agent receives 15% commission on domestic sales. Agent receives 20% commission on foreign sales.

▦ SUSANNA LEA ASSOCIATES

28, rue Bonaparte, 75006 Paris France. E-mail: us-submissions@susannalea.com; uk-submissions@susannalea.com; fr-submissions@susannalea.com (France). Website: www.susannaleaassociates.com. **Contact:** Submissions Department. 331 West 20th Street, New York, NY 10011.

Represents Nonfiction books, novels.

   ☞ "We pride ourselves in keeping our list small: We prefer to focus our energies on a limited number of projects rather than spreading our energies thin. The company is currently developing new international projects: always selective, yet broad in their reach, they all remain faithful to the slogan, 'Published in Europe, Read by the World.'" Does not want to receive poetry, plays, screenplays, science fiction, educational text books, short stories or illustrated works.

How to Contact Send a query letter, brief synopsis, the first three chapters and/or proposal to this agency via e-mail.

Tips "Your query letter should be concise and include any pertinent information about yourself, relevant writing history, etc."

THE NED LEAVITT AGENCY

70 Wooster St., Suite 4F, New York NY 10012. (212)334-0999. Website: www.nedleavittagency.com. **Contact:** Ned Leavitt. Member of AAR. Represents 40 + clients.

Member Agents Ned Leavitt, founder and agent; Britta Alexander, agent; Jill Beckman, editorial assistant.

Represents Nonfiction books, novels.

   ☞ "We are small in size, but intensely dedicated to our authors and to supporting excellent and unique writing."

How to Contact This agency now only takes queries/submissions through referred clients. Do *not* cold query.

Tips "Look online for this agency's recently changed submission guidelines."

▤ ◙ ROBERT LECKER AGENCY

4055 Melrose Ave., Montreal QC H4A 2S5 Canada. (514)830-4818. Fax: (514)483-1644. E-mail: leckerlink@aol.com. Website: www.leckeragency.com. **Contact:** Robert Lecker. Represents 20 clients. 20% of clients are new/unpublished writers. Currently handles: nonfiction books 80%, novels 10%, scholarly books 10%.

- Prior to becoming an agent, Mr. Lecker was the co-founder and publisher of ECW Press and professor of English literature at McGill University. He has 30 years of experience in book and magazine publishing.

Member Agents Robert Lecker (popular culture, music); Mary Williams (travel, food, popular science).

Represents Nonfiction books, novels, scholarly, syndicated material. **Considers these nonfiction areas:** autobiography, biography, cooking, cultural interests, dance, diet/nutrition, ethnic, film, foods, how-to, language, literature, music, popular culture, science, technology, theater. **Considers these fiction areas:** action, adventure, crime, detective, erotica, literary, mainstream, mystery, police, suspense, thriller.

▸ RLA specializes in books about popular culture, popular science, music, entertainment, food and travel. The agency responds to articulate, innovative proposals within 2 weeks. Actively seeking original book mss only after receipt of outlines and proposals.

How to Contact Query first. Only responds to queries of interest. Discards the rest. Accepts simultaneous submissions. Responds in 2 weeks to queries. Responds in 1 month to mss. Obtains most new clients through recommendations from others, conferences, interest in website.

Terms Agent receives 15% commission on domestic sales. Agent receives 15-20% commission on foreign sales. Offers written contract, binding for 1 year; 6-month notice must be given to terminate contract.

◉ LESCHER & LESCHER, LTD.
346 E. 84th St., New York NY 10028. (212)396-1999. Fax: (212)396-1991. **Contact:** Robert Larson; Carolyn Larson. Member of AAR. Represents 150 clients. Currently handles: nonfiction books 80%, novels 20%.

Represents Nonfiction books, novels. **Considers these nonfiction areas:** biography, cooking, current affairs, history, law, memoirs, popular culture, cookbooks/wines, narrative nonfiction. **Considers these fiction areas:** commercial, literary, mystery, suspense.

▸ Does not want to receive screenplays, science fiction or romance.

How to Contact Query with SASE. Obtains most new clients through recommendations from others.

Terms Agent receives 15% commission on domestic sales. Agent receives 10% commission on foreign sales.

LEVINE GREENBERG LITERARY AGENCY, INC.
307 Seventh Ave., Suite 2407, New York NY 10001. (212)337-0934. Fax: (212)337-0948. Website: www.levinegreenberg.com. Member of AAR. Represents 250 clients. 33% of clients are new/unpublished writers. Currently handles: nonfiction books 70%, novels 30%.

• Prior to opening his agency, Mr. Levine served as vice president of the Bank Street College of Education.

Member Agents James Levine, Daniel Greenberg, Stephanie Kip Rostan, Lindsay Edgecombe, Danielle Svetcov, Elizabeth Fisher, Victoria Skurnick.

Represents Nonfiction books, novels. **Considers these nonfiction areas:** New Age, animals, art, biography, business, child, computers, cooking, gardening, gay, health, money, nature, religion, science, self-help, sociology, spirituality, sports, women's. **Considers these fiction areas:** literary, mainstream, mystery, thriller, psychological, women's.

▸ This agency specializes in business, psychology, parenting, health/medicine, narrative nonfiction, spirituality, religion, women's issues, and commercial fiction.

How to Contact See website for full submission procedure at "How to Submit." Or use our e-mail address if you prefer. Do not submit directly to agents. Obtains most new clients through recommendations from others.

Terms Agent receives 15% commission on domestic sales. Agent receives 20% commission on foreign sales. Offers written contract. Charges clients for out-of-pocket expenses—telephone, fax, postage, photocopying—directly connected to the project.

Writers Conferences ASJA Writers' Conference.

Tips "We focus on editorial development, business representation, and publicity and marketing strategy."

◉ PAUL S. LEVINE LITERARY AGENCY
1054 Superba Ave., Venice CA 90291-3940. (310)450-6711. Fax: (310)450-0181. E-mail: paul@paulslevinelit.com. Website: www.paulslevinelit.com. **Contact:** Paul S. Levine. Other memberships include the State Bar of California. Represents over 100 clients. 75% of clients are new/unpublished

writers. Currently handles: nonfiction books 60%, novels 10%, movie scripts 10%, TV scripts 5%, juvenile books 5%.

Member Agents Paul S. Levine (children's and young adult fiction and nonfiction, adult fiction and nonfiction except sci-fi, fantasy, and horror); Loren R. Grossman (archaeology, art/photography/ architecture, gardening, education, health, medicine, science).

Represents Nonfiction books, novels, episodic drama, movie, TV, movie scripts, feature film, TV movie of the week, sitcom, animation, documentary, miniseries, syndicated material, reality show. **Considers these nonfiction areas:** architecture, art, autobiography, biography, business, child guidance, computers, cooking, crafts, cultural interests, current affairs, diet/nutrition, design, economics, education, ethnic, film, foods, gay/lesbian, government, health, history, hobbies, how-to, humor, investigative, language, law, medicine, memoirs, military, money, music, New Age, parenting, photography, popular culture, politics, psychology, science, self-help, sociology, sports, theater, true crime, women's issues, women's studies, creative nonfiction, animation. **Considers these fiction areas:** action, adventure, comic books, confession, crime, detective, erotica, ethnic, experimental, family saga, feminist, frontier, gay, glitz, historical, humor, inspirational, lesbian, literary, mainstream, mystery, police, regional, religious, romance, satire, sports, suspense, thriller, westerns. **Considers these script areas:** action, biography, cartoon, comedy, contemporary, detective, erotica, ethnic, experimental, family, feminist, gay, glitz, historical, horror, juvenile, mainstream, multimedia, mystery, religious, romantic comedy, romantic drama, sports, teen, thriller, western.

○┅ Does not want to receive science fiction, fantasy, or horror.

How to Contact Query with SASE. Accepts simultaneous submissions. Responds in 1 day to queries. Responds in 6-8 weeks to mss. Obtains most new clients through conferences, referrals, listings on various websites and in directories.

Terms Agent receives 15% commission on domestic sales. Offers written contract. Charges for postage and actual, out-of-pocket costs only.

Recent Sales Sold 10 books in the last year and 5 script projects. *Apocalypse Never*, by Tad Daley (Rutgers University Press); movie rights to *Vampire High*, by Douglas Rees (1492 Productions); *Silver*, by Steven Savile (Variance Publishing); *Romancing the Runway*, by Linda Hudson-Smith (Harlequin). Other clients include David Seidman, Patricia Santos, Carol Jones.

Writers Conferences Willamette Writers Conference; San Francisco Writers Conference; Santa Barbara Writers Conference and many others.

Tips "Write good, sellable books."

◎ ROBERT LIEBERMAN ASSOCIATES

400 Nelson Rd., Ithaca NY 14850-9440. (607)273-8801. Fax: (801)749-9682. E-mail: rhl10@cornell. edu. Website: www.people.cornell.edu/pages/rhl10. **Contact:** Robert Lieberman. Represents 30 clients. 50% of clients are new/unpublished writers. Currently handles: nonfiction books 20%.

Represents Nonfiction books, trade, scholarly, college-level textbooks. **Considers these nonfiction areas:** agriculture, anthropology, archeology, architecture, art, business, computers, design, economics, education, environment, film, health, horticulture, medicine, money, music, psychology, science, sociology, technology, theater, memoirs by authors with high public recognition.

○┅ This agency only accepts nonfiction ideas and specializes in university/college-level textbooks, CD-ROM/software for the university/college-level textbook market, and popular trade books in math, engineering, economics, and other subjects. Does not want to receive any fiction, self-help, or screenplays.

How to Contact Prefers to read materials exclusively. Responds in 2 weeks to queries. Responds in 1 month to mss. Obtains most new clients through referrals.

Terms Agent receives 15% commission on domestic sales. Agent receives 20% commission on foreign sales. Offers written contract; 1-month notice must be given to terminate contract. Fees are sometimes charged to clients for shipping and when special reviewers are required.

Tips "The trade books we handle are by authors who are highly recognized in their fields of expertise. Our client list includes Nobel Prize winners and others with high name recognition, either by the public or within a given area of expertise."

▦ ◎ LIMELIGHT CELEBRITY MANAGEMENT LTD.

33 Newman St., London W1T 1PY England. (44)(207)637-2529. E-mail: mary@limelight management.com. Website: www.limelightmanagement.com. **Contact:** Fiona Lindsay. Estab.

1989. Other memberships include AAA. Represents 70 clients. Currently handles: nonfiction books 100%, multimedia.

- Prior to becoming an agent, Ms. Lindsay was a public relations manager at the Dorchester and was working on her law degree.

Member Agents Fiona Lindsay.

Represents Nonfiction books. **Considers these nonfiction areas:** agriculture, architecture, art, cooking, crafts, decorating, diet/nutrition, design, environment, foods, gardening, health, hobbies, horticulture, interior design, medicine, metaphysics, New Age, photography, self-help, sports, travel.

- ⚷ "We are celebrity agents for TV celebrities, broadcasters, writers, journalists, celebrity speakers and media personalities, after dinner speakers, motivational speakers, celebrity chefs, TV presenters and TV chefs." This agency will consider women's fiction, as well.

How to Contact Prefers to read materials exclusively. Query with SASE/IRC via e-mail. Agents will be in contact if they want to see more. No attachments to e-mails. Responds in 1 week to queries. Obtains most new clients through recommendations from others.

Terms Agent receives 15% commission on domestic sales. Agent receives 20% commission on foreign sales. Offers written contract; 2-month notice must be given to terminate contract.

⊠ LINDSTROM LITERARY MANAGEMENT, LLC

871 N. Greenbrier St., Arlington VA 22205. Fax: (703)527-7624. E-mail: submissions@ lindstromliterary.com. Website: www.lindstromliterary.com. **Contact:** Kristin Lindstrom. Other memberships include Author's Guild. Represents 9 clients. 30% of clients are new/unpublished writers. Currently handles: nonfiction books 30%, novels 70%.

- Prior to her current position, Ms. Lindstrom started her career as an editor of a monthly magazine in the energy industry, and was employed as a public relations manager for a national software company before becoming an independent marketing and publicity consultant.

Represents Nonfiction books, novels. **Considers these nonfiction areas:** animals, autobiography, biography, business, current affairs, economics, history, investigative, memoirs, popular culture, science, technology, true crime. **Considers these fiction areas:** action, adventure, crime, detective, erotica, inspirational, mainstream, mystery, police, religious, suspense, thriller, women's.

- ⚷ "In 2006, I decided to add my more specific promotion/publicity skills to the mix in order to support the marketing efforts of my published clients." Actively seeking commercial fiction and narrative nonfiction. Does not want to receive juvenile or children's books, or books of poetry.

How to Contact Query via e-mail only. Submit author bio, synopsis and first four chapters if submitting fiction. For nonfiction, send the first 4 chapters, synopsis, proposal, outline and mission statement. *You will only hear from us again if we decide to ask for a complete manuscript or further information.* Accepts simultaneous submissions. Responds in 6 weeks to queries. Responds in 8 weeks to requested mss. Obtains most new clients through referrals and solicitations.

Terms Agent receives 15% commission on domestic sales. Agent receives 20% commission on performance rights and foreign sales. Offers written contract. This agency charges for postage, UPS, copies and other basic office expenses.

Recent Sales A memoir by Agathe von Trapp (It Books/Harper). Two book deal for Alice Wisler (Bethany House); a thriller by J.C. Hutchins (St. Martin's Press).

Tips "Do your homework on accepted practices; make sure you know what kind of book the agent handles."

LINN PRENTIS LITERARY

155 East 116th St., #2F, New York NY 10029. Fax: (212)875-5565. E-mail: linn@linnprestis.com or righthand@linnprentis.com. Website: www.linnprestis.com. **Contact:** Linn Prentis, agent; Jordana Frankel assistant. Represents 18-20 clients. 25% of clients are new/unpublished writers. Currently handles: nonfiction books 5%, novels 65%, story collections 7%, novella 10%, juvenile books 10%, scholarly books 3%.

- Prior to becoming an agent, Ms. Prentis was a nonfiction writer and editor, primarily in magazines. She also worked in book promotion in New York. Ms. Prentis then worked for and later ran the Virginia Kidd Agency. She is known particularly for her assistance with manuscript development."

Represents Nonfiction books, novels, short story collections, novellas (from authors whose novels I already represent), juvenile (for older juveniles), scholarly, anthology. **Considers these nonfiction areas:** juvenile, animals, art, biography, current affairs, education, ethnic, government, how to, humor, language, memoirs, music, photography, popular culture, sociology, womens. **Considers these fiction areas:** adventure, ethnic, fantasy, feminist, gay, glitz, historical, horror, humor, juvenile, lesbian, literary, mainstream, mystery, thriller.

○→ "Because of the Virginia Kidd connection and the clients I brought with me at the start, I have a special interest in sci-fi and fantasy, but, really, fiction is what interests me. As for my nonfiction projects, they are books I just couldn't resist." Actively seeking hard science fiction, family saga, mystery, memoir, mainstream, literary, women's. Does not want to "receive books for little kids."

How to Contact Query with SASE. Submit synopsis. No phone or fax queries. No snail mail. E-mail queries to ahayden@linnprentis.com. Include first ten pages and synopsis as either attachment or as text in the e-mail. Accepts simultaneous submissions. Obtains most new clients through recommendations from others, solicitations.

Terms Agent receives 15% commission on domestic sales. Agent receives 20% commission on foreign sales. Offers written contract; 60-day notice must be given to terminate contract.

Recent Sales Sold 15 titles in the last year. *The Sons of Heaven*, *The Empress of Mars*, and *The House of the Stag*, by Kage Baker (Tor); the last has also been sold to Dabel Brothers to be published as a comic book/graphic novel; *Indigo Springs* and a sequel, by A.M. Dellamonica (Tor); Wayne Arthurson's debut mystery plus a second series book; *Bone Crossed* and *Cry Wolf* for *New York Times* #1 best-selling author Patricia Briggs (Ace/Penguin). "The latter is the start of a new series."

Tips "Consider query letters and synopses as writing assignments. Spell names correctly."

◎ WENDY LIPKIND AGENCY

120 E. 81st St., New York NY 10028. (212)628-9653. Fax: (212)585-1306. E-mail: lipkindag@aol.com. **Contact:** Wendy Lipkind. Member of AAR. Represents 40 clients. Currently handles: nonfiction books 100%.

Represents Nonfiction books. **Considers these nonfiction areas:** autobiography, biography, current affairs, health, history, medicine, science, technology, women's issues, women's studies, social history; narrative nonfiction.

○→ This agency specializes in adult nonfiction.

How to Contact Prefers to read materials exclusively. Accepts e-mail queries only (no attachments). Obtains most new clients through recommendations from others.

Terms Agent receives 15% commission on domestic sales. Agent receives 20% commission on foreign sales. Sometimes offers written contract. Charges clients for foreign postage, messenger service, photocopying, transatlantic calls, faxes.

Recent Sales Sold 10 titles in the last year. *Master Class*, by Toba Garrett (Wiley); *Vex, Hex, Smash and Smooch*, by Constance Hale (W.W. Norton).

Tips Send intelligent query letter first. Let me know if you've submitted to other agents.

☑ LIPPINCOTT MASSIE MCQUILKIN

27 West 20th Street, Suite 305, New York NY 10011. Fax: (212)352-2059. E-mail: info@lmqlit.com. Website: www.lmqlit.com. **Contact:** Rob McQuilkin. Represents 90 clients. 30% of clients are new/unpublished writers. Currently handles: nonfiction books 40%, novels 40%, story collections 10%, scholarly books 5%, poetry 5%.

Member Agents Maria Massie (fiction, memoir, cultural criticism); Will Lippincott (politics, current affairs, history); Rob McQuilkin (fiction, history, psychology, sociology, graphic material); Jason Anthony (pop culture, memoir, true crime, and general psychology).

Represents Nonfiction books, novels, short story collections, scholarly, graphic novels. **Considers these nonfiction areas:** animals, anthropology, archeology, architecture, art, autobiography, biography, business, child guidance, cultural interests, current affairs, design, economics, ethnic, film, gay/lesbian, government, health, history, inspirational, language, law, literature, medicine, memoirs, military, money, music, parenting, popular culture, politics, psychology, religious, science, self-help, sociology, technology, true crime, women's issues, women's studies. **Considers these fiction areas:** action, adventure, cartoon, comic books, confession, family saga, feminist, gay, historical, humor, lesbian, literary, mainstream, regional, satire.

○┳ "LMQ focuses on bringing new voices in literary and commercial fiction to the market, as well as popularizing the ideas and arguments of scholars in the fields of history, psychology, sociology, political science, and current affairs. Actively seeking fiction writers who already have credits in magazines and quarterlies, as well as nonfiction writers who already have a media platform or some kind of a university affiliation." Does not want to receive romance, genre fiction or children's material.

How to Contact "We accepts electronic queries only. Only send additional materials if requested." Accepts simultaneous submissions. Responds in 1 week to queries. Responds in 1 month to mss. Obtains most new clients through recommendations from others, solicitations, conferences.

Terms Agent receives 15% commission on domestic sales. Agent receives 20% commission on foreign sales. Offers written contract; 30-day notice must be given to terminate contract. Only charges for reasonable business expenses upon successful sale.

Recent Sales Clients include: Peter Ho Davies, Kim Addonizio, Don Lee, Natasha Trethewey, Anatol Lieven, Sir Michael Marmot, Anne Carson, Liza Ward, David Sirota, Anne Marie Slaughter, Marina Belozerskaya, Kate Walbert.

◙ LITERARY AND CREATIVE ARTISTS, INC.

2123 Paris Metz Rd.,, Chattanooga TN 37421. E-mail: southernlitagent@aol.com. **Contact:** Muriel Nellis. Member of AAR. Other memberships include Authors Guild, American Bar Association. Currently handles: nonfiction books 50%, novels 50%.

Member Agents Prior to becoming an agent, Mr. Powell was in sales and contract negotiation.

Represents Nonfiction books, novels, art, biography, business, photography, popular culture, religion, self-help, literary, regional, religious, satire. **Considers these nonfiction areas:** autobiography, biography, business, cooking, diet/nutrition, economics, foods, government, health, how-to, law, medicine, memoirs, philosophy, politics, human drama; lifestyle.

○┳ "We focus on authors that live in the Southern United States. We have the ability to translate and explain complexities of publishing for the Southern author." "Actively seeking quality projects by authors with a vision of where they want to be in 10 years and a plan of how to get there." Does not want to receive unfinished, unedited projects that do not follow the standard presentation conventions of the trade. No Romance.

How to Contact Query via e-mail first and include a synopsis. Accepts simultaneous submissions. Responds in 2-3 months to queries. Responds in 1 week mss. Obtains new clients through recommendations from others.

Terms Agent receives 15% commission on domestic sales. Agent receives 25% commission on foreign sales. Offers written contract. Charges clients for long-distance phone/fax, photocopying, shipping.

Tips "If you are an unpublished author, join a writers group, even if it is on the Internet. You need good honest feedback. Don't send a manuscript that has not been read by at least five people. Don't send a manuscript cold to any agent without first asking if they want it. Try to meet the agent face to face before signing. Make sure the fit is right."

◙ THE LITERARY GROUP INTERNATIONAL

14 Penn Plaza, Suite 925, New York NY 10122. (646)442-5896. E-mail: js@theliterarygroup.com. Website: www.theliterarygroup.com. **Contact:** Frank Weimann. 65% of clients are new/unpublished writers. Currently handles: nonfiction books 50%, other 50% fiction.

Member Agents Frank Weimann.

Represents Nonfiction books, novels, graphic novels. **Considers these nonfiction areas:** animals, anthropology, biography, business, child guidance, crafts, creative nonfiction, current affairs, education, ethnic, film, government, health, history, humor, juvenile nonfiction, language, memoirs, military, multicultural, music, nature, popular culture, politics, psychology, religious, science, self-help, sociology, sports, travel, true crime, women's issues, women's studies. **Considers these fiction areas:** adventure, contemporary issues, detective, ethnic, experimental, family saga, fantasy, feminist, historical, horror, humor, literary, multicultural, mystery, psychic, romance, sports, thriller, young adult, regional, graphic novels.

○┳ This agency specializes in nonfiction (memoir, military, history, biography, sports, how-to).

How to Contact Query with SASE. Prefers to read materials exclusively. Only responds if interested. Obtains most new clients through referrals, writers conferences, query letters.

Terms Agent receives 15% commission on domestic sales. Agent receives 20% commission on foreign sales. Offers written contract; 30-day notice must be given to terminate contract.

Recent Sales *One From the Hart*, by Stefanie Powers with Richard Buskin (Pocket Books); *Sacred Trust, Deadly Betrayal*, by Keith Anderson (Berkley); *Gotti Confidential*, by Victoria Gotti (Pocket Books); Anna Sui's illustrated memoir (Chronicle Books); *Mania*, by Craig Larsen (Kensington); *Everything Explained Through Flowcharts*, by Doogie Horner (HarperCollins); *Bitch*, by Lisa Taddeo (TOR); film rights for *Falling Out of Fashion*, by Karen Yampolsky to Hilary Swank and Molly Smith for 2S Films.

Writers Conferences San Diego State University Writers' Conference; Maui Writers' Conference; Agents and Editors Conference; NAHJ Convention in Puerto Rico, among others.

☙ LITERARY MANAGEMENT GROUP, INC.

(615)812-4445. E-mail: brucebarbour@literarymanagementgroup.com; brb@brucebarbour.com. Website: http//:literarymanagementgroup.com; www.brucebarbour.com. **Contact:** Bruce Barbour.

• Prior to becoming an agent, Mr. Barbour held executive positions at several publishing houses, including Revell, Barbour Books, Thomas Nelson, and Random House.

Represents Nonfiction books, novels. **Considers these nonfiction areas:** biography, Christian living; spiritual growth; women's and men's issues; prayer; devotional; meditational; Bible study; marriage; business; family/parenting.

⚷ "Although we specialize in the area of Christian publishing from an Evangelical perspective, we have editorial contacts and experience in general interest books as well." Does not want to receive gift books, poetry, children's books, short stories, or juvenile/young adult fiction. No unsolicited mss or proposals from unpublished authors.

How to Contact Query with SASE. E-mail proposal as an attachment.

Terms Agent receives 15% commission on domestic sales.

☙ LITERARY SERVICES, INC.

P.O. Box 888, Barnegat NJ 08005. (609)698-7162. Fax: (609)698-7163. E-mail: john@ LiteraryServicesInc.com. Website: www.LiteraryServicesInc.com. **Contact:** John Willig. Other memberships include Author's Guild. Represents 90 clients. 25% of clients are new/unpublished writers. Currently handles: nonfiction books 100%. Beginning to accept and consider crime fiction projects.

Member Agents John Willig (business, personal growth, narratives, history, health); Cynthia Zigmund (personal finance, investments, entrepreneurship).

Represents Nonfiction books. **Considers these nonfiction areas:** architecture, art, biography, business, child guidance, cooking, crafts, design, economics, health, history, politics, how-to, humor, language, literature, metaphysics, money, New Age, popular culture, psychology, satire, science, self-help, sports, technology, true crime.

⚷ "Our publishing experience and 'inside' knowledge of how companies and editors really work sets us apart from many agencies; our specialties are noted above, but we are open to unique presentations in all nonfiction topic areas." Actively seeking business, work/life topics, story-driven narratives. Does not want to receive fiction (except crime fiction), children's books, science fiction, religion or memoirs.

How to Contact Query with SASE. For starters, a one-page outline sent via e-mail is acceptable. See our website and our Submissions section to learn more about our questions. Do not send mss unless requested. Accepts simultaneous submissions. Responds in 3-4 weeks to queries. Responds in 4 weeks to mss. Obtains most new clients through recommendations from others, solicitations, conferences.

Terms Agent receives 15% commission on domestic sales. Agent receives 20% commission on foreign sales. Offers written contract. This agency charges administrative fees for copying, postage, etc.

Recent Sales Sold 32 titles in the last year. *In Pursuit of Elegance* (Doubleday/Currency). A full list of new books are noted on the website.

Writers Conferences Author 101; Publicity Summit; Writer's Digest.

Tips "Be focused. In all likelihood, your work is not going to be of interest to 'a very broad audience' or 'every parent,' so I appreciate when writers put aside their passion and do some homework, i.e. positioning, special features and benefits of your work. Be a marketer. How have you tested your ideas and writing (beyond your inner circle of family and friends)? Have you received any key awards for your work or endorsements from influential persons in your field? What steps, especially social media, have you taken to increase your presence in the market?"

N ☑ LIVING WORD LITERARY AGENCY

PO Box 40974, Eugene OR 97414. E-mail: livingwordliterary@gmail.com. Website: livingwordliterary. wordpress.com. **Contact:** Kimberly Shumate. Estab. 2008. Member, Christian Media Association.

- Kimberly began her employment with Harvest House Publishers as the assistant to the National Sales Manager as well as the International Sales Director.

Represents Fiction and nonfiction. **Considers these nonfiction areas:** health, parenting, self-help, relationships. **Considers these fiction areas:** inspirational, young adult, adult fiction, Christian living.

- ☞ Does not want to receive cookbooks, children's books, science fiction or fantasy, memoirs, or poetry.

How to Contact Submit a query with short synopsis and first chapter via Word document. Agency only responds if interested.

LJK LITERARY MANAGEMENT

708 Third Ave., 16th Floor, New York NY 10018. (212)221-8797. Fax: (212)221-8722. E-mail: submissions@ljkliterary.com. Website: www.ljkliterary.com. Represents 20+ clients.

- Larry Kirschbaum is the former head of Time Warner Book group; Jud Laghi worked for ICM; Susanna Einstein worked for Maria B. Campbell Associates; Meg Thompson worked for Bill Clinton and Charlie Rose before joining Larry in starting LJK; Lisa Leshne co-founded *The Prague Post*.

Member Agents Larry Kirshbaum; Susanna Einstein (contemporary fiction, literary fiction, romance, suspense, historical fiction, middle grade, young adult, crime fiction, narrative nonfiction, memoir and biography); Meg Thompson (new media, narrative nonfiction, politics, pop culture, humor); Lisa Leshne (nonfiction, memoirs, literary and popular fiction, business, politics, pop culture).

Represents Nonfiction books, novels.

- ☞ "We are not considering picture books or poetry collections."

How to Contact Send query letter in the body of an e-mail to submissions@ljkliterary.com with 25-page sample (fiction) or proposal (nonfiction) as an attachment; if sending a paper query, include SASE. E-mail is preferred. No fax queries. Responds in 8 weeks to queries. Responds in 8 weeks to mss.

Recent Sales *Think Big and Kick Ass*, by Donald Trump and Bill Zanker; *The Book of Love*, by Kathleen McGowan; *The Christmas Pearl*, by Dorothea Benton Frank; *The Hidden Man*, by David Ellis; *Maphead*, by Ken Jennings; *Grandma's Dead*, by Ben Schwartz and Amanda McCall; *Found II*, by Davy Rothbart; *Amberville*, by Tim Davys; *Moses Never Closes*, by Jenny Wingfield; *Daily Routines*, by Mason Currey.

Tips "All submissions will receive a response from us if they adhere to our submission guidelines. Please do not contact us to inquire about your submission unless 8 weeks have passed."

☑ JULIA LORD LITERARY MANAGEMENT

38 W. Ninth St., #4, New York NY 10011. (212)995-2333. Fax: (212)995-2332. E-mail: query@ juliallordliterary.com. Website: julialordliterary.com. Member of AAR.

Member Agents Julia Lord, owner.

Represents Nonfiction, fiction. **Considers these nonfiction areas:** autobiography, biography, environment, history, humor, science, sports, travel, African-American; lifestyle; narrative nonfiction; reference. **Considers these fiction areas:** action, adventure, historical, literary, mainstream.

How to Contact Query letter or recommendation. All hard copy query letters will be answered. Query e-mails will only be answered if we are interested. Obtains most new clients through recommendations from others, solicitations.

☑ STERLING LORD LITERISTIC, INC.

65 Bleecker St., 12th Floor, New York NY 10012. (212)780-6050. Fax: (212)780-6095. E-mail: info@ sll.com. Website: www.sll.com. Member of AAR. Signatory of WGA. Represents 600 clients. Currently handles: nonfiction books 50%, novels 50%.

Member Agents Sterling Lord; Peter Matson; Phillippa Brophy (represents journalists, nonfiction writers and novelists, and is most interested in current events, memoir, science, politics, biography,

and women's issues); Chris Calhoun; Claudia Cross (a broad range of fiction and nonfiction, from literary fiction to commercial women's fiction and romance novels, to cookbooks, lifestyle titles, memoirs, serious nonfiction on religious and spiritual topics, and books for the CBA marketplace); Rebecca Friedman (memoir, reportorial nonfiction, history, current events, literary, international and commerical fiction); Robert Guinsler (literary and commercial fiction, journalism, narrative nonfiction with an emphasis on pop culture, science and current events, memoirs and biographies); Laurie Liss (commercial and literary fiction and nonfiction whose perspectives are well developed and unique); Judy Heiblum (fiction and nonfiction writers, looking for distinctive voices that challenge the reader, emotionally or intellectually. She works with journalists, academics, memoirists, and essayists, and is particularly interested in books that explore the intersections of science, culture, history and philosophy. In addition, she is always looking for writers of literary fiction with fresh, uncompromising voices); Neeti Madan (memoir, journalism, history, pop culture, health, lifestyle, women's issues, multicultural books and virtually any intelligent writing on intriguing topics. Neeti is looking for smart, well-written commercial novels, as well as compelling and provocative literary works); George Nicholson (writers and illustrators for children); Jim Rutman; Charlotte Sheedy; Ira Silverberg; Douglas Stewart (literary fiction, narrative nonfiction, and young adult fiction).
Represents Nonfiction books, novels.
How to Contact Query with SASE by snail mail. Include synopsis of the work, a brief proposal or the first three chapters of the manuscript, and brief bio or resume. Does not respond to unsolicited e-mail queries. Responds in 1 month to mss. Obtains most new clients through recommendations from others.
Terms Agent receives 15% commission on domestic sales. Agent receives 20% commission on foreign sales. Offers written contract. Charges clients for photocopying.

☑ NANCY LOVE LITERARY AGENCY
250 E. 65th St., New York NY 10065-6614. (212)980-3499. Fax: (212)308-6405. E-mail: nloveag@aol.com. **Contact:** Nancy Love. Member of AAR. Represents 60-80 clients. 25% of clients are new/unpublished writers. Currently handles: nonfiction books 100%.
Member Agents *This agency is not taking on any new fiction writers at this time.*
Represents Nonfiction books. **Considers these nonfiction areas:** autobiography, biography, child guidance, cooking, cultural interests, current affairs, diet/nutrition, environment, ethnic, foods, government, health, history, how-to, inspirational, law, medicine, parenting, popular culture, politics, psychology, religious, science, self-help, sociology, spirituality, women's issues, travel (arm-chair only, no how-to).
   ☛ This agency specializes in adult nonfiction. Actively seeking narrative nonfiction.
How to Contact Query with SASE. No fax queries. Accepts simultaneous submissions. Responds in 3 weeks to queries. Responds in 6 weeks to mss. Obtains most new clients through recommendations from others, solicitations.
Terms Agent receives 15% commission on domestic sales. Agent receives 20% commission on foreign sales. Offers written contract.
Recent Sales *Reset: Iran, Turkey, and America's Future*, by Stephen Kinzer (Henry Holt); *The Ten Stupidest Mistakes Men Make When Facing Divorce*, by Joseph E. Cordell, Esq. (Crown); *Brazil on the Rise*, by Larry Rohter (Macmillan).
Tips "Nonfiction authors and/or collaborators must be an authority in their subject area and have a platform. Send an SASE if you want a response."

☑ LOWENSTEIN ASSOCIATES INC.
121 W. 27th St., Suite 601, New York NY 10001. (212)206-1630. Fax: (212)727-0280. Website: www.lowensteinassociates.com. **Contact:** Barbara Lowenstein. Member of AAR. Represents 150 clients. 20% of clients are new/unpublished writers. Currently handles: nonfiction books 60%, novels 40%.
Member Agents Barbara Lowenstein, president (nonfiction interests include narrative nonfiction, health, money, finance, travel, multicultural, popular culture and memoir; fiction interests include literary fiction and women's fiction); Kathleen Ortiz, associate agent and foreign rights manager at Lowenstein Associates. She is seeking children's books (chapter, middle grade, and young adult) and young adult nonfiction.

Represents Nonfiction books, novels. **Considers these nonfiction areas:** animals, anthropology, archeology, autobiography, biography, business, child guidance, current affairs, education, ethnic, film, government, health, history, how-to, language, literature, medicine, memoirs, money, multicultural, parenting, popular culture, psychology, science, sociology, travel, music; narrative nonfiction; science; film. **Considers these fiction areas:** crime, detective, erotica, ethnic, fantasy, feminist, historical, literary, mainstream, mystery, police, romance, suspense, thriller, young adult.

⚓ "This agency specializes in health, business, creative nonfiction, literary fiction and commercial fiction—especially suspense, crime and women's issues. We are a full-service agency, handling domestic and foreign rights, film rights and audio rights to all of our books." Barbara Lowenstein is currently looking for writers who have a platform and are leading experts in their field, including business, women's issues, psychology, health, science and social issues, and is particularly interested in strong new voices in fiction and narrative nonfiction.

How to Contact Query with SASE or via electronic form on each agent's page. Submit to only one agent. Prefers to read materials exclusively. For fiction, send outline and first chapter. *No unsolicited mss.* Responds in 4 weeks to queries. Obtains most new clients through recommendations from others, solicitations, conferences.

Terms Agent receives 15% commission on domestic sales. Agent receives 20% commission on foreign sales. Offers written contract. Charges for large photocopy batches, messenger service, international postage.

Writers Conferences Malice Domestic

Tips Know the genre you are working in and read! Also, please see our website for details on which agent to query for your project.

🌐 ◎ ANDREW LOWNIE LITERARY AGENCY, LTD.

36 Great Smith St., London SW1P 3BU England. (44)(207)222-7574. Fax: (44)(207)222-7576. E-mail: lownie@globalnet.co.uk. Website: www.andrewlownie.co.uk. **Contact:** Andrew Lownie. Other memberships include AAA. Represents 130 clients. 20% of clients are new/unpublished writers. Currently handles: nonfiction books 90%, novels 10%.

• Prior to becoming an agent, Mr. Lownie was a journalist, bookseller, publisher, author of 12 books and director of the Curtis Brown Agency.

Represents Nonfiction books. **Considers these nonfiction areas:** autobiography, biography, current affairs, government, history, investigative, law, memoirs, military, popular culture, politics, true crime, war.

⚓ "This agent has wide publishing experience, extensive journalistic contacts, and a specialty in showbiz/celebrity memoir." Showbiz memoirs, narrative histories, and biographies. No poetry, short stories, children's fiction, academic or scripts.

How to Contact Query with SASE and/or IRC. Submit outline, 1 sample chapter. Accepts simultaneous submissions. Responds in 1 week to queries. Responds in 1 month to mss. Obtains most new clients through recommendations from others.

Terms Agent receives 15% commission on domestic sales. Agent receives 15% commission on foreign sales. Offers written contract; 30-day notice must be given to terminate contract.

Recent Sales Sold 50 titles in the last year, with over a dozen top ten bestsellers including two number 1's, as well as the memoirs of actor Warwick Davis, Multiple Personality Disorder sufferer Alice Jamieson, round-the-world yachtsman Mike Perham, poker player Dave 'Devilfish' Ulliott. Other clients: Juliet Barker, Guy Bellamy, Joyce Cary estate, Roger Crowley, Duncan Falconer, Laurence Gardner, Cathy Glass, Timothy Good, Lawrence James, Christopher Lloyd, Sian Rees, Desmond Seward, Daniel Tammet and Christian Wolmar.

🅽 MARSAL LYON LITERARY AGENCY, LLC

PMB 121, 665 San Rodolfo Dr. 124, Solana Beach CA 92075. (858) 492-8009. E-mail: Kevan@MarsalLyonLiteraryAgency.com; Jill@MarsalLyonLiteraryAgency.com. Website: www.marsallyonliteraryagency.com. **Contact:** Kevan Lyon, Jill Marsal.

Represents Nonfiction books, novels. **Considers these nonfiction areas:** animals, biography, business, cooking, current affairs, foods, health, history, memoirs, music, nature, parenting, popular culture, politics, psychology, science, self-help, sports, women's issues, relationships, advice. **Considers these fiction areas:** historical, mainstream, multicultural, mystery, paranormal, romance, suspense, thriller, women's, young adult.

How to Contact Query by e-mail to either Jill Marsal at jill@marsallyonliteraryagency.com or Kevan Lyon at kevan@marsallyonliteraryagency.com. Please visit our website to determine who is best suited for your work. Write 'query' in the subject line of your e-mail. Please allow up to several weeks to hear back on your query.

Tips "Our Agency's mission is to help writers achieve their publishing dreams. We want to work with authors not just for a book but for a career; we are dedicated to building long-term relationships with our authors and publishing partners. Our goal is to help find homes for books that engage, entertain, and make a difference."

☑ LYONS LITERARY, LLC

27 West 20th St., Suite 10003, New York NY 10011. (212)255-5472. Fax: (212)851-8405. E-mail: info@lyonsliterary.com. Website: www.lyonsliterary.com. **Contact:** Jonathan Lyons. Member of AAR. Other memberships include The Author's Guild, American Bar Association, New York State Bar Associaton, New York State Intellectual Property Law Section. Represents 37 clients. 15% of clients are new/unpublished writers. Currently handles: nonfiction books 60%, novels 40%.

Represents Nonfiction books, novels. **Considers these nonfiction areas:** animals, autobiography, biography, cooking, crafts, cultural interests, current affairs, diet/nutrition, ethnic, foods, gay/lesbian, government, health, history, hobbies, how-to, humor, law, medicine, memoirs, military, money, multicultural, popular culture, politics, psychology, science, sociology, sports, technology, translation, travel, true crime, women's issues, women's studies. **Considers these fiction areas:** contemporary issues, crime, detective, fantasy, feminist, gay, historical, humor, lesbian, literary, mainstream, mystery, police, psychic, regional, satire, science fiction, sports, supernatural, suspense, thriller, women's, chick lit.

    ⊶ "With my legal expertise and experience selling domestic and foreign language book rights, paperback reprint rights, audio rights, film/TV rights and permissions, I am able to provide substantive and personal guidance to my clients in all areas relating to their projects. In addition, with the advent of new publishing technology, Lyons Literary, LLC is situated to address the changing nature of the industry while concurrently handling authors' more traditional needs."

How to Contact Only accepts queries through online submission form. Accepts simultaneous submissions. Responds in 8 weeks to queries. Responds in 12 weeks to mss. Obtains most new clients through recommendations from others.

Terms Agent receives 15% commission on domestic sales. Agent receives 20% commission on foreign sales. Offers written contract.

Writers Conferences Agents and Editors Conference.

Tips "Please submit electronic queries through our website submission form."

☑ DONALD MAASS LITERARY AGENCY

121 W. 27th St., Suite 801, New York NY 10001. (212)727-8383. E-mail: info@maassagency.com. Website: www.maassagency.com. Member of AAR. Other memberships include SFWA, MWA, RWA. Represents more than 100 clients. 5% of clients are new/unpublished writers. Currently handles: novels 100%.

    • Prior to opening his agency, Mr. Maass served as an editor at Dell Publishing (New York) and as a reader at Gollancz (London). He also served as the president of AAR.

Member Agents Donald Maass (mainstream, literary, mystery/suspense, science fiction, romance); Jennifer Jackson (commercial fiction, romance, science fiction, fantasy, mystery/suspense); Cameron McClure (literary, mystery/suspense, urban, fantasy, narrative nonfiction and projects with multicultural, international, and environmental themes, gay/lesbian); Ms. J.L. Stermer (fiction, memoir, narrative nonfiction, pop-culture [cooking, fashion, style, music, art], smart humor, upscale erotica/erotic memoir and multi-cultural fiction/nonfiction); Amy Boggs (fantasy and science fiction, especially urban fantasy, paranormal romance, steampunk, YA/children's, and alternate history. historical fiction, multi-cultural fiction, Westerns).

Represents Novels. **Considers these nonfiction areas:** narrative nonfiction (and see J.L's bio for subject interest). **Considers these fiction areas:** crime, detective, fantasy, historical, horror, literary, mainstream, mystery, police, psychic, science fiction, supernatural, suspense, thriller, women's, romance (historical, paranormal, and time travel).

→ This agency specializes in commercial fiction, especially science fiction, fantasy, mystery and suspense. Actively seeking to expand in literary fiction and women's fiction. Does not want to receive nonfiction, picture books, prescriptive nonfiction, or poetry.

How to Contact Query with SASE. Returns material only with SASE. Accepts simultaneous submissions. Responds in 2 weeks to queries. Responds in 3 months to mss.

Terms Agent receives 15% commission on domestic sales. Agent receives 20% commission on foreign sales.

Recent Sales *Codex Alera 5: Princep's Fury*, by Jim Butcher (Ace); *Fonseca 6: Bright Futures*, by Stuart Kaimsky (Forge): *Fathom*, by Cherie Priest (Tor); *Gospel Grrls 3: Be Strong and Curvaceous*, by Shelly Adina (Faith Words); *Ariane 1: Peacekeeper*, by Laura Reeve (Roc); *Execution Dock*, by Anne Perry (Random House).

Writers Conferences Donald Maass: World Science Fiction Convention; Frankfurt Book Fair; Pacific Northwest Writers Conference; Bouchercon. Jennifer Jackson: World Science Fiction Convention; RWA National Conference.

Tips We are fiction specialists, also noted for our innovative approach to career planning. Few new clients are accepted, but interested authors should query with a SASE. Works with subagents in all principle foreign countries and Hollywood. No prescriptive nonfiction, picture books or poetry will be considered.

◎ GINA MACCOBY LITERARY AGENCY

P.O. Box 60, Chappaqua NY 10514. (914)238-5630. **Contact:** Gina Maccoby. Member of AAR. Ethics and Contracts subcommittee; Authors Guild Represents 25 clients. Currently handles: nonfiction books 33%, novels 33%, juvenile books 33%, other illustrators of children's books.

Represents Nonfiction books, novels, juvenile. **Considers these nonfiction areas:** autobiography, biography, cultural interests, current affairs, ethnic, history, juvenile nonfiction, popular culture, women's issues, women's studies. **Considers these fiction areas:** juvenile, literary, mainstream, mystery, thriller, young adult.

How to Contact Query with SASE. If querying by e-mail, put "query" in subject line. Accepts simultaneous submissions. Responds in 3 months to queries. Obtains most new clients through recommendations from clients and publishers.

Terms Agent receives 15% commission on domestic sales. Agent receives 25% commission on foreign sales. Charges clients for photocopying. May recover certain costs, such as legal fees or the cost of shipping books by air to Europe or Japan.

◎ MACGREGOR LITERARY

2373 N.W. 185th Ave., Suite 165, Hillsboro OR 97214. (503)277-8308. E-mail: submissions@ macgregorliterary.com. Website: www.macgregorliterary.com. **Contact:** Chip MacGregor. Signatory of WGA. Represents 40 clients. 10% of clients are new/unpublished writers. Currently handles: nonfiction books 40%, novels 60%.

• Prior to his current position, Mr. MacGregor was the senior agent with Alive Communications. Most recently, he was associate publisher for Time-Warner Book Group's Faith Division, and helped put together their Center Street imprint.

Member Agents Chip MacGregor, Sarah Bishop.

Represents Nonfiction books, novels. **Considers these nonfiction areas:** business, current affairs, economics, history, how-to, humor, inspirational, parenting, popular culture, satire, self-help, sports, marriage. **Considers these fiction areas:** crime, detective, historical, inspirational, mainstream, mystery, police, religious, romance, suspense, thriller, women's, chick lit.

→ "My specialty has been in career planning with authors—finding commercial ideas, then helping authors bring them to market, and in the midst of that assisting the authors as they get firmly established in their writing careers. I'm probably best known for my work with Christian books over the years, but I've done a fair amount of general market projects as well." Actively seeking authors with a Christian worldview and a growing platform. Does not want to receive fantasy, sci-fi, children's books, poetry or screenplays.

How to Contact Query with SASE. Accepts simultaneous submissions. Responds in 3 weeks to queries. Obtains most new clients through recommendations from others. Not looking to add unpublished authors except through referrals from current clients.

Terms Agent receives 15% commission on domestic sales. Agent receives 15% commission on foreign sales. Offers written contract; 30-day notice must be given to terminate contract. Charges for exceptional fees after receiving authors' permission.

Writers Conferences Blue Ridge Christian Writers' Conference; Write to Publish.

Tips "Seriously consider attending a good writers' conference. It will give you the chance to be face-to-face with people in the industry. Also, if you're a novelist, consider joining one of the national writers' organizations. The American Christian Fiction Writers (ACFW) is a wonderful group for new as well as established writers. And if you're a Christian writer of any kind, check into The Writers View, an online writing group. All of these have proven helpful to writers."

☑ RICIA MAINHARDT AGENCY (RMA)

612 Argyle Road, #L5, Brooklyn NY 11230. (718)434-1893. Fax: (718)434-2157. E-mail: ricia@ricia.com. Website: www.ricia.com. **Contact:** Ricia Mainhardt. Represents 10 clients. 50% of clients are new/unpublished writers. Currently handles: nonfiction books 40%, novella 50%, juvenile books 10%.

Represents Nonfiction books, novels, juvenile. **Considers these fiction areas:** action, adventure, confession, crime, detective, erotica, ethnic, family saga, fantasy, feminist, frontier, gay, glitz, historical, horror, humor, juvenile, lesbian, literary, mainstream, mystery, police, psychic, regional, romance, satire, science fiction, sports, supernatural, suspense, thriller, westerns, women's, young adult.

　�☞ "We are a small boutique agency that provides hands-on service and attention to clients." Actively seeking adult and young adult fiction, nonfiction, picture books for early readers. Does not want to receive poetry, children's books or screenplays.

How to Contact Query with SASE or by e-mail. See guidelines on website depending on type of ms. No attachments or diskettes. Accepts simultaneous submissions. Responds in 1 month to queries. Responds in 4 months to mss. Obtains most new clients through recommendations from others, solicitations.

Terms Agent receives 15% commission on domestic sales. Offers written contract; 90-day notice must be given to terminate contract.

Writers Conferences Science Fiction Worldcon; Lunacon, World Fantasy, RWA.

Tips "Be professional; be patient. It takes a long time for me to evaluate all the submissions that come through the door. Pestering phone calls and e-mails are not appreciated. Write the best book you can in your own style and keep an active narrative voice."

☑ KIRSTEN MANGES LITERARY AGENCY

115 West 29th St., Third Floor, New York NY 10001. E-mail: kirsten@mangeslit.com. Website: www.mangeslit.com. **Contact:** Kirsten Manges.

　• Prior to her current position, Ms. Manges was an agent at Curtis Brown.

Represents Nonfiction books, novels. **Considers these nonfiction areas:** cooking, diet/nutrition, foods, history, memoirs, multicultural, psychology, science, spirituality, sports, technology, travel, women's issues, women's studies, journalism, narrative. **Considers these fiction areas:** commercial, women's, chick lit.

　☞ This agency has a focus on women's issues. "Actively seeking high quality fiction and nonfiction. I'm looking for strong credentials, an original point of view and excellent writing skills. With fiction, I'm looking for well written commercial novels, as well as compelling and provocative literary works."

How to Contact Query with SASE. Obtains most new clients through recommendations from others, solicitations.

☑ CAROL MANN AGENCY

55 Fifth Ave., New York NY 10003. (212)206-5635. Fax: (212)675-4809. Website: www.carolmannagency.com/. **Contact:** Eliza Dreier. Member of AAR. Represents roughly 200 clients. 15% of clients are new/unpublished writers. Currently handles: nonfiction books 90%, novels 10%.

Member Agents Carol Mann (health/medical, religion, spirituality, self-help, parenting, narrative nonfiction); Laura Yorke; Gareth Esersky; Myrsini Stephanides (Nonfiction areas of interest: pop culture and music, humor, narrative nonfiction and memoir, cookbooks; fiction areas of interest: offbeat literary fiction, graphic works, and edgy YA fiction).

Represents Nonfiction books, novels. **Considers these nonfiction areas:** anthropology, archeology, architecture, art, autobiography, biography, business, child guidance, cultural interests, current affairs, design, ethnic, government, health, history, law, medicine, money, music, parenting, popular culture, politics, psychology, self-help, sociology, sports, women's issues, women's studies. **Considers these fiction areas:** commercial, literary.

☛ This agency specializes in current affairs, self-help, popular culture, psychology, parenting, and history. Does not want to receive genre fiction (romance, mystery, etc.).

How to Contact Keep initial query/contact to no more than two pages. Responds in 4 weeks to queries.

Terms Agent receives 15% commission on domestic sales. Agent receives 20% commission on foreign sales. Offers written contract.

▥ ◎ SARAH MANSON LITERARY AGENT

6 Totnes Walk, London N2 0AD United Kingdom. (44)(208)442-0396. E-mail: info@sarahmanson. com. Website: www.sarahmanson.com. **Contact:** Sarah Manson. Currently handles: juvenile books 100%.

• Prior to opening her agency, Ms. Manson worked in academic and children's publishing for 10 years and was a chartered school librarian for 8 years.

☛ This agency specializes in fiction for children and young adults. No picture books. Does not want to receive submissions from writers outside the United Kingdom and the Republic of Ireland.

How to Contact See website for full submission guidelines.

Terms Agent receives 10% commission on domestic sales. Agent receives 20% commission on foreign sales. Offers written contract, binding for 1-month.

▨ MANUS & ASSOCIATES LITERARY AGENCY, INC.

425 Sherman Ave., Suite 200, Palo Alto CA 94306. (650)470-5151. Fax: (650)470-5159. E-mail: manuslit@manuslit.com. Website: www.manuslit.com. **Contact:** Jillian Manus, Jandy Nelson, Penny Nelson. Member of AAR. Represents 75 clients. 30% of clients are new/unpublished writers. Currently handles: nonfiction books 70%, novels 30%.

• Prior to becoming an agent, Ms. Manus was associate publisher of two national magazines and director of development at Warner Bros. and Universal Studios; she has been a literary agent for 20 years.

Member Agents Jandy Nelson, jandy@manuslit.com (self-help, health, memoirs, narrative nonfiction, women's fiction, literary fiction, multicultural fiction, thrillers). Nelson is currently on sabbatical and not taking on new clients. Jillian Manus, jillian@manuslit.com (political, memoirs, self-help, history, sports, women's issues, Latin fiction and nonfiction, thrillers); Penny Nelson, penny@manuslit.com (memoirs, self-help, sports, nonfiction); Dena Fischer (literary fiction, mainstream/commercial fiction, chick lit, women's fiction, historical fiction, ethnic/cultural fiction, narrative nonfiction, parenting, relationships, pop culture, health, sociology, psychology); Janet Wilkens Manus (narrative fact-based crime books, religion, pop psychology, inspiration, memoirs, cookbooks); Stephanie Lee (not currently taking on new clients).

Represents Nonfiction books, novels. **Considers these nonfiction areas:** autobiography, biography, business, child guidance, cultural interests, current affairs, economics, environment, ethnic, health, how-to, medicine, memoirs, money, parenting, popular culture, psychology, science, self-help, technology, women's issues, women's studies, Gen X and Gen Y issues; creative nonfiction. **Considers these fiction areas:** literary, mainstream, multicultural, mystery, suspense, thriller, women's, quirky/edgy fiction.

☛ "Our agency is unique in the way that we not only sell the material, but we edit, develop concepts, and participate in the marketing effort. We specialize in large, conceptual fiction and nonfiction, and always value a project that can be sold in the TV/feature film market." Actively seeking high-concept thrillers, commercial literary fiction, women's fiction, celebrity biographies, memoirs, multicultural fiction, popular health, women's empowerment and mysteries. No horror, romance, science fiction, fantasy, Western, young adult, children's, poetry, cookbooks or magazine articles.

How to Contact Query with SASE. If requested, submit outline, 2-3 sample chapters. All queries should be sent to the California office. Accepts simultaneous submissions. Responds in 3 months to queries. Responds in 3 months to mss. Obtains most new clients through recommendations from others, solicitations, conferences.

Terms Agent receives 15% commission on domestic sales. Agent receives 20-25% commission on foreign sales. Offers written contract, binding for 2 years; 60-day notice must be given to terminate contract. Charges for photocopying and postage/UPS.

Recent Sales *Nothing Down for the 2000s* and *Multiple Streams of Income for the 2000s*, by Robert Allen; *Missed Fortune 101*, by Doug Andrew; *Cracking the Millionaire Code*, by Mark Victor Hansen and Robert Allen; *Stress Free for Good*, by Dr. Fred Luskin and Dr. Ken Pelletier; *The Mercy of Thin Air*, by Ronlyn Domangue; *The Fine Art of Small Talk*, by Debra Fine; *Bone Men of Bonares*, by Terry Tamoff.

Writers Conferences Maui Writers' Conference; San Diego State University Writers' Conference; Willamette Writers' Conference; BookExpo America; MEGA Book Marketing University.

Tips "Research agents using a variety of sources."

◙ MARCH TENTH, INC.

4 Myrtle St., Haworth NJ 07641-1740. (201)387-6551. Fax: (201)387-6552. E-mail: hchoron@aol.com; schoron@aol.com. Website: www.marchtenthinc.com. **Contact:** Harry Choron, vice president. Represents 40 clients. 30% of clients are new/unpublished writers. Currently handles: nonfiction books 100%.

Represents Nonfiction books. **Considers these nonfiction areas:** autobiography, biography, current affairs, film, health, history, humor, language, literature, medicine, music, popular culture, satire, theater.

> ✺ "We prefer to work with published/established writers." Does not want to receive children's or young adult novels, plays, screenplays or poetry.

How to Contact Query with SASE. Include your proposal, a short bio, and contact information. Accepts simultaneous submissions. Responds in 1 month to queries.

Terms Agent receives 15% commission on domestic sales. Agent receives 20% commission on foreign sales. Agent receives 20% commission on film sales. Charges clients for postage, photocopying, overseas phone expenses. Does not require expense money upfront.

◎ THE DENISE MARCIL LITERARY AGENCY, INC.

156 Fifth Ave., Suite 625, New York NY 10010. (212)337-3402. Fax: (212)727-2688. Website: www.DeniseMarcilAgency.com. **Contact:** Denise Marcil, Anne Marie O'Farrell. Member of AAR.

- Prior to opening her agency, Ms. Marcil served as an editorial assistant with Avon Books and as an assistant editor with Simon & Schuster.

Member Agents Denise Marcil (women's commercial fiction, thrillers, suspense, popular reference, how-to, self-help, health, business, and parenting).

> ✺ *This agency is currently not taking on new authors.*

Terms Agent receives 15% commission on domestic sales. Agent receives 20% commission on foreign sales. Offers written contract, binding for 2 years. Charges $100/year for postage, photocopying, long-distance calls, etc.

Recent Sales For Denise Marcil: *A Chesapeake Shores Christmas*, by Sherryl Woods; *Prime Time Health*, by William Sears, M.D. and Martha Sears, R.N.; *The Autism Book*, by Robert W. Sears, M.D.; *The Yellow House and The Linen Queen*, by Patricia Falvey; *The 10-Minute Total Body Breakthrough*, by Sean Foy. *For Anne Marie O'Farrell: Think Confident, Be Confident*, by Leslie Sokol Ph.d and Marci G. Fox, Ph.d; *Hell Yes*, by Elizabeth Baskin; *Breaking Into the Boys Club*, by Molly Shepard, Jane K. Stimmler, and Peter Dean.

▓ THE MARSH AGENCY, LTD

50 Albemarle Street, London England W1S 4BD United Kingdom. (44)(207)399-2800. Fax: (44)(207)399-2801. Website: www.marsh-agency.co.uk. Estab. 1994.

Member Agents Paul Marsh (agent), Geraldine Cook (agent), Jessica Woollard (agent), Caroline Hardman (agent), Piers Russell-Cobb (agent).

Represents Nonfiction books, novels.

> ✺ "This agency was founded as an international rights specialist for literary agents and publishers in the United Kingdom, the U.S., Canada and New Zealand, for whom we sell foreign rights on a commission basis. We work directly with publishers in all the major

territories and in the majority of the smaller ones; sometimes in conjunction with local representatives." Actively seeking crime novels.

How to Contact Query with SASE. Obtains most new clients through recommendations from others, solicitations.

Recent Sales A full list of clients and sales is available online.

Tips "Use this agency's online form to send a generic e-mail message."

◙ THE EVAN MARSHALL AGENCY

Six Tristam Place, Pine Brook NJ 07058-9445. (973)882-1122. Fax: (973)882-3099. E-mail: evanmarshall@optonline.net. **Contact:** Evan Marshall. Member of AAR. Other memberships include MWA, Sisters in Crime. Currently handles: novels 100%.

Represents Novels. **Considers these fiction areas:** action, adventure, erotica, ethnic, frontier, historical, horror, humor, inspirational, literary, mainstream, mystery, religious, satire, science fiction, suspense, westerns, romance (contemporary, gothic, historical, regency).

How to Contact Query first with SASE; do not enclose material. No e-mail queries. Responds in 1 week to queries. Responds in 3 months to mss. Obtains most new clients through recommendations from others.

Terms Agent receives 15% commission on domestic sales. Agent receives 20% commission on foreign sales. Offers written contract.

Recent Sales *Blood Vines*, by Erica Spindler (St. Martin's Press); *Breakneck*, by Erica Spindler (St. Martin's Press); *Such a Pretty Face*, by Cathy Lamb (Kensington); *If He's Sinful*, by Hannah Howell (Zebra).

◙ THE MARTELL AGENCY

1350 Avenue of the Americas, Suite 1205, New York NY 10019. Fax: (212)317-2676. E-mail: afmartell@aol.com. **Contact:** Alice Martell.

Represents Nonfiction books, novels. **Considers these nonfiction areas:** business, economics, health, history, medicine, memoirs, multicultural, psychology, self-help, women's issues, women's studies. **Considers these fiction areas:** commercial, mystery, suspense, thriller.

How to Contact Query with SASE. Submit sample chapters. Submit via snail mail. No e-mail or fax queries.

Recent Sales *Peddling Peril: The Secret Nuclear Arms Trade*, by David Albright and Joel Wit (Five Press); *America's Women: Four Hundred Years of Dolls, Drudges, Helpmates, and Heroines*, by Gail Collins (William Morrow). Other clients include Serena Bass, Thomas E. Ricks, Janice Erlbaum, David Cay Johnston, Mark Derr, Barbara Rolls, Ph.D.

◙ MARTIN LITERARY MANAGEMENT

321 High School Rd., Suite D3 #316, Bainbridge Island WA 98110. E-mail: sharlene@ martinliterarymanagement.com. Website: www.MartinLiteraryManagement.com. **Contact:** Sharlene Martin. 75% of clients are new/unpublished writers.

• Prior to becoming an agent, Ms. Martin worked in film/TV production and acquisitions.

Member Agents Sharlene Martin (nonfiction); Bree Ogden (children's books and graphic novels only), Bree@MartinLiteraryManagement.com.

Represents Considers these nonfiction areas: autobiography, biography, business, child guidance, current affairs, economics, health, history, how-to, humor, inspirational, investigative, medicine, memoirs, parenting, popular culture, psychology, satire, self-help, true crime, women's issues, women's studies.

⚬ This agency has strong ties to film/TV. Actively seeking nonfiction that is highly commercial and that can be adapted to film. "We are being inundated with queries and submissions that are wrongfully being submitted to us, which only results in more frustration for the writers."

How to Contact Query via e-mail with MS Word only. No attachments on queries; place letter in body of e-mail. Accepts simultaneous submissions. Responds in 2 weeks to queries. Responds in 3-4 weeks to mss. Obtains most new clients through recommendations from others.

Terms Agent receives 15% commission on domestic sales. Agent receives 25% commission on foreign sales. Offers written contract, binding for 1 year; 1-month notice must be given to terminate contract. Charges author for postage and copying if material is not sent electronically. 99% of materials are sent electronically to minimize charges to author for postage and copying.

Recent Sales *Publish Your Nonfiction Book*, by Keith and Brooke Desserich; *Getting It Through My Thick Skull*, by Mary Jo Buttafuoco; *I Want*, by Jane Velez-Mitchell. Sales are updated weekly on website.

Tips "Have a strong platform for nonfiction. Please don't call. I welcome e-mail. I'm very responsive when I'm interested in a query and work hard to get my clients' materials in the best possible shape before submissions. Do your homework prior to submission and only submit your best efforts. Please review our website carefully to make sure we're a good match for your work. If you read my book, *Publish Your Nonfiction Book: Strategies For Learning the Industry, Selling Your Book and Building a Successful Career* (Writer's Digest Books) you'll know exactly how to charm me."

☑ HAROLD MATSON CO. INC.

276 Fifth Ave., New York NY 10001. (212)679-4490. Fax: (212)545-1224. **Contact:** Jonathan Matson. Member of AAR.

Member Agents Jonathan Matson (literary, adult); Ben Camardi (literary, adult, dramatic).
Represents novels.

JED MATTES, INC.

2095 Broadway, Suite 302, New York NY 10023-2895. (212)595-5228. Fax: (212)595-5232. E-mail: fmorris@jedmattes.com; general@jedmattes.com. Website: www.jedmattes.com. **Contact:** Fred Morris. Member of AAR.

Member Agents Fred Morris.
Represents Nonfiction, fiction.
How to Contact Query with SASE.

☑ MAX AND CO., A LITERARY AGENCY AND SOCIAL CLUB

3929 Coliseum St., New Orleans LA 70115. (201)704-2483. E-mail: mmurphy@maxlit.com. Website: www.maxliterary.org. **Contact:** Michael Murphy.

- Max & Co. was established in the Fall of 2007 by Michael Murphy. Prior to the literary agency, Michael began in book publishing in 1981 at Random House. He left in 1995 as a Vice President and later ran William Morrow as their Publisher. Co-agent Jack Perry joined publishing in 1994 and has been a Vice President in Sales & Marketing for Random House, Source Books, and Scholastic.

Member Agents Michael Murphy; Jack Perry (nonfiction books with a foundation in history, sports, business, politics, narrative nonfiction, math & science).
Represents **Considers these nonfiction areas:** business, history, humor, memoirs, politics, science, sports, narrative nonfiction. **Considers these fiction areas:** commercial, literary, art.

- ⚓ Seeking work in literary or eclectic fiction. In nonfiction, seeks narrative or creative nonfiction. Does not represent romance, science fiction, fantasy, tea-cozy or whodunnit mysteries. Does not represent self-help or prescriptive (how-to) nonfiction. Represents no children's or YA work.

How to Contact Agency desires online submissions and will not accept nor respond to mailed submissions. There are three agents.

☑ MARGRET MCBRIDE LITERARY AGENCY

7744 Fay Ave., Suite 201, La Jolla CA 92037. (858)454-1550. Fax: (858)454-2156. E-mail: staff@mcbridelit.com. Website: www.mcbrideliterary.com. **Contact:** Michael Daley, submissions manager. Member of AAR. Other memberships include Authors Guild. Represents 55 clients.

- Prior to opening her agency, Ms. McBride worked at Random House, Ballantine Books, and Warner Books.

Represents Nonfiction books, novels. **Considers these nonfiction areas:** autobiography, biography, business, cooking, cultural interests, current affairs, dance, diet/nutrition, economics, ethnic, foods, government, health, history, how-to, law, medicine, money, music, popular culture, politics, psychology, science, self-help, sociology, technology, women's issues, women's studies, style. **Considers these fiction areas:** action, adventure, crime, detective, ethnic, frontier, historical, humor, literary, mainstream, mystery, police, satire, suspense, thriller, westerns.

- ⚓ This agency specializes in mainstream fiction and nonfiction. Does not want to receive screenplays, romance, poetry, or children's/young adult.

How to Contact Query with synopsis, bio, SASE. No e-mail or fax queries. Accepts simultaneous submissions. Responds in 4-6 weeks to queries. Responds in 6-8 weeks to mss.
Terms Agent receives 15% commission on domestic sales. Agent receives 25% commission on foreign sales. Charges for overnight delivery and photocopying.

THE MCCARTHY AGENCY, LLC
7 Allen St., Rumson NJ 07660. Phone/Fax: (732)741-3065. E-mail: mccarthylit@aol.com. **Contact:** Shawna McCarthy. Member of AAR. Currently handles: nonfiction books 25%, novels 75%.
Member Agents Shawna McCarthy.
Represents Nonfiction books, novels. **Considers these nonfiction areas:** biography, history, philosophy, science. **Considers these fiction areas:** fantasy, juvenile, mystery, romance, science, womens.
How to Contact Query via e-mail only. Accepts simultaneous submissions.

⬛ ⊘ ANNE MCDERMID & ASSOCIATES, LTD
83 Willcocks St., Toronto ON M5S 1C9 Canada. (416)324-8845. Fax: (416)324-8870. E-mail: info@mcdermidagency.com. Website: www.mcdermidagency.com. **Contact:** Anne McDermid. Estab. 1996. Represents 60+ clients.
Member Agents Anne McDermid, Martha Magor, Monica Pacheco and Chris Bucci.
Represents Nonfiction books, novels. **Considers these nonfiction areas:** The agency represents literary novelists and commercial novelists of high quality, and also writers of nonfiction in the areas of memoir, biography, history, literary travel, narrative science, and investigative journalism. We also represent a certain number of children's and YA writers and writers in the fields of science fiction and fantasy.
How to Contact Query via e-mail or mail with a brief bio, description, and first 5 pages of project only. *No unsolicited manuscripts.* Obtains most new clients through recommendations from others.

⬛ ⊘ THE MCGILL AGENCY, INC.
10000 N. Central Expressway, Suite 400, Dallas TX 75231. (214)390-5970. E-mail: info.mcgillagency@gmail.com. **Contact:** Jack Bollinger. Estab. 2009. Represents 10 clients. 50% of clients are new/unpublished writers.
Member Agents Jack Bollinger (eclectic tastes in nonfiction and fiction); Amy Cohn (nonfiction interests include women's issues, gay/lesbian, ethnic/cultural, memoirs, true crime; fiction interests include mystery, suspense and thriller).
Represents Considers these nonfiction areas: biography, business, child guidance, current affairs, education, ethnic, gay, health, history, how-to, memoirs, military, psychology, self-help, true crime, women's issues. **Considers these fiction areas:** historical, mainstream, mystery, romance, thriller.
How to Contact Query via e-mail. Responds in two weeks to queries and 6 weeks to manuscript. Obtains new clients through conferences

⊘ MCINTOSH & OTIS
353 Lexington Ave., 15th Floor, New York NY 10016. E-mail: info@mcintoshandotis.com. Website: www.mcintoshandotis.net/. **Contact:** Attn: *reference your department*. Estab. 1928. Member of AAR.
Member Agents Eugene H. Winick; Elizabeth Winick (literary fiction, women's fiction, historical fiction, and mystery/suspense, along with narrative nonfiction, spiritual/self-help, history and current affairs. Elizabeth represents numerous New York T); Edward Necarsulmer IV; Rebecca Strauss (nonfiction, literary and commercial fiction, women's fiction, memoirs, and pop culture); Cate Martin; Ina Winick (psychology, self-help, and mystery/suspense); Ian Polonsky (Film/TV/Stage/Radio).
Represents Nonfiction books, novels, movie, movie scripts, feature film, M&O represents a broad range of adult and children's fiction and nonfiction, including many bestsellers, literary icons, Pulitzer Prize and National Book Award winners.
How to Contact Adult Fiction: Please send a query letter, synopsis, author bio, the first two chapters, and a SASE. Adult Nonfiction: Send an outline and all that is required for fiction guidelines above. Children: Middle Grade and YA: Query letter, the first 3 pages of manuscript, and a SASE.

Picture Books: Please send a query letter. One picture book manuscript only, and a SASE. Film and Dramatic Rights: Please send query, synopsis, and a SASE. Does not accept e-mail queries. Responds in 8 weeks to queries.

Tips No phone calls please.

☑ SALLY HILL MCMILLAN & ASSOCIATES, INC.

429 E. Kingston Ave., Charlotte NC 28203. (704)334-0897. **Contact:** Sally Hill McMillan. Member of AAR.

⚷ "We are not seeking new clients at this time. Agency specializes in Southern fiction, women's fiction, mystery and practical nonfiction."

How to Contact *No unsolicited submissions.*

☑ MENDEL MEDIA GROUP, LLC

115 West 30th St., Suite 800, New York NY 10001. (646)239-9896. Fax: (212)685-4717. E-mail: scott@mendelmedia.com. Website: www.mendelmedia.com. Member of AAR. Represents 40-60 clients.

- Prior to becoming an agent, Mr. Mendel was an academic. "I taught American literature, Yiddish, Jewish studies, and literary theory at the University of Chicago and the University of Illinois at Chicago while working on my PhD in English. I also worked as a freelance technical writer and as the managing editor of a healthcare magazine. In 1998, I began working for the late Jane Jordan Browne, a long-time agent in the book publishing world."

Represents Nonfiction books, novels, scholarly, with potential for broad/popular appeal. **Considers these nonfiction areas:** Americana, animals, anthropology, architecture, art, biography, business, child guidance, cooking, current affairs, dance, diet/nutrition, education, environment, ethnic, foods, gardening, gay/lesbian, government, health, history, how-to, humor, investigative, language, medicine, memoirs, military, money, multicultural, music, parenting, philosophy, popular culture, psychology, recreation, regional, religious, science, self-help, sex, sociology, software, spirituality, sports, true crime, war, women's issues, women's studies, Jewish topics; creative nonfiction. **Considers these fiction areas:** action, adventure, contemporary issues, crime, detective, erotica, ethnic, feminist, gay, glitz, historical, humor, inspirational, juvenile, lesbian, literary, mainstream, mystery, picture books, police, religious, romance, satire, sports, thriller, young adult, Jewish fiction.

⚷ "I am interested in major works of history, current affairs, biography, business, politics, economics, science, major memoirs, narrative nonfiction, and other sorts of general nonfiction." Actively seeking new, major or definitive work on a subject of broad interest, or a controversial, but authoritative, new book on a subject that affects many people's lives." I also represent more light-hearted nonfiction projects, such as gift or novelty books, when they suit the market particularly well." Does not want "queries about projects written years ago that were unsuccessfully shopped to a long list of trade publishers by either the author or another agent. I am specifically not interested in reading short, category romances (regency, time travel, paranormal, etc.), horror novels, supernatural stories, poetry, original plays, or film scripts."

How to Contact Query with SASE. Do not e-mail or fax queries. For nonfiction, include a complete, fully edited book proposal with sample chapters. For fiction, include a complete synopsis and no more than 20 pages of sample text. Responds in 2 weeks to queries. Responds in 4-6 weeks to mss. Obtains most new clients through recommendations from others.

Terms Agent receives 15% commission on domestic sales. Agent receives 20% commission on foreign sales.

Writers Conferences BookExpo America; Frankfurt Book Fair; London Book Fair; RWA National Conference; Modern Language Association Convention; Jerusalem Book Fair.

Tips "While I am not interested in being flattered by a prospective client, it does matter to me that she knows why she is writing to me in the first place. Is one of my clients a colleague of hers? Has she read a book by one of my clients that led her to believe I might be interested in her work? Authors of descriptive nonfiction should have real credentials and expertise in their subject areas, either as academics, journalists, or policy experts, and authors of prescriptive nonfiction should have legitimate expertise and considerable experience communicating their ideas in seminars and workshops, in a successful business, through the media, etc."

MENZA-BARRON AGENCY

1170 Broadway, Suite 807, New York NY 10001. (212)889-6850. **Contact:** Claudia Menza, Manie Barron. Member of AAR. Represents 100 clients. 50% of clients are new/unpublished writers.

Represents Nonfiction books, novels, photographic books, especially interested in African-American material. **Considers these nonfiction areas:** current affairs, education, ethnic, especially African-American, health, history, multicultural, music, photography, psychology, film.

☞ This agency specializes in editorial assistance and African-American fiction and nonfiction.

How to Contact Query with SASE. Does not accept e-mail queries. Responds in 2-4 weeks to queries. Responds in 2-4 months to mss.

Terms Agent receives 15% commission on domestic sales. Agent receives 20% (if co-agent is used) commission on foreign sales. Agent receives 20% commission on film sales. Offers written contract.

◐ SCOTT MEREDITH LITERARY AGENCY

200 W. 57th St., Suite 904, New York NY 10019. (646)274-1970. Fax: (212)977-5997. E-mail: info@scottmeredith.com. Website: www.scottmeredith.com. **Contact:** Arthur Klebanoff, CEO. Adheres to the AAR canon of ethics. Represents 20 clients. 5% of clients are new/unpublished writers. Currently handles: nonfiction books 85%, novels 5%, textbooks 5%.

• Prior to becoming an agent, Mr. Klebanoff was a lawyer.

Represents Nonfiction books, textbooks.

☞ This agency's specialty lies in category nonfiction publishing programs. Actively seeking category leading nonfiction. Does not want to receive first fiction projects.

How to Contact Query with SASE. Submit proposal package, author bio. Accepts simultaneous submissions. Responds in 1 week to queries. Responds in 2 weeks to mss. Obtains most new clients through recommendations from others.

Terms Agent receives 15% commission on domestic sales. Offers written contract.

Recent Sales *The Conscience of a Liberal*, by Paul Krugman; *The King of Oil: The Secret Lives of Marc Rich*, by Daniel Ammann; *Ten*, by Sheila Lukins; *Peterson Field Guide to Birds of North America*.

◐ DORIS S. MICHAELS LITERARY AGENCY, INC.

1841 Broadway, Suite 903, New York NY 10023. (212)265-9474. Fax: (212)265-9480. E-mail: query@dsmagency.com. Website: www.dsmagency.com. **Contact:** Doris S. Michaels, President. Member of AAR. Other memberships include WNBA.

Represents Novels. **Considers these nonfiction areas:** specialties are business and self-help books from top professionals in their fields of expertise. We are also looking for books in categories such as current affairs, narrative, biography and memoir, lifestyle, social sciences, gender, history, health, classical music, sports, and women's issues. In the fiction camp, we are currently interested in representing literary fiction that has commercial appeal and strong screen potential. Go to our biography section to find out more. **Considers these fiction areas:** literary, with commercial appeal and strong screen potential., Go to our biography section online to find out more.

☞ Our specialties are business and self-help books from top professionals in their fields of expertise. "We are also looking for books in categories such as current affairs, narrative, biography and memoir, lifestyle, social sciences, gender, history, health, classical music, sports, and women's issues." No romance, coffee table books, art books, trivia, pop culture, humor, westerns, occult and supernatural, horror, poetry, textbooks, children's books, picture books, film scripts, articles, cartoons and professional manuals.

How to Contact Query by e-mail; synopsis of your project in one page or less, and include a short paragraph that details your credentials. Do not send attachments or URL links. See submission guidelines on website. Obtains most new clients through recommendations from others, conferences.

Terms Agent receives 15% commission on domestic sales. Agent receives 20% commission on foreign sales. Offers written contract, binding for 1 year; 1-month notice must be given to terminate contract. Charges clients for office expenses, not to exceed $150 without written permission.

Writers Conferences BookExpo America; Frankfurt Book Fair; London Book Fair; Maui Writers Conference.

Literary Agents

◖ MARTHA MILLARD LITERARY AGENCY

420 Central Park West, #5H, New York NY 10025. (212)787-1030. **Contact:** Martha Millard. Estab. 1980. Member of AAR. Other memberships include SFWA. Represents 50 clients. Currently handles: nonfiction books 25%, novels 65%, story collections 10%.

- Prior to becoming an agent, Ms. Millard worked in editorial departments of several publishers and was vice president at another agency for more than four years.

Represents Nonfiction books, novels. **Considers these nonfiction areas:** architecture, art, autobiography, biography, business, child guidance, cooking, cultural interests, current affairs, design, economics, education, ethnic, film, health, history, how-to, memoirs, metaphysics, money, music, New Age, parenting, photography, popular culture, psychology, self-help, theater, true crime, women's issues, women's studies. **Considers these fiction areas:** fantasy, mystery, romance, science fiction, suspense.

How to Contact No unsolicited queries. **Referrals only.** Obtains most new clients through recommendations from others.

Terms Agent receives 15% commission on domestic sales. Agent receives 20% commission on foreign sales. Offers written contract.

◖ THE MILLER AGENCY

Film Center, 630 Ninth Ave., Suite 1102, New York NY 10036. (212) 206-0913. Fax: (212) 206-1473. E-mail: angela@milleragency.net. **Contact:** Angela Miller, Sharon Bowers, Jennifer Griffin. Represents 100 clients. 5% of clients are new/unpublished writers.

Represents Nonfiction books. **Considers these nonfiction areas:** anthropology, archeology, architecture, art, biography, business, child guidance, cooking, cultural interests, current affairs, diet/nutrition, design, economics, ethnic, foods, gay/lesbian, health, language, literature, medicine, metaphysics, New Age, parenting, psychology, self-help, sports, women's issues, women's studies.

- ⌐ This agency specializes in nonfiction, multicultural arts, psychology, self-help, cookbooks, biography, travel, memoir, and sports. Fiction is considered selectively.

How to Contact Query with SASE. Accepts simultaneous submissions. Responds in 1 week to queries. Obtains most new clients through referrals.

Terms Agent receives 15% commission on domestic sales. Agent receives 20-25% commission on foreign sales. Offers written contract, binding for 2 years; 2-month notice must be given to terminate contract. Charges clients for postage (express mail or messenger services) and photocopying.

◿ MARK B. MILLER MANAGEMENT

PO Box 2442, Warminster PA 18974. (267)988-4226. **Contact:** Mark B. Miller.

Tips "Inquiries welcome, no unsolicited manuscripts accepted."

MOORE LITERARY AGENCY

10 State St., Newburyport MA 01950. (978)465-9015. Fax: (978)465-8817. E-mail: cmoore@moorelit.com. **Contact:** Claudette Moore. Estab. 1989. 10% of clients are new/unpublished writers. Currently handles: nonfiction books 100%.

Represents Nonfiction books. **Considers these nonfiction areas:** computers, technology.

- ⌐ This agency specializes in trade computer books (90% of titles).

How to Contact Query with SASE. Submit proposal package. Query by e-mail. Send proposals by snail mail. Obtains most new clients through recommendations from others, conferences.

Terms Agent receives 15% commission on domestic sales. Agent receives 15% commission on foreign sales. Agent receives 15% commission on film sales. Offers written contract.

◖ PATRICIA MOOSBRUGGER LITERARY AGENCY

2720 Decker Ave. NW, Albuquerque NM 87107. (505)345-9297. E-mail: pm@pmagency.net. Website: www.pmagency.net. **Contact:** Patricia Moosbrugger. Member of AAR.

Represents Nonfiction books.

How to Contact Query with SASE.

◖ HOWARD MORHAIM LITERARY AGENCY

30 Pierrepont St., Brooklyn NY 11201. (718)222-8400. Fax: (718)222-5056. Website: www.morhaimliterary.com/. Member of AAR.

Member Agents Howard Morhaim, Kate McKean, Katie Menick.

☛ Actively seeking fiction, nonfiction and young-adult novels.

How to Contact Query via e-mail with cover letter and three sample chapters. See each agent's listing for specifics.

☑ WILLIAM MORRIS AGENCY, INC.

1325 Avenue of the Americas, New York NY 10019. (212)586-5100. Fax: (212)246-3583. Website: www.wma.com. **Contact:** Literary Department Coordinator. Alternate address: One William Morris Place, Beverly Hills CA 90212. (310)285-9000. Fax: (310)859-4462. Member of AAR.

Member Agents Owen Laster; Jennifer Rudolph Walsh; Suzanne Gluck; Joni Evans; Tracy Fisher; Mel Berger; Jay Mandel; Peter Franklin; Lisa Grubka; Jonathan Pecursky.

Represents Nonfiction books, novels, tv, movie scripts, feature film.

☛ Does not want to receive screenplays.

How to Contact Query with synopsis, publication history, SASE. Send book queries to the NYC address. Accepts simultaneous submissions.

Terms Agent receives 15% commission on domestic sales. Agent receives 20% commission on foreign sales.

Tips "If you are a prospective writer interested in submitting to the William Morris Agency in **London**, please follow these guidelines: For all queries, please send a cover letter, synopsis, and the first three chapters (up to 50 pages) by e-mail only to: dkar@wmeentertainment.com."

☑ HENRY MORRISON, INC.

105 S. Bedford Road, Suite 306A, Mt. Kisco NY 10549. (914)666-3500. Fax: (914)241-7846. **Contact:** Henry Morrison. Signatory of WGA. Represents 54 clients. 5% of clients are new/unpublished writers. Currently handles: nonfiction books 5%, novels 95%.

Represents Nonfiction books, novels. **Considers these nonfiction areas:** anthropology, archeology, autobiography, biography, government, history, law, politics. **Considers these fiction areas:** action, adventure, crime, detective, family saga, historical, police.

How to Contact Query with SASE. Responds in 2 weeks to queries. Responds in 3 months to mss. Obtains most new clients through recommendations from others.

Terms Agent receives 15% commission on domestic sales. Agent receives 25% commission on foreign sales. Charges clients for ms copies, bound galleys, finished books for submissions to publishers, movie producers and foreign publishers.

☐ MORTIMER LITERARY AGENCY

52645 Paui Road, Aguanga CA 92536. E-mail: kmortimer@mortimerliterary.com. Website: www. mortimerliterary.com. **Contact:** Kelly Gottuso Mortimer. Romance Writers of America. Represents 16 clients. 80% of clients are new/unpublished writers. Currently handles: nonfiction books 40%, novels 40%, young adult books 20%.

- Prior to becoming an agent, Ms. Mortimer was a freelance writer and the CFO of Microvector, Inc. She has a degree in contract law, finance and is a winner of The American Christian Fiction Writers Literary Agent of the Year Award in 2008 and the OCC-RAW Volunteer of the Year award. Was Top 5: Publishers marketplace Top 100 Dealmakers—Romance category, 2008.

Represents Nonfiction books, novels, young adult. **Considers these nonfiction areas:** Please refer to submissions page on website, as the list changes. **Considers these fiction areas:** Please refer to submissions page on website, as the list changes.

- ☛ "I keep a short client list to give my writers personal attention. I edit my clients' manuscripts as necessary. I send manuscripts out to pre-selected editors in a timely fashion, and send my clients monthly reports. I only sign writers not yet published, or not published in the last 3 years. Those are the writers who need my help the most."

How to Contact See website for submission guidelines. Accepts simultaneous submissions. Responds in 3 months to mss. Obtains most new clients through query letters.

Terms Agent receives 15% commission on domestic sales. Agent receives 20% commission on foreign sales. Offers written contract. "I charge for postage—only the amount I pay and it comes out of the author's advance. The writer provides me with copies of their manuscripts if needed."

Writers Conferences RWA, several conference. See schedule on website.

Tips "Follow submission guidelines on the website, submit your best work and don't query unless your manuscript is finished. Don't send material or mss that I haven't requested."

☑ DEE MURA LITERARY

269 West Shore Drive, Massapequa NY 11758-8225. (516)795-1616. Fax: (516)795-8797. E-mail: query@deemuraliterary.com. **Contact:** Dee Mura. Signatory of WGA. 50% of clients are new/unpublished writers.

- Prior to opening her agency, Ms. Mura was a public relations executive with a roster of film and entertainment clients and worked in editorial for major weekly news magazines.

Member Agents Dee Mura, Karen Roberts, Bobbie Sokol, David Brozain.

Represents Considers these nonfiction areas: animals, anthropology, biography, business, child guidance, computers, current affairs, education, ethnic, finance, gay, government, health, history, how-to, humor, juvenile nonfiction, law, lesbian, medicine, memoirs, military, money, nature, personal improvement, politics, science, self-help, sociology, sports, technology, travel, true crime, women's issues, women's studies. **Considers these fiction areas:** action, adventure, contemporary issues, crime, detective, ethnic, experimental, family saga, fantasy, feminist, gay, glitz, historical, humor, juvenile, lesbian, literary, mainstream, military, mystery, psychic, regional, romance, science fiction, sports, thriller, westerns, young adult, political. **Considers these script areas:** action, cartoon, comedy, contemporary, detective, (and espionage), family, fantasy, feminist, gay/lesbian, glitz, historical, horror, juvenile, mainstream, mystery, psychic, romantic comedy, romantic drama, science, sports, teen, thriller, western.

- ⚬ "Some of us have special interests and some of us encourage you to share your passion and work with us." Does not want to receive "ideas for sitcoms, novels, films, etc., or queries without SASEs."

How to Contact Query with SASE. Accepts e-mail queries (no attachments). If via e-mail, please include the type of query and your genre in the subject line. If via regular mail, you may include the first few chapters, outline, or proposal. No fax queries. Accepts simultaneous submissions. Only responds if interested; responds as soon as possible. Obtains most new clients through recommendations from others, queries.

Terms Agent receives 15% commission on domestic sales. Agent receives 20% commission on foreign sales. Offers written contract. Charges clients for photocopying, mailing expenses, overseas/long distance phone calls/faxes.

Recent Sales Sold more than 40 titles and 35 scripts in the last year.

Tips "Please include a paragraph on your background, even if you have no literary background, and a brief synopsis of the project."

☑ ERIN MURPHY LITERARY AGENCY

2700 Woodlands Village, #300-458, Flagstaff AZ 86001-7172. (928)525-2056. Fax: (928)525-2480. Website: emliterary.com. **Contact:** Erin Murphy, president; Ammi-Joan Paquette, associate agent.

- ⚬ "This agency only represents children's books. We do not accept unsolicited manuscripts or queries. We consider new clients by referral or personal contact only."

☑ MUSE LITERARY MANAGEMENT

189 Waverly Place, #4, New York NY 10014. (212)925-3721. E-mail: museliterarymgmt@aol.com. Website: www.museliterary.com/. **Contact:** Deborah Carter. Associations: NAWE, International Thriller Writers, Historical Novel Society, Associations of Booksellers for Children, The Authors Guild, Children's Literature Network, and American Folklore Society. Represents 5 clients. 80% of clients are new/unpublished writers.

- Prior to starting her agency, Ms. Carter trained with an AAR literary agent and worked in the music business and as a talent scout for record companies in artist management. She has a BA in English and music from Washington Square University College at NYU.

Represents Novels, short story collections, poetry books. **Considers these nonfiction areas:** narrative nonfiction (no prescriptive nonfiction), children's. **Considers these fiction areas:** adventure, detective, juvenile, mystery, picture books, suspense, thriller, young adult, espionage; middle-grade novels; literary short story collections, literary fiction with popular appeal.

- ⚬ Specializes in manuscript development, the sale and administration of print, performance, and foreign rights to literary works, and post-publication publicity and appearances. Actively seeking "writers with formal training who bring compelling voices and a unique outlook to their manuscripts. Those who submit should be receptive to editorial feedback and willing to revise during the submission provess in order to remain competitive." Does not want "manuscripts that have been worked over by book doctors (collaborative projects ok, but writers must have chops); category romance, chick lit, sci-fi, fantasy, horror, stories about cats and dogs, vampires or serial killers, fiction or nonfiction with religious or spiritual subject matter."

How to Contact Query with SASE. Query via e-mail (no attachments). Discards unwanted queries. Responds in 2 weeks to queries. Responds in 2-3 weeks to mss. Obtains most new clients through recommendations from others, conferences.

Terms Agent receives 15% commission on domestic sales. Agent receives 20% commission on foreign sales. One-year contract offered when writer and agent agree that the manuscript is ready for submission; manuscripts in development are not bound by contract. Sometimes charges for postage and photocopying. All expenses are preapproved by the client.

◖ JEAN V. NAGGAR LITERARY AGENCY, INC.

216 E. 75th St., Suite 1E, New York NY 10021. (212)794-1082. E-mail: jvnla@jvnla.com. Website: www.jvnla.com. **Contact:** Jean Naggar. Member of AAR. Other memberships include PEN, Women's Media Group, Women's Forum. Represents 80 clients. 20% of clients are new/unpublished writers. Currently handles: nonfiction books 35%, novels 45%, juvenile books 15%, scholarly books 5%.

• Ms. Naggar has served as president of AAR.

Member Agents Jean Naggar (mainstream fiction, nonfiction); Jennifer Weltz, director (subsidiary rights, children's books); Alice Tasman, senior agent (commercial and literary fiction, thrillers, narrative nonfiction); Jessica Regel, agent (young adult fiction and nonfiction); Elizabeth Evans.

Represents Nonfiction books, novels. **Considers these nonfiction areas:** biography, child guidance, current affairs, government, health, history, juvenile nonfiction, law, medicine, memoirs, New Age, parenting, politics, psychology, self-help, sociology, travel, women's issues, women's studies. **Considers these fiction areas:** action, adventure, crime, detective, ethnic, family saga, feminist, historical, literary, mainstream, mystery, police, psychic, supernatural, suspense, thriller.

○┐ This agency specializes in mainstream fiction and nonfiction and literary fiction with commercial potential.

How to Contact Query via e-mail. Prefers to read materials exclusively. No fax queries. Responds in 1 day to queries. Responds in 2 months to mss. Obtains most new clients through recommendations from others.

Terms Agent receives 15% commission on domestic sales. Agent receives 20% commission on foreign sales. Offers written contract. Charges for overseas mailing, messenger services, book purchases, long-distance telephone, photocopying—all deductible from royalties received.

Recent Sales *Night Navigation*, by Ginnah Howard; *After Hours At the Almost Home*, by Tara Yelen; *An Entirely Synthetic Fish: A Biography of Rainbow Trout*, by Anders Halverson; *The Patron Saint of Butterflies*, by Cecilia Galante; *Wondrous Strange*, by Lesley Livingston; *6 Sick Hipsters*, by Rayo Casablanca; *The Last Bridge*, by Teri Coyne; *Gypsy Goodbye*, by Nancy Springer; *Commuters*, by Emily Tedrowe; *The Language of Secrets*, by Dianne Dixon; *Smiling to Freedom*, by Martin Benoit Stiles; *The Tale of Halcyon Crane*, by Wendy Webb; *Fugitive*, by Phillip Margolin; *BlackBerry Girl*, by Aidan Donnelley Rowley; *Wild Girls*, by Pat Murphy.

Writers Conferences Willamette Writers Conference; Pacific Northwest Writers Conference; Bread Loaf Writers Conference; Marymount Manhattan Writers Conference; SEAK Medical & Legal Fiction Writing Conference.

Tips "Use a professional presentation. Because of the avalanche of unsolicited queries that flood the agency every week, we have had to modify our policy. We will now only guarantee to read and respond to queries from writers who come recommended by someone we know. Our areas are general fiction and nonfiction—no children's books by unpublished writers, no multimedia, no screenplays, no formula fiction, and no mysteries by unpublished writers. We recommend patience and fortitude: the courage to be true to your own vision, the fortitude to finish a novel and polish it again and again before sending it out, and the patience to accept rejection gracefully and wait for the stars to align themselves appropriately for success."

◖ NAPPALAND LITERARY AGENCY

A Division of Nappaland Communications, Inc., P.O. Box 1674, Loveland CO 80539-1674. Fax: (970)635-9869. Website: www.NappalandLiterary.com. Contact: Mike Nappa, chief agent. Represents 8 clients. 0% of clients are new/unpublished writers. Currently handles: nonfiction books 45%, novels 50%, scholarly books 5%.

- Prior to becoming an agent, Mr. Nappa served as an acquisition editor for three major Christian publishing houses.

Represents Nonfiction books, novels. **Considers these nonfiction areas:** child guidance, current affairs, inspirational, parenting, popular culture, religious, women's issues, women's studies. **Considers these fiction areas:** adventure, crime, detective, literary, police, religious, thriller.

☞ This agency will not consider any new authors unless they come with a recommendation from a current Nappaland client. All queries without such a recommendation are immediately rejected. "Interested in thoughtful, vivid, nonfiction works on religious and cultural themes. Also, fast-paced, well-crafted fiction (suspense, literary, women's) that reads like a work of art. Established authors only; broad promotional platform preferred." Does not want to receive children's books, movie or television scripts, textbooks, short stories, stage plays or poetry.

How to Contact Query with SASE. Submit author bio. Include the name of the person referring you to us. Do *not* send entire proposal unless requested. Send query and bio only. Not currently accepting new clients. To reach either Mike Nappa or Alec Smart at Nappaland Literary Agency, please visit www.NappalandLiterary.com. Accepts simultaneous submissions. Responds in 1 month to queries. Responds in 3 months to mss.

Terms Agent receives 15% commission on domestic sales. Agent receives 20% commission on foreign sales. Offers written contract; 30-day notice must be given to terminate contract.

Recent Sales *Family Matters*, by Dr. Timothy Paul Jones (Wesleyan Publishing House); *Drift*, by Sharon Carter Rogers (Howard Books/Simon & Schuster); *Interactive Illustrations*, by Mike Nappa (Standard Publishing).

Writers Conferences Colorado Christian Writers' Conference in Estes Park.

◙ NELSON LITERARY AGENCY

1732 Wazee St., Suite 207, Denver CO 80202. (303)292-2805. E-mail: query@nelsonagency.com. Website: www.nelsonagency.com. **Contact:** Kristin Nelson, president and senior literary agent; Sara Megibow, associate literary agent. Member of AAR. RWA, SCBWI, SFWA.

- Prior to opening her own agency, Ms. Nelson worked as a literary scout and subrights agent for agent Jody Rein.

Represents Novels, select nonfiction. **Considers these nonfiction areas:** memoirs. **Considers these fiction areas:** commercial, literary, mainstream, women's, chick lit (includes mysteries), romance (includes fantasy with romantic elements, science fiction, fantasy, young adult).

☞ NLA specializes in representing commercial fiction and high caliber literary fiction. Actively seeking Latina writers who tackle contemporary issues in a modern voice (think *Dirty Girls Social Club*). Does not want short story collections, mysteries (except chick lit), thrillers, Christian, horror, or children's picture books.

How to Contact Query by e-mail only.

Recent Sales New York Times Best-selling author of *I'd Tell You I Love You, But Then I'd Have to Kill You*, Ally Carter's fourth novel in the Gallagher Girls series; *Hester* (historical fiction), by Paula Reed; *Proof by Seduction* (debut romance), by Courtney Milan; *Soulless* (fantasy debut), by Gail Carriger; *The Shifter* (debut children's fantasy), by Janice Hardy; *Real Life & Liars* (debut women's fiction), by Kristina Riggle; *Hotel on the Corner of Bitter and Sweet* (debut literary fiction), by Jamie Ford.

Ⓝ ◙ KIRSTEN NEUHAUS LITERARY AGENCY

21 W 38th Street, 13th Floor, New York NY 10018. E-mail: submissions@kirstenneuhausliterary. com. Website: www.kirstenneuhausliterary.com. **Contact:** Kirsten Neuhaus.

- Prior to becoming an agent, Kirsten Neuhaus has worked at Elaine Markson Agency, Sanford J. Greenburger Associates and Vigliano Associates, developing her own client list as well as handling foreign rights. She began her publishing career as an intern at Where Books Begin, a freelance editing company.

Represents Considers these nonfiction areas: cultural interests, current affairs, women's issues, women's studies, international events. **Considers these fiction areas:** , upmarket commercial fiction.

How to Contact "Our preferred method for receiving queries is via e-mail. Please send a query letter, including a bio, and approximately ten sample pages." Paste copy into the e-mail body. No attachments.

NINE MUSES AND APOLLO, INC.

525 Broadway, Suite 201, New York NY 10012. (212)431-2665. **Contact:** Ling Lucas. Represents 50 clients. 10% of clients are new/unpublished writers. Currently handles: nonfiction books 100%.

- Prior to her current position, Ms. Lucas served as vice president, sales/marketing director and associate publisher of Warner Books.

Represents Nonfiction books.

◑ This agency specializes in nonfiction. Does not want to receive children's or young adult material.

How to Contact Submit outline, 2 sample chapters, SASE..Prefers to read materials exclusively.

Terms Agent receives 15% commission on domestic sales. Agent receives 20-25% commission on foreign sales. Offers written contract. Charges clients for photocopying, postage.

Tips "Your outline should already be well developed, cogent, and reveal clarity of thought about the general structure and direction of your project."

◪ NORTHERN LIGHTS LITERARY SERVICES, LLC

2721 Tulip Tree Rd., Suite A, Nashville IN 47448-9128. (888)558-4354. Fax: (208)265-1948. E-mail: queries@northernlightsls.com. Website: www.northernlightsls.com. **Contact:** Sammie Justesen. Represents 25 clients. 35% of clients are new/unpublished writers. Currently handles: nonfiction books 90%, novels 10%.

Member Agents Sammie Justesen (fiction and nonfiction); Vorris Dee Justesen (business and current affairs).

Represents Nonfiction books, novels. **Considers these nonfiction areas:** animals, autobiography, biography, business, child guidance, cooking, crafts, current affairs, diet/nutrition, economics, environment, ethnic, foods, health, inspirational, investigative, memoirs, metaphysics, New Age, parenting, popular culture, psychology, religious, self-help, sports, true crime, women's issues, women's studies. **Considers these fiction areas:** action, adventure, crime, detective, ethnic, family saga, feminist, glitz, historical, inspirational, mainstream, mystery, police, psychic, regional, religious, romance, supernatural, suspense, thriller, women's.

◑ "Our goal is to provide personalized service to clients and create a bond that will endure throughout the writer's career. We seriously consider each query we receive and will accept hardworking new authors who are willing to develop their talents and skills. We enjoy working with healthcare professionals and writers who clearly understand their market and have a platform." Actively seeking general nonfiction—especially if the writer has a platform. Does not want to receive fantasy, horror, erotica, children's books, screenplays, poetry or short stories.

How to Contact Query with SASE. Submit outline/proposal, synopsis, 3 sample chapters, author bio. E-queries preferred. No phone queries. All queries considered, but the agency only replies if interested. If you've completed and polished a novel, send a query letter, a one-or-two page synopsis of the plot, and the first chapter. Also include your biography as it relates to your writing experience. Do not send an entire mss unless requested. If you'd like to submit a nonfiction book, send a query letter, along with the book proposal. Include a bio showing the background that will enable you to write the book. Accepts simultaneous submissions. Responds in 2 months to queries. Responds in 2 months to mss. Obtains most new clients through solicitations, conferences.

Terms Agent receives 15% commission on domestic sales. Agent receives 20% commission on foreign sales. Offers written contract; 30-day notice must be given to terminate contract.

Recent Sales *Intuitive Parenting*, by Debra Snyder, Ph.D. (Beyond Words); *The Confidence Trap*, by Russ Harris (Penguin); *The Never Cold Call Again Toolkit*, by Frank Rumbauskas, Jr. (Wiley); *Thank You for Firing Me*, by Candace Reed and Kitty Martini (Sterling); *The Wal-Mart Cure: Ten Lifesaving Supplements for Under $10* (Sourcebooks).

Tips "If you're fortunate enough to find an agent who answers your query and asks for a printed manuscript, always include a letter and cover page containing your name, physical address, e-mail address and phone number. Be professional!"

◗ HAROLD OBER ASSOCIATES

425 Madison Ave., New York NY 10017. (212)759-8600. Fax: (212)759-9428. Website: www. haroldober.com. **Contact:** Craig Tenney. Member of AAR. Represents 250 clients. 10% of clients are new/unpublished writers. Currently handles: nonfiction books 35%, novels 50%, juvenile books 15%.

- Mr. Elwell was previously with Elwell & Weiser.

Member Agents Phyllis Westberg; Pamela Malpas; Craig Tenney (few new clients, mostly Ober backlist); Jake Elwell (previously with Elwell & Weiser).

How to Contact Submit concise query letter addressed to a specific agent with the first five pages of the manuscript or proposal and SASE. No fax or e-mail. Does not handle scripts. Responds as promptly as possible. Obtains most new clients through recommendations from others.

Terms Agent receives 15% commission on domestic sales. Agent receives 20% commission on foreign sales. Charges clients for photocopying and express mail/package services.

☑ ◎ OBJECTIVE ENTERTAINMENT

265 Canal St., Suite 603 B, New York NY 10013. (212)431-5454. Fax: (917)464.6394. E-mail: ej@objectiveent.com. Website: www.objectiveent.com. **Contact:** Elizabeth Joté.

Member Agents Jarred Weisfeld; Ian Kleinert, IK@objectiveent.com; Fred Borden, Fred@objectiveent.com (fiction and nonfiction related to Middle Eastern politics, sports—especially mixed martial arts—popular culture, and film); Elizabeth Jote, ej@objectiveent.com (commercial fiction (women's fiction, lad lit, thrillers, mysteries, young adult, urban fiction and multicultural books, narrative nonfiction, pop culture, current events, lifestyle books and graphic novels).

Represents Nonfiction books, novels, movie, tv, movie scripts, feature film.

How to Contact Query via e-mail. Send query only unless more information or materials are requested.

ONK AGENCY LTD.

(formerly) ONK Copyright Agency, Ýnönü Caddesi, 23/7 - Taksim, Ýstanbul 34437 Turkey. +90 212 249 86 02. Fax: +90 212 252 51 53. E-mail: info@onkagency.com. Website: www.onkagency.com/english/. Estab. 1959.

☑ FIFI OSCARD AGENCY, INC.

110 W. 40th St., Suite 704, New York NY 10018. (212)764-1100. Fax: (212)840-5019. E-mail: agency@fifioscard.com. Website: www.fifioscard.com. **Contact:** Literary Department. Signatory of WGA.

Member Agents Peter Sawyer; Carmen La Via; Kevin McShane; Carolyn French.

Represents Nonfiction books, novels, stage plays. **Considers these nonfiction areas:** biography, business, cooking, economics, health, history, inspirational, religious, science, sports, technology, women's issues, women's studies, African American, body/mind/spirit, lifestyle, cookbooks.

How to Contact Query through online submission form preferred, though snail mail queries are acceptable. *No unsolicited mss.* Responds in 2 weeks to queries.

Terms Agent receives 15% commission on domestic sales. Agent receives 20% commission on foreign sales. Agent receives 10% commission on film sales. Charges clients for photocopying expenses.

PARAVIEW, INC.

40 Florence Circle, Bracey VA 23919. Phone/Fax: (434)636-4138. E-mail: lhagan@paraview.com. Website: www.paraview.com. **Contact:** Lisa Hagan. Represents 75 clients. 15% of clients are new/unpublished writers. Currently handles: nonfiction books 100%.

Represents Nonfiction books. **Considers these nonfiction areas:** agriculture horticulture, New Age, animals, anthropology, art, biography, business, cooking, current affairs, education, ethnic, gay, government, health, history, how to, humor, language, memoirs, military, money, multicultural, nature, philosophy, popular culture, psychology, recreation, regional, religion, science, self-help, sex, sociology, spirituality, travel, true crime, womens, Americana; creative nonfiction.

    ○┐ This agency specializes in business, science, gay/lesbian, spiritual, New Age, and self-help nonfiction.

How to Contact Submit query, synopsis, author bio via e-mail. Responds in 1 month to queries. Responds in 3 months to mss. Obtains most new clients through recommendations from editors and current clients.

Terms Agent receives 15% commission on domestic sales. Agent receives 20% commission on foreign sales.

Writers Conferences BookExpo America; London Book Fair; E3—Electronic Entertainment Exposition.

Tips "New writers should have their work edited, critiqued, and carefully reworked prior to submission. First contact should be via e-mail."

☑ PARK LITERARY GROUP, LLC

270 Lafayette St., Suite 1504, New York NY 10012. (212)691-3500. Fax: (212)691-3540. Website: www.parkliterary.com.

- Prior to their current positions, Ms. Park and Ms. O'Keefe were literary agents at Sanford J. Greenburger Associates. Prior to 1994, Ms. Park was a practicing attorney.

Member Agents Theresa Park (plot-driven fiction and serious nonfiction); Abigail Koons (quirky, edgy and commercial fiction, as well as superb thrillers and mysteries; adventure and travel narrative nonfiction, exceptional memoirs, popular science, history, politics and art); Amanda Cardinale (commercial fiction and nonfiction); Emily Sweet (not an agent—liaison to film and media industries).

Represents Nonfiction books, novels.

- ⌖ The Park Literary Group represents fiction and nonfiction with a boutique approach: an emphasis on servicing a relatively small number of clients, with the highest professional standards and focused personal attention. Does not want to receive poetry or screenplays.

How to Contact Query with SASE or by e-mail at queries@parkliterary.com. Submit synopsis, 1-3 sample chapters, SASE. Responds in 4-6 weeks to queries.

☑ THE RICHARD PARKS AGENCY

Box 693, Salem NY 12865. (518)854-9466. Fax: (518)854-9466. E-mail: rp@richardparksagency. com. Website: www.richardparksagency.com. **Contact:** Richard Parks. Member of AAR. Currently handles: nonfiction books 55%, novels 40%, story collections 5%.

Represents Nonfiction books, novels. **Considers these nonfiction areas:** animals, anthropology, archeology, art, autobiography, biography, business, child guidance, cooking, crafts, cultural interests, current affairs, dance, diet/nutrition, economics, environment, ethnic, film, foods, gardening, gay/lesbian, government, health, history, hobbies, how-to, humor, language, law, memoirs, military, money, music, parenting, popular culture, politics, psychology, science, self-help, sociology, technology, theater, travel, women's issues, women's studies.

- ⌖ Actively seeking nonfiction. Considers fiction by referral only. Does not want to receive unsolicited material.

How to Contact Query with SASE. Responds in 2 weeks to queries. Obtains most new clients through recommendations/referrals.

Terms Agent receives 15% commission on domestic sales. Agent receives 20% commission on foreign sales. Charges clients for photocopying or any unusual expense incurred at the writer's request.

☑ KATHI J. PATON LITERARY AGENCY

P.O. Box 2236 Radio City Station, New York NY 10101. (212)265-6586. E-mail: kjplitbiz@optonline. net. **Contact:** Kathi Paton. Currently handles: nonfiction books 85%, novels 15%.

Represents Nonfiction books, novels, short story collections, book-based film rights. **Considers these nonfiction areas:** business, child guidance, economics, environment, humor, investigative, money, parenting, psychology, religious, satire, personal investing. **Considers these fiction areas:** literary, mainstream, multicultural, short stories.

- ⌖ This agency specializes in adult nonfiction.

How to Contact Accepts e-mail queries only. Accepts simultaneous submissions. Accepts new clients through recommendations from current clients.

Terms Agent receives 15% commission on domestic sales. Agent receives 20% commission on foreign sales. Offers written contract. Charges clients for photocopying.

Writers Conferences Attends major regional panels, seminars and conferences.

◎ PAVILION LITERARY MANAGEMENT

660 Massachusetts Ave., Suite 4, Boston MA 02118. (617)792-5218. E-mail: jeff@pavilionliterary. com. Website: www.pavilionliterary.com. **Contact:** Jeff Kellogg.

- Prior to his current position, Mr. Kellogg was a literary agent with The Stuart Agency, and an acquiring editor with HarperCollins.

Represents Nonfiction books, novels, memoir. **Considers these nonfiction areas:** , narrative nonfiction (topical and historical) and cutting-edge popular science from experts in their respective fields. **Considers these fiction areas:** adventure, fantasy, juvenile, mystery, thriller, general fiction, genre-blending fiction.

> ⚬ "We are presently accepting fiction submissions only from previously published authors and/ or by client referral. Nonfiction projects, specifically narrative nonfiction and cutting-edge popular science from experts in their respective fields, are most welcome."

How to Contact Query first by e-mail (no attachments). The subject line should specify fiction or nonfiction and include the title of the work. If submitting nonfiction, include a book proposal (no longer than 75 pages), with sample chapters.

☑ PEARSON, MORRIS & BELT

3000 Connecticut Ave., NW, Suite 317, Washington DC 20008. (202)723-6088. E-mail: dpm@ morrisbelt.com; llb@morrisbelt.com. Website: www.morrisbelt.com.

> • Prior to their current positions, Ms. Belt and Ms. Morris were agents with Adler & Robin Books, Inc.

Member Agents Laura Belt (nonfiction and computer books); Djana Pearson Morris (fiction, nonfiction, and computer books. Her favorite subjects are self-help, narrative nonfiction, African-American fiction and nonfiction, health and fitness, women's fiction, technology and parenting).

Represents Nonfiction books, novels, computer books.

> ⚬ This agency specializes in nonfiction, computer books and exceptional fiction. Does not want to receive poetry, children's literature or screenplays. Regarding fiction, this agency does not accept science fiction, thrillers or mysteries.

How to Contact Query with SASE. Submit proposal (nonfiction); detailed synopsis and 2-3 sample chapters (fiction). Only query with a finished ms. Accepts e-mail queries but no attachments. Responds in 6-8 weeks to queries. Obtains most new clients through recommendations from others, solicitations.

Tips "Many of our books come from ideas and proposals we generate in-house. We retain a proprietary interest in and control of all ideas we create and proposals we write."

☑ PELHAM LITERARY AGENCY

PMB 3152650 Jamacha Rd., Suite 147, El Cajon CA 92019. (619)447-4468. E-mail: jmeals@ pelhamliterary.com. Website: pelhamliterary.com. **Contact:** Jim Meals. Currently handles: nonfiction books 10%, novels 90%.

> • Before becoming agents, both Mr. Pelham and Mr. Meals were writers.

Member Agents Howard Pelham; Jim Meals.

Represents Nonfiction books, novels.

> ⚬ "Every manuscript that comes to our agency receives a careful reading and assessment. When a writer submits a promising manuscript, we work extensively with the author until the work is ready for marketing."

How to Contact Query by mail or e-mail first; do not send unsolicited mss.

Terms Agent receives 15% commission on domestic sales. Offers written contract. Charges for photocopying and postage.

Tips "Only phone if it's necessary."

☑ L. PERKINS ASSOCIATES

5800 Arlington Ave., Riverdale NY 10471. (718)543-5344. Fax: (718)543-5354. E-mail: lperkinsagency@yahoo.com. **Contact:** Lori Perkins, Sandy Lu (Sandy@lperkinsagency.com). Member of AAR. Represents 90 clients. 10% of clients are new/unpublished writers.

> • Ms. Perkins has been an agent for 20 years. She is also the author of *The Insider's Guide to Getting an Agent* (Writer's Digest Books), as well as three other nonfiction books. She has also edited 12 erotic anthologies, and is also the Editorial Director of Ravenousromance.com, an e-publisher.

Member Agents Lori Perkins (horror, social science fiction, dark fantasy, dark literary novels and erotica. In nonfiction, she handles books about pop culture such as music, art, film, TV, etc, and she is also interested in architecture and design); Sandy Lu (Fiction areas of interest: literary and commercial fiction, upscale women's fiction, mystery, thriller, psychological horror, and historical fiction. She is especially interested in edgy, contemporary urban fiction. Nonfiction areas of interest: narrative nonfiction, history, biography, memoir, science, psychology, pop culture, and food writing. She also has a particular interest in Asian or Asian-American writing, both original and in translation, fiction and nonfiction); Marisa Iozzi Corvisiero (fiction interests include cross genre romance, science fiction, fantasy and urban fantasy, horror, literary, quality chick lit, young adult and children's books; nonfiction interest include memoirs, how-to, guides and tales about the legal practice, parenting, self-help, and mainstream science).

Represents Nonfiction books, novels. **Considers these nonfiction areas:** how-to, law, memoirs, parenting, popular culture, science, self-help. **Considers these fiction areas:** erotica, fantasy, horror, literary, science fiction, women's, young adult.

    ⚬ "Most of my clients write both fiction and nonfiction. This combination keeps my clients publishing for years. I am also a published author, so I know what it takes to write a good book." Actively seeking a Latino *Gone With the Wind* and *Waiting to Exhale*, and urban ethnic horror. Does not want to receive anything outside of the above categories (westerns, romance, etc.).

How to Contact E-queries only. Accepts simultaneous submissions. Responds in 12 weeks to queries. Responds in 3-6 months to mss. Obtains most new clients through recommendations from others, solicitations, conferences.

Terms Agent receives 15% commission on domestic sales. Agent receives 20% commission on foreign sales. No written contract. Charges clients for photocopying.

Writers Conferences NECON; Killercon; BookExpo America; World Fantasy Convention, RWA, Romantic Times.

Tips "Research your field and contact professional writers' organizations to see who is looking for what. Finish your novel before querying agents. Read my book, *An Insider's Guide to Getting an Agent*, to get a sense of how agents operate. Read agent blogs—agentinthemiddle.blogspot.com and ravenousromance.blogspot.com."

☑ STEPHEN PEVNER, INC.

382 Lafayette St., Eighth Floor, New York NY 10003. (212)674-8403. Fax: (212)529-3692. E-mail: spidevelopment@gmail.com; spevner@aol.com. **Contact:** Stephen Pevner.

Represents Nonfiction books, novels, episodic drama, tv, movie scripts, feature film, tv movie, animation, documentary, miniseries. **Considers these nonfiction areas:** autobiography, biography, dance, ethnic, gay/lesbian, history, humor, inspirational, language, memoirs, metaphysics, music, New Age, photography, popular culture, religious, satire, sociology, travel. **Considers these fiction areas:** cartoon, comic books, contemporary issues, erotica, ethnic, experimental, gay, glitz, horror, humor, lesbian, literary, mainstream, psychic, satire, supernatural, thriller, urban. **Considers these script areas:** comedy, contemporary, detective, gay, glitz, horror, romantic comedy, romantic drama, thriller.

    ⚬ This agency specializes in motion pictures, novels, humor, pop culture, urban fiction, and independent filmmakers.

How to Contact Query with SASE. Submit outline/proposal. Prefers to read materials exclusively. Responds in 2 weeks to queries. Responds in 1 month to mss. Obtains most new clients through recommendations from others.

Terms Agent receives 15% commission on domestic sales. Agent receives 20% commission on foreign sales. Offers written contract, binding for 1 year; 6-week notice must be given to terminate contract.

Tips Be persistent, but civilized.

◓ PFD NEW YORK

Peters Fraser and Dunlop, 34-43 Russell St., London WC2B 5HA United Kingdom. (917)256-0707. Fax: (212)685-9635. Website: www.pfdny.com. **Contact:** Submissions Department.

    • Ms. Pagnamenta was with the Wylie Agency.

Member Agents Zoe Pagnamenta (U.S. authors), zpagnamenta@pfdgroup.com; Michael Sissons.

Represents Nonfiction books, novels, short story collections (if the author has other written works), poetry.

    ⚬ This agency has offices in New York as well as the United Kingdom.

How to Contact Query with SASE. Submit proposal package, synopsis, 2-3 sample chapters, publishing history, author bio, cover letter. Submit via snail mail. See online submission guidelines for more information. Responds in 1 month to queries. Obtains most new clients through recommendations from others, solicitations.

ALISON J. PICARD, LITERARY AGENT

P.O. Box 2000, Cotuit MA 02635. Phone/Fax: (508)477-7192. E-mail: ajpicard@aol.com. **Contact:** Alison Picard. Represents 48 clients. 30% of clients are new/unpublished writers. Currently handles: nonfiction books 40%, novels 40%, juvenile books 20%.

• Prior to becoming an agent, Ms. Picard was an assistant at a literary agency in New York.

Represents Nonfiction books, novels, juvenile. **Considers these nonfiction areas:** animals, autobiography, biography, business, child guidance, cooking, cultural interests, current affairs, diet/nutrition, economics, education, environment, ethnic, foods, gay/lesbian, government, health, history, how-to, humor, inspirational, juvenile nonfiction, law, medicine, memoirs, metaphysics, military, money, multicultural, New Age, parenting, popular culture, politics, psychology, religious, science, self-help, technology, travel, true crime, war, women's issues, women's studies, young adult. **Considers these fiction areas:** action, adventure, contemporary issues, crime, detective, erotica, ethnic, family saga, feminist, gay, glitz, historical, horror, humor, juvenile, lesbian, literary, mainstream, multicultural, mystery, New Age, picture books, police, psychic, romance, sports, supernatural, thriller, young adult.

➤ "Many of my clients have come to me from big agencies, where they felt overlooked or ignored. I communicate freely with my clients and offer a lot of career advice, suggestions for revising manuscripts, etc. If I believe in a project, I will submit it to a dozen or more publishers, unlike some agents who give up after four or five rejections." No science fiction/ fantasy, Western, poetry, plays or articles.

How to Contact Query with SASE. Accepts simultaneous submissions. Responds in 2 weeks to queries. Responds in 4 months to mss. Obtains most new clients through recommendations from others, solicitations.

Terms Agent receives 15% commission on domestic sales. Agent receives 20% commission on foreign sales. Offers written contract, binding for 1 year; 1-week notice must be given to terminate contract.

Recent Sales *Zitface*, by Emily Ormand (Marshall Cavendish); *Totally Together*, by Stephanie O'Dea (Running Press); *The Ultimate Slow Cooker Cookbook*, by Stephanie O'Dea (Hyperion); two untitled cookbooks, by Erin Chase (St. Martin's Press); *A Journal of the Flood Year*, by David Ely (Portobello Books—United Kingdom, L'Ancora—Italy); *A Mighty Wall*, by John Foley (Llewellyn/ Flux); *Jelly's Gold*, by David Housewright (St. Martin's Press).

Tips "Please don't send material without sending a query first via mail or e-mail. I don't accept phone or fax queries. Always enclose an SASE with a query."

◑ PINDER LANE & GARON-BROOKE ASSOCIATES, LTD.

159 W. 53rd St., Suite 14C, New York NY 10019. Member of AAR. Signatory of WGA.

Member Agents Robert Thixton, pinderl@rcn.com; Dick Duane, pinderl@rcn.com.

➤ This agency specializes in mainstream fiction and nonfiction. Does not want to receive screenplays, TV series teleplays, or dramatic plays.

How to Contact Query with SASE. *No unsolicited mss.* Obtains most new clients through referrals.

Terms Agent receives 15% commission on domestic sales. Agent receives 30% commission on foreign sales. Offers written contract.

◎ PIPPIN PROPERTIES, INC.

155 E. 38th St., Suite 2H, New York NY 10016. (212)338-9310. Fax: (212)338-9579. E-mail: info@ pippinproperties.com. Website: www.pippinproperties.com. **Contact:** Holly McGhee. Represents 52 clients. Currently handles: juvenile books 100%.

• Prior to becoming an agent, Ms. McGhee was an editor for 7 years and in book marketing for 4 years. Prior to becoming an agent, Ms. van Beek worked in children's book editorial for 4 years.

Member Agents Holly McGhee, Elena Mechlin.

Represents Juvenile.

☞ "We are strictly a children's literary agency devoted to the management of authors and artists in all media. We are small and discerning in choosing our clientele." Actively seeking middle-grade and young-adult novels.

How to Contact Query via e-mail. Include a synopsis of the work(s), your background and/or publishing history, and anything else you think is relevant. Accepts simultaneous submissions. Responds in 3 weeks to queries if interested. Responds in 10 weeks to mss. Obtains most new clients through recommendations from others.

Terms Agent receives 15% commission on domestic sales. Agent receives 25% commission on foreign sales. Offers written contract; 30-day notice must be given to terminate contract. Charges for color copying and UPS/FedEx.

Tips "Please do not start calling after sending a submission."

☑ ALICKA PISTEK LITERARY AGENCY, LLC

302A W. 12th St., #124, New York NY 10014. Website: www.apliterary.com. **Contact:** Alicka Pistek. Represents 15 clients. 50% of clients are new/unpublished writers. Currently handles: nonfiction books 60%, novels 40%.

- Prior to opening her agency, Ms. Pistek worked at ICM and as an agent at Nicholas Ellison, Inc. Alicka has an M.A. in German Translation and a B.A. in Linguistics from the University of California, San Diego. She has studied and worked in the UK, Germany and Prague, Czech Republic.

Member Agents Alicka Pistek.

Represents Nonfiction books, novels. **Considers these nonfiction areas:** animals, anthropology, autobiography, biography, child guidance, current affairs, environment, government, health, history, how-to, language, law, literature, medicine, memoirs, military, money, parenting, politics, psychology, science, self-help, technology, travel, war, creative nonfiction. **Considers these fiction areas:** crime, detective, ethnic, family saga, historical, literary, mainstream, mystery, police, romance, suspense, thriller.

☞ Does not want to receive fantasy, science fiction or Western's.

How to Contact Send e-query to info@apliterary.com. Include name, address, e-mail, and phone number, title, word count, genre of book, a brief synopsis, and relevant biographical information. Accepts simultaneous submissions. Responds in 2 months to queries. Will only respond if interested. Responds in 8 weeks to mss.

Terms Agent receives 15% commission on domestic sales. Agent receives 20% commission on foreign sales. Offers written contract. This agency charges for photocopying more than 40 pages and international postage.

Tips "Be sure you are familiar with the genre you are writing in and learn standard procedures for submitting your work. A good query will go a long way."

☑ PMA LITERARY AND FILM MANAGEMENT, INC.

45 West 21st St., Suite 4SW, New York NY 10010. (212)929-1222. Fax: (212)206-0238. E-mail: queries@pmalitfilm.com. Website: www.pmalitfilm.com. **Contact:** Peter Miller. Address for packages is P.O. Box 1817, Old Chelsea Station, New York NY 10113 Represents more than 100 clients. 50% of clients are new/unpublished writers. Currently handles: nonfiction books 40%, novels 30%, juvenile books 5%, movie scripts 25%.

- In his time in the literary world, Mr. Miller has successfully managed more than 1,000 books and dozens of motion picture and television properties. He is the author of *Author! Screenwriter!*

Member Agents Peter Miller (big nonfiction, business, true crime, religion); Adrienne Rosado (literary and commercial fiction, young adult).

Represents Nonfiction books, novels, juvenile, movie, tv, tv movie. **Considers these nonfiction areas:** autobiography, biography, business, child guidance, cooking, cultural interests, current affairs, diet/nutrition, economics, ethnic, foods, humor, inspirational, investigative, memoirs, money, parenting, popular culture, religious, satire, self-help, sports, true crime. **Considers these fiction areas:** action, adventure, crime, detective, erotica, ethnic, experimental, gay, historical, humor, inspirational, juvenile, lesbian, literary, mainstream, mystery, police, psychic, religious, romance, satire, supernatural, suspense, thriller, women's, young adult. **Considers these script areas:** action/adventure, comedy, mainstream, romantic comedy, romantic drama, thriller.

⌐ "PMA believes in long-term relationships with professional authors. We manage an author's overall career—hence the name—and have strong connections to Hollywood." Actively seeking new ideas beautifully executed. Does not want to receive poetry, stage plays, picture books and clichés.

How to Contact Query with SASE. Submit publishing history, author bio. Send no attachments or mss of any kind unless requested. Accepts simultaneous submissions. Responds in 5-7 days for e-mail queries; Responds in 4-6 weeks to mss; 6 months for paper submissions. Obtains most new clients through recommendations from others, solicitations, conferences.

Terms Agent receives 15% commission on domestic sales. Agent receives 25% commission on foreign sales. Offers written contract; 30-day notice must be given to terminate contract. This agency charges for approved expenses, such as photocopies and overnight delivery.

Recent Sales *For the Sake of Liberty*, by M. William Phelps (Thomas Dunne Books); *The Haunting of Cambria*, by Richard Taylor (Tor); *Cover Girl Confidential*, by Beverly Bartlett (5 Spot); *Ten Prayers God Always Says Yes To!*, by Anthony DeStefano (Doubleday); *Miss Fido Manners: The Complete Book of Dog Etiquette*, by Charlotte Reed (Adams Media); film rights to *Murder in the Heartland*, by M. William Phelps (Mathis Entertainment); film rights to *The Killer's Game*, by Jay Bonansinga (Andrew Lazar/Mad Chance, Inc.)

Writers Conferences A full list of Mr. Miller's speaking engagements is available online.

Tips "Don't approach agents before your work is ready, and always approach them as professionally as possible. Don't give up."

⊕ PONTAS AGENCY

Sèneca, 31, principal 08006 Barcelona Spain. This agency has other offices in Germany. Website: www.pontas-agency.com.

Member Agents Anna Soler-Pont; Martina Torrades; Carina Brandt; Marc de Gouvenain (represents authors from Scandinavia and the Pacific all over the world, both for publishing and for film rights).

Represents Nonfiction books, novels, movies.

⌐ Does not want original film screenplays.

How to Contact For book submissions send by air mail: Curriculum vitae, with contact details. Details of previously published works. Short synopsis of the work. A printed and bound copy.

⊘ THE POYNOR GROUP

13454 Yorktown Dr., Bowie MD 20715. (301)805-6788. E-mail: jpoynor@aol.com. **Contact:** Jay Poynor, president. Represents 30 clients.

Represents Considers these nonfiction areas: autobiography, biography, business, cooking, cultural interests, diet/nutrition, economics, ethnic, foods, health, inspirational, medicine, multicultural, religious. **Considers these fiction areas:** juvenile, mystery, romance, suspense.

How to Contact Mail: query with SASE; e-mail: query only.

◙ HELEN F. PRATT INC.

1165 Fifth Ave., New York NY 10029. (212)722-5081. Fax: (212)722-8569. E-mail: hfpratt@verizon. net. **Contact:** Helen F. Pratt. Member of AAR. Currently handles: other 100% illustrated books and nonfiction.

Member Agents Helen Pratt (illustrated books, fashion/decorative design nonfiction); Seamus Mullarky (does not accept unsolicited queries).

Represents Nonfiction books, illustrated books. **Considers these nonfiction areas:** Biography, Cookbooks, Gardening, Memoirs, Psychology, and especially gardening. **Considers these fiction areas:** children's and YA.

How to Contact Query with SASE. Include illustrations if possible.

AARON M. PRIEST LITERARY AGENCY

708 Third Ave., 23rd Floor, New York NY 10017-4103. (212)818-0344. Fax: (212)573-9417. Website: www.aaronpriest.com. Estab. 1974. Member of AAR. Currently handles: nonfiction books 25%, novels 75%.

Member Agents Aaron Priest, querypriest@aaronpriest.com (thrillers, commercial fiction, biographies); Lisa Erbach Vance, queryvance@aaronpriest.com (general fiction, international fiction, thrillers, upmarket women's fiction, historical fiction, narrative nonfiction, memoir);

Lucy Childs Baker, querychilds@aaronpriest.com (literary and commercial fiction, memoir, edgy women's fiction); Nicole Kenealy, querykenealy@aaronpriest.com (young adult fiction, narrative nonfiction, how-to, political, and pop-culture, literary and commercial fiction, specifically dealing with social and cultural issues).

⚬ Does not want to receive poetry, screenplays or sci-fi.

How to Contact Query one of the agents using the appropriate e-mail listed on the website. "Please do not submit to more than one agent at this agency. We urge you to check our website and consider each agent's emphasis before submitting. Your query letter should be about one page long and describe your work as well as your background. You may also paste the first chapter of your work in the body of the e-mail. Do not send attachments." Accepts simultaneous submissions. Responds in 3 weeks, only if interested.

Terms Agent receives 15% commission on domestic sales. This agency charges for photocopying and postage expenses.

Recent Sales *Divine Justice*, by David Baldacci; *The White Mary*, by Kira Salak; *Long Lost*, by Harlan Coben; *An Accidental Light*, by Elizabeth Diamond; *Trust No One*, by Gregg Hurwitz; *Power Down*, by Ben Coes.

🖉 PROSPECT AGENCY, LLC

285 Fifth Ave., PMB 445, Brooklyn NY 11215. (718)788-3217. E-mail: esk@prospectagency.com. Website: www.prospectagency.com. **Contact:** Emily Sylvan Kim. Represents 15 clients. 50% of clients are new/unpublished writers. Currently handles: novels 66%, juvenile books 33%.

• Prior to starting her agency, Ms. Kim briefly attended law school and worked for another literary agency.

Member Agents Emily Sylvan Kim; Becca Stumpf (adult and YA literary, mainstream fiction; nonfiction interests include narrative nonfiction, journalistic perspectives, fashion, film studies, travel, art, and informed analysis of cultural phenomena. She has a special interest in aging in America and environmental issues); Rachel Orr (fiction and nonfiction, particularly picture books, beginning readers, chapter books, middle-grade, YA novels); Teresa Kietlinski (artists who both write and illustrate).

Represents Nonfiction books, novels, juvenile. **Considers these nonfiction areas:** art, biography, history, juvenile nonfiction, law, memoirs, popular culture, politics, science, travel, prescriptive guides. **Considers these fiction areas:** action, adventure, detective, erotica, ethnic, frontier, juvenile, literary, mainstream, mystery, picture books, romance, suspense, thriller, westerns, young adult.

⚬ "We are currently looking for the next generation of writers to shape the literary landscape. Our clients receive professional and knowledgeable representation. We are committed to offering skilled editorial advice and advocating our clients in the marketplace." Actively seeking romance, literary fiction, and young adult submissions. Does not want to receive poetry, short stories, textbooks, or most nonfiction.

How to Contact Upload outline and 3 sample chapters to the website. Accepts simultaneous submissions. Responds in 3 weeks to queries. Responds in 1 month to mss. Obtains most new clients through recommendations from others, conferences, unsolicited mss.

Terms Agent receives 15% commission on domestic sales. Agent receives 20% commission on foreign sales. Offers written contract.

Recent Sales *BADD*, by Tim Tharp (Knopf); *Six*, by Elizabeth Batten-Carew (St. Martin's); *Rocky Road*, by Rose Kent (Knopf); *Mating Game*, by Janice Maynard (NAL); *Golden Delicious*, by Aaron Hawkins (Houghton Mifflin Harcourt); *Damaged*, by Pamela Callow (Mira); *Seduced by Shadows*, by Jessica Slade (NAL); *Identity of Ultraviolet*, by Jake Bell (Scholastic); *Quackenstein*, by Sudipta Bardhan-Quallen (Abrams); *Betraying Season*, by Marissa Doyle (Holt); *Sex on the Beach*, by Susan Lyons (Berkley), more.

Writers Conferences "Please see our website for a complete list of attended conferences."

SUSAN ANN PROTTER, LITERARY AGENT

320 Central Park West, Suite 12E, New York NY 10025. Website: SusanAnnProtter.com. **Contact:** Susan Protter. Member of AAR. Other memberships include Authors Guild.

• Prior to opening her agency, Ms. Protter was associate director of subsidiary rights at Harper & Row Publishers.

How to Contact *"We are currently not accepting new unsolicited submissions."*

✐ PSALTIS LITERARY

Post Office: Park West Finance, New York NY 10040. E-mail: psaltsis@mpsaltisliterary.com. **Contact:** Michael Psaltis. Member of AAR. Represents 30-40 clients.

Represents Nonfiction books, novels. **Considers these nonfiction areas:** autobiography, biography, business, cooking, diet/nutrition, economics, foods, health, history, medicine, memoirs, popular culture, psychology, science, technology. **Considers these fiction areas:** mainstream.

How to Contact Query only by e-mail. Unrequested manuscripts will not be read. Responds only to queries of interest.

Terms Agent receives 15% commission on domestic sales. Agent receives 20% commission on foreign sales. Offers written contract.

N ✐ P.S LITERARY AGENCY

520 Kerr St., #20033, Oakville ON L6K 3C7 Canada. E-mail: query@psliterary.com. Website: www.psliterary.com. **Contact:** Curtis Russell. Represents 10 clients. 25% of clients are new/unpublished writers. Currently handles: nonfiction books 50%, novels 50%.

Represents Nonfiction books, novels, juvenile. **Considers these nonfiction areas:** biography, business, child, cooking, current affairs, government, health, how to, humor, memoirs, military, money, nature, popular culture, science, self-help, sports, true crime, women's. **Considers these fiction areas:** adventure, detective, erotica, ethnic, family, historical, horror, humor, juvenile, literary, mainstream, mystery, picture books, romance, sports, thriller, young, women's.

> ⚷ "What makes our agency distinct: We take on a small number of clients per year in order to provide focused, hands-on representation. We pride ourselves in providing industry leading client service." Does not want to receive poetry or screenplays.

How to Contact Query via mail or e-mail. Prefers e-mail. Submit synopsis, author bio. Accepts simultaneous submissions. Responds in 6 weeks to queries. Responds in 6 weeks to mss. Obtains most new clients through solicitations.

Terms Agent receives 15% commission on domestic sales. Agent receives 25% commission on foreign sales. Offers written contract; 30-day notice must be given to terminate contract. "This agency charges for postage/messenger services only if a project is sold."

Tips "Please review our website for the most up-to-date submission guidelines."

N ✐ PUBLISHING RIOT GROUP

E-mail: submissions@priotgroup.com. Website: www.priotgroup.com. **Contact:** Donna Bagdasarian.

> • Prior to being an agent, Ms. Bagdasarian worked as an acquisitions editor. Previously, she worked for the William Morris and Maria Carvainis agencies.

Represents Nonfiction books, novels. **Considers these nonfiction areas:** memoirs, popular culture, politics, science, sociology. **Considers these fiction areas:** ethnic, historical, literary, mainstream, thriller, women's.

> ⚷ "The company is a literary management company, representing their authors in all processes of the entertainment trajectory: from book development, to book sales, to subsidiary sales in the foreign market, television and film." Does not want science fiction and fantasy.

How to Contact Query via e-mail with a short sample.

✐ JOANNA PULCINI LITERARY MANAGEMENT

E-mail: info@jplm.com. Website: www.jplm.com. **Contact:** Joanna Pulcini.

> ⚷ "JPLM is not accepting submissions at this time; however, I do encourage those seeking representation to read the 'Advice to Writers' essay on our website for some guidance on finding an agent."

How to Contact Do not query this agency until they open their client list.

Recent Sales *TV*, by Brian Brown; *The Movies That Changed Us*, by Nick Clooney; *Strange, But True*, by John Searles; *The Intelligencer*, by Leslie Silbert; *In Her Shoes* and *The Guy Not Taken* by Jennifer Weiner.

THE QUADRIVIUM GROUP

7512 Dr. Phillips Boulevard, Suite #50-229, Orlando FL 32819. E-mail: steveblount@ TheQuadriviumGroup.com. Website: www.thequadriviumgroup.com. **Contact:** Steve Blount. Represents 20-30 clients.

○╼ "This agency specializes in Christian titles. Open to a limited number of unpublished authors (with credentials, platform, compelling story/idea), and to new clients (mostly by referral). General agent. Handles Christian and general nonfiction and fiction for all ages, gift books, crossover books."

How to Contact Query with SASE. Already-completed book proposals with sample chapters preferred.

Tips "Recognized in the industry. Other services offered: consulting on book sales and distribution."

◙ QUEEN LITERARY AGENCY

850 Seventh Ave., Suite 704, New York NY 10019. (212)974-8333. Fax: (212)974-8347. Website: www.queenliterary.com. **Contact:** Lisa Queen.

• Prior to her current position, Ms. Queen was a former publishing executive and most recently head of IMG Worldwide's literary division.

Represents Nonfiction books, novels.

○╼ Ms. Queen's specialties: While our agency represents a wide range of nonfiction titles, we have a particular interest in business books, food writing, science and popular psychology, as well as books by well-known chefs, radio and television personalities and sports figures.

How to Contact Query with SASE.

Recent Sales *The Female Brain*, by Louann Brizendine; *Does the Noise in My Head Bother You?* by Steven Tyler; *What I Cannot Change*, by LeAnn Rimes and Darrell Brown.

◙ QUICKSILVER BOOKS: LITERARY AGENTS

508 Central Park Ave., #5101, Scarsdale NY 10583. Phone/Fax: (914)722-4664. E-mail: quickbooks@ optonline.net. Website: www.quicksilverbooks.com. **Contact:** Bob Silverstein. Represents 50 clients. 50% of clients are new/unpublished writers. Currently handles: nonfiction books 75%, novels 25%.

• Prior to opening his agency, Mr. Silverstein served as senior editor at Bantam Books and managing editor at Dell Books/Delacorte Press.

Represents Nonfiction books, novels. **Considers these nonfiction areas:** anthropology, archeology, autobiography, biography, business, child guidance, cooking, cultural interests, current affairs, diet/ nutrition, economics, environment, ethnic, foods, health, history, how-to, inspirational, language, medicine, memoirs, New Age, parenting, popular culture, psychology, religious, science, self-help, sociology, sports, true crime, women's issues, women's studies. **Considers these fiction areas:** action, adventure, glitz, mystery, suspense, thriller.

○╼ This agency specializes in literary and commercial mainstream fiction and nonfiction, especially psychology, New Age, holistic healing, consciousness, ecology, environment, spirituality, reference, self-help, cookbooks and narrative nonfiction. Does not want to receive science fiction, pornography, poetry or single-spaced mss.

How to Contact Query with SASE. Authors are expected to supply SASE for return of ms and for query letter responses. Accepts simultaneous submissions. Responds in 2 weeks to queries. Responds in 1 month to mss. Obtains most new clients through recommendations, listings in sourcebooks, solicitations, workshop participation.

Terms Agent receives 15% commission on domestic sales. Agent receives 20% commission on foreign sales. Offers written contract.

Recent Sales *Simply Mexican*, by Lourdes Castro (Ten Speed Press); *Indian Vegan Cooking*, by Madhu Gadia (Perigee/Penguin); *Selling Luxury*, by Robin Lent & Genevieve Tour (Wiley); *Get the Job You Want, Even When No One's Hiring*, by Ford R. Myers (Wiley); *Matrix Meditations*, by Victor & Kooch Daniels (Inner Traditions Bear & Co.); *Macrobiotics for Dummies* (Wiley); *The Power of Receiving* (Tarcher); *Eat, Drink, Think in Spanish* (Ten Speed Press); *Nice Girls Don't Win at Life* (Broadway).

Writers Conferences National Writers Union.

Tips "Write what you know. Write from the heart. Publishers print, authors sell."

◙ SUSAN RABINER LITERARY AGENCY, INC., THE

315 W. 39th St., Suite 1501, New York NY 10018. (212)279-0316. Fax: (212)279-0932. E-mail: susan@ rabiner.net. Website: www.rabinerlit.com. **Contact:** Susan Rabiner.

- Prior to becoming an agent, Ms. Rabiner was editorial director of Basic Books. She is also the co-author of *Thinking Like Your Editor: How to Write Great Serious Nonfiction and Get it Published* (W.W. Norton).

Member Agents Susan Rabiner; Sydelle Kramer; Helena Schwarz; Holly Bemiss. See the website for individual agent e-mails.

Represents Nonfiction books, novels, textbooks. **Considers these nonfiction areas:** autobiography, biography, business, economics, education, government, health, history, inspirational, law, medicine, philosophy, politics, psychology, religious, science, sociology, sports, technology.

- ⚷ "Representing narrative nonfiction and big-idea books—work that illuminates the past and the present. I look for well-researched, topical books written by fully credentialed academics, journalists, and recognized public intellectuals with the power to stimulate public debate on a broad range of issues including the state of our economy, political discourse, history, science, and the arts."

How to Contact Query by e-mail only, with cover letter and proposal for nonfiction. Accepts simultaneous submissions. Responds in 2 weeks if your project fits the profile of the agency. Obtains most new clients through recommendations from others.

Terms Agent receives 15% commission on domestic sales. Agent receives 20% commission on foreign sales. Offers written contract; 1-month notice must be given to terminate contract.

⬛ LYNNE RABINOFF AGENCY

72-11 Austin St., No. 201, Forest Hills NY 11375. (718)459-6894. E-mail: Lynne@lynnerabinoff. com. **Contact:** Lynne Rabinoff. Represents 50 clients. 50% of clients are new/unpublished writers. Currently handles: nonfiction books 99%, novels 1%.

- Prior to becoming an agent, Ms. Rabinoff was in publishing and dealt with foreign rights.

Represents Nonfiction books. **Considers these nonfiction areas:** anthropology, archeology, autobiography, biography, business, cultural interests, current affairs, economics, ethnic, government, history, inspirational, law, memoirs, military, popular culture, politics, psychology, religious, science, technology, women's issues, women's studies.

- ⚷ "This agency specializes in history, political issues, current affairs and religion."

How to Contact Query with SASE or e-mail. Submit proposal package, synopsis, 1 sample chapter, author bio. Responds in 3 weeks to queries. Responds in 1 month to mss. Obtains most new clients through recommendations from others.

Terms Agent receives 15% commission on domestic sales. Agent receives 20% commission on foreign sales. Offers written contract; 60-day notice must be given to terminate contract. This agency charges for postage.

Recent Sales *The Confrontation*, by Walid Phares (Palgrave); *Flying Solo*, by Robert Vaughn (Thomas Dunne); *Thugs*, by Micah Halpern (Thomas Nelson); *Size Sexy*, by Stella Ellis (Adams Media); *Cruel and Usual*, by Nonie Darwish (Thomas Nelson); *Now they Call Me Infidel*, by Nonie Darwish (Sentinel/Penguin); *34 Days*, by Avid Issacharoff (Palgrave).

⬛ RAINES & RAINES

103 Kenyon Road, Medusa NY 12120. (518)239-8311. Fax: (518)239-6029. **Contact:** Theron Raines (member of AAR); Joan Raines; Keith Korman. Member of AAR. Represents 100 clients.

Represents Nonfiction books, novels. **Considers these nonfiction areas:** Action/Adventure, Autobiography/Biography, Finance/Investing, History, Military/War, NarrativePsychology, All subjects. **Considers these fiction areas:** action, adventure, crime, detective, fantasy, frontier, historical, mystery, picture books, police, science fiction, suspense, thriller, westerns, whimsical.

How to Contact Query with SASE. Responds in 2 weeks to queries.

Terms Agent receives 15% commission on domestic sales. Agent receives 20% commission on foreign sales. Charges for photocopying.

⬛ ⬛ RED SOFA LITERARY

2163 Grand Avenue, #2, St. Paul MN 55105. (651)224-6670. E-mail: dawn@redsofaliterary.com. Website: www.redsofaliterary.com. **Contact:** Dawn Frederick, Agent and Owner. Represents 10 clients. 60% of clients are new/unpublished writers. Currently handles: nonfiction books 97%, novels 2%, story collections 1%.

- Prior to her current position, Ms. Frederick spent five years at Sebastian Literary Agency. In addition, Ms. Frederick worked over ten years in indie and chain book stores, and at an independent children's book publisher. Ms. Frederick has a Master's Degree in Library and Information Sciences from an ALA-Accredited institution.

Represents Nonfiction books and YA fiction. **Considers these nonfiction areas:** animals, anthropology, archeology, cooking, crafts, cultural interests, current affairs, diet/nutrition, ethnic, foods, gay/lesbian, government, health, history, hobbies, humor, investigative, law, medicine, popular culture, politics, satire, sociology, true crime, women's issues, women's studies, extreme sports.

How to Contact Query by e-mail or mail with SASE. No attachments, please. Submit full proposal plus 3 sample chapters and any other pertinent writing samples. Accepts simultaneous submissions. Responds in 3 weeks to queries. Responds in 6 weeks to mss. Obtains most new clients through recommendations from others, and solicitations.

Terms Agent receives 15% commission on domestic sales. Agent receives 20% commission on foreign sales. Offers written contract. May charge a one-time $100 fee for partial reimbursement of postage and phone expenses incurred if the advance is below $15,000.

Writers Conferences SDSU Writers' Conference.

Tips "Truly research the agents you query. Avoid e-mailing and/or snail mailing every literary agent your book idea. Due to the large volume of queries received, the process of reading queries for unrepresented categories (by the agency) becomes tedious. Investigate online directories, printed guides like *Writer's Market*, individual agent websites, and more, before assuming every literary agent in this industry would represent your book idea. Each agent has a vision of what he/she wants to represent and will communicate this information accordingly; we're simply waiting for those specific book ideas to come in our direction."

☑ THE REDWOOD AGENCY

4300 SW 34th Avenue, Portland OR 97239. (503)219-9019. E-mail: info@redwoodagency.com. Website: www.redwoodagency.com. **Contact:** Catherine Fowler, founder. Adheres to AAR canon of ethics. Currently handles: nonfiction books 100%.

- Prior to becoming an agent, Ms. Fowler was an editor, subsidiary rights director and associate publisher for Doubleday, Simon & Schuster and Random House for her 20 years in NY Publishing. Content exec for web startups Excite and WebMD.

Represents Nonfiction books, novels. **Considers these nonfiction areas:** business, cooking, diet/nutrition, environment, gardening, health, humor, medicine, memoirs, parenting, popular culture, psychology, satire, self-help, women's issues, women's studies, narrative, parenting, aging, reference, lifestyle, cultural technology. **Considers these fiction areas:** literary, mainstream, suspense, women's, quirky.

- ⌐ "Along with our love of books and publishing, we have the desire and commitment to work with fun, interesting and creative people, to do so with respect and professionalism, but also with a sense of humor." Actively seeking high-quality, nonfiction works created for the general consumer market, as well as projects with the potential to become book series. Does not want to receive fiction. Do not send packages that require signature for delivery.

How to Contact Query via e-mail only. While we redesign website, submit "quick query" to: query@redwoodagency.com. See all guidelines online. Obtains most new clients through recommendations from others, solicitations.

Terms Offers written contract. Charges for copying and delivery charges, if any, as specified in author/agency agreement.

RED WRITING HOOD INK

2075 Attala Road 1990, Kosciusko MS 39090. (662)674-0636. Fax: (662)796-3095. E-mail: rwhi@bellsouth.net. Website: www.redwritinghoodink.net. **Contact:** Sheri Ables. Other memberships include adheres to AAR canon. Currently handles: nonfiction books 100%.

- Prior to her current position, Ms. Ables was an agent of the Williams Agency. In addition, she worked for an agency in Oregon from 1996-1997. Collectively, the staff of RWHI has more than 25 years experience in the publishing industry.

Member Agents Sheri Ables, agent; Terri Dunlap, literary assistant (terri@redwritinghoodink.net).

Represents Nonfiction books.

- ⌐ Biography, Children's, Crime & Thrillers, Entertainment, General Fiction, Health, History, Inspirationa, Mystery/Suspense, Romantic Fiction, General nonfiction, Self-help

How to Contact Send cover letter and 2-page synopsis only to e-mail. If mailing, include SASE.
Terms Agent receives 15% commission on domestic sales. Agent receives 20% commission on foreign sales.
Tips Writers: View submission guidelines prior to making contact.

HELEN REES LITERARY AGENCY

14 Beacon St., Suite 710, Boston MA 02108. (617)227-9014. Fax: (617)227-8762. E-mail: reesagency@reesagency.com. **Contact:** Joan Mazmanian, Ann Collette, Helen Rees, Lorin Rees. Estab. 1983. Member of AAR. Other memberships include PEN. Represents more than 100 clients. 50% of clients are new/unpublished writers. Currently handles: nonfiction books 60%, novels 40%.
Member Agents Ann Collette (literary, mystery, thrillers, suspense, vampire, and women's fiction; in nonfiction, she prefers true crime, narrative nonfiction, military & war, work to do with race & class, and work set in or about Southeast Asia. Ann can be reached at: Agent10702@aol.com). Lorin Rees (literary fiction, memoirs, business books, self-help, science, history, psychology and narrative nonfiction. lorin@reesagency.com).
Represents Nonfiction books, novels. **Considers these nonfiction areas:** autobiography, biography, business, current affairs, economics, government, health, history, law, medicine, money, politics, women's issues, women's studies. **Considers these fiction areas:** historical, literary, mainstream, mystery, suspense, thriller.
How to Contact Query with SASE, outline, 2 sample chapters. No unsolicited e-mail submissions. No multiple submissions. Responds in 3-4 weeks to queries. Obtains most new clients through recommendations from others, conferences, submissions.
Terms Agent receives 15% commission on domestic sales. Agent receives 20% commission on foreign sales.
Recent Sales Sold more than 35 titles in the last year. *Get Your Ship Together*, by Capt. D. Michael Abrashoff; *Overpromise and Overdeliver*, by Rick Berrara; *Opacity*, by Joel Kurtzman; *America the Broke*, by Gerald Swanson; *Murder at the B-School*, by Jeffrey Cruikshank; *Bone Factory*, by Steven Sidor; *Father Said*, by Hal Sirowitz; *Winning*, by Jack Welch; *The Case for Israel*, by Alan Dershowitz; *As the Future Catches You*, by Juan Enriquez; *Blood Makes the Grass Grow Green*, by Johnny Rico; *DVD Movie Guide*, by Mick Martin and Marsha Porter; *Words that Work*, by Frank Luntz; *Stirring It Up*, by Gary Hirshberg; *Hot Spots*, by Martin Fletcher; *Andy Grove: The Life and Times of an American*, by Richard Tedlow; *Girls Most Likely To*, by Poonam Sharma.

REGAL LITERARY AGENCY

1140 Broadway, Penthouse, New York NY 10001. (212)684-7900. Fax: (212)684-7906. E-mail: info@regal-literary.com. Website: www.regal-literary.com. **Contact:** Barbara Marshall. London Office: Studio One, 7 Chalcot Road, Primrose Hill, London NW1 8LH, UNITED KINGDOM, uk@regal-literary.com Estab. 2002. Member of AAR. Represents 70 clients. 20% of clients are new/unpublished writers.
Member Agents Markus Hoffmann joined Regal Literary in 2006. He had been a literary scout and foreign rights agent on both sides of the Atlantic, most recently as Foreign Rights Manager at Aitken Alexander Associates in London and then Director of International Scouting at Maria Campbell Associates in New York. His main interests are international and literary fiction, crime, (pop) cultural studies, current affairs, economics, history, music, popular science, and travel literature. He also looks after foreign rights for the agency, and the London and Frankfurt Book Fairs every year. He's the trumpeter of Half on Signature, the finest R & B band on the international publishing circuit. Lauren Pearson started her career at the Russell & Volkening Literary Agency, and after stints at Tina Brown's *Talk* magazine and the Chicago-based *Modern Luxury* magazine group, she joined Regal Literary in 2004. In 2007, she moved across the pond to set up our London office. In addition to handling UK rights for the agency, she is looking to represent European-based writers of literary and commercial fiction, memoir, narrative nonfiction, and young adult and children's books. If it makes sense for your primary agent to be based in London, she's your gal. She likes anything pop-culture or crime-related, and is an avid late-night watcher of *Law & Order* reruns and the British detective drama *Dalziel and Pascoe*. She is a graduate of Duke University and the Radcliffe Publishing Course. With over a decade of experience in the book publishing industry, Michael Psaltis is a partner in The Culinary Cooperative, as well as the head

of his own agency, Psaltis Literary. Michael began his book publishing career working with an independent book marketing company, then with a book publicist and then at a small press before becoming an agent at a boutique literary agency. For nine years he worked with the Book Industry Study Group (BISG), a non-profit organization that studies and reports on all aspects of the book industry. Joseph Regal got his first job in publishing at the Russell & Volkening Literary Agency in 1991. There he worked with Pulitzer Prize-winning best-selling authors Anne Tyler, Eudora Welty, Annie Dillard, Howell Raines, and Peter Taylor, as well as Tony Award-winner Ntozake Shange, Nobel Prize-winner Nadine Gordimer, and TV anchorman and novelist Jim Lehrer. After leaving music for publishing, he founded Regal Literary Inc. in 2002. He graduated from Columbia College magna cum laude. His primary interests are literary fiction, international thrillers, history, science, photography, music, culture, and whimsy. After graduating from Middlebury College, Michael Strong was a sailing instructor at the Hurricane Island Outward Bound School, a carpenter in Berkeley, California, an English teacher at a school for dyslexic students, and a graduate student in English at UNC-Chapel Hill, where he read for Carolina Quarterly. He was a PhD candidate at the Program in Comparative Literature and Literary Theory at the University of Pennsylvania, where he taught classes on technology and ethics, wrote a dissertation on FINNEGANS WAKE, and was Assistant Director of the Penn National Commission. After 7 years in digital marketing at Sotheby's, he now handles marketing and publicity at Regal Literary. He yearns for fine literary fiction and ambitious thrillers, and for nonfiction about art, politics, science, business, sports, and he loves boats and the oceans.

′ Actively seeking literary fiction and narrative nonfiction. Does not want romance, science fiction, horror, or screenplays.

How to Contact Query with SASE. No phone calls. Submissions should consist of a one-page query letter detailing the book in question as well as the qualifications of the author. For fiction, submissions may also include the first ten pages of the novel or one short story from a collection. We do not consider romance, science fiction, poetry, or screenplays. Accepts simultaneous submissions. Responds in 2-3 weeks to queries. Responds in 4-12 weeks to mss.

Terms Agent receives 15% commission on domestic sales. Agent receives 20% commission on foreign sales. We charge no reading fees.

Recent Sales Audrey Niffenegger's *The Time Traveler's Wife* (Mariner) and *Her Fearful Symmetry* (Scribner), Gregory David Roberts' *Shantaram* (St. Martin's), Josh Bazell's *Beat the Reaper* (Little, Brown), John Twelve Hawks' *The Fourth Realm Trilogy* (Doubleday), James Reston, Jr.'s *The Conviction of Richard Nixon* (Three Rivers) and *Defenders of the Faith* (Penguin), Michael Psilakis' *How to Roast a Lamb: New Greek Classic Cooking* (Little, Brown), Colman Andrews' *Country Cooking of Ireland* (Chronicle) and *Reinventing Food: Ferran Adria and How He Changed the Way We Eat* (Phaidon).

Tips "We are deeply committed to every aspect of our clients' careers, and are engaged in everything from the editorial work of developing a great book proposal or line editing a fiction manuscript to negotiating state-of-the-art book deals and working to promote and publicize the book when it's published. We are at the forefront of the effort to increase authors' rights in publishing contracts in a rapidly changing commercial environment. We deal directly with co-agents and publishers in every foreign territory and also work directly and with co-agents for feature film and television rights, with extraordinary success in both arenas. Many of our clients' works have sold in dozens of translation markets, and a high proportion of our books have been sold in Hollywood. We have strong relationships with speaking agents, who can assist in arranging author tours and other corporate and college speaking opportunities when appropriate. We also have a staff publicist and marketer to help promote our clients' and their work."

Ⓢ JODY REIN BOOKS, INC.
7741 S. Ash Ct., Centennial CO 80122. (303)694-4430. Fax: (303)694-0687. Website: www.jodyreinbooks.com. **Contact:** Winnefred Dollar. Member of AAR. Other memberships include Authors' Guild. Currently handles: nonfiction books 70%, novels 30%.

• Prior to opening her agency, Ms. Rein worked for 13 years as an acquisitions editor for Contemporary Books and as executive editor for Bantam/Doubleday/Dell and Morrow/Avon.

Represents Nonfiction books, novels. **Considers these nonfiction areas:** business, child guidance, cultural interests, current affairs, dance, economics, environment, ethnic, film, government, history, humor, law, music, parenting, popular culture, politics, psychology, satire, science, sociology, technology, theater, women's issues, women's studies. **Considers these fiction areas:** literary, mainstream.

   ☞ *This agency is no longer actively seeking new clients.*

Terms Agent receives 15% commission on domestic sales. Agent receives 25% commission on foreign sales. Agent receives 20% commission on film sales. Offers written contract. Charges clients for express mail, overseas expenses, photocopying mss.

Recent Sales *How to Remodel a Man*, by Bruce Cameron (St. Martin's Press); *8 Simple Rules for Dating My Teenage Daughter*, by Bruce Cameron (ABC/Disney); *Unbound*, by Dean King (Little, Brown); *Halfway to Heaven*, by Mark Obmascik (The Free Press); *The Rhino with Glue-On Shoes*, by Dr. Lucy Spelman (Random House); *When She Flew*, by Jennie Shortridge (NAL).

Tips "Do your homework before submitting. Make sure you have a marketable topic and the credentials to write about it. We want well-written books on fresh and original nonfiction topics that have broad appeal, as well as novels written by authors who have spent years developing their craft. Authors must be well established in their fields and have strong media experience."

☑ THE AMY RENNERT AGENCY

98 Main St., #302, Tiburon CA 94920. E-mail: queries@amyrennert.com. **Contact:** Amy Rennert.

Represents Nonfiction books, novels. **Considers these nonfiction areas:** autobiography, biography, health, history, medicine, memoirs, sports, lifestyle, narrative nonfiction. **Considers these fiction areas:** literary, mystery.

   ☞ "The Amy Rennert Agency specializes in books that matter. We provide career management for established and first-time authors, and our breadth of experience in many genres enables us to meet the needs of a diverse clientele."

How to Contact We now prefer to receive submissions by e-mail. For nonfiction, send cover letter and attach a Word file with proposal/first chapter. For fiction—and sometimes memoir—send cover letter and attach a Word file with 10-20 pages.

Tips Due to the high volume of submissions, it is not possible to respond to each and every one. Please understand that we are only able to respond to queries that we feel may be a good fit with our agency.

☑ JODIE RHODES LITERARY AGENCY

8840 Villa La Jolla Drive, Suite 315, La Jolla CA 92037-1957. Website: jodierhodesliterary.com. **Contact:** Jodie Rhodes, president. Member of AAR. Represents 74 clients. 60% of clients are new/unpublished writers. Currently handles: nonfiction books 45%, novels 35%, juvenile books 20%.

   • Prior to opening her agency, Ms. Rhodes was a university-level creative writing teacher, workshop director, published novelist, and vice president/media director at the N.W. Ayer Advertising Agency.

Member Agents Jodie Rhodes; Clark McCutcheon (fiction); Bob McCarter (nonfiction).

Represents Nonfiction books, novels. **Considers these nonfiction areas:** autobiography, biography, child guidance, cultural interests, ethnic, government, health, history, law, medicine, memoirs, military, parenting, politics, science, technology, war, women's issues, women's studies. **Considers these fiction areas:** ethnic, family saga, historical, literary, mainstream, mystery, suspense, thriller, women's, young adult.

   ☞ "Actively seeking witty, sophisticated women's books about career ambitions and relationships; edgy/trendy YA and teen books; narrative nonfiction on groundbreaking scientific discoveries, politics, economics, military and important current affairs by prominent scientists and academic professors." Does not want to receive erotica, horror, fantasy, romance, science fiction, religious/inspirational, or children's books (does accept young adult/teen).

How to Contact Query with brief synopsis, first 30-50 pages, SASE. Do not call. Do not send complete ms unless requested. This agency does not return unrequested material weighing a pound or more that requires special postage. Include e-mail address with query. Accepts simultaneous submissions. Responds in 3 weeks to queries. Obtains most new clients through recommendations from others, agent sourcebooks.

Terms Agent receives 15% commission on domestic sales. Agent receives 20% commission on foreign sales. Offers written contract; 1-month notice must be given to terminate contract. Charges

Literary Agents

clients for fax, photocopying, phone calls, postage. Charges are itemized and approved by writers upfront.

Recent Sales Sold 42 titles in the last year. *The Ring*, by Kavita Daswani (HarperCollins); *Train to Trieste*, by Domnica Radulescu (Knopf); *A Year With Cats and Dogs*, by Margaret Hawkins (Permanent Press); *Silence and Silhouettes*, by Ryan Smithson (HarperCollins); *Internal Affairs*, by Constance Dial (Permanent Press); *How Math Rules the World*, by James Stein (HarperCollins); *Diagnosis of Love*, by Maggie Martin (Bantam); *Lies, Damn Lies, and Science*, by Sherry Seethaler (Prentice Hall); *Freaked*, by Jeanne Dutton (HarperCollins); *The Five Second Rule*, by Anne Maczulak (Perseus Books); *The Intelligence Wars*, by Stephen O'Hern (Prometheus); *Seducing the Spirits*, by Louise Young (The Permanent Press), and more.

Tips "Think your book out before you write it. Do your research, know your subject matter intimately, and write vivid specifics, not bland generalities. Care deeply about your book. Don't imitate other writers. Find your own voice. We never take on a book we don't believe in, and we go the extra mile for our writers. We welcome talented, new writers."

JONNE RICCI LITERARY AGENCY

P.O. Box 13410, Palm Desert CA 92255. Website: jonnericciliteraryagency.net/. **Contact:** Jonne Ricci. Other memberships include Better Business Bureau of Southland (California). Follows AAR guidelines. Currently handles: novels, juvenile books.

○┐ "We represent authors who have special writing skills and want to see their books published. We encourage first-time writers to contact us. Our Agency is committed to finding new talent and we don't charge fees for reading or evaluating material. We urge you to learn more about our Agency. Explore our Webscape and see if your work fits with us." "Our agency represents writers of literary fiction. We are most interested in Crime, Mystery, Romance, Westerns, Thrillers and Adventure. We also specialize in Christian themes. If you feel your work fits with us, please send (in hard copy only, no submissions via e-mail) a query with Synopsis (3 pages or less) and the first few chapters (30 pages or less), all of which should be double-spaced. SASE."

▦ THE LISA RICHARDS AGENCY

108 Upper Leeson St., Dublin 4 Republic of Ireland Ireland. (03)(531)637-5000. Fax: (03)531)667-1256. E-mail: info@lisarichards.ie. Website: www.lisarichards.ie. **Contact:** Chairman: Alan Cook; Managing Director: Miranda Pheifer, Fergus Cronin, Patrick Sutton; Actors' Agents: Lisa Cook, Richard Cook, Jonathan Shankey, Lorraine Cummins: Comedy Agents: Caroline Lee, Christine Dwyer; Literary Agent: Faith O'Grady; Voice Overs & Corp. Bookings: Eavan Kenny. Estab. 1989.

Member Agents Faith O'Grady (literary).

Represents Movie, TV, Broadcast. **Considers these nonfiction areas:** biography, current affairs, history, memoirs, popular culture, travel, Politics. **Considers these script areas:** comedy, General Scipts.

How to Contact Submit proposal package, synopsis, 2-3 sample chapters, query letter with SAE.

Recent Sales Clients include Denise Deegan, Arlene Hunt, Roisin Ingle, Declan Lynch, Jennifer McCann, Sarah O'Brien, Kevin Rafter.

▦ ☻ RICHARDS LITERARY AGENCY

P.O. Box 31-240, Milford, North Shore City 0741 New Zealand (64)(9)410-0209. E-mail: rla.richards@clear.net.nz. **Contact:** Ray Richards. Other memberships include NZALA. Represents 100 clients. 20% of clients are new/unpublished writers. Currently handles: nonfiction books 20%, novels 15%, story collections 5%, juvenile books 40%, scholarly books 5%, other 15% movie rights.

• Prior to opening his agency, Mr. Richards was a book publisher, managing director and vice chairman.

○┐ We offer a high quality of experience, acceptances and client relationships. Does not want to receive short stories, articles or poetry.

How to Contact Submit outline/proposal. Do not send full ms until requested. Responds in 1 week to queries. Responds in 1 month to mss. Obtains most new clients through referrals.

Terms Agent receives 15% commission on domestic sales. Agent receives 20% commission on foreign sales. Offers written contract. Charges clients for overseas postage and photocopying.

Tips We first need a full book proposal, outline of 2-10 pages, author statement of experience and published works.

◙ ANGELA RINALDI LITERARY AGENCY

P.O. Box 7877, Beverly Hills CA 90212-7877. (310)842-7665. Fax: (310)837-8143. E-mail: amr@ rinaldiliterary.com. Website: www.rinaldiliterary.com. **Contact:** Angela Rinaldi. Member of AAR. Represents 50 clients. Currently handles: nonfiction books 50%, novels 50%.

- Prior to opening her agency, Ms. Rinaldi was an editor at NAL/Signet, Pocket Books and Bantam, and the manager of book development for *The Los Angeles Times*.

Represents Nonfiction books, novels, TV and motion picture rights (for clients only). **Considers these nonfiction areas:** biography, business, health books that address specific issues, career, personal finance, self-help, true crime, women's issues/studies, current issues, psychology, popular reference, prescriptive and proactive self-help,, books by journalists, academics, doctors and therapists, based on their research, motivational. **Considers these fiction areas:** Commercial/ Literary fiction, upmarket contemporary women's fiction, suspense, literary historical thrillers like Elizabeth Kostova's *The Historian*, gothic suspense like Diane Setterfield's *The Thirteenth Tale* and Matthew Pearl's *The Dante Club*, women's book club fiction—novels where the story lends itself to discussion like Kim Edwards' *The Memory Keeper's Daughter*.

- ⚮ Actively seeking commercial and literary fiction. Does not want to receive humor, techno thrillers, KGB/CIA espionage, drug thrillers, *Da Vinci*-code thrillers, category romances, science fiction, fantasy, horror, westerns, film scripts, poetry, category romances, magazine articles, religion, occult, supernatural.

How to Contact For fiction, send first 3 chapters, brief synopsis, SASE or brief e-mail inquiry with the first 10 pages pastsed into the e-mail—no attachments unless asked for. For nonfiction, query with detailed letter or outline/proposal, SASE or e-mail—no attachments unless asked for. Do not send certified or metered mail. Responds in 6 weeks to queries that are posted; e-mail queries 2-3 weeks.

Terms Agent receives 15% commission on domestic sales. Agent receives 25% commission on foreign sales. Offers written contract.

◙ ANN RITTENBERG LITERARY AGENCY, INC.

30 Bond St., New York NY 10012. (212)684-6936. Fax: (212)684-6929. Website: www.rittlit.com. **Contact:** Ann Rittenberg, President, and Penn Whaling, Associate. Member of AAR. Currently handles: fiction 75%, nonfiction 25%.

Represents Considers these nonfiction areas: memoirs, women's issues, women's studies. **Considers these fiction areas:** literary, thriller, upmarket fiction.

- ⚮ This agent specializes in literary fiction and literary nonfiction. Does not want to receive screenplays, straight genre fiction, poetry, self-help.

How to Contact Query with SASE. Submit outline, 3 sample chapters, SASE. Query via postal mail *only*. Accepts simultaneous submissions. Responds in 6 weeks to queries. Responds in 2 months to mss. Obtains most new clients through referrals from established writers and editors.

Terms Terms: Agent receives 15% commission on domestic sales. Agent receives 20% commission on foreign sales. Offers written contract. This agency charges clients for photocopying only.

Recent Sales *The Given Day*, by Dennis Lehane; *My Cat Hates You*, by Jim Edgar; *Never Wave Goodbye*, by Doug Magee; *House and Home*, by Kathleen McCleary; *Nowhere to Run*, by CJ Box; and *Daughter of Kura*, by Debra Austin.

RIVERSIDE LITERARY AGENCY

41 Simon Keets Road, Leyden MA 01337. (413)772-0067. Fax: (413)772-0969. E-mail: rivlit@sover. net. Website: www.riversideliteraryagency.com. **Contact:** Susan Lee Cohen. Represents 40 clients. 20% of clients are new/unpublished writers.

- ⚮ nonfiction

How to Contact Query with SASE. Responds in 2 weeks to queries. Obtains most new clients through referrals.

Terms Agent receives 15% commission on domestic sales. Offers written contract. Charges clients for foreign postage, photocopying large mss, express mail deliveries, etc.

◙ LESLIE RIVERS, INTERNATIONAL (LRI)

P.O. Box 940772, Houston TX 77094-7772. (281)493–5822. Fax: (281)493–5835. E-mail: LRivers@ LeslieRivers.com. Website: www.leslierivers.com. **Contact:** Judith Bruni. Adheres to AAR's canon of ethics. Represents 20 clients. 80% of clients are new/unpublished writers. Currently handles: novels 90%.

- Prior to becoming agents, members were in marketing, sales, project management, customer satisfaction, writers, and publishing assistants.

Member Agents Judith Bruni, literary agent and founder; Mark Bruni, consulting editor.

Represents Novels. **Considers these nonfiction areas:** "Open to all genres, as long as the author is established with a platform.". **Considers these fiction areas:** All fiction genres, but no children's.

- ➤ "LRI collaborates with creative professionals and offers a customized, boutique service, based on the client's individual requirements. LRI maintains flexible hours to accommodate specific client needs. Its primary focus since 2005 is a high-end, no-fee based literary agency for authors. LRI provides high quality service, feedback, and recommendations at no charge, which include readings, proofreading, editing—including content editing, analysis, feedback, and recommendations. Send only your finest work." Actively seeking fiction/novels only— all subgenres. Does not want to receive children's books or poetry or nonfiction.

How to Contact Query via e-mail with Microsoft Word attachments. Submit synopsis, author bio, 3 chapters or 50 pages, whichever is longer. Prefers an exclusive read, but will consider simultaneous queries. Responds in 1-2 months to queries. Responds in 4-6 months to mss. Obtains most new clients through recommendations from others or solicitations.

Terms Agent receives 15% commission on domestic sales. Agent receives 25% commission on foreign sales. Offers written contract; 90-day notice must be given to terminate contract. This agency charges for postage, printing, copying, etc. If no sale is made, no charges are enforced.

Recent Sales *Secrets of the Sands*, by Leona Wisoker (Mercury Retrograde Press). Other clients include Brinn Colenda, Carol Gambino, Don Armijo and Fred Stawitz: co-authors of *Homeboy's Soul: Pride, Terror & Street Justice in America*, Fletcher F. Cockrell, author of *Dismissed With Prejudice*, Kathy J. Keller, author of *The Butterfly Clinic*, Leona Wisoker, author of *Secrets of the Sands, Book 1 of The Children of the Desert*, Michael Eldrige, Patricia Forehand, RC (Ruth) White, author of *Devil's Trace*, also *The Ascension at Antioch*, Rhiannon Lynn, Skott Darlow.

◙ RLR ASSOCIATES, LTD.

Literary Department, 7 W. 51st St., New York NY 10019. (212)541-8641. Fax: (212)262-7084. E-mail: sgould@rlrassociates.net. Website: www.rlrliterary.net. **Contact:** Scott Gould. Member of AAR. Represents 50 clients. 25% of clients are new/unpublished writers. Currently handles: nonfiction books 70%, novels 25%, story collections 5%.

Represents Nonfiction books, novels, short story collections, scholarly. **Considers these nonfiction areas:** animals, anthropology, archeology, art, autobiography, biography, business, child guidance, cooking, cultural interests, current affairs, decorating, diet/nutrition, economics, education, environment, ethnic, foods, gay/lesbian, government, health, history, humor, inspirational, interior design, language, law, memoirs, money, multicultural, music, parenting, photography, popular culture, politics, psychology, religious, science, self-help, sociology, sports, technology, translation, travel, true crime, women's issues, women's studies. **Considers these fiction areas:** action, adventure, cartoon, comic books, crime, detective, ethnic, experimental, family saga, feminist, gay, historical, horror, humor, lesbian, literary, mainstream, multicultural, mystery, police, satire, sports, suspense.

- ➤ "We provide a lot of editorial assistance to our clients and have connections." Actively seeking fiction, current affairs, history, art, popular culture, health and business. Does not want to receive screenplays.

How to Contact Query by either e-mail or mail. Accepts simultaneous submissions. Responds in 4-8 weeks to queries. Obtains most new clients through recommendations from others.

Terms Agent receives 15% commission on domestic sales. Agent receives 20% commission on foreign sales. Offers written contract.

Recent Sales Clients include Shelby Foote, The Grief Recovery Institute, Don Wade, Don Zimmer, The Knot.com, David Plowden, PGA of America, Danny Peary, George Kalinsky, Peter Hyman, Daniel Parker, Lee Miller, Elise Miller, Nina Planck, Karyn Bosnak, Christopher Pike, Gerald Carbone, Jason Lethcoe, Andy Crouch.

Tips "Please check out our website for more details on our agency."

◙ B.J. ROBBINS LITERARY AGENCY

5130 Bellaire Ave., North Hollywood CA 91607-2908. E-mail: Robbinsliterary@gmail.com. **Contact:**

(Ms.) B.J. Robbins. Member of AAR. Represents 40 clients. 50% of clients are new/unpublished writers. Currently handles: nonfiction books 50%, novels 50%.

Represents Nonfiction books, novels. **Considers these nonfiction areas:** autobiography, biography, cultural interests, current affairs, dance, ethnic, film, health, humor, investigative, medicine, memoirs, music, popular culture, psychology, self-help, sociology, sports, theater, travel, true crime, women's issues, women's studies. **Considers these fiction areas:** crime, detective, ethnic, literary, mainstream, mystery, police, sports, suspense, thriller.

How to Contact Query with SASE. Submit outline/proposal, 3 sample chapters, SASE. Accepts e-mail queries (no attachments). Accepts simultaneous submissions. Responds in 2-6 weeks to queries. Responds in 6-8 weeks to mss. Obtains most new clients through conferences, referrals.

Terms Agent receives 15% commission on domestic sales. Agent receives 20% commission on foreign sales. Offers written contract; 3-month notice must be given to terminate contract. This agency charges clients for postage and photocopying (only after sale of ms).

Recent Sales Sold 15 titles in the last year. *Getting Stoned With Savages*, by J. Maarten Troost (Broadway); *Hot Water*, by Kathryn Jordan (Berkley); *Between the Bridge and the River*, by Craig Ferguson (Chronicle); *I'm Proud of You*, by Tim Madigan (Gotham); *Man of the House*, by Chris Erskine (Rodale); *Bird of Another heaven*, by James D. Houston (Knopf); *Tomorrow They Will Kiss*, by Eduardo Santiago (Little, Brown); *A Terrible Glory*, by James Donovan (Little, Brown); *The Writing on My Forehead*, by Nafisa Haji (Morrow); *Seen the Glory*, by John Hough Jr. (Simon & Schuster); *Lost on Planet China*, by J. Maarten Troost (Broadway).

Writers Conferences Squaw Valley Writers Workshop; San Diego State University Writers' Conference.

THE ROBBINS OFFICE, INC.

405 Park Ave., New York NY 10022. (212)223-0720. Fax: (212)223-2535. Website: www.robbinsoffice. com. **Contact:** Kathy P. Robbins, owner.

Member Agents Kathy P. Robbins; David Halpern.

Represents Nonfiction books, novels. **Considers these nonfiction areas:** hitory, poliitics, journalism, regional interest, memoirs.

○┐ This agency specializes in selling serious nonfiction as well as commercial and literary fiction.

How to Contact Accepts submissions by referral only.

Terms Agent receives 15% commission on domestic sales. Agent receives 15% commission on foreign sales. Agent receives 15% commission on film sales. Bills back specific expenses incurred in doing business for a client.

⃞ ☑ RODEEN LITERARY MANAGEMENT

3501 N. Southport #497, Chicago IL 60657. E-mail: info@rodeenliterary.com. Website: www. rodeenliterary.com. **Contact:** Paul Rodeen. Estab. 2009.

• Paul Rodeen established Rodeen Literary Management in 2009 after seven years of experience with the literary agency Sterling Lord Literistic, Inc.

Represents Nonfiction books, novels, juvenile books, illustrations, graphic novels. **Considers these fiction areas:** picture books, young adult, middle grade fiction.

○┐ Actively seeking "writers and illustrators of all genres of children's literature including picture books, early readers, middle-grade fiction and nonfiction, graphic novels and comic books as well as young adult fiction and nonfiction." This is primarily an agency devoted to children's books.

How to Contact Unsolicited submissions are accepted by e-mail only to submissions@rodeenliterary. com. Cover letters with contact information should be included, and a maximum of 50 sample pages. Accepts simultaneous submissions. Response time varies.

⊕ ☑ ROGERS, COLERIDGE & WHITE

20 Powis Mews, London England W11 1JN United Kingdom. (44)(207)221-3717. Fax: (44)(207)229-9084. E-mail: info@rcwlitagency.co.uk. Website: www.rcwlitagency.co.uk. **Contact:** David Miller, agent. Estab. 1987.

• Prior to opening the agency, Ms. Rogers was an agent with Peter Janson-Smith; Ms. Coleridge worked at Sidgwick & Jackson, Chatto & Windus, and Anthony Sheil Associates; Ms. White was an editor and rights director for Simon & Schuster; Mr. Straus worked at Hodder and

Stoughton, Hamish Hamilton, and Macmillan; Mr. Miller worked as Ms. Rogers' assistant and was treasurer of the AAA; Ms. Waldie worked with Carole Smith.

Member Agents Deborah Rogers; Gill Coleridge; Pat White (illustrated and children's books); Peter Straus; David Miller; Zoe Waldie (fiction, biography, current affairs, narrative history); Laurence Laluyaux (foreign rights); Stephen Edwards (foreign rights); Peter Robinson; Sam Copeland; Catherine Pellegrino; Hannah Westland; Jenny Hewson.

Represents Nonfiction books, novels, juvenile. **Considers these nonfiction areas:** biography, cooking, current affairs, diet/nutrition, foods, humor, satire, sports, narrative history. **Considers these fiction areas:** Considers most fiction categories.

> ⊶ YA and Children's fiction should be submitted via e-mail to clairewilson@rcwlitagency.com. We do not accept any other e-mail submissions unless by prior arrangement with individual agents. Does not want to receive plays, screenplays, technical books or educational books.

How to Contact Submit synopsis, proposal, sample chapters, bio, SAE by mail. Submissions should include a covering letter telling us about yourself and the background to the book. In the case of fiction they should consist of the first 3 chapters or approximately the first 50 pages of the work to a natural break, and a brief synopsis. Nonfiction submissions should take the form of a proposal up to 20 pages in length explaining what the work is about and why you are best placed to write it. Material should be printed out in 12 point font, in double-spacing and on one side only of A4 paper. We cannot acknowledge receipt of material and nor can we accept responsibility for anything you send us, so please retain a copy of material submitted. Material will be returned only if sent with an adequately stamped and sized SASE; if return postage is not provided the material will be recycled. We do not accept e-mail submissions unless by prior arrangement with individual agents. We will try to respond within 6-8 weeks of receipt of your material, but please appreciate that this isn't always possible as we must give priority to the authors we already represent. Please note that we do not represent scripts for theatre, film or television. Responds in 6-8 weeks to queries. Obtains most new clients through recommendations from others, solicitations, conferences.

Terms Agent receives 15% commission on domestic sales. Agent receives 20% commission on foreign sales. Offers written contract.

⊘ LINDA ROGHAAR LITERARY AGENCY, LLC

133 High Point Drive, Amherst MA 01002. (413)256-1921. E-mail: contact@lindaroghaar.com. Website: www.lindaroghaar.com. **Contact:** Linda L. Roghaar. Represents 50 clients. 10% of clients are new/unpublished writers. Currently handles: nonfiction books 100%.

- Prior to opening her agency, Ms. Roghaar worked in retail bookselling for 5 years and as a publishers' sales rep for 15 years.

Represents Nonfiction books. **Considers these nonfiction areas:** animals, anthropology, archeology, autobiography, biography, education, environment, history, inspirational, popular culture, self-help, women's issues, women's studies.

How to Contact Query with SASE. Accepts simultaneous submissions. Responds in 3 months to queries. Responds in 4 months to mss.

Terms Agent receives 15% commission on domestic sales. Agent receives negotiable commission on foreign sales. Offers written contract.

Recent Sales *Handmade Home*, by Amanda Soule (Shambhala); *Vintage Knits*, by Debbie Brisson (aka Stitchy McYarnpants) and Carolyn Sheridan (Wiley); *TYV Ccrafting For Kids*, by Jennifer Casa (Wiley); *The White Hand Society*, by Peter Conners (City Lights); *The Writing Warrior*, by Laraine Herring (Shambhala); *All Wound Up*, by Stephanie Pearl-McPhee (Andrews McMeel).

⊘ THE ROSENBERG GROUP

23 Lincoln Ave., Marblehead MA 01945. (781)990-1341. Fax: (781)990-1344. Website: www.rosenberggroup.com. **Contact:** Barbara Collins Rosenberg. Estab. 1998. Member of AAR. Other memberships include recognized agent of the RWA. Represents 25 clients. 15% of clients are new/unpublished writers. Currently handles: nonfiction books 30%, novels 30%, scholarly books 10%, other 30% college textbooks.

- Prior to becoming an agent, Ms. Rosenberg was a senior editor for Harcourt.

Represents Nonfiction books, novels, textbooks, college textbooks only. **Considers these nonfiction areas:** current affairs, foods, popular culture, psychology, sports, women's issues, women's studies, women's health, wine/beverages. **Considers these fiction areas:** romance, women's.

☞ Ms. Rosenberg is well-versed in the romance market (both category and single title). She is a frequent speaker at romance conferences. Actively seeking romance category or single title in contemporary romantic suspense, and the historical subgenres. Does not want to receive inspirational, time travel, futuristic or paranormal.

How to Contact Query with SASE. No e-mail or fax queries; will not respond. See guidelines online at website. Responds in 2 weeks to queries. Responds in 4-6 weeks to mss. Obtains most new clients through recommendations from others, solicitations, conferences.

Terms Agent receives 15% commission on domestic sales. Agent receives 15% commission on foreign sales. Offers written contract; 1-month notice must be given to terminate contract. Charges maximum of $350/year for postage and photocopying.

Recent Sales Sold 24 titles in the last year.

Writers Conferences RWA National Conference; BookExpo America.

☑ RITA ROSENKRANZ LITERARY AGENCY

440 West End Ave., Suite 15D, New York NY 10024-5358. (212)873-6333. **Contact:** Rita Rosenkranz. Member of AAR. Represents 35 clients. 30% of clients are new/unpublished writers. Currently handles: nonfiction books 99%, novels 1%.

- Prior to opening her agency, Ms. Rosenkranz worked as an editor at major New York publishing houses.

Represents Nonfiction books. **Considers these nonfiction areas:** animals, anthropology, art, autobiography, biography, business, child guidance, computers, cooking, crafts, cultural interests, current affairs, dance, decorating, economics, ethnic, film, gay, government, health, history, hobbies, how-to, humor, inspirational, interior design, language, law, lesbian, literature, medicine, military, money, music, nature, parenting, personal improvement, photography, popular culture, politics, psychology, religious, satire, science, self-help, sports, technology, theater, war, women's issues, women's studies.

☞ "This agency focuses on adult nonfiction, stresses strong editorial development and refinement before submitting to publishers, and brainstorms ideas with authors." Actively seeks authors who are well paired with their subject, either for professional or personal reasons.

How to Contact Send query letter only (no proposal) via regular mail or e-mail. Submit proposal package with SASE only on request. No fax queries. Accepts simultaneous submissions. Responds in 2 weeks to queries. Obtains most new clients through directory listings, solicitations, conferences, word of mouth.

Terms Agent receives 15% commission on domestic sales. Agent receives 20% commission on foreign sales. Offers written contract, binding for 3 years; 3-month written notice must be given to terminate contract. Charges clients for photocopying. Makes referrals to editing services.

Recent Sales Sold 35 titles in the last year. *29 GIFTS: How a Month of Giving Can Change Your Life*, by Cami Walker (DaCapo Press), *Writers Gone Wild: The Feuds, Frolics and Follies of Literature's Great Adventurers, Drunkards, Lovers, Iconoclasts, and Misanthropes*, by Bill Peschel (Perigee), *Study Your Brains Out!* by Anne Crossman (Ten Speed Press).

Tips "Identify the current competition for your project to make sure the project is valid. A strong cover letter is very important."

▦ MERCEDES ROS LITERARY AGENCY

Castell 38, 08329 Teia, Barcelona Spain. (34)(93)540-1353. Fax: (34)(93)540-1346. E-mail: info@mercedesros.com. Website: www.mercedesros.com. **Contact:** Mercedes Ros.

Member Agents Mercedes Ros; Mercé Segarra.

Represents juvenile.

☞ "Gemser Publications publishes nonfiction and religious illustrated books for the 0-7 age group. Our products, basically aimed to convey concepts, habits, attitudes and values that are close to the child's environment, always adopt an open mentality in a globalized world. We combine excellent quality with competitive prices and good texts and beautiful illustrations to educate and inspire our young readers."

How to Contact Accepts submissions by e-mail or on disc.

Writers Conferences Frankfurt Book Fair; London Book Fair; Bologna Book Fair; BookExpo of America; Tokyo Book Fair; Beijing International Book Fair; Frankfurt Book Fair 2007.

Tips Try to read or look at as many books a publisher has published before sending in your material, to get a feel for their list and whether your manuscript, idea or style of illustration is likely to fit.

☻ ANDY ROSS LITERARY AGENCY

767 Santa Ray Ave, Oakland CA 94610. (510)238-8965. E-mail: andyrossagency@hotmail.com. Website: www.andyrossagency.com. **Contact:** Andy Ross. Represents 30 clients. 20% of clients are new/unpublished writers. Currently handles: nonfiction books 100%.

Represents Nonfiction books, scholarly. **Considers these nonfiction areas:** anthropology, autobiography, biography, child guidance, cultural interests, current affairs, education, environment, ethnic, government, history, language, law, literature, military, parenting, popular culture, politics, psychology, science, sociology, technology, war.

> ☙ "This agency specializes in general nonfiction, politics and current events, history, biography, journalism and contemporary culture." Actively seeking narrative nonfiction. Does not want to receive personal memoir, fiction, poetry, juvenile books.

How to Contact Query via e-mail only. Accepts simultaneous submissions. Responds in 1 week to queries.

Terms Agent receives 15% commission on domestic sales. Agent receives 20% commission on foreign sales through a sub-agent. Offers written contract.

☻ THE GAIL ROSS LITERARY AGENCY

1666 Connecticut Ave. NW, #500, Washington DC 20009. (202)328-3282. Fax: (202)328-9162. E-mail: jennifer@gailross.com; submissions@gailross.com. Website: www.gailross.com. **Contact:** Jennifer Manguera. Member of AAR. Represents 200 clients. 75% of clients are new/unpublished writers. Currently handles: nonfiction books 95%.

Member Agents Gail Ross (represents important commercial nonfiction in a variety of areas and counts top doctors, CEO's, prize-winning journalists, and historians among her clients. She and her team work closely with first-time authors. gail@gailross.com) Howard Yoon (nonfiction topics ranging from current events and politics to culture to religion and history, to smart business. He is also looking for commercial fiction by published authors. howard@gailross.com).

Represents Nonfiction books. **Considers these nonfiction areas:** anthropology, archeology, autobiography, biography, business, cultural interests, economics, education, environment, ethnic, gay/lesbian, government, health, inspirational, investigative, law, medicine, money, politics, psychology, religious, science, self-help, sociology, sports, technology, true crime. **Considers these fiction areas:** , occasional commercial fiction.

> ☙ "This agency specializes in adult trade nonfiction." Actively seeking sci-fi, fantasy, romance, or children's books

How to Contact Send proposals by e-mail with a cover letter, résumé, brief synopsis of your work, and several sample chapters. We also accept query letters. No longer accepting submissions by mail. Accepts simultaneous submissions. Responds in 4-6 weeks to queries. Obtains most new clients through recommendations from others.

Terms Agent receives 15% commission on domestic sales. Agent receives 25% commission on foreign sales. Charges for office expenses.

THE ROTHMAN BRECHER AGENCY

9250 Wilshire Blvd., Penthouse, Beverly Hills CA 90212. (310)247-9898. E-mail: reception@ rothmanbrecher.com. **Contact:** Andrea Kavoosi. Signatory of WGA.

Represents movie, tv, movie scripts, feature film.

How to Contact *Referrals only.*

☻ JANE ROTROSEN AGENCY LLC

318 E. 51st St., New York NY 10022. (212)593-4330. Fax: (212)935-6985. E-mail: lcohen@janerotrosen. com. Website: www.janerotrosen.com. Estab. 1974. Member of AAR. Other memberships include Authors Guild. Represents over 100 clients. Currently handles: nonfiction books 30%, novels 70%.

Member Agents Jane R. Berkey; Andrea Cirillo; Annelise Robey; Margaret Ruley; Christina Hogrebe; Suzanna Best; Peggy Gordijn, director of rights.

Represents Nonfiction books, novels. **Considers these nonfiction areas:** autobiography, biography, business, child guidance, cooking, current affairs, diet/nutrition, economics, environment, foods, health, how-to, humor, investigative, medicine, money, parenting, popular culture, psychology, satire, self-help, sports, true crime, women's issues, women's studies. **Considers these fiction areas:** crime, family saga, historical, mystery, police, romance, suspense, thriller, women's.

How to Contact Query with SASE to the attention of Submissions. Responds in 2 weeks to writers who have been referred by a client or colleague. Responds in 2 months to mss. Obtains most new clients through recommendations from others.

Terms Agent receives 15% commission on domestic sales. Agent receives 20% commission on foreign sales. Offers written contract, binding for 3 years; 2-month notice must be given to terminate contract. Charges clients for photocopying, express mail, overseas postage, book purchase.

◎ THE DAMARIS ROWLAND AGENCY

420 E 23rd St., Suite 6F, New York NY 10010-5040. **Contact:** Damaris Rowland. Member of AAR. **Represents** Nonfiction books, novels.

○ͫ This agency specializes in women's fiction, literary fiction and nonfiction, and pop fiction.

How to Contact Query with synopsis, SASE. Obtains most new clients through recommendations from others, solicitations, conferences.

Terms Agent receives 15% commission on domestic sales. Agent receives 20% commission on foreign sales. Offers written contract.

◎ ◎ THE RUDY AGENCY

825 Wildlife Lane, Estes Park CO 80517. (970)577-8500. Fax: (970)577-8600. E-mail: mak@rudyagency.com. Website: www.rudyagency.com. **Contact:** Maryann Karinch. Other memberships include adheres to AAR canon of ethics. Represents 15 clients. 50% of clients are new/unpublished writers. Currently handles: nonfiction books 100%.

- Prior to becoming an agent, Ms. Karinch was, and continues to be, an author of nonfiction books—covering the subjects of health/medicine and human behavior. Prior to that, she was in public relations and marketing: areas of expertise she also applies in her practice as an agent.

Member Agents Maryann Karinch (nonfiction: health/medicine, culture/values, history, biography, memoir, science/technology, military/intelligence).

Represents Nonfiction books, textbooks, with consumer appeal. **Considers these nonfiction areas:** anthropology, archeology, autobiography, biography, business, child guidance, computers, cultural interests, current affairs, economics, education, ethnic, gay/lesbian, government, health, history, how-to, language, law, literature, medicine, memoirs, military, money, music, parenting, popular culture, politics, psychology, science, sociology, sports, technology, true crime, war, women's issues, women's studies.

○ͫ "We support authors from the proposal stage through promotion of the published work. We work in partnership with publishers to promote the published work and coach authors in their role in the marketing and public relations campaigns for the book." Actively seeking projects with social value, projects that open minds to new ideas and interesting lives, and projects that entertain through good storytelling. Does not want to receive poetry, children's/juvenile books, screenplays/plays, art/photo books, novels/novellas, religion books, and joke books or books that fit in to the impulse buy/gift book category.

How to Contact "Query us. If we like the query, we will invite a complete proposal. No phone queries." Accepts simultaneous submissions. Responds in 8 weeks to mss. Obtains most new clients through recommendations from others, solicitations.

Terms Agent receives 15% commission on domestic sales. Offers written contract, binding for 1 year.

Recent Sales Sold 11 titles in the last year. *Live from Jordan: Letters Home from My Journal Through the Middle East*, by Benjamin Orbach (Amacom); *Finding Center: Strategies to Build Strong Girls & Women*, by Maureen Mack (New Horizon Press); *Crossing Fifth Avenue to Bergdorf Goodman: An Insider's Account on the Rise of Luxury Retailing*, by Ira Neimark (SPI Books); *Hamas vs. Fatah: The Struggle for Palestine*, by Jonathan Schanzer (Palgrave Macmillan); *The New Rules of Etiquette and Entertaining*, by Curtrise Garner (Adams Media); *Comes the Darkness, Comes the Light*, by Vanessa Vega (Amacom); *Murder in Mayberry*, by Mary and Jack Branson (New Horizon Press); *Not My Turn to Die*, by Savo Heleta.

Writers Conferences BookExpo of America; industry events.

Tips "Present yourself professionally. I tell people all the time: Subscribe to *Writer's Digest* (I do), because you will get good advice about how to approach an agent."

☑ MARLY RUSOFF & ASSOCIATES, INC.

P.O. Box 524, Bronxville NY 10708. (914)961-7939. E-mail: mra_queries3@rusoffagency.com. Website: www.rusoffagency.com. **Contact:** Marly Rusoff.

- Prior to her current position, Ms. Rusoff held positions at Houghton Mifflin, Doubleday and William Morrow.

Member Agents Marly Rusoff.

Represents Nonfiction books, novels. **Considers these nonfiction areas:** architecture, art, autobiography, biography, business, design, economics, health, history, medicine, memoirs, popular culture, psychology. **Considers these fiction areas:** commercial, historical, literary.

- ⦿ "While we take delight in discovering new talent, we are particularly interested in helping established writers expand readership and develop their careers."

How to Contact Query with SASE. Submit synopsis, publishing history, author bio, contact information. For e-queries, include no attachments or pdf files. "We cannot read DOCXs." This agency only responds if interested. Responds to queries. Obtains most new clients through recommendations from others.

Recent Sales *The Thieves of Manhattan*, by Adam Langer (fiction, Spiegel & Grau); *The Kabul Beauty School*, by Deborah Rodriguez & Kristen Ohlson (memoir, Random House); *The Death of Santini*, by Pat Conroy (memoir, Nan Talese/Doubleday); *31 Bond Street*, by Ellen Horan (historical fiction, Harper); *My Name is Mary Sutter*, by Robin Oliveira (historical fiction, Viking); *Sweet Blasphemy*, by Elif Shafak (fiction). Other clients include: Thrity Umrigar, Elif Shafak, Arthur Phillips, Ron Rash, and Roland Merullo.

☑ RUSSELL & VOLKENING

50 W. 29th St., #7E, New York NY 10001. (212)684-6050. Fax: (212)889-3026. Website: www.randvinc.com. **Contact:** Jesseca Salky (adult, general fiction & nonfiction, memoirs: jesseca@randvinc.com) Carrie Hannigan (children's & YA), Josh Getzler (mysteries, thrillers, literary and commercial fiction, young adult and middle grade (particularly adventures and mysteries for boys). E-mail queries only with cover letter & first 5 pages: josh@randvinc.com), Joy Azmitia (Chicklit, multicultural fiction, romance, humor, and nonfiction in the areas of travel, pop-culture, and philosophy; joy@randvinc.com.). Member of AAR. Represents 140 clients. 20% of clients are new/unpublished writers. Currently handles: nonfiction books 45%, novels 50%, story collections 3%, novella 2%.

Represents Nonfiction books, novels, short story collections. **Considers these nonfiction areas:** anthropology, architecture, art, autobiography, biography, business, cooking, cultural interests, current affairs, design, education, environment, ethnic, film, gay/lesbian, government, health, history, language, law, military, money, music, photography, popular culture, politics, psychology, science, sociology, sports, technology, true crime, war, women's issues, women's studies, creative nonfiction. **Considers these fiction areas:** action, adventure, crime, detective, ethnic, literary, mainstream, mystery, picture books, police, sports, suspense, thriller.

- ⦿ This agency specializes in literary fiction and narrative nonfiction.

How to Contact Query only with SASE to appropriate person. Responds in 4 weeks to queries.

Terms Agent receives 15% commission on domestic sales. Agent receives 20% commission on foreign sales. Charges clients for standard office expenses relating to the submission of materials.

Tips If the query is cogent, well written, well presented, and is the type of book we'd represent, we'll ask to see the manuscript. From there, it depends purely on the quality of the work.

☑ REGINA RYAN PUBLISHING ENTERPRISES, INC.

251 Central Park W., 7D, New York NY 10024. (212)787-5589. E-mail: queryreginaryanbooks@rcn.com. **Contact:** Regina Ryan. Currently handles: nonfiction books 100%.

- Prior to becoming an agent, Ms. Ryan was an editor at Alfred A. Knopf, editor-in-chief of Macmillan Adult Trade, and a book producer.

Represents Nonfiction books. **Considers these nonfiction areas:** animals, architecture, gardening, government, history, law, memoirs, parenting, politics, psychology, travel, women's issues, women's studies, narrative nonfiction; natural history (especially birds and birding); popular science, adventure, lifestyle, business, sustainability, mind-body-spirit, relationships.

How to Contact Query by e-mail or mail with SASE. No telephone queries. Does not accept queries for juvenile or fiction. Accepts simultaneous submissions. Tries to respond in 1 month to queries. Obtains most new clients through recommendations from others.

Terms Agent receives 15% commission on domestic sales. Agent receives 15% commission on foreign sales. Offers written contract. Charges clients for all out-of-pocket expenses (e.g., long distance calls, messengers, freight, copying) if it's more than just a nominal amount.

Recent Sales *Backyard Bird Feeding*, by Randi Minetor (Globe Pequot Press); *In Search of Sacco and Vanzetti*, by Susan Tejada (Univ. Press of New England); *Trouble Shooting the Vegetable Garden*, by David Deardorff and Kathryn Wadsworth (Timber Press); *When Johnny Comes Marching Home: What Vets Need, What They Don't Need and What All of Us Can Do to Help*, by Paula Caplan (MIT Press); Everything Changes: The Insider's Guide to Cancer in Your 20's and 30's, by Kairol Rosenthal (Wiley); *Angel of Death Row: My Life as a Death Penalty Defense Lawyer*, by Andrea Lyon (Kaplan Publishing).

Tips "An analysis of why your proposed book is different and better than the competition is essential; a sample chapter is helpful."

⬛ THE SAGALYN AGENCY

4922 Fairmont Ave., Suite 200, Bethesda MD 20814. (301)718-6440. Fax: (301)718-6444. E-mail: query@sagalyn.com. Website: www.sagalyn.com. Estab. 1980. Member of AAR. Currently handles: nonfiction books 85%, novels 5%, scholarly books 10%.

Member Agents Raphael Sagalyn; Bridget Wagner, Shannon O'Neill.

Represents Nonfiction books. **Considers these nonfiction areas:** autobiography, biography, business, economics, history, inspirational, memoirs, popular culture, science, technology, journalism.

  ⚮ Does not want to receive stage plays, screenplays, poetry, science fiction, fantasy, romance, children's books or young adult books.

How to Contact Please send e-mail queries only (no attachments). Include 1 of these words in the subject line: query, submission, inquiry.

Tips "We receive 1,000-1,200 queries a year, which in turn lead to 2 or 3 new clients. Query via e-mail only. See our website for sales information and recent projects."

⬛ SALKIND LITERARY AGENCY

Part of Studio B, 734 Indiana St., Lawrence KS 66044. (913)538-7113. Fax: (516)706-2369. E-mail: neil@studiob.com. Website: www.salkindagency.com. **Contact:** Neil Salkind. Represents 200 clients. 25% of clients are new/unpublished writers. Currently handles: nonfiction books 60%, scholarly books 20%, textbooks 20%.

  • Prior to becoming an agent, Mr. Salkind authored numerous trade and textbooks.

Member Agents Greg Aunapu, Lynn Haller, Jennifer Lawler, Malka Margolies, Neil J. Salkind.

  ⚮ Greg Aunapu represents both fiction and nonfiction including true crime, technology, biography, history, narrative nonfiction, memoir (by people who have accomplished something great in their fields), finance, current affairs, politics, pop-culture, psychology, relationships, science and travel. Fiction includes suspense/thrillers, mystery, detective, adventure, humor, science-fiction and modern urban fantasy. Submission guidelines can be found at www.gregaunapu.com. Nonfiction queries should be in book-proposal format; fiction queries should include a complete book synopsis and the first 25 pages of the manuscript, and an author biography. He can be reached at greg@studiob.com. Lynn Haller represents nonfiction authors, with a special interest in business, technology, and how-to. Queries should include a book proposal, a bio, and writing samples. She can be reached at lynn@studiob.com. Jennifer Lawler represents fiction and nonfiction authors. Her nonfiction interests include narrative nonfiction, self-help and some how-to. She is interested in genre fiction, including mystery and science fiction/fantasy. She does NOT represent children's or young adult. Please query with a book proposal (for nonfiction) and the first chapter of the manuscript (for fiction). She can be reached at jennifer@studiob.com. Malka Margolies represents predominantly nonfiction. Her interests include history, current events, cultural issues, religion/spirituality, nutrition and health, women's issues, parenting and the environment. She is not interested in science fiction, fantasy, how-to or children's books. She can be reached at malka@studiob.

com. Neil J. Salkind represents these nonfiction areas: business, cooking, crafts, health, how-to, photography and visual arts, science and self-help. He also represents textbooks and scholarly books. Does not want "to receive book proposals based on ideas where potential authors have not yet researched what has been published."

How to Contact Query electronically. Obtains most new clients through recommendations from others.

Terms Agent receives 15% commission on domestic sales. Agent receives 15% commission on foreign sales.

SALOMONSSON AGENCY

Svartensgatan 4, 116 20 Stockholm Sweden. E-mail: info@salomonssonagency.com. Website: www.salomonssonagency.com. **Contact:** Niclas Salomonsson. Estab. 2000. Currently handles: novels 100%.

Member Agents Niclas Salomonsson, Szilvia Monar, Leyla Belle Drake.

Represents Novels.

⚬┯ "Salomonsson Agency is one of the leading literary agencies in Scandinavia. We focus on fiction from the Nordic countries."

How to Contact This agency focuses on Scandinavian authors.

Recent Sales 9-book deal with Random House Canada regarding Liza Marklund; 2-book deal with HarperCollins US regarding Sissel-Jo Gazan; 8 book deal with Doubleday UK regarding Liza Marklund.

VICTORIA SANDERS & ASSOCIATES

241 Avenue of the Americas, Suite 11 H, New York NY 10014. (212)633-8811. Fax: (212)633-0525. E-mail: queriesvsa@hotmail.com. Website: www.victoriasanders.com. **Contact:** Victoria Sanders, Diane Dickensheid. Estab. 1992. Member of AAR. Signatory of WGA. Represents 135 clients. 25% of clients are new/unpublished writers. Currently handles: nonfiction books 30%, novels 70%.

Member Agents Tanya McKinnon, Victoria Sanders, Chris Kepner (open to all types of books as long as the writing is exceptional. include the first three chapters in the body of the e-mail. At the moment, he is especially on the lookout for quality nonfiction.).

Represents Nonfiction books, novels. **Considers these nonfiction areas:** autobiography, biography, cultural interests, current affairs, dance, ethnic, film, gay/lesbian, government, history, humor, language, law, literature, music, popular culture, politics, psychology, satire, theater, translation, women's issues, women's studies. **Considers these fiction areas:** action, adventure, contemporary issues, ethnic, family saga, feminist, gay, lesbian, literary, thriller.

How to Contact Query by e-mail only.

Terms Agent receives 15% commission on domestic sales. Agent receives 20% commission on foreign sales. Offers written contract. Charges for photocopying, messenger, express mail. If in excess of $100, client approval is required.

Recent Sales Sold 20+ titles in the last year.

Tips "Limit query to letter (no calls) and give it your best shot. A good query is going to get a good response."

SANDUM & ASSOCIATES

144 E. 84th St., New York NY 10028-2035. (212)737-2011. **Contact:** Howard E. Sandum.

⚬┯ This agency specializes in general nonfiction and occasionally literary fiction.

How to Contact Query with synopsis, bio, SASE. Do not send full ms unless requested.

Terms Agent receives 15% commission on domestic sales. Charges clients for photocopying, air express, long-distance telephone/fax.

LENNART SANE AGENCY

Hollandareplan 9, S-374 34, Karlshamn Sweden. E-mail: info@lennartsaneagency.com. Website: www.lennartsaneagency.com. **Contact:** Lennart Sane. Represents 20+ clients.

Member Agents Lennart Sane, agent; Philip Sane, agent; Lina Hammarling, agent.

Represents Nonfiction books, novels, juvenile.

⚬┯ Lennart Sane Agency AB "represents the literary rights of authors, agents and publishers, in the markets of fiction, nonfiction, and film." This European agency deals in a lot of translation rights, and North American authors are best *not* to query this agency without a strong referral.

How to Contact Query with SASE.

☺ SCHIAVONE LITERARY AGENCY, INC.

236 Trails End, West Palm Beach FL 33413-2135. (561)966-9294. Fax: (561)966-9294. E-mail: profschia@aol.com. Website: www.publishersmarketplace.com/members/profschia; Blog Site: www.schiavoneliteraryagencyinc.blogspot.com. **Contact:** Dr. James Schiavone. CEO, corporate offices in Florida; Jennifer DuVall, president, New York office. New York office: 3671 Hudson Manor Terrace, No. 11H, Bronx, NY, 10463-1139, phone: (718)548-5332; fax: (718)548-5332; e-mail: jendu77@aol.com Other memberships include National Education Association. Represents 60 + clients. 2% of clients are new/unpublished writers. Currently handles: nonfiction books 50%, novels 49%, textbooks 1%.

- Prior to opening his agency, Dr. Schiavone was a full professor of developmental skills at the City University of New York and author of 5 trade books and 3 textbooks. Jennifer DuVall has many years of combined experience in office management and agenting.

Represents Nonfiction books, novels, juvenile, scholarly, textbooks. **Considers these nonfiction areas:** animals, anthropology, archeology, autobiography, biography, child guidance, cultural interests, current affairs, education, environment, ethnic, gay/lesbian, government, health, history, how-to, humor, investigative, juvenile nonfiction, language, law, literature, medicine, military, parenting, popular culture, politics, psychology, satire, science, sociology, spirituality, true crime. **Considers these fiction areas:** ethnic, family saga, historical, horror, humor, juvenile, literary, mainstream, science fiction, young adult.

- ⚬ₜ This agency specializes in celebrity biography and autobiography and memoirs. Does not want to receive poetry.

How to Contact Query with SASE. Do not send unsolicited materials or parcels requiring a signature. Send no e-attachments. Accepts simultaneous submissions. Responds in 2 weeks to queries. Responds in 6 weeks to mss. Obtains most new clients through recommendations from others, solicitations, conferences.

Terms Agent receives 15% commission on domestic sales. Agent receives 20% commission on foreign sales. Offers written contract. Charges clients for postage only.

Writers Conferences Key West Literary Seminar; South Florida Writers' Conference; Tallahassee Writers' Conference, Million Dollar Writers' Conference; Alaska Writers Conference.

Tips "We prefer to work with established authors published by major houses in New York. We will consider marketable proposals from new/previously unpublished writers."

HAROLD SCHMIDT LITERARY AGENCY

415 W. 23rd St., #6F, New York NY 10011. (212)727-7473. Fax: (212)807-6025. **Contact:** Harold Schmidt. Member of AAR. Represents 3 clients.

Represents nonfiction, fiction. **Considers these fiction areas:** contemporary issues, gay, literary, original fiction with unique narrative voices, high quality psychological suspense and thrillers, likes offbeat/quirky.

- ⚬ₜ Novels

How to Contact Query with SASE; do not send material without being asked. No telephone or e-mail queries.

☑ ◎ SUSAN SCHULMAN LITERARY AGENCY

454 West 44th St., New York NY 10036. (212)713-1633. Fax: (212)581-8830. E-mail: queries@ schulmanagency.com. **Contact:** Susan Schulman. Estab. 1980. Member of AAR. Signatory of WGA. Other memberships include Dramatists Guild. 10% of clients are new/unpublished writers. Currently handles: nonfiction books 50%, novels 25%, juvenile books 15%, stage plays 10%.

Member Agents Linda Kiss, director of foreign rights; Katherine Stones, theater; Emily Uhry, submissions editor.

Represents Considers these nonfiction areas: anthropology, archeology, autobiography, biography, business, child guidance, cooking, cultural interests, current affairs, dance, diet/ nutrition, economics, education, environment, ethnic, foods, gay/lesbian, government, health, history, how-to, inspirational, investigative, language, law, literature, medicine, memoirs, money, music, parenting, popular culture, politics, psychology, religious, self-help, sociology, sports, true crime, women's issues, women's studies. **Considers these fiction areas:** action, adventure, crime, detective, feminist, historical, humor, inspirational, juvenile, literary, mainstream, mystery, picture books, police, religious, suspense, women's, young adult.

> ☞ "We specialize in books for, by and about women and women's issues including nonfiction self-help books, fiction and theater projects. We also handle the film, television and allied rights for several agencies as well as foreign rights for several publishing houses." Actively seeking new nonfiction. Considers plays. Does not want to receive poetry, television scripts or concepts for television.

How to Contact Query with SASE. Submit outline, synopsis, author bio, 3 sample chapters, SASE. Accepts simultaneous submissions. Responds in 6 weeks to queries. Responds in 6 weeks to mss. Obtains most new clients through recommendations from others, solicitations, conferences.

Terms Agent receives 15% commission on domestic sales. Agent receives 20% commission on foreign sales. Offers written contract; 30-day notice must be given to terminate contract.

Recent Sales Sold 50 titles in the last year; hundred of subsidiary rights deals.

Writers Conferences Geneva Writers' Conference (Switzerland); Columbus Writers' Conference; Skidmore Conference of the Independent Women's Writers Group.

Tips "Keep writing!"

▦ THE SCIENCE FACTORY

Scheideweg 34C, 20253 Hamburg, Germany. 44 (0)207 193 7296. E-mail: info@sciencefactory. co.uk. Website: www.sciencefactory.co.uk. **Contact:** Peter Tallack. Estab. 2008.

> • Prior to his current position, Mr. Tallack was a director of the UK agency Conville & Walsh.

Represents Considers these nonfiction areas: Considers all areas of serious popular nonfiction, particularly science, history and current affairs. **Considers these fiction areas:** Does not consider fiction unless especially related to science.

> ☞ "This agency specializes in representing authors aiming to satisfy the public's intellectual hunger for serious ideas. Experience of dealing directly in all markets, media and languages across the world." Actively seeking popular science nonfiction.

Tips The Science Factory is the trading name of The Science Factory Limited. Registered Office: The Courtyard, Shoreham Road, Upper Beeding, Steyning, West Sussex BN44 3TN, UK. Registered in England and Wales: Company No. 06498410. VAT Registration No. 938 1678 84.

☑ JONATHAN SCOTT, INC

933 West Van Buren, Suite 510, Chicago IL 60607. (847)557-2365. Fax: (847)557-8408. E-mail: jon@jonathanscott.us; scott@jonathanscott.us. Website: www.jonathanscott.us. **Contact:** Jon Malysiak, Scott Adlington. Estab. 2005. Represents 40 clients. 75% of clients are new/unpublished writers. Currently handles: nonfiction books 90%, novels 10%.

Member Agents Scott Adlington (narrative nonfiction, sports, health, wellness, fitness, environmental issues); Jon Malysiak (narrative nonfiction and fiction, current affairs, history, memoir, business).

Represents Nonfiction books. **Considers these fiction areas:** No fiction.

> ☞ "We are very hands-on with our authors in terms of working with them to develop their proposals and manuscripts. Since both of us come from publishing backgrounds—editorial and sales—we are able to give our authors a perspective of what goes on within the publishing house from initial consideration through the entire development, publication, marketing and sales processes." Categories of health/fitness, cooking, sports history, narrative nonfiction, memoir, parenting, general business, and travel essay, and all other nonfiction categories. We also represents books to be sold into film, television, and other subsidiary channels. To find out about literary representation, please contact Jon Malysiak, with a query e-mail describing your book idea and/or a proposal.

How to Contact We only accept electronic submissions. Query e-mail describing your book idea and/or a proposal. Accepts simultaneous submissions. Responds in 1-2 weeks to queries. Responds in 4-6 weeks to mss. Obtains most new clients through recommendations from others, solicitations, contacting good authors for representation.

Terms Agent receives 15% commission on domestic sales. Agent receives 20% commission on foreign sales. Offers written contract; 30-day notice must be given to terminate contract.

Tips "Platform, platform, platform. We can't emphasize this enough. Without a strong national platform, it is nearly impossible to get the interest of a publisher. Also, be organized in your thoughts and your goals before contacting an agent. Think of the proposal as your business plan. What do you hope to achieve by publishing your book. How can your book change the world?"

◙ SCOVIL GALEN GHOSH LITERARY AGENCY, INC.

276 Fifth Ave., Suite 708, New York NY 10001. (212)679-8686. Fax: (212)679-6710. E-mail: info@ sgglit.com. Website: www.sgglit.com. **Contact:** Russell Galen. Estab. 1992. Member of AAR. Represents 300 clients. Currently handles: nonfiction books 60%, novels 40%.

Member Agents Jack Scovil, jackscovil@sgglit.com; Russell Galen, russellgalen@sgglit.com (novels that stretch the bounds of reality; strong, serious nonfiction books on almost any subject that teach something new; no books that are merely entertaining, such as diet or pop psych books; serious interests include science, history, journalism, biography, business, memoir, nature, politics, sports, contemporary culture, literary nonfiction, etc.); Anna Ghosh, annaghosh@sgglit. com (strong nonfiction proposals on all subjects as well as adult commercial and literary fiction by both unpublished and published authors; serious interests include investigative journalism, literary nonfiction, history, biography, memoir, popular culture, science, adventure, art, food, religion, psychology, alternative health, social issues, women's fiction, historical novels and literary fiction); Ann Behar, annbehar@sgglit.com (juvenile books for all ages).

Represents Nonfiction books, novels.

How to Contact E-mail queries required. Accepts simultaneous submissions.

◙ SCRIBBLERS HOUSE, LLC LITERARY AGENCY

P.O. Box 1007, Cooper Station, New York NY 10276-1007. (212)714-7744. E-mail: query@ scribblershouse.net. Website: www.scribblershouse.net. **Contact:** Stedman Mays, Garrett Gambino. 25% of clients are new/unpublished writers.

Member Agents Stedman Mays, Garrett Gambino.

Represents Nonfiction books, novels, occasionally. **Considers these nonfiction areas:** biography, business, diet/nutrition, economics, health, history, how-to, language, literature, medicine, memoirs, money, parenting, popular culture, politics, psychology, self-help, sex, spirituality, the brain; personal finance; writing books; relationships; gender issues. **Considers these fiction areas:** crime, historical, literary, suspense, thriller, women's.

How to Contact Query via e-mail. Put "nonfiction query" or "fiction query" in the subject line followed by the title of your project (send to our submissions e-mail on our website). Do not send attachments or downloadable materials of any kind with query. We will request more materials if we are interested. Usually respond in 2 weeks to 2 months to e-mail queries if we are interested (if we are not interested, we will not respond due to the overwhelming amount of queries we receive). We are only accepting e-mail queries at the present time. Accepts simultaneous submissions.

Terms Agent receives 15% commission on domestic sales. Charges clients for postage, shipping and copying.

Tips "If you must send by snail mail, we will return material or respond to a U.S. Postal Service-accepted SASE. (No international coupons or outdated mail strips, please.) Presentation means a lot. A well-written query letter with a brief author bio and your credentials is important. For query letter models, go to the bookstore or online and look at the cover copy and flap copy on other books in your general area of interest. Emulate what's best. Have an idea of other notable books that will be perceived as being in the same vein as yours. Know what's fresh about your project and articulate it in as few words as possible. Consult our website for the most up-to-date information on submitting."

▢ SCRIBE AGENCY, LLC

5508 Joylynne Dr., Madison WI 53716. E-mail: queries@scribeagency.com. Website: www. scribeagency.com. **Contact:** Kristopher O'Higgins. Represents 11 clients. 18% of clients are new/ unpublished writers. Currently handles: novels 98%, story collections 2%.

- "We have 17 years of experience in publishing and have worked on both agency and editorial sides in the past, with marketing expertise to boot. We love books as much or more than anyone you know. Check our website to see what we're about and to make sure you jive with the Scribe vibe."

Member Agents Kristopher O'Higgins; Jesse Vogel.

Represents Nonfiction books, novels, short story collections, novellas, anthologies. **Considers these nonfiction areas:** cooking, diet/nutrition, ethnic, foods, gay/lesbian, humor, memoirs, popular culture, satire, women's issues, women's studies. **Considers these fiction areas:** detective, erotica, experimental, fantasy, feminist, gay, horror, humor, lesbian, literary, mainstream, mystery, psychic, science fiction, thriller.

🖙 Actively seeking excellent writers with ideas and stories to tell.

How to Contact E-queries only: submissions@scribeagency.com. See the website for submission info, as it may change. Responds in 3-4 weeks to queries. Responds in 5 months to mss.

Terms Agent receives 15% commission on domestic sales. Agent receives 20% commission on foreign sales. Offers written contract. Charges for postage and photocopying.

Recent Sales Sold 3 titles in the last year.

Writers Conferences BookExpo America; The Writer's Institute; Spring Writer's Festival; WisCon; Wisconsin Book Festival; World Fantasy Convention.

SECRET AGENT MAN

P.O. Box 1078, Lake Forest CA 92609-1078. (949)698-6987. E-mail: scott@secretagentman.net. Website: www.secretagentman.net. **Contact:** Scott Mortenson.

Represents Novels. **Considers these fiction areas:** detective, mystery, religious, thriller.

🖙 Actively seeking selective mystery, thriller, suspense and detective fiction. Does not want to receive scripts or screenplays.

How to Contact Query with SASE. Query via e-mail or snail mail; include sample chapter(s), synopsis and/or outline. Prefers to read the real thing rather than a description of it. Obtains most new clients through recommendations from others, solicitations.

LYNN SELIGMAN, LITERARY AGENT

400 Highland Ave., Upper Montclair NJ 07043. (973)783-3631. **Contact:** Lynn Seligman. Other memberships include Women's Media Group. Represents 32 clients. 15% of clients are new/unpublished writers. Currently handles: nonfiction books 60%, novels 40%.

• Prior to opening her agency, Ms. Seligman worked in the subsidiary rights department of Doubleday and Simon & Schuster, and served as an agent with Julian Bach Literary Agency (which became IMG Literary Agency). Foreign rights are represented by Books Crossing Borders, Inc.

Represents Nonfiction books, novels. **Considers these nonfiction areas:** interior, anthropology, art, biography, business, child, cooking, current affairs, education, ethnic, government, health, history, how to, humor, language, money, music, nature, photography, popular culture, psychology, science, self-help, sociology, film, true crime, womens. **Considers these fiction areas:** detective, ethnic, fantasy, feminist, historical, horror, humor, literary, mainstream, mystery, romance, contemporary, gothic, historical, regency, science fiction.

🖙 "This agency specializes in general nonfiction and fiction. I also do illustrated and photography books and have represented several photographers for books."

How to Contact Query with SASE. Prefers to read materials exclusively. Accepts simultaneous submissions. Responds in 2 weeks to queries. Responds in 2 months to mss. Obtains most new clients through referrals from other writers and editors.

Terms Agent receives 15% commission on domestic sales. Agent receives 25% commission on foreign sales. Charges clients for photocopying, unusual postage, express mail, telephone expenses (checks with author first).

Recent Sales Sold 15 titles in the last year. Lords of Vice series, by Barbara Pierce; Untitled series, by Deborah Leblanc.

⌧ SERENDIPITY LITERARY AGENCY, LLC

305 Gates Ave., Brooklyn NY 11216. (718)230-7689. Fax: (718)230-7829. E-mail: rbrooks@ serendipitylit.com; info@serendipitylit.com. Website: www.serendipitylit.com. **Contact:** Regina Brooks. Represents 50 clients. 50% of clients are new/unpublished writers. Currently handles: nonfiction books 50%, other 50% fiction.

• Prior to becoming an agent, Ms. Brooks was an acquisitions editor for John Wiley & Sons, Inc. and McGraw-Hill Companies.

Member Agents Regina Brooks; Guichard Cadet (sports, pop culture, fiction, Caribbean writers).

Represents Nonfiction books, novels, juvenile, scholarly, children's books. **Considers these nonfiction areas:** biography, business, cooking, crafts, cultural interests, current affairs, design, economics, education, ethnic, foods, health, history, inspirational, juvenile nonfiction, medicine, memoirs, metaphysics, money, multicultural, New Age, popular culture, politics, psychology, religious, science, self-help, sports, technology, women's issues, women's studies, narrative; popular science, contemporary culture. **Considers these fiction areas:** action, adventure, confession, ethnic, historical, juvenile, literary, multicultural, mystery, picture books, romance, suspense, thriller.

    ⚭ African-American nonfiction, commercial fiction, young adult novels with an urban flair and juvenile books. No stage plays, screenplays or poetry.

How to Contact Prefers to read materials exclusively. For nonfiction, submit outline, 1 sample chapter, SASE. Write the field on the back of the envelope. See guidelines online. For adult fiction, please send a query letter that includes basic information that describes your project. Your query letter should include the title, premise, and length of the manuscript. See our guidelines onine. Write the genre of your book on the back of your envelope. Based on your initial query letter and synopsis, our office may request sample chapters, or your ms in its entirety. Responds in 2 months to queries. Responds in 3 months to mss. Obtains most new clients through conferences, referrals.

Terms Agent receives 15% commission on domestic sales. Agent receives 20% commission on foreign sales. Offers written contract; 2-month notice must be given to terminate contract. Charges clients for office fees, which are taken from any advance.

Tips "We are eagerly looking for young adult books. We also represent illustrators."

⬙ ◙ SEVENTH AVENUE LITERARY AGENCY

1663 West Seventh Ave., Vancouver British Columbia V6J 1S4 Canada. (604)734-3663. Fax: (604)734-8906. E-mail: info@seventhavenuelit.com. Website: www.seventhavenuelit.com. **Contact:** Robert Mackwood, director. Currently handles: nonfiction books 100%.

Represents Nonfiction books. **Considers these nonfiction areas:** autobiography, biography, business, computers, economics, health, history, medicine, science, sports, technology, travel, lifestyle.

    ⚭ Seventh Avenue Literary Agency is one of Canada's largest and most venerable literary and personal management agencies. (The agency was originally called Contemporary Management.) Actively seeking nonfiction. Does not want to receive poetry, screenplays, children's books, young adult titles, or genre writing such as science fiction, fantasy or erotica.

How to Contact Query with SASE. Submit outline, synopsis, 1 (nonfiction) sample chapters, publishing history, author bio, table of contents with proposal or query. Send 1-2 chapters and submission history if sending fiction. No e-mail attachments. Provide full contact information. For fiction queries only contact Gloria Goodman: hettyphil@sympatico.ca. Obtains most new clients through recommendations from others, solicitations.

Tips "If you want your material returned, please include an SASE with adequate postage; otherwise, material will be recycled. (U.S. stamps are not adequate; they do not work in Canada.)"

◙ THE SEYMOUR AGENCY

475 Miner St., Canton NY 13617. (315)386-1831. E-mail: marysue@twcny.rr.com. Website: www.theseymouragency.com. **Contact:** Mary Sue Seymour. Member of AAR. Signatory of WGA. Other memberships include RWA, Authors Guild. Represents 50 clients. 5% of clients are new/unpublished writers. Currently handles: nonfiction books 50%, other 50% fiction.

    • Ms. Seymour is a retired New York State certified teacher.

Represents Nonfiction books, novels. **Considers these nonfiction areas:** business, health, how-to, self-help, Christian books; cookbooks; any well-written nonfiction that includes a proposal in standard format and 1 sample chapter. **Considers these fiction areas:** religious, Christian books, romance, any type.

How to Contact Query with SASE, synopsis, first 50 pages for romance. Accepts e-mail queries. Accepts simultaneous submissions. Responds in 1 month to queries. Responds in 3 months to mss.

Terms Agent receives 12-15% commission on domestic sales.

Recent Sales Dinah Bucholz's *The Harry Potter Cookbook* to Adams Media.com; Vannetta Chapman's *A Simple Amish Christmas* to Abingdon Press; Shelley Shepard Gray's current book deal to Harper Collins; Shelley Galloway's multibook deal to Zondervan; Beth Wiseman's Christmas two novellas and multibook deal to Thomas Nelson; Mary Ellis's multibook deal to Harvest House, Barbara Cameron's novellas to Thomas Nelson and multibook deal to Abingdon Press.

DENISE SHANNON LITERARY AGENCY, INC.

20 W. 22nd St., Suite 1603, New York NY 10010. (212)414-2911. Fax: (212)414-2930. E-mail: info@ deniseshannonagency.com. Website: www.deniseshannonagency.com. **Contact:** Denise Shannon. Estab. 2002. Member of AAR.

- Prior to opening her agency, Ms. Shannon worked for 16 years with Georges Borchardt and International Creative Management.

Represents Nonfiction books, novels. **Considers these nonfiction areas:** biography, business, health, narrative nonfiction; politics; journalism; memoir; social history. **Considers these fiction areas:** literary.

- ☛ "We are a boutique agency with a distinguished list of fiction and nonfiction authors."

How to Contact Query by e-mail to: submissions@deniseshannonagency.com, or mail with SASE. Submit query with description of project, bio, SASE. See guidelines online.

Tips "Please do not send queries regarding fiction projects until a complete manuscript is available for review. We request that you inform us if you are submitting material simultaneously to other agencies."

☑ THE ROBERT E. SHEPARD AGENCY

4804 Laurel Canyon Blvd., PMB 592, Valley Village CA 91607-3717. (818)508-0056. E-mail: mail@shepardagency.com. Website: www.shepardagency.com. **Contact:** Robert Shepard. Other memberships include Authors Guild. Represents 70 clients. 15% of clients are new/unpublished writers. Currently handles: nonfiction books 90%, scholarly books 10%.

- Prior to opening his agency, Mr. Shepard was an editor and a sales and marketing manager in book publishing; he now writes, teaches courses for nonfiction authors, and speaks at many writers' conferences.

Represents Nonfiction books, scholarly, appropriate for trade publishers. **Considers these nonfiction areas:** business, cultural interests, current affairs, economics, gay/lesbian, government, health, history, law, parenting, popular culture, politics, psychology, sports, Judaica; narrative nonfiction; science for laypeople.

- ☛ This agency specializes in nonfiction, particularly key issues facing society and culture. Actively seeking works by experts recognized in their fields whether or not they're well-known to the general public, and books that offer fresh perspectives or new information even when the subject is familiar. Does not want to receive autobiographies, art books, memoir, spirituality or fiction.

How to Contact Query either by e-mail or by regular mail with SASE (if you want material to be returned). Accepts simultaneous submissions. Responds in 2-3 weeks to queries; 6 weeks to proposals. Do not send ms unless specifically requested to do so. Obtains most new clients through recommendations from others, solicitations.

Terms Agent receives 15% commission on domestic sales. Agent receives 20% commission on foreign sales. Offers written contract, binding for term of project or until canceled; 30-day notice must be given to terminate contract. Charges clients for phone/fax, photocopying, postage (if and when the project sells).

Recent Sales Sold 10 titles in the last year. *A Few Seconds of Panic*, by Stefan Fatsis (Penguin); *Big Boy Rules*, by Steve Fainaru (Da Capo Press); *The Fois Gras Wars*, by Mark Caro (Simon & Schuster).

Tips "We pay attention to detail. We believe in close working relationships between the author and agent, and in building better relationships between the author and editor. Please do your homework! There's no substitute for learning all you can about similar or directly competing books and presenting a well-reasoned competitive analysis in your proposal. Be sure to describe what's new and fresh about your work, why you are the best person to be writing on your subject, everything editors will need to know about your work, and how the book will serve the needs or interests of your intended readers. Don't work in a vacuum: Visit bookstores, talk to other writers about their experiences, and let the information you gather inform the work that you do as an author."

⬛ WENDY SHERMAN ASSOCIATES, INC.

27 W. 24th St., New York NY 10010. (212)279-9027. Website: www.wsherman.com. **Contact:** Wendy Sherman. Member of AAR. Represents 50 clients. 30% of clients are new/unpublished writers. Currently handles: nonfiction books 50%, novels 50%.

- Prior to opening the agency, Ms. Sherman served as vice president, executive director, associate publisher, subsidiary rights director, and sales and marketing director for major publishers.

Member Agents Wendy Sherman (board member of AAR).

Represents nonfiction, fiction. **Considers these nonfiction areas:** memoirs, psychology, narrative; practical. **Considers these fiction areas:** literary, suspense, women's.

- ⚷ "We specialize in developing new writers, as well as working with more established writers. My experience as a publisher has proven to be a great asset to my clients."

How to Contact Query via e-mail to submissions@wsherman.com Accepts simultaneous submissions. Responds in 1 month to queries. Obtains most new clients through recommendations from others.

Terms Agent receives 15% commission on domestic sales. Agent receives 20% commission on foreign and film sales. Offers written contract.

Recent Sales *Daughters of the Witching Hill*, by Mary Sharratt; *The Measure of Brightness*, by Todd Johnson; *Supergirls Speak Out*, by Liz Funk; *Love in 90 Days*, by Diana Kirschner; *A Long Time Ago and Essentially*, by Brigid Pasulka; *Changing Shoes*, by Tina Sloan.

Tips "The bottom line is: Do your homework. Be as well prepared as possible. Read the books that will help you present yourself and your work with polish. You want your submission to stand out."

⬛ ROSALIE SIEGEL, INTERNATIONAL LITERARY AGENCY, INC.

1 Abey Dr., Pennington NJ 08543. (609)737-1007. Fax: (609)737-3708. **Contact:** Rosalie Siegel. Member of AAR. Represents 35 clients. 10% of clients are new/unpublished writers. Currently handles: nonfiction books 45%, novels 45%, other 10% young adult books; short story collections for current clients.

How to Contact Obtains most new clients through referrals from writers and friends.

Terms Agent receives 15% commission on domestic sales. Agent receives 20% commission on foreign sales. Offers written contract; 2-month notice must be given to terminate contract. Charges clients for photocopying.

🌐 ⬛ JEFFREY SIMMONS LITERARY AGENCY

15 Penn House, Mallory St., London NW8 8SX England. (44)(207)224-8917. E-mail: jasimmons@unicombox.co.uk. **Contact:** Jeffrey Simmons. Represents 43 clients. 40% of clients are new/unpublished writers. Currently handles: nonfiction books 65%, novels 35%.

- Prior to becoming an agent, Mr. Simmons was a publisher. He is also an author.

Represents Nonfiction books, novels. **Considers these nonfiction areas:** autobiography, biography, current affairs, film, government, history, language, memoirs, music, popular culture, sociology, sports, translation, true crime. **Considers these fiction areas:** action, adventure, confession, crime, detective, family saga, literary, mainstream, mystery, police, suspense, thriller.

- ⚷ "This agency seeks to handle good books and promising young writers. My long experience in publishing and as an author and ghostwriter means I can offer an excellent service all around, especially in terms of editorial experience where appropriate." Actively seeking quality fiction, biography, autobiography, showbiz, personality books, law, crime, politics, and world affairs. Does not want to receive science fiction, horror, fantasy, juvenile, academic books, or specialist subjects (e.g., cooking, gardening, religious).

How to Contact Submit sample chapter, outline/proposal, SASE (IRCs if necessary).Prefers to read materials exclusively. Responds in 1 week to queries. Responds in 1 month to mss. Obtains most new clients through recommendations from others, solicitations.

Terms Agent receives 10-15% commission on domestic sales. Agent receives 15% commission on foreign sales. Offers written contract, binding for lifetime of book in question or until it becomes out of print.

Tips "When contacting us with an outline/proposal, include a brief biographical note (listing any previous publications, with publishers and dates). Preferably tell us if the book has already been offered elsewhere."

▣ ◙ BEVERLEY SLOPEN LITERARY AGENCY

131 Bloor St. W., Suite 711, Toronto ON M5S 1S3 Canada. (416)964-9598. Fax: (416)921-7726. E-mail: beverly@slopenagency.ca. Website: www.slopenagency.ca. **Contact:** Beverley Slopen. Represents 70 clients. 20% of clients are new/unpublished writers. Currently handles: nonfiction books 60%, novels 40%.

• Prior to opening her agency, Ms. Slopen worked in publishing and as a journalist.

Represents Nonfiction books, novels, scholarly, textbooks, college. **Considers these nonfiction areas:** anthropology, archeology, autobiography, biography, business, current affairs, economics, investigative, psychology, sociology, true crime, women's issues, women's studies. **Considers these fiction areas:** literary, mystery, suspense.

   ○┅ "This agency has a strong bent toward Canadian writers." Actively seeking serious nonfiction that is accessible and appealing to the general reader. Does not want to receive fantasy, science fiction, or children's books.

How to Contact Query with SAE and IRCs. Returns materials only with SASE (Canadian postage only). Accepts simultaneous submissions. Responds in 2 months to queries.

Terms Agent receives 15% commission on domestic sales. Agent receives 10% commission on foreign sales. Offers written contract, binding for 2 years; 3-month notice must be given to terminate contract.

Recent Sales *Solar Dance*, by Modris Eksteins (Knopf Canada); *God's Brain*, by Lionel Tiger & Michael McGuire (Prometheus Books); *What They Wanted*, by Donna Morrissey (Penguin Canada, Premium/DTV Germany); *The Age of Persuasion*, by Terry O'Reilly & Mike Tennant (Knopf Canada, Counterpoint US); *Prisoner of Tehran*, by Marina Nemat (Penguin Canada, Free Press US, John Murray UK); *Race to the Polar Sea*, by Ken McGoogan (HarperCollins Canada, Counterpoint US); *Transgression*, by James Nichol (HarperCollins US, McArthur Canada, Goldmann Germany); *Vermeer's Hat*, by Timothy Brook (HarperCollins Canada, Bloomsbury US); *Distantly Related to Freud*, by Ann Charney (Cormorant).

Tips "Please, no unsolicited manuscripts."

◎ SLW LITERARY AGENCY

4100 Ridgeland Ave., Northbrook IL 60062. (847)509-0999. Fax: (847)509-0996. E-mail: shariwenk@gmail.com. **Contact:** Shari Wenk. Currently handles: nonfiction books 100%.

Represents Nonfiction books. **Considers these nonfiction areas:** sports.

   ○┅ "This agency specializes in representing books written by sports celebrities and sports writers."

How to Contact Query via e-mail, but note the agency's specific specialty.

VALERIE SMITH, LITERARY AGENT

1746 Route 44-55, Modena NY 12548. **Contact:** Valerie Smith. Represents 17 clients. Currently handles: nonfiction books 2%, novels 75%, story collections 1%, juvenile books 20%, scholarly books 1%, textbooks 1%.

Represents Nonfiction books, novels, juvenile, textbooks. **Considers these nonfiction areas:** agriculture horticulture, cooking, how to, self-help. **Considers these fiction areas:** fantasy, historical, juvenile, literary, mainstream, mystery, science, young, women's/chick lit.

   ○┅ "This is a small, personalized agency with a strong long-term commitment to clients interested in building careers. I have strong ties to science fiction, fantasy and young adult projects. I look for serious, productive writers whose work I can be passionate about." Does not want to receive unsolicited mss.

How to Contact Query with synopsis, bio, 3 sample chapters, SASE. Contact by snail mail only. Obtains most new clients through recommendations from others.

Terms Agent receives 15% commission on domestic sales. Agent receives 20% commission on foreign sales. Offers written contract; 6-week notice must be given to terminate contract.

▦ ☑ ROBERT SMITH LITERARY AGENCY, LTD.

12 Bridge Wharf, 156 Caledonian Rd., London NI 9UU England. (44)(207)278-2444. Fax: (44)(207)833-5680. E-mail: robertsmith.literaryagency@virgin.net. **Contact:** Robert Smith. Other memberships include AAA. Represents 40 clients. 10% of clients are new/unpublished writers. Currently handles: nonfiction books 80%, syndicated material 20%.

• Prior to becoming an agent, Mr. Smith was a book publisher.

Represents Nonfiction books, syndicated material. **Considers these nonfiction areas:** autobiography, biography, cooking, diet/nutrition, film, foods, health, investigative, medicine, memoirs, music, popular culture, self-help, sports, theater, true crime, entertainment.

☞ "This agency offers clients full management service in all media. Clients are not necessarily book authors. Our special expertise is in placing newspaper series internationally." Actively seeking autobiographies.

How to Contact Submit outline/proposal, SASE (IRCs if necessary). Prefers to read materials exclusively. Responds in 2 weeks to queries. Obtains most new clients through recommendations from others, direct approaches to prospective authors.

Terms Agent receives 15% commission on domestic sales. Agent receives 20% commission on foreign sales. Offers written contract, binding for 3 months; 3-month notice must be given to terminate contract. Charges clients for couriers, photocopying, overseas mailings of mss (subject to client authorization).

Recent Sales *Lawro*, by Mark Lawrenson (Penguin); *Enter the Dragon*, by Theo Paphitis (Orion); *Strong Women*, by Roberta Kray (Little, Brown); *Home From War*, by Martyn and Michelle Compton (Mainstream); *Diary of a Japanese P.O.W*, by John Baxter (Aurum Press); *A Different Kind of Courage*, by Gretel Wachtel and Claudia Strachan (Mainstream); *Drawing Fire*, by Len Smith (HarperCollins); *Mummy Doesn't Love You*, by Alexander Sinclair (Ebury Press); *Forgotten*, by Les Cummings (Macmillan); *Suffer the Little Children*, by Frances Reilly (Orion).

MICHAEL SNELL LITERARY AGENCY

P.O. Box 1206, Truro MA 02666-1206. (508)349-3718. E-mail: snell.patricia@gmail.com. Website: www.michaelsnellagency.com. **Contact:** Michael Snell. Represents 200 clients, 25% of clients are new/unpublished writers. Currently handles: nonfiction books 90%, novels 10%.

• Prior to opening his agency, Mr. Snell served as an editor at Wadsworth and Addison-Wesley for 13 years.

Member Agents Michael Snell (business, leadership, pets, sports).

Represents Nonfiction books. **Considers these nonfiction areas:** agriculture horticulture, crafts, interior, New Age, animals, pets, anthropology, art, business, child, computers, cooking, current affairs, education, ethnic, gardening, gay, government, health, history, how to, humor, language, military, money, music, nature, photography, popular culture, psychology, recreation, religion, science, self-help, sex, spirituality, sports, fitness, film, travel, true crime, womens, creative nonfiction.

☞ This agency specializes in how-to, self-help, and all types of business and computer books, from low-level how-to to professional and reference. Especially interested in business, health, law, medicine, psychology, science, and women's issues. Actively seeking strong book proposals in any nonfiction area where a clear need exists for a new book—especially self-help and how-to books on all subjects, from business to personal well-being. Does not want to receive fiction, children's books, or complete mss (considers proposals only).

How to Contact Query by mail with SASE, or e-mail. Prefers to read materials exclusively. Responds in 1 week to queries. Responds in 2 weeks to mss. Obtains most new clients through unsolicited mss, word of mouth, *Literary Market Place, Guide to Literary Agents*.

Terms Agent receives 15% commission on domestic sales. Agent receives 15% commission on foreign sales.

Recent Sales *How Did That Happen? Holding Other People Accountable for Results the Positive, Principled Way*, by Roger Connors and Tom Smith (Portfolio/Penguin); *Recovering the Lost River: Rewilding Salmon, Recivilizing Humans, Removing Dams*, by Steve Hawley (Beacon Press); *You, Him and Her: Coping With Infidelity in Your Marriage*, by Dr. Paul Coleman (Adams Media); *Strategic Customer Service*, by John Goodman (Amacom Books).

Tips "Send a maximum 1-page query with SASE. Brochure on 'How to Write a Book Proposal' is available on request with SASE. We suggest prospective clients read Michael Snell's book, *From Book Idea to Bestseller* (Prima 1997), or purchase a model proposal directly from the company."

☑ SPECTRUM LITERARY AGENCY

320 Central Park W., Suite 1-D, New York NY 10025. Fax: (212)362-4562. Website: www.spectrumliteraryagency.com. **Contact:** Eleanor Wood, president. Estab. 1976. SFWA Represents 90 clients. Currently handles: nonfiction books 10%, novels 90%.

Member Agents Eleanor Wood, Justin Bell.

Represents Nonfiction books, novels. **Considers these fiction areas:** fantasy, historical, mainstream, mystery, romance, science fiction, suspense.

How to Contact Query with SASE. Submit author bio, publishing credits. No unsolicited mss will be read. Snail mail queries **only**. Eleanor and Lucienne have different addresses—see the website for full info. Responds in 1-3 months to queries. Obtains most new clients through recommendations from authors.

Terms Agent receives 15% commission on domestic sales. Deducts for photocopying and book orders.

Tips "Spectrum's policy is to read only book-length manuscripts that we have specifically asked to see. Unsolicited manuscripts are not accepted. The letter should describe your book briefly and include publishing credits and background information or qualifications relating to your work, if any."

◪ SPENCERHILL ASSOCIATES

P.O. Box 374, Chatham NY 12037. (518)392-9293. Fax: (518)392-9554. E-mail: submissions@spencerhillassociates.com. Website: www.spencerhillassociates.com. **Contact:** Karen Solem or Jennifer Schober (and please refer to our website for the latest information). Member of AAR. Represents 96 clients. 10% of clients are new/unpublished writers.

- Prior to becoming an agent, Ms. Solem was editor-in-chief at HarperCollins and an associate publisher.

Member Agents Karen Solem; Jennifer Schober.

Represents Novels. **Considers these fiction areas:** crime, detective, historical, inspirational, literary, mainstream, police, religious, romance, thriller, young adult.

- ⌐ "We handle mostly commercial women's fiction, historical novels, romance (historical, contemporary, paranormal, urban fantasy), thrillers, and mysteries. We also represent Christian fiction only—no nonfiction." No nonfiction, poetry, science fiction, children's picture books, or scripts.

How to Contact Query submissions@spencerhillassociates.com with synopsis and first three chapters attached as a .doc or .rtf file. Please note we no longer accept queries via the mail. Responds in 6-8 weeks to queries if we are interested in pursuing.

Terms Agent receives 15% commission on domestic sales. Agent receives 20% commission on foreign sales. Offers written contract; 3-month notice must be given to terminate contract.

◪ THE SPIELER AGENCY

154 W. 57th St., Suite 135, New York NY 10019. E-mail: eric@spieleragency.com. **Contact:** Katya Balter. Represents 160 clients. 2% of clients are new/unpublished writers.

- Prior to opening his agency, Mr. Spieler was a magazine editor.

Member Agents Joe Spieler.

Represents Nonfiction books, novels, children's books. **Considers these nonfiction areas:** autobiography, biography, business, child guidance, current affairs, economics, environment, film, gay/lesbian, government, history, law, memoirs, money, music, parenting, politics, sociology, spirituality, theater, travel, women's issues, women's studies. **Considers these fiction areas:** detective, feminist, gay, lesbian, literary, mystery, children's books, Middle Grade and Young Adult novels.

How to Contact Accepts electronic submissions (spieleragency@spieleragency.com), or send query letter and sample chapters. Prefers to read materials exclusively. Returns materials only with SASE; otherwise materials are discarded when rejected. Accepts simultaneous submissions. Responds in 2 weeks to queries. Responds in 2 months to mss. Obtains most new clients through recommendations, listing in *Guide to Literary Agents*.

Terms Agent receives 15% commission on domestic sales. Charges clients for messenger bills, photocopying, postage.

Writers Conferences London Book Fair.

Tips "Check http://www.publishersmarketplace.com/members/spielerlit/."

◪ PHILIP G. SPITZER LITERARY AGENCY, INC

50 Talmage Farm Ln., East Hampton NY 11937. (631)329-3650. Fax: (631)329-3651. E-mail: luc. hunt@spitzeragency.com. Website: www.spitzeragency.com. **Contact:** Luc Hunt. Member of AAR.

Represents 60 clients. 10% of clients are new/unpublished writers. Currently handles: nonfiction books 35%, novels 65%.
- Prior to opening his agency, Mr. Spitzer served at New York University Press, McGraw-Hill, and the John Cushman Associates literary agency.

Represents Nonfiction books, novels. **Considers these nonfiction areas:** biography, history, investigative, sports, travel, true crime. **Considers these fiction areas:** crime, detective, literary, mainstream, mystery, police, sports, suspense, thriller.
- ⚬ This agency specializes in mystery/suspense, literary fiction, sports and general nonfiction (no how-to).

How to Contact Query with SASE. Responds in 2 weeks to queries. Responds in 6 weeks to mss. Obtains most new clients through recommendations from others.
Terms Agent receives 15% commission on domestic sales. Agent receives 20% commission on foreign sales. Charges clients for photocopying.
Writers Conferences London Bookfair, Frankfurt, BookExpo America.

⬛ ☑ P. STATHONIKOS AGENCY

146 Springbluff Heights SW, Calgary Alberta T3H 5E5 Canada. (403)245-2087. Fax: (403)245-2087. E-mail: pastath@telus.net. **Contact:** Penny Stathonikos.
- Prior to becoming an agent, Ms. Stathonikos was a bookstore owner and publisher's representative for 10 years.

Represents Nonfiction books, novels, juvenile.
- ⚬ Children's literature, some young adult. Does not want to receive romance, fantasy, historical fiction, plays, movie scripts or poetry.

How to Contact Query with SASE. Submit outline. Responds in 1 month to queries. Responds in 2 months to mss.
Terms Agent receives 10% commission on domestic sales. Agent receives 15% commission on foreign sales. Charges for postage, telephone, copying, etc.
Tips "Do your homework—read any of the Writer's Digest market books, join a writers' group and check out the local bookstore or library for similar books. Know who your competition is and why your book is different."

☑ NANCY STAUFFER ASSOCIATES

P.O. Box 1203, 1540 Boston Post Road, Darien CT 06820. (203)202-2500. Fax: (203)655-3704. E-mail: StaufferAssoc@optonline.net. Website: publishersmarketplace.com/members/nstauffer. **Contact:** Nancy Stauffer Cahoon. Other memberships include Authors Guild. 5% of clients are new/unpublished writers. Currently handles: nonfiction books 15%, novels 85%.
Represents Considers these nonfiction areas: cultural interests, current affairs, ethnic, creative nonfiction (narrative). **Considers these fiction areas:** contemporary, literary, regional.
How to Contact Obtains most new clients through referrals from existing clients.
Terms Agent receives 15% commission on domestic sales. Agent receives 20% commission on foreign sales. Agent receives 15% commission on film sales.
Recent Sales *The Magic and Tragic Year of My Broken Thumb*, by Sherman Alexie; *Bone Fire*, by Mark Spragg; *Claiming Ground*, by Laura Bell; *The Best Camera is the One That's With You*, by Chase Jarvis.

☑ STEELE-PERKINS LITERARY AGENCY

26 Island Ln., Canandaigua NY 14424. (585)396-9290. Fax: (585)396-3579. E-mail: pattiesp@aol.com. **Contact:** Pattie Steele-Perkins. Member of AAR. Other memberships include RWA. Currently handles: novels 100%.
Represents Novels. **Considers these fiction areas:** romance, women's. All genres: category romance, romantic suspense, historical, contemporary, multi-cultural, and inspirational.
How to Contact Submit synopsis and one chapter via e-mail (no attachments) or snail mail. Snail mail submissions require SASE. Accepts simultaneous submissions. Responds in 6 weeks to queries. Obtains most new clients through recommendations from others, queries/solicitations.
Terms Agent receives 15% commission on domestic sales. Offers written contract, binding for 1 year; 1-month notice must be given to terminate contract.
Recent Sales Sold 130 titles last year. This agency prefers not to share specific sales information.

Writers Conferences RWA National Conference; BookExpo America; CBA Convention; Romance Slam Jam.

Tips "Be patient. E-mail rather than call. Make sure what you are sending is the best it can be."

◖ STERNIG & BYRNE LITERARY AGENCY

2370 S. 107th St., Apt. #4, Milwaukee WI 53227-2036. (414)328-8034. Fax: (414)328-8034. E-mail: jackbyrne@hotmail.com. Website: www.sff.net/people/jackbyrne. **Contact:** Jack Byrne. Other memberships include SFWA, MWA. Represents 30 clients. 10% of clients are new/unpublished writers. Currently handles: nonfiction books 5%, novels 90%, juvenile books 5%.

Represents Nonfiction books, novels, juvenile. **Considers these fiction areas:** fantasy, horror, mystery, science fiction, suspense.

> ⚬⌐ "Our client list is comfortably full and our current needs are therefore quite limited." Actively seeking science fiction/fantasy and mystery by established writers. Does not want to receive romance, poetry, textbooks, or highly specialized nonfiction.

How to Contact Query with SASE. Prefers e-mail queries (no attachments); hard copy queries also acceptable. Responds in 3 weeks to queries. Responds in 3 months to mss.

Terms Agent receives 15% commission on domestic sales. Agent receives 20% commission on foreign sales. Offers written contract; 2-month notice must be given to terminate contract.

Tips "Don't send first drafts, have a professional presentation (including cover letter), and know your field. Read what's been done—good and bad."

◖ STIMOLA LITERARY STUDIO, INC.

306 Chase Court, Edgewater NJ 07020. Phone/Fax: (201)945-9353. E-mail: info@stimolaliterary studio.com. Website: www.stimolaliterarystudio.com. **Contact:** Rosemary B. Stimola. Member of AAR.

How to Contact Query via e-mail (no unsolicited attachments). Responds in 3 weeks to queries "we wish to pursue further." Responds in 2 months to requested mss. Obtains most new clients through referrals. Unsolicited submissions are still accepted.

Terms Agent receives 15% commission on domestic sales. Agent receives 20% (if subagents are employed) commission on foreign sales.

Recent Sales *The Hunger Games Trilogy*, by Suzanne Collins (Scholastic); *Another Brother, by Matt Cordell* (Feiwel & Friends/Macmillan); *Don't Stop Now*, by Julie Halpern (Feiwel & Friends/Macmillan); *The Anti-Prom*, by Abby McDonald (Candlewick Press); *Not That Kind of Girl*, by Siobhan Vivian (Scholastic, Push); *Courage Has No Color*, by Tanya Lee Stone (Candlewick); *Crossing Lines*, by Paul Voponi (Viking/Penguin).

◖ STRACHAN LITERARY AGENCY

P.O. Box 2091, Annapolis MD 21404. E-mail: query@strachanlit.com. Website: www.strachanlit.com. **Contact:** Laura Strachan.

> • Prior to becoming an agent, Ms. Strachan was (and still is) an attorney.

Represents Nonfiction books, novels. **Considers these nonfiction areas:** narrative. **Considers these fiction areas:** literary and up-market commercial.

> ⚬⌐ "This agency specializes in literary fiction and narrative nonfiction."

How to Contact E-mail queries only with brief synopsis and bio.; no attachments or samples unless requested.

Recent Sales *The Interventionist* (Hazelden); The Golden Bristled Boar (UVA Press); *Poser* (Walker).

◖ ROBIN STRAUS AGENCY, INC.

229 E. 79th St., Suite 5A, New York NY 10075. (212)472-3282. Fax: (212)472-3833. E-mail: info@robinstrausagency.com. Website: www.robinstrausagency.com/. **Contact:** Ms. Robin Straus. Estab. 1983. Member of AAR.

> • Prior to becoming an agent, Robin Straus served as a subsidary rights manager at Random House and Doubleday and worked in editorial at Little, Brown.

Represents Represents high quality adult fiction and nonfiction including literary and commercial fiction, narrative nonfiction, women's fiction, memoirs, history, biographies, books on psychology, popular culture and current affairs, science, parenting, and cookbooks. **Considers these nonfiction areas:** , ays.

☞ We do not represent juvenile, young adult, science fiction/fantasy, horror, romance, westerns, poetry or screenplays.

How to Contact If you prefer to submit your queries electronically, please note that we do not download manuscripts. All materials must be included in the body of the e-mail. We do not respond to any submissions that do not include a SASE. No metered postage.

Terms Agent receives 15% commission on domestic sales. Agent receives 20% commission on foreign sales. Offers written contract. Charges for photocopying, express mail services, messenger and foreign postage, etc. as incurred.

◙ PAM STRICKLER AUTHOR MANAGEMENT

1 Water St., New Paltz NY 12561. (845)255-0061. E-mail: pam302mail-aaaqueries@yahoo.com; pdsnewyork-query@yahoo.com. Website: www.pamstrickler.com. **Contact:** Pamela Dean Strickler. Member of AAR.

• Prior to opening her agency, Ms. Strickler was senior editor at Ballantine Books.

Represents Novels. **Considers these fiction areas:** historical, romance, women's.

☞ Does not want to receive nonfiction or children's books.

How to Contact Please, no unsolicited manuscripts. PREFER EMAIL queries, including a one-page letter with a brief description of your plot, plus the first ten pages of your novel ALL PASTED IN to the body of the e-mail. Sorry, unknown attachments will not be opened.

◉ REBECCA STRONG INTERNATIONAL LITERARY AGENCY

235 W. 108th St., #35, New York NY 10025. (212)865-1569. E-mail: info@rsila.com. Website: www.rsila.com. **Contact:** Rebecca Strong. Estab. 2004.

• Prior to opening her agency, Ms. Strong was an industry executive with experience editing and licensing in the US and UK. She has worked at Crown/Random House, Harmony/Random House, Bloomsbury, and Harvill.

Represents Nonfiction books, novels. **Considers these nonfiction areas:** biography, business, health, history, memoirs, science, travel.

☞ "We are a consciously small agency selectively representing authors all over the world." Does not want to receive poetry, screenplays or any unsolicited mss.

How to Contact E-mail submissions only; subject line should indicate "submission query"; include cover letter with proposal. For fiction, include 1-2 complete chapters only. Accepts simultaneous submissions. Responds in 6-8 weeks to queries. Obtains most new clients through recommendations from others, conferences.

Terms Agent receives 15% commission on domestic sales. Agent receives 20% commission on foreign sales. Offers written contract, binding for 10 years; 30-day notice must be given to terminate contract.

Tips "I represent writers with prior publishing experience only: journalists, magazine writers or writers of fiction who have been published in anthologies or literary magazines. There are exceptions to this guideline, but not many."

◙ THE STROTHMAN AGENCY, LLC

Six Beacon St., Suite 810, Boston MA 02108. (617)742-2011. Fax: (617)742-2014. E-mail: info@strothmanagency.com. Website: www.strothmanagency.com. **Contact:** Wendy Strothman, Lauren MacLeod. Member of AAR. Other memberships include Authors' Guild. Represents 50 clients. Currently handles: nonfiction books 70%, novels 10%, scholarly books 20%.

• Prior to becoming an agent, Ms. Strothman was head of Beacon Press (1983-1995) and executive vice president of Houghton Mifflin's Trade & Reference Division (1996-2002).

Member Agents Wendy Strothman; Lauren MacLeod.

Represents Nonfiction books, novels, scholarly, young adult and middle grade. **Considers these nonfiction areas:** current affairs, environment, government, history, language, law, literature, politics. **Considers these fiction areas:** literary, young adult, middle grade.

☞ "Because we are highly selective in the clients we represent, we increase the value publishers place on our properties. We specialize in narrative nonfiction, memoir, history, science and nature, arts and culture, literary travel, current affairs, and some business. We have a highly selective practice in literary fiction, young adult and middle grade fiction, and nonfiction. We are now opening our doors to more commercial fiction but ONLY from authors who have a platform. If you have a platform, please mention it in your query letter." "The Strothman

Agency seeks out scholars, journalists, and other acknowledged and emerging experts in their fields. We are now actively looking for authors of well written young-adult fiction and nonfiction. Browse the Latest News to get an idea of the types of books that we represent. For more about what we're looking for, read Pitching an Agent: The Strothman Agency on the publishing website www.strothmanagency.com." Does not want to receive commercial fiction, romance, science fiction or self-help.

How to Contact Open to e-mail (strothmanagency@gmail.com) and postal submissions. See submission guidelines. Accepts simultaneous submissions. Responds in 4 weeks to queries. Responds in 6 weeks to mss. Obtains most new clients through recommendations from others.

Terms Agent receives 15% commission on domestic sales. Agent receives 20% commission on foreign sales. Offers written contract; 30-day notice must be given to terminate contract.

THE STUART AGENCY

260 W. 52 St., #24C, New York NY 10019. (212)586-2711. Fax: (212)977-1488. Website: http://stuartagency.com. **Contact:** Andrew Stuart. Estab. 2002.

- Prior to his current position, Mr. Stuart was an agent with Literary Group International for five years. Prior to becoming an agent, he was an editor at Random House and Simon & Schuster.

Represents Nonfiction books, novels. **Considers these nonfiction areas:** biography, ethnic, government, history, memoirs, multicultural, psychology, science, sports, narrative nonfiction. **Considers these fiction areas:** ethnic, literary.

How to Contact Query by e-mail or mail with SASE. Do not send any materials besides query/SASE unless requested.

SUBIAS

One Union Square West, # 913, New York NY 10003. (212)445-1091. Fax: (212)898-0375. E-mail: mark@marksubias.com. **Contact:** Mark Subias. Represents 35 clients. Currently handles: stage plays 100%.

Represents stage plays.

⊶ This agency is not currently representing movie scripts.

How to Contact Query with SASE.

☑ EMMA SWEENEY AGENCY, LLC

245 East 80th St., Suite 7E, New York NY 10075. E-mail: queries@emmasweeneyagency.com. Website: www.emmasweeneyagency.com. **Contact:** Eva Talmadge. Member of AAR. Other memberships include Women's Media Group. Represents 80 clients. 5% of clients are new/unpublished writers. Currently handles: nonfiction books 50%, novels 50%.

- Prior to becoming an agent, Ms. Sweeney was director of subsidiary rights at Grove Press. Since 1990, she has been a literary agent.

Member Agents Emma Sweeney, president; Eva Talmadge, rights manager and agent (Represents literary fiction, young adult novels, and narrative nonfiction. Considers these nonfiction areas: popular science, pop culture and music history, biography, memoirs, cooking, and anything relating to animals. Considers these fiction areas: literary (of the highest writing quality possible), young adult. eva@emmasweeneyagency.com); Justine Wenger, junior agent/assistant (justine@emmasweeneyagency.com).

Represents Nonfiction books, novels.

⊶ "We specialize in quality fiction and nonfiction. Our primary areas of interest include literary and women's fiction, mysteries and thrillers; science, history, biography, memoir, religious studies and the natural sciences." Does not want to receive romance and westerns or screenplays.

How to Contact Send query letter and first ten pages in body of e-mail (no attachments) to queries@emmasweeneyagency.com. No snail mail queries.

Terms Agent receives 15% commission on domestic sales. Agent receives 10% commission on foreign sales.

Writers Conferences Nebraska Writers' Conference; Words and Music Festival in New Orleans.

☑ THE SWETKY AGENCY

2150 Balboa Way, No. 29, St. George UT 84770. E-mail: fayeswetky@amsaw.org. Website: www.

amsaw.org/swetkyagency/index.html. **Contact:** Faye M. Swetky. Other memberships include American Society of Authors and Writers. Represents 20+ clients. 90% of clients are new/unpublished writers. Currently handles: nonfiction books 45%, novels 45%, movie scripts 10%, TV scripts 20%.

- Prior to becoming an agent, Ms. Swetky was an editor and corporate manager. She has also raised and raced thoroughbred horses.

Represents Nonfiction books, novels, short story collections, juvenile, movie, TV, movie scripts, feature film, MOW, sitcom, documentary. **Considers these nonfiction areas:** , All major genres. **Considers these fiction areas:** , All major genres. **Considers these script areas:** action, biography, cartoon, comedy, contemporary, detective, erotica, ethnic, experimental, family, fantasy, feminist, gay, glitz, historical, horror, juvenile, mainstream, multicultural, multimedia, mystery, psychic, regional, religious, romantic comedy, romantic drama, science, sports, teen, thriller, western.

❖ "We handle only book-length fiction and nonfiction and feature-length movie and television scripts. Please visit our website before submitting. All agency-related information is there, including a sample contract, e-mail submission forms, policies, clients, etc." Actively seeking marketable full-length material. Do not send unprofessionally prepared mss and/or scripts.

How to Contact See website for submission instructions. Accepts e-mail queries only. Accepts simultaneous submissions. Response time varies. Obtains most new clients through queries.

Terms Agent receives 15% commission on domestic sales. Agent receives 20% commission on foreign sales. Agent receives 20% commission on film sales. Offers written contract, binding for 6 months; 30-day notice must be given to terminate contract.

Recent Sales *DOC—The Life and Legend of the Man Behind Wyatt Earp*; *Growing Fruit and Vegetables in Pots*; *Doc Holliday*. Others in negotiation.

Tips "Be professional. Have a professionally prepared product."

▣ TALCOTT NOTCH LITERARY

276 Forest Road, Milford CT 06460. (203)877-1146. Fax: (203)876-9517. E-mail: editorial@talcottnotch.net. Website: www.talcottnotch.net. **Contact:** Gina Panettieri, president. Represents 35 clients. 25% of clients are new/unpublished writers. Currently handles: nonfiction books 25%, novels 55%, story collections 5%, juvenile books 10%, scholarly books 5%.

- Prior to becoming an agent, Ms. Panettieri was a freelance writer and editor.

Member Agents Gina Panettieri (nonfiction, mystery); Rachel Dowen (children's fiction, mystery); Ann Rought (romance, women's fiction, paranormal).

Represents Nonfiction books, novels, juvenile, scholarly, textbooks. **Considers these nonfiction areas:** animals, anthropology, art, biography, business, computers, cooking, current affairs, decorating, education, environment, ethnic, gay/lesbian, government, health, history, interior design, investigative, juvenile nonfiction, memoirs, metaphysics, military, money, music, New Age, popular culture, psychology, science, sociology, sports, technology, true crime, women's issues, women's studies. **Considers these fiction areas:** action, adventure, crime, detective, fantasy, juvenile, mystery, police, romance, suspense, thriller, young adult.

How to Contact Query via e-mail (preferred) with first ten pages of the ms within the body of the e-mail, not as an attachment, or with SASE. Accepts simultaneous submissions. Responds in 1 week to queries. Responds in 4-6 weeks to mss.

Terms Agent receives 15% commission on domestic sales. Agent receives 20% commission on foreign sales. Offers written contract, binding for 1 year.

Recent Sales Sold 36 titles in the last year. *Delivered from Evil*, by Ron Franscell (Fairwinds); *Outlaw Texas: The Crime Buff's Guide to Texas*, by Ron Franscell (Globe Pequot); *God Goes to Work*, by Tom Zender (John Wiley & Sons); *CPR For Your Plants*, by Sandra Dark and Dean Hill (University Press of Florida); *Now Is The Time To Do What You Love: How To Make The Career Move That Will Change Your Life*, by Nancy Whitney-Reiter (Adams Media Corp); *Green Collar Jobs*, by Scott Deitche (Praeger/Greenwood), and more. Other clients include Tracy Tamborra, William Brennan, Melissa Ellis, Nancy Hawks-Miller, Koos Verkaik, Kim Bookout, Karen Williams, Kevin Wolf, Jay (Dr. J) Stratoudakis, and more.

Tips "Present your book or project effectively in your query. Don't include links to a Web page rather than a traditional query, and take the time to prepare a thorough but brief synopsis of the material. Make the effort to prepare a thoughtful analysis of comparison titles. How is your work different, yet would appeal to those same readers?"

N ✐ TDP LITERARY AGENCY & NOTARY

612 Ziegler Ave, Suite 16, Linden NJ 07036. (908)205-2793. Fax: (801)443-8968. E-mail: tdpliteraryagency@yahoo.com. Website: tdp-literaryagency.tripod.com/. **Contact:** Takesha D. McKenzie. Represents 15 clients. 50% of clients are new/unpublished writers. Currently handles: nonfiction books 25%, novels 75%.

How to Contact Query via e-mail only per guidelines on website. Include one-paragraph synopsis, one-paragraph bio, up to one sample chapter. No attachments. Responds in 4-6 weeks to queries. Responds in 6-8 weeks to mss. Obtains most clients through recommendations from others, solicitations, conferences.

Terms Agent receives 15% commission on domestic sales. Agent receives 20% commission on foreign sales. Offers written contract; 30-day notice must be given to terminate contract. This agency charges for postage and photocopying. Author is consulted before any charges are incurred.

Recent Sales *It's In the Rhythm,* by Sammie Ward (Genesis Press).

✐ TESSLER LITERARY AGENCY, LLC

27 W. 20th St., Suite 1003, New York NY 10011. (212)242-0466. Fax: (212)242-2366. E-mail: michelle@tessleragency.com. Website: www.tessleragency.com. **Contact:** Michelle Tessler. Member of AAR.

- Prior to forming her own agency, Ms. Tessler worked at Carlisle & Co. (now a part of Inkwell Management). She has also worked at the William Morris Agency and the Elaine Markson Literary Agency.

Represents Nonfiction books, novels.

- ⛏ "The Tessler Agency is a full-service boutique agency that represents writers of literary fiction and high quality nonfiction in the following categories: popular science, reportage, memoir, history, biography, psychology, business and travel."

How to Contact Submit query through website only.

N BENT AGENCY, THE

204 Park Place, Number 2, Brooklyn NY 11238. E-mail: info@thebentagency.com. Website: www.thebentagency.com. **Contact:** Jenny Bent. Estab. 2009.

- Prior to forming her own agency, Ms. Bent was an agent at Trident Media.

Member Agents Jenny Bent (all adult fiction except for science fiction); Susan Hawk (young adult and middle grade books; within the realm of kids stories, she likes fantasy, science fiction, historical fiction and mystery).

Represents Considers these fiction areas: commercial, crime, historical, horror, mystery, picture books, romance, suspense, thriller, women's, young adult.

How to Contact E-mail queries@thebentagency.com, or if you're writing for children or teens, kidsqueries@thebentagency.com. "Tell us briefly who you are, what your book is, and why you're the one to write it. Then include the first ten pages of your material in the body of your e-mail. We regret that we cannot respond to each and every query, although we do our best. Rest assured that we read each one and we will certainly follow-up when we have interest." Accepts simultaneous submissions.

Recent Sales *Worst Laid Plans,* by Laura Kindred and Alexandra Lydon; *The Dark Ink Chronicles,* by Elle Jasper; *What We Don't Tell,* by Desiree Washington.

N ✐ THE MCVEIGH AGENCY

345 West 21st Street, New York NY 10011. E-mail: queries@themcveighagency.com. Website: www.themcveighagency.com. **Contact:** Linda Epstein. Estab. 2009.

Represents Considers these nonfiction areas: biography, history, memoirs. **Considers these fiction areas:** commercial, crime, literary, mainstream, picture books, young adult, graphic novels, middle grade.

- ⛏ Actively seeking genre mashups, a book that combines two common but disparate themes and combines them to comic or dramatic effect. As far as MG and YA, this agency seeks everything, but especially scary books, historical steampunk, and books that would appeal to children of color.

How to Contact E-query. In the subject line of your e-mail, please write: "Query," then the type of manuscript (e.g. YA, MG, PB, adult, nonfiction), and then the title of your book. The body of your e-mail should consist of your query letter, followed by the first 20 pages of your manuscript (for fiction) or your full proposal (for nonfiction). Please do not add your manuscript as an attachment. If the agency is interested in reading more, they'll request that you e-mail the full manuscript.

ⓝ THE RIGHTS FACTORY

PO Box 499, Station C, Toronto Canada M6J 3P6. (416)966-5367.
Member Agents Sam Hiyate, Alisha Sevigny, Kelvin Kong, Ali McDonald.

○━ "The Rights Factory is an agency that deals in intellectual property rights to entertainment products, including books, comics & graphic novels, film, television, and video games. We license rights in every territory by representing three types of clients"

How to Contact There is a submission form on this agency's website.
Recent Sales *Beauty, Pure & Simple*, by Kristen Ma; *Why Mr. Right Can't Find You*, by J.M. Kearns; *Tout Sweet: Hanging Up My High Heels for a New Life in France*, by Karen Wheeler; *The Orange Code*, by Arkadi Kuhlmann and Bruce Philp.

ⓝ ⓐ THE STRINGER LITERARY AGENCY, LLC

E-mail: stringerlit@comcast.net. Website: www.stringerlit.com. **Contact:** Marlene Stringer.
Represents Considers these nonfiction areas: history, military, music, parenting, science, sports. **Considers these fiction areas:** fantasy, historical, mystery, romance, science fiction, thriller, women's, young adult.

○━ This agency specializes in fiction. Does not want to receive picture books, plays, short stories or poetry.

How to Contact E-query. Accepts simultaneous submissions.
Recent Sales *Bloodfeud*, *Hunt the Day* and *Stolen*, by Alyxandra Harvey (Walker Books); *Change of Heart*, by Shari Maurer (WestSide Books); *Zelda From the Stars*, by Gary Ghislain (Chronicle Books).
Tips "If your manuscript falls between categories, or you are not sure of the category, query and we'll let you know if we'd like to take a look. We strive to respond as quickly as possible. If you have not received a response in the time period indicated, please re-query."

ⓝ ⓐ THE UNTER AGENCY

310 W. 71st St., Ground floor, New York NY 10023. (212)579-5688. E-mail: jennifer@theunteragency. com. Website: www.theunteragency.com. **Contact:** Jennifer Unter. Estab. 2008.

• Ms. Unter began her book publishing career in the editorial department at Henry Holt & Co. She later worked at the Karpfinger Agency while she attended law school. She then became an associate at the entertainment firm of Cowan, DeBaets, Abrahams & Sheppard LLP where she practiced primarily in the areas of publishing and copyright law.

Represents Considers these nonfiction areas: biography, foods, memoirs, popular culture, nature subjects. **Considers these fiction areas:** commercial, mainstream, picture books, young adult.

○━ This agency specializes in children's and nonfiction, but does take some fiction.

How to Contact Send an e-query.

ⓐ THREE SEAS LITERARY AGENCY

P.O. Box 8571, Madison WI 53708. (608)221-4306. E-mail: queries@threeseaslit.com. Website: www.threeseaslit.com. **Contact:** Michelle Grajkowski, Cori Deyoe. Estab. 2000. Other memberships include RWA, Romance Writers of America Represents 55 clients. 10% of clients are new/ unpublished writers. Currently handles: nonfiction books 5%, novels 80%, juvenile books 15%.

• Since starting her agency, Ms. Grajkowski has sold more than 350 titles worldwide. Her authors have appeared on all the major lists including the *New York Times* and *USA Today*. Prior to joining the agency in 2006, Ms. Deyoe was a multi-published author. She represents a wide-range of authors and has sold many projects at auction.

Member Agents Michelle Grajkowski; Cori Deyoe.
Represents nonfiction, novels, juvenile.

○━ 3 Seas focuses primarily on romance (including contemporary, romantic suspense, paranormal, fantasy, historical and category), women's fiction, mysteries, nonfiction, young adult and children's stories. "Currently, we are looking for fantastic authors with a voice of their own." 3 Seas does not represent poetry, screenplays or novellas.

How to Contact E-mail queries only. For fiction titles, query with first chapter and synopsis embedded in the e-mail. For nonfiction, query with complete proposal attached. For picture books, query with complete text. Illustrations are not necessary. Accepts simultaneous submissions. Responds in 1 month to queries. Obtains most new clients through recommendations from others, conferences.

Terms Agent receives 15% commission on domestic sales. Agent receives 20% commission on foreign sales. Offers written contract.

Recent Sales Clients include New York Times Best-selling Authors: Katie MacAlister, Kerrelyn Sparks and C.L. Wilson. Other award-winning authors include: Alexis Morgan, Donna MacMeans, Anna DeStefano, Laura Marie Altom, Cathy McDavid, Trish Milburn, Winnie Griggs, Carla Capshaw, Lisa Mondello, Tricia Mills, Tracy Madison, Keri Mikulski, Lori McDonald, R. Barri Flowers, Jennifer Brown, Kristi Gold and Susan Gee Heino.

⊚ ANN TOBIAS: A LITERARY AGENCY FOR CHILDREN'S BOOKS

520 E. 84th St., Apt. 4L, New York NY 10028. E-mail: AnnTobias84@hotmail.com. **Contact:** Ann Tobias. Represents 25 clients. 10% of clients are new/unpublished writers. Currently handles: juvenile books 100%.

- Prior to opening her agency, Ms. Tobias worked as a children's book editor at Harper, William Morrow and Scholastic.

Represents juvenile and young adult. **Considers these nonfiction areas:** juvenile nonfiction, young adult. **Considers these fiction areas:** picture books, poetry, poetry in translation, young adult, illustrated mss; mid-level novels.

- ☛ This agency specializes in books for children.

How to Contact For all age groups and genres: Send a one-page letter of inquiry accompanied by a one-page writing sample, double-spaced. No attachments will be opened. Responds in 2 months to mss. Obtains most new clients through recommendations from editors.

Terms Agent receives 15% commission on domestic sales. Agent receives 20% commission on foreign sales. This agency charges clients for photocopying, overnight mail, foreign postage, foreign telephone.

Tips "Read at least 200 children's books in the age group and genre in which you hope to be published. Follow this by reading another 100 children's books in other age groups and genres so you will have a feel for the field as a whole."

⊡ ◖ TRANSATLANTIC LITERARY AGENCY

72 Glengowan Road, Toronto Ontario M4N 1G4 Canada. E-mail: info@tla1.com. Website: www. tla1.com. **Contact:** Lynn Bennett. Represents 250 clients. 10% of clients are new/unpublished writers. Currently handles: nonfiction books 30%, novels 15%, juvenile books 50%, textbooks 5%.

Member Agents Lynn Bennett, Lynn@tla1.com, (juvenile and young adult fiction); Shaun Bradley, Shaun@tla1.com (literary fiction and narrative nonfiction); Marie Campbell, Marie@tla1.com (literary juvenile and young adult fiction); Andrea Cascardi, Andrea@tla1.com (literary juvenile and young adult fiction); Samantha Haywood, Sam@tla1.com (literary fiction, narrative nonfiction and graphic novels); Don Sedgwick, Don@tla1.com (literary fiction and narrative nonfiction).

Represents Nonfiction books, novels, juvenile. **Considers these nonfiction areas:** autobiography, biography, business, current affairs, economics, environment. **Considers these fiction areas:** juvenile, literary, mainstream, mystery, suspense, young adult.

- ☛ "In both children's and adult literature, we market directly into the United States, the United Kingdom and Canada." Actively seeking literary children's and adult fiction, nonfiction. Does not want to receive picture books, poetry, screenplays or stage plays.

How to Contact Submit E-query with synopsis, 2 sample chapters, bio. Always refer to the website as guidelines will change. Responds in 2 weeks to queries. Obtains most new clients through recommendations from others.

Terms Agent receives 15% commission on domestic sales. Agent receives 20% commission on foreign sales. Offers written contract; 45-day notice must be given to terminate contract. This agency charges for photocopying and postage when it exceeds $100.

Recent Sales Sold 250 titles in the last year.

◖ TRIADA U.S. LITERARY AGENCY, INC.

P.O. Box 561, Sewickley PA 15143. (412)401-3376. E-mail: uwe@triadaus.com. Website: www.

triadaus.com. **Contact:** Dr. Uwe Stender. Member of AAR. Represents 65 clients. 20% of clients are new/unpublished writers.
Represents fiction, nonfiction. **Considers these nonfiction areas:** biography, business, cooking, diet/nutrition, economics, education, foods, health, how-to, memoirs, popular culture, science, sports, advice, relationships, lifestyle. **Considers these fiction areas:** action, adventure, crime, detective, ethnic, historical, horror, juvenile, literary, mainstream, mystery, occult, police, romance, women's, young adult.

> ⚬ "We are looking for great writing and story platforms. Our response time is fairly unique. We recognize that neither we nor the authors have time to waste, so we guarantee a 5-day response time. We usually respond within 24 hours." Actively looking for both fiction and nonfiction in all areas.

How to Contact E-mail queries preferred; otherwise query with SASE. Accepts simultaneous submissions. Responds in 1-5 weeks to queries. Responds in 2-6 weeks to mss. Obtains most new clients through recommendations from others, conferences.
Terms Agent receives 15% commission on domestic sales. Agent receives 20% commission on foreign sales. Offers written contract; 30-day notice must be given to terminate contract.
Recent Sales *Whatever Happened To Pudding Pops*, by Gael Fashingbauer Cooper and Brian Bellmont (Penguin/Perigee); *86'd*, by Dan Fante (Harper Perennial); *Hating Olivia*, by Mark SaFranko (Harper Perennial); *Everything I'm Not Made Me Everything I Am*, by Jeff Johnson (Smiley Books).
Tips "I comment on all requested manuscripts that I reject."

☑ TRIDENT MEDIA GROUP

41 Madison Ave., 36th Floor, New York NY 10010. (212)262-4810. Website: www.tridentmediagroup. com. **Contact:** Ellen Levine. Member of AAR.
Member Agents Kimberly Whalen, whalen.assistant@tridentmediagroup (commercial fiction and nonfiction, women's fiction, suspense, paranormal and pop culture); Eileen Cope, ecope@ tridentmediagroup.com (narrative nonfiction, history, biography, pop culture, health, literary fiction and short story collections); Scott Miller, smiller@tridentmediagroup.com (thrillers, crime, mystery, young adult, children's, narrative nonfiction, current events, military, memoir, literary fiction, graphic novels, pop culture); Alex Glass aglass@tridentmediagroup (thrillers, literary fiction, crime, middle grade, pop culture, young adult, humor and narrative nonfiction); Melissa Flashman, mflashman@tridentmediagroup.com (narrative nonfiction, serious nonfiction, pop culture, lifstyle); Alyssa Henkin, ahenkin@tridentmediagroup.com (juvenile, children's, YA); Stephanie Maclean (Romance, Women's Fiction and Young Adult); Don Fehr (literary and commercial novelists, narrative nonfiction, memoirs, biography, travel, as well as science/medical/ health related titles); Alanna Ramirez (literary fiction, narrative nonfiction, memoir, pop culture, food and wine, and lifestyle books); John Silbersack (commercial and literary fiction, science fiction and fantasy, narrative nonfiction, young adult, and thrillers).
Represents Nonfiction books, novels, short story collections, juvenile. **Considers these nonfiction areas:** autobiography, biography, current affairs, government, humor, law, memoirs, military, multicultural, popular culture, politics, true crime, war, women's issues, women's studies, young adult. **Considers these fiction areas:** crime, detective, humor, juvenile, literary, military, multicultural, mystery, police, short story collections, suspense, thriller, women's, young adult.

> ⚬ Actively seeking new or established authors in a variety of fiction and nonfiction genres.

How to Contact Query with SASE or via e-mail. Check website for more details.
Tips "If you have any questions, please check FAQ page before e-mailing us."

Ⓝ ☑ UPSTART CROW LITERARY

P.O. Box 25404, Brooklyn NY 11202. E-mail: michael (at) upstartcrowliterary (dot) com. Website: www.upstartcrowliterary.com. **Contact:** Michael Stearns. Estab. 2009.
Member Agents Michael Stearns; Chris Richman (special interest in books for boys, books with unforgettable characters, and fantasy that doesn't take itself too seriously); Danielle Chiotti (books ranging from contemporary women's fiction to narrative nonfiction, from romance to relationship stories, humorous tales and young adult fiction); Ted Malawer (accepting queries only through conference submissions and client referrals).
Represents Considers these fiction areas: women's, young adult, middle grade.

How to Contact This agency likes submissions sent through its online form, rather than e-mails to agents.

☐ VANGUARD LITERARY AGENCY

81 E. Jefryn Blvd., Suite E, Deer Park NY 11729. (718)710-3662. Fax: (917)591-7088. E-mail: sandylu@ vanguardliterary.com; sandy@lperkinsagency.com. Website: www.vanguardliterary.com. **Contact:** Sandy Lu. Represents 15 clients. 60% of clients are new/unpublished writers. Currently handles: nonfiction books 20%, novels 80%.

- Prior to becoming an agent, Ms. Lu held managerial positions in commercial theater. "Ms. Lu is also an associate agent at the L. Perkins Agency. Please only send queries to one of her e-mail addresses."

Represents Nonfiction books, novels, short story collections, novellas. **Considers these nonfiction areas:** anthropology, archeology, autobiography, biography, cooking, cultural interests, diet/ nutrition, ethnic, foods, gay/lesbian, history, investigative, memoirs, music, popular culture, psychology, science, sociology, technology, translation, true crime, women's issues, women's studies. **Considers these fiction areas:** action, adventure, confession, crime, detective, ethnic, historical, horror, humor, literary, mainstream, mystery, police, regional, short story collections, suspense, thriller, women's, urban fantasy.

- ⚷ "Very few agents in the business still edit their clients' manuscripts, especially when it comes to fiction. Vanguard Literary Agency is different. I care about the quality of my clients' works and will not send anything out to publishers without personally going through each page first to ensure that when the manuscript is sent out, it is in the best possible shape." Actively seeking literary and commercial fiction with a unique voice. Does not want to receive movie or TV scripts, stage plays or poetry; unwanted fiction genres include science fiction/fantasy, Western, YA, children's; unwanted nonfiction genres include self-help, how-to, parenting, sports, dating/relationship, military/war, religion/spirituality, New Age, gift books.

How to Contact Only accepts e-mail queries. No fax queries. Accepts simultaneous submissions. Responds in 2 weeks to queries. Responds in 6-8 weeks to mss. Obtains most new clients through recommendations from others, solicitations, conferences.

Terms Agent receives 15% commission on domestic sales. Agent receives 20% commission on foreign sales. Offers written contract, binding for 1 year; 30-day notice must be given to terminate contract. This agency charges for photocopying and postage, and discusses larger costs (in excess of $100) with authors prior to charging.

Tips "Do your research. Do not query an agent for a genre he or she does not represent. Personalize your query letter. Start with an interesting hook. Learn how to write a succinct yet interesting synopsis or proposal."

☑ RALPH M. VICINANZA LTD.

303 W. 18th St., New York NY 10011. (212)924-7090. Fax: (212)691-9644. Member of AAR.

Member Agents Ralph M. Vicinanza; Chris Lotts; Christopher Schelling, Matthew Mahoney.

How to Contact This agency takes on new clients by professional recommendation only.

Terms Agent receives 15% commission on domestic sales. Agent receives 20% commission on foreign sales.

☑ WALES LITERARY AGENCY, INC.

P.O. Box 9426, Seattle WA 98109-0426. (206)284-7114. E-mail: waleslit@waleslit.com. Website: www.waleslit.com. **Contact:** Elizabeth Wales, Neal Swain. Member of AAR. Other memberships include Book Publishers' Northwest, Pacific Northwest Booksellers Association, PEN. Represents 60 clients. 10% of clients are new/unpublished writers. Currently handles: nonfiction books 60%, novels 40%.

- Prior to becoming an agent, Ms. Wales worked at Oxford University Press and Viking Penguin.

Member Agents Elizabeth Wales; Neal Swain.

- ⚷ This agency specializes in quality fiction and nonfiction. Does not handle screenplays, children's literature, genre fiction, or most category nonfiction.

How to Contact Accepts queries sent with cover letter and SASE, and e-mail queries with no attachments. No phone or fax queries. Accepts simultaneous submissions. Responds in 2 weeks to queries, 2 months to mss.

Terms Agent receives 15% commission on domestic sales. Agent receives 20% commission on foreign sales.

Recent Sales *The Dirty Doll Diaries,* A novel by Cinthia Ritchie (Grand Central/Hachette, 2011); *Heat: A Natural and Unnatural History,* by Bill Streever (Little, Brown, 2012); *Cheesemonger: A Life on the Wedge, by Gordon Edgar (Chelsea Green, 2010); Special Exits: My Parents,* A Memoir by Joyce Farmer (Fantagraphics, 2010); *Unterzakhn: A Graphic Novel,* by Leela Corman (Schocken/Pantheon, 2010).

Writers Conferences Pacific Northwest Writers Conference, annually; and others.

Tips "We are especially interested in work that espouses a progressive cultural or political view, projects a new voice, or simply shares an important, compelling story. We also encourage writers living in the Pacific Northwest, West Coast, Alaska, and Pacific Rim countries, and writers from historically underrepresented groups, such as gay and lesbian writers and writers of color, to submit work (but does not discourage writers outside these areas). Most importantly, whether in fiction or nonfiction, the agency is looking for talented storytellers."

CHRISTINA WARD LITERARY AGENCY

PO Box 7144, Lowell MA 01852. (978)656-8389. E-mail: christinawardlit@mac.com.

Represents books and proposals, and novels. **Considers these nonfiction areas:** biography, health, history, medicine, memoirs, nature, alternative and "green" lifestyle, psychology, science, literary nonfiction, including narrative nonfiction. **Considers these fiction areas:** literary, mystery, suspense, thriller.

☑ JOHN A. WARE LITERARY AGENCY

392 Central Park W., New York NY 10025-5801. (212)866-4733. Fax: (212)866-4734. **Contact:** John Ware. Represents 60 clients. 40%% of clients are new/unpublished writers. Currently handles: nonfiction books 75%, novels 25%.

- Prior to opening his agency, Mr. Ware served as a literary agent with James Brown Associates/Curtis Brown, Ltd., and as an editor for Doubleday.

Represents Nonfiction books, novels. **Considers these nonfiction areas:** Americana, anthropology, biography, current affairs, history, investigative journalism sports, language, music, nature, popular culture, psychology (academic credentials required), true crime, women's issues, social commentary, folklore. **Considers these fiction areas:** detective, mystery, thriller, accessible literary noncategory fiction.

- Does not want personal memoirs.

How to Contact Query with SASE. Send a letter only. Responds in 2 weeks to queries.

Terms Agent receives 15% commission on domestic sales, 20% commission on foreign sales, film. Charges clients for courier and messenger service and photocopying.

Recent Sales *Where Men Win Glory: The Odyssey of Pat Tillman,* by Jon Krakauer (Doubleday); *Abundance of Valor* (military history), by Will Irwin (Ballantine); *Velva Jean Learns to Drive* (novel), by Jennifer Niven (Plume); *The Art of the Game* (basketball), by Chris Ballard (Sports Illustrated/Simon & Schuster); *The Aquanet Diaries: Big Hair, Big Dreams, Small Town* (high school memoir), by Jennifer Niven (Gallery); *Spent: A Memoir of Shopaholism,* by Avis Cardella (Little, Brown); *To Kill a Page: A Memoir of Becoming Literate,* by Travis Hugh Culley (Random House); *The Pledge (of Allegiance),* by Jeffrey Jones and Peter Mayer (Thomas Dunne/St. Martin's Press); Conversions (religious), by Craig Harline (Yale).

Tips "Writers must have appropriate credentials for authorship of proposal (nonfiction); no publishing track record required. I am open to good writing and interesting ideas by new or veteran writers."

◐ WATKINS LOOMIS AGENCY, INC.

P.O. Box 20925, New York NY 10025. (212)532-0080. Fax: (646)383-2448. Website: www.watkinsloomis.com/. Estab. 1980. Represents 50+ clients.

Member Agents Gloria Loomis, president, Julia Masnik, junior agent.

Represents nonfiction, novels, short story collections. **Considers these nonfiction areas:** autobiography, biography, cultural interests, current affairs, environment, ethnic, history, popular culture, technology, investigative journalism. **Considers these fiction areas:** literary, short story collections.

- This agency specializes in literary fiction and nonfiction.

How to Contact *No unsolicited mss.* This agency does not guarantee a response to queries.

Terms Agent receives 15% commission on domestic sales. Agent receives 20% commission on foreign sales.

◙ WAXMAN LITERARY AGENCY, INC.

80 Fifth Ave., Suite 1101, New York NY 10011. Website: www.waxmanagency.com. **Contact:** Scott Waxman. Represents 60 clients. 50% of clients are new/unpublished writers. Currently handles: nonfiction books 80%, novels 20%.

- Prior to opening his agency, Mr. Waxman was an editor at HarperCollins.

Member Agents Scott Waxman (all categories of nonfiction, commercial fiction-specifically suspense/thriller), Byrd Leavell, Farley Chase, Holly Root.

Represents Considers these nonfiction areas: prescriptive, historical, sports, narrative, pop culture, humor, memoir, biography, celebrity. **Considers these fiction areas:** literary, contemporary, commercial, young adult.

- ⊶ We're looking for new novelists with non-published works.

How to Contact Please visit our website at www.waxmanagency.com. Accepts simultaneous submissions.

Terms Agent receives 15% commission on domestic sales. Agent receives 10% commission on foreign sales. Offers written contract; 2-month notice must be given to terminate contract.

Ⓝ ◙ WEED LITERARY

27 West 20th St., New York NY 10011. E-mail: stephanie@weedliterary.com. Website: www. weedliterary.com. **Contact:** Elisabeth Weed. Estab. 2007.

- Prior to forming her own agency, Ms. Weed was an agent at Curtis Brown and Trident Media Group.

Represents nonfiction, fiction, novels. **Considers these fiction areas:** literary, women's.

- ⊶ This agency specializes in upmarket women's fiction. Does not want to receive picture books, mysteries, thrillers, romance or military.

How to Contact Send a query letter.

Recent Sales *Life Without Summer*, by Lynne Griffin (St. Martin's Press); *Time of My Life*, by Allison Winn Scotch (Shaye Areheart Books); and *The Last Will of Moira Leahy*, by Therese Walsh (Shaye Areheart Books).

Writers Conferences Muse and the Marketplace (Boston, annual).

◙ CHERRY WEINER LITERARY AGENCY

28 Kipling Way, Manalapan NJ 07726-3711. (732)446-2096. Fax: (732)792-0506. E-mail: cherry8486@ aol.com. **Contact:** Cherry Weiner. Represents 40 clients. 10% of clients are new/unpublished writers. Currently handles: nonfiction books 10-20%, novels 80-90%.

Represents Nonfiction books, novels. **Considers these nonfiction areas:** self-help. **Considers these fiction areas:** action, adventure, contemporary issues, crime, detective, family saga, fantasy, frontier, historical, mainstream, mystery, police, psychic, romance, science fiction, supernatural, thriller, westerns.

- ⊶ *This agency is currently not accepting new clients except by referral or by personal contact at writers' conferences.* Specializes in fantasy, science fiction, Western's, mysteries (both contemporary and historical), historical novels, Native-American works, mainstream and all genre romances.

How to Contact Query with SASE. Prefers to read materials exclusively. Responds in 1 week to queries. Responds in 2 months to mss.

Terms Agent receives 15% commission on domestic sales. Agent receives 15% commission on foreign sales. Offers written contract. Charges clients for extra copies of mss, first-class postage for author's copies of books, express mail for important documents/mss.

Recent Sales Sold 60 titles in the last year. This agency prefers not to share information on specific sales.

Tips "Meet agents and publishers at conferences. Establish a relationship, then get in touch with them and remind them of the meeting and conference."

◙ THE WEINGEL-FIDEL AGENCY

310 E. 46th St., 21E, New York NY 10017. (212)599-2959. **Contact:** Loretta Weingel-Fidel. Currently handles: nonfiction books 75%, novels 25%.

- Prior to opening her agency, Ms. Weingel-Fidel was a psychoeducational diagnostician.

Represents Nonfiction books, novels. **Considers these nonfiction areas:** art, autobiography, biography, dance, memoirs, music, psychology, science, sociology, technology, women's issues, women's studies, investigative journalism. **Considers these fiction areas:** literary, mainstream.

> ⚷ This agency specializes in commercial and literary fiction and nonfiction. Actively seeking investigative journalism. Does not want to receive genre fiction, self-help, science fiction, or fantasy.

How to Contact Accepts writers by referral only. *No unsolicited mss.*

Terms Agent receives 15% commission on domestic sales. Agent receives 20% commission on foreign sales. Offers written contract, binding for 1 year with automatic renewal. Bills sent back to clients are all reasonable expenses, such as UPS, express mail, photocopying, etc.

Tips "A very small, selective list enables me to work very closely with my clients to develop and nurture talent. I only take on projects and writers about which I am extremely enthusiastic."

◙ TED WEINSTEIN LITERARY MANAGEMENT

307 Seventh Ave., Suite 2407, Dept. GLA, New York NY 10001. Website: www.twliterary.com. **Contact:** Ted Weinstein. Member of AAR. Represents 75 clients. 50% of clients are new/unpublished writers. Currently handles: nonfiction books 100%.

Represents Considers these nonfiction areas: biography, business, current affairs, economics, government, health, history, investigative, law, medicine, popular culture, politics, science, self-help, technology, travel, true crime, lifestyle, narrative journalism, popular science.

How to Contact Please visit website for detailed guidelines before submitting. E-mail queries **only**. Other Responds in 3 weeks to queries.

Terms Agent receives 15% commission on domestic sales. Agent receives 20% commission on foreign sales. Agent receives 20% commission on film sales. Offers written contract, binding for 1 year. Charges clients for photocopying and express shipping.

Tips "Accepts e-mail queries ONLY; paper submissions are discarded. See agency's website (www.twliterary.com) for full guidelines."

◙ LARRY WEISSMAN LITERARY, LLC

526 8th St., #2R, Brooklyn NY **Contact:** Larry Weissman. Represents 35 clients. Currently handles: nonfiction books 80%, novels 10%, story collections 10%.

Represents Nonfiction books, novels, short story collections. **Considers these fiction areas:** literary.

> ⚷ "Very interested in established journalists with bold voices. Interested in anything to do with food. Fiction has to feel 'vital' and short stories are accepted, but only if you can sell us on an idea for a novel as well." Nonfiction, including food & lifestyle, politics, pop culture, narrative, cultural/social issues, journalism. No genre fiction, poetry or children's.

How to Contact Send e-queries only. If you don't hear back, your project was not right for our list.

Terms Agent receives 15% commission on domestic sales. Agent receives 20% commission on foreign sales.

◻ WHIMSY LITERARY AGENCY, LLC

New York/Los Angeles E-mail: whimsynyc@aol.com. **Contact:** Jackie Meyer. Other memberships include Center for Independent Publishing Advisory Board. Represents 30 clients. 20% of clients are new/unpublished writers. Currently handles: nonfiction books 100%.

- Prior to becoming an agent, Ms. Meyer was with Warner Books for 19 years; Ms. Vezeris and Ms. Legette have 30 years experience at various book publishers.

Member Agents Jackie Meyer; Olga Vezeris (fiction and nonfiction); Nansci LeGette, senior associate in LA.

Represents Nonfiction books. **Considers these nonfiction areas:** agriculture, art, biography, business, child guidance, cooking, education, health, history, horticulture, how-to, humor, interior design, memoirs, money, New Age, popular culture, psychology, religious, self-help, true crime, women's issues, women's studies. **Considers these fiction areas:** mainstream, religious, thriller, women's.

○━ "Whimsy looks for projects that are concept- and platform-driven. We seek books that educate, inspire and entertain." Actively seeking experts in their field with good platforms.

How to Contact Send a query letter via e-mail. Send a synopsis, bio, platform and proposal. No snail mail submissions. Responds "quickly, but only if interested" to queries. Obtains most new clients through recommendations from others, solicitations.

Terms Agent receives 15% commission on domestic sales. Agent receives 20% commission on foreign sales. Offers written contract. Charges for posting and photocopying.

☐ WOLFSON LITERARY AGENCY

P.O. Box 266, New York NY 10276. E-mail: query@wolfsonliterary.com. Website: www. wolfsonliterary.com/. **Contact:** Michelle Wolfson. Other memberships include Adheres to AAR canon of ethics. Currently handles: nonfiction books 70%, novels 30%.

- Prior to forming her own agency, Michelle spent two years with Artists & Artisans, Inc. and two years with Ralph Vicinanza, Ltd.

Represents Nonfiction books, novels. **Considers these nonfiction areas:** business, child guidance, economics, health, how-to, humor, medicine, memoirs, parenting, popular culture, satire, self-help, women's issues, women's studies. **Considers these fiction areas:** action, adventure, crime, detective, family saga, mainstream, mystery, police, romance, suspense, thriller, women's, young adult.

○━ Actively seeking commercial fiction, mainstream, mysteries, thrillers, suspense, women's fiction, romance, YA, practical nonfiction (particularly of interest to women), advice, medical, pop culture, humor, business.

How to Contact E-queries only! Accepts simultaneous submissions. Responds only if interested. Positive response is generally given within 2-4 weeks. Responds in 3 months to mss. Obtains most new clients through recommendations from others, solicitations.

Terms Agent receives 15% commission on domestic sales. Agent receives 25% commission on foreign sales. Offers written contract; 30-day notice must be given to terminate contract.

Writers Conferences SDSU Writers' Conference; New Jersey Romance Writers of America Writers' Conference; American Independent Writers Conference in Washington DC.

Tips "Be persistent."

☑ WOLGEMUTH & ASSOCIATES, INC

8600 Crestgate Circle, Orlando FL 32819. (407)909-9445. Fax: (407)909-9446. E-mail: ewolgemuth@ wolgemuthandassociates.com. **Contact:** Erik Wolgemuth. Member of AAR. Represents 60 clients. 10% of clients are new/unpublished writers. Currently handles: nonfiction books 90%, novella 2%, juvenile books 5%, multimedia 3%.

- "We have been in the publishing business since 1976, having been a marketing executive at a number of houses, a publisher, an author, and a founder and owner of a publishing company."

Member Agents Robert D. Wolgemuth; Andrew D. Wolgemuth; Erik S. Wolgemuth.

Represents Material used by Christian families.

○━ "We are not considering any new material at this time."

Terms Agent receives 15% commission on domestic sales. Offers written contract, binding for 2-3 years; 30-day notice must be given to terminate contract.

☑ ◎ WORDSERVE LITERARY GROUP

10152 S. Knoll Circle, Highlands Ranch CO 80130. (303)471-6675. Website: www.wordserveliterary. com. **Contact:** Greg Johnson; Rachelle Gardner. Represents 100 clients. 20% of clients are new/ unpublished writers. Currently handles: nonfiction books 50%, novels 35%, juvenile books 10%, multimedia 5%.

- Prior to becoming an agent in 1994, Mr. Johnson was a magazine editor and freelance writer of more than 20 books and 200 articles.

Member Agents Greg Johnson; Rachelle Gardner; Caleb Seeling.

Represents **Considers these nonfiction areas:** biography, child guidance, inspirational, memoirs, parenting, self-help. **Considers these fiction areas:** historical, inspirational, mainstream, spiritual, suspense, thriller, women's.

☞ Materials with a faith-based angle.

How to Contact Please address queries to: admin@wordserveliterary.com. In the subject line, include the word "query." All queries should include the following three elements: a pitch for the book, information about you and your platform (for nonfiction) or writing background (for fiction), and the first 5 (or so) pages of the manuscript pasted into the e-mail. Accepts simultaneous submissions. Responds in 4 weeks to queries. Responds in 2 months to mss. Obtains most new clients through recommendations from others.

Terms Agent receives 15% commission on domestic sales. Agent receives 10-15% commission on foreign sales. Offers written contract; up to 60-day notice must be given to terminate contract.

Recent Sales Sold 1,500 titles in the last 15 years. *Redemption* series, by Karen Kingsbury (Tyndale); *Loving God Up Close*, by Calvin Miller (Warner Faith); *Christmas in My Heart,* by Joe Wheeler (Tyndale). Other clients include Doug Fields, Wanda Dyson, Catherine Martin, David Murrow, Leslie Haskin, Gilbert Morris, Robert Wise, Jim Burns, Wayne Cordeiro, Denise George, Susie Shellenberger, Tim Smith, Athol Dickson, Patty Kirk, John Shore, Marcus Bretherton, Rick Johnson.

Tips "We are looking for good proposals, great writing, and authors willing to market their books, as appropriate. Also, we're only looking for projects with a faith element bent. See the website before submitting."

⊘ YATES & YATES

1100 Town & Country Road, Suite 1300, Orange CA 92868. Website: www.yates2.com. Represents 60 clients.

Represents Nonfiction books, novels. **Considers these nonfiction areas:** animals, autobiography, biography, business, current affairs, dance, economics, gay/lesbian, government, health, history, how-to, investigative, language, law, literature, medicine, memoirs, money, music, politics, psychology, science, self-help, sports, technology, true crime, women's issues, women's studies. **Considers these fiction areas:** contemporary issues, crime, detective, ethnic, feminist, gay, historical, lesbian, literary, mainstream, mystery, police, regional, religious, suspense, thriller.

Recent Sales *No More Mondays*, by Dan Miller (Doubleday Currency).

☑ ZACHARY SHUSTER HARMSWORTH

1776 Broadway, Suite 1405, New York NY 10019. (212)765-6900. Fax: (212)765-6490. E-mail: kfleury@zshliterary.com. Website: www.zshliterary.com. **Contact:** Kathleen Fleury. Alternate address: 535 Boylston St., 11th Floor. (617)262-2400. Fax: (617)262-2468. Represents 125 clients. 20%% of clients are new/unpublished writers. Currently handles: nonfiction books 45%, novels 45%, story collections 5%, scholarly books 5%.

• Our principals include two former publishing and entertainment lawyers, a journalist, and an editor/agent. Lane Zachary was an editor at Random House before becoming an agent.

Member Agents Esmond Harmsworth (commercial mysteries, literary fiction, history, science, adventure, business); Todd Shuster (narrative and prescriptive nonfiction, biography, memoirs); Lane Zachary (biography, memoirs, literary fiction); Jennifer Gates (literary fiction, nonfiction); Colleen Rafferty; Janet Silver; Mary Beth Chappell; Joanne Wyckoff. You can e-mail any agent on the website online form.

Represents Nonfiction books, novels. **Considers these nonfiction areas:** animals, autobiography, biography, business, current affairs, economics, gay/lesbian, government, health, history, how-to, investigative, language, law, literature, memoirs, money, music, politics, psychology, science, self-help, sports, technology, true crime, women's issues, women's studies. **Considers these fiction areas:** detective, ethnic, feminist, gay, historical, lesbian, literary, mainstream, mystery, suspense, thriller.

☞ This agency is still no longer accepting unsolicited work. Check the website for updated info.

How to Contact *Cannot accept unsolicited submissions.* Query with SASE. Obtains most new clients through recommendations from others.

Terms Agent receives 15% commission on domestic sales. Agent receives 20% commission on foreign sales. Offers written contract, binding for 1 work only; 30-day notice must be given to terminate contract.

⦿ KAREN GANTZ ZAHLER LITERARY MANAGEMENT AND ATTORNEY AT LAW

860 Fifth Ave., Suite 7J, New York NY 10065. (212)734-3619. E-mail: karen@karengantzlit.com. Website: www.karengantzlit.com. **Contact:** Karen Gantz Zahler. Currently handles: nonfiction books 95%, novels 5%, film, TV scripts.

- Prior to her current position, Ms. Gantz Zahler practiced law at two law firms, wrote two cookbooks, *Taste of New York* (Addison-Wesley) and *Superchefs* (John Wiley & Sons). She also participated in a Presidential Advisory Committee on Intellectual Property, U.S. Department of Commerce. She currently chairs Literary and Media Committee at Harmone Club NYC.

Represents Nonfiction books, novels, very selective.

- ⚲ "We are hired for two purposes, one as lawyers to negotiate publishing agreements, option agreements and other entertainment deals and two as literary agents to help in all aspects of the publishing field. Ms. Gantz is both a literary agent and a literary property lawyer. Thus, her firm involves themselves in all stages of a book's development, including the collaboration agreement with the writer, advice regarding the book proposal, presentations to the publisher, negotiations including the legal work for the publishing agreement and other rights to be negotiated, and work with the publisher and public relations firm so that the book gets the best possible media coverage. We do extensive manuscript reviews for a few." Actively seeking nonfiction. "We assist with speaking engagements and publicity."

How to Contact Accepting queries and summaries by e-mail only. Check the website for complete submission information. Responds in 4 weeks to queries. Obtains most new clients through recommendations from others, solicitations.

Recent Sales *A Promise to Ourselves,* by Alec Baldwin (St. Martin's Press 2008); *Take the Lead, Lady! Kathleen Turner's Life Lessons,* by Kathleen Turner in collaboration with Gloria Feldt (Springboard Press 2007); *Tales of a Neo-Con*, by Benjamin Wattenberg (Tom Dunne 2008); *Beyond Control*, by Nancy Friday (Sourcebooks 2009); more sales can be found online.

Tips "Our dream client is someone who is a professional writer and a great listener. What writers can do to increase the likelihood of our retainer is to write an excellent summary and provide a great marketing plan for their proposal in an excellent presentation. Any typos or grammatical mistakes do not resonate well. If we want to review your project, we will ask you to send a copy by snail mail with an envelope and return postage enclosed. We don't call people unless we have something to report.

⦿ SUSAN ZECKENDORF ASSOC., INC.

171 W. 57th St., New York NY 10019. (212)245-2928. **Contact:** Susan Zeckendorf. Estab. 1979. Member of AAR. Represents 15 clients. 25% of clients are new/unpublished writers. Currently handles: nonfiction books 50%, novels 50%.

- Prior to opening her agency, Ms. Zeckendorf was a counseling psychologist.

Represents Nonfiction books, novels. **Considers these nonfiction areas:** biography, child guidance, health, history, medicine, music, parenting, psychology, sociology, technology, women's issues, women's studies. **Considers these fiction areas:** crime, detective, ethnic, historical, literary, mainstream, mystery, police, suspense, thriller.

- ⚲ Actively seeking mysteries, literary fiction, mainstream fiction, thrillers, social history, classical music, and biography. Does not want to receive science fiction, romance, or children's books.

How to Contact Query with SASE. No emai or fax. Accepts simultaneous submissions. Responds in 10 days to queries. Responds in 3 weeks to mss.

Terms Agent receives 15% commission on domestic sales. Agent receives 20% commission on foreign sales. Charges for photocopying and messenger services.

Writers Conferences Frontiers in Writing Conference; Oklahoma Festival of Books.

Tips "We are a small agency giving lots of individual attention. We respond quickly to submissions."

⦿ HELEN ZIMMERMANN LITERARY AGENCY

3 Emmy Lane, New Paltz NY 12561. (845)256-0977. Fax: (845)256-0979. E-mail: helen@zimmagency.com. Website: www.zimmermannliterary.com. **Contact:** Helen Zimmermann. Estab. 2003. Represents 25 clients. 50% of clients are new/unpublished writers. Currently handles: nonfiction books 80%, other 20% fiction.

- Prior to opening her agency, Ms. Zimmermann was the director of advertising and promotion at Random House and the events coordinator at an independent bookstore.

Represents Nonfiction books, novels. **Considers these nonfiction areas:** animals, child guidance, diet/nutrition, how-to, humor, memoirs, popular culture, sports. **Considers these fiction areas:** family saga, historical, literary, mystery, suspense.

- ⚬⇥ "As an agent who has experience at both a publishing house and a bookstore, I have a keen insight for viable projects. This experience also helps me ensure every client gets published well, through the whole process." Actively seeking memoirs, pop culture, women's issues and accessible literary fiction. Does not want to receive horror, science fiction, poetry or romance.

How to Contact Accepts e-mail queries only. E-mail should include a short description of project and bio, whether it be fiction or nonfiction. Accepts simultaneous submissions. Responds in 2 weeks to queries. Responds in 1 month to mss. Obtains most new clients through recommendations from others, solicitations.

Terms Agent receives 15% commission on domestic sales. Offers written contract; 30-day notice must be given to terminate contract. Charges for photocopying and postage (reimbursed if project is sold).

Recent Sales *She Bets Her Life: Women and Gambling*, by Mary Sojourner (Seal Press); *Seeds: One Man's Quest to Preserve the Trees of America's Mot Famous People*, by Rick Horan (HarperCollins); *Saddled*, by Susan Richards (Houghton Mifflin Harcourt); *Final Target*, by Steven Gore (HarperPerennial); *Liberated Body, Captive Mind: A WWII POW Memoir*, by Normal Bussel (Pegasus Books).

Writers Conferences BEA/Writer's Digest Books Writers' Conference, Portland, ME Writers Conference, Berkshire Writers and Readers Conference

☐ RENEE ZUCKERBROT LITERARY AGENCY

115 West 29th St., Third Floor, New York NY 10001. (212)967-0072. Fax: (212)967-0073. E-mail: submissions@rzagency.com. Website: rzagency.com. **Contact:** Renee Zuckerbrot. Member of AAR. Represents 30 clients. Currently handles: novels, other 30& nonfiction and 70% fiction.

- Prior to becoming an agent, Ms. Zuckerbrot worked as an editor at Doubleday as well as in the editorial department at Putnam.

Represents Nonfiction books, novels, short story collections.

- ⚬⇥ Literary fiction, short story collections, mysteries, thrillers, women's fiction, slipstream/ speculative, narrative nonfiction (focusing on science, history and pop culture). No business books, self-help, spirituality or romance. No screenplays.

How to Contact Query by mail, e-mail at: submissions@rzagency.com. Include a description of your manuscript or proposal. Include your publishing history, if applicable. Include a brief personal bio. Include a SASE or an e-mail address. Accepts simultaneous submissions. Responds in 4 weeks.

Terms Agent receives 15% commission on domestic sales. Agent receives 25% commission on foreign sales.

Recent Sales *Pretty Monster*, by Kelly Link (Penguin); *Manhattan Primeval*, by Eric Sanderson (Abrams); *Everything Asian*, by Sung Woo (Dunne/St. Martin's); *The Dart League King*, by Keith Lee Morris (Tin House); *Pleasure Bound: Victorian Sex Rebels and the New Eroticism* by Deborah Lutz (W.W. Norton)]; *Clinton St. Baking Company Cookbook: Breakfast, Brunch and Beyond from New York's Favorite Neighborhood Restaurant*, by DeDe Lahman & Neil Kleinberg (Little Brown).

Conferences

Attending a writers' conference that includes agents gives you the opportunity to learn more about what agents do as well as pitching agents in person. Ideally, a conference should include a panel or two with a number of agents to give writers a sense of the variety of personalities and tastes of different agents.

Not all agents are alike: Some are more personable, and sometimes you simply click better with one agent versus another. When only one agent attends a conference, there is a tendency for every writer at that conference to think, "Ah, this is the agent I've been looking for!" When the number of agents attending is larger, you have a wider group from which to choose, and you may have less competition for the agent's time.

Besides including panels of agents discussing what representation means and how to go about securing it, many of these gatherings also include time—either scheduled or impromptu—to meet briefly with an agent to discuss your work.

If they're impressed with what they see and hear about your work, they will invite you to submit a query, a proposal, a few sample chapters, or possibly your entire manuscript. Some conferences even arrange for agents to review manuscripts in advance and schedule one-on-one sessions during which you can receive specific feedback or advice regarding your work. Such meetings may cost a small fee, but the input you receive is usually worth the price.

Ask writers who attend conferences and they'll tell you that, at the very least, you'll walk away with new knowledge about the industry. At the very best, you'll receive an invitation to send your material to an agent (or several)!

Many writers try to make it to at least one conference a year, but cost and location can count as much as subject matter when determining which one to attend. There are conferences in almost every state and province that can provide answers to your questions about writing and the publishing industry. Conferences also connect you with a community of other writers. Such connections help you learn about the pros and cons of different agents, and they can also give you a renewed sense of purpose and direction in your own writing. (For more information, consult this book's article on conferences on page 64.)

SUBHEADS

Each listing is divided into subheads to make locating specific information easier. In the first section, you'll find contact information for conference contacts. You'll also learn conference dates, specific focus, and the average number of attendees. Finally, names of agents who will be speaking or have spoken in the past are listed along with details about their availability during the conference. Calling or e-mailing a conference director to verify the names of agents in attendance is always a good idea.

Costs: Looking at the price of events, plus room and board, may help writers on a tight budget narrow their choices.

Accommodations: Here conferences list overnight accommodations and travel information. Often conferences held in hotels will reserve rooms at a discount rate and may provide a shuttle bus to and from the local airport.

Additional Information: This section includes information on conference-sponsored contests, individual meetings, the availability of brochures, and more.

Quick Reference Icons

At the beginning of some listings, you will find one or more of the following symbols:

  Conference new to this edition

  Canadian conference

  International conference

Find a pull-out bookmark with a key to symbols on the inside cover of this book.

AMERICAN INDEPENDENT WRITERS (AIW) SPRING WRITERS CONFERENCE

1001 Connecticut Ave. NW, Suite 701, Washington DC 20036. (202)775-5150. Fax: (202)775-5810. E-mail: info@amerindywriters.org. Website: www.amerindywriters.org. **Contact:** Taryn Carrino. Estab. 1975. Annual conference held in June. Average attendance: 350. Focuses on fiction, nonfiction, screenwriting, poetry, children's writing, and technical writing. Gives participants the chance to hear from and talk with dozens of experts on book and magazine publishing, as well as on the craft, tools, and business of writing. Speakers have included Erica Jong, John Barth, Kitty Kelley, Vanessa Leggett, Diana McLellan, Brian Lamb, and Stephen Hunter. New York and local agents attend the conference.

Additional Information See the website or send a SASE in mid-February for brochures/guidelines and fees information.

ANHINGA WRITERS' STUDIO WORKSHOPS

P.O. Box 357154, Gainesville FL 32635. (352) 379-8782. Fax: (352) 380-0018. E-mail: info@anhingawriters.org. Website: www.anhingawriters.org. Estab. 1997. Formerly *Writing the Region*. Annual conference held in summer. Conference duration: 4 days. Average attendance: 250. Conference concentrates on fiction, narrative non-fiction, poetry, and consultations with agents, edtitors, and publishers.

Costs available online. Lower costs for half-day and one-day registration.

ASJA WRITERS CONFERENCE

American Society of Journalists and Authors, 1501 Broadway, Suite 302, New York NY 10036. (212)997-0947. Fax: (212)937-2315. E-mail: asjaoffice@asja.org; director@asja.org. Website: www.asja.org/wc. **Contact:** Alexandra Owens, exec. director. Estab. 1971. Annual conference held in April. Conference duration: 2 days. Average attendance: 600. Covers nonfiction and screenwriting. Held at the Grand Hyatt in New York. Speakers have included Arianna Huffington, Kitty Kelley, Barbara Ehrenreich, Stefan Fatsis. Largest gathering of nonfiction freelance authors in the country.

Costs $200 + , depending on when you sign up (includes lunch). Check website for updates.

Accommodations The hotel holding our conference always blocks out discounted rooms for attendees.

Additional Information Brochures available in February. Registration form is on the website. Inquire by e-mail or fax. Sign up for conference updates on website.

⊞ AUSTRALIAN POETRY FESTIVAL

Poets Union and the Australian Poetry Centre, P.O. Box 755, Potts Point NSW 1335 Australia. (61)(2)9357 6602. Fax: (61)(2)9818-5377. E-mail: info@poetsunion.com; martinlangford@bigpond.com. Website: www.poetsunion.com. Estab. 1998. "The Australian Poetry Festival is a joint festival to be hosted by the Poets Union and the Australian Poetry Centre on September 3-5, 2010, in Sydney, and in other locations." The Australian Poetry Festival is a joint festival to be hosted by the Poets Union and the Australian Poetry Centre.

▓ BLOODY WORDS

64 Shaver Ave., Toronto ON M9B 3T5 Canada. E-mail: carosoles@rogers.com; cheryl@freedmanandsister.com; amummenhoff@rogers.com; info@bloodywords.com. Website: www.bloodywords.com. **Contact:** Caro Soles. Estab. 1999. Annual conference usually held in June. 2010 dates: May 28-30. Conference duration: 3 days. Average attendance: 250. Focuses on mystery fiction and aims to provide a showcase for Canadian mystery writers and readers, as well as provide writing information to aspiring writers. We will present 3 tracks of programming: Just the Facts, where everyone from coroners to toxicologists to tactical police units present how things are done in the real works; and What's the Story—where panelists discuss subjects of interest to readers; and the Mystery Cafe, where 12 authors read and discuss their work. Bloody Words is Canada's oldest and largest gathering of mystery readers and authors. The conference has become *the* June event to look forward to for people who enjoy genre conventions.

Costs $175. Includes banquet.

Accommodations A special rate will be available at The Downtown Hilton Hotel in Toronto, Ontario.

Additional Information Registration is available online. Send inquiries via e-mail.

◉ BLUE RIDGE "AUTUMN IN THE MOUNTAINS" NOVEL RETREAT

(800)588-7222. E-mail: ylehman@bellsouth.net. Website: www.lifeway.com/novelretreat. **Contact:** Yvonne Lehman, director. Estab. 2007. Annual retreat held in October at Ridgecrest/LifeWay Conference Center near Asheville, NC. Retreat duration: Sunday through lunch on Thursday. Average attendance: 55. All areas of novel writing is included. For beginning and advanced novelists. Site: LifeWay/Ridgecrest Conference Center, 20 miles east of Asheville, NC. Faculty: Dr. Dennis Hensley, Dr. Angela Hunt, Jeff Gerke, Deborah Raney, DiAnn Mills, Ray Blackstock, Ann Tatlock, Yvonne Lehman. No editors or agents. Mornings: large group class. Afternoons: writing time and workshops. Evening: discussion and faculty panel.
Costs Retreat Fee: $375.
Accommodations $84 in Mountain Laurel Hotel on campus - Meals: $96.

◉ BRISBANE WRITERS FESTIVAL

P.O. Box 3453, 12 Merivale St., South Brisbane QLD 4101 Australia. (61)(7)3255-0254. Fax: (61) (7)3255-0362. E-mail: info@brisbanewritersfestival.com.au. Website: www.brisbanewritersfestival. com.au. **Contact:** Jane O'Hara, Artistic Director. Annual festival held in September. This event draws on local, national, and international guests for an eclectic mix of panels, discussions, debates, launches and interviews.

◉ BYRON BAY WRITERS FESTIVAL

Northern Rivers Writers' Centre, P.O. Box 1846, 69 Johnson St., Byron Bay NSW 2481 Australia. 040755-2441. E-mail: jeni@nrwc.org.au. Website: www.byronbaywritersfestival.com. **Contact:** Jeni Caffin, director. Estab. 1997. Annual festival held the first weekend in August at Byron's Bay Belongil Fields. Festival duration: 3 days. Celebrate and reflect with over 100 of the finest writers from Australia and overseas. Workshops, panel discussions, and literary breakfasts, lunches, and dinners will also be offered. The Byron Bay Writers Festival is organised by the staff and Committee of the Northern Rivers Writers' Centre, a member based organisation receiving core funding from Arts NSW.
Costs See costs online under Tickets. Early bird, NRWC members and students, kids.
Additional Information "2010 Festival dates are August 6-8 with workshops beginning August 2 and discounted Early Bird 3 day passes are on sale from March 26 at our website. Full program on sale June 4.

CALIFORNIA CRIME WRITERS CONFERENCE

Cosponsored by Sisters in Crime/Los Angeles and the Southern California Chapter of Mystery Writers of America, No public address available, E-mail: sistersincrimela@yahoo.com. Website: www.sistersincrimela.com. Estab. 1995. Annual conference held June, 2011. TBO. Average attendance: 150. Conference on mystery and crime writing. Offers craft and forensic sessions, a keynote speaker, a luncheon speaker, author and agent panels, and book signings.
Additional Information Conference information is available on the website. Website might be down temporarily.

CLARION WEST WRITERS WORKSHOP

P.O. Box 31264, Seattle WA 98103-1264. (206)322-9083. E-mail: info@clarionwest.org. Website: www.clarionwest.org. Clarion West is an intensive 6-week workshop for writers preparing for professional careers in science fiction and fantasy, held annually in Seattle, Washington, USA. Usually goes from mid-June through end of July. Conference duration: 6 weeks. Average attendance: 18. Held near the University of Washington. Deadline for applications is March 1. Instructors are well-known writers and editors in the field. This year's workshop will be held from June 21–July 31.
Costs $3200 (for tuition, housing, most meals). $100 discount if application received prior to February 1. Limited scholarships are available based on financial need.
Additional Information This is a critique-based workshop. Students are encouraged to write a story every week; the critique of student material produced at the workshop forms the principal activity of the workshop. Students and instructors critique mss as a group. Students must submit 20-30 pages of ms to qualify for admission. Conference guidelines are available for a SASE. Visit the website for updates and complete details.

DESERT DREAMS

Phoenix Desert Rose Chapter No. 60, PO Box 27407, Tempe AZ 85285. (866)267-2249. E-mail: info@desertroserwa.org; desertdreams@desertroserwa.org. Website: www.desertroserwa.org. Estab. 1986. Conference held every other April. Conference duration: 3 days. Average attendance: 250. Covers marketing, fiction, screenwriting, and research. Keynote speakers: *New York Times* best-selling Author Linda Lael Miller; and Brad Schreiber, VP of Storytech (*The Writer's Journey* with Chris Vogler).
Costs $218 + (includes meals, seminars, appointments with agents/editors).
Accommodations Discounted rates for attendees is negotiated at the Crowne Plaza San Marcos Resort in Chandler, Ariz.
Additional Information Send inquiries via e-mail. Visit website for updates and complete details.

EAST OF EDEN WRITERS CONFERENCE

P.O. Box 3254, Santa Clara CA 95055. E-mail: eastofeden@southbaywriters.com; press@southbaywriters.com. Website: www.southbaywriters.com. Estab. 1987. Biennial conference held in September of even years. Average attendance: 300. Writers of all levels are welcome. Pitch-sessions to agents and publishers are available, as are meetings with authors and editors. Workshops address the craft and the business of writing and publishing. Location: Salinas, Calif.— Steinbeck Country.
Costs Costs vary. The full conference (Friday through Sunday noon) is approximately $350; Saturday only is approximately $200. The fee includes meals, workshops and pitch/meeting sessions. Contests require attendance and additional nominal fee.
Accommodations Negotiated rates at local hotels—$85-110 per night, give or take.
Additional Information The East of Eden conference is run by writers/volunteers from the nonprofit California Writers Club, South Bay Branch. The Salinas Community Center's Sherwood Hall has been reserved for September 24-26, 2010. Luis Valdez heads the list of seven keynote speakers. Some thirty-five professional presenters will lead workshops touching the 2010 theme "Why do I write?" For details, please visit website or send an SASE.

EAST TEXAS CHRISTIAN WRITERS CONFERENCE

The School of Humanities, Dr. Jerry L. Summers, Dean, Scarborough Hall, East Texas Baptist Univ., 1209 N. Grove, Marshall TX 75670. (903)923-2269. E-mail: jhopkins@etbu.edu. Website: www.etbu.edu/News/CWC. Estab. 2002. Annual conference held second weekend of April. Average attendance: 125. Conference offers: contact, conversation, and exchange of ideas with other aspiring writers; outstanding presentations and workshop experiences with established authors, agents, editors, and publishers; potential publishing and writing opportunities; networking with other writers with related interests; promotion of both craft and faith; and one-on-one consultations with agents, editors, and publishers. Speakers have included Vickie Phelps, Terry Burns, Robert Darden, Bill Keith, Miriam Hees, Lenora Worth, Donn Taylor, and Mary Lou Redding. Offers an advanced track and teen track beginner, intermediate, and advanced level contest. Partial scholarships available for students only.
Costs Visit website.
Accommodations Visit website for a list of local hotels offering a discounted rate.

ENVIRONMENTAL WRITERS' CONFERENCE & WORKSHOP IN HONOR OF RACHEL CARSON

New-Cue, Inc., Methodist College, Clark Hall, 5300 Ramsey St., Fayetteville NC 28311. (845)630-7047 or (910)630-7046. Fax: (910)630-7221. E-mail: info@new-cue.org. Website: www.new-cue.org. Estab. 1999. Biennial conference held in June. Next one will be in 2010. Conference duration: 4 days. Average attendance: 100. This interdisciplinary event is a blend of scholarly presentations, readings, informal discussions, and writing workshops. Held at The Spruce Point Inn in Boothbay Harbor, Maine. Speakers have included Lawrence Buell, Bill McKibben, Carl Safina, Linda Lear and Verlyn Klinkenborg.
Costs Registration costs include sessions, meals and keynote reception.
Accommodations Special rates are available for participants at the Spruce Point Inn. Transportation and area information is available through the Boothbay Harbor Chamber of Commerce.

FESTIVAL OF FAITH AND WRITING

Department of English, Calvin College, 1795 Knollcrest Circle SE, Grand Rapids MI 49546. (616)526-6770. E-mail: ffw@calvin.edu. Website: www.calvin.edu/festival. Estab. 1990. Biennial festival held in April. Conference duration: 3 days. The festival brings together writers, editors, publishers, musicians, artists, and readers to discuss and celebrate insightful writing that explores issues of faith. Focuses on fiction, nonfiction, memoir, poetry, drama, children's, young adult, academic, film, and songwriting. Past speakers have included Joyce Carol Oates, Salman Rushdie, Patricia Hampl, Thomas Lynch, Leif Enger, Marilynne Robinson and Michael Chabon. Agents and editors attend the festival.

Costs Consult website.

Accommodations Shuttles are available to and from local hotels. Shuttles are also available for overflow parking lots. A list of hotels with special rates for conference attendees is available on the festival website. High school and college students can arrange on-campus lodging by e-mail.

Additional Information Online registration opens in October. Accepts inquiries by e-mail and phone

FLATHEAD RIVER WRITERS CONFERENCE

P.O. Box 7711, Kalispeil MT 59904-7711. E-mail: answers@authorsoftheflathead.org. Website: www.authorsoftheflathead.org. Estab. 1990. Annual conference held in early mid-October. Average attendance: 100. We provide several small, intense 3-day workshops before the general weekend conference. Workshops, panel discussions, and speakers focus on novels, nonfiction, screenwriting, short stories, magazine articles, and the writing industry. Formerly held at the Grouse Mountain Lodge in Whitefish, Montana. Past speakers have included Sam Pinkus, Randy Wayne White, Donald Maass, Ann Rule, Cricket Pechstein, Marcela Landres, Amy Rennert, Ben Mikaelsen, Esmond Harmsworth, Linda McFall, and Ron Carlson. Agents will be speaking and available for meetings with attendees.

Accommodations Rooms are available at a discounted rate.

Additional Information "Our 20th Annual Flathead River Writers' Conference will be reduced in scope and duration. It will be a one-day conference on October 2nd and 3rd, 2010 at Flathead Valley Community College. There will be no pre-conference workshops this year. It is our hope that by doing this we can relieve some of the pressures on your pocketbooks and still make it possible for you to enjoy and learn from top-notch speakers. We will soon announce the agenda for our conference and the particulars. Watch our website for details. Send inquiries via e-mail."

FLORIDA CHRISTIAN WRITERS CONFERENCE

2344 Armour Ct., Titusville FL 32780. (321)269-5831. Fax: (321)264-0037. E-mail: billiewilson@cfl.rr.com. Website: www.flwriters.org. Estab. 1988. Annual conference held in March. Conference duration: 4 days. Average attendance: 275. Covers fiction, nonfiction, magazine writing, marketing, Internet writing, greeting cards, and more. Conference is held at the Christian Retreat Center in Brandenton, Florida.

Costs $575 (includes tuition, meals).

Accommodations We provide a shuttle from the Orlando airport. $725/double occupancy; $950/single occupancy.

Additional Information "Each writer may submit 2 works for critique. We have specialists in every area of writing. Brochures/guidelines are available online or for a SASE."

GOTHAM WRITERS' WORKSHOP

WritingClasses.com, 555 Elghth Ave., Suite 1402, New York NY 10018. (212)974-8377. Fax: (212)307-6325. E-mail: dana@write.org. Website: www.writingclasses.com. Estab. 1993. Online classes are held throughout the year. There are four terms of NYC classes, beginning in January, April, June/July, and September/October. Offers craft-oriented creative writing courses in general creative writing, fiction writing, screenwriting, nonfiction writing, article writing, stand-up comedy writing, humor writing, memoir writing, novel writing, children's book writing, playwriting, poetry, songwriting, mystery writing, science fiction writing, romance writing, television writing, article writing, travel writing, business writing and classes on freelancing, selling your screenplay, hot to blog, nonfiction book proposal, and getting published. Also, the Workshop offers a teen program, private instruction, mentoring program, and classes on selling your work. Classes are held at various schools in New York City as well as online at www.writingclasses.com. Agents and editors participate in some workshops.

Costs $395/10-week workshops; $125 for the four-week online selling seminars and 1-day intensive courses; $295 for 6-week creative writing and business writing classes.

THE GREAT AMERICAN PITCHFEST & SCREENWRITING CONFERENCE

Twilight Pictures, 12400 Ventura Blvd. #735, Studio City CA 91604. (877)255-2528. E-mail: info@pitchfest.com. Website: pitchfest.com/index.shtml. Conference duration: 2 days (one day conference, one day pitchfest). "Our companies are all carefully screened, and only the most credible companies in the industry are invited to hear pitches. They include: agents, managers, and production companies." Annual.

Costs Saturday is free, with a full day of industry classes, workshops, and panels, all led by industry professionals. The Sunday Pitchfest is $250.

Accommodations All activities will be held at the Burbank Marriott Hotel & Convention Center, 2500 N. Hollywood Way, Burbank, CA 91505.

Additional Information June 26-27, 2010.

GREEN MOUNTAIN WRITERS CONFERENCE

47 Hazel St., Rutland VT 05701. (802)236-6133. E-mail: ydaley@sbcglobal.net. Website: www.vermontwriters.com. Estab. 1999. "Annual conference held in the summer; 2010 dates are Aug. 2–6. Covers fiction, creative nonfiction, poetry, journalism, nature writing, essay, memoir, personal narrative, and biography. Held at an old dance pavillion on on a remote pond in Tinmouth, Vermont. Speakers have included Stephen Sandy, Grace Paley, Ruth Stone, Howard Frank Mosher, Chris Bohjalian, Joan Connor, Yvonne Daley, David Huddle, David Budbill, Jeffrey Lent, Verandah Porche, Tom Smith, and Chuck Clarino."

Costs $500 before July 1; $525 after July 1. Partial scholarships are available.

Accommodations "We have made arrangements with a major hotel in nearby Rutland and 3 area bed and breakfast inns for special accommodations and rates for conference participants. You must make your own reservations."

HEART TALK

Women's Center for Ministry, Western Seminary, 5511 SE Hawthorne Blvd., Portland OR 97215-3367. (800)517-1800, ext. 1931. Fax: (503)517-1889. E-mail: wcm@westernseminary.edu. Website: www.westernseminary.edu/women. Estab. 1998. Biannual conference held in March. Conference alternates between writing one year and speaking the next. Provides inspirational training for beginning and advanced writers/speakers. Workshops may include writing fiction, nonfiction, children's books, publishing, trends, dialogue, book proposals, websites, blogs, etc. Editors/publicists available for one-on-one consultations. Past speakers have included Robin Jones Gunn, Deborah Hedstrom-Page, Patricia Rushford, Sally Stuart, and many more.

Additional Information Conference information is available online, by e-mail, phone, or fax.

HIGHLAND SUMMER CONFERENCE

Box 7014, Radford University, Radford VA 24142-7014. (540)831-5366. Fax: (540)831-5951. E-mail: rbderrick@radford.edu; jasbury@radford.edu. Website: www.radford.edu/arsc. **Contact:** Ruth Derrick. Estab. 1978. Annual conference held in June. 2010 date: June 7-18. Conference duration: 2 weeks. Average attendance: 25. Covers fiction, nonfiction, poetry, and screenwriting. This year's Highland Summer Conference will be conducted the first week by Pamela Duncan. The second week of the Conference will be conducted by author George Ella Lyon. Special evening readings by Dot Jackson and Charles Swanson. Go to website for more information.

Costs The cost is based on current Radford tuition for 3 credit hours, plus an additional conference fee. On-campus meals and housing are available at additional cost. In 2009, conference tuition was $815/in-state undergraduates, $1,944/for out-of-state undergraduates, $900/in-state graduates, and $1,728/out-of-state graduates.

Accommodations "We do not have special rate arrangements with local hotels. We do offer accommodations on the Radford University campus in a recently refurbished residence hall." The 2009 cost was $26-36/night.

Additional Information Conference leaders typically critique work done during the 2-week conference, but do not ask to have any writing submitted prior to the conference. Conference brochures/guidelines are available in March for a SASE.

HIGHLIGHTS FOUNDATION WRITERS WORKSHOP AT CHAUTAUQUA

814 Court St., Honesdale PA 18431. (570)253-1192. Fax: (570)253-0179. E-mail: contact@ highlightsfoundation.org. Website: www.highlightsfoundation.org. Estab. 1985. Annual conference held July 16-23, 2011. Average attendance: 100. Workshops are geared toward those who write for children at the beginner, intermediate, and advanced levels. Offers seminars, small group workshops, and one-on-one sessions with authors, editors, illustrators, critics, and publishers. Workshop site is the picturesque community of Chautauqua, New York. Speakers have included Bruce Coville, Candace Fleming, Linda Sue Park, Jane Yolen, Patricia Gauch, Jerry Spinelli, Eileen Spinelli, Joy Cowley and Pam Munoz Ryan.
Costs 2009 was $2,400 (includes all meals, conference supplies, gate pass to Chautauqua Institution).
Accommodations We coordinate ground transportation to and from airports, trains, and bus stations in the Erie, Pennsylvania and Jamestown/Buffalo, New York area. We also coordinate accommodations for conference attendees.
Additional Information "We offer the opportunity for attendees to submit a manuscript for review at the conference. Workshop brochures/guidelines are available upon request."

INTERNATIONAL MUSEUM PUBLISHING SEMINAR

University of Chicago, Graham School of General Studies, 1427 E. 60th St., Chicago IL 60637. (773)702-1682. Fax: (773)702-6814. E-mail: spesin@uchicago.edu. kjaffe@uchicago.edu. Website: grahamschool.uchicago.edu. Sarah Pesin **Contact:** Kineret Jaffe. Estab. 1988. Biennial conference. Conference duration: 2.5 days. Average attendance: 250. Primarily covers nonfiction, writing, and editing in museums. Recent themes have included selecting an attractive books cover, artful strategies for cutting costs, digital imaging, a survival guide, and more. The conference moves to a new city each year and is co-sponsored by the university with different museums.
Costs $600-650.
Accommodations See website for hotel options.
Additional Information Send a SASE in January for brochure/guidelines. Inquire via e-mail or fax.

IWWG EARLY SPRING IN CALIFORNIA CONFERENCE

International Women's Writing Guild, P.O. Box 810, Gracie Station, New York NY 10028-0082. (212)737-7536. Fax: (212)737-9469. E-mail: iwwg@iwwg.org. Website: www.iwwg.org. Estab. 1982. Annual conference held the second week in March. Average attendance: 50. Conference promotes creative writing, personal growth, and voice. Site is a redwood forest mountain retreat in Santa Cruz, California.
Costs $350/members; $380/nonmembers for weekend program with room and board; $125 for weekend program without room and board.
Accommodations All participants stay at the conference site or may commute.
Additional Information Brochures/guidelines are available online or for a SASE. Inquire via e-mail or fax.

JACKSON HOLE WRITERS CONFERENCE

PO Box 1974, Jackson WY 83001. (307)413-3332. E-mail: tim@jacksonholewritersconference.com. Website: www.jacksonholewritersconference.com. Estab. 1991. Annual conference held in June. For 2010: June 24-27. Conference duration: 4 days. Average attendance: 110. Covers fiction, creative nonfiction, and young adult and offers ms critiques from authors, agents, and editors. Agents in attendance will take pitches from writers. Paid manuscript critique programs are available.
Costs $355-385, includes all workshops, speaking events, cocktail party, BBQ, and goodie bag with dining coupons.
Additional Information Held at the Center for the Arts in Jackson, Wyoming.

KARITOS CHRISTIAN ARTS CONFERENCE

1122 Brentwood Ln., Wheaton IL 60189. (847)925-8018. E-mail: bob@karitos.com. Website: www. karitos.com. Estab. 1996. Annual conference held each summer in July. 2010: July 15-17. Average

attendance: 200-300. Karitos is a celebration and teaching weekend for Christian artists and writers. Literary arts track focuses on practical instruction in the craft of writing. Site for this year's conference is Living Waters Community Church in the Chicago suburb of Bolingbrook. Past faculty has included Lori Davis, John DeJarlais, Eva Marie Everson, Lin Johnson, Patricia Hickman, Elma Photikarm, Rajendra Pillai, Jane Rubietta, Travis Thrasher and Chris Wave.
Costs See website for costs.

KILLER NASHVILLE
P.O. Box 680686, Franklin TN 37068-0686. (615)599-4032. E-mail: contact@killernashville. com. Website: www.killernashville.com. Estab. 2006. Annual conference held in August. Next conference: Aug. 20-22, 2010. Conference duration: 3 days. Average attendance: 180 + . Conference designed for writers and fans of mysteries and thrillers, including fiction and nonfiction authors, playwrights, and screenwriters. There are many opportunities for authors to sign books. 2010 guest of honor is Jeffery Deaver. Authors/panelists have included Michael Connelly, Bill Bass, J.A. Jance, Carol Higgins Clark, Hallie Ephron, Greg Hurwitz, Chris Grabenstein, Rhonda Pollero, P.J. Parrish, Reed Farrel Coleman, Kathryn Wall, Mary Saums, Don Bruns, Bill Moody, Richard Helms, Brad Strickland and Steven Womack. Literary agents and acquisitions editors attend and take pitches from writers. The conference is sponsored by American Blackguard, Barnes and Noble, Mystery Writers of America, Sisters in Crime and the Nashville Scene, among others. Representatives from the FBI, TBI, ATF, police department and sheriff's department present on law enforcement procedures to the general public.

THE MACDOWELL COLONY
100 High St., Peterborough NH 03458. (603)924-3886. Fax: (603)924-9142. E-mail: admissions@ macdowellcolony.org. Website: www.macdowellcolony.org. Estab. 1907. Open to writers, playwrights, composers, visual artists, film/video artists, interdisciplinary artists and architects. Applicants send information and work samples for review by a panel of experts in each discipline. Application form submitted online at www.macdowellcolony.org/apply.html. Work samples and completed application forms must still be mailed. See application guidelines for details.
Costs Travel reimbursement and stipends are available for participants of the residency, based on need. There are no residency fees.

MARYMOUNT MANHATTAN COLLEGE WRITERS' CONFERENCE
Marymount Manhattan College, 221 E. 71st St., New York NY 10021. (212)774-4810. E-mail: lfrumkes@mmm.edu. Estab. 1993. "Annual conference held in June. Keynote speakers for this year's conference held on June 3, 2010 will be David Baldacci and Cathy Black. Conference duration: 1 day. Average attendance: 200. We present workshops on several different writing genres and panels on fiction and nonfiction, literary agents, memoir and more. Over 60 distinguished authors, agents, and publicists attend. Keynote speakers have included Lewis Lapham and Joyce Carol Oates."
Costs $165 before June 1; $185 after June 1 (includes lunch, reception).

MONTROSE CHRISTIAN WRITERS' CONFERENCE
5 Locust St., Montrose PA 18801. (570)278-1001 or (800)598-5030. Fax: (570)278-3061. E-mail: mbc@montrosebible.org. Website: www.montrosebible.org. Estab. 1990. "Annual conference held in July. Offers workshops, editorial appointments, and professional critiques. We try to meet a cross-section of writing needs, for beginners and advanced, covering fiction, poetry, and writing for children. It is small enough to allow personal interaction between attendees and faculty. Speakers have included William Petersen, Mona Hodgson, Jim Fletcher, and Terri Gibbs."
Costs $150/tuition; $35/critique for 2008.
Accommodations Housing and meals are available on site.

MOUNT HERMON CHRISTIAN WRITERS CONFERENCE
37 Conference Drive, Mount Hermon CA 95041. E-mail: info@mounthermon.org. Website: www. mounthermon.org/writers. Estab. 1970. Annual professional conference. Always held over the Palm Sunday weekend, Friday noon through Tuesday at noon. 2011 dates are April 15-19. Average attendance: 450. Sponsored by and held at the 440-acre Mount Hermon Christian Conference Center near San Jose, CA in the heart of the coastal redwoods, we are a broad-ranging conference for all areas of Christian writing, including fiction, nonfiction, fantasy, children's, teen, young adult,

poetry, magazines, inspirational and devotional writing. This is a working, how-to conference, with Major Morning tracks in all genres (including a track especially for teen writers), and as many as 20 optional workshops each afternoon. Faculty-to-student ratio is about 1 to 6. The bulk of our more than 70 faculty members are editors and publisher representatives from major Christian publishing houses nationwide. Speakers have included T. Davis Bunn, Debbie Macomber, Jerry Jenkins, Bill Butterworth, Dick Foth and others.

Accommodations Registrants stay in hotel-style accommodations. Meals are buffet style, with faculty joining registrants.

Additional Information "The residential nature of our conference makes this a unique setting for one-on-one interaction with faculty/staff. There is also a decided inspirational flavor to the conference, and general sessions with well-known speakers are a highlight. Registrants may submit 2 works for critique in advance of the conference, then have personal interviews with critiquers during the conference. All conference information is online by December 1 of each year. All conference information is online by December 1 of each year. Send inquiries via e-mail. Tapes of past conferences are also available online."

NATCHEZ LITERARY AND CINEMA CELEBRATION

P.O. Box 1307, Natchez MS 39121-1307. (601)446-1208. Fax: (601)446-1214. E-mail: carolyn.smith@ colin.edu. Website: www.colin.edu/NLCC. Estab. 1990. Annual conference held in February. Conference duration: 5 days. Conference focuses on all literature, including film scripts. Each year's conference deals with some general aspect of Southern history. Speakers have included Eudora Welty, Margaret Walker Alexander, William Styron, Willie Morris, Ellen Douglas, Ernest Gaines, Elizabeth Spencer, Nikki Giovanni, Myrlie Evers-Williams, and Maya Angelou.

NATIONAL WRITERS ASSOCIATION FOUNDATION CONFERENCE

P.O. Box 4187, Parker CO 80134. (303)841-0246. Fax: (303)841-2607. E-mail: natlwritersassn@ hotmail.com. Website: www.nationalwriters.com. **Contact:** Sandy Whelchel. Estab. 1926. Annual conference held the second week of June in Denver. Conference duration: 1 day. Average attendance: 100. Focuses on general writing and marketing.

Costs Approximately $100.

Additional Information Awards for previous contests will be presented at the conference. Brochures/ guidelines are online, or send a SASE.

NEW JERSEY ROMANCE WRITERS PUT YOUR HEART IN A BOOK CONFERENCE

P.O. Box 513, Plainsboro NJ 08536. E-mail: njrwconfchair@yahoo.com; njrw@njromance writers. org. Website: www.njromancewriters.org. Estab. 1984. Annual conference held in October. Average attendance: 500. Workshops are offered on various topics for all writers of romance, from beginner to multi-published. Speakers have included Nora Roberts, Kathleen Woodiwiss, Patricia Gaffney, Jill Barnett and Kay Hooper. Appointments are offered with editors/agents.

Accommodations Special rate available for conference attendees at the Sheraton at Renaissance Woodbridge Hotel in Iselin, New Jersey.

Additional Information Conference brochures, guidelines, and membership information are available for SASE. Massive bookfair is open to the public with authors signing copies of their books.

NIMROD AWARDS CELEBRATION & WRITING WORKSHOP

University of Tulsa, 800 S. Tucker Drive, Tulsa OK 74104-3189. (918)631-3080. Fax: (918)631-3033. E-mail: nimrod@utulsa.edu. Website: www.utulsa.edu/nimrod. Estab. 1978. Annual conference held in October. Conference duration: 1 day. Offers one-on-one editing sessions, readings, panel discussions, and master classes in fiction, poetry, nonfiction, memoir, and fantasy writing. Speakers have included Myla Goldberg, B.H. Fairchild, Colleen McElroy, Gina Ochsner, Kelly Link, Rilla Askew, Matthew Galkin, and A.D. Coleman.

Additional Information Full conference details are online in August.

NORTH CAROLINA WRITERS' NETWORK FALL CONFERENCE

P.O. Box 954, Carrboro NC 27510-0954. (919)251-9140. Fax: (919)929-0535. E-mail: mail@ncwriters. org. Website: www.ncwriters.org. Estab. 1985. "Annual conference held in November in different NC venues. Average attendance: 250. This organization hosts two conferences: one in the spring and one in the fall. Each conference is a weekend full of workshops, panels, book signings, and readings (including open mic). There will be a keynote speaker, along with sessions on a variety of genres, including fiction, poetry, creative nonfiction, journalism, children's book writing, screenwriting, and playwriting. We also offer craft, editing, and marketing classes. We hold the event at a conference center with hotel rooms available. Speakers have included Donald Maass, Noah Lukeman, Joe Regal, Jeff Kleinman, and Evan Marshall. Some agents will teach classes and some are available for meetings with attendees."

Costs Approximately $250 (includes 2 meals).

Accommodations Special rates are usually available at the conference hotel, but conferees must make their own reservations.

Additional Information Brochures/guidelines are available online or by sending your street address to mail@ncwriters.org. You can also register online.

ODYSSEY FANTASY WRITING WORKSHOP

P.O. Box 75, Mont Vernon NH 03057. E-mail: jcavelos@sff.net. Website: www.odysseyworkshop. org. Estab. 1996. Annual workshop held in June (through July). Conference duration: 6 weeks. Average attendance: 16. A workshop for fantasy, science fiction, and horror writers that combines an intensive learning and writing experience with in-depth feedback on students' mss. Held on the campus of Saint Anselm College in Manchester, New Hampshire. Speakers have included George R.R. Martin, Elizabeth Hand, Jane Yolen, Harlan Ellison, Melissa Scott and Dan Simmons.

Costs $1,900/tuition; $775-1,550/on-campus apartment; approximately $500/on-campus meals.

Additional Information Prospective students must include a 4,000-word writing sample with their application. Accepts inquiries by SASE, e-mail, fax and phone. Application deadline April 8.

WILLIAM PATERSON UNIVERSITY SPRING WRITER'S CONFERENCE

English Department, Atrium 232, 300 Pompton Rd., Wayne NJ 07470. (973)720-3067. Fax: (973)720-2189. E-mail: parrasj@wpunj.edu. Website: http://euphrates.wpunj.edu/writersconference. Annual conference held in April. Conference duration: 1 day. Average attendance: 100-125. Small writing workshops and panels address topics such as writing from life, getting your work in print, poetry, playwriting, fiction, creative nonfiction, and book and magazine editing. Sessions are led by William Paterson faculty members and distinguished guest writers and editors of verse and prose. Speakers have included Alison Lurie, Russell Banks, Terese Svoboda, and Anthony Swofford.

Costs $50 (includes lunch).

PIKES PEAK WRITERS CONFERENCE

Pikes Peak Writers, 427 E. Colorado Ave., #116, Colorado Springs CO 80903. (719)531-5723. E-mail: info@pikespeakwriters.com. Website: www.pikespeakwriters.com. Estab. 1993. Annual conference held in April. Conference duration: 3 days. Average attendance: 400. Workshops, presentations, and panels focus on writing and publishing mainstream and genre fiction (romance, science fiction/fantasy, suspense/thrillers, action/adventure, mysteries, children's, young adult). Agents and editors are available for meetings with attendees on Saturday.

Costs $300-500 (includes all meals).

Accommodations Marriott Colorado Springs holds a block of rooms at a special rate for attendees until late March.

Additional Information Readings with critiques are available on Friday afternoon. Also offers a contest for unpublished writers; entrants need not attend the conference. Deadline: November 1. Registration and contest entry forms are online; brochures are available in January. Send inquiries via e-mail.

PNWA SUMMER WRITERS CONFERENCE

PMB 2717, 1420 NW Gilman Blvd., Issaquah WA 98027. (425)673-2665. E-mail: pnwa@pnwa. org. Website: www.pnwa.org. Estab. 1955. All conferences are held in July. Conference duration: 4 days. Average attendance: 400. Attendees have the chance to meet agents and editors, learn craft from authors and uncover marketing secrets. Speakers have included J.A. Jance, Sheree Bykofsky, Kimberley Cameron, Jennie Dunham, Donald Maass, Jandy Nelson, Robert Dugoni and Terry Brooks. Annual.

Accommodations The conference is held at the Hilton Seattle Airport & Conference Center.

Additional Information "PNWA also holds an annual literary contest every February with more than $12,000 in prize money. Finalists' manuscripts are then available to agents and editors at our summer conference. Visit the website for further details."

REMEMBER THE MAGIC

International Women's Writing Guild, P.O. Box 810, Gracie Station, New York NY 10028-0082. (212)737-7536. Fax: (212)737-9469. E-mail: iwwg@iwwg.org. Website: www.iwwg.org. Estab. 1978. Annual conference held in July-August. Average attendance: 400. Conference to promote creative writing and personal growth, professional know-how and contacts, and networking. Over 50 workshops are offered each day. Conferees have the freedom to make their own schedule.

Costs $1,399 single for members; $1,419 double for nonmembers. These fees include the 7-day program and room and board for the week. Rates for a 5-day stay and a weekend stay, as well as commuter rates, are also available.

Additional Information Conference brochures/guidelines are available online or for a SASE. Inquire via e-mail or fax.

RETREAT FROM HARSH REALITY

Mid-Michigan RWA, P.O. Box 2725, Kalamazoo MI 49003-2725. E-mail: retreat@midmichiganrwa. org. Website: www.midmichiganrwa.org/retreat.html. Estab. 1985. Annual conference held in April. Average attendance: 50. Conference focusing on romance and fiction writing. Speakers have included Rosanne Bittner, Debra Dixon, Bettina Krahn, Ruth Ryan Langan, Elizabeth Bevarly, Julie Kistler, Merline Lovelace, and Elizabeth Grayson.

RT BOOKLOVERS CONVENTION

55 Bergen St., Brooklyn NY 11201. (718)237-1097 or (800)989-8816, ext. 12. Fax: (718)624-2526. E-mail: jocarol@rtconvention.com. Website: www.rtconvention.com. Annual conference held in April. Features 125 workshops, agent and editor appointments, a book fair, and more.

Costs See website for pricing and other information.

SANDHILLS WRITERS CONFERENCE

Augusta State University, Department of Communications and Professional Writing, 2500 Walton Way, Augusta GA 30904-2200. E-mail: akellman@aug.edu. Website: www.sandhills.aug.edu. Annual conference held the fourth weekend in March. Covers fiction, poetry, children's literature, nonfiction, plays, and songwriting. Located on the campus of Augusta State University in Georgia. Agents and editors will be speaking at the event.

Accommodations Several hotels are located near the university.

SAN FRANCISCO WRITERS CONFERENCE

1029 Jones St., San Francisco CA 94109. (415)673-0939. Fax: (415)673-0367. E-mail: sfwriterscon@ aol.com. Website: www.sfwriters.org. **Contact:** Michael Larsen, director. Estab. 2003. "Annual conference held President's Day weekend in February. Average attendance: 400 +. Top authors, respected literary agents, and major publishing houses are at the event so attendees can make face-to-face contact with all the right people. Writers of nonfiction, fiction, poetry, and specialty writing (children's books, cookbooks, travel, etc.) will all benefit from the event. There are important sessions on marketing, self-publishing, technology, and trends in the publishing industry. Plus, there's an optional 4-hour session called Speed Dating for Agents where attendees can meet with 20 + agents. Speakers have included Jennifer Crusie, Richard Paul Evans, Jamie Raab, Mary Roach, Jane Smiley, Debbie Macomber, Firoozeh Dumas, Zilpha Keatley Snyder, Steve Berry, Jacquelyn Mitchard. More than 20 agents and editors participate each year, many of whom will be available for meetings with attendees."

Costs $600 + with price breaks for early registration (includes all sessions/workshops/keynotes, Speed Dating with Editors, opening gala at the Top of the Mark, 2 continental breakfasts, 2 lunches). Optional Speed Dating for Agents is $50.

Accommodations The Intercontinental Mark Hopkins Hotel is a historic landmark at the top of Nob Hill in San Francisco. Elegant rooms and first-class service are offered to attendees at the rate of $159/night. The hotel is located so that everyone arriving at the Oakland or San Francisco airport can take BART to either the Embarcadero or Powell Street exits, then walk or take a cable car or taxi directly to the hotel.

Conferences

Additional Information "Present yourself in a professional manner and the contact you will make will be invaluable to your writing career. Brochures and registration are online."

SCBWI SOUTHERN BREEZE FALL CONFERENCE

P.O. Box 26282, Birmingham AL 35260. E-mail: jskittinger@bellsouth.net. Website: www.southern-breeze.org. Estab. 1992. Annual conference held on the third Saturday in October (2010: Oct. 16). Conference duration: 1 day. The Society of Children's Book Writers and Illustrators is geared toward the production and support of quality children's literature. Offers approximately 28 workshops on craft and the business of writing, including a basic workshop for those new to the children's field. Manuscript and portfolio critiques are offered. Speakers typically include editors, agents, art directors, authors and illustrators.

Accommodations "We have a hotel room block with a conference rate. The conference is held at a nearby school. Pre-registration is required."

SCENE CONFERENCE

Kansas Writers Association, P.O. Box 2236, Wichita KS 67201. E-mail: info@kwawriters.org. Website: www.kwawriters.org/sceneofthecrime.htm. Biennual conference held in April. Features agent/editor consultations, banquet and speaker sessions with editors, agents and authors. A full list of each year's speakers is available on the website. Annual.

Accommodations Wichita Airport Hilton.

◪ THE SCHOOL FOR WRITERS SUMMER WORKSHOP

The Humber School for Writers, Humber Institute of Technology & Advanced Learning, 3199 Lake Shore Blvd. W., Toronto ON M8V 1K8 Canada. (416)675-6622. E-mail: antanas.sileika@humber.ca; hilary.higgins@humber.ca. Website: www.creativeandperformingarts.humber.ca/content/writers.html. Annual workshop held second week in July. Conference duration: 1 week. Average attendance: 100. New writers from around the world gather to study with faculty members to work on their novel, short stories, poetry, or creative nonfiction. Agents and editors participate in conference. Include a work-in-progress with your registration. Faculty has included Martin Amis, David Mitchell, Rachel Kuschner, Peter Carey, Roddy Doyle, Tim O'Brien, Andrea Levy, Barry Unsworth, Edward Albee, Ha Jin, Mavis Gallant, Bruce Jay Friedman, Isabel Huggan, Alistair MacLeod, Lisa Moore, Kim Moritsugu, Francine Prose, Paul Quarrington, Olive Senior, and D.M. Thomas, Annabel Lyon, Mary Gaitskill, M. G. Vassanji.

Costs $949/Canadian residents before June 12; $1,469/non-Canadian residents before June 12; $999/Canadian residents after June 12; $1,519/non-Canadian residents after June 12 (includes panels, classes, lunch). Scholarships are available.

Accommodations Approximately $60/night. See www.conference.humber.ca for a modest college dorm room. Nearby hotels are also available.

Additional Information Accepts inquiries by e-mail, phone, and fax.

SEAK: FICTION WRITING FOR PHYSICIANS CONFERENCE

P.O. Box 729, Falmouth MA 02541. (508)548-7023. Fax: (508)540-8304. E-mail: mail@seak.com. Website: www.seak.com. Estab. 1980. Annual conferences held on Cape Cod. The medical seminar is taught by *New York Times* best-selling authors Michael Palmer, MD and Tess Gerritsen, MD. Session topics include writing fiction that sells, screenwriting, writing riveting dialogue, creating memorable characters, getting your first novel published, and more. Agents will be speaking and available for one-on-one meetings. 11th Annual Conference is Oct. 22-24, 2010.

SLEUTHFEST

MWA Florida Chapter, E-mail: sleuthfestlinda@gmail.com. Website: www.mwa-florida.org/sleuthfest.htm. **Contact:** Linda Hengerer, chairperson. Annual conference held in Feb/March, at the Deerfield Beach Hilton, Florida. Conference duration: 4 days. Hands-on workshops, 4 tracks of writing and business panels, and 2 keynote speakers for writers of mystery and crime fiction. 2010 Guests of Honor were David Morrell and Stephen J. Cannell. Also offers agent and editor appointments and paid ms critiques. A full list of attending speakers as well as agents and editors is online. This event is put on by the local chapter of the Mystery Writers of America.

Accommodations The Deerfield Beach Hilton.

SOCIETY OF CHILDREN'S BOOK WRITERS & ILLUSTRATORS ANNUAL SUMMER CONFERENCE ON WRITING AND ILLUSTRATING FOR CHILDREN

8271 Beverly Blvd., Los Angeles CA 90048-4515. (323)782-1010. Fax: (323)782-1892. E-mail: scbwi@scbwi.org. Website: www.scbwi.org. Estab. 1972. Annual conference held in early August. Conference duration: 4 days. Average attendance: 1,000. Held at the Century Plaza Hotel in Los Angeles. Speakers have included Andrea Brown, Steven Malk, Scott Treimel, Ashley Bryan, Bruce Coville, Karen Hesse, Harry Mazer, Lucia Monfried, and Russell Freedman. Agents will be speaking and sometimes participate in ms critiques.

Costs Approximately $400 (does not include hotel room).

Accommodations Information on overnight accommodations is made available.

Additional Information Ms and illustration critiques are available. Brochure/guidelines are available in June online or for SASE.

SOUTH COAST WRITERS CONFERENCE

Southwestern Oregon Community College, P.O. Box 590, 29392 Ellensburg Avenue, Gold Beach OR 97444. (541)247-2741. Fax: (541)247-6247. E-mail: scwc@socc.edu. Website: www.socc.edu/ scwriters. Estab. 1996. Annual conference held President's Day weekend in February. Conference duration: 2 days. Covers fiction, historical, poetry, children's, nature, and marketing. John Daniel is the next scheduled keynote speaker and presenters include John Daniel, Linda Barnes, Jayel Gibson, Kim Griswell, Diane Hammond, Leigh Anne Jasheway, Marianne Monson, Rebecca Olson, Dennis Powers, Keith Scales, Erica Wheeler, Jaimal Yogis.

Additional Information See website for cost and additional details.

SPACE COAST WRITERS GUILD ANNUAL CONFERENCE

No public address available, (321)956-7193. E-mail: scwg-jm@cfl.rr.com. Website: www.scwg.org/ conference.asp. Annual conference held last weekend of January along the east coast of central Florida. Conference duration: 2 days. Average attendance: 150+. This conference is hosted each winter in Florida and features a variety of presenters on all topics writing. Critiques are available for a price, and agents in attendance will take pitches from writers. Previous presenters have included Debra Dixon, Davis Bunn (writer), Ellen Pepus (agent), Jennifer Crusie, Mike Resnick, Christina York, Ben Bova, Elizabeth Sinclair.

Accommodations The conference is hosted on a beachside hotel, with special room rates available.

STEAMBOAT SPRINGS WRITERS CONFERENCE

Steamboat Springs Arts Council, P.O. Box 774284, Steamboat Springs CO 80477. (970)879-8138. E-mail: info@steamboatwriters.com. Website: www.steamboatwriters.com. **Contact:** Susan de Wardt. Estab. 1982. Annual conference held in mid-July. Conference duration: 1 day. Average attendance: approximately 35. Attendance is limited. Featured areas of instruction change each year. Held at the restored train depot. Speakers have included Carl Brandt, Jim Fergus, Avi, Robert Greer, Renate Wood, Connie Willis, Margaret Coel and Kent Nelson.

Costs $50 prior to May 21; $60 after May 21 (includes seminars, catered lunch). A pre-conference dinner is also available.

Additional Information Brochures are available in April for a SASE. Send inquiries via e-mail.

STONY BROOK SOUTHAMPTON SCREENWRITING CONFERENCE

Stony Brook Southampton, 239 Montauk Highway, Southampton NY 11968. (631)632-5007. E-mail: southamptonwriters@notes.cc.sunysb.edu. Website: www.sunysb.edu/writers/screenwriting/. **Contact:** Conference Coordinator. "The Southampton Screenwriting Conference welcomes new and advanced screenwriters, as well as all writers interested in using the language of film to tell a story. The five-day residential conference will inform, inspire, challenge, and further participants' understanding of the art of the screenplay and the individual writing process. Our unique program of workshops, seminars, panel presentations, and screenings will encourage and motivate attendees under the professional guidance of accomplished screenwriters, educators, and script analysts." Annual.

Costs $1,200+.

Additional Information Space is limited.

TENNESSEE WRITERS ALLIANCE WORDFEST

Tennessee Writers Alliance, Inc., P.O. Box 120396, Nashville TN 37212. E-mail: inquiries@tn-writers.org. Website: www.tn-writers.org/Workshops.asp. Annual conference held in June near Nashville, TN. Conference duration: 1 day. Previous speakers have included Robert Hicks, Tama Kieves, Richard Goodman, Ted Swindley and Carl Harris. The conference features a variety of sessions on fiction, nonfiction, playwriting, creative nonfiction, inspiring writers and more.
Costs Costs available online.
Accommodations Hotel accommodations available not far from the conference site.

THE WRITERS' WORKSHOP

387 Beaucatcher Rd., Asheville NC 28805. (828)254-8111. E-mail: writersw@gmail.com. Website: www.twwoa.org. Estab. 1984. Held throughout the year. Sites are in Asheville and Charlotte, NC. Past facilitators: Laine Cunningham, Karen Ackerson, Anne Barnhill. Upcoming: Creative Nonfiction Workshop with Jeremy B. Jones. Techniques will be taught on making nonfiction stories come alive, such as creating a sense of place, inserting dialogue, and more. Students may bring five pages (double-spaced) to the class for review. Jones received his MFA in nonfiction writing from the University of Iowa. His essays have been published in various literary magazines including *Crab Orchard Review*, and he has recently won Honorable Mention in Best American Essays 2009. Classes are held at 387 Beaucatcher Road in Asheville. Registration is in advance only by mailing check or money order to The Writers' Workshop, 387 Beaucatcher Rd., Asheville, NC 28805. Financial aid in exchange for volunteering is available. For more information please email or call . All classes meet Saturdays, 10-4 p.m. and cost $75 / $70 with membership, unless otherwise noted. For printable directions, go to our website.
Costs Vary. Financial assistance available to low-income writers. Information on overnight accommodations is made available.
Additional Information We also sponsor these contests, open to all writers: Words of Love Contest, Prizes from $100-300 (Deadline: Feb. 20, 2010); Annual Poetry Contest, Prizes from $100-300 (Deadline: Apr. 30, 2010); Hard Times Writing Contest, Prizes from $100-300, (Deadline: June 30, 2010); Fiction Contest, Prizes from $150-350 (Deadline: Aug. 30, 2010); Annual Memoirs Competition, Prizes from $150-350 (Deadline: Oct. 30, 2010). Contests for young writers are posted at our website.

THRILLERFEST

PO Box 311, Eureka CA 95502. E-mail: infocentral@thrillerwriters.org. Website: www.thrillerwriters.org/thrillerfest/. **Contact:** Shirley Kennett. Estab. 2006. 2010 conference: July 7-10 in Manhattan. Conference duration: 4 days. Average attendance: 700. Conference "dedicated to writing the thriller and promoting the enjoyment of reading thrillers." Speakers have included David Morrell, Sandra Brown, Eric Van Lustbader, David Baldacci, Brad Meltzer, Steve Martini, R.L. Stine, Katherine Neville, Robin Cook, Andrew Gross, Kathy Reichs, Brad Thor, Clive Cussler, James Patterson, Donald Maass, and Al Zuckerman. Two days of the conference is CraftFest, where the focus is on writing craft, and two days is ThrillerFest, which showcase the author-fan relationship. Also featured are AgentFest, a unique event where authors can pitch their work face-to-face to forty top literary agents; and the international Thriller Awards and Banquet. Annual.
Costs Price will vary from $200 to $1,000 dollars depending on which events are selected. Various package deals are available offering savings, and Early Bird pricing is offered beginning August of each year.
Accommodations Grand Hyatt in New York City.

UNIVERSITY OF NORTH DAKOTA WRITERS CONFERENCE

Department of English, 110 Merrifield Hall, 276 Centennial Drive, Stop 7209, Grand Forks ND 58202. (701)777-3321. E-mail: writersconference@und.nodak.edu. Website: www.undwritersconference.org. Estab. 1970. Annual conference held in March. Offers panels, readings, and films focused around a specific theme. Almost all events take place in the UND Memorial Union, which has a variety of small rooms and a 1,000-seat main hall. Past speakers include Art Spiegelman, Truman Capote, Sir Salman Rushdie, Allen Ginsberg, Alice Walker, and Louise Erdrich.
Costs All events are free and open to the public. Donations accepted.

VIRGINIA FESTIVAL OF THE BOOK
Virginia Festival of the Book Foundation for the Humanities, 145 Ednam Dr., Charlottesville VA 22903-4629. (434)924-7548. Fax: (434)296-4714. E-mail: vabook@virginia.edu. Website: www.vabook.org. **Contact:** Nancy Coble Damon, Program Director. Estab. 1995. 16th Annual Virginia Festival of the Book, March 17-21. Average attendance: 20,000. Festival held to celebrate books and promote reading and literacy.

WINTER POETRY & PROSE GETAWAY IN CAPE MAY
18 N. Richards Ave., Ventnor NJ 08406. (888)887-2105. E-mail: info@wintergetaway.com. Website: www.wintergetaway.com. **Contact:** Peter Murphy. Estab. 1994. Annual conference. Join Peter E. Murphy and friends for the 18th annual Winter Poetry & Prose Getaway on the oceanfront in historica Cape May, NJ, January 14-17, 2011. This is not your typical writers' conference. Energize your writing with challenging and supportive workshos thpfocus on at starting new material. Advance your craft with feedback from our award-winning faculty including Pulitzer Prize & National Book Award winners. Thousands of people have enjoyed the getaway over the past 17 years, developing their craft as writers and making lifelong friends. The focus isn't on our award-winning faculty, it's on helping you improve and advance your skills." Features a variety of poetry and prose workshops, each with 10 or fewer participants. Choose from poetry, memoir, creative nonfiction, novel, short story, children's market, songwriting, and more.
Accommodations Please see website or call for current fee information.
Additional Information Previous faculty has included Julianna Baggott, Christian Bauman, Laure-Anne Bosselaar, Kurt Brown, Mark Doty (National Book Award Winner), Stephen Dunn (Pulitzer Prize Winner), Carol Plum-Ucci, James Richardson, Mimi Schwartz, Terese Svoboda, and more.

WISCONSIN BOOK FESTIVAL
222 S. Bedford St., Suite F, Madison WI 53703. (608)262-0706. Fax: (608)263-7970. E-mail: alison@wisconsinbookfestival.org. Website: www.wisconsinbookfestival.org. Estab. 2002. Annual festival held in October. Conference duration: 5 days. The festival features readings, lectures, book discussions, writing workshops, live interviews, children's events, and more. Speakers have included Michael Cunningham, Grace Paley, TC Boyle, Marjane Satrapi, Phillip Gourevitch, Myla Goldberg, Audrey Niffenegger, Harvey Pekar, Billy Collins, Tim O'Brien and Isabel Allende.
Costs All festival events are free.

WRITE ON THE SOUND WRITERS' CONFERENCE
Edmonds Arts Commission, 700 Main St., Edmonds WA 98020. (425)771-0228. Fax: (425)771-0253. E-mail: wots@ci.edmonds.wa.us. Website: www.ci.edmonds.wa.us/ArtsCommission/wots.stm. Estab. 1985. Annual conference held in October. Conference duration: 2.5 days. Average attendance: 200. Features over 30 presenters, a literary contest, ms critiques, a reception and book signing, onsite bookstore, and a variety of evening activities. Held at the Frances Anderson Center in Edmonds, just north of Seattle on the Puget Sound. Speakers have included Elizabeth George, Dan Hurley, Marcia Woodard, Holly Hughes, Greg Bear, Timothy Egan, Joe McHugh, Frances Wood, Garth Stein and Max Grover.
Costs See website for more information.
Additional Information Brochures are available Aug. 1. Accepts inquiries via phone, e-mail and fax.

2010 WRITERS' LEAGUE OF TEXAS AGENTS CONFERENCE
Writers' League of Texas, 611 S. Congress Ave., Suite 130, Austin TX 78704. (512)499-8914. Fax: (512)499-0441. E-mail: wlt@writersleague.org. Website: www.writersleague.org. Estab. 1982. Annual conference held in the summer. Conference duration: 3 days. Average attendance: 300. "The Writers' League of Texas Agents Conference is the place to meet agents and editors to learn the latest trends in publishing. This event provides writers iwth the opportunity to meet top literary agents and editors from New York and the West Coast. Topics include: finding and working with agents and publishers, writing and marketing fiction and nonfiction, dialogue, characterization, voice, research, basica and advanced fiction writing, the business of writing, and workshops for genres." Speakers have included Malaika Adero, Stacey Barney, Sha-Shana Crichton, Jessica Faust, Dena Fischer, Mickey Freiberg, Jill Grosjean, Anne Hawkins, Jim Hornfischer, Jennifer Joel, David Hale Smith and Elisabeth Weed.

Costs $309 member/$439 nonmember.

Accommodations 2010 event is at the Hyatt Regency Austin, 208 Barton Springs Road, Austin, TX 78704. Check back often for new information.

Additional Information June 25-27, 2010. Contests and awards programs are offered separately. Brochures are available upon request.

WRITERS WEEKEND AT THE BEACH

P.O. Box 877, Ocean Park WA 98640. (360)262-0160. E-mail: bhansen6@juno.com. Website: www.writersweekend.wordpress.com. Estab. 1992. Annual conference held in March. Conference duration: 2 days. Average attendance: 50-60. A retreat for writers with an emphasis on poetry, fiction, and nonfiction. Held at the Ocean Park Methodist Retreat Center & Camp. Speakers have included Wayne Holmes, Jim Whiting, Colette Tennant, and Linda Clare.

Costs $195-205 (includes lodging, meals, full workshop); $145/everything but lodging; $95/Saturday only (includes lunch); $25/Sunday critique session (includes brunch); $10/Saturday evening only.

Accommodations Offers on-site overnight lodging.

WRITERS WORKSHOP IN SCIENCE FICTION

English Department/University of Kansas, Lawrence KS 66045-2115. (785)864-3380. Fax: (785)864-1159. E-mail: jgunn@ku.edu. Website: www.ku.edu/~sfcenter. Estab. 1985. Annual workshop held in late June/early July (2010: July 5-16). Average attendance: 10. Conference for writing and marketing science fiction. Classes meet in university housing on the University of Kansas campus. Workshop sessions operate informally in a lounge. Speakers have included Frederik Pohl, Kij Johnson, James Gunn, and Chris McKitterick.

Costs See website for tuition rates, dormitory housing costs, and deadlines.

Accommodations Housing information is available. Several airport shuttle services offer reasonable transportation from the Kansas City International Airport to Lawrence.

Additional Information Admission to the workshop is by submission of an acceptable story. Two additional stories should be submitted by the middle of June. These 3 stories are distributed to other participants for critquing and are the basis for the first week of the workshop. One story is rewritten for the second week. Send SASE for brochure/guidelines. This workshop is intended for writers who have just started to sell their work or need that extra bit of understanding or skill to become a published writer.

WRITE-TO-PUBLISH CONFERENCE

WordPro Communication Services, 9118 W Elmwood Dr., #1G, Niles IL 60714-5820. (847)296-3964. Fax: (847)296-0754. E-mail: lin@writetopublish.com. Website: www.writetopublish.com. Estab. 1971. Annual conference held June 8-11, 2011. Conference duration: 4 days. Average attendance: 250. Conference on writing fiction, nonfiction, devotions, and magazine articles for the Christian market. Held at Wheaton College in Wheaton, Illinois. Speakers have included Dr. Dennis E. Hensley, agent Chip MacGregor, David Long (Bethany House), Carol Traver (Tyndale House), Dave Zimmerman (InterVarsity Press), Ed Gilbreath (Urban Ministries), Ken Peterson (WaterBrook Multnomah).

Costs $475 (includes all sessions, Saturday night banquet, 1 ms evaluation); $105/meals.

Accommodations Campus residence halls: $260/double; $340/single. A list of area hotels is also on the website.

WRITING FOR THE SOUL

Jerry B. Jenkins Christian Writers Guild, 5525 N. Union Blvd., Suite 200, Colorado Springs CO 80918. (866)495-5177. Fax: (719)495-5181. E-mail: leilani@christianwritersguild.com. Website: www.christianwritersguild.com/conferences. **Contact:** Leilani Squiers, admissions manager. Annual conference held in February. Workshops and continuing classes cover fiction, nonfiction, magazine writing, children's books, and teen writing. Appointments with more than 30 agents, publishers, and editors are also available. The keynote speakers are nationally known, leading authors. The conference is hosted by Jerry B. Jenkins.

Costs $649/guild members; $799/nonmembers.

Accommodations $159/night at the Grand Hyatt in Denver.

Glossary

#10 Envelope. A standard, business-size envelope.

Acquisitions Editor. The person responsible for originating and/or acquiring new publishing projects.

Adaptation. The process of rewriting a composition (novel, story, film, article, play) into a form suitable for some other medium, such as TV or the stage.

Advance. Money a publisher pays a writer prior to book publication, usually paid in installments, such as one-half upon signing the contract and one-half upon delivery of the complete, satisfactory manuscript. An advance is paid against the royalty money to be earned by the book. Agents take their percentage off the top of the advance as well as from the royalties earned.

Adventure. A genre of fiction in which action is the key element, overshadowing characters, theme and setting.

Auction. Publishers sometimes bid for the acquisition of a book manuscript with excellent sales prospects. The bids are for the amount of the author's advance, guaranteed dollar amounts, advertising and promotional expenses, royalty percentage, etc. Auctions are conducted by agents.

Author's Copies. An author usually receives about 10 free copies of his hardcover book from the publisher; more from a paperback firm. He can obtain additional copies at a price that has been reduced by an author's discount (usually 40 percent of the retail price).

Autobiography. A book-length account of a person's entire life written by the subject himself.

Backlist. A publisher's list of books that were not published during the current season, but that are still in print.

Backstory. The history of what has happened before the action in your script takes place, affecting a character's current behavior.

Bible. The collected background information on all characters and story lines of all existing episodes, as well as projections of future plots.

Bio. A sentence or brief paragraph about the writer; includes work and educational experience.

Blurb. The copy on paperback book covers or hardcover book dust jackets, either promoting the book and the author or featuring testimonials from book reviewers or well-known people in the book's field. Also called flap copy or jacket copy.

Boilerplate. A standardized publishing contract. Most authors and agents make many changes on the boilerplate before accepting the contract.

Book Doctor. A freelance editor hired by a writer, agent or book editor who analyzes problems that exist in a book manuscript or proposal and offers solutions to those problems.

Book Packager. Someone who draws elements of a book together-from the initial concept to writing and marketing strategies-and then sells the book package to a book publisher and/or movie producer. Also known as book producer or book developer.

Bound Galleys. A prepublication-often paperbound-edition of a book, usually prepared from photocopies of the final galley proofs. Designed for promotional purposes, bound galleys serve as the first set of review copies to be mailed out. Also called bound proofs.

Category Fiction. A term used to include all types of fiction. See genre.

Clips. Samples, usually from newspapers or magazines, of your published work. Also called tearsheets.

Commercial Fiction. Novels designed to appeal to a broad audience. These are often broken down into categories such as western, mystery and romance. See genre.

Concept. A statement that summarizes a screenplay or teleplay-before the outline or treatment is written.

Confession. A first-person story in which the narrator is involved in an emotional situation that encourages sympathetic reader identification, concluding with the affirmation of a morally acceptable theme.

Contributor's Copies. Copies of the book sent to the author. The number of contributor's copies is often negotiated in the publishing contract.

Co-Publishing. Arrangement where author and publisher share publication costs and profits of a book. Also called co-operative publishing.

Copyediting. Editing of a manuscript for writing style, grammar, punctuation and factual accuracy.

Copyright. A means to protect an author's work.

Cover Letter. A brief letter that accompanies the manuscript being sent to an agent or publisher.

Coverage. A brief synopsis and analysis of a script provided by a reader to a buyer considering purchasing the work.

Creative Nonfiction. Type of writing where true stories are told by employing the techniques usually reserved for novelists and poets, such as scenes, dialogue and detailed descriptions. Also called literary journalism.

Critiquing Service. An editing service offered by some agents in which writers pay a fee for comments on the salability or other qualities of their manuscript. Sometimes the critique includes suggestions on how to improve the work. Fees vary, as does the quality of the critique.

Curriculum Vitae (CV). Short account of one's career or qualifications.

D Person. Development person; includes readers, story editors and creative executives who work in development and acquisition of properties for TV and film.

Deal Memo. The memorandum of agreement between a publisher and author that precedes the actual contract and includes important issues such as royalty, advance, rights, distribution and option clauses.

Development. The process in which writers present ideas to producers who oversee the developing script through various stages to finished product.

Division. An unincorporated branch of a company.

Docudrama. A fictional film rendition of recent news-making events or people.

Electronic Rights. Secondary or subsidiary rights dealing with electronic/multimedia formats (the Internet, CD-ROMs, electronic magazines).

Elements. Actors, directors and producers attached to a project to make an attractive package.

El-Hi. Elementary to high school. A term used to indicate reading or interest level.

Episodic Drama. An hour-long, continuing TV show, often shown at 10 p.m.

Erotica. A form of literature or film dealing with the sexual aspects of love. Erotic content ranges from subtle sexual innuendo to explicit descriptions of sexual acts

Ethnic. Stories and novels whose central characters are African American, Native American, Italian American, Jewish, Appalachian or members of some other specific cultural group. Ethnic fiction usually deals with a protagonist caught between two conflicting ways of life: mainstream American culture and his ethnic heritage.

Evaluation Fees. Fees an agent may charge to evaluate material. The extent and quality of this evaluation varies, but comments usually concern the salability of the manuscript.

Exclusive. Offering a manuscript, usually for a set period of time, to just one agent and guaranteeing that agent is the only one looking at the manuscript.

Experimental. Type of fiction that focuses on style, structure, narrative technique, setting and strong characterization rather than plot. This form depends largely on the revelation of a character's inner being, which elicits an emotional response from the reader.

Family Saga. A story that chronicles the lives of a family or a number of related or interconnected families over a period of time.

Fantasy. Stories set in fanciful, invented worlds or in a legendary, mythic past that rely on outright invention or magic for conflict and setting.

Film Rights. May be sold or optioned by the agent/author to a person in the film industry, enabling the book to be made into a movie.

Floor Bid. If a publisher is very interested in a manuscript, he may offer to enter a floor bid when the book goes to auction. The publisher sits out of the auction, but agrees to take the book by topping the highest bid by an agreed-upon percentage (usually 10 percent).

Foreign Rights. Translation or reprint rights to be sold abroad.

Foreign Rights Agent. An agent who handles selling the rights to a country other than that of the first book agent. Usually an additional percentage (about 5 percent) will be added on to the first book agent's commission to cover the foreign rights agent.

Genre. Refers to either a general classification of writing, such as a novel, poem or short story, or to the categories within those classifications, such as problem novels or sonnets. Genre fiction is a term that covers various types of commercial novels, such as mystery, romance, Western, science fiction and horror.

Ghostwriting. A writer puts into literary form the words, ideas, or knowledge of another person under that person's name. Some agents offer this service; others pair ghostwriters with celebrities or experts.

Gothic. Novels characterized by historical settings and featuring young, beautiful women who win the favor of handsome, brooding heroes while simultaneously dealing with some life-threatening menace—either natural or supernatural.

Graphic Novel. Contains comic-like drawings and captions, but deals more with everyday events and issues than with superheroes.

High Concept. A story idea easily expressed in a quick, one-line description.

Hi-Lo. A type of fiction that offers a high level of interest for readers at a low reading level.

Historical. A story set in a recognizable period of history. In addition to telling the stories of ordinary people's lives, historical fiction may involve political or social events of the time.

Hook. Aspect of the work that sets it apart from others and draws in the reader/viewer.

Horror. A story that aims to evoke some combination of fear, fascination and revulsion in its readers—either through supernatural or psychological circumstances.

How-To. A book that offers the reader a description of how something can be accomplished. It includes both information and advice.

Imprint. The name applied to a publisher's specific line of books.

Independent Producers. Self-employed entrepreneurs who assemble scripts, actors, directors and financing for their film concepts.

IRC. International Reply Coupon. Buy at a post office to enclose with material sent outside the country to cover the cost of return postage. The recipient turns them in for stamps in their own country.

Joint Contract. A legal agreement between a publisher and two or more authors that establishes provisions for the division of royalties the book generates.

Juvenile. Category of children's writing that can be broken down into easy-to-read books (ages 7-9), which run 2,000-10,000 words, and middle-grade books (ages 8-12), which run 20,000-40,000 words.

Literary. A book where style and technique are often as important as subject matter. Also called serious fiction.

Logline. A one-line description of a plot as it might appear in TV Guide.

Mainstream Fiction. Fiction on subjects or trends that transcend popular novel categories like mystery or romance. Using conventional methods, this kind of fiction tells stories about people and their conflicts.

Marketing Fee. Fee charged by some agents to cover marketing expenses. It may be used to cover postage, telephone calls, faxes, photocopying or any other expense incurred in marketing a manuscript.

Mass Market Paperbacks. Softcover books, usually 4 × 7, on a popular subject directed at a general audience and sold in groceries, drugstores and bookstores.

Memoir. An author's commentary on the personalities and events that have significantly influenced one phase of his life.

MFTS. Made for TV series.

Midlist. Those titles on a publisher's list expected to have limited sales. Midlist books are mainstream, not literary, scholarly or genre, and are usually written by new or relatively unknown writers.

Miniseries. A limited dramatic series written for television, often based on a popular novel.

MOW. Movie of the week. A movie script written especially for television, usually seven acts with time for commercial breaks. Topics are often contemporary, sometimes controversial, fictional accounts. Also called a made-for-TV movie.

Multiple Contract. Book contract with an agreement for a future book(s).

Mystery. A form of narration in which one or more elements remain unknown or unexplained until the end of the story. Subgenres include: amateur sleuth, caper, cozy, heist, malice domestic, police procedural, etc.

Net Receipts. One method of royalty payment based on the amount of money a book publisher receives on the sale of the book after the booksellers' discounts, special sales discounts and returned copies.

Novelization. A novel created from the script of a popular movie and published in paperback. Also called a movie tie-in.

Novella. A short novel or long short story, usually 25,000-50,000 words. Also called a novelette.

Occult. Supernatural phenomena, including ghosts, ESP, astrology, demonic possession and witchcraft.

One-Time Rights. This right allows a short story or portions of a fiction or nonfiction book to be published again without violating the contract.

Option. Instead of buying a movie script outright, a producer buys the right to a script for a short period of time (usually six months to one year) for a small down payment. If the movie has not begun production and the producer does not wish to purchase the script at the end of the agreed time period, the rights revert back to the scriptwriter. Also called a script option.

Option Clause. A contract clause giving a publisher the right to publish an author's next book.

Outline. A summary of a book's content (up to 15 double-spaced pages); often in the form of chapter headings with a descriptive sentence or two under each one to show the scope of the book. A script's outline is a scene-by-scene narrative description of the story (10-15 pages for a 1/2-hour teleplay; 15-25 pages for 1-hour; 25-40 pages for 90 minutes; 40-60 pages for a 2-hour feature film or teleplay).

Picture Book. A type of book aimed at ages 2-9 that tells the story partially or entirely with artwork, with up to 1,000 words. Agents interested in selling to publishers of these books often handle both artists and writers.

Pitch. The process where a writer meets with a producer and briefly outlines ideas that could be developed if the writer is hired to write a script for the project.

Platform. A writer's speaking experience, interview skills, website and other abilities which help form a following of potential buyers for his book.

Proofreading. Close reading and correction of a manuscript's typographical errors.

Property. Books or scripts forming the basis for a movie or TV project.

Proposal. An offer to an editor or publisher to write a specific work, usually a package consisting of an outline and sample chapters.

Prospectus. A preliminary written description of a book, usually one page in length.

Psychic/Supernatural. Fiction exploiting—or requiring as plot devices or themes—some contradictions of the commonplace natural world and materialist assumptions about it (including the traditional ghost story).

Query. A letter written to an agent or a potential market to elicit interest in a writer's work.

Reader. A person employed by an agent or buyer to go through the slush pile of manuscripts and scripts and select those worth considering.

Regional. A book faithful to a particular geographic region and its people, including behavior, customs, speech and history.

Release. A statement that your idea is original, has never been sold to anyone else, and that you are selling negotiated rights to the idea upon payment.

Remainders. Leftover copies of an out-of-print or slow-selling book purchased from the publisher at a reduced rate. Depending on the contract, a reduced royalty or no royalty is paid on remaindered books.

Reprint Rights. The right to republish a book after its initial printing.

Romance. A type of category fiction in which the love relationship between a man and a woman pervades the plot. The story is told from the viewpoint of the heroine, who meets a man (the hero), falls in love with him, encounters a conflict that hinders their relationship, and then resolves the conflict with a happy ending.

Royalties. A percentage of the retail price paid to the author for each copy of the book that is sold. Agents take their percentage from the royalties earned and from the advance.

SASE. Self-addressed, stamped envelope. It should be included with all correspondence.

Scholarly Books. Books written for an academic or research audience. These are usually heavily researched, technical, and often contain terms used only within a specific field.

Science Fiction. Literature involving elements of science and technology as a basis for conflict, or as the setting for a story.

Screenplay. Script for a film intended to be shown in theaters.

Script. Broad term covering teleplay, screenplay or stage play. Sometimes used as a shortened version of the word manuscript when referring to books.

Serial Rights. The right for a newspaper or magazine to publish sections of a manuscript.

Simultaneous Submission. Sending the same manuscript to several agents or publishers at the same time.

Sitcom. Situation comedy. Episodic comedy script for a television series. The term comes from the characters dealing with various situations with humorous results.

Slice of Life. A type of short story, novel, play or film that takes a strong thematic approach, depending less on plot than on vivid detail in describing the setting and/or environment, and the environment's effect on characters involved in it.

Slush Pile. A stack of unsolicited submissions in the office of an editor, agent or publisher.

Spec Script. A script written on speculation without confirmation of a sale.

Standard Commission. The commission an agent earns on the sales of a manuscript or script. For literary agents, the commission percentage (usually 10-20 percent) is taken from the advance and royalties paid to the writer. For script agents, the commission (usually 15-20 percent) is taken from script sales. If handling plays, agents take a percentage from the box office proceeds.

Subagent. An agent handling certain subsidiary rights, usually working in conjunction with the agent who handled the book rights. The percentage paid the book agent is increased to pay the subagent.

Subsidiary. An incorporated branch of a company or conglomerate (e.g., Knopf Publishing Group is a subsidiary of Random House, Inc.).

Subsidiary Rights. All rights other than book publishing rights included in a book publishing contract, such as paperback rights, book club rights and movie rights. Part of an agent's job is to negotiate those rights and advise you on which to sell and which to keep.

Syndication Rights. The right for a station to rerun a sitcom or drama, even if the show originally appeared on a different network.

Synopsis. A brief summary of a story, novel or play. As a part of a book proposal, it is a comprehensive summary condensed in a page or page and a half, single-spaced. See outline.

Teleplay. Script for television.

Terms. Financial provisions agreed upon in a contract.

Textbook. Book used in a classroom at the elementary, high school or college level.

Thriller. A story intended to arouse feelings of excitement or suspense. Works in this genre are highly sensational, usually focusing on illegal activities, international espionage, sex and violence.

TOC. Table of Contents. A listing at the beginning of a book indicating chapter titles and their corresponding page numbers. It can also include brief chapter descriptions.

Trade Book. Either a hardcover or softcover book sold mainly in bookstores. The subject matter frequently concerns a special interest for a general audience.

Trade Paperback. A soft-bound volume, usually 5 × 8, published and designed for the general public; available mainly in bookstores.

Translation Rights. Sold to a foreign agent or foreign publisher.

Treatment. Synopsis of a television or film script (40-60 pages for a two-hour feature film or teleplay).

Unsolicited Manuscript. An unrequested manuscript sent to an editor, agent or publisher.

Westerns/Frontier. Stories set in the American West, almost always in the 19th century, generally between the antebellum period and the turn of the century.

Young Adult (YA). The general classification of books written for ages 12-17. They run 50,000-60,000 words and include category novels—adventure, sports, career, mysteries, romance, etc.

Literary Agents Specialties Index

FICTION

Action

Adventure

Specialties Index

Frontier

Gay

Glitz

Gothic

Historical

Horror

Humor

Inspirational

Juvenile

Lesbian

Literary

Mainstream

Military

Multicultural

Occult

Picture Books

Plays

Police

Psychic

Psychological

Regency

Regional

Supernatural

Suspense

Thriller

Young Adult

NONFICTION

Agriculture/Horticulture

Americana

Animals

Autobiography/Biography

Business

Child Guidance

Crafts

Creative Nonfiction

Cultural Interests

Current Affairs

Specialties Index

Dance

Decorating

Education

Film

Finance

Foods

Specialties Index

Health

History

Humor

Inspirational

Interior Design

Investigative

Juvenile

Language

Law

Memoirs

Specialties Index

Metaphysics

Military

Personal Improvement

Philosophy

Photography

Politics

Popular Culture

Psychology

Satire

Science

Self-Help

Sports

Specialties Index

Technology

Theater

Women's Studies

Young Adult

Agents Index

Agents Index

General Index